BORN TO REBEL

BORN TO REBEL

BIRTH ORDER, FAMILY DYNAMICS, AND CREATIVE LIVES

FRANK J. SULLOWAY

PANTHEON BOOKS
NEW YORK

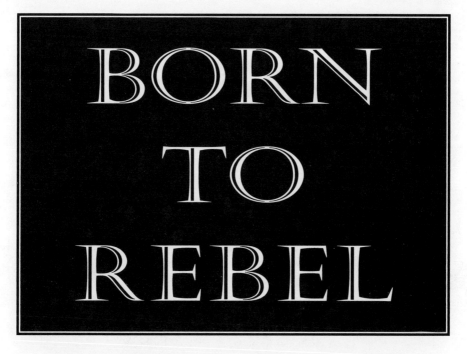

Published in the United States by Pantheon Books, a division of Random House, Inc., New York, and simultaneously in Canada by Random House of Canada Limited, Toronto.

Illustration credits are on pages 445–50.

A cataloging-in-publication record has been established for this title by the Library of Congress.

ISBN 0-679-44232-4

Library of Congress Catalog Card Number: 96-5382

Random House Web Address: http://www.randomhouse.com/

Book design by Fearn Cutler
Chart design by Bonnie Scranton

Printed in the United States of America
First Edition
2 4 6 8 9 7 5 3 1

TO JEROME KAGAN

Charles Darwin in 1840, four years after his circumnavigation of the world aboard HMS *Beagle* (1831–36). The fifth of six children from a landed gentry family, Darwin revolutionized the science of biology with his theory of evolution, which he set forth in the *Origin of Species by Means of Natural Selection* (1859). Owing to the family dynamics that shaped his personality, Darwin was born to rebel. When Darwin's own theories are applied to the science of human behavior—particularly the development of personality—they offer the single best guide to the origins of creative achievement.

I have been speculating last night what makes a man a discoverer of undiscovered things; and a most perplexing problem it is. Many men who are very clever—much cleverer than the discoverers—never originate anything.

—Charles Darwin, 1871 letter to his son Horace
(E. Darwin, 1915, 2:207)

CONTENTS

APPENDICES

INTRODUCTION

This book is inspired by a perplexing puzzle. Why do some people have the genius to reject the conventional wisdom of their day and to revolutionize the way we think? Copernicus, Newton, and Darwin are just three of the bold visionaries who have radically transformed our understanding of the world. No matter how radical the idea, and no matter how fierce the opposition, some people have quickly recognized the brilliance of the innovation and come to its defense.

When Darwin proposed his theory of evolution by natural selection, he plunged the scientific community into acrimonious debate that has continued even to this day. In spite of intense opposition to Darwin's ideas, some scientists quickly recognized Darwin as the greatest scientific revolutionary since Isaac Newton. Others, deeply disturbed by the possibility of humankind's descent from apes, branded him as a misguided atheist who had forsaken the true methods of scientific inference. Eventually the minority viewpoint prevailed over the majority, and Darwin lies buried in Westminster Abbey, not far from Isaac Newton.

Darwin's success as a revolutionary thinker raises a second critical question. Why, during radical revolutions, do some people rapidly discard their old, erroneous ways of thinking whereas others hold tenaciously to the prevailing dogma? Historians, sociologists, philosophers, and psychologists have all proposed answers to the questions I am raising. In spite of numerous hypotheses, and considerable empirical research, there is no satisfactory answer to the question of why some people rebel and why others, just as zealously, defend the status quo.

In the case of Darwin's theory of evolution, religious convictions clearly played a part in the reception. But many revolutions in science have been fiercely contested on technical rather than ideological grounds. For example, Alfred Wegener's theory of continental drift was resisted for half a century before finally gaining acceptance among geologists.

Age has sometimes been suggested as a relevant factor, but this influence cannot explain why parents have sometimes championed new ideas and why their own offspring have sometimes opposed the same innovation.[1] The great naturalist Étienne Geoffroy Saint-Hilaire believed in evolution a quarter of a century before Darwin announced his theory of natural selection. Yet Étienne's son Isidore, who was also a naturalist, opposed these heterodox ideas. In the political domain, Benjamin Franklin's eldest son, William, opposed the American Revolution and was expelled from the country as a Loyalist. Many further examples could be given to show that age is surprisingly independent of revolutionary proclivities.

Another fashionable hypothesis about radical thinking involves Freud's notion of oedipal rivalry. Revolutionary thinkers are often said to have experienced a difficult relationship with a parent.[2] Using a case history approach, it is not hard to find corroborative evidence for this thesis. Using the same approach, it is just as easy to find evidence to the contrary. It is true that young Darwin experienced somewhat greater conflict with his father than most scientists. But Alfred Russel Wallace, who codiscovered the theory of natural selection, had excellent relationships with both parents. Other famous scientists who have managed to revolutionize the thinking of their disciplines without having experienced appreciable oedipal conflict include Francis Bacon, René Descartes, Louis Pasteur, and Max Planck. Even Sigmund Freud had a better relationship with his parents than most scientists.

Wealth and social status have frequently been called upon to explain differences in revolutionary allegiances.[3] Appeals to social class fail to elucidate one of the most puzzling features about revolutionary controversies. More often than not, major revolutions tend to polarize family members, including siblings who have grown up together. As one witness to the French Revolution commented during the Reign of Terror, "The worst part of this deplorable revolution is the discord sown by it in private circles, among families and friends and even between lovers. Nothing is free from the contagion."[4] Consistent with this verdict, historians have repeatedly failed to find meaningful socioeconomic differences among the members of the French National Convention (1792–94). Yet bitter feuding among these predominantly middle-class deputies led to the harsh policies of the Terror and also caused these politicians to send more than fifty of their colleagues to the guillotine. For compelling evidence on this score, one need look no further than the sixteen brothers who were elected to the convention. More often than not, these brothers affiliated themselves with *rival* political factions. The Protestant Reformation had a similar impact on family members, turning husbands against their wives, parents against their offspring, and siblings fratricidally against one another.[5]

What is missing from these and other attempts to explain radical thought is a simple but startling observation about human behavior: most individual differences in personality, including those that underlie the propensity to rebel, arise *within* the family. The question of why some people rebel, including why a few particularly far-sighted individuals initiate radical revolutions, is synonymous with the question of why siblings are so different.

Born to Rebel is organized into four parts, each of which adds a new layer to the basic argument. Part One sets forth a central problem: Why do some scientists, but not others, readily accept radical ideas? The story of Charles Darwin's conversion to the theory of evolution illustrates a frequent feature about revolutionary ideas. Most people, including scientists, *resist radical innovations.* Faced with the same biological evidence that caused Darwin to accept evolution, his closest colleagues refused to abandon their creationist convictions. Far more than evidence was required to transform Darwin into a radical revolutionary. The biographical circumstances that paved Darwin's way exemplify some of the insights I have garnered from the study of 6,000 lives in Western history. Some people, it seems, are born to rebel.

The crux of my argument stems from a remarkable discovery. Siblings raised together are almost as different in their personalities as people from different families.[6] This finding, firmly established by studies in personality psychology, raises the question of how the family experience can be so different for each child. Do siblings differ because of random influences and experiences within the family, or are some of these influences systematically linked to variables that partition the family environment? Certainly gender is a relevant consideration, but is gender the only one or even the most important?

What about birth order, which is different for each sibling? Although a review of the birth-order literature strongly underscores the relevance of this variable, these findings have generally been dismissed because they are often contradictory. As it turns out, these inconsistencies are largely methodological. In addition to methodological problems, the voluminous birth-order literature has lacked an adequate theoretical perspective to make sense out of the results. Properly reinterpreted, the literature on birth order reveals striking trends and allows a crucial first step toward resolving the problem of why siblings are so different.

Darwinian theory, and the nascent field of evolutionary psychology, provide useful guidelines for understanding family life, including the question of why siblings are so different. One particularly important source of sibling differences is competition over family resources. Disputes over these resources, especially over parental affection, create rivalries. In nature, any recurring cause of conflict tends to promote adaptations that increase the odds of coming out on top. In their efforts to gain a competitive edge, siblings use physical advantages in size and strength. These disparities dictate many of the tactics that siblings employ in mutual competition. The crucial factor for measuring these physical differences, as well as for determining status within the family, is order of birth. Over time, the strategies perfected by firstborns have spawned counterstrategies by laterborns. The result has been an evolutionary arms race played out within the family. Even the Bible concurs with evolutionary theory regarding the primacy of sibling strife: the first biblical murder—that of Abel by his elder brother, Cain—was fratricidal.

It is natural for firstborns to identify more strongly with power and authority. They arrive first within the family and employ their superior size and strength to defend their special status. Relative to their younger siblings, firstborns are more assertive, socially dominant, ambitious, jealous of their status, and defensive. As underdogs within the family system, younger siblings are inclined to question the status quo and in some cases to develop a "revolutionary personality." In the name of revolution, laterborns have repeatedly challenged the time-honored assumptions of their day. From their ranks have come the bold explorers, the iconoclasts, and the heretics of history.

The influence of birth order, like that of gender, can be traced throughout history with clear and dramatic consequences. For most of recorded history, birth order has often determined who lived and who died, who possessed political power and who lacked it, and who was successful in efforts to find a mate and to reproduce. In prior centuries, parents often invested more heavily in firstborns to guarantee that at least one offspring would successfully perpetuate the family lineage.

Historically, firstborns have tended to have more offspring. Even before the advent of primogeniture, scarce resources exerted a constant restraining influence on family size, causing the incidence of infanticide, as well as parental neglect, to be most frequent among younger siblings. In their efforts to survive childhood, and to pass on their genes to the next generation, laterborns have perennially been in conflict with their elder siblings.[7]

The evolution of behavior is a separate issue from how behaviors are individually learned. Children do not inherit special genes for being firstborns or laterborns, only genes for engaging successfully in competition for parental investment. The family environment determines how these competitive tendencies are expressed. In terms of personality, every firstborn is a potential laterborn, and vice versa. The psychological consequences of birth order provide compelling evidence for the role of the family environment.

Part Two of the book explores a variety of influences, besides birth order, that affect personality. Siblings become different for the same reason that species do over time: divergence minimizes competition for scarce resources. For example, children can increase the amount of nurturing and attention they receive from parents if they avoid direct competition and instead appeal to whichever parent is unencumbered. The story of sibling differences is the story of family structure and how niches are partitioned within it. It is also the story of parental investment and any perceived biases in it. In spite of their best efforts to the contrary, parents occasionally exhibit favoritism toward some of their children. No social injustice is felt more deeply than that suffered within one's own family. When unassuaged, such feelings undermine respect for authority, laying the foundations for a revolutionary personality.

Particular factors such as gender, temperament, parent-offspring conflict, and parental loss add to our ability to predict revolutionary personality. Together these and other variables shape *sibling strategies* that are aimed at maximizing parental investment. Even only children employ sibling strategies. This seeming paradox is explained by the threat of unborn siblings, whose Darwinian influence on family life is as real as the ova and sperm in which they reside.

Sibling strategies typically entail *emergent* properties. Birth order, gender, and temperament all interact to produce personality characteristics that could not be anticipated based on a simple aggregate of these influences. A theory of sibling strategies serves to highlight these emergent features of personality and also seeks to delineate their links with family structure and dynamics.

Part Three considers the role of social influences, especially social attitudes and social class. To a significant extent, social influences encompass *between*-family differences. Although such disparities exert little direct effect on personality, they do shape social attitudes and values, which have substantial influence on behavior. A variety of biographical paradoxes are resolved by understanding the relative independence of personality and social attitudes. A person with a "conforming" personality may espouse liberal attitudes that have been learned from parents or other authority figures. Social attitudes also reflect sibling differences, not only among offspring but also among their immediate forebears. The social attitudes of mates are highly correlated. Over the generations, sibling differences in worldviews become compounded by the process of assortative mating, or "like marrying like." The worldviews endorsed by families are substantially sibling differences in another guise. To explain radical thinking, much of what we need to know are, or once were, sibling differences.

Much of Part Three is devoted to general history. Without the application of scientific criteria, the correct and incorrect hunches of historians cannot easily be differentiated. Methods heretofore employed by historians are excellent for hypothesis generation, but they are inadequate for hypothesis testing. In connection with this study I have computerized more than half a million biographical data points, culled from tens of thousands of biographies. To integrate and analyze so much information, I have availed myself of computer technologies and hypothesis testing. Most people think of science as a subject, such as physics or chemistry. Science is not a subject but a *method*. Much of history can be studied scientifically.[8]

Are the principal sources of rebelliousness the same in social life as they are in science? As an arena for the expression of sibling strategies, politics is complicated by violence. Left-wing terrorism and egalitarianism are very different political inclinations. Historically, such movements reveal correspondingly different characteristics of siblings.

To elucidate the role of family dynamics in political life, I have studied the Protestant Reformation and the French Revolution. These two radical social revolutions provide both a check on my general thesis and a further illumination of it. The best predictors of attitudes toward social change during these two radical events are differences between siblings. The French Revolution is the story of Cain and Abel writ large. To the extent that social class helps to explain the Reign of Terror, it illustrates how and why the shared family background forges such disparate political opinions among siblings.

Conflict between spouses reflects the rules of sibling strife. Most spouses have grown up with siblings and have learned adaptive strategies in their efforts to establish a family niche of their own. Social revolutions bring these sibling differences to the fore. Not every Reformation spouse had the good fortune to marry someone with the same birth order. As a result, Reformation couples often became embroiled over religious and political issues. Henry VIII is not the only husband whose authority was tested by a discontented spouse. Having embraced the Protestant heresy, some of these royal wives were imprisoned by their husbands. Others met with the executioner's blade. Birth order is an excellent predictor of these marital conflicts, including those experienced by Henry VIII and his six wives.

In the fourth and last part of the book I synthesize my findings about the propensity to rebel. In doing so I wrestle with the highly contingent nature of history. What is unique about history is the diversity of the situations it presents. Human behavior is predictable, but only when the context has been adequately specified. The detection of recurring patterns requires that we give historical context just as much explanatory weight as individual biographical influences. Although historians have rightly appreciated the role of historical context, they have failed to investigate this issue scientifically. Owing to the plethora of interactions between individual dispositions and behavioral contexts, this problem is too complex to be resolved by narrative methods.

Using independent criteria, innovations can be analyzed and classified. Once innovations have been properly classified, they exhibit remarkable cross-revolution consistency in the type of supporters they recruit. In science, firstborns are sympathetic to conservative innovations, which laterborns generally oppose. "Vitalist" doctrines in biology have provided repeated examples of this firstborn predilection. In contrast to conservative innovations, the proposals of radical revolutionaries have typically clashed with accepted social beliefs, especially with prevailing religious dogma. Copernican theory and Darwinism were both radical revolutions, led by laterborns and strenuously opposed by firstborns.

Because different types of revolutions inspire different individual responses by the same person, no single episode of historical change will suffice to explain who will play a leadership role in history. It is essential to study many historical events and to classify these events in terms of their defining features. Once historical events are properly categorized, consistency in human behavior can often be demonstrated.

At the outset of this study, my goal was to explain just one aspect of human behavior—the propensity to rebel. Nothing prepared me for what I encountered. Behavioral solutions to the dilemmas of family life preadapt people to the merits of change. To accept or reject the status quo is a fundamental decision that we must all sometimes make. We first learn to make such decisions within the family. As the great forge of individual tendencies toward revolution and counterrevolution, the family is one of the foremost engines of historical change. In ways that I did not suspect when I began, the causes of rebellion reside within every family. This story is about us all.

PART ONE

BIRTH ORDER AND REVOLUTIONARY PERSONALITY

I

OPENNESS TO SCIENTIFIC INNOVATION

In Charles Darwin's day evolution was a heretical notion, contradicting both the Bible and common sense. Most of his contemporaries rejected the idea outright. But Darwin took it seriously, even though it made him sick with worry. He once commented that it was "like confessing a murder" to acknowledge his belief in evolution.[1]

This book is about the numerous "Darwins" in the history of Western thought who have tried to revolutionize the thinking of their day. Some of these people, like sixteenth-century philosopher Giordano Bruno, were burned at the stake. Others, more mercifully, were strangled or beheaded for their heretical beliefs. Still others, like Galileo, were strongly censured by the powerful social institutions of their time. Many radical thinkers sought protection through anonymous publication. The ever-clever Voltaire employed over a hundred different pseudonyms. This tactic did not prevent his being exiled from his beloved Paris, and later from his country, for much of his life. Despite the threat of banishment, beheading, and burning, some of these courageous people refused to be silenced.

Why do some people, like Darwin, accept new ideas, and yet others oppose the same innovation? In Darwin's case, compelling scientific evidence was hardly the deciding factor. He was converted to a belief in evolution by findings that, within just a few years, had been widely disseminated among his colleagues. Only Darwin was sufficiently disturbed by this evidence to consider a revolutionary explanation for it. This story is worth telling.

On 27 December 1831 HMS *Beagle* departed England on a five-year circumnavigation of the world. The *Beagle*'s orders were to survey the southern coast of South America and to conduct longitudinal measurements of the globe. On board, as the ship's naturalist, sailed Charles

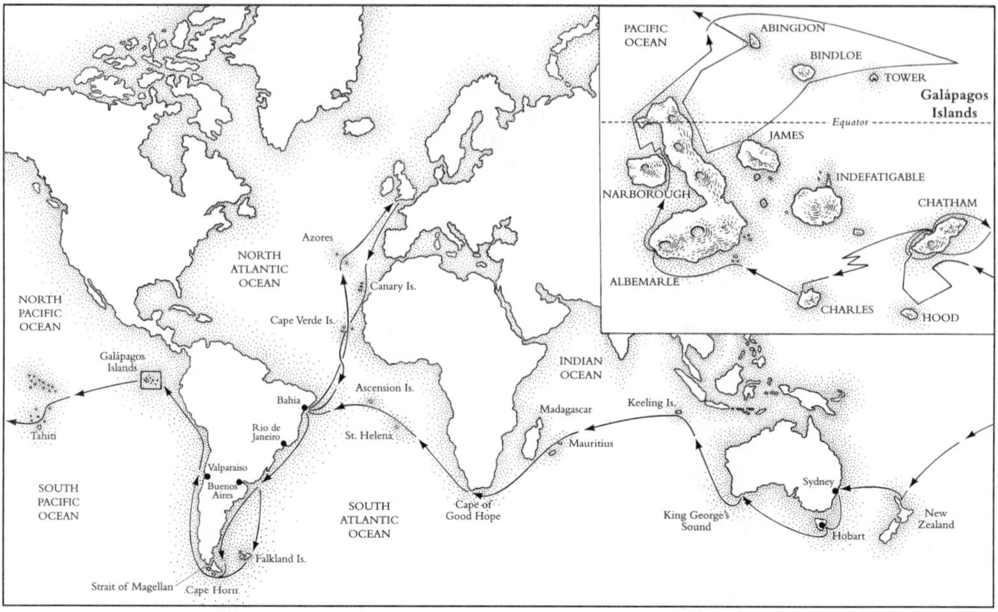

FIGURE 1.1. The route of HMS *Beagle* during her circumnavigation of the globe (1831–36). *Inset, upper right:* The Galápagos Islands, 600 miles west of Ecuador, which the *Beagle* visited in September and October 1835. Although Darwin spent only five weeks in this archipelago, the evidence he encountered there revolutionized his thinking about the origin of species. Darwin landed on four of the major islands: Chatham, Charles, Albemarle, and James, where he collected specimens for nine days, including three days in the highlands.

Darwin. At twenty-two, he had recently graduated from Cambridge University in preparation for a career as a clergyman. Darwin was an amiable person with a passionate interest in geology and natural history. His uncle aptly described him as "a man of enlarged curiosity."[2] Darwin left England a creationist believing that God had designed each creature for its intended place in the world. "Whilst on board the Beagle," he recalled in his *Autobiography,* "I was quite orthodox, and I remember being heartily laughed at by several of the officers (though themselves orthodox) for quoting the Bible as an unanswerable authority on some point of morality."[3]

All this changed as a result of the *Beagle* voyage and especially Darwin's visit to the Galápagos Islands (Fig. 1.1).[4] Composed of sixteen major islands 600 miles west of Ecuador, the Galápagos Archipelago is built up from volcanic eruptions over the last several million years. The oldest portions of the present-day Galápagos Islands date back about three million years, but the chain includes several submerged seamounts (or "drowned" islands) that are up to nine million years old.[5] This

Volcanic cones near Stephens Bay, Chatham Island. Darwin commented about this region in his *Journal:* "One night I slept on shore on part of the island, where black truncated cones were extraordinarily numerous: from one small eminence I counted sixty of them, all surmounted by craters more or less perfect. . . . The entire surface of this part of the island seems to have been permeated, like a sieve, by the subterranean vapours. . . . From the regular form of the many craters, they gave to the country an artificial appearance, which vividly reminded me of those parts of Staffordshire, where the great iron-foundaries are most numerous. The day was glowing hot, and the scrambling over the rough surface and through intricate thickets, was very fatiguing; but I was well repaid by the strange Cyclopean scene" (Darwin 1845:374).

amount of time is only 1/400 of the age of the earth and just 1/20 of the period since dinosaurs ruled the world. Still, it has been enough time for evolution to produce a veritable showcase of results.

The entire Galápagos Archipelago is contained within an oval area that extends only 250 miles, and most of the islands are within sight of each other. Originally uninhabited by man, the islands were named by the Spanish buccaneers after the giant land tortoises (*galápagos*) that live there. Straddling the equator, the islands have a hot, dry climate, except at higher altitudes where clouds collect on the volcanic peaks and support milder temperatures and a luxuriant vegetation. In contrast, the lowlands are desert-like, covered with cactus and leafless thickets. Darwin compared these arid parts of the landscape to something one might expect to see in "the cultivated parts of the Infernal regions."[6]

"THAT MYSTERY OF MYSTERIES"

The most remarkable feature about the Galápagos Islands is their living inhabitants, as Darwin pointed out in his *Journal of Researches:*

> The natural history of these islands is eminently curious, and well deserves attention. Most of the organic productions are aboriginal creations, found nowhere else. . . . Considering the small size of these islands, we feel the more astonished at the number of their aboriginal beings, and at their confined range. Seeing every height crowned with its crater, and the boundaries of most of the lava-streams still distinct, we are led to believe that within a period, geologically recent, the unbroken ocean was here spread out. Hence, both in space and in time, we seem to be brought somewhat near to that great fact—that mystery of mysteries—the first appearance of new beings on this earth.[7]

The recent geological origins of the Galápagos group was the key to Darwin's "mystery of mysteries." According to the theory of creationism, God had placed various species on the earth at different epochs. The doctrine of separate creations, which Darwin accepted at the time of his Galápagos visit, attempted to explain why various "centers" of creation possessed their own distinct animals and plants. Such geographic differences, as Darwin noted in his voyage diary, seemed to indicate that "the periods of Creation have been distinct & remote the one from the other; that the Creator rested in his labor."[8] The theory of Design provided the backbone of creationism and explained why organisms tend to be so well suited to their local environments. According to this theory, the Creator had anticipated the needs of every species, providing them with appropriate adaptations for their place in the economy of nature.

Because Galápagos organisms are both unique to these islands and of recent origin, they appeared to Darwin to represent evidence of a "separate creation." Otherwise the islands ought to have been inhabited by some of the same species found in western South America, from which colonists might occasionally have strayed.

Darwin was particularly struck by the fact that the different islands in the Galápagos group were inhabited by closely related but nonidentical species. The vice-governor of the islands first told Darwin about these local variations, saying that he could tell "with certainty" from which island any tortoise was brought. Although Darwin did not initially pay much attention to this claim, the more he pondered the evidence, the more important such facts became in his mind.

Darwin was intrigued by the many forms of closely related finches found in the Galápagos—thirteen species with beaks ranging in size from that of a large-billed grosbeak to that of a wren. There are four ground species that feed mostly on seeds, two cactus-eating finches, a leaf-eating form, and six insectivorous tree species, which include "warbler" and "woodpecker" finches (Fig. 1.2). Darwin later remarked about this unusual ornithological group in his *Journal:* "Seeing this

FIGURE 1.2 Darwin's Galápagos finches. Figured are four of the thirteen species: (1) the large-beaked ground finch (*Geospiza magnirostris*), (2) the medium-beaked ground finch (*G. fortis*), (3) the small insectivorous tree finch (*Camarhynchus parvulus*), and (4) the warbler finch (*Certhidea olivacea*). Darwin was so impressed with the evolutionary implications of these different forms of finch that he added this illustration to the second edition of his *Journal of Researches* (1845:379). "Darwin's finches" are one of the best-known examples of evolution in action.

Galápagos tortoises. *Left:* The James Island tortoise (*Geochelone elephantopus darwini*), a dome-shaped form from an island that has lush highlands and hence plentiful food and water. *Right:* The Hood Island tortoise (*G. elephantopus hoodensis*), an extreme saddleback form similar to the now extinct Charles Island race. On the lower and drier islands, an upturn of the carapace has evolved to allow tortoises to stretch their necks higher in search of food and water, which is obtained from cactus pads.

gradation and diversity of structure in one small, intimately related group of birds, one might really fancy that from an original paucity of birds in this archipelago, one species had been taken and modified for different ends."[9]

Another remarkable aspect of the Galápagos fauna, Darwin recognized, was the presence of two species of large lizards, one seagoing and one confined to land. Both species were new to science and yet both were also closely allied to one another. The marine form, Darwin observed, was usually to be found in large groups basking on the lava rocks near the shore. They appeared to feed exclusively on algae beneath the sea, making them the world's only oceangoing lizard. Previous visitors had dubbed these hideous-looking creatures "imps of darkness."[10] According to the experiments of one *Beagle* crew member,

Galápagos iguanas, unique to these islands. *Left:* a marine iguana (*Amblyrhynchus cristatus*), basking on the lava rocks near the shoreline. *Right:* a large adult land iguana (*Conolophus subcristatus*). Land iguanas are now extinct on James Island, where Darwin observed them, and they are threatened with extinction on two other islands. When the *Beagle* made its visit in 1835, the land form of iguana was extraordinarily numerous. "I cannot give a more forcible proof of their numbers," Darwin commented, "than by stating that when we were left at James Island, we could not for some time find a spot free from their burrows on which to pitch our single tent" (1845:388).

who tied a rock to one of these iguanas and tried to drown it, the creatures were capable of submerging for over an hour.

Unlike the marine form, the land form of iguana was highly territorial, Darwin discovered, and lived in underground burrows. Although the marine species was found throughout the archipelago, the land form was curiously restricted to just four central islands. "It is very interesting," Darwin remarked, "to find a well-characterized genus, having its marine and terrestrial species, belonging to so confined a portion of the world."[11] But how had these unique forms, found nowhere else, first appeared in the Galápagos? Were they *created* there? And if so, why did God create distinct species for islands within sight of each other?

As he pondered these questions, Darwin increasingly began to wonder whether the organisms inhabiting the Galápagos were descended from creatures arriving long ago from the mainland of the Americas. This would explain why so many of them bore an "American stamp," like the mockingbirds and flycatchers. As he later observed in his voyage *Journal:*

> It is probable that the islands of the Cape de Verd group [off the coast of northwestern Africa] resemble, in all their physical conditions, far more closely the Galapagos Islands than these latter physically resemble the coast of America; yet the aboriginal inhabitants of the two groups are totally unlike; those of the Cape de Verd Islands bearing the impress of Africa, as the inhabitants of the Galapagos Archipelago are stamped with that of America.[12]

Why was this the case, he wondered, unless the island colonists were descended from the nearest mainland forms? Furthermore, the presence of distinct but closely allied species on the separate islands appeared to represent a continuation of evolution within the archipelago itself. Much of Darwin's revolutionary genius lies in his recognition that the evidence from the Galápagos Islands was inconsistent with creationist theory.

Although his Galápagos visit had piqued Darwin's doubts about the immutability of species, he was not an expert at judging what is, and what is not, a distinct species.[13] This was the province of taxonomists whose conclusions were crucial to answering the questions that the Galápagos Islands had raised.

The *Beagle* completed her circumnavigation of the globe on 2 October 1836. Darwin soon arranged for various taxonomists to name and describe his voyage specimens. He gave the birds to the London Zoological Society, where they were handed over to the society's taxidermist, John Gould. Five years older than Darwin, Gould was one of the great nineteenth-century ornithologists.[14] During his lifetime, Gould depicted more than three thousand bird species, or about a third of the world's known forms. Today Gould's beautifully illustrated works are collector's items valued in the tens of thousands of dollars. Particularly adept at attracting birds by imitating their songs, he identified so closely with these creatures that he asked to have as his epitaph: "Here lies John Gould, the 'Bird Man.' "[15]

Upon receiving Darwin's *Beagle* specimens, in early January 1837, Gould was immediately drawn to the Galápagos portion of the collec-

John Gould, the "Bird Man," in 1849 (age forty-five).

tion, which he recognized as being largely new to science. The finches, of which Gould identified thirteen species, were "so peculiar in form" that he was "induced to regard them as constituting an entirely new group . . . strictly confined to the Galapagos Islands."[16] In addition, Gould confirmed Darwin's suspicion that closely allied species in the Galápagos group were often confined to single islands. This curious fact, Gould concluded, was true not only of the mockingbirds but also of the flycatchers and possibly some of the finches. Gould also determined that the bulk of the Galápagos land birds were unique to this archipelago. This was an important fact that Darwin had not fully appreciated during the *Beagle* voyage.

Gould's various reports on Darwin's Galápagos birds, delivered before the London Zoological Society during the first two months of 1837, were of sufficient interest that they made the London newspapers.[17] When Darwin first learned of Gould's conclusions in early

March 1837, he was stunned by the implications. *Almost overnight, Darwin was converted, becoming an enthusiastic evolutionist.*[18] His new beliefs prompted the following famous entry in a private journal: "In July [1837] opened first notebook on 'Transmutation of Species'—Had been greatly struck from about Month of previous March on character of S. American fossils—& species on Galapagos Archipelago. These facts origin (especially latter) of all my views."[19]

Darwin was the *only* scientist who found his *Beagle* evidence sufficiently compelling to adopt an evolutionary explanation for it. None of the experts, including John Gould, who helped him to classify and interpret his *Beagle* specimens were swayed by this remarkable evidence. Nor were any of the numerous naturalists persuaded who personally examined Darwin's Galápagos species at various meetings of the London Zoological Society. Darwin brought the Galápagos evidence to the attention of several of his closest scientific friends, including fellow geologist Charles Lyell, but none of these colleagues felt impelled to question their creationist beliefs.[20] In rejecting creationism Darwin did not invent the notion of evolution. Earlier theories had preceded his own. His major contribution was the theory of natural selection.

NATURAL SELECTION

Approximately fifteen months after Darwin had begun his formal inquiry into the transmutation of species, he happened across Thomas Malthus's *Essay on the Principle of Population* (1798). In his essay, Malthus had pointed out that human populations have the tendency to increase "geometrically" (or exponentially). This growth rate can never be maintained, however, because the food supply expands only arithmetically. Population growth is continually held in check, Malthus argued, by famine, disease, and war, or by reproductive restraint. Part of Darwin's genius was to realize that these Malthusian principles applied to all populations, not just to human beings. In his *Autobiography* Darwin later recalled his reaction upon reading Malthus's essay:

> Being well prepared to appreciate the struggle for existence which everywhere goes on from long-continued observation of the habits of animals and plants, it at once struck me that under these circumstances favourable variations would tend to be preserved,

> and unfavourable ones to be destroyed. The result of this would be the formation of new species. Here, then, I had at last got a theory by which to work.[21]

Darwin spent the next fifteen years publishing his scientific results from the *Beagle* voyage. His Galápagos evidence became well publicized in the process, receiving a prominent place in his *Journal of Researches* (1839) and in a subsequent zoological monograph (1841). Darwin did take time out, in 1842, to write a 35-page sketch of his evolutionary theory. Two years later he expanded this sketch into a 230-page essay. He also took the precaution of writing a letter to his wife asking her to arrange publication of his essay in case of his premature death.[22] Darwin was determined not to let an untoward incident thwart his revolutionary plans.

It was not until 1854 that Darwin began to work on his "Big Book," *Natural Selection*.[23] The writing of this evolutionary treatise was interrupted in July 1858 when a stunned Darwin received a brief manuscript from Alfred Russel Wallace, sent from Malaysia. Wallace's essay contained the same theory of natural selection that Darwin had developed twenty years earlier! Like Darwin, Wallace had found the evidence of geographic distribution, especially from the Malay Archipelago, a powerful argument for evolution.

Joint honor for the theory was assured for both discoverers by the amicable publication of Wallace's manuscript together with extracts from Darwin's essay of 1844.[24] The resulting announcement of their theory by the prestigious Linnean Society of London created surprisingly little stir. The effect of the Darwin-Wallace papers on Thomas Bell, president of that society, is typical. He concluded a review of the society's activities for 1858 with the classic understatement: "The year . . . has not, indeed, been marked by any of those striking discoveries which at once revolutionize, so to speak, the department of science on which they bear."[25] Two decades earlier, Bell had provided the taxonomic descriptions of Darwin's two Galápagos iguanas. Then, as later, Bell was impervious to an evolutionary interpretation of this evidence.

Following the reading at the Linnean Society of their joint papers, Darwin felt the necessity of bolstering his ideas with additional evidence. Instead of finishing his big book, which was only half written, he hastened to get a briefer version of his argument into print. This work appeared in November 1859 as *On the Origin of Species by Means of*

Natural Selection. The *Origin* was indeed "the book that shook the world" and it inaugurated perhaps the most important revolution in the history of modern science.[26]

Most of Darwin's contemporary readers were appalled by the conclusions of his book. Louis Agassiz, who was generally considered the world's most eminent living naturalist in 1859, blasted Darwin's theory as "a scientific mistake, untrue in its facts, unscientific in its method, and mischievous in its tendency."[27] Darwin's old geology teacher, Cambridge University professor Adam Sedgwick, wrote to him in bitter dismay: "I have read your book with more pain than pleasure. . . . Parts I read with absolute sorrow, because I think them utterly false and grievously mischievous. You have *deserted*—after a start in that tram-road of all solid physical truth—the true method of induction."[28] To another correspondent Sedgwick commented even more disdainfully about the *Origin:* "From the first to the last it is a dish of rank materialism cleverly cooked and served up."[29] Pierre Flourens, the Perpetual Secretary of the French Academy of Sciences, devoted a whole book to refuting Darwin's theory. "What unclear ideas, what false ideas!" he exhorted. "What metaphysical jargon clumsily hurled into natural history! What pretentious and empty language! What childish and out-of-date personifications! Oh lucidity! Oh French stability of mind, where art thou?"[30]

It was even possible for some individuals to see Darwin's evidence as proof of creationism, not evolution. The captain of the *Beagle,* Robert FitzRoy, commented on the Galápagos finches in just such a creationist vein in his *Narrative* of the voyage. In contrast to his own ship's naturalist, he wrote: "All the small birds that live on these lava-covered islands have short beaks, very thick at the base, like that of a bullfinch. This appears to be one of these admirable provisions of Infinite Wisdom by which each created thing is adapted to the place for which it was intended."[31]

In 1872, a year before his death, Louis Agassiz decided to retrace Darwin's footsteps in South America as a critical test of Darwin's evolutionary claims.[32] Agassiz was so convinced that evolution could not be true that he managed to find facts from the Galápagos to support this viewpoint. Surveying the recent lava flows that abound in this archipelago, he concluded that sufficient geological time was lacking for such a slow process as evolution. Agassiz never bothered to visit the Galápagos highlands, as Darwin had done. There Agassiz would have encountered a very different story. These elevated regions show evidence of extensive erosion and of relatively ancient volcanic structures. One glance at

Three distinct ecological zones in the Galápagos Archipelago. *Above:* The arid zone, covered with recent lava flows, on James Island. The prominent "Pinnacle Rock," in Sulivan's Bay, is the remains of a volcanic tuff cone, the outsides of which have eroded away, leaving the harder basalt lava plug. This barren volcanic landscape impressed Louis Agassiz with the geologically recent age of the Galápagos Islands and led him to conclude that there was not enough time for evolution to have taken place. *Below, left:* The highest ecological zone in the Galápagos (the fern and sedge belt), on Indefatigable Island. The old volcanic cones have largely eroded away into rolling hillocks. The prominent feature to the left is, like Pinnacle Rock, the remaining basalt interior of an old volcanic cone. *Below, right:* The author photographing Darwin's finches in the humid zone, which is dominated by forests of *Scalesia* trees, and by numerous epiphytic ferns, orchids, and mosses. Had Agassiz, like Darwin, visited the Galápagos highlands, he might have been more impressed with the amount of geological time actually available for evolutionary change in this archipelago.

the terrain of the Galápagos highlands is sufficient to tell an experienced naturalist that several million years are available to explain evolutionary change. It seems that Agassiz found in the Galápagos only the evidence he had been anxiously seeking.

These and other contemporary reactions to Darwin's evidence for evolution tell us something important: No matter how compelling this evidence was in *Darwin's* mind, it was not convincing to others. This circumstance underscores the deep-seated ideological commitments that most naturalists were unwilling to abandon. Such commitments included a belief in a constant world, the theory of Design, and the presumption of man's unique status in the Creation.[33] The diverse reactions to Darwin's evidence for evolution underscore an important principle about science. "Facts" in science do not speak for themselves but assume their meaning based on theoretical and ideological commitments. The practice and the beliefs of scientists are embedded in a greater social context.

The profoundly social character of science is what prompted Thomas Kuhn, in his *Structure of Scientific Revolutions,* to stress that an intellectual "crisis" is required to bring about most scientific revolutions.[34] Without a crisis, Kuhn argued, scientists are inclined to dismiss anomalous findings, attributing them to error.[35] Only when scientists are repeatedly unable to make anomalous evidence harmonize with their current theoretical assumptions do they finally admit that their theories may be wrong. During this state of growing crisis, innovation finally becomes acceptable and science enters a period of revolution.[36]

As some historians of science have pointed out, anomalous evidence—the stuff that supposedly spawns most scientific revolutions—is usually recognized as anomalous only after the fact.[37] The human mind finds it much easier to assimilate facts into existing cognitive structures than to accommodate these structures to anomalous findings. The history of science is replete with evidence that confirms the observation that *most scientists resist innovation.*[38]

Copernicus's claim that the earth revolves around the sun required more than a century to be fully endorsed. The Newtonian revolution in celestial mechanics took six decades to replace Descartes's rival theory of gravitation based on swirling vortices. And Alfred Wegener's theory of continental drift, proposed in 1912, was not accepted until the mid 1960s—more than half a century after its announcement. The doctrine of evolution was clearly enunciated by de Maillet and Maupertuis in the 1740s, fully a century before Darwin's ideas finally prevailed on this topic.[39] Resistance to Darwin's evolutionary ideas reflects a general phenomenon that has occurred over and over again in the history of science. Darwin himself once remarked on this topic: "It seems to me a very striking fact that the Newtonian theory of gravitation, which seems to every one now so certain and plain, was rejected by a man so extraordinarily able as Leibnitz. The truth will not penetrate a preoccupied mind."[40]

Kuhn's notion of intellectual crisis posits that scientists respond as a community to innovation. How well does Kuhn's sociological perspective apply to Darwin's own case? In some ways it seems to fit, especially given the near unanimity with which fellow naturalists assimilated Darwin's Galápagos findings into a creationist framework. There is little indication, moreover, that a state of crisis existed in natural history during the 1830s, or even during the decade immediately preceding the publication of Darwin's *Origin*.[41] In his *Autobiography* Darwin remarked in this connection:

> I occasionally sounded out not a few naturalists, and never happened to come across a single one who seemed to doubt about the permanence of species. Even Lyell and Hooker, though they would listen with interest to me, never seemed to agree. I tried once or twice to explain to able men what I meant by natural selection, but signally failed.[42]

In the 1840s, evolutionary thinking was considered a sign of scientific incompetence rather than a solution to widespread problems in interpreting the existing data. To dabble in evolution was to dabble in pseudoscience, which for many scientists was even worse than entertaining a heresy. Robert Chambers, the Edinburgh publisher and geologist who influenced so many naturalists, took elaborate steps to conceal his identity as the author of the anonymously published *Vestiges of the Natural History of Creation* (1844). This speculative work claimed that the solar system had developed from "a universal Fire Mist," and that life had subsequently arisen on earth by a natural process of "development." Chambers's book was widely read and just as widely criticized. Darwin's mentor in geology, Adam Sedgwick, spoke for many other scientists when he exclaimed: "From the bottom of my soul I loathe and detest the Vestiges."[43]

Only in 1884, thirteen years after Robert Chambers's death, did his authorship finally become known. Seeking anonymity for a "history-making" innovation would seem like an odd precaution if science had really reached a stage of crisis. Similarly, in a recognized state of crisis, Darwin would not have felt that divulging his views to a fellow scientist was "like confessing a murder."[44]

Given the lack of a community-wide crisis during the pre-*Origin* period, evolutionists had a difficult time getting anyone to listen to their ideas. Most scientists believed that the theory of creation was in good shape, so they were uninterested in radical alternatives and inclined to ridicule those colleagues who dared to propose them. Yet, Kuhn's approach fails to explain why Chambers, Darwin, Wallace, and various other scientific radicals were prompted to challenge orthodoxy in the absence of a general crisis. As one critic has observed: "Kuhn accords far too passive a role to individual scientists in bringing about a revolution."[45] Other customary approaches to scientific innovation, such as the appeal to "genius," are equally inadequate to explain why some scientists ultimately rebel against entrenched dogmas. It may have taken a genius like Darwin to write the *Origin of Species,* but superior intelligence was not enough. Other equally intelligent scientists failed to see the problem, much less the need for a solution.[46]

Reception of the *Origin of Species* illustrates another important phenomenon. Individual attitudes toward Darwin's theories varied enormously. For every die-hard critic of evolution who could not see the light, just as many zealous converts found it hard to believe that they had not come around sooner. Thomas Henry Huxley's famous line, upon first mastering the central idea of the *Origin,* comes to mind: "How extremely stupid not to have thought of that!"[47] Similarly, Hewett Cottrell Watson, who had become an evolutionist in the 1830s, wrote to Darwin shortly after reading the *Origin:* "You are the greatest revolutionist in natural history in this century, if not of all centuries. . . . Now [that] these novel views are brought fairly before the public, it seems truly remarkable how so many of them could have failed to see their right road sooner."[48] Watson's perceptive observation reinforces my basic point. What made Darwin a revolutionary thinker was not facts but rather a certain type of personality—a *revolutionary* personality.

To be sure, innovation involves a strong social component, as does the process by which new ideas compete for support. Still, the initiators of scientific revolutions are never scientific communities, even when communities happen to be in a state of crisis. The initiators—unconventional people like Darwin—are always individuals with a vision.

Like artistic creativity, scientific innovation is not well understood at the level of the individual. The Darwinian revolution reveals the full magnitude of the problem. Some people, it would appear, are inclined to challenge established truths. The question is *why.*

2

BIRTH ORDER AND SCIENTIFIC REVOLUTIONS

What differentiates revolutionary thinkers from nonrevolutionary ones is almost never a greater knowledge of the facts. Darwin knew far less about the various species he collected on the *Beagle* voyage than did the experts back in England who later classified these organisms for him. Yet expert after expert missed the revolutionary significance of what Darwin had collected. Darwin, who knew less, somehow understood more.[1]

Examples such as Darwin suggest that the capacity for radical innovation requires more than just exposure to anomalous findings. One must also be willing to act upon these anomalous facts, by taking them seriously and by developing new theories to explain them. This crucial aspect of the creative process requires what psychologists term *openness to experience.* People who exhibit openness are described as imaginative, flexible, creative, independent, and liberal.[2] Such people enjoy exposure to novel situations and experiences.

Research on siblings, including twins reared together or apart, indicates that openness is heritable. About 30 to 40 percent of the variance in this and other personality traits is now thought to be genetic. The big surprise from this research is the discovery that environmental influences on personality are largely specific to the individual.[3] For openness to experience, the shared family environment explains only 5 percent of the variance in test scores. By comparison, nonshared environmental influences appear to explain 35 percent of the variance—a sevenfold difference!

For siblings growing up within the same family, nonshared experiences have two general sources. The first source is *chance experiences,* many of which occur outside the family—at school, for example. The second source is *systematic influences,* most of which occur within the family. The concept of "niches" is useful in this regard and describes how individuals develop differing roles within the family system. The concept of niches derives from the field of ecology, where it exemplifies how different species use available resources within their environments.[4] Family niches may be conceptualized in a similar manner. Siblings compete with one another in an effort to secure physical, emotional, and intellectual resources from parents. Depending on differences in birth order, gender, physical traits, and aspects of temperament, siblings create differing roles for themselves within the family system. These differing roles in turn lead to disparate ways of currying parental favor. Eldest children, for example, are likely to seek parental favor by acting as surrogate parents toward their younger siblings. Younger siblings are not in a position to ingratiate themselves with parents in the same manner. Their niche is typically less parent identified, less driven by conscientious behavior, and more inclined toward sociability. As children become older and their unique interests and talents begin to emerge, siblings become increasingly diversified in their niches. One sibling may become recognized for athletic prowess, whereas another may manifest artistic talents. Yet another sibling may be good at mediating arguments and become the family diplomat. Because siblings—even identical twins—occupy different niches, they experience the family in diverse ways.

To the extent that personality can be traced to systematic differences in family niches, rather than to idiosyncratic experiences, the task of explaining personality is made considerably more manageable. One candidate for partitioning the family environment into niches is birth order. Ordinal position sums up several important considerations, not just one. It is a proxy for differences in age, size, power, and privilege within the family system. For these reasons, birth order provides a potential Rosetta stone for deciphering some of the basic principles that govern family niches.

Differences in personality have been reported by birth order for a wide variety of traits.[5] These differences are sufficiently large that firstborns appear to be more similar in their personalities to other firstborns than they are to their own younger siblings. In particular, eldest children tend to identify more closely with parents and authority.[6] This well-documented tendency is consistent with the general profile of firstborns as ambitious, conscientious, and achievement oriented. Relative to their younger siblings, eldest children are also more conforming, conventional, and defensive—attributes that are all *negative* features of openness to experience.

These birth-order trends hold true not only in personality psychology but also throughout recorded history, as I shall argue in this book. History is itself a "personality test," and it possesses distinct advantages in this regard. In the course of history, people engage in behaviors that are difficult or impossible to study in the psychological laboratory, in part because these behaviors are sometimes illegal. Even when experimental studies are possible, psychologists are often unsure whether their findings hold true for real-life behavior.[7] By contrast, historians need not worry whether the burning of heretics was ever relevant to the real world. For these and other reasons, the causes of openness to radical change are best studied by means of the historical record.

BIOLOGICAL VERSUS FUNCTIONAL BIRTH ORDER

Birth order can be assessed as a *biological* as well as a *functional* category.* What matters for personality is not only what biological dispositions individuals are endowed with at birth, but what kind of environment they are born into. The key to birth-order effects is family niches, so functional birth order is my concern throughout this book.[8] In many cases, biological and functional birth order are the same. Still, functional birth order does change owing to sibling mortality, adoption, remarriage, and other circumstances. The existence of these ambiguous cases does not negate the fact that most individuals have spent their childhood and adolescence in stable sibling positions. I employ evidence from *these* families to test for possible birth-order differences.

Whenever information on age gaps between siblings is available, I have recorded it.[9] In conjunction with birth order, this information is moderately predictive of openness to experience and other features of personality. For example, firstborns whose closest siblings are six or more years younger are functionally similar to only children. Singletons

---

* Throughout this book I distinguish the term *birth order* from *birth rank*. *Birth order* is the more general term, which I use to distinguish firstborns (who include only children) from laterborns. The term *birth rank* refers to specific differences by ordinal position, such as being a first, second, or third child. I frequently employ the term *sibship size* to denote the number of children in a given family, preferring this term to *family size,* which is ambiguous.

represent a kind of "controlled experiment"—what it is like to grow up unaffected by birth order or sibling rivalry. Although singletons tend to score somewhere between firstborns and laterborns on most personality measures, they are typically closer to firstborns on openness to experience. The reason is that only children, like other firstborns, tend to identify with parents and authority. In the course of this book I consider some of the behavioral differences between these two sibling positions. Although these differences are typically small, they can be demonstrated with large samples. When analyzing attitudes toward scientific innovation, I group the only children with other firstborns, unless I specify otherwise.[10]

Much of the fascination of history lies in its strange details, many of which involve the family. Such bizarre happenings provide dramatic evidence for birth order as a functional construct. Darwin's American critic Louis Agassiz was his parents' fifth child but the first to survive infancy. Three younger siblings lived to adulthood.[11] Functionally, Agassiz was the eldest of four children, which is how I code him.

Like Agassiz, the French naturalist Georges Cuvier grew up as an eldest child owing to the death of an older brother. Although Cuvier's legal name was Jean-Léopold, his parents always called him Georges, after his deceased brother. Cuvier had one other sibling, Frédéric, who was four years his junior. Functionally, Georges Cuvier was the elder of two children.[12]

Cases like those of Louis Agassiz and the elder Cuvier underscore the importance of how people are raised. In spite of being "biological" laterborns, neither of these two scientists was known for his open-mindedness. About Agassiz, one historian of science has asserted: "He seemed constitutionally incapable to entertain honest doubts of his judgment and too proud to admit his own errors."[13] Another historian reaffirms this verdict, noting that Agassiz demanded "unquestioning loyalty" from his coworkers and was "driven by a perpetual passion that tolerated no opposition."[14]

As for Cuvier, his political ideal was enlightened despotism. One historian of science has summed up this eminent firstborn's mental framework:

> He was . . . convinced that a peaceful and orderly mind was a correct mind, just as the peaceful and orderly society was the correct society. . . . In order to assure peace, men must adhere to accepted and traditional practices. . . . [15]

Louis Agassiz in 1861 (age fifty-four). About this time Agassiz was asked his opinion on the future of the Negro race in the United States. He replied: "There is no more one-sided doctrine concerning human nature than the idea that all men are equal, in the sense of being equally capable of fostering human progress and advancing civilization, especially in the various spheres of intellectual and moral activity. . . . Social equality I deem at all times impracticable,—a natural impossibility, from the very character of the Negro race . . ." (E. Agassiz 1885, 2:603–605).

Another Cuvier scholar observes: "He had a somewhat Germanic mentality and envisioned society as a sort of organism in which subordination was the rule. Although he was very pliant toward his 'superiors,' he was authoritarian toward those he deemed his 'inferiors.' . . ."[16]

Cuvier served faithfully under Napoleon Bonaparte and three Restoration monarchs, one of whom made him a baron. Nicknamed the Mammoth owing to his imposing physique, Cuvier saw himself as a "bishop of science."[17] As councilor of state after 1814, he oversaw the French scientific establishment, pursuing radical evolutionists as if they were heretics. Cuvier's "vanity was boundless, as was his hunger for honors and praise."[18] Stendhal once remarked of him: "What servility and baseness has not been shown toward those in power by M. Cuvier."[19]

Cuvier's younger brother, Frédéric, who also became a naturalist, was the antithesis of his famous elder sibling. One biographer describes

Georges Cuvier, in his early sixties, from a posthumous portrait. When he died in May 1832, at the age of sixty-four, Cuvier had just begun drafting a sustained critique of evolutionary theory. In his last lecture, "having pronounced an anathema on useless scientific theories and upon the pantheism of Kielmeyer, Lamarck, and Geoffroy [Saint-Hilaire], he rendered solemn homage to Divine Intelligence, the Creator of all things, before an audience overcome by emotion" (Bourdier 1971b:527).

That same month a young naturalist named Charles Darwin arrived in Rio de Janeiro. He was on the first leg of the five-year voyage that would turn him against Cuvier's creationist teachings.

him as "modest and gentle" and notes that he attracted "loyal friends."[20] Beneath his modest exterior, however, Frédéric was "often audacious" in his scientific ideas.[21] One of his most important discoveries was that primate social groups tend to be hierarchical, with one dominant male at the top. He could easily have been describing his brother's place in French natural history.

Alfred Russel Wallace, who became a socialist, provides another instructive contrast with functional firstborns like Agassiz and the elder Cuvier. As codiscoverer of the theory of natural selection, Wallace's scientific originality has always suffered in comparison with Darwin's, causing one biographer to refer to him as "Darwin's Moon."[22] A younger son, Wallace was the eighth of his parents' nine offspring.

Three older sisters died before he was born, so Wallace grew up, like Darwin, as the fifth of six children.[23] Wallace's younger brother Edward died at the age of twenty-two, while helping him collect specimens in the Amazon. By my guidelines, Edward's death is too late to affect his older brother's functional birth rank or his status as a middle child.

The famous Danish astronomer Tycho Brahe was the eldest male and the second of twelve children born to a noble Danish family. A twin brother was stillborn. Three of Tycho's younger siblings died in infancy. Except for a quirk of family history, Tycho would have grown up as the second of eight offspring. Sibling conflict, in this case involving the previous Brahe generation, thwarted this scenario.

Tycho's father, Otto, had an elder brother, George, who was "cut from the ancient warrior pattern."[24] Although married, George was childless. As an eldest son, George was anxious to perpetuate the family line. He therefore informed his younger brother that, given the fertile condition of Otto's wife, "it was only fitting and proper for them to share their wealth, so to speak."[25] Otto and his wife did not agree, and negotiations on the subject broke down sometime after Tycho's birth. When Otto's wife gave birth to a second son, twelve months later, George took matters into his own hands. While the parents were away from home, he kidnapped young Tycho. Otto Brahe threatened murder in response, but he eventually cooled down and accepted the arrangement, which ensured his son a considerable inheritance.

As a result of being kidnapped by his uncle, Tycho Brahe grew up as an only child living on an estate 50 miles from his natural parents' home. During his childhood he had little contact with his biological siblings. Had Tycho not been kidnapped and raised separately by his aunt and uncle, I would have recorded him as (1) a laterborn, (2) a second child, (3) an eldest son, and (4) one of eight surviving siblings. Instead I record him as an only child.

Tycho turned out to be an "arrogant" and "uncompromising" fellow, more like a firstborn than a laterborn.[26] He seems to have taken after his foster father, who had a reputation for keeping underlings in their place and was known as a "peasant baiter."[27] Although Tycho was an innovator in some important aspects of astronomy, he was hardly a radical revolutionary, and he thought Copernicus's ideas about a moving earth to be "physically absurd."[28]

Tycho eventually precipitated his own death, at the age of fifty-five, owing to his reluctance to commit a breach of etiquette. While dining out one night in polite society and drinking "a bit overgenerously," he

Tycho Brahe in 1586 (age forty). A hot-tempered individual who was notorious for his quarrels over scientific priority, Tycho had part of his nose sliced off in a duel when he was twenty. As a result of his injury, he was forced to wear a cosmetic nosepiece of gold and silver alloy (shown in the portrait). The argument may have involved an erroneous astrological prediction on Tycho's part. Two months before the duel, he had forecast the death of the Turkish sultan Suleiman the Great, based on the occurrence of a lunar eclipse. Soon afterward, news arrived that the sultan had died, six weeks *before* the eclipse. Tycho was widely ridiculed for his blunder. In later life he was reluctant to cast horoscopes.

declined to excuse himself from the table in order to relieve his bladder.[29] As a result of retaining his urine for most of the evening, he developed a bladder obstruction and died nine days later. A man who was incapable of setting aside table manners for a call of nature was hardly suited to challenging, as Copernicus did, the foundations of cosmology.

REVOLUTIONS IN SCIENCE

The history of science has been punctuated by more than a dozen conceptual battles that are now recognized as "revolutions" and that were often regarded as such at the time.[30] The Copernican, Newtonian, and Darwinian revolutions are three prominent examples. These and other major intellectual transformations in science have been diligently studied by historians. The resulting secondary literature has enabled me to assemble a database that includes 3,890 scientists who passed judgment on 28 such innovations. My survey includes 16 events that are widely considered to be "revolutions" in science, along with another 12 innovations entailing less radical consequences.

Before I present my findings about birth order and scientific innovation, I must first explain how these samples were gathered. In collecting historical evidence, I have tried to follow three basic rules: (1) samples should be *representative;* (2) assessments of scientific stance should be *accurate;* and (3) because they involve judgment, assessments also require a demonstration of *reliability.*

I have documented participation in scientific innovations in two steps. By reading through the secondary literature, I developed *preliminary samples* for each debate, making a record of each individual reported to have spoken out.[31] In most instances, I was able to classify scientists as "supporters" or "opponents" of innovation, based on explicit statements by historians.[32]

The *final samples* were arrived at in consultation with more than a hundred experts in the history of science. These historians assisted me by validating my preliminary samples and by rating the participants on various scales (including a formal scale of "scientific stance").[33] Experts were also asked to nominate any individuals they thought were missing from my preliminary lists. About two hundred participants, mostly minor figures, were nominated in this manner. All nominated individuals whose scientific views could be confirmed by a published source were added to the final lists. Owing to changes in allegiances over time, some individuals are entered more than once in my database.

Assessing Attitudes toward Scientific Innovation

In deciding what constitutes acceptance of a scientific theory, I have used two scales—one binary and one continuous. My binary scale records whether an individual supported or opposed a given innova-

Charles Lyell in 1865 (age sixty-seven), during the height of debate over Darwin's theories. Lyell had long been disturbed by the possibility that mankind might be descended from brutes, and he stopped short of endorsing this controversial theory in his *Antiquity of Man* (1863). Having expected Lyell to announce his conversion, Darwin was greatly dismayed. After reading Lyell's *Antiquity of Man,* Darwin commented to Joseph Hooker: "The best joke is that he thinks he has acted with the courage of a martyr of old" (Darwin 1887, 3:9).

tion, which is how the secondary literature typically reports this information. The continuous scale assesses attitudes from 1 (extreme opposition) to 7 (extreme support). To be a supporter of Darwin's theories on a binary scale, one had to accept (1) that evolution occurs and (2) that natural selection is a plausible, although not necessarily an exclusive, cause of evolution.[34] Charles Lyell, who was the eldest of ten children, rejected both of these propositions until 1868. He is classified as an opponent before this date and as a guarded convert afterward.

Whenever sufficient information has been provided in the secondary literature, I have classified attitudes toward evolution using a 7-point scale for scientific stance. As an added precaution, I have asked ten historians of science—all experts on the Darwinian revolution—to provide independent ratings using the same scale.[35] The use of a continuous rating scale provides more leeway for assessing individual differences in how scientists responded to Darwinism (Table 1).

For his initially hesitant reaction to Darwin's *Origin of Species* (1859), Charles Lyell is rated 3.75, which places him just below the midpoint of the scale. As a close personal friend of Darwin's, Lyell was anxious to ensure a fair hearing for Darwin's evolutionary views. Along with Joseph Hooker, Lyell communicated the famous Darwin-Wallace papers to the Linnean Society in July 1858, where the theory of natural selection was first announced. Darwin was grateful to Lyell for his intervention and commented to Asa Gray in 1860: "Considering his age, his former views and position in society, I think his conduct has been heroic on this subject."[36]

In spite of Lyell's actions on Darwin's behalf, he was not immediately converted to a belief in evolution. Indeed, he agonized over the problem, remarking to Darwin in 1863: "I have spoken out to the utmost extent of my tether, so far as my reason goes, and farther than my imagination and sentiment can follow."[37] Darwin grew increasingly exasperated by his friend's refusal to endorse the fact of evolution.[38] More than one biographer has attributed Darwin's severe ill health around this time to his bitter disappointment over Lyell's withholding of public support.[39]

By 1868, when Lyell finally endorsed an evolutionary view of life, he is rated 4.8. This rating places him somewhat above a "neutral" stance (4.0) but below the level of "moderate" support (5.0). Lyell died in 1875, the final year covered by my survey. During the last seven years of his life he never accepted the sufficiency of natural selection or any other purely natural process of evolution. He adhered instead to a form of evolutionary change in which God preordained creative steps, especially for the evolutionary leap from apes to man. One might call Lyell's position "creative evolution," a common stance among formerly staunch creationists who eventually became evolutionists.

On the same 7-point scale, Darwin's old geology teacher Adam Sedgwick is rated 1.3 owing to his bitter opposition to Darwin's theories, which "greatly shocked" his "moral taste."[40] Louis Agassiz receives an identical rating. Shortly after publication of the *Origin,* Agassiz denounced Darwin's book as a colossal scientific blunder, and he spearheaded the opposition to Darwinism in America.[41]

TABLE 1

Examples of "Scientific Stance" During the Darwinian Revolution

Rating[a]	*Interpretation*	*Individual Examples, with Birth-Order Information* (FB = *firstborn*, LB = *laterborn*)
1.0	**EXTREME OPPOSITION** often emotional in nature	Louis Agassiz **(FB)** Karl Friedrich Schimper **(FB)** Adam Sedgwick **(LB)**
2.0	**STRONG OPPOSITION** generally reasoned in nature	Léonce Élie de Beaumont **(FB)** John Herschel **(FB)** Roderick Murchison **(FB)** William Whewell **(FB)**
3.0	**MODERATE OPPOSITION** often respectful and even sympathetic	James Dwight Dana **(FB)** John Stevens Henslow **(FB)** Fleeming Jenkin **(FB)** Richard Owen **(LB)**
4.0	**NEUTRAL OR AMBIVALENT**	Charles Lyell *(before 1868)* **(FB)** *(rated 3.75)*
5.0	**MODERATE SUPPORT** but with important qualifications	George Bentham **(LB)** William Carpenter **(LB)** Charles Lyell *(after 1868)* **(FB)** Jeffries Wyman **(LB)**
6.0	**STRONG SUPPORT** but with fewer qualifications	Asa Gray **(FB)** Joseph Dalton Hooker **(LB)** Thomas Henry Huxley **(LB)** Alfred Russel Wallace *(after 1867)* **(LB)**
7.0	**EXTREME SUPPORT** sometimes bordering on zealousness	Charles Robert Darwin **(LB)** Ernst Haeckel **(LB)** Alfred Russel Wallace *(before 1868)* **(LB)** August Weismann **(FB)**

a. Based on ratings by ten historians of science. For the purposes of this table, ratings have been averaged and rounded off to the nearest whole integer.

In contrast to these prominent opponents of evolution, Darwin is rated 6.9. All but one of my expert raters gave Darwin the highest possible score (7.0). In order to distinguish Darwin from fanatical followers like Ernst Haeckel, one judge assigned Darwin a rating of 6.0. No scientist in my sample received a rating of 7.0 from every judge. It seems as if there were no pure Darwinians—even Charles Darwin—a view that has been maintained by some historians of science.[42]

Evolution Before Darwin

My historical survey of evolutionary thinking covers the period from 1700 to 1875. This scientific revolution includes two distinct phases, demarcated by Darwin's *Origin of Species* (1859). The first person to present a genuine argument for evolution was the French geologist and diplomat Benoît de Maillet (1656–1738).[43] De Maillet believed that all life had evolved from germs in the sea. Because of the atheistic implications of his theory, de Maillet waited more than two decades before publishing it. In 1735, three years before his death, he finally presented his ideas in a book called *Telliamed*. The work was published anonymously, and without an official license, clear indications of its heterodox nature. De Maillet was not one to forgo all credit. His book's title spells his name backward.[44]

Between de Maillet's *Telliamed* and Darwin's *Origin,* more than two hundred scientists spoke out on the issue of evolution. The majority of these commentators were strongly opposed to the idea. After correcting for the fact that laterborns are more numerous than firstborns in the population we are considering, laterborns are still markedly overrepresented as champions of evolutionary theory, beginning with de Maillet himself. Other notable advocates of evolutionary ideas include Erasmus Darwin (Darwin's grandfather), Jean-Baptiste Lamarck, and Étienne Geoffroy Saint-Hilaire, each of whom was the last child in a large family. (Collectively, these three evolutionary pioneers had 29 older siblings.)

During the period prior to publication of the *Origin of Species,* 56 of the 117 laterborns, or 48 percent of those who took a published position, were favorable to some form of evolutionary theory. During this same period, firstborns were pronounced in their opposition. Of the 103 firstborns whose opinions I have been able to document, only 9 (or 9 percent) were sympathetic to evolution, and 5 of these individuals were converted between 1850 and 1859. (Fig. 2.1).[45]*

A simple statistic called the "odds ratio" provides an effective way of

Receptivity to Evolutionary Theory by Year and Birth Order

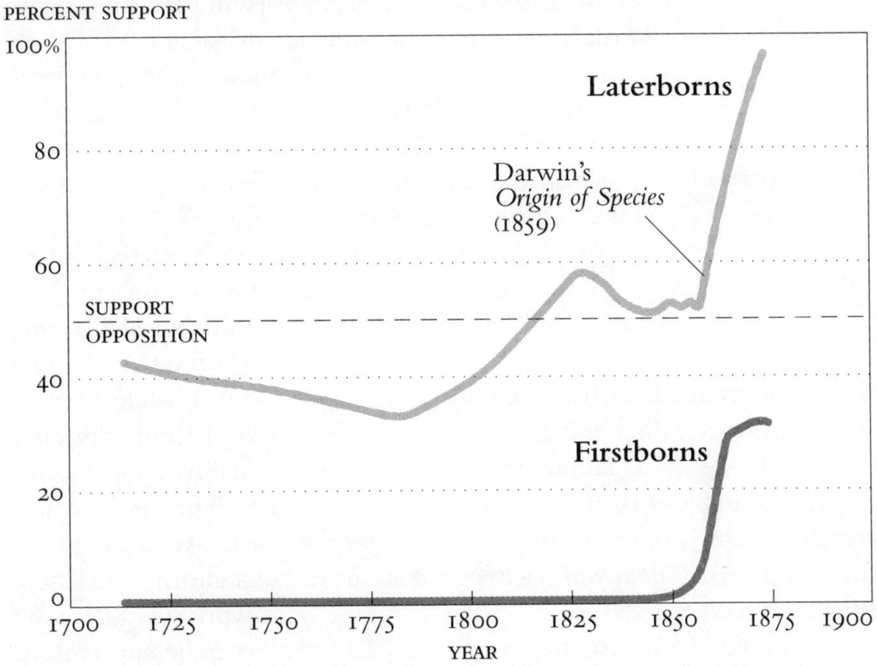

FIGURE 2.1. The reception of evolutionary theory from 1700 to 1875 by birth order ($N = 433$). During the long period of debate preceding publication of Darwin's *Origin of Species* (1859), individual laterborns were 9.7 times more likely than individual firstborns to endorse evolution. These group differences are corrected for the greater frequency of laterborns in the population. The likelihood of these birth-order differences arising by chance is less than one in a billion.

Note that firstborn conversions to Darwinism peaked soon after publication of the *Origin*. Those firstborns capable of being converted to Darwin's theories were converted quickly, leaving fewer open-minded firstborns to be converted later on.

---

* Formal statistical results for this and other charts are supplied in notes to the text, following the first reference to each chart. Most statistics in this book are presented in the form of correlations, which makes it easy to compare different effects. For readers who are unfamiliar with correlations and other basic statistical concepts, I review this topic in Appendix 1: "A Brief Introduction to Statistics (or Correlations Made Easy)."

Figure 2.1 employs a distance-weighted least squares algorithm to plot smoothed averages in support levels over time (Wilkinson and Hill 1994:380–91). Such smoothing algorithms provide a visual equivalent of regression procedures and have the virtue of emphasizing "effect sizes" rather than statistical significance.

summing up these birth-order findings. This statistic corrects for the differing frequencies of firstborns and laterborns in the population and compares the two populations on an individual-by-individual basis. During the period prior to 1859, the odds ratio was *9.7 to 1*. This means that individual laterborns, such as Darwin and Wallace, were *9.7 times more likely* than individual firstborns, such as Lyell or Agassiz, to advocate evolutionary ideas. It is unnecessary to know anything about statistics to realize that something extraordinary is going on here.

A temporary downturn in support for evolution occurred during the 1830s and early 1840s. This decline reflects the domineering influence of two firstborns, Georges Cuvier and Charles Lyell, who mounted effective campaigns against evolution at this time. Lyell's critique was set forth in his *Principles of Geology* (1830–33) while Darwin was circumnavigating the globe. In a notebook that Darwin kept after the *Beagle* voyage to record his growing ideas about evolution, he reminded himself that "Lyells Principles must be abstracted & answered."[46] One important reason why Darwin waited so long to publish his evolutionary ideas was his concern about the objections of eminent firstborns such as Lyell.

A revival of interest in evolutionary theory during the late 1840s is due largely to Robert Chambers's anonymous publication of the *Vestiges of Creation* (1844). During this period, the odds ratio in favor of laterborn evolutionists peaked at *17.5 to 1*.[47] Given odds like these, it is not surprising that Chambers was a younger son, as was his most notable convert—Alfred Russel Wallace.

The Reception of Darwinism

I have conducted a separate analysis of responses to Darwin's *Origin of Species* (1859), which substantially changed the nature of debate on this topic. Compared with individual firstborns, individual laterborns were *4.4* times more likely to support Darwin's ideas. One measure of Darwin's success was his ability to win over many firstborns who had resisted previous theories on the subject.[48] Still, a majority of firstborns had not accepted evolution by 1875, the last year of my survey. The French biologist Jean-Louis-Armand Quatrefages de Bréau—the eldest of two children—campaigned against Darwinism until his death in 1892. His last anti-Darwinian work appeared posthumously, in 1894, under the title *Les Émules de Darwin* (Darwin's Rivals). Another first-

Receptivity to Evolutionary Theory by Age and Birth Order

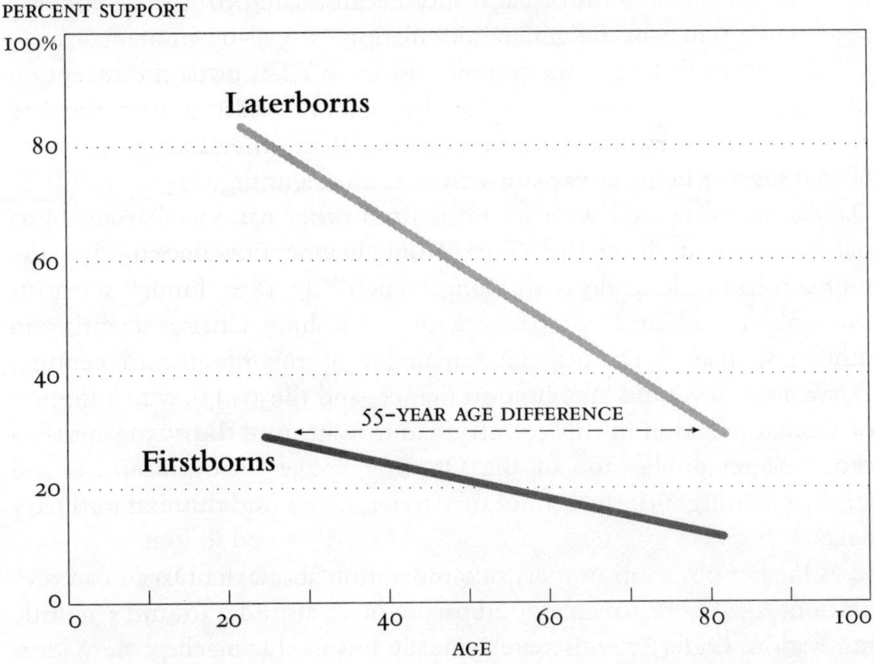

FIGURE 2.2. The reception of evolutionary theory from 1700 to 1875, stratified by age and birth order (N=405). Owing to the influence of birth order, an 80-year-old laterborn was as open to evolutionary theory as a 25-year-old firstborn.

There is a significant interaction effect between birth order and age. Because firstborns were generally hostile to evolution, they tended to oppose this theory regardless of age. To become close-minded with age, it is necessary to be open-minded during youth. Among laterborns, age exerts a substantially greater influence on attitudes toward evolution.

born, Canadian geologist John William Dawson, went to his grave in 1899 defending creationist theory.

The nineteenth century has sometimes been called "Darwin's Century" owing to the dramatic impact that Darwin's ideas had on science and social thought.[49] So great is the disparity in the reception of evolutionary ideas by birth order that the adoption process occurred in two waves that were nearly a century apart. By 1875, firstborns had achieved the same support level for evolution (40 percent) that laterborns first achieved around 1775. Simple arithmetic tells us that "Darwin's Century" only became a historical reality because laterborns outnumbered firstborns 2.6 to 1 in the general population.[50]

A curious fact of demographic history is relevant to the reception of Darwinism. France began the demographic shift during the late eighteenth century, about 50 years earlier than other European countries. This fact helps to explain why French scientists were so hostile to Darwinism compared with scientists from other nations. Darwin himself complained about the "horrid unbelieving Frenchmen," but the problem had little to do with being French.[51] In 1859, French scientists had only 1.1 siblings compared with 2.8 siblings among scientists in other countries.[52] During the remainder of the nineteenth century, Darwinism never did take hold in France, and the widespread adoption of natural selection in this country had to wait until the 1950s, nearly a century after publication of the *Origin of Species*.[53] Contraception and family planning, not the school of Cuvier, lie behind this extraordinary delay.[54]

One last observation merits consideration about the Darwinian revolution. Age is a reasonably good predictor of attitudes toward scientific innovation. Older scientists are typically less likely to accept new ideas than are younger scientists.[55] This circumstance provides a convenient yardstick for measuring the influence of birth order. Throughout the debates over evolution, 80-year-old laterborns were as open to this theory as were 25-year-old firstborns. During the Darwinian revolution, being laterborn was equivalent to a 55-year dose of the open-mindedness that typically resides in youth (Fig. 2.2).[56]

Other Scientific Controversies

It is natural to wonder whether other scientific transformations have been initiated and supported by laterborns. To answer this question, I have analyzed 28 innovations that have punctuated the history of science during the last five centuries.[57] Sixteen of these 28 innovations were selected based on their frequent citation as major "revolutions." Besides the Darwinian revolution, my list of highly cited events includes the Copernican revolution, Newtonian physics, and Einstein's theories of special and general relativity.[58]

Some scientific revolutions have been more heavily imbued with ideological implications than others.[59] Therefore, it is useful to subdivide these 16 innovations into two groups—Radical Ideological Revolutions and Technical Revolutions.[60] Newton was knighted for his scientific efforts, whereas Galileo was tried for heresy.

To be classified as a Radical Ideological Revolution, a theory must have provoked widespread religious controversy. I have employed formal indicators of this criterion, such as whether books on the subject were placed on the Catholic Church's *Index Librorum Prohibitorum*. Another sign of a Radical Ideological Revolution is the tendency for scientists to publish their ideas anonymously, as did de Maillet, Chambers, and half a dozen other pre-Darwinian evolutionists. By these guidelines, only 4 of my 16 major breakthroughs are Radical Ideological Revolutions, namely, Copernican theory, James Hutton's theory of the earth, pre-Darwinian theories of evolution, and Darwinism.[61]

Hutton's theory of the earth is less well known than other radical revolutions, but it was no less heterodox. In contrast to contemporary scientists who emphasized catastrophic mechanisms of geological change—including the Mosaic Deluge—Hutton proposed the doctrine of "uniformitarianism." This approach allowed no geological processes other than those observable today, such as erosion and weathering. To explain major changes in the earth's crust, Huttonians required immense amounts of time—millions of years. In a well-known phrase, Hutton described the world as having "no vestige of a beginning,—no prospect of an end."[62] By drastically lengthening the geological timescale from the biblically allotted 6,000 years, Hutton prepared the way for Darwin.[63] Because Hutton's geological ideas clashed with biblical chronology, they were widely criticized for their atheistic implications. Like Darwin, Hutton was a laterborn.

In addition to the 16 events that historians of science have judged to be major revolutions in science, I have investigated another 12 innovations of a less profound nature. Like revolutions, these 12 breakthroughs can be divided into two groups. One group—Controversial Innovations—encompasses 7 of the 12 inventions. This category includes Ignaz Semmelweis's ideas about childbed fever and Joseph Lister's introduction of antiseptic surgery. Although these two medical developments represent important advances, historians of science have not generally viewed them as major "revolutions."

I call the fourth and last group of inventions Conservative Theories. This category comprises five doctrines that lent support to established religion or to upper-class values. Historically, the life sciences have served as a fertile spawning ground for conservative doctrines. During the seventeenth century various mechanistic explanations of life began to invade biology, seriously threatening the explanatory role of the Creator. "Vitalists" were strongly opposed to "materialist" theories of life, and vitalistic doctrines were often bolstered with appeals to religious considerations.[64] In 1766 Albrecht von Haller explained this conservative agenda in a letter to a fellow naturalist: "Beware that it is very dangerous to admit the formation of a finger by chance. If a finger can form itself, a hand will form itself, and an arm, and a man."[65] Most of Haller's scientific battles, notes one historian of biology, "turn on the theme of reverence for God and condemnation for atheists and materialists."[66]

Conservative Theories can be thought of as the antithesis of Radical Ideological Revolutions. From Linnaeus to Darwin, most systems of biological classification were based on creationist theory, which they sought to promote. These naturalists developed a variety of new systems of classification that reflected their beliefs about Divine Wisdom. Some of these "idealistic" systems involved numerological assumptions.[67] "Quinarians," for example, thought that species were designed according to five overlapping groups, each arranged in a circle. Within each circle, quinarians identified five more circles. Other biologists preferred the number seven, coinciding with the seven days of creation. For these pious exponents of idealist zoology, God was a mathematician, somewhat more clever than Euclid. Zoological idealists were at distinct odds with the radical faction that engineered the Darwinian revolution. As one science historian has remarked, the two groups championed different "social and natural worlds" and were often "bitterly antagonistic" toward one another.[68]

I provide a complete listing of the 28 controversies in my survey, along with information about birth order, in Table 2. For each controversy, my findings are summed up by the odds ratio (printed in **boldface type**). The first event in the table is the Copernican revolution. During the early stages of this controversy, the odds ratio was *5.4 to 1* in favor of laterborns. This means that *individual laterborns* were *5.4* times more likely than *individual firstborns* to support Copernicus's claim that the earth revolves around the sun. Copernicus himself was the youngest of four children.

TABLE 2
Birth-Order Data on 28 Scientific Controversies

Controversy	*Years Surveyed*	*Known Birth Orders*	*Correlation*[a]	*Relative Likelihood of Laterborn Support*[b]
RADICAL IDEOLOGICAL REVOLUTIONS (*N* = 4)				
Copernican revolution (to 1609)	1543–1609	30	.38*	**5.4 to 1**
Copernican revolution (after 1609)	1610–1649	51	.00	**1.0 to 1**
Evolution prior to Darwin	1700–1859	221	.43***	**9.7 to 1**
Hutton's theory of the earth	1788–1829	46	.31*	**5.2 to 1**
Darwinian revolution	1859–1875	228	.36***	**4.6 to 1**
Subtotals[c]	*1543–1875*	*576*	*.36****	*4.8 to 1*
TECHNICAL REVOLUTIONS (*N* = 12)				
Bacon and Descartes (the scientific method)	1600–1685	82	.09	**1.7 to 1**
Harvey and the circulation of the blood	1628–1653	37	.34*	**5.8 to 1**
Newtonian revolution (in celestial mechanics)	1687–1750	65	.24	**3.1 to 1**
Lavoisier's chemical revolution	1778–1795	85	.25*	**3.1 to 1**

a. A positive correlation denotes greater laterborn support. All correlations (*phi*) have been computed from birth order and scientific stance coded dichotomously. Levels of statistical significance, using Fisher's exact test, are indicated by asterisks: * ($p < .05$), ** ($p < .01$), and *** ($p < .001$). Tests are two tailed.

b. The odds ratio corrects for the fact that laterborns are more numerous than firstborns in the population.

c. For subtotals, correlations are mean-weighted values. The odds ratio for each class of events is based on the Mantel-Haenszel statistic (also a weighted average).

Controversy	*Years Surveyed*	*Known Birth Orders*	*Correlation*	*Relative Likelihood of Laterborn Support*
TECHNICAL REVOLUTIONS *(cont.)*				
Glaciation theory[d]	1815–1849	42	.00	**1.0 to 1**
Lyell and uniformitarianism[e]	1830–1850	32	.06	**1.3 to 1**
Freudian psychoanalysis (to 1919)	1900–1919	90	.30**	**3.8 to 1**
Freudian psychoanalysis (after 1919)	1920–1930	36	−.04	**0.86 to 1**
Planck's quantum hypothesis	1900–1919	59	.05	**1.2 to 1**
Einstein and special relativity	1905–1914	48	.30*	**3.6 to 1**
Einstein and general relativity	1915–1930	67	.06	**1.3 to 1**
Continental drift	1912–1967	57	.24	**2.7 to 1**
Indeterminacy in physics	1918–1927	40	.18	**2.1 to 1**
Subtotals	***1600–1967***	***740***	***.18****	***2.2 to 1***
CONTROVERSIAL INNOVATIONS (*N* = 7)				
Preformation theory[f]	1600–1699	20	.41	**6.0 to 1**
Epigenesis theory	1700–1820	45	.21	**2.3 to 1**

d. Based on its affirmation of catastrophism and creationism, Louis Agassiz's concept of the ice ages is a Conservative Theory, but not all advocates of glaciation theory adopted Agassiz's catastrophist version.

e. Lyell's doctrine of uniformitarianism can also be seen as a later stage of Hutton's Radical Ideological Revolution about earth history.

f. After 1700, preformation is the conservative alternative to epigenesis.

Controversy	*Years Surveyed*	*Known Birth Orders*	*Correlation*	*Relative Likelihood of Laterborn Support*
CONTROVERSIAL INNOVATIONS *(cont.)*				
Mesmerism[g]	1780–1800	42	−.03	**0.89 to 1**
Phrenology[h]	1796–1840	98	.45***	**9.0 to 1**
Devonian controversy	1830–1840	15	.22	**2.5 to 1**
Semmelweis and puerperal fever	1842–1862	37	.22	**2.6 to 1**
Lister and antisepsis	1867–1880	45	.14	**1.9 to 1**
Subtotals	***1600–1880***	***302***	***.28****	***3.5 to 1***
CONSERVATIVE THEORIES (N = 5)[i]				
Refutations of spontaneous generation (= vitalism)	1640–1859	67	−.24*	**0.36 to 1**
Idealistic systems of classification	1809–1859	43	−.41**	**0.08 to 1**
Modern spiritualism	1848–1920	110	−.09	**0.68 to 1**
Germ theory	1859–1880	33	−.19	**0.30 to 1**
Eugenics	1864–1949	142	−.06	**0.76 to 1**
Subtotals	***1640–1949***	***395***	***−.14****	***0.54 to 1***

g. Mesmerism could perhaps be classified as a Conservative Theory owing to its status as a "fashionable parlor game for the wealthy and the well-bred" (Darnton 1968:74).

h. Phrenology is a Radical Ideological Revolution that failed. If phrenology is classified as a Radical Ideological Revolution, then the mean-weighted birth-order correlation for Controversial Innovations becomes .17, whereas that for Radical Revolutions becomes .37.

i. Doctrines about *innate racial differences* represent Conservative Theories, especially versions emphasizing the inferiority of blacks and other minority groups. Sherwood and Nataupsky (1968) report that firstborn psychologists are more likely than laterborns to believe that IQ differences between blacks and whites are innate. The odds ratio, which I have computed from their Table 2, is 0.35 to 1 in favor of greater firstborn support ($r = -.24$, $N = 82$, $p < .05$).

Overview of Results

Laterborns are consistently overrepresented among the champions of conceptual change. For the 28 innovations included in my survey, the odds are *2.0 to 1* in favor of greater laterborn adoption. The likelihood of this difference arising by chance is substantially less than one in a billion.[69] Even when the initiators of new theories turn out to be firstborn—as was the case with Newton, Lavoisier, Einstein, and Freud—the supporters are still predominantly laterborn. Among radical scientific innovators, firstborns are the exception, just as they are among scientists who welcome radical innovations.[70]

Because these findings do not distinguish between different kinds of innovations, they minimize the influence of birth order. We are justified in considering scientific innovations in terms of subgroups owing to a crucial statistical circumstance. The findings in Table 2 are significantly *heterogeneous,* which means that birth-order effects are significantly different across events.[71] Whenever findings from multiple studies are significantly different, we need to consider the possibility of "moderator" variables. In history, moderator variables tend to involve the nature of the event.

Ideological Radicalism

The importance of ideological factors in theory adoption becomes apparent when we consider each class of innovations separately. During Radical Ideological Revolutions, individual laterborns are *4.8* times more likely than individual firstborns to endorse the heterodox alternative. During Technical Revolutions, there are *2.2* times as many laterborn as firstborn adopters, an overrepresentation that is significantly smaller than for radical innovations but significantly greater than chance.

With Conservative Theories, the outcome is reversed. Individual firstborns are *1.9* times more likely than individual laterborns to adopt this class of ideas, a disparity that is also significantly different from chance. In science, firstborns are the champions of *reactionary* ideas. The more reactionary the innovation, the more firstborns are overrepresented in support of it (Fig. 2.3).

One statistical surprise involves Controversial Innovations, or new theories that are not usually ranked as revolutions. The odds ratio for this class of events is *3.4 to 1* in favor of laterborns, significantly greater

Receptivity to Scientific Innovations by Birth Order and Type of Innovation

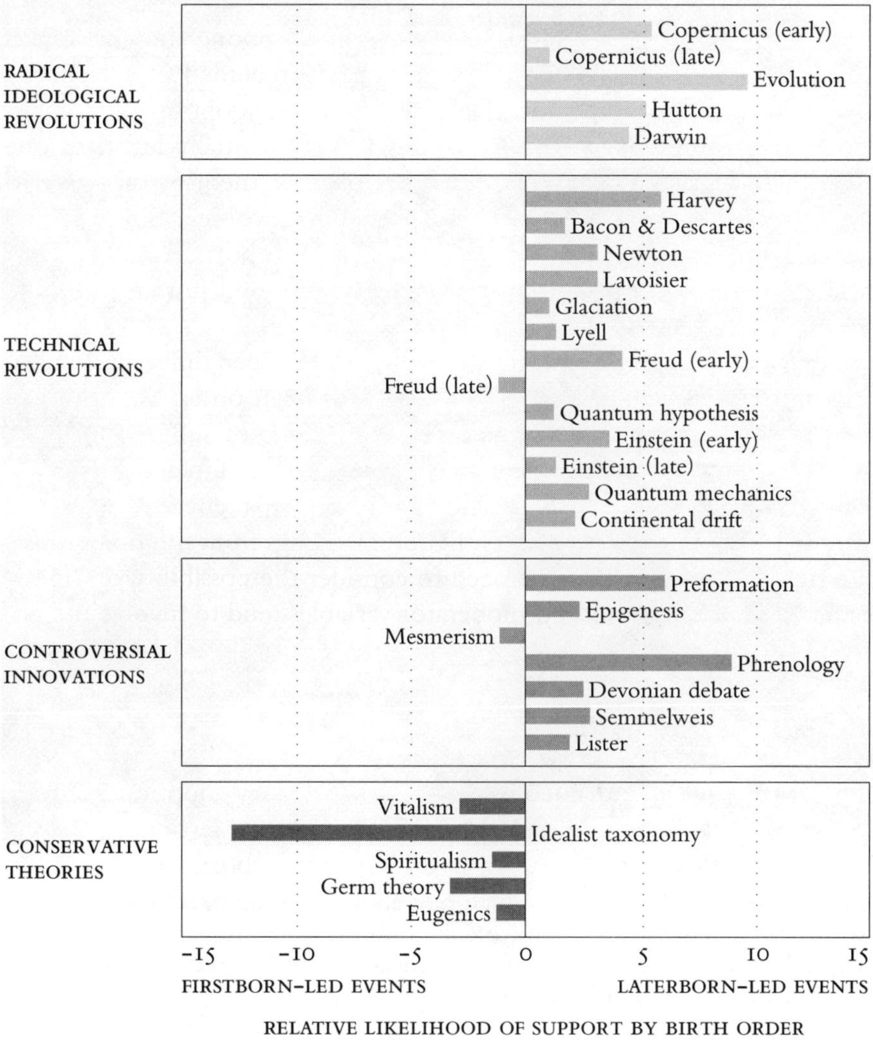

FIGURE 2.3. Birth-order effects for 28 innovations in science. For each of the four classes of innovations, a positive likelihood of support (depicted here as the odds ratio) means greater endorsement by laterborns than by firstborns, whereas a negative value means greater endorsement by firstborns. During the early stages of the Copernican revolution, prior to Galileo's telescopic discoveries, laterborns were 5.4 times more likely to uphold this theory than were firstborns. The greatest propensity for laterborns to adopt new theories ahead of firstborns is observed during Radical Ideological Revolutions. Conservative Theories are typically supported by firstborns and opposed by laterborns.

Franz Joseph Gall, holding a discussion about phrenology with some of his sympathizers, amidst his extensive collection of skulls and model heads. This satirical etching dates from 1808, and reflects the hostile reception that Gall's ideas received within orthodox medicine.

than the odds ratio for Technical Revolutions (*2.2 to 1*). I would not have predicted this difference.

The explanation for this anomaly is simple. One of the seven Controversial Innovations—phrenology—is misclassified. This doctrine posited that cognitive ability and character could be assessed via "bumps" on the skull. Developed in 1796 by Franz Joseph Gall, phrenology was based on the assumption that mental functioning could be traced to specific regions within the brain. Owing to this blatantly materialist supposition, Gall's theory seemed to deny the existence of the soul and was bitterly opposed by orthodox scientists, including Georges Cuvier. In 1801 Austrian emperor Franz Josef, in a personal letter to Gall, prohibited him from giving further public lectures on the subject, on the grounds that Gall's theories were "conducive to materialism, immorality, and atheism."[72] Upon Gall's death in 1828, Catholic authorities denied him a church burial. In addition, his phrenological writings were placed on the *Index,* meeting one of my formal criteria for status as a Radical Ideological Revolution. Consistent with the strong birth-order trend among his supporters, Gall was a laterborn—the sixth of ten children.

The case of phrenology shows that any attempt to classify scientific innovations as "revolutions" should not rely too heavily on retrospective judgments, such as being cited as a revolution by present-day historians of science.[73] At the time of their announcement, some Controversial Innovations were thought to be revolutionary achievements, including mesmerism and phrenology. To the extent that ideological heterodoxy, rather than success, is the appropriate indicator of a Radical Ideological Revolution, phrenology belongs in this radical class of events.[74]

Another difficulty that arises in classifying scientific controversies involves changes in the nature of what is being contested at different points in time. Radical revolutions that succeed eventually become technical ones. This circumstance has important consequences for birth-order effects, which become attenuated as debates make the transition from one class of events to the other. A diminution in the role of birth order occurred during the later stages of debate over Copernican theory, Hutton's theory of the earth, evolutionary theory, Freudian psychoanalysis, and relativity theory.[75] The moderating influence of time is detectable within each class of innovations, although it is significantly more pronounced during Radical Ideological Revolutions than it is during other events (Fig. 2.4).[76]

Although birth-order effects often diminish over time *within* individual controversies, these effects have not tended to diminish over time in general. In other words, birth-order effects are just as substantial during twentieth-century disputes as they were four centuries ago, after being controlled for the type of innovation.[77]

This last finding tends to rule out the possibility that birth-order differences owe themselves to the practice of primogeniture.[78] Primogeniture—the custom of leaving whole estates to eldest sons—was

Differences in Support for Scientific Innovations by Birth Order, as Related to the Phase and Type of Innovation

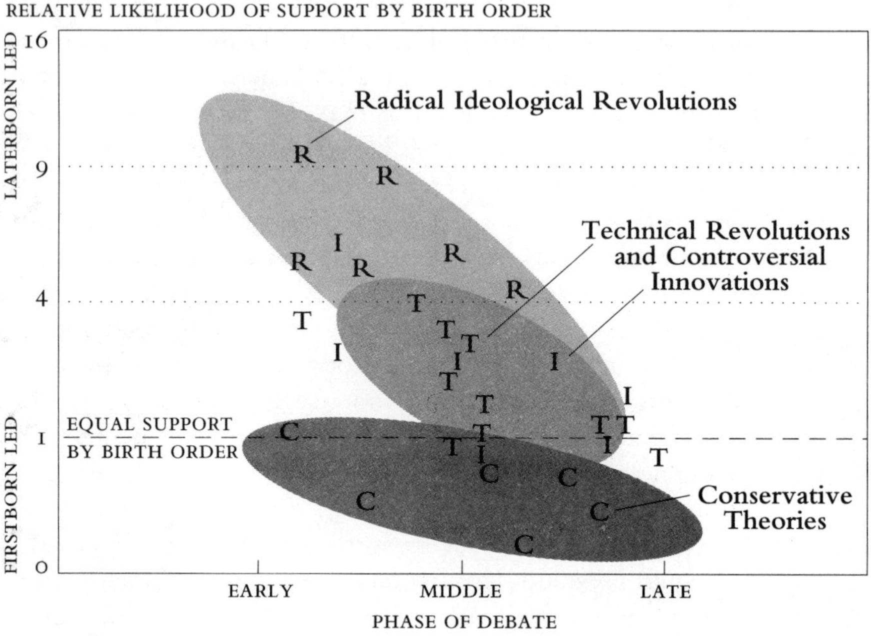

FIGURE 2.4. Birth-order differences in receptivity to scientific innovation in 28 events, represented according to phase of debate and type of innovation. Innovations are represented in terms of the relative likelihood of support by birth order (the odds ratio). An odds ratio greater than 1.0 indicates stronger support by laterborns than by firstborns. An odds ratio below 1.0 indicates the opposite trend. During the early phases of Radical Ideological Revolutions, laterborns have been 10 times more likely than firstborns to support innovation. During the late stages of Conservative Theories, firstborns have been 2 to 3 times more likely than laterborns to endorse the new point of view.

Within each class of scientific innovations, firstborns are more likely to convert during the later stages of debate. The moderating role of time is significantly greater during Radical Ideological Revolutions than it is during other kinds of scientific innovations.

abolished in most European countries in the wake of the French Revolution.[79] This change in inheritance practices has had no measurable influence on the size of birth-order effects. It is also noteworthy that laterborns who were eldest sons, and who were generally favored by primogeniture, were just as likely to support innovations as were laterborns who were younger sons.[80] What causes people to oppose radical change is being a functional firstborn, not inheriting the family estate.[81]

Because Conservative Theories entail different adoption patterns compared with other scientific developments, I analyze these innovations separately throughout this book. For convenience I use the term "liberal theories" to refer to the 23 innovations that are not associated with conservative implications. In response to these liberal innovations, laterborns have been *3.1* times more likely than firstborns to lend their support.[82] The likelihood of this finding arising by chance is less than one in a billion billion. If we compare support for theories that fall into these two opposing categories (conservative versus liberal), laterborns have been *5.7* times more likely than firstborns to endorse the liberal alternative. When the choice has been between supporting a conservative and a *radical* alternative, the disparity by birth order is *8.9 to 1* in favor of laterborn advocacy for the radical point of view.[83]

In chapters 9 and 14 I present additional evidence to support the distinction between conservative and liberal innovations. Social attitudes provide a particularly good way of corroborating this distinction. After controlling for differences in theory adoption by birth order, conservative innovations attract people whose social views contrast significantly with those of people who accept liberal innovations. Conservative theories appeal to social conservatives, whereas liberal theories appeal to social liberals. In addition, liberal theories are likely to be adopted by young people, something that is not the case among the advocates of conservative ideas. To lump these two classes of innovations together obscures virtually all of the predisposing factors—such as age, social attitudes, and birth order—that influence openness to innovation.

Other considerations, besides ideology and technical content, moderate birth-order effects in science. In general, these moderating factors are proxies for controversy.[84] Laterborns are especially overrepresented among the supporters of innovations that have met with little initial support, that have attracted many combatants, and that have taken a long time to resolve.[85] If we combine these three indicators of controversy, their collective role in promoting birth-order differences is impressive. For scientific innovations that have been controversial in all three respects, the odds ratio in favor of laterborn support is 4.2 to 1. Where there is little indication of controversy according to these three measures, the odds ratio is only 1.4 to 1 in favor of laterborn support—a modest difference that is not statistically significant.

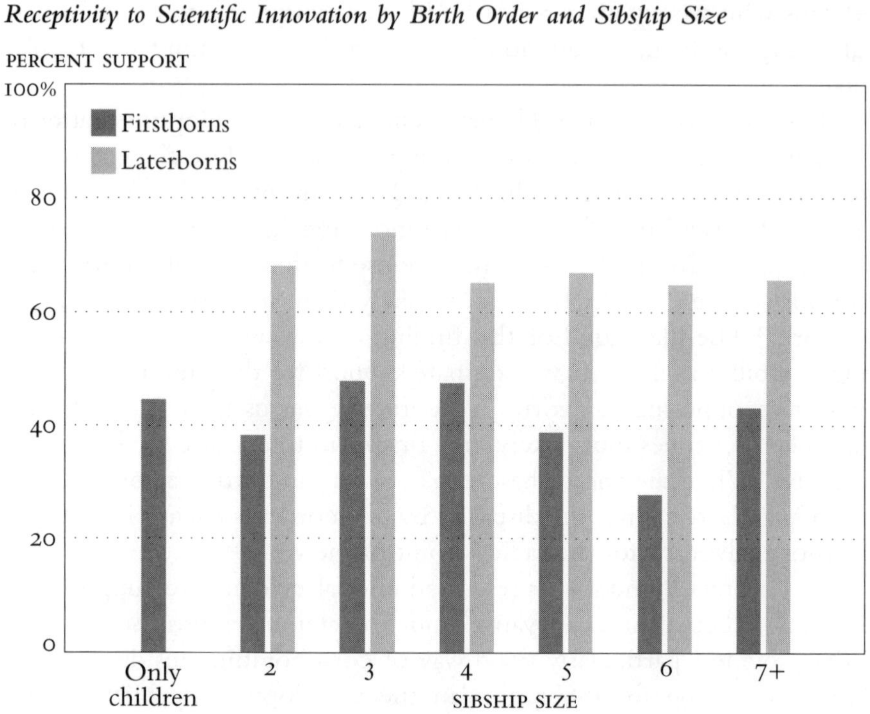

FIGURE 2.5. Birth-order differences in the adoption of 23 liberal theories in science, stratified by sibship size (N= 1,218). The difference in support by birth order is statistically significant within every sibship size from 2 to 7 and above.

CONFRONTING THE BIRTH-ORDER CRITICS

A potential source of error in birth-order studies has been noted by two Swiss psychologists, Cécile Ernst and Jules Angst, in a comprehensive critique of the birth-order literature. Most birth-order research, Ernst and Angst point out, is inadequately controlled for background variables.[86] As an example, lower-class families tend to be larger than upper-class families, so lower-class families are biased for laterborns. The discovery of a significant birth-order trend, without adequate controls for social class and sibship size, does not substantiate the influence of birth order. Differences between families may be the cause.

Receptivity to Scientific Innovation by Birth Order and Socioeconomic Class

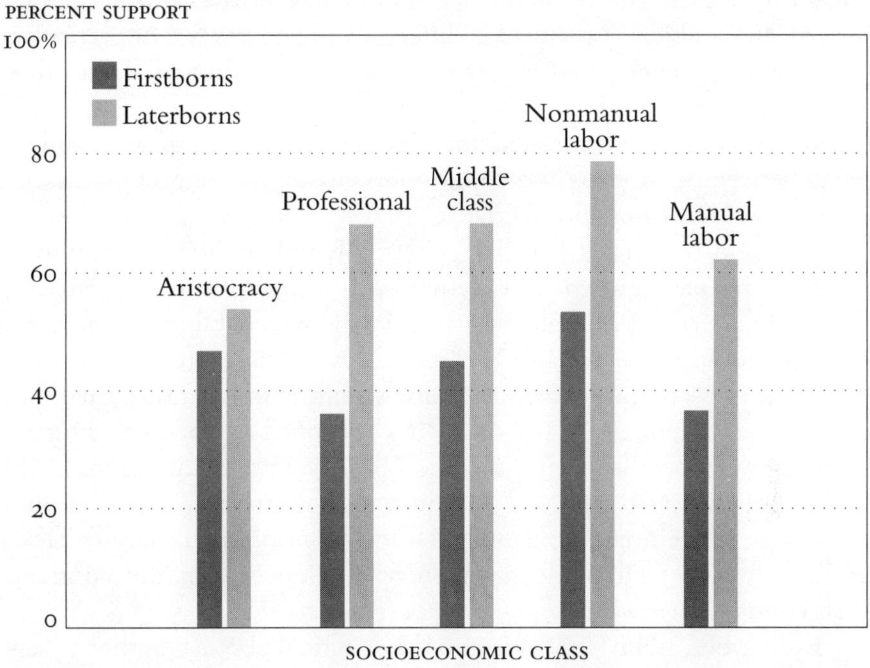

FIGURE 2.6. Birth-order differences in the adoption of 23 liberal theories in science, stratified by social class (N = 1,502). The influence of birth order is statistically significant within every social class except the aristocracy. Social class has no overall influence on scientific stance. Socioeconomic status is based on the father's occupation.

In response to these methodological concerns, I have collected data on all the variables that Ernst and Angst consider to be serious confounders in birth-order research. The most crucial of these confounding variables is sibship size. In my sample, the tendency for laterborns to be overrepresented among the adopters of new ideas is observed within every sibship size from 2 to 20. Family size is not a confounding factor in these findings (Fig. 2.5).[87]

Stratified by social class, laterborns are more likely to endorse new theories at every socioeconomic level, from aristocracy to manual labor. Only in the aristocracy does the trend fail to reach statistical significance. Surprisingly, socioeconomic class itself exerts no detectable influence on the acceptance of scientific innovations (Fig. 2.6).[88]

The situation among aristocrats, where the birth-order trend is not statistically significant, bears further comment. Relative to other members of my sample, aristocrats are different in several ways. In particular, they are underrepresented in debates that were controversial. In other words, aristocrats are biased for participation in controversies that lack birth-order effects. Controlled for this and other background differences between aristocrats and commoners, aristocrats exhibit just as impressive differences by birth order.[89]

The acid test of birth-order effects is whether they occur among siblings who have grown up together within the same family. Among the members of my sample, 105 individuals were siblings of one another, including Georges and Frédéric Cuvier. Three-quarters of these siblings expressed opinions on the same scientific innovations. Birth order is an excellent predictor of their conceptual preferences. During disputes over liberal theories, the laterborns were *7.3* times more likely than the firstborns to support the innovative alternative, twice the disparity observed among unrelated scientists. Controlling for family background does not eliminate birth-order differences. On the contrary, such controls *augment* these differences (Fig. 2.7).[90]

Even when siblings in my study have agreed about whether to accept or reject new scientific theories, they have often differed in the strength of their opinions. The two Cuviers provide an instructive example. Based on ratings by historical experts, Frédéric Cuvier receives 3.3 points out of a possible 7 for his cautious but moderately sympathetic attitude toward evolution. His elder brother, Georges, who campaigned vigorously against this theory, is rated 1.0. The difference between the two Cuviers—2.3 points—is somewhat larger than the average birth-order difference for sibling-scientists.[91] What ultimately counts in assessing birth order is the *relative* difference between siblings from the same family. In comparison to Georges, Frédéric Cuvier took a typical "laterborn" stance toward evolution.

Frédéric Cuvier's ideas on the species question reflect another scientific disparity between the two Cuviers and exemplify an important principle about sibling differences. In 1797, Georges Cuvier summoned his younger brother to Paris. Initially Frédéric, who was just twenty-six, worked at the Museum of Natural History as his brother's assistant, but Georges appointed Frédéric in 1804 as head of the museum's zoo. Frédéric took advantage of his new job to study animal behavior, a field then in its infancy. In this scientific domain—where laterborns have historically pioneered—Frédéric's own researches turned out to be

Sibling Scientists: Receptivity to Liberal Theories by Birth Order

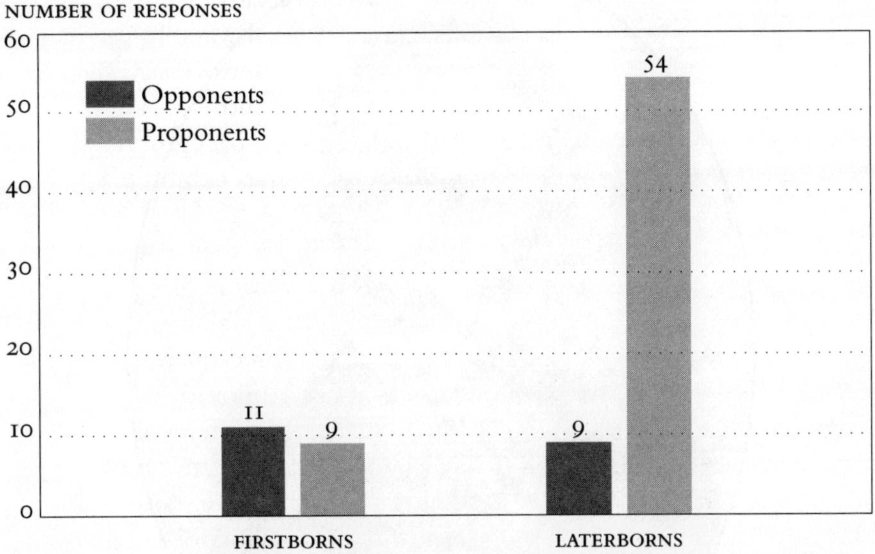

FIGURE 2.7. The reception of liberal theories by scientists who were siblings of one another ($N = 83$). The difference in support by birth order is substantial. On an individual-by-individual basis, a laterborn was 7.3 times more likely to support scientific innovation than was his own eldest sibling.

This figure also illustrates the principle of odds ratios. The odds of a laterborn supporting scientific innovation are 54/9 (or 6.0 to 1). The odds of a firstborn doing so are only 9/11 (or .8 to 1). The odds ratio is 54/9 divided by 9/11, which equals 7.3 to 1 in favor of laterborn adoption.

"most original" and "ahead of his time."[92] Impressed by the intelligence of the mammals he studied, Frédéric concluded that animal instincts are hereditary forms of learning. Such conclusions were particularly heterodox because instincts were considered proof of Design. Frédéric even suggested that moral conscience in man had its origins in the animal instinct of sociability.

Although Frédéric Cuvier did not endorse transmutation in his brother's sphere of expertise—animal morphology and physiology—his views about animal behavior put him squarely in the evolutionary camp. "Despite his fraternal devotion," remarks historian Robert Richards, "Cuvier . . . was a behavioral evolutionist, if a modest one."[93] From a purely logical point of view, Frédéric's scientific views about species were oddly contradictory, and Richards calls them "very

Frédéric Cuvier in 1826 (age fifty-two). This portrait suggests the sympathetic disposition that made Frédéric so different from his brother Georges, whose authoritarian manner was legendary. Although not an outright evolutionist like his colleagues Lamarck and Geoffroy Saint-Hilaire, Frédéric was remarkably open to this idea in the behavioral realm.

Shortly after he became an evolutionist in 1837, Darwin studied Cuvier's ideas about behavioral evolution, copying an extract from Cuvier's writings into his first notebook on the transmutation of species. Twenty-two years later, in the *Origin of Species* (1859), Darwin called attention to Frédéric Cuvier's pioneering views.

strange."[94] Frédéric's logic was that of a laterborn, not a logician. In the awesome shadow of his brother, he cultivated his own scientific niche. And within this niche—the science of animal behavior—he respectfully defied his brother's teachings about the fixity of species. Frédéric died in 1838, too early to express an opinion on Darwin's theories.

Modest to the end, his tombstone reads "Frédéric Cuvier, brother of Georges Cuvier."[95]

CONCLUSIONS

Most innovations in science, especially radical ones, have been initiated and championed by laterborns. Firstborns tend to reject new ideas, especially when the innovation appears to upset long-accepted principles. During the early stages of radical revolutions, laterborns are 5 to 15 times more likely than firstborns to adopt the heterodox point of view. During technical revolutions, laterborns are 2 to 3 times more likely to lend their support. For their own part, firstborns are drawn to reactionary innovations, a domain in which they are also the principal pioneers. Firstborns typically welcome conservative doctrines as potential bulwarks against radical change, supporting them 2 to 1 over laterborns.

Sibling differences in openness to innovation are not artifacts of uncontrolled background variables, such as social class and sibship size. Differences by birth order occur within each of the more than twenty countries represented in my historical survey. Such differences hold true of women as well as men, as I demonstrate in Chapter 6. Finally, the influence of birth order has held steady since the time of the Protestant Reformation, a period of nearly five centuries. Few aspects of human behavior can claim such generalizability across class, nationality, gender, and time.

The influence of birth order is particularly striking when we contrast individuals living during the same historical period and facing the same conceptual choices. Before 1859, most firstborns believed, with Voltaire's character Dr. Pangloss, that "All is for the best in the best of all possible worlds." In biology, firstborns consistently supported doctrines promoting the Wisdom and Power of God. Their worldview was premised on the need for stability and a faith in Divine Providence. Like Georges Cuvier and Charles Lyell, firstborn naturalists extolled the "balance of nature," which everywhere seemed to keep creatures in their intended place.

So powerful is the influence of birth order on scientific worldviews, that pre-Darwinian laterborns were a staggering 124 times more likely than firstborns to support a "radical" innovation over a "conservative" one. This statistic follows from the circumstance that only one laterborn in my historical survey supported biological theories celebrating Divine Wisdom for every 12.8 firstborns who lent their support. By comparison, for every 12.8 firstborns who supported the idea of evolution, 124 laterborns did.[96]

Such strong links between birth order and scientific worldviews challenge us to provide an explanatory framework. As it turns out, one of the theories in my survey is directly relevant to this problem. Siblings are in conflict because their Darwinian interests do not always coincide. Sibling strategies, including personality differences in openness to experience, are Darwinian adaptations for enhancing parental love and attention. Younger siblings face different developmental challenges than do their older siblings, and their personalities develop in correspondingly disparate ways.

That birth order has implications for evolutionary theory did not escape the notice of Darwin. In 1864 he remarked to Alfred Russel Wallace: "But oh, what a scheme is primogeniture for destroying natural selection!"[97] To Joseph Hooker he reiterated the same sentiment: "Primogeniture is dreadfully opposed to natural selection; suppose the first-born bull was necessarily made by each farmer the begetter of his stock!"[98] As it turns out, Darwin's theories explain far more than why primogeniture is anti-Darwinian and unlikely to produce the best filet mignon. Darwin's evolutionary framework elucidates a wide variety of problems in psychology that are only now beginning to be understood. When applied to family life, Darwin's principles clarify the vexing problem of why siblings are so different. In addition, evolutionary psychology explains why laterborns tend to welcome radical change, and why their older siblings generally cling to the status quo. Change favors the underdog. Younger siblings seem instinctively to appreciate this behavioral logic. So do their elder siblings, who just as zealously champion the rival worldview of Dr. Pangloss.

3

BIRTH ORDER AND PERSONALITY

Psychologists have been studying birth order for more than a century and have documented many intriguing results. Firstborns are reported to be more responsible and achievement oriented than laterborns, who are in turn reported to be more socially successful than their older siblings.[1] Although numerous explanations have been offered to account for these findings, no theory has commanded general acceptance. Alfred Adler, an early follower of Freud's who broke away in 1911 to found his own school of "individual psychology," had a strong interest in birth order.[2] The firstborn child, Adler argued, is "dethroned" by the birth of the next sibling.[3] Firstborns who manage to overcome this trauma try to emulate parents. In their role as surrogate parents, firstborns may overemphasize the importance of law and order and become "power-hungry conservatives."[4] As Adler reasoned, "Sometimes a child who has lost his power, the small kingdom he ruled, understands better than others the importance of power and authority."[5] If firstborns are unable to regain parental favor, Adler claimed, they sometimes rebel.

A secondborn himself, Adler considered individuals from this birth rank to be more cooperative than firstborns. Secondborns try harder than their older siblings, he maintained, because they are always playing catch-up. The secondborn "behaves as if he were in a race, is under full steam all the time, and trains continually to surpass his older brother and conquer him."[6] As a result, secondborns are "rarely able to endure the strict leadership of others."[7]

Youngest children are not subject to dethronement and are said to become lazy and spoiled. "A spoiled child can never be independent," Adler insisted.[8] Those lastborns who feel particularly overshadowed by their older siblings may experience a sense of inferiority. When last-

Sigmund Freud (*left*), age fifty, and **Alfred Adler**, in his forties, about the time of their break. According to Ansbacher (1959), Freud's and Adler's initial choice of patients, and the theories they developed based on this clinical evidence, were influenced by their birth orders. Freud, his mother's undisputed favorite and a typical firstborn, was conscious of his social status, valued authority and power over his fellowman, and once wrote that "the unworthiness of human beings, even of analysts, has always made a deep impression on me." Consistent with such attitudes, Freud assumed man to possess an innate evil component that must be constantly controlled by a higher authority (the superego). Freud dealt largely with an upper-class clientele, in contrast to Adler, who saw less-affluent patients.

Adler, according to Ansbacher, was influenced by his status as a second son to discount Freud's "firstborn" notion of the Oedipus complex (with its overemphasis on parent-child relations). In elaborating on the psychological significance of birth order, Adler saw his patients as victims of their struggles for greater power (the fate of many younger siblings).

borns do decide to compete with older siblings, Adler argued, they are often successful in later life.

Adler's hypotheses can accommodate themselves to almost any psychological outcome. Adlerian firstborns can be conservative or rebellious. Adlerian laterborns can be competitive or lazy. To be useful, these hypotheses need to be stated in ways that are refutable. Psychoanalytic approaches to human behavior have largely foundered on their propensity to forgo hypothesis testing.[9] Systematic studies, not clinical anecdotes, are required to validate such claims.[10] Anecdotal evidence plays a different role in science. For example, it helps to generate hypotheses and can illustrate tendencies that have already been validated through statistical testing.

DARWINIAN GUIDANCE

Evolutionary Conflicts

Evolutionary theory offers a compelling answer to the question of why birth order should affect personality. Evolution is governed by a small number of biological conflicts. Organisms are in continual conflict with their environments, including predators and pathogens. This insight led Charles Darwin to his celebrated theory of natural selection. In the relentless struggle for existence, even minor individual differences can alter the balance between survival and death. Individuals who possess advantageous traits have a greater chance of passing them on to their progeny. Over time, natural selection adapts species to the dangers that lurk within their environments.

Darwin recognized a second principle, sexual selection, as a powerful mechanism of evolutionary change. In the *Origin of Species* (1859) and especially in the *Descent of Man* (1871), he used this principle to explain secondary sexual characteristics. The peacock has evolved his beautiful tail in response to competition for mates. Although peacocks suffer greater predation owing to this cumbersome objet d'art, the discerning preferences of peahens have overridden the pressures of natural selection. Structures such as the peacock's tail, which detract from classical Darwinian "fitness," demonstrate that natural and sexual selection are independent processes.

It took more than a century for biologists to go beyond Darwin's two fundamental insights. In recent years, biologists have begun to rethink the subject of evolution from the point of view of the gene. In 1963 William Hamilton, a graduate student, proposed a resolution to a problem that had stymied the greatest minds in biology since Darwin.[11] Because natural selection acts only for the good of the individual, the

TABLE 3

Five Principles of Darwinian Evolution
(Each principle explains a specific class of biological adaptations, which have evolved in response to the designated conflicts.)

Principle	*Conflict*	*Evolved Adaptations*
CLASSIC PRINCIPLES (CHARLES DARWIN, 1859)		
1. Natural Selection	Organism versus environment	Adaptations for survival
2. Sexual Selection	Between, and within, sexes	Secondary sexual characteristics, mating strategies
RECENT THEORIES (1963 TO THE PRESENT)		
3. Kin Selection	Between nonkin and kin (and among kin, by degree of relatedness)	Altruism and cooperation, parental investment
CONSEQUENCES OF KIN SELECTION: FAMILY DYNAMICS		
4. Parent-Offspring Conflict	Between parents and offspring	Weaning conflicts, infanticide, parental discrimination
5. Sibling Conflict	Between siblings	Sibling rivalry, sibling strategies, sibling differences in personality

outcome is inherently selfish. Why, then, do organisms sometimes cooperate? Hamilton's solution to this problem was the theory of "kin selection." Copies of an altruist's genes are typically present in close kin. Because kin benefit from altruistic acts, genes coding for these behaviors will tend to spread within the population, despite occasional costs to the altruist (Table 3).

This line of reasoning led Hamilton to the notion of "inclusive fitness." This measure of fitness is calculated as an individual's own reproductive success, together with his contribution to the reproductive success of relatives, discounted according to their coefficient of related-

Charles Darwin about 1857 (age forty-eight), as he was writing the *Origin of Species.* After publishing the *Origin* in 1859, Darwin waited a decade to articulate his ideas on human evolution. His *Descent of Man* (1871) was followed a year later by *The Expression of the Emotions in Man and Animals* (1872). The latter topic had originally been intended as a chapter in the *Descent of Man,* but Darwin found the subject so rich in evolutionary implications that his researches filled an entire book.

ness.[12] Based on the logic of inclusive fitness, J. B. S. Haldane once quipped that he would lay down his life for more than two brothers, four half-brothers, or eight cousins—a formula that closely approximates the genetic costs of sacrificing oneself for close kin.[13]

Hamilton's solution to this problem has been called "the most important advance in evolutionary theory since Charles Darwin and Gregor Mendel."[14] Curiously, Hamilton's ideas were not immediately appreciated, and they were judged insufficient for a doctoral degree at the University of London.[15] His theory of kin selection has inspired a staggering amount of empirical research, which has confirmed and extended his central idea. Foremost among the extensions of Hamilton's principle are those explaining conflicts over parental investment.

Based on a cost-benefit approach to kin selection, Robert Trivers developed the principle of "parent-offspring conflict."[16] In most organisms that reproduce sexually, parents and offspring share only one-half their genes. As a consequence, parents will sometimes disagree with offspring about the optimum level of investment. One prominent manifestation of these disagreements is conflict over weaning. At the time of weaning, the offspring wants to continue being fed. The parents' genetic interests are usually better served by having, and nurturing, other offspring. In many species, weaning conflicts involve considerable physical violence as parents inflict prohibitive costs on offspring who resist this process.[17] When these costs become high enough, the offspring finally agrees with the parent.

Implicit in the theory of parent-offspring conflict is another basic evolutionary principle. Because siblings share, on average, only one-half their genes, altruism among siblings—while considerable—has its limits. Siblings will tend to disagree about the allocation of shared resources. Whereas parents will normally encourage equal sharing among their offspring, offspring will generally prefer to acquire more of any scarce resource than they give to a sibling. As a rule, an offspring's idea of "fairness" is to give a sibling only one-third of any shared item, not half. This allocation follows from the fact that offspring are twice as related to themselves as they are to their siblings.[18]

The notion of "sibling conflict" is generally subsumed under the principle of parent-offspring conflict. Although these two principles are biologically inseparable, treating them as a single process obscures an important point: Parent-offspring conflict is driven by conflict between siblings. If parents could have only one offspring, their genetic interests would coincide with their offspring's and there would be no parent-offspring conflict in the Darwinian sense of the term. It is not necessary for an individual to have a sibling in order to experience sibling conflict. As disputes over weaning demonstrate, future siblings represent a powerful source of conflict over parental investment.[19] When resisting the weaning process, only children are engaged in sibling competition.

Infanticide

Hamilton's theory of kin selection, together with the conflicts it predicts among close relatives, explains a particularly grim side of animal behavior. Under some circumstances, it is adaptive for organisms to kill their closest kin. Infanticide, long considered a rare and aberrant phenomenon, has turned out to be widespread among insects, fish, birds, and mammals. Competition between siblings is also observed throughout the animal kingdom and sometimes ends in siblicide. Consider the case of sand sharks. The young devour one another inside the oviducts of the mother until only one well-fed shark is left alive. Such unrestrained siblicide is rare, but unbridled altruism is equally rare.

Siblicide is especially common among seabirds and predatory birds. These species regularly lay one egg more than the parents can successfully rear. What happens next depends upon the species and the available food supply. Among blue-footed boobies, siblicide is triggered when the eldest chick's body weight drops below 80 percent of normal for a good year. The older chick pecks the younger to death or excludes it from the nest, causing it to die from exposure and starvation.[20] "In all siblicidal species studied to date," reports one team of biologists, "there is a striking tendency for the victim to be the youngest member of the brood."[21] Parents do nothing to intervene in these lethal sibling conflicts, and it is not in their genetic interests to do so. Indeed, parents often participate. Once the elder booby chick has evicted the younger one from the nest, the parents steadfastly oppose the younger chick's efforts to recross the guano ring that defines the nest. In this species, "siblicide" is a team effort.[22]

If siblicidal species can be said to have a champion, it is surely the cuckoo. Female cuckoos lay their eggs in other birds' nests, depositing one egg per nest. Because the cuckoo chick is unrelated to its stepsiblings, it has no reason to share parental care. When the cuckoo hatches, its first act is to eject all eggs, and even live chicks, from the nest. The baby cuckoo possesses a special hollow in its back, which helps it to scoop up round objects between its shoulder blades and to push them over the rim of the nest. This behavior is dictated by instinct, and the cuckoo goes about its deadly work even though it is blind when hatched (Fig. 3.1).

Siblicide can be costly to parents, whose Darwinian interests do not always coincide with their offsprings'. Natural selection has tended to push such conflicts back to the earliest stages of development, before the parents have invested heavily in the offspring. In some mammals, siblicide occurs in utero as fetuses compete for a small number of implantation sites on the wall of the womb.[23] In other species, mothers have evolved counterstrategies to check siblicidal behavior after birth.

FIGURE 3.1. The dunnock, a European sparrow, is confronted with a nest parasite. "Soon after hatching the cuckoo chick, still naked and blind, ejects the dunnock's eggs out of the nest, one by one. The dunnock never interferes, even as its reproductive success is destroyed in front of its own eyes" (Davies 1992:217).

In the *Origin of Species,* Darwin called attention to the "strange and odious instinct" that causes the cuckoo chick to eject its foster-siblings from the nest. "This has been boldly called a beneficent arrangement, in order that the young cuckoo may get sufficient food, and that its foster-brothers may perish before they had acquired much feeling!" (1872b:236). Natural selection, Darwin argued, provides a much better explanation for nest parasitism than does the doctrine of Design.

Canaries have found an ingenious method to protect their later-hatched chicks. Over a period of several days, female canaries lay four or five eggs. Chicks hatch on successive days, and the earlier-hatched chicks tend to monopolize food resources. Female canaries equalize the odds by lacing each successive egg with greater amounts of testosterone. The last chick may receive twenty times the dose of testosterone given to the first chick. Testosterone makes hatchlings pugnacious and also accelerates growth.[24] An equivalent tactic among humans would be for mothers to give their laterborn offspring a set of brass knuckles.

The case of canaries brings up the important distinction between different kinds of biological causation. Darwinian theory illuminates the *ultimate* causes of behavior.[25] These ultimate causes explain *why* certain behaviors occur. Insectivorous birds migrate in winter, whereas owls do not. Evolution explains why this is so, given differences in the ecological requirements among these species. Evolutionary theory does not tell us *how* the migratory instinct is triggered as winter approaches, any more than it explains how testosterone in canary eggs equalizes the odds among rivalrous offspring. The science of animal physiology supplies the *proximate* causes to these physiological questions, telling us how they achieve their effects.

In the study of human development, psychological theories provide proximate-causal explanations of behavior, analogous to those derived from animal physiology. These theories help us to understand how people develop the personality traits that they do, given differing genetic endowments and family histories. Evolutionary psychology deals with different questions: not *how* family dynamics shape personality, but *why* they do. It is important to recognize that neither proximate nor ultimate causes alone provide a full account of behavior. Nor is the story simply the sum of its causal parts. The more a species, such as our own, is capable of lifelong learning, the more individual behavior needs to be explained as the product of complex interactions between proximate and ultimate causes. This kind of interactionist perspective lies at the heart of this book.

In Darwinian theory, siblicide, parental infanticide, lactational contraception, and nutritional neglect are related phenomena.[26] Breast-feeding suppresses ovulation, which prevents conception. When mothers are nutritionally stressed, the contraceptive protection from lactation is particularly effective. Although ova are not thereby lost, any delay in their use is associated with cellular degeneration, which amounts to genetic death. Breast-feeding therefore combines, in the resulting process of contraception, both infanticide and siblicide.

Spontaneous abortions also reflect Darwinian principles. The frequency of such abortions is increased by stress and inadequate diet. When the costs of reproduction threaten the life of the mother, nature often steps in to end the pregnancy. Among humans, "infanticide" also occurs in utero. A substantial proportion of twins, visible in early sonograms, are never born. In most cases the smaller of the twins is reabsorbed by the mother before the beginning of the third trimester.

In traditional societies, parents sometimes resort to infanticide when siblings are too closely spaced or when resources are scarce. "The classic example," reports anthropologist Sarah Hrdy, "involves killing the youngest of two closely spaced children, withholding investment from a new infant in order to invest in a healthy, older child already past the perilous first years of life."[27] Traditional societies routinely condone infanticide, but never against the elder of two siblings.[28] As a form of natural selection, "sibling selection" tends to occur at the expense of laterborns.

Even when parents do not kill unwanted offspring at birth, subsequent nutritional neglect often does the job for them. Birth order and birth spacing are important moderators in these forms of "masked infanticide."[29] In Latin America, infant mortality is two to three times higher for children having birth orders five or higher than it is among firstborns. Even among secondborns, infant mortality is significantly higher when spacing is close. These findings have been documented in many countries and are independent of the mother's age.[30] One anthropologist, who studied women in rural Brazil, found that mothers were cognizant of the bias against laterborns:

> Some older women were explicit about their feelings toward the birth of their late-born and supernumerary children: they had had enough, the children were an unwanted burden, and the mothers were grateful when some of the children died in infancy.[31]

In developing societies, folk beliefs legitimate the practice of infanticide through neglect, reinforcing the notion that some children are "doomed" from birth and hence "better off dead."[32] When unwanted children become sick, they are frequently denied medical attention and "allowed to die."[33]

In most developing countries the odds of dying during childhood are 1 in 2, although the likelihood of survival is substantially lower among individuals having a high birth rank. If laterborns succeed in defying these odds, they still face an uphill struggle in their efforts to reverse parental discrimination. Throughout human evolution, older siblings have typically possessed greater reproductive prospects than their younger siblings. Because they have survived more childhood diseases, older children are more likely to live to adulthood. In terms of parental investment, firstborns are like "blue chip" securities. Their younger siblings are more like "penny stocks." Firstborns also tend to reproduce sooner than their younger siblings. Parents often favor their firstborn offspring, even as adults, as a means of favoring their firstborn grandchildren.[34]

Most cultures honor the Darwinian logic that links birth order to reproductive success and accord higher status to firstborns. Reflecting this fact, the two sons of Britain's Prince Charles and Princess Diana have sometimes been called the "heir" and the "spare." A survey of 39 non-Western societies found that in every culture firstborns received greater status and respect than laterborns. In ancient Japan, the lesser status of younger siblings was exemplified by their nickname—"cold rice"—which derived from the custom of feeding them leftovers after the parents and firstborn had eaten their fill.[35]

Inheritance Practices

Inheritance is a form of parental investment. As a rule, these practices accord with evolutionary principles. This does not mean that specific inheritance strategies, such as primogeniture, are innate tendencies.[36] Few aspects of human behavior work in such a genetically predetermined fashion. What is innate is a propensity for parents to invest wisely in offspring, which tends to result in their maximizing their inclusive fitness. Culture determines how this goal is fulfilled.

Properly understood, inheritance systems underscore an insufficiently appreciated truth about Darwinian principles: *they are context dependent.*[37] That parents should avail themselves of *flexible* inheritance strategies makes decided Darwinian sense. Once offspring have survived the vulnerable period of childhood, their reproductive potential becomes largely independent of birth rank. For this reason, parents ought to invest more or less equally in their surviving offspring. Given the role that chance plays in the survival of any lineage, an equal distribution of parental investment reduces the risk that family lineages will go extinct. In the Italian city-states of medieval Europe, wealth was based on financial speculation and could be won or lost in a single generation. Parents hedged their genetic bets, distributing their assets equally among their children.[38]

From a Darwinian point of view, primogeniture (along with sex-biased inheritance) is a strategy for long-term lineal success in a saturated agrarian habitat. According to the theory of inclusive fitness, wealthy parents ought to invest more heavily in their male offspring.[39] There are fewer physiological limitations on a male's capacity to sire offspring, and wealth can magnify this capacity far beyond that attainable by a female. If a wife dies in childbirth, a wealthy male is likely to remarry. In polygynous societies, wealthy males acquire a disproportionate share of wives. Whenever wealth is tied to land, parents will tend to adopt primogeniture to avoid diminishing the family's socioeconomic status.

In nonelite families, sons are at a disadvantage compared with daughters. Landless sons cannot compete successfully against wealthy sons, but a sister can marry upward in social station. Under these circumstances, parents ought to invest in daughters, using dowries to improve their daughters' social status.

Several large-scale studies have tested this culture-sensitive theory of inheritance practices. One study of medieval Portugal encompasses the twenty-five highest houses of the aristocracy from 1380 to 1580.[40] This study included more than 3,700 people and, using genealogical records, documented information on birth order, marital patterns, and reproductive histories. As expected, elite dynasties invested more heavily in sons than daughters. In allocating their resources to sons, parents did so largely according to birth rank. It was the story of heirs and spares.

In contrast, the nontitled nobility of Portugal invested heavily in daughters. By providing daughters with a dowry, nonelite parents were able to ensure that one offspring—usually the eldest daughter—continued the family line.

Regardless of socioeconomic status, younger sons had little prospect of marriage. Because these landless males represented a threat to political stability, the Portuguese state encouraged them to vent their aggressions upon other states. Ever hopeful of raising their social position, younger sons participated in expansionist wars, crusades, and geographic explorations. Compared with their elder brothers, younger sons were much more likely to die in warfare, usually in faraway India.[41]

In medieval Portugal, birth order had "a catastrophic effect on the probability of marriage."[42] In the course of two centuries, eldest males left 50 percent more descendants than their younger brothers. The fecundity of sisters exhibited a similar disparity by birth order. Many younger sons, unable to marry, were limited to fathering the occasional illegitimate child.[43]

Western history can be seen as an often nasty contest over the right to reproduce.[44] More often than we realize, these battles have been fought *within the family.* In some societies, laterborns are raised from birth to become servants in the household of their eldest sibling.[45] Under these circumstances, sibling conflict is "class struggle."

ADAPTIVE STRATEGIES FOR SIBLINGS

In all societies, parents make discriminations about the potential of their children and invest in them accordingly. When confronted by parental discrimination, siblings respond in strategic ways. One well-established finding about siblings is how exquisitely sensitive they are to any favoritism by parents.[46] Siblings can spend hours debating who got the better gift. No evolutionary psychologist should be surprised by such behavior. Sibling rivalry is Darwinian common sense. To keep parents on their toes, siblings even compete when parents have no intention of treating them differently. The *anticipatory* nature of sibling rivalry betrays its evolutionary roots.

In their efforts to maximize parental investment, siblings avail themselves of certain basic strategies. First, offspring can try to promote parental favor directly—for instance, by helping and obeying parents.

"Mom always liked you and Pinkie and Spike and Custard and Fluffy best."

Offspring can also attempt to dominate their rivals, reducing their demands for parental investment. Finally, offspring who find that they are being dominated can adopt various countermeasures, including appeasement, rebellion, or a combination of both tactics. Depending on age and physical size, some of these strategies are more effective than others. Here is where birth order comes in.[47]

Birth Order and the "Big Five" Personality Dimensions

To determine whether birth order is a proximate cause of sibling differences, it is useful to consider a general taxonomy for personality traits. Most personality traits can be grouped under five global "dimensions." These five dimensions emerge consistently in personality tests administered in different countries and languages around the world.[48] Called the "Big Five," these dimensions encompass (1) Extraversion, (2) Agreeableness, (3) Conscientiousness, (4) Neuroticism, and (5) Openness to Experience.[49]

Using the Big Five as my guide, I offer here a psychodynamic account of birth-order differences. Although more research is needed to validate some of these hypotheses, they are reasonably consistent with the evidence. My hypotheses take the form of answers to a question: In competing for parental investment, what strategies are children most likely to employ, given differences in their birth orders? Although my hypotheses are informed by a Darwinian perspective, they must stand or fall on their own empirical merits.

1. Extraversion. As a dimension of personality, Extraversion involves at least six facets, which can be grouped under the dual headings of temperamental and interpersonal traits. The three temperamental facets of extraversion include activity level, excitement-seeking, and positive emotions such as self-confidence. Shyness is closely associated with these temperamental features of extraversion. The three interpersonal attributes of extraversion are warmth, friendliness, and gregariousness—all aspects of sociability.[50] The birth-order prediction that one might make for temperamental features of extraversion is not the same prediction that one might make for the interpersonal features.

I first address the issue of birth order and temperament. Throughout most of childhood, firstborns enjoy the advantages of being bigger, stronger, and smarter than their younger siblings. The possession of these attributes makes it natural for firstborns to feel more self-assured than laterborns. Firstborns are also likely to try to minimize the costs of having siblings by dominating them. Firstborns should therefore score higher than laterborns on those behaviors that tend toward "assertiveness" and "dominance." With some qualifications to be discussed later in this chapter, the existing research supports these expectations. For example, firstborns are reported to be more self-confident than laterborns, and they are overrepresented among political leaders, including American presidents and British prime ministers.[51]

When extraversion is measured as sociability, an attribute that is associated with lower social status, laterborns ought to score higher than firstborns. For this reason, one cannot make a global prediction about birth order and extraversion, although one can make predictions with regard to some of this dimension's six facets.

2. Agreeableness/Antagonism. Again based on physical superiority, firstborns ought to be more antagonistic than laterborns, and firstborns are rated higher, by themselves and their siblings, in the physical uses of power.[52] Among laterborns, lesser physical size suggests strategies that minimize physical confrontations. Prudent laterborn strategies include acquiescing to firstborn demands, cooperating, pleading and whining, and appealing to parents for protection. These "low-power" strategies are well documented in studies of laterborn behavior.[53] Relative to firstborns, laterborns are also reported to be more altruistic, empathetic, and peer-oriented.[54]

3. Conscientiousness. Given their special place within the family constellation, firstborns should be more amenable than laterborns to their parents' wishes, values, and standards. One effective way for firstborns to retain parental favor is by assisting with child-rearing tasks and by trying to be the "responsible" child of the family. As a consequence, firstborns should score higher than laterborns on Conscientiousness. The tendency for firstborns to excel in school and in other forms of intellectual achievement is consistent with their strong motivation to satisfy parental expectations.[55] Studies have repeatedly found that firstborns are "more strongly identified with parents and readier to accept their authority."[56]

4. Neuroticism. My psychodynamic hypotheses for Neuroticism are more restricted than for other Big Five dimensions. The reason is that Neuroticism (or Emotional Instability) does not apply across the board. Firstborns are not likely to be more "nervous" or "neurotic" than laterborns.[57] Still, Neuroticism is closely tied to jealousy, a trait that is instrumental to the preservation of valued resources.[58] From a Darwinian point of view, siblings are a threat to survival. One of the most common causes of childhood mortality is malnourishment, which tends to increase with sibship size. Negative emotions, including jealousy, are natural responses to this threat.

Firstborns have more reason than laterborns to be jealous of their siblings. Every firstborn begins life with 100 percent of parental investment. For laterborns, who share parental investment from the beginning, the reduction in parental care owing to a new sibling is never suffered to the same degree. Parents try to discourage jealousy, and firstborns may often suppress this trait. Still, when parents are not watching, a firstborn's display of jealous rage can be an effective means of intimidating younger siblings.

The literature on birth order is consistent with these expectations. For example, firstborns are described as being more anxious about their status.[59] They are also more emotionally intense than laterborns and slower to recover from upsets.[60] Among males, firstborns are more likely than laterborns to exhibit anger and vengefulness.[61] The Bible tells the same story. It was Cain, not his younger brother Abel, whose jealousy precipitated the first biblical murder.

5. *Openness to Experience.* Laterborns should score higher than firstborns on Openness to Experience, a dimension that is associated with being unconventional, adventurous, and rebellious. This prediction stems from the lesser identification that laterborns have with parents, as well as their history of domination by older siblings. As family "underdogs," laterborns should empathize with other downtrodden individuals and generally support egalitarian social change. Effecting social change usually requires taking risks, so we would expect laterborns to be more adventurous than firstborns.[62]

The literature on birth order accords closely with these expectations. Laterborns are more inclined than firstborns to question authority and to resist pressure to conform to a consensus. Firstborns, in contrast, tend to endorse conventional morality. Studies also reveal that laterborns are more risk oriented than firstborns. For instance, laterborns are more likely to engage in dangerous physical activities, such as contact sports.[63]

Although the literature on birth order is generally consistent with these five trends, this body of research has not compelled widespread agreement. Indeed, accomplished psychologists have vigorously contested the existence of any general trends. The reasons for their objections need to be considered.

"I knew Darwin. Nice guy."

Charles Darwin possessed an agreeable personality, as his biographers have generally acknowledged.

TESTING BIRTH-ORDER CLAIMS

It has been more than two decades since Carmi Schooler published his damning review of the birth-order literature under the title "Birth Order Effects: Not Here, Not Now!"[64] Since then several other reputable scholars have reached the same conclusion: birth-order effects are a mirage. In a noteworthy 1983 book, Cécile Ernst and Jules Angst reviewed more than a thousand publications on the subject. Most birth-order effects, they concluded, are artifacts of poor research design.[65]

According to Ernst and Angst, birth-order researchers have consistently failed to control for important background factors, such as social class and family size. On average, lower-class families are larger than upper-class families, creating spurious cross-correlations with birth order. Ernst and Angst have summed up their assessment of the literature with the blunt conclusion: *"Birth order influences on personality and IQ have been widely overrated."*[66] Other careful scholars, working with independent data, have agreed. Birth order, assert Dunn and Plomin, "plays only a bit-part in the drama of sibling differences."[67]

Conflicting Findings: A Meta-analytic Overview

Ernst and Angst's sweeping critique overlooks an important methodological issue in behavioral research, namely, how to interpret contradictory findings. Conflicting results abound in the behavioral sciences, even in areas where general trends are no longer in dispute. The question we need to ask about any topic of research is whether significant results exceed "chance" expectations, especially in well-designed studies. *Meta-analysis* allows us to answer this question.[68]

Meta-analysis involves pooling studies to gain statistical power.[69] Small studies are less reliable than large studies. The typical behavioral study involves about 70 subjects.[70] Owing to statistical error, studies routinely fail to confirm relationships that are known to be true for larger populations. In addition, standard safeguards against "chance" findings cause statistical conclusions to err on the side of rejecting a truth rather than accepting a falsehood. Everyone knows that girls, at age eighteen, are taller than they are at age fourteen. In samples of only 70 subjects, this lawful relationship will be validated statistically less than half the time! Common sense dictates that findings should count more if they are based on 10,000 subjects than if they are based on 100.

If we ignore all birth-order findings that lack controls for social class or sibship size, 196 controlled studies remain in Ernst and Angst's survey, involving 120,800 subjects. The numerous birth-order effects reported in these studies are not likely to be artifacts of poor research design. In order to test my own hypotheses about birth order, I have classified each controlled study under the Big Five personality dimension to which it is most relevant. The bulk of these 196 studies are already grouped by Ernst and Angst under categories corresponding closely with the Big Five, including extraversion, aggression, responsibility, neuroticism, and conformity. In all such instances, I have followed their own classifications (Table 4).

Within this carefully controlled literature, 72 of the 196 studies display significant birth-order results that are consistent with my psychodynamic hypotheses. Fourteen studies yield contrary results. The remaining 110 studies are not statistically significant in either direction. What does this mean? In any group of 196 studies, chance will produce about 10 spurious confirmations, give or take a random fluctuation in the error rate. We can be 99 percent confident that chance will produce no more than 21 spurious confirmations. The likelihood of obtaining 72 spurious findings is less than 1 in a billion billion! In spite of occa-

TABLE 4

Summary of 196 Controlled Birth-Order Studies, Classified According to the Big Five Personality Dimensions

Behavioral Domain (by Degree of Confirmation)	*Outcome*[a]	*Likelihood of Outcome by Chance*[b]
OPENNESS TO EXPERIENCE		
Firstborns are more conforming, traditional, and closely identified with parents	*21 confirming (2.2 expected)* *2 negating* *20 no difference*	*Less than 1 in a billion*
CONSCIENTIOUSNESS		
Firstborns are more responsible, achievement oriented, organized, and planful	*20 confirming (2.3 expected)* *0 negating* *25 no difference*	*Less than 1 in a billion*
AGREEABLENESS/ANTAGONISM		
Laterborns are more easygoing, cooperative, and popular	*12 confirming (1.6 expected)* *1 negating* *18 no difference*	*Less than 1 in a billion*
NEUROTICISM (OR EMOTIONAL INSTABILITY)		
Firstborns are more jealous, anxious, neurotic, fearful, and likely to affiliate under stress	*14 confirming (2.4 expected)* *5 negating* *29 no difference*	*Less than 1 in a billion*
EXTRAVERSION		
Firstborns are more extraverted, assertive, and likely to exhibit leadership	*5 confirming (1.5 expected)* *6 negating* *18 no difference*	*Less than 1 in a million (but studies conflict)*[c]
All Results Pooled	*72 confirming (9.8 expected)* *14 negating* *110 no difference*	*Less than 1 in a billion billion*

NOTE: Data are tabulated from Ernst and Angst (1983:93–189), using only those studies controlled for social class or sibship size. Each reported finding constitutes a "study."

a. Based on a "chance" confirmation rate of 5 percent.

b. Based on the meta-analytic procedure of counting confirming studies versus all other outcomes (Rosenthal 1987:213); one-tailed tests. With the expected number of confirming studies set to a minimum of 5, all statistical comparisons are significant at $p < .005$. For Openness, $z = 13.19$; for Conscientiousness, $z = 12.14$; for Agreeableness, $z = 8.44$; for Neuroticism, $z = 7.68$; for Extraversion, $z = 5.01$; for all results pooled, $z = 20.39$.

c. In this one instance I have compared positive and negative studies together, versus those showing no difference, and employ a two-tailed test.

sional negative findings, the literature on birth order exhibits consistent trends that overwhelmingly exceed chance expectations.[71]

Four of the Big Five personality dimensions display particularly impressive trends. The most striking trend occurs for Openness to Experience, a domain where confirming studies are 10 times more numerous than refuting ones. Relative to firstborns, laterborns are more nonconforming, adventurous, and unconventional. For Conscientiousness, there are 20 confirming studies and no disconfirming ones.[72] Firstborns appear to be "goody-goodies."

Only Extraversion yields an ambiguous result. For this Big Five dimension, both confirming and disconfirming studies occur more often than expected by chance, an intriguing result. The source of the confusion appears to reside in the construct of Extraversion, not with birth order. Research on this topic tends to lump "sociability," a laterborn trait, with "assertiveness," a firstborn tendency. When findings on birth order and Extraversion are analyzed in terms of various subscales for this dimension, they make reasonable sense.[73]

Degrees of Influence

Meta-analysis clarifies other inconsistencies in the birth-order literature. The degree to which birth order shapes personality varies significantly, depending on the domain being analyzed—an important finding.[74] For example, birth order exerts significantly greater influence on Openness to Experience, and on Conscientiousness, than it does on the other Big Five dimensions. In addition, birth order has substantially more impact on Agreeableness and Neuroticism than it does on Extraversion. Birth order tells us a great deal about the propensity to rebel, but it does not tell us much about shyness. The following chapter will consider why Openness to Experience is associated more consistently with birth-order differences than are the other Big Five dimensions.

Another striking finding about birth order involves the contrast between research on personality variables and research on intellectual abilities. The influence of birth order is *5 to 10 times greater* for most personality traits than it is for academic achievement and IQ.[75] Ernst and Angst were fully justified in emphasizing the consistently small birth-order effects for intellectual ability. Firstborns are smarter than laterborns, but the typical difference in IQ (one point for each increase in birth rank) has little practical significance for individuals.[76]

Based on well-designed studies, birth-order correlations for personality attributes range from .40 (for Openness to Experience) down to about .10 (for Extraversion).[77] How big is a correlation of .40? A correlation this size is equivalent to a medicine that raises one's chances of surviving a life-threatening disease from 30 percent to 70 percent (*a doubling of the survival rate*). Birth-order correlations for other personality variables are typically about half this size, but these are still impressive effects. By way of comparison, the mean correlation between gender and the Big Five personality dimensions is .14, which is smaller than many reported birth-order differences.[78]

INTERACTION EFFECTS

In spite of all the criticisms, the literature on birth order exhibits consistent behavioral trends. Closer analysis leads to an even more positive verdict: The literature consistently underestimates the influence of birth order. One important reason is *interaction effects.* An interaction effect occurs whenever two or more variables have nonadditive properties. The joint effect is synergistic and "emergent," just like the properties of water from its constituents—hydrogen and oxygen.

The emergent nature of birth-order effects is nicely demonstrated by the most comprehensive study ever conducted. Beginning in 1954 Helen Koch, a psychologist at the University of Chicago, published ten articles on birth order, testing its influence on dozens of psychological traits.[79] Koch's study is noteworthy for its sophisticated design. Even today, no study has approached its efforts to control for so many confounding variables. Koch selected 384 children for her research, all five- and six-year-olds from schools near Chicago. Each child was from a white, intact, two-child family. Her subjects were carefully divided into matched subgroups to facilitate controls for every combination of birth order, sex, and sex of sibling. In addition, Koch matched each subgroup for three categories of age gaps between siblings. Technically, her study involved a $2 \times 2 \times 2 \times 3$ design, yielding 24 subgroups (each containing 16 children). Finally, Koch matched each subgroup by social class. Even Gregor Mendel, the Austrian monk whose careful breeding experiments allowed him to discover the laws of genetics, would have been impressed by such a thoughtful research design.

Koch had teachers rate her subjects, using 58 behavioral measures. Relative to laterborns, firstborns were judged to be more self-confident, competitive, insistent on rights, emotionally intense, and upset by defeat.[80] Koch summed up these personality differences by noting that firstborns, in spite of their veneer of self-confidence, were "intense, anxious, on the defensive, and concerned about status."[81] The various trends I have already described in this chapter concur with her findings.

The most striking feature about Koch's study is the astonishing number of interaction effects that she documented. These nonadditive effects involved birth order, subject's sex, sibling's sex, and age spacing—interacting in pairs, triplets, and even foursomes. Overall, birth order participated in 31 significant interaction effects, compared with only 5 main effects. (A "main effect" is one that holds across the board, and not just for subgroups.) Age spacing and sex of sibling contributed another 36 interaction effects in Koch's study. Directly or indirectly, birth order, age spacing, and sex of sibling produced 72 significant effects. The likelihood of this happening by chance is less than 1 in a million.[82]

Interaction Effects as "Sibling Strategies"

Here are some typical interaction effects from Koch's study. Compared with laterborn boys, firstborn boys were judged to be more angry, vengeful, and cruel. Among girls, these trends did not reach statistical significance.[83] Girls, however, made up for these missing differences by manifesting a significant birth-order disparity in quarrelsome tendencies.[84] Firstborn boys, it would seem, assert their dominance in aggressive and punitive ways, whereas firstborn girls do so verbally. The common denominator is that firstborns are more "antagonistic" than laterborns, a trend that coincides with a Big Five personality dimension.

Most of the interaction effects in Koch's study can be explained analogously. Siblings possess a sophisticated understanding of gender-based norms of behavior, and they mold these norms to their own strategic ends. What is consistent about birth order is the *general gist of strategies,* not the specific behaviors employed to achieve these ends. The same conclusion applies to other causes of differences between siblings, including gender.[85]

One reason why birth order interacts so frequently with gender is that both variables promote similar strategies. Social organisms seek access to valued resources in two basic ways—domination and cooperation. Status-enhancing behavior is a firstborn tendency. It is also a "male" tendency. Cooperation is a laterborn tendency, and it is also a "female" tendency.[86]

The close relationship between birth order and gender is underscored in a reanalysis of Helen Koch's data undertaken by Orville Brim.[87] Guided by Talcott Parsons's sociological model of the family, Brim divided Koch's behavioral measures into "instrumental" and "expressive" traits based on their congruence with masculine and feminine roles.[88] Brim's list of "masculine" tendencies encompasses traits such as leadership, self-confidence, assertiveness, competitiveness, and aggression. His list of "feminine" tendencies includes traits such as affection, cooperation, and flexibility.

In coding these behavioral tendencies, Brim assessed each of Koch's 24 sibling groups according to its participation in interaction effects. This unusual method of scoring enabled him to analyze, and to contrast, synergistic behaviors promoting status and dominance with those promoting love and cooperation.[89]

Based on Brim's analysis, firstborns of both sexes emerge as the "alpha males" of their sibling system. The gender of siblings, Brim found, was also a significant predictor of instrumental behavior. Individuals who had a brother were more competitive and assertive than those who had a sister.[90]

In contrast to instrumental tendencies, expressive ones were manifested predominantly by girls and by laterborns.[91] Laterborn boys (especially those having an older sister) were considered particularly "effeminate" by their teachers. Girls, judged flexible and agreeable as a whole, were deemed even more so if they were younger siblings.[92]

As Brim's findings demonstrate, birth order determines many traits that are stereotypically associated with gender. The study of gender is therefore the study of birth order, and vice versa. Although sex differences were numerous in Koch's study, birth order frequently overrode these differences. In dyads that included a firstborn girl and a laterborn boy, the girls were actually more "masculine" than the boys.[93] Overall, the influence of birth order on traits related to gender is *two-thirds as large as the influence of sex!* The field of women's studies should take heed of these findings, which have important implications for how gender expresses itself in individual lives. Just like birth-order effects, much of gender-related behavior is an "emergent" product of the family system as a whole (Fig. 3.2).

The Influence of Birth Order and Gender on Selected Personality Traits

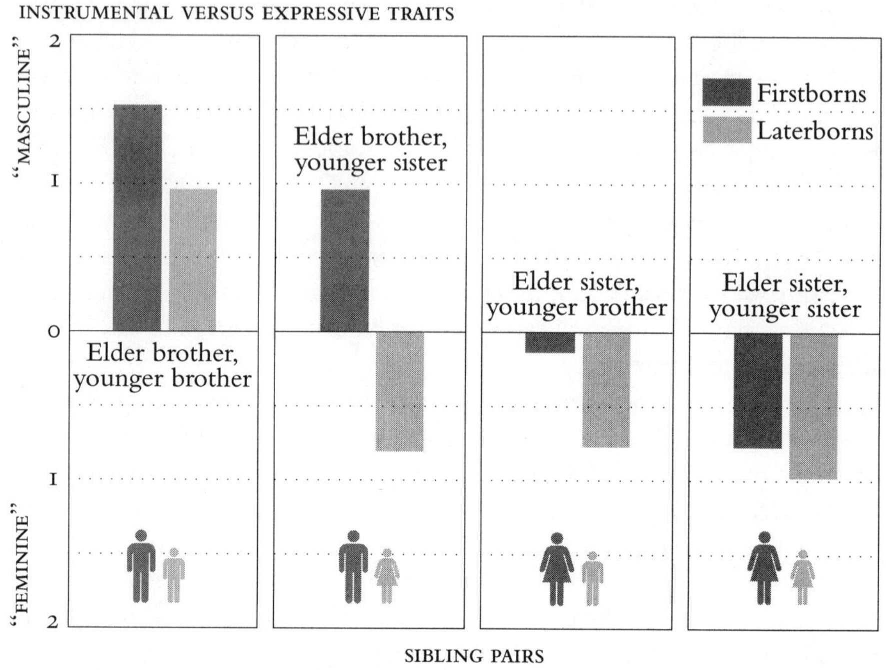

FIGURE 3.2. Gender-related traits, as documented by Helen Koch ($N = 384$). Standardized scores for each sibling pair are presented in terms of birth order, gender, and the gender of siblings. As expected, males are more likely than females to exhibit conventionally masculine traits. Siblings having a brother also exhibit more "masculine" tendencies. Finally, birth order exerts a significant influence on gender-related behavior. In each of the four pairs, firstborns are more conventionally masculine than laterborns. The effect is greatest among males. In one pair—that of a firstborn sister having a younger brother—the female actually scored higher in masculine traits than did the brother. To sum up, the influence of birth order on gender-related traits is pervasive and about two-thirds as extensive as gender itself.

CONCLUSIONS

Helen Koch's pioneering study proves, incontrovertibly, that birth order shapes personality. Just as importantly, her findings indicate that gender and other systematic sibling differences are vital to the story of human development. This story involves numerous interaction effects—a phenomenon that underscores the "emergent" nature of personality. Besides gender, the most common sources of interaction effects are age gaps between siblings and the sex of siblings. In subsequent chapters I shall expand on this list, which, properly constituted, encompasses a wide variety of influences that define a child's family niche.

Like the alpha males of primate societies, firstborns covet status and power. They specialize in strategies designed to subordinate rivals. The Big Five dimensions of personality provide us with a convenient means of summarizing these strategies. Firstborns tend to be *dominant, aggressive, ambitious, jealous,* and *conservative.* At these five levels of behavior, the influence of birth order is consistent and unmistakable.

Like low-status primates, laterborns are at a disadvantage in direct confrontations with older siblings. Although laterborns often manifest a decided inclination to rebel, they also work hard to improve their lot through good-natured sociability and cooperation. Dominance and cooperation are timeworn strategies, created and perpetuated by different forms of Darwinian selection.[94] Success can be achieved by either route.

In the drama of sibling competition, birth order and gender appear to be the two most important players in the choice of sibling strategies. There is evolutionary aptness to this conclusion. As ancestral siblings tailored their competitive strategies to the cognitive and physical dictates of age, they increasingly conducted the business of sibling rivalry like a game of chess, coordinating tactics in age- and gender-sensitive ways. Today's offspring continue to play out this evolutionary drama. All over the world, offspring strive to maximize parental investment, adapting their strategies to their own particular family niche. Ultimately, sibling rivalry is about surviving childhood. Even after this Darwinian hurdle has been cleared, siblings continue to compete over the right to reproduce. In attempting to achieve these two fundamental Darwinian goals, siblings become astute strategists. The end result is called personality.

PART TWO

ALL IN THE FAMILY

4

FAMILY NICHES

DARWIN'S "PRINCIPLE OF DIVERGENCE"

During the last two decades, studies of personality have shown that siblings raised in the same family are almost as different as unrelated individuals. To the modest extent that biological siblings are more similar in their personalities than adoptees, these resemblances are attributable to shared genes, not to the shared family environment. The longer siblings live with one another, the more different they become. One of the most pressing questions confronting personality psychology is why siblings are so different. Resolving this problem is important for numerous allied disciplines, including biography and history.[1]

That brothers and sisters are remarkably different has been noted by siblings themselves, often with surprise. Charles Darwin observed about his older brother, Erasmus, who was four years his senior: "Our minds and tastes were . . . so different that I do not think that I owed much to him intellectually—nor to my four sisters, who possessed very different characters."[2]

The eminent linguist Wilhelm von Humboldt made a similar observation about himself and his younger brother, Alexander, who became a naturalist:

> I sometimes wish I had my brother's temperament. It is true he complains of being dull, but on the whole he seems to amuse himself pretty well. He is forever on the move, and continually joking. . . . We continue to live together as we used to do, and are always the best of friends, though rarely of the same mind; our characters differ too widely.[3]

Alexander von Humboldt (*standing, at the right*) and his traveling companion, Aimé Bonpland (*seated next to Humboldt*), in 1800. This illustration shows them camped beside the Orinoco River, in Venezuela, with their native guides. The two naturalists traveled more than a thousand miles on the Orinoco and discovered its connection with the Amazon. During their six-month expedition on this river they were constantly threatened by jaguars, crocodiles, and boa constrictors.

Wilhelm was not much of a traveler, whereas Alexander—"forever on the move"—soon became famous for his explorations in Central and South America (1799–1804). In the course of five years Alexander walked, rode, canoed, and sailed through more than 40,000 miles of largely unexplored territory.[4] He and his traveling companion, Aimé Bonpland, risked their lives many times over. At the age of sixty Humboldt fulfilled his ambition to visit Siberia, where he logged another 8,000 miles. His brother Wilhelm's idea of an adventurous trip was to spend his winters in Italy.

Siblings are sometimes so strikingly different that commentators have found themselves at a complete loss for an explanation. Voltaire's nineteenth-century biographer James Parton was so astonished at the contrast between the irreverent François and his sanctimonious elder brother Armand that he asked: "What Darwin will explain to us so mysterious a fact in the natural history of our race?"[5]

A Darwinian Theory of Personality

In mentioning Darwin, Voltaire's biographer was closer than he knew to an answer. Siblings are different because they exemplify Darwin's "principle of divergence." Throughout organic nature, diversity is a useful strategy that allows species to compete for scarce resources. This insight of Darwin's, which he hit upon during a carriage ride in the 1850s, resolved a nagging evolutionary puzzle. As species evolve, why do they diverge in character? Neither evolution nor speciation requires divergence. "The solution," Darwin realized, "is that the modified offspring of all dominant and increasing forms tend to become adapted to many and highly diversified places in the economy of nature."[6] Darwin was so impressed by the power of this idea that, along with natural selection, he deemed it the "key-stone" of the *Origin*.[7]

Even when species seem indistinguishable morphologically, they usually differ in their ecological requirements. These cases—biologists generally call them "sibling species"—represent evolution in its earliest stages.[8] Given enough time, species tend to evolve multiple forms that diverge in character, a process called "adaptive radiation." One of the best-known examples is Darwin's finches, which live in the Galápagos Islands. By occupying different ecological niches, the members of this subfamily coexist in far greater numbers than would otherwise be possible.

Because some species of Darwin's finches overlap in their feeding habits, they regularly exclude each other from the same island.[9] Known as the principle of "competitive exclusion," this biological rule holds that no two species can coexist in the same habitat if their ecological requirements are identical.[10] When similar species do live side by side, they exhibit a phenomenon known as "character displacement." Differences in bill size, for example, are accentuated, reducing competition for the same foods.[11] Only through evolutionary diversification is coexistence possible.

As children grow up, they undergo adaptive radiation in their efforts to establish their own individual niches within the family. By pursuing disparate interests and abilities, siblings minimize direct competition. This well-known evolutionary principle allows me to recast the topic of birth order and its influence on personality. We have seen that laterborns are especially open to experience, as evidenced by personality tests and by history. *But why?* Openness helps younger siblings in their quest to find an unoccupied family niche. This psychological capacity is the engine that drives Darwin's principle of divergence.[12]

From a Darwinian point of view, personality is the repertoire of strategies that each individual develops in an effort to survive childhood. The bulk of these strategies are *sibling* strategies. In proposing a theory of sibling strategies, I do not mean to exclude only children. Singletons are a special case in the theory of sibling strategies. Like all children, singletons seek to maximize parental investment. In traditional societies they do so by resisting the mother's efforts at weaning, which in turn affects the mother's likelihood of conceiving another child. Like the cuckoo, only children represent an instance in which sibling strategies have accomplished their goal.

Besides birth order, other relevant considerations for a theory of sibling strategies include parent-offspring conflict, available parental resources, family size, gender, and temperament.

GENETIC SOURCES OF SIBLING DIVERSITY

Owing to the laws of genetics, brothers and sisters are already remarkably different when they are first conceived. On average, siblings share only half of each other's genes.[13] In addition to differences in physical attributes, genetics is responsible for numerous disparities in personality. Even at birth, children differ temperamentally.[14] As one researcher has commented: "All parents are environmentalists until they have their second child."[15]

One would think a 50 percent overlap in genes would cause substantial resemblances in personality, but this is not the case. Sexual reproduction not only halves the genetic contribution of each parent, but it also rearranges the sequence of genes through a process called "recombination." Twin researcher David Lykken has provided a useful metaphor to elucidate this process.[16] Siblings are like people who receive similar digits in a telephone number. Just as with a scrambled telephone number and its resulting connection, genes that have been scrambled express themselves disparately. For this reason, many genetic influences are unique to the individual and cannot be passed on through inheritance.[17] Such traits are said to be "emergent."

The famous race horse Secretariat is thought to have possessed such emergent abilities.[18] Secretariat won the Triple Crown in 1973—the last horse to do so. To say that Secretariat "broke" course records is an understatement: he smashed them. Most of Secretariat's racing achievements, such as winning the Belmont stakes by 31 lengths, have never been approached to this day. Of Secretariat's 400-odd foals, only one (Risen Star) came close to matching Secretariat's racing abilities. Risen Star won two of the three contests that make up the Triple Crown, but even in these victories he was several seconds behind his sire's record-setting paces. For horse owners who paid handsomely for Secretariat's stud services, the problem was simple: once genetically scrambled, half of Secretariat was never really half.

One reason why identical twins have such similar personalities is their possession of the same emergent traits. This circumstance explains why identical twins reared apart often exhibit strikingly similar behavioral quirks, including unusual habits and hobbies. Even though some of these similarities would be expected by chance, they are significantly more common when twins are identical than when they are fraternal.[19]

There has been considerable debate over whether the genetic variability underlying most personality traits is adaptive. A good case can be made in the affirmative.[20] Nonvarying traits, such as the number of chambers in the human heart, represent evolutionary battles that were fought and resolved long ago. Traits that vary represent the playing field for evolutionary battles that are still being contested.[21] These battles are unresolved because no single genetic solution has proved optimal. Sensation seeking, which is heritable, provides a good example.[22] There is

Separated at birth, the Mallifert twins meet accidentally.

no ideal propensity for this behavior, which is adaptive in some contexts but not in others. Most behavioral problems can be surmounted in different ways. When hungry, for example, we can satisfy our needs by forcibly taking food from others. We can also negotiate for food, promising to repay any assistance with future acts of reciprocity.

Genetics represents the Darwinian wisdom of the ages. We are born into this world equipped with an extensive genetic tool kit that facilitates previously successful strategies. Individual family experience prompts us to develop the behavioral repertoires that are most relevant to our own lives. Although genetics is an ever-present part of this story, the environment is just as crucial. The relationship between nature and nurture is like that between artists and their tools. Genetics supplies the equivalent of canvas and paints. The environment, which guides the process of individual development, provides the equivalent of the artist's brush strokes. In a similar vein, our species has an "instinct" for language—one that other primates lack—but culture determines which particular language we learn to speak.[23]

Darwinian theory is often mistakenly allied with the doctrine of genetic determinism. Ample evidence demonstrates that nature and nurture represent a two-way street, and evolutionary biologists have supplied much of this evidence. In many species, environmental contexts trigger the release of hormones that regulate behavior. When a primate becomes the alpha male, his testosterone level rises. Give a low-ranking primate an injection of testosterone and this animal will rise to the top of the dominance hierarchy. As a result of being displaced, the previous alpha male suffers a reduction in his testosterone level. Antidepressant drugs such as Prozac have a similar effect. After being put on Prozac, beta males become alpha males.[24]

Properly understood, evolutionary accounts of human behavior are far from deterministic. A Darwinian approach calls attention to the constant interaction between nature and nurture, doing so, moreover, within a *developmental* framework.[25] In addition, Darwinian evolution highlights *the uniqueness of the individual.* Sibling differences represent perhaps the single most important source of evidence for this Darwinian perspective. When the developmental interactions between genetics and the environment are finally given their due, the distinction between nature and nurture is no longer particularly useful.

ENVIRONMENTAL INFLUENCES ON PERSONALITY

Relative to other species, human beings possess remarkably "open" genetic programs that facilitate learning.[26] Such open programs have been strongly favored during evolution by lengthy parental care. Extensive parental investment has in turn increased the adaptive consequences of behavioral strategies for maximizing such care. Because the environment is capable of facilitating this process in myriad ways, siblings are receptive to its influence. Openness to experience is the personality dimension that most reflects this distinctly human attribute.[27]

Chance Events

Environmental influences on personality can be subdivided into chance events and systematic experiences. Charles Darwin has asserted that the offer to sail as ship's naturalist on the *Beagle* was "by far the most important event in my life and has determined my whole career; yet it depended on so small a circumstance as my uncle offering to drive me 30 miles to Shrewsbury, which few uncles would have done."[28] Darwin's uncle made this trip in order to convince Darwin's father and older sisters, who initially opposed the idea, that Darwin should be allowed to accompany the *Beagle.* The uncle's opinion prevailed and Darwin's life was changed.[29] As much as chance played a role in Darwin's presence on the *Beagle,* the fact remains that Darwin was already organizing a voyage of his own to the Canary Islands. Given his natural history interests and his burning desire to travel, he was an obvious choice for the *Beagle* post, which is why his teacher Henslow nominated him.

From a Darwinian point of view, one would expect systematic experiences, especially those occurring within kin groups, to be more important for personality development than idiosyncratic influences. By "systematic experiences" I mean those that regularly reoccur as a result of attributes within individuals or their local environments. Although the precise degree to which personality is shaped by systematic experiences, rather than by chance events, cannot be resolved based on current evidence, the findings I present in this book confirm the overwhelming importance of systematic experiences.[30] The bulk of these systematic experiences occur *within the family.*

Systematic Experiences: Parental Discrimination

To their surprise, parents often discover that they prefer one child over another. Parents exhibit such preferences despite their own best efforts to treat children equally.[31] In one study, two-thirds of the children being interviewed claimed that mothers exhibited partiality.[32] Siblings also report greater parental discrimination than parents report. Indeed, children are exquisitely alert to favoritism by parents.

That children are sensitive to signs of parental discrimination makes Darwinian sense.[33] A child who cannot count on parental investment must come to terms with this fact of life and consider alternative options. This topic has long fascinated novelists, none of whom wrote about it more passionately than Charles Dickens. His literary career was haunted by the theme.

At the age of eleven Dickens became "chagrinned and depressed" when his impoverished parents allowed his elder sister to attend the Royal School of Music, leaving him at home "to black his father's boots, look after the younger children, and do small errands."[34] Soon afterward, his father was committed to debtors' prison. Just two days after his twelfth birthday, Dickens was sent to work in a boot-blacking factory. When his elder sister won a silver medal at the Royal Academy,

Charles Dickens in 1839 (age twenty-seven). His second novel, *Oliver Twist,* had appeared the previous year. He built his career on a simple truth known to children everywhere and summed up by him in *Great Expectations* (1861): "In the little world in which children have their existence, whosoever brings them up, there is nothing so finely perceived and so finely felt, as injustice."

Dickens was "deeply humiliated by the contrast with his own position, though incapable of envying her success."[35] He later recalled about the prize-day ceremony:

> I could not bear to think of myself—beyond the reach of all such honourable emulation and success. The tears ran down my face. . . . I prayed, when I went to bed that night, to be lifted out of the humiliation and neglect in which I was. I never had suffered so much before.[36]

After emerging from debtors' prison, Dickens's father quarreled with his son's employer, resulting in his son's dismissal. Dickens's mother tried to patch things up so that Dickens could be sent back to the factory. The mother's wishes were overruled, and Dickens was allowed to remain at home. With a bitterness unmitigated by the passage of time, Dickens later asserted: "I never afterwards forgot, I never shall forget, I never can forget that my mother was warm for my being sent back."[37]

Dickens was so embarrassed at having been temporarily "cast away" by his parents that he never told his wife or his children about this episode.[38] Two decades after his experience at the blacking factory, he finally penned a brief account about it:

> No words can express the secret agony of my soul as . . . I felt my early hopes of growing up to be a learned and distinguished man, crushed in my breast. . . . My whole nature was so penetrated with the grief and humiliation of such considerations, that even now, famous and caressed and happy, I often forget in my dreams that I have a dear wife and children; even that I am a man; and wander desolate back to that time in my life.[39]

This autobiographical fragment formed the basis for *David Copperfield* (1849–50), which Dickens once described as "a very complicated interweaving of truth and fiction."[40] For young Dickens, the response to being abandoned by his parents was to become obsessed by the problem and its diverse remedies. "Practically all of his novels," comments one biographer, "are concerned with the life within families . . . , specifically in the degradation and unsatisfactoriness of familial relationships."[41]

Dickens's poignant experience helps to explain why within-family differences are so influential in personality development. Children may not know if they are loved less than the children of other parents, but they are painfully aware when they are loved less than a sibling.[42] Children are especially sensitive to injustices within their own families because the psychological mechanisms for detecting these inequities have evolved within this social context.[43] This is why social class is a surprisingly poor predictor of social radicalism. The motives for rebellion generally arise *within* families, not *between* them.

Sibling Relationships

Siblings introduce substantial differences into each other's environments. In one study, more than three-quarters of siblings reported differing levels of attachment to each other.[44] Judy Dunn and Robert Plomin provide an instructive example from interviews with one sibling pair:

> I think I'd be very lonely without Carl [a ten-year-old sister comments about her six-year-old brother]. He comes and meets me at the gate after school and I think that's very friendly. . . . Don't really know what I'd do without a brother.
>
> [Carl, talking about his sister, remarks:] She's pretty disgusting and we don't talk to each other much. I don't really know much about her. [Interviewer: What is it you particularly like about her?] Nothing. Sometimes when I do something wrong she tells me off cruelly.[45]

Not all siblings perceive their relationship as disparately as these two, but agreement is also rare.

Because siblings are so different, they engage in frequent social comparisons. A shy child may feel socially inept compared with an extraverted sibling. When one sibling excels at school, or in a particular sport, other siblings carefully consider their chances of measuring up to these achievements.

Younger siblings are especially sensitive to adverse comparisons with their older siblings. For this reason they are drawn to interests and activities that older siblings have not already cultivated. Younger siblings

Voltaire in his later years. He responded to his brother's religious fanaticism by becoming the leading Enlightenment critic of the Catholic Church.

Voltaire subjected his elder brother to ridicule in his play *Le Dépositaire* (The Trustee, 1772). In a thinly disguised scene of the play, Voltaire has two brothers face off in dialogue. The elder brother is described as "a serious fool" who has formed "the extravagant design of being a perfect man." The younger brother "lives to please and to be pleased; a little wild, perhaps, but entirely amiable and honorable,—a universal favorite" (Parton 1881 , 1:56–57).

also relish those pursuits in which they manage to achieve competitive superiority. This is how Voltaire got his start as a poet. "I wrote verses from my cradle," he once commented. It seems that to amuse themselves, his family used to pit him in verse making against his elder brother Armand. Voltaire won easily. Comments one biographer: "The verses of the younger were so good as at first to please and afterwards to alarm the father, who was a man of judgment, and dreaded the development of so unprofitable a talent."[46] Voltaire's father, François Arouet, underestimated his prodigal son, whose literary works made him one of the richest men in Europe.

The example of Voltaire is instructive from another point of view. His whole personality was a mirror image of his brother's. The eldest son, Armand, has been described as "reserved and a little clumsy."[47] He was a "dutiful" son whose father favored him with the bequest of his lucrative office as royal notary.[48] At the age of seventeen Armand was converted to Jansenism, a fanatical Catholic sect. Armand's religious zeal led him "to condemn every sort of amusement, and to seek greedily for all apparent manifestations of divine favor."[49] Voltaire recoiled "with loathing and contempt" from his brother's pious example, "which made conscientious living ridiculous and offensive."[50] He turned to literature, a profession that his family considered "useless to society," because it allowed him to perfect the art of satire and to direct this formidable talent against bigotry and injustice.[51] His favorite target was the Catholic Church.

FINDING A NICHE

Sibling Contrast Effects

Among siblings, dramatic differences are commonplace. They arise because siblings cultivate distinct niches within the family. My favorite example of "niche picking" involves the family of Ralph Nader, the American crusader for consumer rights. When Nader and his three siblings were adolescents, they decided to divide up the world. Each sibling specialized in the languages, culture, and history related to his or her portion of the globe. The eldest, Shafeek, took the United States and Canada, and he later received his bachelor's degree at a Canadian university. The second sibling, Claire, specialized in the Middle East and wrote a master's thesis on the subject. The third sibling, Laura, selected Mexico and Latin America. At the University of California, Berkeley, she wrote her undergraduate thesis on how Mexican novels have portrayed leadership in the Mexican revolution. Her topic was considered so exotic by her department—sociology—that it refused to grant her a degree. Fortunately, an enlightened dean intervened, awarding her the first (and still the only) undergraduate degree at Berkeley in Latin American studies. Laura Nader subsequently became an anthropologist and is a member of the faculty at Berkeley.

The youngest of the four Nader siblings, Ralph chose to study China and the Far East. As an undergraduate at Princeton University, he learned Chinese, Russian, and Arabic. After Princeton, Ralph's interests turned to consumer safety in the United States, where he took on "Big Brother" in the form of General Motors and other large American corporations. None of the four Nader siblings picked Europe as their personal sphere of expertise because they had all studied this subject in school. By selecting other regions to study, they were able to learn more about different parts of the globe while also minimizing direct competition with one another.*

The term *contrast effects* has been used to describe these kinds of systematic sibling differences. Although the phenomenon is now well documented, the psychological mechanisms that underlie it are only beginning to be understood. One intriguing study was conducted by Frances Schachter et al., who surveyed the interests and personalities of college students from two- and three-child families.[52] Schachter's study is unusual because she and her associates had subjects assess both themselves and their siblings. Within each family, the first two siblings manifested the greatest disparities, followed by the second and third. Differences were significantly smaller for nonadjacent siblings. Gender also played a part, with dissimilarities being greatest for same-sex pairs. Schachter has proposed the term "deidentification" in discussing these sibling differences.[53]

These findings are part of a more complex pattern revealed by Schachter's elegant study. Siblings differed systematically in their identification with parents. If one sibling identified strongly with one parent, the adjacent sibling identified strongly with the other parent. Within each family, "split-parent" identifications were particularly pronounced for the first sibling pair.

* I thank Laura Nader for these personal details. I invite readers to send me stories about sibling competition and efforts to establish family niches. Such information may shed further light on some of the theoretical issues raised in this chapter. Please address any accounts to me, care of Pantheon Books, 201 East 50th Street, New York, NY 10022.

"And then, as soon as I had carved out my niche, they went and had another kid."

Theoretical Considerations

Everything that is known about siblings indicates that they go out of their way to be different. But why? Schachter explained her own results in psychoanalytic terms. Deidentification, she argued, is a "defense" against sibling rivalry—an attempt to deal with disruptive emotions arising from the "Cain Complex."[54] According to psychoanalytic theory, siblings are unconsciously preoccupied with the wish to kill other family members. When the intended victim is not a parent, it is a sibling.[55]

A Darwinian psychologist would turn Schachter's psychoanalytic interpretation on its head: the primary reason why siblings seek to be different is not defensive, but offensive. Siblings are motivated to exploit unoccupied niches because they stand to gain something in the process: greater parental investment. If deidentification facilitates a reduction in "intrapsychic conflict," as Schachter has proposed, this outcome is merely a by-product of a more fundamental Darwinian goal. Although this evolutionary explanation is hypothetical, it is consistent with considerable evidence from animal biology, where the phenomenon is well documented.[56] Should the hypothesis prove incorrect, *Homo sapiens* will be a remarkable exception to such a fundamental evolutionary principle.

The primary benefit of diversifying from one's siblings is the likelihood of increasing parental investment. Laterborns stand to gain more from this strategy than firstborns, who already tend to be favored and who also have first pick of a family niche. For younger siblings, diversification offers three advantages. First, given differences in age, laterborns will typically lag behind older siblings in the development of similar skills. To the extent that they cultivate different skills, laterborns will tend to minimize adverse comparisons with their older siblings. Second, to the extent that children differ in their abilities, parents will find it more difficult to compare them. Any ambiguity will generally work to the advantage of the younger offspring. Third and most important, the addition that each child makes to the parents' inclusive fitness will tend to be proportional to the development of skills not already represented among other family members. The benefits associated with novel abilities would have been especially useful within the small social groups that characterized ancestral life. When older siblings were uniformly accomplished at spear throwing, it was time to invent the bow and arrow. When older siblings already excelled at hunting, it was time to develop an aptitude for fishing. Diversification of talents would have provided our hominid ancestors with a considerable hedge against harsh and unpredictable environments, just as diversification in financial investments today helps to reduce the risk-adjusted return. In short, laterborns tend to become "radicals" in part because they are trying to cultivate novel approaches to the problem of family niches.[57]

That siblings jockey for family niches, including that of "the family radical," is evident from the interdependent relationship between birth rank, sibship size, and radicalism. Firstborns tend to respect the status quo, but the second of two children is distinctly radical. As sibship size increases, lastborns continue to be the most radical family members. Siblings having intermediate birth ranks tend to adopt intermediate degrees of radicalism (Fig. 4.1).[58]

Many Darwinian hypotheses about human behavior, including my explanation of why siblings seek to be different, agree with intuition. By agreeing with intuition, I mean that such hypotheses could easily have been formulated without a knowledge of Darwinian theory. For example, Darwin's theories explain why we tend to run away from large predators; but common sense provides the same explanation. Not every evolutionary explanation of human behavior is self-evident, but many of them tend to be so.[59] This circumstance raises an interesting

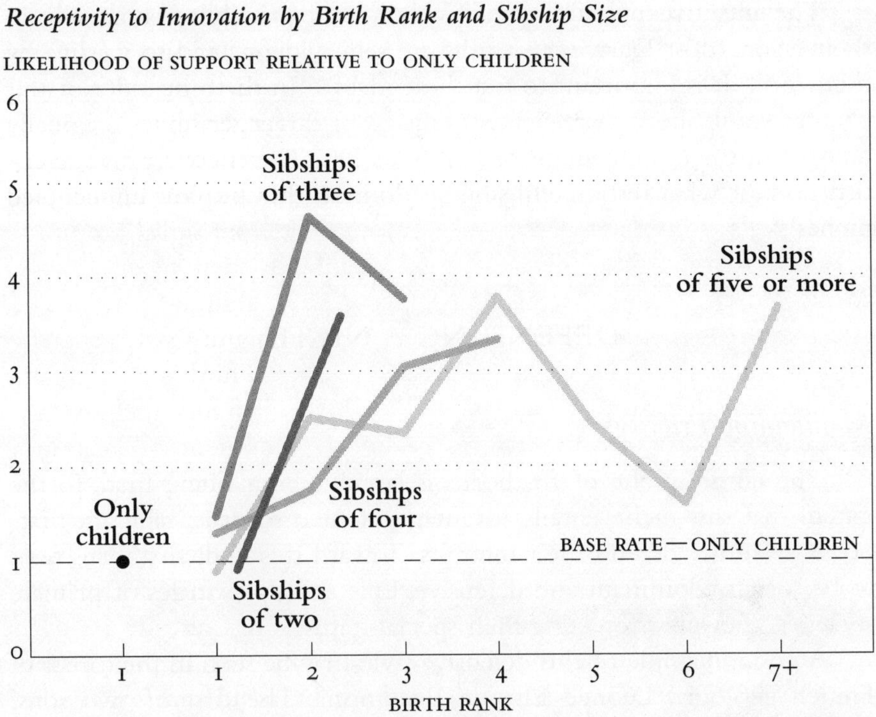

FIGURE 4.1. Birth rank and sibship size, as they relate to receptivity to 23 liberal scientific theories.The likelihood of support for each ordinal position is relative to the base rate for only children. In sibships of three children, secondborns are 4.6 times more likely than only children to support radical innovations. Because they have no siblings, only children represent a "controlled experiment" in birth-order studies.

In general, radicalism is proportional to *relative birth rank* (from first to last). This finding suggests that siblings jockey for family niches. Once occupied, niches preclude occupation by other siblings. In large sibships, laterborns are significantly less radical than they are in small sibships (an interaction effect). This finding invites a number of speculations about how family relationships change with increasing sibship size. For example, larger families may encourage greater cooperation among siblings.

question about evolutionary psychology: "Who needs it?" One of the great appeals of psychoanalytic theory has been its bold departure from intuition. Before Freud, who would have guessed that we all harbor an unconscious wish to kill our same-sex parent? Certainly no Darwinian! By comparison with psychoanalytic theory, evolutionary explanations of human behavior might seem lackluster.

The intuitive plausibility of evolutionary principles is actually in their favor. Most Darwinian truths are self-evident because we live by them. Still, it is important to test these ideas.[60] In the remainder of this chapter I will show that scientists engage in career strategies originally tailored to the advancement of family niches. The most creative scientists do best what resourceful siblings do best: they exploit unoccupied niches.

DEFENDING A NICHE

Maintaining Priority

The family niche of firstborns is largely about being first. To the extent that this niche entails advantages denied to other siblings, firstborns zealously defend their interests. Toward this end, firstborns tend to be socially dominant and defensive. Like the alpha males of primate societies, they are protecting their special status.

A good example of this defensive style may be seen in the career of French geologist Léonce Élie de Beaumont. The first of two sons, de Beaumont has been described as "dogmatic, cold, and distant."[61] Throughout his life he stuck fast to his own original but misguided theories of mountain formation. The innovations of others were anathema to him. In the 1850s he dismissed Boucher de Perthes's pioneering discovery of prehistoric tools. "The vacuous science" was how he referred to Darwin's evolutionary doctrines. When he died, in 1874, de Beaumont was the last surviving opponent of the theory of glaciation, proposed four decades earlier.[62] "Retraction," comments one historian about de Beaumont, "was not in his intellectual repertoire."[63]

Another of Darwin's firstborn critics, William Whewell, displayed a similar propensity for defending his own infallibility. As one Whewell biographer reports: "There can be no doubt about his quick-tempered resentment of criticism, his autocratic and often arbitrary exercise of academic power, and his jealous defense of his own position."[64] Whewell, who knew Darwin when the latter was a student at Cambridge University, dissented from the *Origin of Species* in a practical way. As the master of Trinity College at Cambridge, Whewell refused to allow a copy of Darwin's book to be placed in the college library.[65]

Priority disputes provide a particularly conspicuous manifestation of territorial behavior in science. The essence of such disputes is the need to be first. Firstborns ought to reflect this need more strongly than laterborns. To test this hypothesis, I have analyzed more than a hundred episodes in which scientists disputed priority.[66] In most instances, participants can be reliably subdivided into aggressors and their victims. A third relevant subgroup includes scientists who avoided priority disputes by agreeing to share credit or by renouncing their claims.

Among the 200 individuals included in this survey, firstborns were 3.2 times more likely than laterborns to initiate priority disputes or to pursue them in an uncompromising manner.[67] Galileo, Newton, Leibniz, and Freud are some of the firstborns who vigorously asserted their priority and sought to tarnish the careers of any scientists who got in their way. Many of the laterborns involved in these disputes were dragged into them by firstborns, whose charges of plagiarism forced the accused to defend a valid priority.

Isaac Newton was particularly well known for his disputes over priority. He was an arrogant man who ruled over the Royal Society "with an iron hand."[68] In his bitter quarrel with Leibniz over the invention of the calculus, Newton handpicked a committee of inquiry from among his supporters in the Royal Society, directed the self-serving investigation, and anonymously wrote the committee's published report.[69] Not content with this subterfuge, Newton then published an anonymous review extolling his own anonymous report! "By any normal standards," I. Bernard Cohen has asserted of Newton and Leibniz, "the behavior of both men was astonishing."[70] Like Newton, Leibniz was a firstborn, which helps to account for the acrimony of this dispute. Firstborns do not like being second best, and they readily forsake amicable forms of discourse to forestall this outcome.

Some social historians have linked the formation of the Royal Society, and the emergence of the experimental method, to the adoption of "polite" styles of scientific discourse. "The experimental philosophers of the Royal Society," assert Steven Shapin and Simon Schaffer, "were 'modest, humble, and friendly'; they were tolerant of differing opinions and worked collectively toward attainable and solid goals."[71] In making their argument, Shapin and Schaffer steer clear of Isaac Newton—a decidedly cantankerous genius—and instead build their case around Robert Boyle, a chemist who was a brilliant exponent of the experimental method. Boyle was also the youngest of fourteen children and is described by one biographer as possessing a "friendly and modest" personality typical of laterborns.[72] As one of his British contemporaries remarked about him, Boyle was "civil rather to excess."[73] No one

Left: **Humphry Davy** in 1821 (age forty-two), the renowned chemist whose character was flawed by arrogance and jealousy. *Right:* **Michael Faraday** in 1842 (age fifty). His brilliant experimental studies surpassed those of his former employer, Davy. A modest and gentle person, Faraday enjoyed teaching children about the mysteries of science.

would have made the same charge against Boyle's elder brother Roger, a military leader under Cromwell, who wrote poetry on the side. He is best remembered for the couplet: "Poets are sultans, if they had their will; / For every author would his brother kill."[74]

Humphry Davy's behavior toward his young assistant Michael Faraday provides another poignant example of uncivil behavior in science. In 1821 Faraday discovered electromagnetic induction and, based on this principle, showed how electricity could be transformed into mechanical motion. Every electrical motor in use today incorporates this revolutionary principle. Some scientists thought that Faraday should have given more credit to William Hyde Wollaston, who had overlooked the radical consequences of his own idea, but Wollaston did not bother to dispute the matter. Both Wollaston and Faraday were younger sons.

Humphry Davy, the first of five children, convinced himself that Faraday had stolen Wollaston's ideas. How else, Davy reasoned, could his former laboratory assistant make such an important discovery? More than just a suspicion of wrongdoing was behind Davy's jealous reaction:

> The discovery of electromagnetic rotations in 1821 had raised Faraday's reputation to the point of international renown. Davy . . . saw his pre-eminence in English science gradually fading before the achievements of his former laboratory helper. Davy was not a vicious man, but he was vain and the rise of Faraday's reputation could not be accepted by him with good grace.[75]

Faraday was an unusually modest individual who had no taste for scientific polemics, and he felt deeply wounded by Davy's accusations.[76] Matters came to a head in 1824 when Faraday was proposed for membership in the Royal Society. As president of this prestigious body, Davy campaigned strenuously against his former assistant. When it looked like Faraday would be elected, Davy tried to block the voting. Despite Davy's opposition, Faraday was elected. Davy cast the only opposing vote.[77]

Magnanimity in Science

Faced with the prospect of losing credit for their discoveries, some scientists have behaved surprisingly magnanimously. In 1799, twenty-five-year-old Jean-Baptiste Biot developed a method for solving difference-differential equations. Pierre Simon de Laplace encouraged him to present his ideas before the Institut de France. Together with Sylvestre Lacroix and Napoleon Bonaparte (who dabbled in mathematics before conquering Europe), Laplace wrote a favorable memoir discussing Biot's discovery. "Only some time afterward did Laplace show Biot a paper he had put away in a drawer, a paper in which Laplace had himself arrived at much the same method years before."[78] Laplace's many students became, in Biot's words, "so many adopted children of his thought. . . . He looked after us so actively that we did not have to think of it ourselves."[79] Laplace was a lastborn.

Another potentially bitter priority dispute was avoided by two particularly chivalrous younger sons. In June 1858 Charles Darwin received a manuscript from Alfred Russel Wallace, who was collecting natural history specimens in Malaysia. Wallace's brief essay completely anticipated Darwin's theory of natural selection. Darwin was stunned. Although Wallace had not specifically asked Darwin to submit the essay for publication, he had asked Darwin to forward it to Charles Lyell.[80] After receiving Wallace's bombshell, Darwin honored Wallace's request, remarking to Lyell:

> Your words have come true with a vengeance that I sh^{d}. be forestalled. . . . I never saw a more striking coincidence. [If] Wallace had my M.S. sketch written out in 1842 he could not have made a better short abstract! Even his terms now stand as Heads of my Chapters. . . . So all my originality, whatever it may amount to, will be smashed.[81]

Although distressed at the prospect of losing his priority, Darwin offered to step aside in favor of the younger naturalist. "I would far rather burn my whole book," he informed Lyell, "than that he [Wallace] or any man sh^{d}. think that I had behaved in a paltry spirit."[82] Together with Joseph Hooker, Lyell persuaded Darwin that it was honorable for him to publish simultaneously. Wallace's paper appeared in the July 1858 issue of the Linnean Society's journal, preceded by extracts from Darwin's unpublished writings.[83]

Wallace responded to this "delicate situation" in a most amiable manner, stating that "it would have caused me much pain & regret had Mr. Darwin's excess of generosity led him to make public my paper unaccompanied by his own much earlier & I doubt not much more complete views on the same subject."[84] In response to Wallace's glowing praise of the *Origin of Species,* Darwin replied that "most persons would in your position have felt some envy or jealousy. How nobly free you seem to be of this common failing of mankind."[85]

After Wallace's return to England, in 1862, he and Darwin became good friends. Some years later Darwin commented to Wallace that "very few things in my life have been more satisfactory to me—that we have never felt any jealousy towards each other, though in one sense rivals."[86] In 1889, seven years after Darwin's death, Wallace reissued a series of evolutionary essays under the title *Darwinism.* He always referred to the theory of natural selection as Darwin's. As sociologist Robert Merton has commented, the Darwin-Wallace affair is a remarkable instance in which two scientists tried "to outdo one another in giving credit to the other for what each had separately worked out."[87] It is hard to imagine two firstborns reacting so magnanimously under the same circumstances. Nothing about the firstborn niche is conducive to relinquishing priority.

OPENNESS AND DIVERSIFICATION

Hypotheses

Faced with older siblings who are superior in age and expertise (and inclined to claim priority for good ideas), younger siblings do well to seek out interests of their own. The more interests, the better. Having broad interests increases the likelihood of discovering personal talents that parents deem worthy of support. Broad interests are a prominent manifestation of openness to experience, so this hypothesis is consistent with many other common findings about birth order.[88]

The strong link between birth order and openness to experience is no accident. For laterborns, openness and versatility are tactical responses to firstborn priority, facilitating "adaptive radiation" within the family system. Unlike the thirteen species of Darwin's finches, which have required several million years to evolve their distinctive forms, we human beings achieve the same adaptive end by using our minds. As Jonathan Weiner has expressed this point in his Pulitzer Prize–winning *The Beak of the Finch,* "The mind is our beak."[89] Everything about laterborns—their interests, their attitudes, and their cognitive styles—tends toward "divergence."

Psychologists have used the term "divergent thinking" to describe this psychological style.[90] The aim of divergent thinking is to generate a large number of potential solutions to a problem. In testing for this ability, psychologists sometimes ask people how many uses they can think of for an object, such as a paper clip. Originality, mental flexibility, and resourcefulness are hallmarks of divergent thinking. Divergent thinking may be contrasted with convergent thinking, which aims to find a single fixed answer to questions. Convergent thinking is emphasized on IQ tests. Divergent thinking is tested most effectively by life, especially life under difficult circumstances.

The conditions that promote diversity in organic evolution are all present in the normal course of family life. Divergence is adaptive whenever competition exists for a scarce resource, such as parental investment. Diversification provides three benefits: it minimizes direct competition between siblings; it tends to increase parental investment (for reasons I shall explain); and it makes offspring less dependent on parents. A Darwinian perspective on family life suggests a number of testable hypotheses about sibling diversification. I state these hypotheses in the form of four "rules" for optimizing parental investment.

Rule 1: If you are laterborn, diversify. All things being equal, it is wise for laterborns to adopt multiple interests. As a rule, parents invest heavily in eldest children. Whether they invest as much in subsequent offspring may depend on the prospects of a superior "return" on investment. The more talents a laterborn offspring exhibits, the more parents are likely to nurture the most promising ones.

Rule 2: If parents have limited resources, diversify. Whenever parents are unable to nurture all of their children's interests and abilities, they are likely to invest more in those offspring who display the greatest talent and zeal. When resources are limited, the benefits of diversification ought to apply to all offspring—firstborns and laterborns alike.

Rule 3: Diversify in proportion to the number of your siblings. The same logic that dictates diversification by laterborns, and when family resources are limited, also applies whenever numerous rivals are competing for parental investment.

Rule 4: Under certain circumstances, disregard the previous three rules and specialize. When family resources are limited, it may be wise to consider specialization. If other siblings are striving to be generalists, specialization is a "divergent" strategy that may work to one's advantage. Paradoxically, by demanding less from parents, offspring may end up receiving more. Several conditions favor success with this "contrarian" strategy. First, interests must be chosen *very carefully*. Second, mastery of these interests should be enhanced by study or practice. Third, specialization is likely to be a good strategy for enhancing parental investment whenever siblings closest in age have opted for generalist niches.

Career Strategies in Science

To test these four hypotheses I have analyzed the career histories of the 3,890 scientists in my database.[91] My dependent variable is the tendency for scientists to specialize or generalize. Fifty-two percent of these scientists confined their research to a single field, such as astronomy. Another 35 percent made significant contributions in two fields, such as geology and paleontology. Only 9 percent did notable work in three fields, and only 3 percent did so in four fields. Charles Darwin was a premier "generalist," achieving distinction in five fields—geographic exploration, geology, zoology, botany, and psychology. In the course of the last four centuries, only 1 percent of scientists have matched Darwin's breadth.[92] He was a very "divergent" fellow indeed, which is perhaps why he grasped the evolutionary significance of this principle.

The pursuit of multiple disciplines is associated with scientific eminence.[93] Were diversification the only requirement for success in science, every scientist would push this strategy to extremes, like seventeenth-century Jesuit Athanasius Kircher. With publications in ten different disciplines, he holds the record for polymathy in my study, but he spread himself too thin to achieve lasting fame. By confining himself to five disciplines, and by relating them all to the unifying principle of evolution, Darwin was far more successful.

Findings

Rule 1 ("If laterborn, diversify"). This rule is confirmed. The higher an individual's birth rank, the more intellectual diversity he or she achieved. Within each family, youngest children tended to be the most diversified individuals.[94] Voltaire, the youngest of three children, is a good example. He achieved distinction in five fields: physics (as a popularizer of Newtonian theory), natural history, moral philosophy, history, and literature. As the fifteenth of seventeen children, Benjamin Franklin distinguished himself in six fields. Athanasius Kircher, who sought to out-diversify all diversifiers, was the youngest of six sons in a family of nine children.

Rule 2 ("When parental resources are scarce, diversify"). This rule is also confirmed. Lower-class scientists (including firstborns) pursued more interests than upper-class scientists.[95] This finding is noteworthy because it goes counter to socioeconomic expectation. Scientists from well-to-do families had ample resources to branch out in their researches, but they were less likely to do so than lower-class individuals. Scientists typically accomplished diversification in the face of socioeconomic hardship.

Rule 3 ("Diversify in large sibships"). This third rule is confirmed, although the confirmation includes an unanticipated twist. In general, individuals having many siblings were more scientifically diverse than those who had few siblings.[96] Social class substantially modifies this trend. In upper-class families, having multiple siblings was especially conducive to having multiple scientific interests, and laterborns led the way in this respect. In middle- and lower-class families, sibship size is negatively correlated with number of scientific interests, a contradiction of Rule 2. Laterborns were the most affected by this trend, in large part because firstborns seem to have cornered the available family resources. Significant findings related to Rule 3 therefore involve three different effects: family size acting as a main effect; a two-way interaction between family size and social class; and a three-way interaction involving family size, social class, and birth order.[97] Sibling strategies are a complicated business!

The precise proximate-causal mechanisms that are responsible for these interaction effects are open to question. One plausible explanation is that middle- and lower-class parents tend to concentrate investment in the eldest son, to the detriment of younger siblings. Sigmund Freud, a firstborn, provides a good illustration of this bias in parental investment. "In spite of his youth," his sister Anna later wrote about her brother, "Sigmund's word and wish were respected by everyone in the family."[98] When Freud was eleven, Anna began to play the piano. Although her brother's room was nowhere near the piano, Sigmund insisted that the noise was disturbing his ability to study. "The piano disappeared," Anna lamented, "and with it all opportunities for his [five] sisters to become musicians."[99] In Freud's case, firstborn priority won out over laterborn efforts at diversification. The money that might have been spent on piano lessons went instead into the many books that, even when he was a child, lined Sigmund's study.

Rule 4 ("Whenever expedient, disregard Rules 1–3 and specialize"). Faced with limited family resources, some laterborns will inevitably resort to Rule 4. This contrarian rule manifests itself in subtle ways, making its influence easy to miss. In any given family, the optimal strategy depends in part on the strategies employed by other offspring. Firstborns typically preempt the best strategy given the amount of available family resources. Firstborn strategies then dictate secondborn strategies, and so on down the line.[100]

The greater the number of rivals for parental investment, the more firstborns responded by developing diverse interests. Lastborns also pursued this strategy, doing so even more zealously than firstborns. Surrounded by would-be Leonardo da Vincis, middle children often resorted to Rule 4. Their tendency to limit their interests was often decided in conjunction with age spacing. The larger the age gap between them and the next older sibling, the more middle children were likely to pursue the usual lastborn strategy. Within each family of a given size, these trends in diversification involve U-shaped patterns by birth rank. These findings are best appreciated visually (Fig. 4.2).[101]

Number of Scientific Fields as Related to Birth Rank and Sibship Size

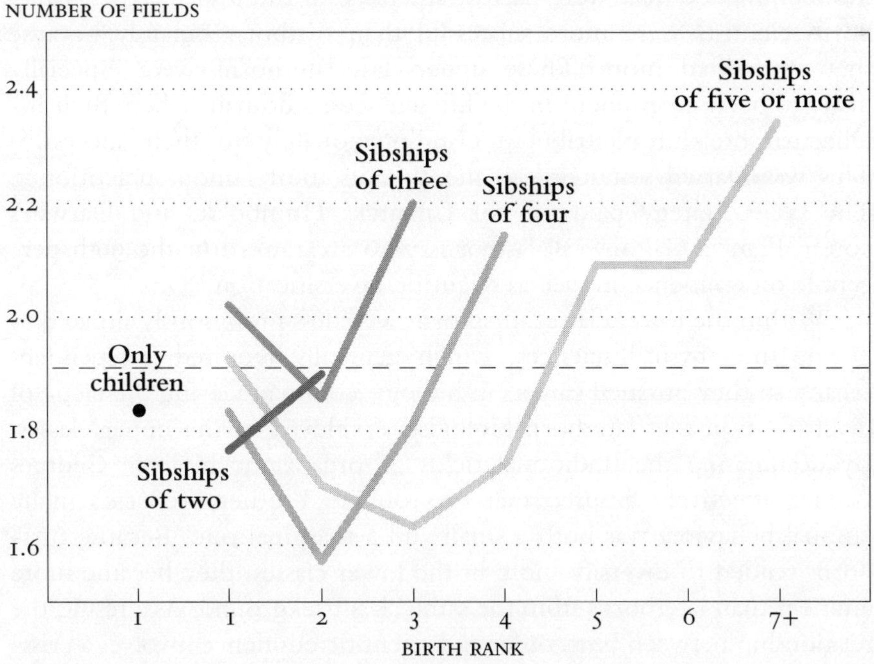

FIGURE 4.2. Birth rank and sibship size, as they relate to number of fields in which a scientist does research. Lastborns tend to work in the largest number of fields. Although less diversified than lastborns, firstborns work in more fields than middle children—especially those middle children who follow firstborns immediately in birth rank.

The interactive relationship between birth rank and sibship size is illustrated by the pattern of diversification in small sibships. In a sibship of two children, the second child diversifies. In a sibship of three, the second child specializes, thereby achieving maximum contrast with the other two siblings.

Career Strategies and Scientific Eminence

To what extent are sibling strategies relevant to scientific success? Being firstborn is associated with eminence, although the effect is modest. Once eminence is controlled for family size and social class, differences by birth order generally disappear (as they do in my own study). Intriguing differences remain, however, in *how* people become eminent. Because there are many sibling strategies, there are many roads to Stockholm.[102]

Historically, multiple scientific interests were more likely to promote eminence than were narrow interests. In the upper classes, laterborn scientists were more successful than firstborns, mainly because they diversified more. These upper-class laterborns were especially likely to become eminent in the life sciences, a domain where their intellectual breadth contributed disproportionately to their success.[103] This was Darwin's strategy, to mention its most famous practitioner. The same strategy paid off for Lamarck, Humboldt, and Darwin's cousin Francis Galton—all lastborns who are ranked in the 99th percentile on eminence as well as scientific diversification.[104]

Within the lower classes, firstborns were less propitiously situated to pursue the physical sciences, which generally required independent means, so they pursued careers in biology, commandeering the tactic of diversification that laterborn biologists employed in the upper classes. By dominating the traditional fields of organismic biology, Georges Cuvier effectively ensured that his younger brother Frédéric's niche (animal behavior) was both a small and a marginal one! Because firstborns tended to diversify more in the lower classes, they became more eminent than laterborns from the same class background. As a result, the relationship between birth order and scientific eminence involves a crisscrossing relationship by social class. One constant, however, stands out: Within each class, firstborns generally chose the most straightforward route to eminence. Laterborns pursued more unconventional paths.[105]

These findings about social class and eminence are typical of the association between sibling strategies and intellectual success. Among people who go into the sciences, social class exerts almost no direct influence on achievement. Still, social class manifests itself indirectly, causing siblings in the same family to adopt different strategies. Paradoxically, social class expresses itself as a *within-family* difference.

One other point about scientific eminence deserves emphasis. Controlled for levels of parental investment, middle children were unusually adept at becoming eminent by working in just one field.[106] Gregor Mendel, who discovered the laws of genetics, provides a good illustration of this tendency.

The second of three children, Mendel came from a family of peasant farmers. He received a university education only because his younger sister renounced her share in the family estate.[107] Lacking the means to continue his education, Mendel entered a monastery. Teaching duties at a local high school, along with other obligations at the monastery, limited his free time for research. During his entire career,

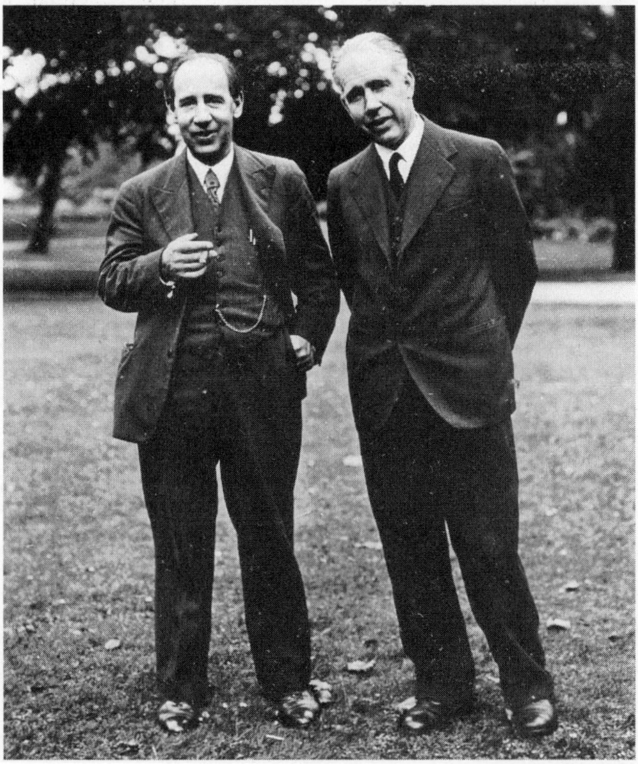

Niels and Harald Bohr, about 1950. They were the second and third of the three Bohr children. Niels (*right*), an eldest son, was serious and reserved, whereas Harald, eighteen months younger, was more outgoing. In their youth, the two brothers played soccer for the Danish national team. Niels was a goalie on the backup squad. Harald diagnosed his brother's weak point by noting that Niels "did not charge out fast enough" (Moore 1966:17). Harald played halfback on the first squad and led his team to an Olympic silver medal in 1908. Not to be outdone, Niels won the Nobel Prize in physics (1922). Harald, who became a mathematician, never equaled his brother's scientific accomplishments.

Mendel published only thirteen papers. One of these papers was all that he needed to achieve lasting fame.

The essence of Mendel's genius was his ability to discover profound truths by the simplest of experimental means. In 1855, the year before he began his hybridization experiments with ordinary garden peas, the headmaster at his secondary school wrote a brief report about his gentle monk. "Herr Mendel," he noted, "is a good experimentalist, and can give excellent demonstrations with rather scanty equipment, both in physics and in natural history."[108] Between 1856 and 1863 Mendel hybridized thousands of garden peas according to a simple research design. Hundreds of better-known biologists, all favored with greater resources, failed to accomplish what Mendel achieved in a small monastery garden. They lacked the revolutionary genius characteristic of his family niche.

RISK TAKING

Laterborns are inclined to take risks. From a Darwinian point of view, the evolutionary costs of risk taking are low whenever the prospects of survival or reproduction are also low. Risk taking is a useful strategy in the quest to find an unoccupied niche, and it is an important component of openness to experience. People who are open are often described as "adventurous" and "daring."[109]

A variety of research findings support these assertions. Compared with firstborns, laterborns are more likely to rate themselves as "physically daring."[110] Laterborns are also more likely to engage in dangerous sports such as rugby, football, boxing, and parachute jumping. By contrast, firstborns favor swimming, tennis, golf, and other noncontact sports. The inclination to participate in dangerous sports increases with birth rank and family size.[111] Two timeworn rules of the sibling road!

Scientist-Explorers

In an effort to determine the antecedents of risk-taking behavior, I have made a special study of scientific explorers.[112] Prior to the mid-nineteenth century, travel to faraway places was a good way to shorten one's lifespan. The voyage of the *Beagle* cost the lives of five men, through accidents and disease, and Darwin himself risked death on several occasions. Humboldt's traveling companion, Aimé Bonpland, was imprisoned for nine years by a Paraguayan dictator, who feared losing his monopoly on maté.[113] As Darwin himself discovered in South America, naturalists were often suspected of being spies.

To better understand the relationship between world travel and family niches, I have coded every member of my sample for the farthest distance they traversed from their place of birth.[114] Most naturalists who journeyed to remote parts of the world were younger sons, like Darwin, Wallace, Humboldt, and Bonpland (Fig. 4.3).[115]

World Travel as Related to Ordinal Position

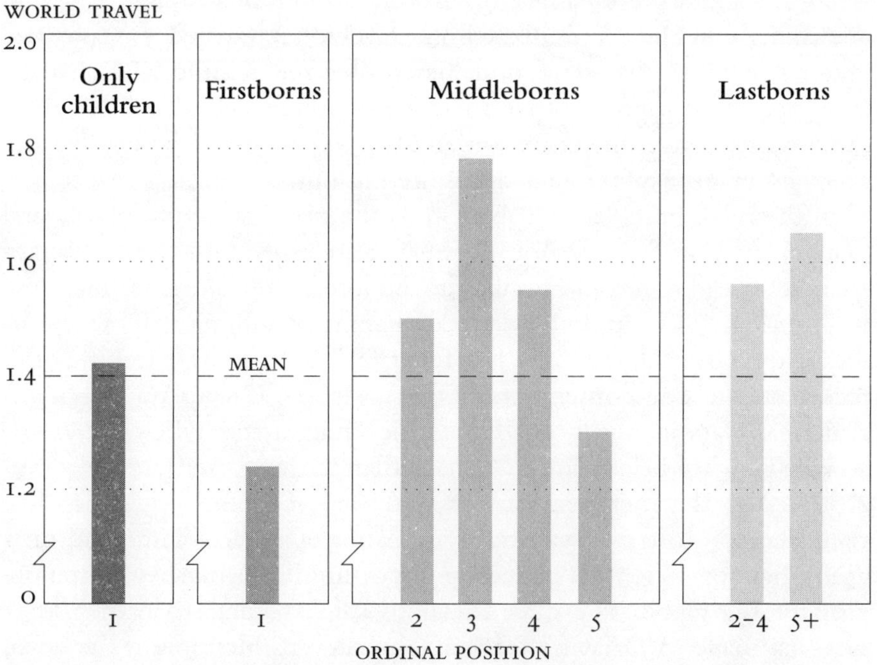

FIGURE 4.3. Birth order and world travel, coded from 0 (no travel to another country) to 4 (circumnavigation of the globe). The dotted line indicates the mean level of travel for the sample. Controlled for social class and sibship size, laterborns were significantly more likely than firstborns to undertake extensive travel to remote regions of the globe. Degree of world travel peaks with birth ranks two through four, although it is almost as pronounced among lastborns from birth ranks five and higher. Compared with firstborns, laterborns were 2.0 times more likely to circumnavigate the globe. Lastborns were 3.0 times more likely to do so.

World travel reflects sibling differences independently of socioeconomic considerations such as primogeniture. For example, only children and laterborn eldest sons both engaged in significantly more travel than eldest sons who were firstborns. It might be argued that firstborns, who are older than their siblings, are more likely to have families of their own, which would limit their ability to travel. Firstborns are no older, however, than the average laterborn in the general population, and this is the relevant issue. Controlling for the age of parents relative to their offspring, which might influence available resources, does not diminish these birth-order differences.

Darwin's story illustrates an important tendency among explorers. Even as a child, he dreamed of making an oceanic voyage.[116] So did Alexander von Humboldt, for whom travel to faraway places was a "secret fascination" that he found "irresistible" as a child.[117] Conveyed from one laterborn to another, these childhood fantasies became contagious realities. As a university student, Darwin read Humboldt's *Personal Narrative* of his exploits, which inspired in him a "burning zeal to add even the most humble contribution to the noble structure of Natural Science."[118] Darwin was soon organizing an expedition to the Canary Islands. "I read & reread Humboldt," he informed his teacher Henslow in July 1831. "Do you do the same, & I am sure nothing will prevent us seeing the Great Dragon tree [of Tenerife]."[119] A month later, the offer to sail on the *Beagle* interrupted Darwin's plans. On his way to South America, Darwin finally got to see the Dragon tree when the *Beagle* weighed anchor briefly in the Canary Islands.

Because the members of my study are predominantly scientists, their decision to travel was mostly a matter of choice. Time and time again, firstborn scientists passed up opportunities to journey to remote parts of the globe. The offer to sail as ship's naturalist on the *Beagle* was first made to Darwin's teacher John Stevens Henslow, a firstborn. Henslow declined the invitation, recommending Darwin instead. Another famous firstborn, the Swedish botanist Carolus Linnaeus, turned down multiple offers to broaden his botanical knowledge through travel. In rejecting the enticements of Hermann Boerhaave, who had offered to arrange free passage for him on Dutch ships, "Linnaeus excused himself on the grounds that the heat would be intolerable to one brought up in a cold climate." Linnaeus's biographer explains his true motives: "In fact the Swede disliked extreme cold almost as much as he disliked extreme heat, and [a visit to nearby] Lapland had taught him that he did not care for 'roughing it' anywhere."[120] When Napoleon Bonaparte organized his Egyptian campaign, he requested assistance from various French scientists. Georges Cuvier "avoided leaving [Paris], but Geoffrey [Saint-Hilaire, a lastborn] accepted enthusiastically, and from 1798 to 1801, in the midst of adventures in which he often risked his life, he made many scientific observations."[121]

When firstborns did journey to remote parts of the globe, they often did so because they were able to travel in relative comfort. Darwin's American opponent Louis Agassiz followed in Darwin's South American footsteps in 1865. His trip was made aboard a luxurious steamship, hardly the kind of primitive accommodations that laterborns generally

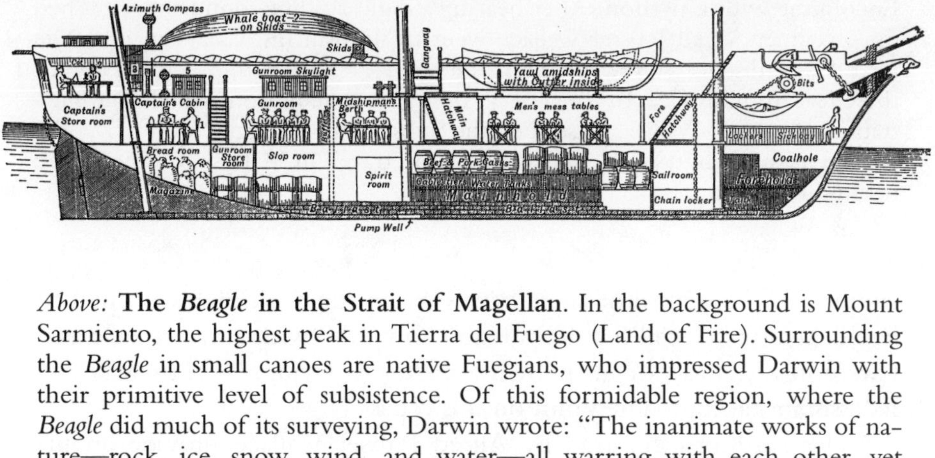

Above: **The *Beagle* in the Strait of Magellan**. In the background is Mount Sarmiento, the highest peak in Tierra del Fuego (Land of Fire). Surrounding the *Beagle* in small canoes are native Fuegians, who impressed Darwin with their primitive level of subsistence. Of this formidable region, where the *Beagle* did much of its surveying, Darwin wrote: "The inanimate works of nature—rock, ice, snow, wind, and water—all warring with each other, yet combined against man—here reigned in absolute sovereignty" (1845:241).

Below: **Plan of the *Beagle*,** as sketched by one of Darwin's shipmates in 1890. Shown are (1) Darwin's seat in the captain's cabin, (2) his seat in the poop cabin, and (3) his drawers for storing specimens.

Darwin suffered dreadfully from seasickness during the *Beagle* voyage, especially in Tierra del Fuego. "I loathe, I abhor the sea, & all ships which sail on it," he proclaimed to his sister Susan near the end of the five-year voyage (Darwin 1985–, 1:503). In spite of his problems with seasickness, Darwin contemplated undertaking another voyage after his return to England.

Encounter with a python. After hearing a slight rustling sound above his bed one evening, Alfred Russel Wallace went to sleep in his Malaysian hut. The next day he discovered the source of the noise—a large python, curled up just three feet from his face. In *The Malay Archipelago* (1869), from which this illustration is taken, Wallace describes the subsequent struggle to remove the python from the hut. Wallace's account of his travels in Malaysia was dedicated to another famous voyager—Charles Darwin.

endured in the course of their travels. From the deck of his steamer in Brazil Agassiz boasted that he was able to work "with as much ease as if I were in my study, or in the Museum at Cambridge."[122] His wife and six assistants accompanied him on this cruise.

The hardships endured by Alfred Russel Wallace provide an instructive contrast with Louis Agassiz's mode of travel. From 1848 to 1852 Wallace explored the tributaries of the Amazon basin with Henry Walter Bates. On his return home from South America in 1852 Wallace's ship caught fire and sank. He lost the fruits of four years of collecting, his diary, and most of his scientific papers. He also lost his youngest brother, Edward, who had joined him on the Amazon and died there of yellow fever at the age of twenty-two.[123]

Setting out again to Malaysia in 1854, Wallace contracted malaria. It was while resting during a malarial attack that he thought of the theory of natural selection.[124] Like Wallace, scientists who brave the dangers of faraway places are generally inclined toward radical ideas. When they are not risking their necks in dangerous explorations, they are braving intellectual storms at home. Among participants in the Darwinian revolution, world travel predicts support for Darwinism. Besides Wallace and Darwin, prominent laterborn explorers who backed the theory of evolution include Joseph Hooker, Thomas Henry Huxley, and Ernst Haeckel. Birth order, not travel, explains most of the relationship. When world travel is controlled for the fact that explorers were usually laterborn, travel is no longer a significant predictor.[125]

Like diversity of interests, world travel obeys the four rules of the sibling road that I have outlined earlier in this chapter. The people who risked their lives in faraway places were (1) laterborns, (2) from large families, (3) from the lower classes, and (4) individuals who made exploration their personal family niche. This last conclusion follows from a significant zigzag pattern that can be observed between world travel and birth rank. Firstborns were unlikely to travel, but second sons were especially likely to do so. Other middle sons were less likely to travel, apparently because the "explorer" niche was already taken. The failure of these other middle sons to exploit this niche made it more attractive to lastborns, who were typically inveterate travelers.[126]

The inclination to travel, with its "irresistible" roots in childhood daydreams, bears all the hallmarks of a sibling strategy. Like intellectual diversity, travel to faraway places is an effective way of finding an unoccupied niche. Most younger siblings are explorers, which is how they find their niche. For some of them, the process of discovery becomes a niche of its own.[127]

CONCLUSIONS

It is not widely known, but Darwin had a lifelong interest in biography.[128] He read countless biographies and he also wrote three: one of his grandfather Erasmus Darwin; an *Autobiography;* and a biography of his eldest son's psychological development during his first three years.[129] In addition, a substantial portion of Darwin's *Autobiography* is devoted to his father.[130] In all, Darwin's biographical efforts cover four generations of his own family. Why did Darwin value biography so highly? His theories are about *individuals* and especially about their development over the lifespan. Natural selection, as Darwin fully appreciated, acts on the entire life course. Properly told, Darwinian narratives are biographies.

Childhood and the family are central to the story of human behavior because they provide the immediate causal context for these developmental scenarios. Childhood is about the search for a family niche. The first rule of the sibling road is to be different from one's brothers and sisters, especially if one happens to be a laterborn. Sibling diversity is testimony to the powerful role that the environment plays in personality development. Although evolutionary principles guide this process, the story is one of seamless interactions between genetic potentials and environmental opportunities.

Siblings go out of their way to be different because it is in their Darwinian interests to do so. Diversity reduces competition for scarce resources. It is also a good way of finding an unoccupied niche. Unlike other species, we human beings diverge with our minds. In the course of individual development, we accomplish what other species achieve more gradually over the generations.

Darwin's theories provide a surprisingly useful road map for biography. In particular, Darwin's principle of divergence helps to resolve the question that so puzzled Voltaire's nineteenth-century biographer James Parton: Why was Voltaire so different from his pious elder brother? Voltaire's whole career was a divergent response to the problems of "Voltairian" family life. His solution to these problems was so radical that his own family failed to see the genius of it. Confronted with an elder brother who worshipped God and the status quo, Voltaire devoted his life to criticizing "the best of all possible worlds." He sent his stinging barbs of social criticism dressed in poetry so pleasing that his victims could never be sure whether to laugh or cry. The day that François Arouet's family invited him to compete with his elder brother in composing verses, the future "Voltaire" discovered his niche. His genius was that of a typical younger sibling: *versatility,* and in verse!

5

DEVELOPMENTAL GLITCHES

Voltaire was right. Ours is not the best of all possible worlds. As Voltaire's Candide discovered, the optimistic philosophy of Dr. Pangloss is contradicted by imperfection and suffering all over the globe. The unfortunate Candide had to endure robbery, floggings, and enslavement before he finally rejected his teacher's platitudes.

Life's miseries fall disproportionately on children. In most developing countries, children are afflicted by chronic malnutrition and disease. Throughout history, half of all children have failed to reach adulthood. Even when life is not seriously threatened, childhood involves developmental glitches. When children encounter adversity, they do their best to make things better. We may not live in Pangloss's "best of all possible worlds," but we usually make the best of the world in which we live. The grain of truth in Dr. Pangloss's philosophy reflects the teachings of his greatest adversary—Charles Darwin: Evolution promotes adaptation. More than any other species, *Homo sapiens* possesses "open" genetic programs that allow adaptation to occur during the course of individual development.

Developmental glitches affect family members differently. For example, parental loss rarely has the same impact on siblings because they are at different ages. Parental loss may induce an eldest child to forgo further education in order to help support younger siblings, whose likelihood of attending college may actually increase. In closing a window of opportunity for one offspring, misfortune may open a window for another.

To understand such disparate developmental outcomes, we need to relate sibling strategies, and the niches they promote, to the family system. Besides birth order, a theory of sibling strategies must consider available parental resources, bias in their allocation, and conflicts over these allocations. Gender, temperament, and birth order all contribute to sibling strategies. In developing a theory of sibling strategies, I do not mean to exclude only children. Singletons are a special case in this theory. Like other children, singletons do their best to maximize parental investment. In traditional societies they do so by resisting the mother's efforts at weaning, which in turn affects her likelihood of conceiving a rival for parental investment. Like the cuckoo, only children exemplify sibling strategies that have accomplished their goal. There is an "only child" in all of us. Among children with siblings, the strategies typical of singletons are supplemented by others for dealing with brothers and sisters.

CONFLICT WITH PARENTS

Sibling conflict and parent-offspring conflict are flip sides of the same Darwinian coin. For this reason, conflict with parents is part of the dynamic that promotes birth-order differences. Parent-offspring conflict is closely allied to the concept of *attachment.* Attachment behavior has become an important field of research following the pioneering work of British psychiatrist John Bowlby.[1] Bowlby rejected the conventional thinking of his profession, which interpreted attachment behavior as neurotic dependency on the mother's breast. Observation of children separated from their parents convinced Bowlby that attachment was more than a conditioned reflex based on feeding. In 1952, he learned about ethological studies of imprinting in birds. Imprinting is a process by which young animals learn to restrict their social preferences to members of their own species. Newly hatched goslings imprint on the first moving object they encounter, which is usually their mother. Thereafter the young birds faithfully follow this object—which can even be a human being—wherever it goes. From this research and a related body of observations on primates, Bowlby inferred that attachment is an adaptive system rooted in Darwinian principles. By remaining close to the mother, goslings are less likely to succumb to predators and more likely to learn the skills needed to survive and reproduce.[2] Subsequent research has amply confirmed this insight. In most animal species, infants face a significant risk of death from predators. Among primates, infanticide by unrelated males is well documented.[3] A nursing infant is an effective birth-control device. Like the Catholic Church, alpha males take a dim view of contraception. After taking over a new troop, a male benefits from infanticidal acts, because the loss of a nursing infant brings females back into estrus. Infanticidal males employ Darwinian common sense, killing only those infants who are too old to be their own.

Owing to the dangers posed by predators and infanticidal adults, most animals have evolved a variety of mechanisms—physiological and behavioral—that keep mothers and offspring in proximity. A female sea lion can distinguish her pup from among hundreds of others in the rookery by its distinctive call. The pup shows equal discrimination for the call of its mother.

In the late 1950s, experiments by Harry Harlow showed that monkeys raised without mothers did not develop normally. Harlow devised surrogate mothers made of wood, sponge rubber, and a terry-cloth covering. Infants were fed from a bottle attached to the terry-cloth mother. Although the infants became strongly attached to their terry-cloth mothers and developed in a physically normal manner, their social skills were severely impaired. When placed among their peers, these infants often cowered in fear and were unable to engage in play. As adults such individuals were abusive and even murderous parents.[4]

The disruption of attachment behavior is just as consequential in humans as it is in other primates. For this reason, I have included parent-offspring conflict in my study of why people rebel. Excessive conflict leads to developmental glitches. All told, I have obtained descriptions of parent-offspring relationships for 989 members of my study, based on autobiographical and biographical accounts. I have used three independent judges to rate whether relationships were warm, ambivalent, or conflict-ridden.[5]

The Influence of Parental Conflict

Substantial conflict with parents increases the likelihood that an offspring will reject authority. In science, high levels of parental conflict predict openness to innovation. The most striking aspect of this finding is that it is confined mostly to firstborns. As part of the firstborn niche, eldest children tend to identify with parents, who generally favor them in return. Conflict disrupts the usual repertoire of firstborn strategies, causing some firstborns to behave like laterborns (Fig. 5.1).[6]

High levels of parent-offspring conflict make laterborns somewhat more radical than they would otherwise have been, but the effect is significantly smaller than it is for firstborns. Who needs to have Attila the

Receptivity to Scientific Innovation by Parent-Offspring Conflict and Birth Order

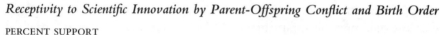

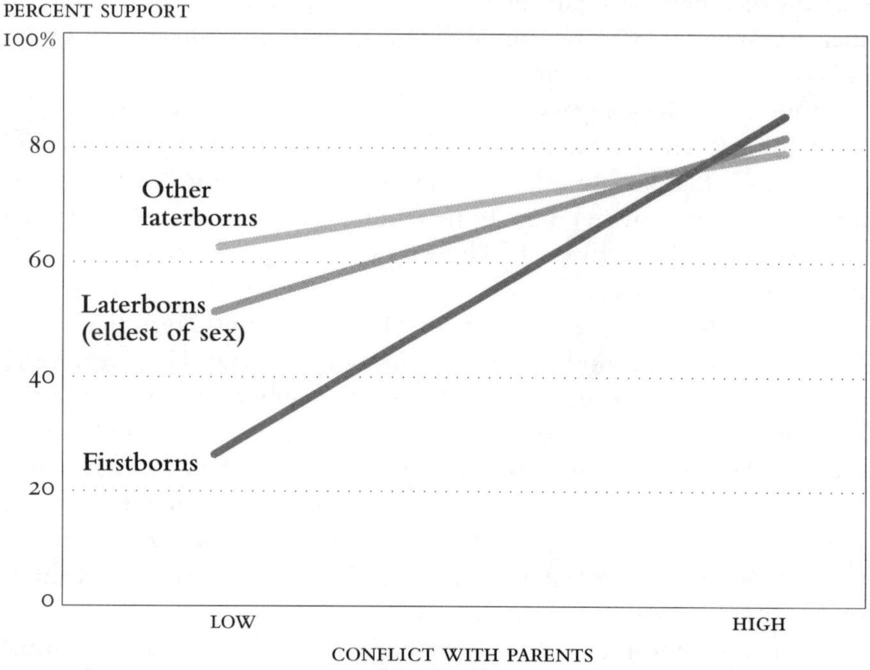

FIGURE 5.1 Parent-offspring conflict and birth order, as they relate to receptivity to scientific innovation. Conflict with parents causes offspring to become more open to innovation. Birth order and parental conflict interact: firstborns are particularly affected by parental conflict, as are laterborns who are the eldest of their sex.

Hun for a father, or the Wicked Witch of the West for a mother, if you already have a domineering older sibling?

Birth order contributes substantially more to revolutionary personality than does parent-offspring conflict. Comparing the two variables directly, birth order is more than twice as important. This finding is surprising from a psychoanalytic point of view.[7] Psychohistory is largely based on Freud's notion of the Oedipus complex, a topic on which Darwinian and Freudian approaches offer very different interpretations.[8] Conflict with parents does play an important role in personality development, as Freud believed, but parent-offspring conflict is not typically sex linked, as Freud also claimed. Freud convinced himself that children harbor murderous wishes against the same-sex parent. Darwinian theory strenuously disagrees. For a young child to kill a parent is tantamount to committing evolutionary suicide. To *wish* to kill a parent, if one never acts on this wish, is a blatant waste of time. Owing to natural selection, Freudian genes coding for patricidal wishes would soon vanish from any population.[9]

As a test of Freud's claims, I have analyzed my sample of scientists for levels of conflict with each parent. Contrary to the psychoanalytic expectation, offspring experienced just as much conflict with their mothers as they did with their fathers. In addition, both sources of conflict contribute equally to scientific radicalism.[10]

Parent-offspring conflict and openness to experience have a reciprocal relationship. Just as conflict with a parent tends to induce greater openness (together with independence from parental authority), the degree of independence regulates parent-offspring conflict. It is noteworthy that parent-offspring conflict is minimized when firstborns adopt a "closed" or conforming intellectual style and laterborns adopt a moderately "open" or independent style. When both siblings adopt the same style, parent-offspring conflict increases. It is also noteworthy that the price of independence is different for firstborns and laterborns. Parents tolerate independent thinking among their laterborn offspring. The same level of independence in a firstborn is associated with significantly greater parental conflict. In short, individuals who occupy a favored niche seem to pay a higher price for asserting their independence.[11]

Based on these findings about parental conflict, a biographical rule of thumb presents itself. Whenever one encounters a firstborn radical (and family life does occasionally produce them), such individuals are likely to have experienced substantial conflict with a parent. Parent-offspring conflict makes honorary laterborns out of some firstborns.

The tendency for firstborns to adopt laterborn strategies is most common in lower-class families. Children are more likely to accept parental authority in the upper and middle classes, probably because parents are good role models.[12] When parents are impoverished, they provide less reason for emulation. Under such circumstances, firstborns are sometimes pressured to invest in their younger siblings at the expense of their own reproductive potential. Such pressures deny them the usual advantages that stem from their firstborn niche. The value of family niches is always relative to the investment capabilities of parents.

A good example of the tendency for lower-class firstborns to experience conflict with parents is provided by Gideon Lincecum

(1793–1874). He was an American entomologist who resided in the deep South. It is hard to find anyone more iconoclastic than Lincecum. A self-proclaimed atheist, he led a colorful life in Texas, where he tried to found an "Infidel Society" in 1859. For a time he lived among various Indian tribes and learned their languages, preferring Indians, he once said, to white men.[13] Immediately after reading Darwin's *Origin of Species,* he announced himself a convert. As he informed Darwin in an enthusiastic letter of praise, he had independently accepted the truth of evolution even before 1859. In fact, he had long been an advocate of the evolutionary views of Darwin's grandfather Erasmus.[14]

As the first of ten children, Lincecum overcame 20 to 1 odds when he became an evolutionist. Parent-offspring conflict helps to explain Lincecum's unusual achievement. He got on poorly with his father, an itinerant farmer and drunkard who boasted a "notorious temper."[15] Before he was twenty, Lincecum had run away from home to escape his father's "ill-natured" ways.[16] Owing to high parental conflict, Lincecum's probability of accepting new scientific ideas was 80 percent.

Another radical firstborn in my sample is Johannes Kepler (1571–1630). An ardent Copernican, he published his views on this topic thirteen years before Galileo. In 1597 Kepler entreated Galileo to endorse this theory. Although privately a Copernican, Galileo preferred to play it safe until he had better evidence, which came in 1609 as a result of the newly invented telescope. Kepler needed no such empirical edge. It was he who took the radical step of substituting elliptical for circular planetary orbits. Even Galileo, for all his staunch anti-Aristotelianism, did not accept this conceptual break with the past.[17]

Kepler had a difficult relationship with both of his parents, who had "a quarrelsome marriage."[18] In a family horoscope that he drew up when he was twenty-six, Kepler described his father as being "vicious, inflexible, quarrelsome, and doomed to a bad end."[19] Although the father was away much of the time fighting as a mercenary, he still managed to disgrace his Protestant family by fighting on the Catholic side in Holland. When Kepler was seventeen, his father abandoned the family and was never heard from again.

Kepler has described his mother as "small, thin, swarthy, gossiping, and quarrelsome, of a bad disposition."[20] She was an annoying busybody who alienated her neighbors. Eventually the neighbors retaliated, accusing her of witchcraft. Put on trial, Kepler's mother would have been executed but for her son's intervention. There is something so absurd about Kepler's family background that it is good he possessed a

Johannes Kepler, about 1620 (age forty-eight), at the height of his career.

sense of humor about it. In a continuation of his family horoscope, he writes about himself (in the third person):

> That man [Kepler] has in every way a doglike nature. His appearance is that of a little lap dog. . . . He is bored with conversation, but greets visitors just like a little dog; yet when the least thing is snatched away from him, he flares up and growls. He tenaciously persecutes wrongdoers—that is, he barks at them. He is malicious and bites people with his sarcasms. He hates many people exceedingly and they avoid him, but his masters are fond of him. . . . His recklessness knows no limits.[21]

I have studied the lives of over a thousand firstborns in Western history, and Johannes Kepler's description of himself is hardly that of a typical firstborn. Recklessness and sarcasm, for example, are traits more likely to occur among laterborns than firstborns. These traits are consistent with the conclusion that Kepler's attachment to his parents was disrupted. Because of his difficult childhood, Kepler possessed an unusually high likelihood, for a firstborn, of supporting new ideas.[22]

Isaac Newton (1642–1727) is another case of a firstborn who, because of his atypical family background, had an unusually high likelihood of becoming a radical thinker.[23] Newton was a posthumous child. His mother remarried when he was three and lived thereafter with her husband, a minister named Barnabas Smith. Isaac was left to the care of his elderly grandparents. Newton's biographer Richard Westfall has commented on this formative period in Newton's life:

> The loss of his mother must have been a traumatic event in the life of the fatherless boy of three. . . . As we shall see, Newton was a tortured man, an extremely neurotic personality who teetered always, at least through middle age, on the verge of breakdown. No one has to stretch his credulity excessively to believe that the second marriage and departure of his mother could have contributed enormously to the inner torment of a boy already perhaps bewildered by the realization that he, unlike others, had no father. . . . He formed no bond with any of his numerous relations that can be traced in his later life. The lonely boyhood was the first chapter in a long career of isolation.[24]

Regarding Barnabas Smith's rejecting attitude toward his stepson Isaac,

Isaac Newton in 1689 (age forty-six), two years after publication of his monumental *Mathematical Principles of Natural Philosophy.* He was remembered by a childhood acquaintance as "a sober, silent, thinking lad" and was "never known scarce to play with the boys abroad" (Westfall 1980:59).

Westfall concludes: "His actions speak clearly enough. . . . While the child of three grew up to be a boy of ten, he did not take him to live in the rectory in North Witham."[25] There, three half-siblings were born and enjoyed the affections of Newton's mother.

Newton's stepfather died when Isaac was ten. Only then was Isaac allowed to live with his mother and three half-siblings. Manuscript evidence reveals his resentment at having previously been excluded from his stepfather's household. When he was nineteen, Newton drew up a list of his sins, which included: "Threatening my father and mother Smith to burne them and the house over them."[26] Almost no firstborn from a happy family background would utter such a threat (or go on to become such a revolutionary thinker). Newton fits the profile of a radical firstborn who did not identify with parents and authority. In his voluminous writings, Newton never recorded a single affectionate sentiment about his mother, whose death went unnoticed.

To the extent that firstborns fail to identify with their parents, they are more likely to join forces with their younger siblings. A Dickensian example of this strategy is provided by William and Robert Chambers, who together founded the W & R Chambers Publishing Company. They were the first two children in a large Edinburgh family. Robert, the younger of the two brothers, was a pre-Darwinian evolutionist and author of the *Vestiges of the Natural History of Creation* (1844). After 1859 he supported Darwin's theories.

When the Chambers brothers were in their early teens, their father's ineptitudes forced the family into bankruptcy. The brothers were forced to quit school. "On winter nights," a biographer relates, "the two used to haunt that grim old jail the Tolbooth, with other unfortunates, in search of warmth."[27] Some years later, William and Robert were saddled with their father's debts. William later wrote an admiring biography of his brother, whose intellectual abilities surpassed his own. In this biography William remarked: "Literature abounds with instances . . . of fathers being pulled down by sons. Wonderfully little is said of the many ingenious ways in which sons and daughters are pulled down by fathers."[28] At the age of eighteen, William financed Robert's start in a small bookselling business, giving him four years' savings. This fraternal gesture blossomed into the world-famous Chambers publishing house. As business partners, the two brothers worked together harmoniously the whole of their adult lives. When upward mobility is the name of the game, and especially when parents fail to provide adequate support, sibling cooperation is a good strategy. Although sibling strategies follow certain formal rules, they are also remarkably flexible because they draw their inspiration from the specific family environments that offspring actually experience.

A Radical Monarch

Among laterborns, conflict with parents has the greatest effect on individuals who are early in birth rank. Laterborn eldest sons are particularly susceptible to this developmental glitch, especially when they are secondborns in large families.[29] A good example is Voltaire's benefactor Frederick the Great. We tend to think of monarchs as being socially

Frederick the Great's parents, Frederick William I and Sophia Dorothea. Frederick's mother was the daughter of George, elector of Hanover and later King George I of England. Her older brother became King George II of England.

conservative. What truth there is to this generalization is largely inherent in the fact that kings and queens are typically firstborns, or the eldest of their sex. An eldest son, Frederick was second of the ten children of Frederick William I of Prussia. In spite of his early birth rank, Frederick proved to be an unusually open-minded monarch. He scoffed at most religious beliefs, but as monarch permitted them all. One of his first acts as king was to issue the simple order: "All religions must be tolerated, . . . for in this country every man must get to heaven in his own way."[30] Throughout his reign he befriended many freethinkers. From 1750 to 1752, Voltaire, who had been exiled from France by Louis XV, found refuge at Frederick's lively Prussian court.

How did a king become so open-minded? The principal exception to conservative monarchs involves offspring who have experienced substantial conflict with their parents. Frederick's father was a rigid, volatile, and brutal man who had no respect for learning. Frederick's mother was little better—a selfish and formidable woman who encouraged strife between her children and their father as a means of protesting her own unhappiness. One story nicely captures Frederick William's nasty temperament and suggests what life was like for his eldest son. The king had a habit of buttonholing his subjects so he could question them at length. As a result, they usually ran on sight of him. One day the king captured a man who was desperately trying to hide. The king demanded to know why the man had tried to avoid him. Shaking with fear, the prisoner confessed that he was afraid. "Afraid? Afraid?" the king bellowed as he poked at his captive with a walking stick. "You are supposed to love me! Love me, you scum!"[31]

The king commanded Frederick's tutor to educate his son for life as a professional soldier. Frederick was to earn honor and glory with "the sword." In spite of his father's intentions, Frederick became everything that his father despised. He was a sensitive boy who hated the German language and instead loved everything French. The father tried to beat "manly" interests into his son. The more the king persisted, the more his son hated him for it. Frederick's elder sister recalled that "the king could not bear my brother; he abused him whenever he laid eyes on him, so that Frederick became obsessed with a fear of him." The king, she reported, "never saw my brother without threatening him with his stick."[32] Frederick and his sister were banished from the king's presence except for mealtimes, when the king would often "hit out at us with his crutch."[33] One time the king threw a plate at his son's head, narrowly missing him.[34]

In 1730, when Frederick was eighteen, the crazed king tried to murder him:

> He sent for me one morning. As I entered the room he seized me by the hair and threw me to the ground. After having beaten me with his fists he dragged me to the window and tied the curtain cord around my throat. I had fortunately time to get up and seize his hands, but as he pulled with all his might at the cord around my throat, I felt I was being strangled, and screamed for help. A page rushed to my assistance, and had to use force to free me.[35]

Fearing for his life, Frederick determined to flee to England. When the king learned of the plot, Frederick and a fellow conspirator were arrested and court-martialed. The military court sentenced the conspir-

Frederick II, with his younger brothers in 1730. *From left to right:* Frederick (age twenty-eight), Ferdinand (age ten), Augustus William (age eighteen), and Henry (age fourteen). Prince Henry was acutely envious of his eldest brother and, as a boy, refused to speak to him for months on end. The artist has captured Prince Henry's feelings toward Frederick, especially in his eyes.

ator to life imprisonment, but it refused to pronounce sentence on Frederick. Furious at the court's lenient verdict, the king overruled its judgment and sentenced both deserters to death. From the prison where he was being held, Frederick was forced to watch the beheading

Voltaire and Frederick the Great (*right*) at Sans-Souci, Frederick's summer palace near Potsdam, seventeen miles southwest of Berlin. After his arrival at Frederick's freethinking court Voltaire wrote to a good friend of the "grandeur and graces, grenadiers and muses, trumpets and violins, a meal of Plato, society, and liberty. Who would believe it? Nevertheless it is true" (quoted in Asprey 1986:396).

of his friend, who had also been his homosexual lover.[36] For a time the king seriously considered beheading his own son. He finally changed his mind, after concluding that the international repercussions would be too great.

Frederick remained imprisoned for over a year until he pledged loyalty to his father. He gradually earned his way back into the royal line of succession by doing his father's bidding. When his father died ten years later in 1740, Frederick succeeded to the throne at the young age of twenty-eight. One of his first acts as king was to establish freedom of the press. "He bore with contemptuous silence a thousand diatribes that were published against him. Once, on seeing a lampoon against him posted in the street, he had it removed to a position where it could be more easily read."[37] When Voltaire published a scurrilous volume detailing Frederick's homosexual affairs, Frederick was unperturbed. "No ruler yet has escaped poisonous treatment," he remarked, and he did "not want to be an exception to the rule."[38]

It is truly fitting that Voltaire and Frederick the Great were such kindred spirits and partners in the Enlightenment. One survived a brutal childhood, a murder attempt, and even a sentence of death by his unbalanced father, to become king of Prussia; the other, driven to rebel by his reactionary family, became the uncrowned king of the Enlightenment. Even the differences between king and subject could not override what similar family dynamics had forged. As Frederick himself once remarked: "Impressions received in childhood cannot be erased from the soul."[39]

AGE GAPS

For an immediately older sibling, the arrival of a younger brother or sister constitutes a developmental glitch. How significant a glitch this arrival represents is influenced by the age difference between offspring. Siblings entail costs and benefits, which vary in proportion to the birth interval. Every sibling represents a genetic insurance policy. Even if a child dies before reproducing, half of its genes continue to reside, on average, in each of its surviving siblings and will be represented in nieces and nephews. Substantially older offspring—no longer dependent on parental care—experience minimal costs owing to additional siblings. They ought to adopt a protective attitude toward a new arrival, like the three brothers of Austrian biologist Paul Kammerer. Two decades Kammerer's senior, these siblings "adored the new baby, and throughout the years remained loving and loyal brothers."[40]

By increasing competition for parental investment, close age spacing promotes greater parent-offspring conflict as well as increased sibling rivalry. The costs represented by a younger sibling are greatest when both offspring are infants. In traditional societies, birth intervals of less than five years are associated with increased infant mortality.[41] It follows that the influence of birth order on sibling strategies should be greatest for offspring who are spaced within five years. Under these circumstances, older siblings should tend to derogate their rivals, a tactic that tends to foster resentment and rebellion. Younger siblings ought to respond by trying to minimize direct comparisons with their older siblings—that is, by diverging in their interests.

To test this last hypothesis, I have collected data on age spacing for scientists included in my study. Openness to experience is the psychological engine behind Darwin's principle of divergence, which is a direct expression of competition for scarce resources. For this reason, openness should be affected by birth intervals. This hypothesis is confirmed. The greatest disparities in revolutionary personality occur among offspring who are separated by moderate differences in age. Siblings who are closely or distantly spaced are significantly less polarized by episodes of revolutionary change (Fig. 5.2).[42]

These findings are corroborated by a more comprehensive measure of openness to experience. This measure combines three indicators: openness to scientific change, broad interests, and travel. Age spacing exerts significantly greater influence on this composite measure than it does on scientific stance alone.[43] Laterborn scientists who were separated from their next older sibling by three to five years achieved the highest scores on this index. Darwin and Wallace are good examples. Both were four years younger than their next older sibling. Owing to their predilection for world travel and their wide range of interests, Darwin and Wallace are tied for third on openness, out of the 2,458 scientists in my sample for whom this information is available.[44]

Why are sibling contrast effects so pronounced at middle age spacings? Intuition suggests a different result. Survival is most threatened by siblings who are near in age. Close spacing, not intermediate spacing, should therefore promote the greatest sibling differences. The evidence I have presented about personality development seems to contradict a Darwinian approach to the problem.

One answer to this question, even if speculative and in need of further testing, illustrates the kinds of assumptions that guide a Darwinian approach to human development. According to Hamilton's theory of inclusive fitness, the costs of having siblings must be adjusted by the benefits arising through kinship. For an older sibling, the benefits are

Receptivity to Scientific Innovation by Birth Order and Age Spacing

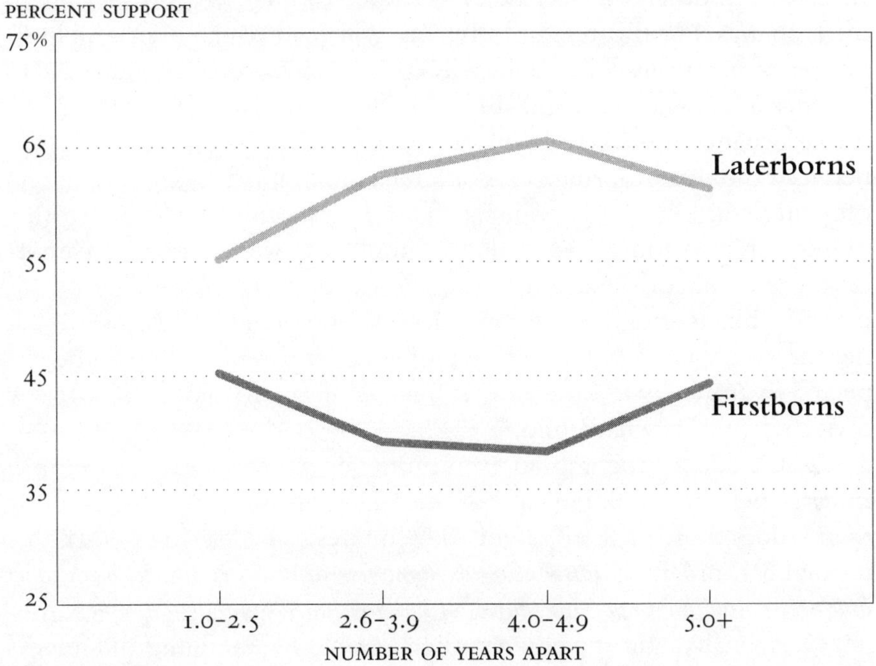

FIGURE 5.2. Acceptance of scientific innovation by birth order and age gaps between siblings. The two variables interact: birth-order differences are significantly greater for middle spacings than for other spacings. Only children are counted here as large-age-gap "firstborns," whom they resemble.

in proportion to the younger sibling's likelihood of survival. These adjusted benefits must also be weighed against the older sibling's prospects of survival. The operative factor is relative differences in the likelihood of survival. The closer that siblings are in age, the more equal these prospects will be, in which case siblings will not tend to discount the benefits of altruism. Twins—even fraternal twins—have good reason to behave altruistically toward one another because they are in the same Darwinian boat.[45] For substantially older siblings, the costs of investing in a newborn are so low that the benefits, even when discounted by the uncertainty of a newborn's ever reproducing, generally outweigh these costs. At middle age spacings the *adjusted* costs of having a younger sibling are elevated in relation to the benefits.[46]

This hypothesis leads to a testable inference. Parents are equally related to all of their offspring. Although offspring are also equally related to each other, they are twice as related to themselves as they are to their siblings. For this reason, offspring will tend to discount a sibling's prospects of survival more heavily than parents do. The degree to which parents and offspring differ in how they discount another offspring's chances of survival will vary as a function of the age difference between the two offspring. This difference in evaluations by parents and offspring will follow a curvilinear trend. In particular, firstborns with a sibling three to four years younger should experience greater parent-offspring conflict than at other spacings. In contrast, the younger of this pair of siblings should experience less parental conflict because his or her interests will often tend to be protected by parents, who can be expected to compensate for excessive aggression by the older child. In my own study, this is what I find.[47]

This evidence suggests an even more general conclusion. The birth interval between children affects their Darwinian interests differently than it does those of their parents. The interests of offspring in turn differ by birth order. *By introducing asymmetries in inclusive fitness, birth order and age spacing are important sources of the nonshared family environment.*

Darwinian logic suggests another testable idea. Sibling differences should be less extensive among fraternal twins, who do not differ in age, than among nontwin siblings, even though both kinds of offspring share approximately half their genes. Based on a composite of personality traits from several different studies, the average correlation among fraternal twins is .25, or twice that for nontwin siblings (.11).[48] One might argue that the greater similarity among fraternal twins is due to greater shared experiences, not just to similarity in age (and hence in inclusive fitness). Given the modest role that the shared environment typically exerts on personality development, this alternative explanation is not particularly compelling, although it is not ruled out.[49]

PARENTAL LOSS

Siblings compete for a purpose: to win greater parental investment. This conclusion leads to another test of my claims. If parental investment drives birth-order effects, then lack of investment should modify the results. To take an extreme example, siblings who have grown up in an orphanage should not behave like typical firstborns and laterborns.

Birth-order effects are indeed mediated by parental loss. Social class

Receptivity to Innovation by Birth Order, Parental Loss, and Social Class

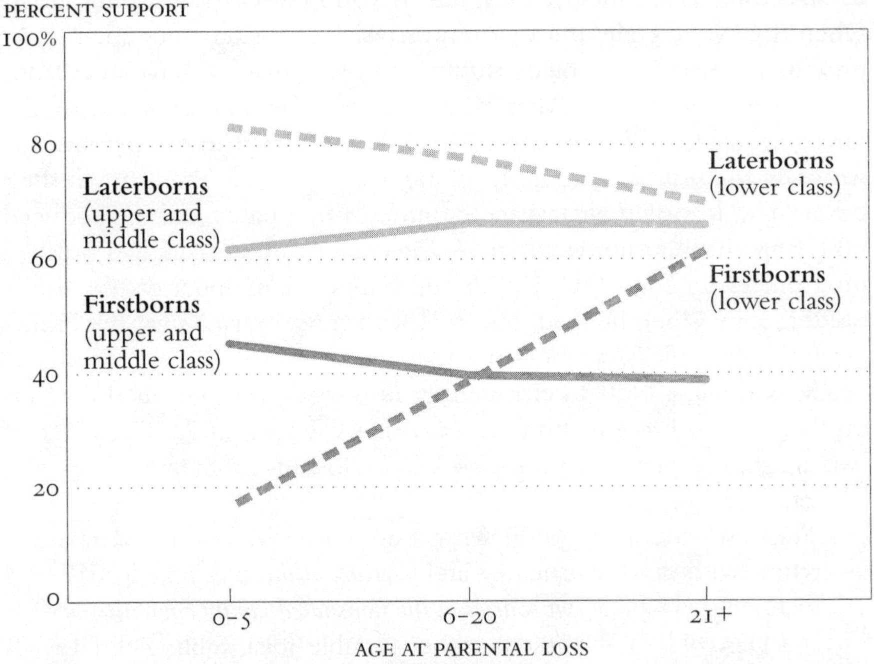

FIGURE 5.3. Openness to scientific innovation by birth order, social class, and parental loss. The figure displays a three-way interaction effect.

Birth order influences openness to innovation, but social class and parental loss do not (at least directly). The latter two variables interact, however, with birth order. In the upper and middle classes, early parental loss causes a reduction in birth-order effects. In the lower classes, early parental loss has the opposite effect, magnifying birth-order differences. This three-way interaction effect reflects changes in family niches, as explained in the text.

plays an important role in this relationship. In upper- and middle-class families, the early loss of a parent reduces the typical sibling differences in radicalism. In lower-class families, parental loss has the *opposite* effect. Early loss turns firstborns into staunch conservatives. In these families, the firstborns' pronounced conservatism drives their younger siblings to rebel more than ever (Fig. 5.3).[50]

These crisscrossing outcomes suggest that parental loss affects personality indirectly through its influence on family roles and niches. Following the loss of a parent, siblings typically become more supportive of one another as they grieve the loss. This closeness is sometimes maintained, especially when the death does not lead to changes in family structure.[51] Alexander and Wilhelm von Humboldt lost their father when they were eight and ten, respectively. Thereafter they spent their time in "inseparable companionship."[52] In large part, this closeness may be attributed to the fact that Wilhelm never became the man of the house. Instead, a faithful tutor named Kunth acted *in loco parentis,* instructing them in various subjects and accompanying them on all their trips. "The loss of their father," comments one biographer, "produced no change in their mode of life."[53] Even after the brothers had finished their university education, Kunth continued as a member of the Humboldt family. When he died, the loyal Kunth was buried near the Humboldt family vault.

Max Born, a Nobel Prize winner in physics, has described how his mother's death brought him closer to his younger sister. The elder of two children, Born was just four when he lost his mother:

> There was never anybody with whom we children could take refuge with our little sorrows and joys, as other children did with their mothers. This made us all the closer. We shared our games and play, and we developed a kind of private language, distorted expressions for everything, with which we could converse in the presence of grown-ups without being understood.[54]

Born's "twinning" experience with his younger sister would surely not have occurred had he adopted a role of authority over her. Instead, their grandmother "took over supreme command" and a full-time servant "acted as her lieutenant" (Born's words).[55] These two military mothers effectively preempted the parental role, allowing Born and his sister to become "army buddies."[56]

In middle- and lower-class families, the burden of caring for younger siblings is not likely to be assumed by other adults, such as housekeepers and private tutors. Firstborns therefore tend to become surrogate parents.[57] Theodor Billroth, a famous nineteenth-century surgeon, provides a good example. He lost his father when he was five, and his mother, who was ill with tuberculosis, ran the house from her sickbed. "Theodor," notes one biographer, "had little choice but to assume responsibility and become an advisor to his younger brothers."[58] Younger siblings typically begrudge the firstborn's heightened authority as a surrogate parent and rebel even more than usual, as clinical observa-

Max Born in the 1920s, a leader in the new quantum mechanics. A shy person, Born later remarked on this trait in his autobiography: "There was no mother in whom I could confide [as a child], and who could restore my confidence. So it happened that I became a somewhat odd fellow. I did not know this myself, but after I was married and, for the first time, became intimate with another human being, I learned from my wife what was wrong with me" (Born 1975:9).

tion shows.[59] The earlier the loss, the more it polarizes siblings from lower-class backgrounds.

Parental loss exerts much the same effect on parent-offspring conflict as it does on radicalism. Following early parental loss, conflict increases between offspring and the surviving parent. The bulk of this effect occurs among laterborns. Under such circumstances, firstborns actually experience *less* conflict with the surviving parent. Becoming a surrogate parent has certain prerogatives. In upper-class families, where the power structure is different, the loss of a parent does not change levels of parental conflict.[60] In short, when family roles change, so do patterns of parent-offspring conflict. Sibling conflict follows suit. A famous case history helps to illuminate this point.

Darwin's Loss of His Mother

Psychiatrist John Bowlby structured a biography of Darwin around the loss of his mother, which occurred when Darwin was eight.[61] What was unusual about his experience, Bowlby argues, is Darwin's lack of opportunity for mourning. Out of grief, Darwin's father and sisters refused to talk about his mother's death or to mention her name. To this "wall of silence" Darwin later attributed his inability to remember much about his mother, even what she looked like! Yet Darwin had an excellent memory for other childhood experiences, as his *Autobiography* amply demonstrates.

A striking story reinforces the conclusion that Darwin largely "repressed" his mother's memory.[62] The family used to play a word game in which words could be taken from another player by adding letters to form new words. After observing someone insert the letter M in front of the word OTHER, Darwin stared at it for a long time. He then objected: "MOE—THER; there's no word MOE—THER."[63]

The loss of Darwin's mother changed the family dynamics, and this, according to Bowlby, injured Darwin's self-esteem. Darwin's father reacted to his wife's death by becoming depressed and by resorting to "sarcasm and bullying." Darwin's cousin Emma, who later became Darwin's wife, knew the doctor as a child. "He was a fidgety man," she remarked, "and the noise and untidiness of a boy were unpleasant to him."[64]

Robert Darwin's irritability and depression added to a somewhat troubled relationship with his son, whom he considered "a very ordinary boy." In his *Autobiography,* Darwin recalled that his father did not think much of his natural history pursuits. "To my deep mortification my father once said to me, 'You care for nothing but shooting, dogs, and rat-catching, and you will be a disgrace to yourself and all your family.' "[65] Darwin's daughter Henrietta remembered him once saying, "I think my father was a little unjust to me when I was young, but afterwards I am thankful to think I became a prime favourite with him."[66] Given Darwin's mild manner and forgiving temperament, this remark probably minimizes his resentment.

Left: **Robert Waring Darwin** (1766–1848), Darwin's father. He was a huge man; the last time he weighed himself he was 288 pounds. Afterward, according to his son, he "increased much in weight." *Right:* **Susannah Wedgwood Darwin** (1765–1817), Darwin's mother, who died when he was eight (probably from an abdominal cancer). Darwin remembered almost nothing about her, but others have described her as having a "gentle, sympathising nature." According to one source: "She entered zealously into all her husband's pursuits; and as he took almost as much interest in botany and zoology as his father, Erasmus Darwin, their gardens and grounds became known for the choicest shrubs and flowers. They petted and reared birds and animals; and the beauty, variety, and tameness of 'The Mount pigeons' were well known in the town and far beyond" (quoted in Bowlby 1990:46).

Another major consequence of Susannah Darwin's death was her son's altered relationship with his two immediately older sisters, especially Caroline, who was nine years his senior. Although she tried to become a second mother to him, she was much too dedicated in her efforts. In his *Autobiography* Darwin recalled a telling sentiment. Whenever he was about to enter a room where Caroline was present, he would say to himself: " 'What will she blame me for now?' and I made myself dogged so as not to care what she might say."[67] Darwin never

Four of the six Darwin siblings. *Above left:* Erasmus, who was four years older than Charles. *Above right:* Caroline, who was nine years older than Charles and tried to be a second mother to him after the death of their own mother, Susannah. *Below:* Charles and his sister Catherine, the two youngest members of the family. This portrait was done in 1816, the year before their mother died, when Charles was seven and Catherine was six. The fact that Darwin is holding a plant probably reflects his mother's interest in flowers and gardening.

outgrew this subordinate relationship with his older sisters, to whom he wrote during the last year of the *Beagle* voyage: "[Upon my return] you must undertake the task of scolding, as in years long gone past, & of civilizing me."[68] What was remarkably absent in Darwin's childhood was a feeling of secure attachment to anyone.

According to Bowlby, Darwin's lack of opportunity to discuss his mother's loss, his difficult childhood relationship with his father, and his ambivalent feelings toward his overzealous sisters combined to make him vulnerable to anxiety, depression, and the protean symptoms of "hyperventilation syndrome." Recent epidemiological studies have indeed shown that early parental loss increases the likelihood of such disorders.[69]

Following Darwin's return from the *Beagle* voyage (during which he exhibited mostly robust health and tireless energy), he developed "violent shivering and vomiting attacks" generally brought on by the excitement of conversing with people. For the remainder of his life, he was often prostrated by dizziness, vomiting, and hysterical crying. In 1841, at the age of thirty-two, he wrote to a cousin that he was "forced to live . . . very quietly and am able to see scarcely anybody & cannot even talk long with my nearest relations."[70] He was, as he commented pathetically, "confined to a living grave."[71]

Darwin's symptoms are remarkably consistent with a diagnosis of hyperventilation syndrome. Sufferers from this disorder experience excessive arousal of the autonomic nervous system, which triggers an unconscious increase in breathing. Without a simultaneous increase in energetic action, the victim's carbon dioxide level drops, precipitating the symptoms. These typically include those experienced by Darwin, such as faintness and nausea. The cure is to have the patient breathe into a paper bag for several minutes. This restores the carbon dioxide level to a symptom-free level.

Hyperventilation syndrome, Bowlby argues, was a physiological expression of Darwin's sensitivity to criticism. His work habits were another manifestation of this tendency. In his efforts to defend himself from his ever-anticipated shortcomings, he became a workaholic. "The word holiday," Darwin confided to his friend Joseph Hooker, "is written in a dead language for me, and much I grieve at it."[72] In his *Autobiography* Darwin described the gradual loss of his taste for poetry and music. "My mind," he lamented, "seems to have become a kind of machine for grinding general laws out of large collections of facts."[73] He would push himself until his attacks of vomiting became so severe that his wife, Emma, would force him to take a "rest cure" at one of several health spas. Over and over again this awful cycle of prostration and misery was repeated. Bowlby continues:

> Darwin's scientific work . . . served also as an indispensable refuge from the troubles that beset him. Small wonder he overworked. He was a workaholic who pursued his studies according to a daily routine seven days a week, week in and week out, until he could continue no longer.[74]

Darwin's study at Down House, the year of his death (1882). To his son Leonard, Darwin once confessed that he "was *never* quite comfortable except when utterly absorbed in his writing" (quoted in Bowlby 1990:12).

Darwin's vulnerable self-esteem also influenced distinctive features of his "scientific style." A hallmark of this style was chronic self-doubt. In particular, Darwin's constant questioning of his own judgment made him a genius at hypothesis testing. Unfortunately this obsession with possible error exacted a continuous emotional cost.

Darwin's propensity toward self-doubt was a powerful asset in his work only because it was counterbalanced by another distinctive feature of his personality. In the face of opposition, Darwin was remarkably persistent.[75] It will be recalled that he made himself "dogged" as a boy so as not to care about his sister Caroline's reproaches. Such scolding from a mother might have been received differently, but coming from an elder sister it made Darwin defiant.

Properly directed, doggedness is a useful quality. In Darwin's case it was fundamental to his lifelong researches on evolution. Darwin himself thought particularly highly of this quality, which was his personal explanation for genius.[76] He was especially fond of the expression "It's dogged as does it."[77] "Doggedness," Francis Darwin commented about this saying of his father's, "expresses his frame of mind almost better than perseverance. Perseverance seems hardly to express his almost fierce desire to force the truth to reveal itself."[78] As a scientist, Darwin approached the most controversial issues of his day with the same stoic determination with which he had previously faced his elder sister's reproaches. Genius, at least as Darwin seems to have conceived of it, was synonymous with one of his most characteristic sibling strategies. Although there was considerably more to Darwin's genius than his dogged persistence in defiance of established authority, his intellectual brilliance would have counted for little, without this attribute, in accomplishing the revolution that now bears his name.

Darwin's life and revolutionary achievements reinforce an important conclusion about parental loss. Changes in sibling relationships—not the loss per se—dictate the changes in personality that follow. After a loss, social class enters the picture because it is a good proxy for the likelihood of substitute parenting. Like inadequate parenting, inadequate substitute parenting increases the propensity to rebel.

CONCLUSIONS

Ours is not the best of all possible worlds, as Darwin discovered in the course of his scientific career. Like Voltaire's Candide, he initially believed what he had been taught about a perfect world. God, said William Paley (a famous British Panglossian), had wisely adapted every creature to its intended place within the economy of nature. Just two days before publication of the *Origin of Species,* Darwin remarked: "I hardly ever admired a book more than Paley's Natural Theology. I could almost formerly have said it by heart."[79]

Evolution by natural selection, not the doctrine of Design, explains why creatures are adapted to their environments. Evolution also explains why creatures are never *perfectly* adapted to the world around them. Pain and suffering are two notable consequences of an imperfect world. "To my imagination," Darwin argued in the *Origin,* "it is far more satisfactory to look at such instances as the young cuckoo ejecting its foster-brothers,—ants making slaves,—the larvæ of ichneumonidæ feeding within the live bodies of caterpillars,—not as specially endowed or created instincts, but as small consequences of one general law."[80] A century later, evolution by natural selection remains the single greatest unifying principle within the life sciences. As American geneticist Theodosius Dobzhansky has remarked: "Nothing in biology makes sense except in the light of evolution."[81]

Human development accords with Darwin's basic principles, although most of the details are accomplished through learning. This process involves potential snags, some of which Darwin experienced firsthand. His personal difficulties included a high birth rank in a large family, a four-year age gap between himself and his next older sibling, a troubled relationship with his father, his mother's death when he was eight, and an elder sister who mothered him too zealously. Based on these childhood experiences, Darwin was loaded to the gills with the kinds of developmental glitches that promote radical tendencies. His own theories, which provide the general framework for relating ultimate causes to the proximate ones that determine individual human development, offer a comprehensive guide to such biographical outcomes.

Parental loss illustrates the way in which family experiences, including developmental glitches, typically impact on family members. The consequences of parental loss are never the same for siblings because they occupy different niches within the family system. Even social class, to the modest extent that it influences personality, does so largely because its ramifications for siblings are different. After the death of a parent, social class lies behind changes in family niches. In lower-class families, an eldest child often becomes a surrogate parent, whereas younger siblings are rarely thrust into a parental role. In upper-class families, parental loss has a different impact; the niches in these families are structured differently.

This kind of evidence clashes with Marxist claims about class conflict as the engine of history. Revolutionaries owe their radicalism to competition for limited family resources—and to the niches that characterize such competition—not to class consciousness.[82] Similarly, Freud's notion of the Oedipus complex makes little sense in a Darwinian world. Offspring are not trying to kill one parent in order to take sole possession of the other. Childhood is about maximizing parental investment, not reducing it by half. Freud's disregard for Darwinian principles doomed his developmental claims from the start. The failures of psychoanalysis—both theoretical and therapeutic—are largely footnotes to this fundamental misreading of the family experience.

Sibling strategies are not set in stone. Nor are they predetermined in any simple way by genetics. Owing to obstacles encountered during development, evolution has equipped us all to be versatile strategists. Problematic family niches sometimes make honorary laterborns out of firstborns. In a Darwinian world, personality development reflects the indelible imprint of family niches and developmental glitches.

6

GENDER

The nature and extent of gender differences in personality have long been controversial. For most of recorded history, women have been considered inferior to men, destined as the "weaker sex" to be assigned subordinate social status. Compared with men, women have smaller brains, a finding that was long considered proof of female inferiority. When scientists finally realized that brain size is correlated with body size, they also realized that male and female brains have proportionately the same volume.[1] With the advent of more reliable psychological tests, it has been possible to distinguish many imagined gender differences from reality. Even so, the literature on sex differences continues to display seemingly contradictory findings. For example, some studies report that women conform more than men. Other studies report the opposite.[2] What is one to believe?

For many psychological attributes, gender differences have proved modest or nonexistent, and gender itself is not as relevant a factor as *gender roles.* As one expert has concluded: "Gender differences in intellectual and psychosocial tasks are relatively small compared with the massive differences in participation of males and females in powerful, remunerative, satisfying, and secure careers."[3]

Some psychological differences between the sexes have survived repeated scrutiny. The most important of these include aggression, assertiveness, conformity, and tender-mindedness.[4] Another difference between the sexes involves the values most desired in a mate. Males value youth and attractiveness in a mate more than females do. Females seek economic success in a mate more than males do. Both sexes place similar value on attributes like honesty and kindness.[5]

Many gender differences are specific to situations and tasks.[6] Males typically outperform females on test items involving knowledge of the physical sciences. When it comes to information about health practices, women outperform men.[7] Conforming behavior reveals similar interactions with tasks. In experimental studies involving adults, women generally conform more than men. The demands of the experiment are often crucial to the outcome. When women are especially knowledgeable about the topic being considered (such as women's fashions), men conform more than women.[8] Such interactions between persons, situations, and tasks are commonplace. Even when interaction effects are recognized, there is a tendency to interpret them as "contradictory" findings, thereby underestimating the real influence of gender.

Most of these interactions have precursors within the family system. Siblings face differing behavioral contexts in their different family niches. Paradoxically, gender can help us to understand why sisters are so different. Being female does not constitute the same experience for a firstborn as it does for a laterborn. The same conclusion is true about brothers, whose personalities vary according to the dictates of family niches. In the development of personality—including gender-related traits—family niches often override biology, just as they often transcend cultural stereotypes. Research on conformity helps to illustrate this point.

BIRTH ORDER AND CONFORMITY

In terms of a birth-order expectation, gender introduces a striking anomaly in conforming behavior. Among "sister dyads," some firstborns are distinctly nonconforming, whereas some laterborns are distinctly conforming.[9] These findings are restricted to pairs of sisters in two-child sibships. In larger sibships, firstborn women tend to conform and laterborn women tend to rebel, as they also do when brothers are present in the sibship. These findings highlight the need for an interactionist viewpoint about gender, especially one that includes a role for family niches (Fig. 6.1).[10]

Some psychologists have employed role theory to explain these conformity findings.[11] According to these researchers, siblings learn gender-appropriate behavior from one another, a process influenced by the model's gender.[12] The younger of two sisters grows up with a model exemplifying feminine behavior. As a result, she learns to emulate sisterly virtues, including cooperation and conformity to group wishes.[13]

Conformity by Birth Order among Females in Two-Child Sibships

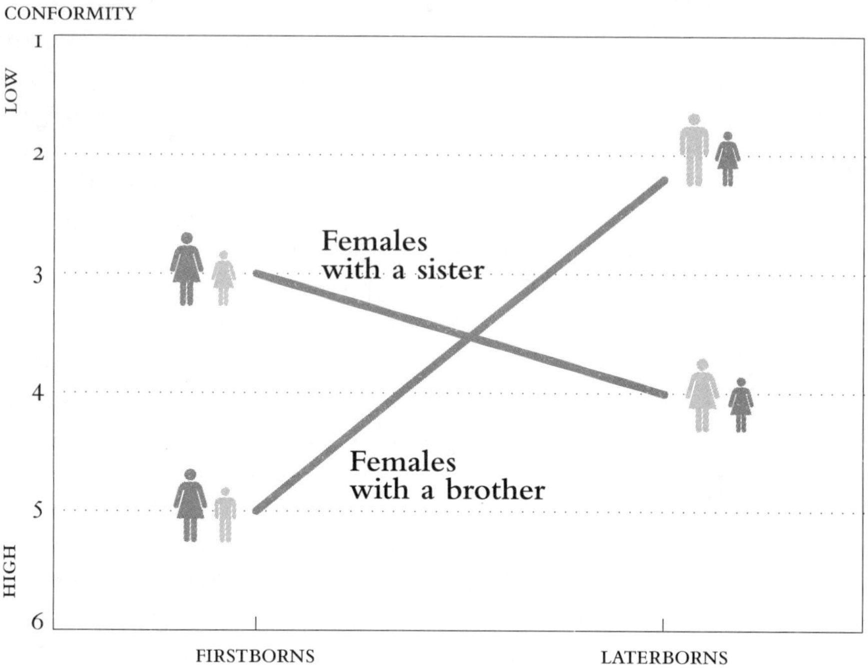

FIGURE 6.1. Birth order and conformity among females in two-child sibships. The vertical scale records the mean rank order for conformity among the four sibships, scored together with the four analogous male sibships (not shown here).

Within pairs of sisters, laterborns are more likely to conform than firstborns. Among sisters who have brothers, the usual birth-order relationship prevails: firstborns conform and laterborns do not. The most nonconforming sibling position of the four consists of laterborn sisters who have elder brothers. Among women, neither birth order nor sex of sibling is a significant predictor of conformity. But the interaction between birth order and sex of sibling is significant.

The notion of "niche partitioning" is helpful in explaining the behavior of sibling dyads composed of sisters. In the absence of brothers, sisters appear to assign themselves instrumental (masculine) and expressive (feminine) niches. Being displaced as the mother's sole object of attention, the elder sister tends to shift her principal identification to her father, a process that encourages the development of instrumental traits.[14] Sibling contrast effects seem to reinforce these differences in identification. Although the precise psychological mechanisms responsible for niche partitioning are not fully understood, the evidence for their occurrence is considerable. This evidence is typically manifested as interactions between birth order, gender, and the gender of siblings.[15]

The studies I have just reviewed are based on two-child families. In larger sibships, the situation is different because niche partitioning appears to follow somewhat different rules. Large sibships reinforce the firstborn's duties as a surrogate parent. Parenting responsibilities increase the likelihood that eldest sisters will become mother-identified, and hence conforming to parental authority. As family size increases, so does the statistical probability that sisters will grow up with brothers. The presence of brothers boosts the likelihood that sisters will adopt traditional sex roles. When siblings assume traditional sex roles, birth order asserts its usual influence on conformity.[16]

One of the most noteworthy features about gender is its complex links with other sibling differences. For most personality traits, sibling differences dwarf gender differences. Gender-related traits typically emerge on an individual-by-individual basis as interaction effects involving variables that help to define family niches.[17] Historical data reinforce these conclusions. Indeed, they provide some of the best evidence in support of them.

WOMEN REFORMERS

In an effort to understand the causes of radicalism among women, I have assembled a database that includes 504 notable reformers drawn from American history.[18] As a control group, I have included another 110 Americans who have distinguished themselves as advocates of conservative causes. Women constitute 35 percent of this combined sample.[19]

My survey encompasses 61 different types of reform, which include issues such as health care, food, clothing, housing, politics, racial equality, and women's rights. For purposes of simplification, I have classified these 61 movements into five categories: (1) religious and political reforms, (2) the struggle for racial equality, (3) women's rights, (4) health-related issues, and (5) other social reforms (housing, education, temperance, and the like).[20] These distinctions are important because reform movements recruit adherents based on "person by situation" interaction effects, which in turn depend on sibling differences.

In addition to differing by type of reform interests, reformers differ markedly in their radicalism. As one scholar has remarked: "Some reformers made their case with sweet reasonableness, seeking only modest changes in social arrangements, while others called for basic structural alternations, sometimes in strong language."[21] What I call "moderate reformers" have generally sought to ameliorate the system rather than to overthrow it. They have focused their efforts on improving living conditions, health care, and education. "Radical reformers" have directed their efforts toward culturally sensitive topics—particularly politics, religion, and race relations. Examples of radical reformers include socialists, communists, antislavery crusaders, and anarchists. In Western history, people have consistently died for these causes, which have helped to promote egalitarian ideals around the world.

Compared with moderate reformers, those of a more radical persuasion have tended to be members of racial minorities and the lower classes. Laterborns have also been consistent champions of radical reforms. These trends hold for both sexes. Gender itself is not significantly correlated with social radicalism.[22] Still, gender influences reform tendencies in indirect ways. This story involves a panoply of interactions with birth order, sex of siblings, and other aspects of family structure. I begin with the role of birth order.

Based on the criterion of attracting social underdogs, the most radical reform movement in American history is abolitionism.[23] This cause, which divided a nation and catapulted it into armed conflict, illustrates a general principle about civil wars: they often polarize siblings from the same family. Abolitionism attracted the highest proportion of laterborns of any reform movement in my survey. Prominent abolitionists—men and women alike—were typically younger siblings.[24] Harriet Beecher Stowe, who wrote *Uncle Tom's Cabin* (1852), is a good example. She was the seventh of thirteen children. Her poignant tale about the slave system and its appalling cruelties sold more than 300,000 copies in its first year and was eventually translated into fifty-five languages. When Abraham Lincoln met Stowe in 1863, he declared: "So this is the little lady that made the big war."[25]

The ranks of laterborn abolitionists were bolstered by several particularly courageous black women, among them Harriet Tubman. Born near the tail end of a family having eleven children (her exact birth rank is unknown), Tubman experienced brutal treatment as a slave.[26] While she was still a child, two of her older siblings were sold away. Tubman became a fugitive in 1849, when she was about thirty. She traveled alone and by night from Maryland to Philadelphia, navigating

HARRIET TUBMAN.

Harriet Tubman (ca. 1820–1913). She was trained in tracking and scouting by her father. After her escape from the South in 1849, she worked in Philadelphia as a servant, cook, and laborer in order to finance her trips to free other slaves. Like the militant John Brown, Tubman disdained other abolitionists who fought with words rather than deeds. Only illness prevented her from joining Brown, in October 1859, during his ill-fated raid on Harpers Ferry. Because of her unusual courage and determination, Tubman has often been called "the Moses of her people" (Wrench 1985b).

by the North Star. Several of her brothers, who commenced the escape with her, turned back out of fear. Over the next decade Tubman returned to the South nineteen times, leading an estimated 300 slaves along the Underground Railroad to their freedom in the North. She rescued seven of her siblings, along with her aged parents. In a vain effort to stop Tubman's raids, Maryland slaveholders put a substantial price on her head. Notes one biographer: "She treated each journey as a military campaign, enforcing strict discipline—even, when necessary, threatening her 'passengers' with death if they tried to turn back. In ten years of rescue work she never lost an escaping slave through capture or surrender."[27] A contemporary remarked that Tubman "seemed wholly devoid of personal fear."[28] Once, when she and several fugitive slaves were threatened with capture, she boarded a train heading south, surmising that no one would challenge a party of blacks traveling in this direction. John Brown, who led the raid on Harpers Ferry, admired Tubman and dubbed her "The General."[29] During the Civil War, she was active in the South as a Union spy.

In contrast to laterborn women, firstborn women have tended to defend the status quo.[30] Former beauty queen Anita Bryant is a good example. She became an outspoken critic of homosexuality during the 1960s, a stance that eventually cost her her position as spokesperson for the Florida citrus industry. Later Bryant underwent a conversion to born-again Christianity, which helped to free her from her homophobic views. Phyllis Schlafly is another prominent firstborn conservative. A zealous Goldwater supporter in 1964, Schlafly campaigned vigorously against the Equal Rights Amendment and "saw her war against Women's Rights as a religious issue."[31] Still another firstborn in my sample, Ayn Rand, developed her philosophy of Objectivism to unmask "altruism, cooperation, humanity, benevolence, and all variations thereof."[32] The key to happiness, Rand argued, was to satisfy the ego and self-esteem. Rand's personal philosophy reflects an extreme of antagonism on the Big Five personality dimension of Agreeableness/Antagonism. Birth order is an excellent predictor of differences on this dimension.

When firstborn women endorse social reforms, they usually confine their activities to domains such as health care and social work. Firstborns are motivated to reform by high moral conscience, not by rebellion against the status quo. A good example of this reform style is Catherine Esther Beecher, the eldest sibling of Harriet Beecher Stowe. Stimulated by her reformist father, the Reverend Lyman Beecher, Catherine pioneered in women's education, but her reformist inclinations had limits. In response to the efforts of Angelina Grimké, a lastborn, to recruit women to the abolitionist cause, Catherine Beecher maintained that "females were naturally subordinate to men in social relations . . . and above meddling in politics."[33] She opposed woman suffrage. Two of Catherine Beecher's younger siblings, Isabella Beecher and Henry Ward Beecher, strongly supported the same cause. Different family niches, different styles of reform!

The contrast between the various Beecher siblings is reflected in my sample as a whole. Laterborn women were significantly more likely than firstborns to engage in gender-incongruent behavior.[34] For most of the nineteenth century, "meddling in politics" was considered inappropriate for women, who were often prohibited by law from addressing mixed audiences. This circumstance did not stop *laterborn* women from crossing gender lines and participating in various political reforms.

Laterborn women also tended to defy regional loyalties. The Grimké sisters, Sarah and Angelina, were the first two Southern women to join the abolition movement. Sarah was the sixth child in an aristocratic family from Charleston. Her younger sister Angelina was the fourteenth and last child of the family. Distressed by the plight of slaves, the two Grimké sisters left the South in the 1820s and settled in Philadelphia. Soon afterward they made contact with radical abolitionist William Lloyd Garrison and became active in the antislavery movement. The Grimké sisters lectured widely on the evils of slavery, occasionally to mixed audiences, and they were criticized by many Northerners for overstepping the proprieties of their sex. The sisters' home state of South Carolina was more emphatic, threatening them with imprisonment if they ever returned! In 1838 Angelina Grimké became the first woman to address an American legislative body when she defended the right of women's petitions before the Massachusetts legislature. More radical than her elder sister Sarah, Angelina commented at the time, "We Abolition Women are turning the world upside down."[35]

In keeping with their radical tendencies, laterborn women have been more likely than firstborns to advocate reforms associated with the lower classes. Birth control and anarchism are examples of reforms that attracted strong lower-class support. Upper-class firstborns tended to stay clear of these two movements, but upper-class laterborns supported them. Child welfare and temperance are good examples of upper-class concerns that appealed to firstborn women.[36]

Race and Gender as Moderating Variables

My study of American reformers underscores the importance of variables, including race and gender, that moderate reformist tendencies by interacting with birth order. Consider the behavior of people who belonged to religious or racial minorities. Minority status tends to increase support for radical reforms. Controlled for this tendency, firstborns and laterborns from minority backgrounds were more likely to concur in the struggle for radical reform than were firstborns and laterborns from the white Protestant majority. This interaction effect holds for both sexes.[37] The main reason for this interaction involves the manner in which minority status affected firstborns. Laterborns tend to rebel regardless of race, but ethnic oppression makes firstborns behave like laterborns. Slavery, in particular, tended to make true brothers out of brothers.

Among the women in my study, a good example of a firstborn who became a radical reformer is Sojourner Truth. Born a slave to Dutch-speaking parents in New York State, Sojourner was the second youngest child in a large family. All of her siblings but one—a younger brother—had been sold away prior to her birth, so she grew up as a functional firstborn. In 1806, at the age of nine, Sojourner was sold at auction. Freed by state law in 1828, she joined the abolition movement. She was an imposing figure and a brilliant lecturer who "brought rowdy and skeptical audiences to spellbound attention with the quiet forcefulness of her descriptions of life under slavery."[38] In 1851 she attended a national convention in Ohio on the question of woman suffrage. In response to several male speakers who brought up a woman's need to be pampered, Sojourner made her famous "Ain't I a Woman" speech:

> That man over there says that women need to be helped into carriages, and lifted over ditches, and to have the best place everywhere. Nobody ever helps me into carriages, or over mud puddles, or gives me any best place, and ain't I a woman? Look at me! Look at my arm! I have plowed and planted, and gathered into barns, and no man could head me—and ain't I a woman? I could work as much and eat as much as a man (when I could get it), and bear the lash as well—and ain't I a woman?[39]

When firstborns such as Sojourner Truth support radical reforms, their radicalism often reflects a developmental glitch. Owing to slavery, the lives of blacks were filled with developmental glitches.

Charlotte Forten Grimké, also a firstborn abolitionist, illustrates another way in which race sometimes interacts with birth order. Charlotte came from a black family that had been prominent in the abolition movement for three generations. She grew up amidst abolitionist relatives, including her father and several aunts. Firstborns tend to identify with their parents and to absorb their parents' social values. In Charlotte's case, to do so was to identify with rebellion against the status quo. Although most eldest children are not born to rebel, they can be coaxed into doing so by radical role models.[40]

Firstborn women are overrepresented in the battle for women's rights.[41] This finding represents a seeming refutation of my thesis. The inconsistency is explained by yet another interaction effect. The disenfranchisement of women made it easier for firstborns to rebel over *this* issue, just as slavery made it easier for firstborn blacks to fight for freedom. Support for women's rights was especially prevalent among firstborns in the upper classes. High social status and superior education made their restriction to the home particularly galling.[42] Because firstborns are more achievement oriented than laterborns, they were especially motivated to protest their plight.

Additional light is thrown on this last interaction effect by considering the range of reforms espoused by each woman in my study. Some suffragists confined their reform efforts to women's rights, whereas others were active in a variety of radical reforms. Among suffragists who campaigned for these other issues, including racial reforms, laterborn women are overrepresented.[43] In short, the most radical suffragists were laterborns. They used the women's rights issue as a springboard for even more iconoclastic reforms, not as an end in itself.

To recount my findings: Whenever laterborn women have taken to reforming, they have transcended social conventions based on gender, class, geography, and race. Firstborn women have favored genteel reforms—activities deemed appropriate to their social background. Among individuals who have a *personal stake* in reform, the likelihood of support typically increases, while also reducing the role of birth order. What typically differentiates laterborn reformers from their elder siblings is their willingness to support radical changes independently of any personal stake. They reform out of empathy, not high moral conscience or the need for achievement.

WOMEN IN SCIENCE

Thirty-six women in my study of scientific advancement were active in liberal scientific innovations.[44] Although this is a small proportion of the total sample, what is noteworthy about these women is their distinctly radical stance: *all but one of them (or 97 percent) supported the innovative alternative!* By comparison, only 57 percent of the men in this sample supported new ideas—a significant difference.[45] This disparity by gender is part of a larger story involving recruitment effects in science: it took *radical* women to break into this profession. The biggest revolution faced by these women was getting into "the academy." For such iconoclasts, revolutions in science were a repeat performance for which they were already well prepared.

Although gender is strongly associated with radical thought, correlation does not in this case signify causation. Other aspects of family niches, besides gender, are largely responsible for making women into radical scientists. The women in my study are heavily biased for being lastborns as well as for having at least one older brother.[46] These findings contrast with the situation among men. For them, being firstborn was a strong stimulus to a scientific career.[47] Firstborns are attracted by knowledge domains that stress certainty and that offer the potential for high achievement. As science has become more open to women, firstborn women have become increasingly overrepresented in this profession.[48] Firstborns tend to show up en masse once revolutions are largely over.

Being laterborn is just one of several attributes that serve to distinguish early women pioneers in science. These pioneers also grew up in liberal families and espoused liberal social attitudes.[49] In addition, they were significantly more likely than men to experience conflict with a parent.[50] Closer analysis reveals that conflict occurred disproportionately with mothers.[51] Discord between mothers and offspring tends to encourage a stronger identification with the father. In sum, the family dynamics experienced by these women favored instrumental, not expressive, tendencies, which helps to explain their gender-incongruent behavior.

Conservative ideas attract conservative people—men and women alike. Among the women in my study who participated in debates over conservative scientific innovations, firstborns are overrepresented.[52] Believing in communication with the dead was different, ideologically, from believing in Darwin's theory of evolution. The first standpoint reaffirmed the existence of God (and appealed to firstborns). The second standpoint denied God's role in the Creation (and appealed to laterborns). These ideological differences are best illustrated through biographical examples.

Margaret Mead and Samoa

The one woman in my sample who opposed a liberal scientific revolution is Margaret Mead. A firstborn, she was hostile to psychoanalysis in the late 1920s.[53] When psychoanalysis had become more fashionable, Mead changed her mind and accepted many of Freud's ideas. After the feminist revolution got under way and women began attacking psychoanalysis, Mead "would not allow herself to join in the chorus of vituperation against Freud."[54] She chastised Karen Horney, one of Freud's most important critics, because she felt that Horney should have "prevented schisms rather than initiating divisions within the psychoanalytic movement."[55]

Mead's attitude toward deviation was consistent with her autocratic role in her own family. At an early age she became a surrogate mother toward her younger siblings, who included two sisters and a brother. In her autobiography Mead asserts: "I thought of the babies as my children, whom I could observe and teach and cultivate."[56] Another biographical source reports: "At the age of eight . . . , firstborn Margaret kept notes on the small natives in her own household. Protective and domineering with the best of intentions, she made plans for her siblings' futures. . . . All of her life Margaret continued to be the protective, dictatorial big sister."[57] These qualities spilled over into her scientific work and led to a controversy that captured media attention worldwide.

The opposite of a revolutionary personality is someone who perceives the world in terms of the expected. Such people assimilate evidence into existing cognitive schemes, which are often provided by parents and mentors. Mead's anthropological career was dedicated to extending the environmentalist paradigm of her teacher, "Papa" Franz Boas. In 1925 Boas sent Mead, who was just twenty-three, off to American Samoa. Her assignment was to show that culture, not biology, determines human behavior in these idyllic South Sea islands. Mead chose to investigate adolescence in order to refute G. Stanley Hall's biologically based theory on the subject. Just before her departure, Boas gave her half an hour's instruction in field methods.[58]

After arriving in Samoa, Mead spent six weeks in the port of Pago Pago, on the central island of Tutuila. She then moved to the smaller island of Ta'u, where she lived for seven months with the family of a naval pharmacist. A gift for languages "was never one of Mead's strong suits," a colleague later observed, and she picked up only a smattering of the Samoan language during her stay.[59] For her information about Samoan life, Mead relied mostly on adolescent girls. Samoa, she concluded from their reports, was a "very simple society" whose fundamental structure could be mastered "in a few months."[60]

In her best-selling book *Coming of Age in Samoa* (1928), Mead portrayed Samoan life as idyllic, peaceful, noncompetitive, and "replete with easy solutions for all conflicts."[61] Sexual activity, she argued, was considered "play," and adolescents were free to indulge their sexual yearnings before marriage. In such a promiscuous society, she reported, "the capacity for intercourse only once in a night is counted as senility."[62] Promiscuity, she suggested, somehow protected young Samoans against pregnancy, although she provided no evidence for this extraordinary claim. Among Samoans, Mead also insisted, there was no sexual jealousy because children were only weakly bonded to parents, eliminating oedipal conflict.[63] Samoa, she concluded, was a society without rivalries because it refused to take life seriously. These unexpected findings, which delighted her teacher Franz Boas, gave rise to "the most widely promulgated myth of twentieth-century anthropology."[64]

Thirty years after Mead's visit to Samoa, anthropologist Lowell Holmes conducted a follow-up study on the same island where Mead had done her own field research. Although Mead considered Samoans to be free of rivalry, she personally was not immune from this emotion. When Holmes wrote to introduce himself, he received a reply that was "extremely skeptical and uncooperative." Holmes reports: "She wrote back that she didn't know who I was, and that I should have had the courtesy to clear my study with her before I left."[65]

To Holmes's surprise, he soon discovered a host of discrepancies with Mead's classic account. Samoans appeared to be bitterly rivalrous, aggressive, preoccupied with rank, punitive against transgressions, and puritanical about sex! Forcible rape, considered by Mead to be "completely foreign to the Samoan mind," was widespread.[66] In the government-kept statistics for 1953, rape proved to be the fifth most common crime. So prized was virginity in Samoan culture that men would sometimes creep into an adolescent girl's hut at night in order to deflower her manually while she slept. Once deflowered, women were considered tarnished and unsuitable for marriage to high-ranking males. Such acts of *moetotolo* (or sleep crawling) often enabled the rapist to claim the victim as his wife.[67] A young scholar, Holmes did his best

Margaret Mead, at a news conference in 1971 (age seventy). A typical firstborn, Mead was once described by a college roommate as "goal-oriented even when there wasn't any special goal." During her long and distinguished career, she produced 39 books and 1,397 articles, not to mention more than 40 films and records. Marvin Harris, a fellow anthropologist, considered her "the busiest, hardest-working incarnation of the Protestant ethic since Calvin." Not long before her death, in 1978, Mead told a nurse that she was dying. "Yes," the nurse replied in a gentle tone, adding: "We all will someday." "But this is different," Mead retorted (Howard 1984:47, 424, 439).

to minimize the contradictions between his own findings and those of the world-famous Mead.

Firstborns find it particularly hard to admit their mistakes. Margaret Mead reacted to Holmes's 1958 book on Samoa with great umbrage and wrote an unfavorable review of it. Later she ran into Holmes at a meeting of the American Anthropological Association, where she vented her outrage against the young scholar. Holmes has recounted:

> [She] cornered me and laced me up and down, said how dishonest I was, and what a poor job I had done. I was a brand new Ph.D. then, and this was tough for me to take. . . . She's nobody to have as an enemy, I can tell you that.[68]

Holmes was not alone in questioning Mead's anthropological claims. By the end of Mead's life, a wealth of accumulated evidence had called into question her idyllic portrait of Samoan society. Seemingly oblivious to the objections of other researchers, Mead refused to revise the text of her famous book, which had become the most widely read work in her field.

Margaret Mead died in 1978. Five years later a New Zealand anthropologist published a book on Samoa that made headlines around the world. The author, Derek Freeman, had lived in the Samoan islands since 1940 and was fluent in the Samoan language. He had been adopted by a tribal chief and had eventually become a chief himself. He was thus able to attend tribal councils and to learn many details about Samoan society that were kept from outsiders. In the years since Mead's visit many Samoans had learned to read English. Some of them had come across Mead's book and had been flabbergasted by what they read. Her portrait of Samoan life, they concurred, was a "mind-boggling" distortion of their society.[69] Freeman was repeatedly asked by these native Samoans to correct the record. His book, based on decades of research, constituted a relentless exposé of Mead's errors and also offers an intriguing explanation for Mead's mistake, which was suggested to him by native Samoans.

It seems that Mead was deliberately misled by her adolescent informants. Sex is a taboo subject among Samoans, and adolescents are tight-lipped on the subject. For a woman to be revealed as a nonvirgin at the time of her marriage was to cause disgrace to herself and her family. For daughters of rank, virginity was tested in a special ceremony that could not, as Mead believed, be circumvented. Because Mead kept pushing for details, her informants finally manufactured lies "in order to tease her."[70] Duping, it turns out, is something of a pastime that "greatly appeals to the Samoans as a respite from the severity of their authoritarian society."[71]

"Anthropologists! Anthropologists!"

In Mead's later anthropological researches, she generally collaborated with other investigators. This strategy helped to protect against the kinds of misconceptions that marred her earliest field study.[72] All scientists make mistakes, so Mead's youthful error is understandable. What is instructive about this example is the *nature* of Mead's error. The mistakes of firstborns tend to be those of their teachers—in Mead's case, "Papa" Franz Boas. In contrast, the mistakes of laterborns often arise from an excess of rebellious zeal.

Radical Women in Science

A high proportion of the women in my study were closely associated with other revolutionary figures, including Voltaire, Darwin, and Freud. Some of these women served as translators or expositors of revolutionary ideas. Others made scientific contributions that went beyond

Madame Émilie du Châtelet, an early French Newtonian.

the achievements of the revolutionary thinkers they zealously supported. Some biographical examples will help to illustrate the varied contributions these women made to radical thought.

Émilie du Châtelet. Madame Émilie du Châtelet is one of the most iconoclastic women in my study. The fourth of five children, she was strongly encouraged by her father, who recognized her intellectual talents and tutored her himself. She received instruction at home in English, Latin, Italian, mathematics, and the sciences. By her late twenties Mme. du Châtelet was studying mathematics with Maupertuis, and she was soon corresponding with other eminent mathematicians of her day, including Alexis-Claude Clairaut and Leonhard Euler. An ardent feminist, she once remarked: "If I were king . . . I would redress an abuse which cuts back, as it were, one half of human kind. I would have women participate in all human rights, especially those of the mind."[73]

In 1740 Mme. du Châtelet published her *Institution de physique,* which defended Newtonian doctrines in defiance of established Cartesian physics. Later she translated Newton's *Principia* into French, a work to which Clairaut added an extensive commentary. Reports one biographer:

> Mme du Châtelet's mansion, the famous Cirey, became the setting for the Newtonian camp waging battle against the old Cartesian order. A laboratory was set up, scientists were invited from Paris and from abroad and everyone "Newtonised."[74]

To Charles Dufay, a French physicist who was still a Cartesian, Mme. du Châtelet wrote of Descartes's system of swirling vortices: "It is a house collapsing in ruins, propped up on every side. I think it would be prudent to leave." One historian of science, who has also cited this passage, adds: "But the residents of the crazy tenement declined to move."[75] The continuing efforts of Mme. du Châtelet—along with Clairaut, Maupertuis, and Voltaire—finally ended the reign of Cartesian physics in France.

Besides her role in the Newtonian revolution, Mme. du Châtelet engaged in other radical crusades. In 1735 she translated Bernard Mandeville's *Fable of the Bees: or, Private Vices, Publick Benefits* (1723). The message of Mandeville's controversial book was that greed promotes prosperity, that prostitution keeps husbands happy, and that filth indicates a prosperous society. Mme. du Châtelet liked a book that "turned accepted notions on their head."[76] The French government did not. Her translation was publicly burned by the executioner.

In 1737 Mme. du Châtelet secretly competed for a prize, offered by the Académie des Sciences, for the best essay on the nature of fire. To surprise Voltaire, who shared her house and was also competing for the prize, she composed her essay by night. Each night for a month she forced herself to get by with only an hour's sleep. The prize was won by Leonhard Euler, a firstborn representing the Cartesian opposition. The Académie was sufficiently impressed by the submissions of Mme. du Châtelet and Voltaire that it printed them together with the winning essay. Comparing the scientific work of Mme. du Châtelet with that of Voltaire, historian Ira Wade has concluded that "she had a wider outlook on the science of her time and was more open to other, non-Newtonian scientists, more original in her investigations, and more imaginative."[77] When she was forty-three, a late pregnancy ended Mme. du Châtelet's life from childbed fever. Voltaire was devastated. In his eulogy he remarked: "We have witnessed two miracles; one, that Newton wrote this work [the *Principia*], the other, that a lady has translated and explained it."[78]

Harriet Martineau. The sixth of eight children, Harriet Martineau endorsed mesmerism, phrenology, and Darwinism. She also enjoyed a distinguished career as a social critic. Martineau was good friends with Darwin's older brother, Erasmus, who was such a frequent caller at Martineau's house in London that it was rumored they were lovers. In 1838, Darwin made the following comment about Martineau: "She is a wonderful woman: when Lyell called, he found Rogers, L^{d}. Jeffrys, & Empson [all well-known writers for the *Edinburgh Review*] calling on her.—what a person she is thus to collect together all the geniuses."[79] In her *Autobiography,* Martineau returned the compliment. Reminiscing about "eminent men who were not vain," she described "the simple, childlike, painstaking, effective Charles Darwin, who established himself presently at the head of living English naturalists."[80]

Martineau's life illustrates the tendency for radical women to have experienced difficult relationships with their parents, especially with a mother. In her *Autobiography* Martineau spoke bitterly of "the bondage of my early life."[81] In particular, she characterized the cold maternal authority to which she was subjected as a child as "a tyranny of the mind." This experience, she claimed, bred an "interior rebellion." "The well-meant but rigid discipline of her parents, and the thoughtless roughness of the elder children," observes one biographer, "injured her temper and made her gloomy, jealous, and morbid." Martineau was sent to live with an aunt at the age of seventeen, and "here for the first time she found . . . a 'human being of whom she was not afraid.' "[82]

During the early 1830s Martineau became interested in Thomas Robert Malthus's controversial theory of population growth. In the spirit of Voltaire's *Candide,* Malthus wrote his *Essay on the Principle of Population* (1798) to demonstrate that the world was not infinitely perfectible. His intent was to awaken utopian dreamers to the ever-present reality of struggle, poverty, and death.[83] Many of Martineau's contemporaries considered it indecent for a woman to write about the issue

Harriet Martineau, around 1834 (in her early thirties). Her interest in population growth led her to study the radical writings of Thomas Robert Malthus, whom she met in 1834. Two years later she became acquainted with Charles Darwin, shortly after his return from the *Beagle* voyage.

of sexual reproduction, and she was "held in horror" for endorsing Malthus's "dismal" views. From this experience she concluded that "the reformers of morality, personal and social, are always subject at the outset to the imputation of immorality from those interested in the continuance of corruption."[84]

Martineau may have been responsible for Charles Darwin's exposure to Malthusian thinking, and hence to the formulation of his theory of natural selection. Malthus himself was the second youngest of seven children, so we are confronted by a web of laterborn revolt against Panglossian beliefs. This web leads from Malthus to Harriet Martineau, from Martineau to Erasmus Darwin (the fourth of six children), and from Erasmus to his younger brother Charles. It was Erasmus's copy of Malthus's *Essay* that Darwin borrowed and read in September 1838 with such revolutionary consequences.[85]

Women and Psychoanalysis

Psychoanalysis has attracted a substantial number of radical women. Among these psychoanalytic pioneers were Karen Horney (the second of two children), Helene Deutsch and Melanie Klein (both the youngest of four), and Freud's own daughter Anna (the youngest of six). Of these four women, Freud's daughter was the most conservative. It is now known that Freud analyzed his daughter—a particularly effective way of minimizing "resistance" to his theories.[86] Anna, who got along poorly with her mother, loyally defended her father's views and acted as his secretary. After Freud developed cancer of the mouth, Anna took over as his nurse. A shy person, she lacked the temperament of a rebel.

Karen Horney overcame much of her own shyness to become a "gentle rebel."[87] During the 1920s, two controversial issues emerged within psychoanalysis and caused serious schisms within the movement. The first issue centered around the Oedipus complex. Freud considered oedipal conflicts to be the "nuclear" complex of the neuroses, but some of his followers were not so sure. The second major controversy involved female sexual development, which Freud portrayed as a stunted form of male development. Women, according to Freud, were "wounded" men—reacting to their lack of a phallus with "penis envy" and repudiation of their mother (whom they typically blame for this deficiency).[88]

Horney rejected the centrality of the Oedipus complex as well as Freud's phallocentric views on female sexuality.[89] Penis envy, she argued, is not primary in women. She also dismissed Freud's claim that little girls lack vaginal sensations. Femininity, she maintained, was spontaneous in girls, not the result of a flight from masculinity. "Her woman," comments one historian of psychoanalysis, "is a rebel, not the passive, submissive type whom Freud . . . saw as the 'normal' woman."[90]

Sigmund and Anna Freud in 1917, walking together in the Dolomites. Freud was sixty-one that year. Anna was twenty-one.

In 1932 Horney emigrated to the United States. A decade later, the American Psychoanalytic Association responded to her growing heterodoxy by restricting her right to train candidates. Horney resigned and founded a rival organization, the Association for the Advancement of Psychoanalysis.[91] Her successful insurrection against Freud inspired the school of interpersonal psychiatry in the United States.

Perhaps the most radical of these psychoanalytic revisionists was Melanie Klein—considered a "heretic" by many.[92] Virginia Woolf described her as "a woman of character & force," and others have noted her "grande dame quality" and her combative nature.[93] Klein was so taken with her own ideas that Donald Winnicott, a fellow analyst, called her a "eureka shrieker."[94] She pioneered child analysis and extended psychoanalytic theory to the pre-oedipal phases, pushing Freud's ideas into "speculative depths from which even Freud had retreated. This was her offense: for daring to branch out on her own paths of investigation, she was branded, vilified, and mocked."[95]

Like Horney, Klein discounted Freud's notion of the Oedipus complex. She also disagreed with Freud's ideas about female sexuality. Klein was particularly interested in the role of the mother, something that Freud tended to minimize given his preoccupation with the father-son rivalry of the oedipal conflict. Klein boldly traced neuroses back to the first months of life, locating the seeds of psychopathology in traumas such as weaning, and the infant's schizophrenic conceptions of good and bad breasts.[96] Freud's reaction to these heterodox ideas was predictable: he "abhorred the direction Melanie Klein took."[97]

Klein's ideas on "object relations" succeeded in becoming the dominant psychoanalytic paradigm in Great Britain, and her views are still influential today. John Bowlby, who developed attachment theory, trained under Melanie Klein. Bowlby had the wisdom to realize that, for all of Klein's iconoclasm, "she was totally unaware of the scientific method."[98] Owing to Bowlby's decision to study attachment scientifically, some of Klein's speculations have earned a place in scientific psychology.[99]

CONCLUSIONS

For many personality traits the influence of gender is surprisingly indirect and does not coincide with sexual stereotypes. Being female makes some women more agreeable, empathetic, and liberal. Because of family niches, being female has the opposite effect on other women. In particular, firstborns of both sexes tend to be "alpha males." For this reason, the topic of gender is best approached on an individual-by-individual basis.

To understand why some women rebel, we must answer the question "Why are sisters so different?" The answer involves the ways in which family niches promote sibling differences in risk taking and openness to experience. Only modest gender differences exist for these personality attributes. In contrast, sibling differences in these traits are substantial and reflect the diversity of the family niches that forge them. Because laterborns are more open than firstborns to challenging the status quo, they have often championed heterodox reforms. In American history, the most radical women reformers have tended to be younger siblings. In politics, religion, and race relations these laterborn women have typically transgressed the barriers of gender and class in their efforts to promote egalitarian causes. Firstborn women have tended to reject radical reforms and have generally confined their own reforming efforts to improving the system, not to overthrowing it. Owing to the powerful role of sibling differences, birth order is a much better predictor of reform tendencies than either gender or class.

In past centuries, women in science were a distinct minority, and radical proclivities were almost a prerequisite for their entry into this profession. This circumstance explains why women scientists were consistently more open to scientific change than the men in my study. Owing to personal experiences associated with family niches, these radical women were generally born to rebel. When we control for the attributes of family niches, gender per se does not predict scientific radicalism.[100] Gender's contribution to radicalism is typically *indirect*—a product of "gender by niche" interactions within the family system.

Because radicals (including radical women) are usually open to experience, they possess greater sensitivity to anomalous evidence and the need for conceptual pluralism. Some feminist scholars consider these qualities to be goals for "gender-free" science.[101] Because gender differences are closely entwined with sibling differences, the goals of gender-free science are largely prescriptions about birth order and other aspects of family niches. It is not just men who cause science to be dogmatic, impersonal, and competitive. Science and letters have always been dominated by firstborns, who excel at traditional forms of learning. Owing to the numerous interactions between gender and family niches, even a science that managed to exclude males would never be gender free. It is only by coming to terms with this paradox, and with the role that family niches play in its resolution, that we can understand why some people—women as well as men—decide to rebel.

7

TEMPERAMENT

Most features of personality are moderately heritable.[1] The fact that many behaviors are under partial genetic control does not mean they are predetermined. Within the normal range of potential variations in physical and psychological characteristics, the environment affects how observed traits express themselves. Biological predispositions do tend to set limits. For instance, it is difficult to become a professional basketball star if one is genetically predestined to be only five feet tall. Similarly, it is not possible to be a world-class marathoner if one lacks the aerobic capacity. Certain aspects of personality present analogous limitations for social behavior.

Those features of personality that emerge early, and that are associated with the emotions, are said to represent "temperament." Individual differences in mood and activity level are already distinguishable in newborns.[2] Similarly, a tendency toward shyness is evident in a one-year-old child, whereas many aspects of personality, such as conscientiousness, do not emerge until a later developmental stage. Most aspects of temperament appear to be heritable. Temperament may be subdivided into three components: activity level, sociability, and emotionality.[3]

The topic of temperament is especially important in the context of why siblings are so different. Depending on differences in family niches, individual disparities in temperament have highly varied consequences for the rest of personality. Individual differences that can be attributed to biology are often magnified by the environment. This conclusion is especially true of the inclination to rebel. Shyness, for example, either promotes or inhibits revolutionary personality, depending on one's family niche. Such contrary outcomes arise because most personality traits are the product of complex interactions between genetic dispositions and environmental experiences. Many of these experiences are non-shared and arise within the family system.

SHYNESS AND INTROVERSION

Shyness is closely associated with Introversion/Extraversion, one of the Big Five personality dimensions. But shyness and introversion are not synonymous. Shyness also reflects social anxiety, an attribute associated with Neuroticism.[4] Shyness therefore transects two major dimensions of personality. Because shyness can be classified as a kind of "nervous introversion," it is helpful to define introversion.

According to the British psychologist Hans Eysenck,

> The typical extravert is sociable, likes parties, has many friends, needs to have people to talk to, and does not like reading or studying by himself. He craves excitement, takes chances, often sticks his neck out, acts on the spur of the moment, and is generally an impulsive individual. . . . [He] tends to be aggressive and loses his temper quickly.
>
> The typical introvert is a quiet, retiring sort of person, introspective, fond of books rather than people; he is reserved and distant except to intimate friends. He tends to plan ahead, "looks before he leaps," and mistrusts the impulse of the moment. He does not like excitement, takes matters of everyday life with proper seriousness, and likes a well-ordered mode of life.[5]

Not all psychologists would agree with the details of this definition of introversion/extraversion, but most would concur with Eysenck's basic claim: Extraverts are characterized by a lively sociability that contrasts with the introvert's reserved and quiet manner. Shy people are *anxiously* introverted, which is why they are uneasy in the presence of strangers.[6] As shy children are growing up, their disposition to social timidity is a source of small but recurrent developmental glitches. This behavioral handicap limits the kinds of strategies that offspring may comfortably employ in competition with siblings. In particular, shy firstborns have more difficulty establishing social dominance over other siblings. Given this and other variations in temperament, siblings must adjust their competitive strategies.

The Biology of Shyness

Shyness is one of the most heritable personality traits. Research in behavioral genetics suggests that as much as 50 percent of the variance in shyness is heritable, compared with 30 to 40 percent for most other personality traits.[7] Although most basic features of personality are heritable, direct evidence for their physiological substratum is still limited. In the case of shyness, the physiological substratum has been amply documented.

Psychologist Jerome Kagan has established many of the physiological findings on this topic. He and his coworkers have followed children who were selected at two years of age, on the basis of being particularly shy or outgoing. The behavioral signs of shyness that were employed in Kagan's study included clinging to the mother, lack of vocalization, and avoidance of unfamiliar objects or experiences.[8] Shy children also have more nightmares and phobias than not-so-shy children.

Shyness is reliably associated with five physiological indicators. Compared with children who are uninhibited, shy children possess high and stable heart rates. A high and stable heart rate is an indicator of vigilance. Because shy children are more fearful of their environment, they monitor it more closely than other children. It is particularly striking that, even before they are born, children who turn out to be shy possess higher-than-average heart rates.

Other physiological markers of shyness include greater pupillary dilation during cognitive tasks, higher blood pressure, greater muscle tension in the vocal cords (as measured by sound analysis), and elevated levels of salivary cortisol. (Secreted by the adrenal gland, cortisol is a response to stress.) An aggregate measure of these physiological indicators is strongly correlated with shyness. Several of these physiological indicators have been studied in connection with introversion, and they also correlate highly with this personality trait. Physiological evidence therefore reinforces the close connection between shyness and introversion.[9]

Nature and nurture cooperate in determining who is shy and who is not. Two-thirds of Kagan's shy children were laterborns, whereas two-thirds of his extraverted children were firstborns. Kagan has hypothesized that older siblings, who sometimes terrorize their younger siblings with aggressive behavior, might transform an innate temperamental disposition into the personality trait that is later recognized as shyness.[10]

Biographical Examples

I have systematically collected biographical information on the personalities of scientists in my study, especially in connection with the traits of social apprehensiveness and introversion/extraversion.[11] My approach may be illustrated by some of the descriptions of shyness I have encountered.

Charles Darwin. Darwin is a good example because, like most of us, he is somewhere in the middle on shyness. His son Francis observed about him:

> The transparent goodness and simplicity of his nature gave to his manner a vivid personal charm, which has impressed so many of those who came in contact with him. In society he was bright and animated, and he had a quiet ease and naturalness arising from a complete absence of *pose* or pretension. His natural tendency was to express his feelings warmly and frankly; and on any subject that aroused his indignation—such as cruelty—his anger easily broke forth. Conversation was a keen enjoyment to him, and he had in a striking degree the pleasant quality of being a good listener.[12]

This biographical description makes Darwin seem like an extravert. But Darwin also displayed an aloofness in his character. Francis Darwin noted that his father's "manner toward strangers was marked by something of a formal politeness, a habit heightened perhaps by his retired life at Down." Other observers have commented on Darwin's reserve toward people he did not know well.[13]

Darwin's secluded life at Down, sixteen miles south of London, reflects his strong predilection for privacy. In this rural hamlet, he relished the solitude that enabled him to get on with his work. "Few persons," he remarked in his *Autobiography,* "can have lived a more retired life than we have done."[14] His daily work schedule went like clockwork, and he disliked being interrupted without warning. To prevent this, he installed a small mirror outside his study window so he could see people coming up the driveway.[15] Still, Darwin frequently invited guests to come to Down for weekends, usually arriving on a Friday afternoon and departing on Sunday. To the extent that Darwin was an extravert, it was on his own terms.

Darwin's case exemplifies a common problem in assessing traits

Down House (from the rear), where Darwin lived and worked for forty years. At his home in Down Darwin felt sufficiently secluded from the distractions of London and society, but he could still entertain guests and make day trips to London by train.

such as extraversion. In some contexts, we are all extraverted. Darwin himself recognized this point. In his *Expression of the Emotions in Man and Animals* (1872), he noted that "persons who are exceedingly shy are rarely shy in the presence of those with whom they are quite familiar and of whose good opinion and sympathy they are perfectly assured."[16] The true extravert is *consistently* outgoing. Darwin displayed a mix of the two characteristics. My raters agree, giving Darwin a mean score of 4.5 on a 7-point extraversion scale—just above the midpoint.

Louis Agassiz. In contrast to Darwin, Louis Agassiz was a consistent extravert, and I know of no scientist who was more sociable or self-confident. A brilliant lecturer, Agassiz captivated his audiences with his effortless charm. He made friends "easily and quickly," and he was a natural leader.[17] A fellow student once commented about him: "He was always ready to demonstrate and speak on any subject. If it was a subject he was not familiar with, he would study and rapidly master it; and on the next occasion he would speak in such brilliant terms and with such profound erudition that he was a constant source of wonder to us."[18]

In spite of his studious nature, Agassiz amazed his friends by his capacity for pleasure seeking. At social events "he was always the first to

Louis Agassiz in 1844 (age thirty-five). He is standing in the glacial fields near Neuchâtel, Switzerland, where he did much of his pioneering work on the geology of glaciers. At this time Agassiz was still an expert fencer and "appeared at a public fencing exhibition given by a tall and powerful negro fencing master, with success and credit" (Marcou 1896, 1:23). Sixteen years later, after he had emigrated to America to become a professor at Harvard University, Agassiz found himself in an intellectual fencing match with Darwin's American supporters. This was one match that he finally lost, but not without a strong public defense of his creationist views.

come and the last to go, his strong constitution requiring an absorption of food and drink which left all the others far behind him." It was in these student years that he adopted as his personal motto, "First at work and first at play," and he honored this motto "through all his life, with rare interruptions."[19]

A brilliant fencer, Agassiz was president of his student fencing club. When the Swiss club to which he belonged was insulted by a German club, Agassiz issued a challenge and was selected to defend his club's honor. The rival club also picked its best swordsman, but Agassiz would not accept such conditions, saying: "It is not with one of you that I want to fight, but with all, one after another." Agassiz quickly dispatched his first four opponents with sword cuts to the face and was prepared to take on the rest. The German club, having exhausted its best swordsmen, decided that matters had gone far enough and persuaded the swashbuckling Louis that honor had been restored. Agassiz fought other sword duels "to his credit and always successfully."[20] Independent raters give Agassiz the highest possible rating on my scale (7.0).

Percy Williams Bridgman. We may contrast the highly sociable and brazen Agassiz with Percy Bridgman. An American physicist and philosopher, Bridgman invented operational analysis. According to the philosophy of "operationalism," the meaning of a scientific term lies entirely in measurement. A biographer has described how Bridgman's shyness limited his social functioning:

> Despite a strong competitive drive, he was a modest and private person. Those who have never experienced shyness rarely appreciate the psychic energy required to overcome the barrier it imposes. . . . Bridgman's shyness . . . caused him extreme discomfort in public speaking situations; in fact, not only did he dislike lecturing, he was not very good at it.[21]

As a young scientist, Bridgman was asked to discuss his research at a conference. After he had seen some of the other presentations, he withdrew out of timidity. As a teacher, Bridgman was always helpful to students, but he was happiest when they left him alone. Bridgman is an exception to the rule that firstborns reject scientific revolutions. He supported two of them—the quantum hypothesis and relativity theory. Independent raters give Bridgman a 1.5 on my extraversion scale, the lowest rating that anyone has received.

SHYNESS AND REVOLUTIONARY PERSONALITY

There is no direct relationship between shyness and revolutionary personality. Shy scientists are just as likely to support innovations as are extraverted scientists. There is, however, a curious relationship lurking behind these findings, and it involves birth order.

Receptivity to Scientific Innovation by Birth Order and Shyness

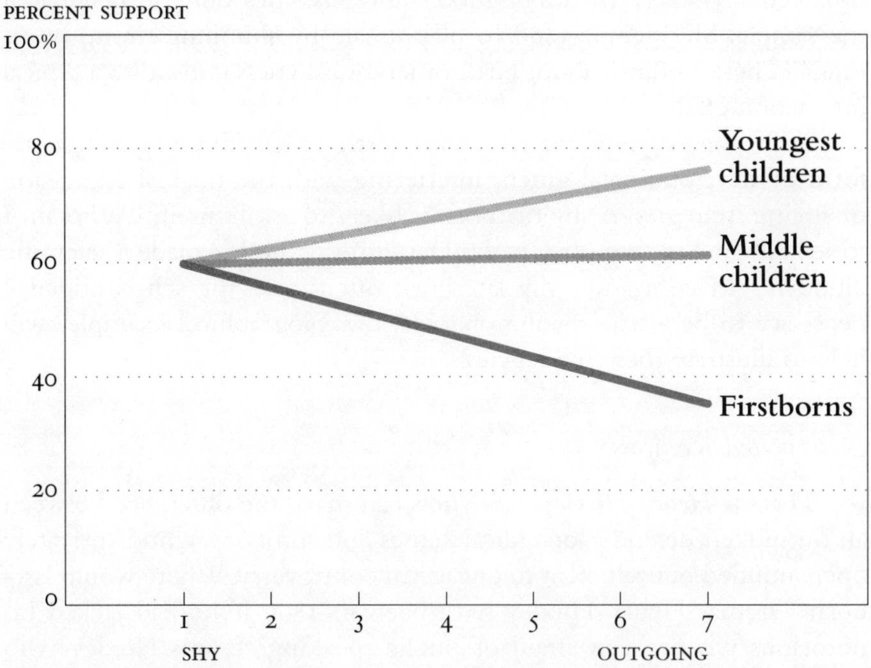

FIGURE 7.1 Receptivity to scientific innovation by birth order and shyness. A shy disposition keeps individuals from expressing the tendencies they would otherwise express according to their birth orders. It is difficult for a shy laterborn to be a staunch proponent of radical thinking. In contrast, shy firstborns are more likely than not-so-shy firstborns to accept new theories.

These findings entail a significant interaction effect: birth rank and shyness have *nonadditive* consequences. Although birth order exerts a significant main effect on scientific stance, shyness only does so in conjunction with birth order.

Extraverted individuals tend to respond to new ideas in accordance with their birth orders (Fig. 7.1).[22] Extraverted firstborns, like Louis Agassiz, generally reject radical innovations—doing so with zeal. From the bottom of his soul, Agassiz believed that Darwin was wrong about evolution. In contrast to extraverted firstborns, extraverted laterborns are just as strongly convinced that radical innovations are justified, defending heterodox ideas with a self-confidence that shy revolutionaries lack. In predicting radical thinking among particularly extraverted individuals, the success of birth order is impressive—correctly classifying nine scientists out of ten. Revolutionaries and their most vocal opponents are rarely timid people. Among scientists burdened by pronounced shyness, birth order successfully classifies only 56 percent of the sample. Shy people tend to play it safe by shunning strong opinions.[23] These findings about birth order and shyness constitute a typical interaction effect.

Why does shyness interact with birth order? Shyness is a subtle form of developmental glitch, interfering with the normal expression of sibling strategies. A shy firstborn is likely to ask himself, "Who am I to tell Albert Einstein (or Charles Darwin) that he has made a scientific blunder?" In contrast, a shy laterborn often lacks the self-confidence necessary to be a true revolutionary. A few biographical examples will help to illustrate these tendencies.

Extraverted Radicals

Thomas Henry Huxley. Shyness can make the difference between an outspoken defender of radical causes and someone who is privately open-minded but reluctant to engage in controversy. Where would lastborn Thomas Henry Huxley have been in 1860 if he had lacked his notorious wit or been afraid of public speaking? It was Huxley who faced off against bishop "Soapy" Sam Wilberforce in the famous Oxford debates over Darwin's theories. At the end of Wilberforce's speech, which had ridiculed the notion of evolution, the bishop contemptuously asked Huxley whether it was through his grandmother or his grandfather that he claimed his descent from an ape. Huxley blurted out to the person sitting next to him: "The Lord hath delivered him into mine hands." He then took the platform and dissected the poor bishop, demonstrating the bishop's utter ignorance of the facts, and delivering one of the most memorable retorts in the entire history of science:

> If then, said I, the question is put to me "would I rather have a miserable ape for a grandfather or a man highly endowed by nature and possessed of great means of influence & yet who employs those faculties & that influence for the mere purpose of introducing ridicule into a grave scientific discussion"—I unhesitatingly affirm my preference for the ape.[24]

One lady in the audience fainted and had to be carried out. Mild-mannered Darwin, safely ensconced back at Down House, wrote to

Thomas Henry Huxley in 1857 (age thirty-two), just two years before the *Origin of Species* was published. Upon receiving his presentation copy of the *Origin* he wrote to Darwin in thanks: "Depend upon it you have earned the lasting gratitude of all thoughtful men—And as to the curs which will bark & yelp—you must recollect that some of your friends at any rate are endowed with an amount of combativeness which (though you have often & justly rebuked it) may stand you in good stead—I am sharpening up my claws & beak in readiness" (Darwin 1985– , 7:391; letter of 23 November 1859).

Huxley with taunting delight: "But how durst you attack a live bishop in that fashion? I am quite ashamed of you! Have you no reverence . . . ? By Jove, you seem to have done it well!" Darwin himself never publicly debated his ideas on evolution. He confessed to Joseph Hooker: "I would as soon have died as tried to answer the Bishop in such an assem-

Voltaire in 1718 (age twenty-four), shortly after his first imprisonment in the Bastille. Only a few years earlier he was described as "tall for his age, not handsome, having only one decided beauty,—brilliant piercing eyes, which strangers always remarked" (Parton 1881, 1:50).

bly."[25] The pugnacious Huxley repeatedly defended Darwin's ideas in public, earning himself the nickname "Darwin's Bulldog."

François-Marie Arouet (Voltaire). The inimitable Voltaire is one of the most extraverted individuals in my sample. A lastborn to boot, he represents an eighteenth-century analogue of Thomas Henry Huxley. Indeed, Voltaire's brilliant literary career is an exemplar of the kind of militant radicalism that emerges in people who combine pronounced self-confidence with lastborn status. Naturalist Charles Bonnet—a firstborn—spoke for most other conservative souls of his generation when he asserted that "providence had permitted earthquakes, floods, heresy, and Voltaire."[26]

Voltaire has been called "one of the century's liveliest minds," and he was an undisputed master of irony.[27] As a young literary figure in Paris, "François was a success in every drawing-room into which he was invited."[28] "The flashing quickness of his mind," another biographer remarks, "rendered his conversation at all times interesting, and gave him a talent for repartee."[29] This talent was so extraordinary that it led to his being physically assaulted by several of his outraged victims. Remarks one biographer: "This agile spirit lived among the monarchies and hierarchies of the time, familiar and fearless, courting and avoiding the crushing strokes of power, and answering saucily from remote and comfortable nooks which his masters could not reach."[30]

The following story, which involves his irascible father, conveys Voltaire's talent for repartee. Voltaire has recounted: "One day, after he had horribly and without cause scolded his gardener, and had almost beaten him, he said to him, 'Get out, you rascal! I wish you may find a master as patient as I am.' " This ridiculous speech reminded Voltaire of a character he had seen in a recent play, so he took his father to see the play. Beforehand, Voltaire secretly visited the actor who was playing the part and asked him to replace his usual lines with the *exact words* that his father had said to the gardener! Voltaire noted of this episode: "My good father corrected himself a little."[31]

Voltaire's unrestrained wit, combined with his penchant for radical viewpoints, made his life difficult. As a young man he was imprisoned twice in the Bastille for satirizing members of the nobility. One indignant nobleman had him publicly beaten by his henchman. Voltaire sought revenge by taking fencing lessons and by challenging this noble to a duel.[32] Before dawn the next morning, when the duel was to have taken place, Voltaire found himself back in the Bastille. He was then exiled from the country as a public nuisance.

After a three-year absence, Voltaire returned to Paris in 1729. He was soon up to his neck in trouble again for expressing various radical opinions. The remainder of his life was spent in banishment or exile, or dodging orders for his arrest. In his later years he concluded most of his communications with the phrase *"Écrasez l'Infâme"* (Crush the infamous thing).[33] To Voltaire, the most "infamous thing" of all was the deleterious influence of religious fanatics, including his older brother the Jansenist.

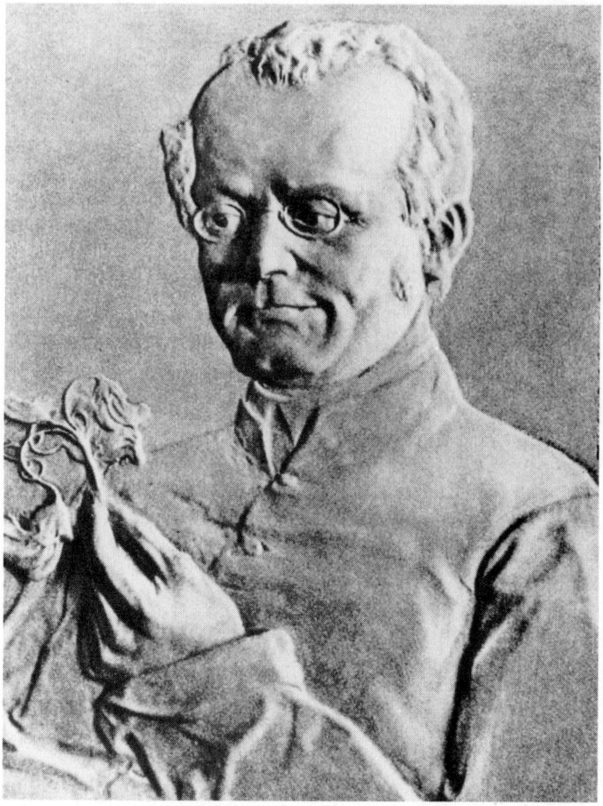

Gregor Mendel, examining a variety of the common garden pea. Mendel was elected prelate of his monastery in 1868, two years after publication of his famous paper on the laws of inheritance. He was forty-six years old. His new duties interfered with his ability to conduct further scientific research.

Reluctant Revolutionaries

Sometimes shy people make radical breakthroughs without having intended to do so, or without having fully considered the consequences. The result is a *reluctant* revolutionary. Even when shy people intend to be radical, their timidity often undermines their ability to get their message across. A classic instance of a timid revolutionary involves Gregor Mendel, the Austrian monk who discovered the laws of heredity. Mendel was the second of three children and an only son.

Over a ten-year period the meticulous Mendel bred almost 30,000 pea plants and studied their seeds for the inheritance of genetic traits. For example, some seeds are smooth whereas others are wrinkled—a difference that is controlled by a single gene. Mendel published his laws of inheritance in 1866. Unfortunately his communication appeared in a relatively obscure journal, the proceedings of the Brno Natural Sciences Society. For the next thirty-four years no one recognized the importance of Mendel's discoveries. In 1900 Mendel's laws were rediscovered by three different biologists, working independently, which finally allowed Mendel's own publication on the subject to be understood.[34] Scholars have long puzzled over this egregious case of conceptual neglect.

Mendel was an intellectual revolutionary, but he lacked the right personality for the role. Twice, while studying at the university, he had nervous breakdowns owing to anxiety over his examinations, and once he was forced to return home for a year. He is described as "extremely sensitive" and "overcome by fear and shyness," traits that occasionally made him depressed to the point of illness.[35] Mendel's worries about coping in the real world were ultimately what prompted this mild-mannered man to become a monk.[36]

After Mendel published his famous paper on peas, he did little to promote his ideas. Although receptive to Darwin's theories, he does not appear to have written to Darwin or to any of the other leaders in the Darwinian crusade. More important, Mendel never presented his findings in book form. Until recently, books, not articles, have been necessary to inaugurate a scientific revolution. In 1858, the famous Darwin-Wallace papers announcing the theory of natural selection had almost no impact. It took the *Origin of Species* (1859) to launch the Darwinian revolution.

Other examples of scientific revolutionaries whose shyness limited their effectiveness typically involve laterborns. Nicholas Copernicus, the last of three children, was decidedly reserved, and one biographer calls him "the timid canon."[37] Copernicus, comments another scholar, "long refused to publish his masterly work *On the Revolutions of the Heavenly Spheres* . . . because it might involve him in controversy."[38] Privately Copernicus did circulate a manuscript known as the *Commentariolus* (Brief Outline), which described his heterodox theory. In 1533, Pope Clement VII's secretary, Johann Albrecht Widmannstetter, explained Copernicus's theory to the pontiff. "The explanation pleased Clement VII so much that he presented to Widmannstetter a valuable Greek manuscript, which still survives."[39] Clement died the following

Nicholas Copernicus, called by Martin Luther the "new astrologer" and the "fool [who] will overturn the whole science of astronomy" (Stimson 1917:39).

year and was succeeded by Paul III. Widmannstetter then entered into the service of one of the new pope's most trusted cardinals, Nicholas Schönberg. Schönberg was so impressed by Widmannstetter's report about the new theory that he personally wrote to Copernicus in 1536 to urge him to publish his ideas. Still Copernicus resisted![40] Copernicus, it seems, did not withhold publication of his heterodox theories because of fear of persecution by the Catholic Church. What he wished to avoid was the ridicule of his disbelieving colleagues.[41]

Radical ideas tend to attract extraverted laterborns, and this propensity saved Copernicus from scientific obscurity. In 1540, only three years before his death, Copernicus was persuaded by a young and daring lastborn, Georg Joachim Rheticus, to publish his theory of the cosmos. Rheticus was just the kind of intellectual "bulldog" to accomplish this task. A Lutheran, he risked a personal visit to Frombork, in Catholic Poland, in order to learn about the new cosmology directly from the master. At this time, the attitude toward Lutherans was decidedly hostile, and the local bishop in Frombork had recently banned all Lutheran sympathizers from his diocese. The bishop had also issued an order recalling all sons of nobles who were attending universities in "the poisoned places of heretical Lutheranism."[42] Rheticus himself was a professor at one of these places, namely Luther's own Wittenberg! Unlike the cautious Copernicus, Rheticus was a man of "enthusiasm" and even "excessive zeal."[43] He soon pushed some of Copernicus's ideas further than the timid canon from Frombork had ever dared to do.

Upon his arrival in Frombork, Rheticus was warmly greeted by Copernicus. Neither astronomer seems to have been bothered by their confessional differences or the fact that Copernicus was a canon in the Catholic Church. Copernicus allowed Rheticus to study all his unpublished manuscripts, and Rheticus soon mastered the new cosmology. Rheticus published a *First Report* on it in 1540, and he spent the next three years overseeing publication of Copernicus's magnum opus. Copernicus received a copy of his book on the day of his death, "just before he closed his eyes for the last time."[44] By revolutionary standards, this was cutting it close.

Nearly four decades later, Rheticus, who had moved to Hungary, received a visitor who had traveled all the way from Wittenberg to discuss one of his works. He greeted his guest warmly and then remarked: "You come to see me at the same age as I myself went to Copernicus. If I had not visited him, none of his works would have seen the light."[45] The story of Rheticus and his relationship with Copernicus suggests a practical application for career strategies in science. If you happen to be a shy individual and have radical aspirations, consider collaborating with a lastborn extravert.

Another timid revolutionary, Max Planck, set forth one of the most radical ideas of modern physics. Planck's "quantum of action" brought an end to the principle of continuity that had guided classical physics.

Not every innovator intends to start a revolution or wishes to be pivotally involved in one. In 1931, Planck explained to an American physicist how he had reached his radical notion of the quantum:

> Briefly summarized, what I did can be described as simply an act of desperation. By nature I am peacefully inclined and reject all doubtful adventures. But by then [1900] I had been wrestling unsuccessfully for six years . . . with the problem of equilibrium between radiation and matter. . . . A theoretical interpretation therefore *had* to be found at any cost, no matter how high. It was clear to me that classical physics could offer no solution to this problem.[46]

By his own account, Planck was *driven* to make his radical suggestion, responding to what Thomas Kuhn has called a "crisis" in science.[47] Even so, Planck was never fully comfortable with this heterodox step. He later found himself trying to reconcile his radical hypothesis with classical mechanics. One historian has commented about Planck's efforts to salvage the old physics: "In 1910 he expressed himself in the manner of a protector of a menaced and even losing cause. . . . By then conservatism, always congenial, had become a duty for Planck under a general rule of his own devising. As scientists age and gain authority, he said, they must display 'an increased caution and reticence in entering into new paths.' "[48]

CAUSES OF SHYNESS

The environmental sources of shyness are not as well understood as the physiological attributes that serve as markers for it. Birth order has been implicated in shyness, but the published findings conflict.[49] Such contradictory results arise because birth order interacts with other features of the family system (especially its diverse niches). Among the scientists included in my own study, shyness is influenced by birth order and sibship size, whose joint effects interact as opposed to combining additively. In small sibships, shyness is not related to birth order. As sibship size increases, firstborns become more outgoing and laterborns become more reserved (Fig. 7.2).[50]

A psychological explanation for these findings involves three considerations: (1) the effects of birth order on personality; (2) the socializ-

Boldness Versus Shyness as Related to Birth Order and Sibship Size

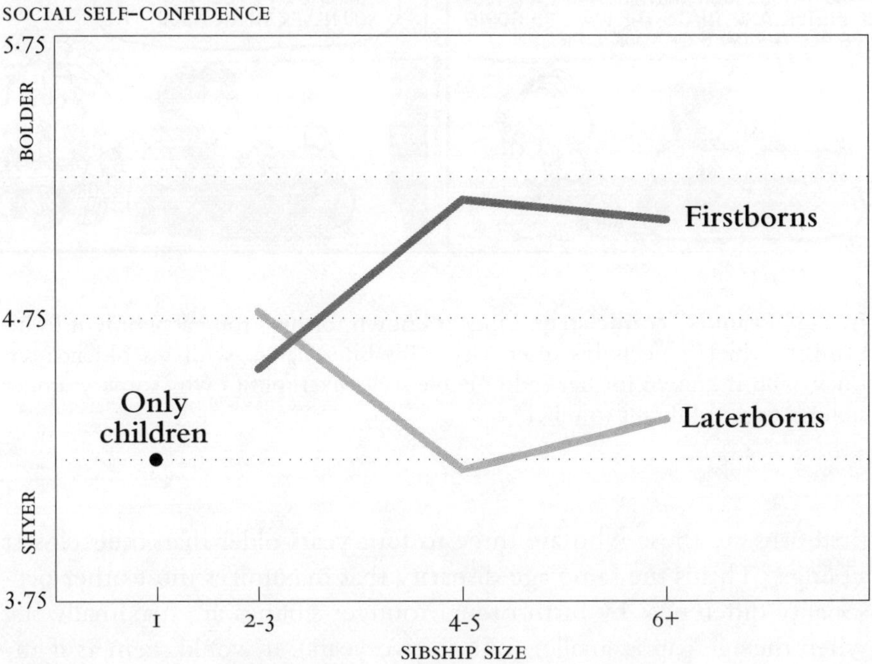

FIGURE 7.2. The relationship between birth order, sibship size, and shyness. In small sibships, birth order is not a significant predictor of shyness. In large sibships, laterborns are shyer than firstborns. Overall, birth order exerts a significant main effect on shyness, but sibship size does not. However, the interaction between birth order and sibship size is significant.

ing effects of siblings; and (3) the interaction between birth order and sibship size, which reflects the politics of dominance hierarchies. In assessing the environmental causes of shyness, we may consider only children as a controlled experiment. Singletons are somewhat less extraverted than other firstborns. The presence of siblings seems to facilitate extraversion by giving offspring more practice at socializing.[51]

Birth order is an important precursor of shyness, but its consequences change with age and are also dependent on age spacing and sibship size. Research indicates that, as *young* children, laterborns are more reserved than older siblings.[52] A two-year-old is easily intimidated by a four-year-old, but the same age difference between teenagers is not nearly as intimidating. Age spacing moderates this developmental trend and affects laterborns differently from firstborns. The most extraverted

In the "Peanuts" comic strip, Linus is known for his strong attachment to his blanket, which reflects his insecurity. This interchange with his older sister, Lucy, who is known for her indomitable style, exemplifies why some younger siblings find it difficult to rebel.

firstborns are those who are three to four years older than their closest sibling.[53] This is the same age disparity that maximizes most other personality differences by birth order. Younger siblings are maximally shy when the age gap is smaller (one to two years). It would seem as if inequality in age, which typically fosters rebellion in younger siblings, also fosters a measure of extraversion.

Laterborns often outgrow their early shyness, especially as they learn effective strategies for dealing with their older siblings. Time also assists laterborns by gradually redressing the physical disparities that handicap them during childhood. Finally, the degree to which laterborns overcome shyness is influenced by sibship size. Small sibships offer greater opportunity for laterborns to achieve cognitive and physical parity with their elders. Birth order therefore tends to create greater disparities in shyness in large families, where laterborns are more likely to be lost in the shuffle.

Childhood dispositions to shyness are sometimes reinforced by the early loss of a parent. Family niches determine how this experience affects siblings. In the middle and especially the upper classes, early parental loss is associated with decreased extraversion. Early loss of the mother, not the father, is responsible for this effect.[54] As Bowlby and other psychologists have demonstrated, disrupted attachments, especially to the mother, tend to make children insecure.[55] But this is not always so. Among lower-class families, early parental loss is associated with *increased* extraversion! This counterintuitive effect probably owes itself to the practice of surrogate parenting, because the effect is most pronounced among firstborns.[56] By assuming a greater share of parental duties following the death of a parent, lower-class firstborns tend to gain in personal power. Instead of becoming insecure, such children gain in self-confidence. Based on my own findings, Bowlby's account of Darwin's illness, which Bowlby attributed to early parental loss, is plausible for laterborns like Darwin.[57] The same explanation for the same disorder would not always hold true for firstborns, especially those from the lower classes. The key to these discrepancies is the nature of family niches: different niches, different consequences arising from developmental glitches.

Several anecdotal examples from my study illustrate the generalizations I have just made. Georg Groddeck, an early Freudian, called himself a "wild analyst" for his deviations from orthodox psychoanalysis. He was the youngest of five children. According to biographers, his shyness was closely linked to his relationship with his siblings:[58]

> As the youngest, he bore the brunt of their jokes. He was their favorite object of ridicule, the baby who mispronounced words, who misquoted, misunderstood, and made all sorts of comical mistakes. His idiocies were detailed at mealtime, his stupidities recalled, his ignorance hooted at. There was, of course, a defense against all of this. He became cautious and silent.[59]

Writer Harriet Martineau gave a similar explanation for her own shyness: "I was almost the youngest of a large family, and subject, not only to the rule of severity to which all were liable, but also to the rough and contemptuous treatment of the elder children, who meant no harm but injured me irreparably." As a child, Martineau was morbid and depressed. Her mother once described her as "the most timid child she had ever known."[60] As she got older, Martineau overcame much of her shyness and often hosted lively parties at her home in London.

Overcoming shyness generally represents a personal "revolution." These kinds of individual transformations are most likely to occur among laterborns who have successfully rebelled against domination by older siblings. In many cases, these rebellious laterborns overcome timidity by systematically cultivating openness to experience. A good example of such a personality transformation involves evolutionary biologist Ernst Mayr. No one who has ever met him would describe Mayr as quiet or introspective, but he possessed such traits as a child.

Ernst Mayr (*right*) in New Guinea in 1928, with his Malay *mantri,* or guide. Mayr was twenty-three at the time. During a two-year period he collected over 4,500 bird skins. Much of his success as a collector stemmed from his ability to work with local tribesmen, who acted as his assistants and were instrumental in obtaining rare specimens. One time Mayr sought to impress his native coworkers, using a trick employed by Mark Twain in *A Connecticut Yankee in King Arthur's Court.* From an almanac, Mayr had learned of an upcoming lunar eclipse, and he announced to the tribesmen that the full moon would soon darken almost completely. An elderly chief replied, "Don't worry, my son, it will soon get light again" (Mayr 1995).

The second of three sons, Mayr resented his elder brother's domineering manner. Throughout childhood he fantasized about becoming a famous explorer. He fulfilled this dream in 1928 when he took part in a zoological expedition to New Guinea. He later wrote about the impact of his travels: "The daily fight with unknown difficulties, the need for initiative, the contact with the strange psychology of the primitive people, and the other odds and ends of such an expedition, accomplish a development of character that cannot be had in the routine of civilized life."[61]

When Mayr returned to Germany in 1930, he encountered his childhood nanny and informed her that he would soon be going to New York to accept an appointment at the American Museum of Natural History. After hearing this, the nanny replied in astonishment, "You were such a quiet and dreamy child!"[62] By thriving on openness to experience, Mayr's "laterborn" style gradually changed him from an introverted youngster into a remarkably extraverted adult. Traveling through jungles filled with headhunters and poisonous snakes, and having to communicate with other people in languages such as Malay, will do that to you. Exploration—geographic or otherwise—changes people.

CONCLUSIONS

Shyness illustrates how the same innate behavioral disposition can have very different effects on personality depending upon an individual's family niche. Shyness makes firstborns more open to experience—the opposite effect to that which it has on laterborns. These contrary outcomes occur because temperament is not a behavioral end in itself. Within the context of the family system, temperament is drafted into the service of sibling strategies, which revolve around the politics of family dominance hierarchies and the niches that characterize them. These niches, not just innate dispositions, determine the final form of personality. What nature commences in the form of temperament, the family environment completes with strategic twists that are as varied as the niches that inspire them.

In terms of family-niche theory, shyness is both a cause and an effect—a focus for ceaseless interactions between the strategies of siblings and the contingencies of family life. Certain features of the family system reinforce shyness, which is most common among laterborns in large sibships and among people who have lost a parent during early childhood. Owing to interactions between genetic dispositions and the environment, being laterborn can have contradictory consequences, causing some people to become rebellious and timid at the same time! This is a good formula for radical worriers such as Copernicus, Darwin, and Mendel. Such individuals have sought to tread a fine line between revolutionary scientific discovery and crippling self-doubt. Some cautious laterborns, such as Max Planck, have spent a lifetime resisting their own radical insights. Other gentle rebels, such as Mendel, have failed to assert their innovations with sufficient force to achieve acceptance for their ideas in their own lifetime. Rescued from potential obscurity by a laterborn more extraverted than himself, Copernicus was plain lucky. Scientific discovery would not be characterized by so many interesting biographical scenarios were it not for the continual developmental interactions that occur between family niches and temperament.

8

EXCEPTIONS TO THE RULE

INTEGRATING FAMILY INFLUENCES

In an effort to secure valued resources from parents, siblings carve out adaptive niches for themselves within the family system. Older siblings tend to preempt the most readily available niches, such as those associated with scholastic achievement and adultlike responsibility. As a consequence, younger siblings are impelled to make more unconventional choices that lead them down ever more radical pathways. Radicalism is also shaped by a variety of influences that come from *outside* the family. Family dynamics alone do not always explain individual behavior, although such influences go a considerable way toward this end.

In previous chapters I have documented more than a dozen variables that are developmental antecedents of revolutionary personality. The task of understanding the combined influence of these factors is formidable. For example, how radical should we expect a shy laterborn boy to be if he is from a lower-class family and has lost a parent at age seven? Will this boy's shy disposition cancel out the typical radicalizing influence of birth order? Does parental loss, which tends to radicalize lower-class laterborns owing to surrogate parenting by older siblings, do so just as strongly among shy laterborns? If so, does the typical increase in radicalism associated with surrogate parenting by older siblings compensate for the typical reduction in radicalism due to shyness? Given this and other biographical scenarios, predictions about radical behavior are far from self-evident.

Fortunately, causal modeling techniques allow us to combine multiple biographical variables into predictions for single individuals. Although each variable may contribute only moderately to a model's overall prediction, the combined power of multiple predictors can be impressive. Counterintuitively, statistical models are sometimes indispensable in making sense out of individual behavior. Forecasts made by such models can be expressed as "predicted probabilities" ranging from 0 to 100 percent. In making predictions about the behavior of some individuals, we can be 90 percent, or even 95 percent, confident about the outcome. What does such a statistic mean? It means that, given 100 individuals all sharing a particular biographical profile, we can be reasonably confident that 95 of them will have endorsed radical opinions on issues that evenly divided the rest of the population. We can also be 95 percent confident that some people with other kinds of biographical profiles will have *opposed* radical innovations. Although these kinds of statistical generalizations cannot be made for everyone, they can often be made for the most important figures in history. People who leave their mark on history have a tendency to be extremists, especially in attributes such as openness to experience.[1]

This chapter has two main goals. The first is to combine all of the significant trends I have already documented about family dynamics and revolutionary personality into a single predictive model. My second goal is to do everything I can think of to break this model. I will therefore try to be my own worst critic by emphasizing the model's greatest shortcomings. By focusing on the model's mistakes—particularly the individuals who most defy its predictions—we can begin to appreciate the limitations of a family dynamics model *and to highlight the kinds of influences it fails to include.* It is the model's errors, not its success stories, that provide useful insights for further understanding.

I have employed eight predictors in a family dynamics model of radical behavior. The most important of these predictors are *birth order* and *parent-offspring conflict.* The model is also informed by seven significant interaction effects. These interaction effects involve six additional predictors: *sibship size, gender, age gaps between siblings, age at parental loss, social class,* and *temperament.* For example, parent-offspring conflict is more predictive of radicalism among firstborns than laterborns. The model also recognizes that shyness and parental loss have divergent consequences for personality development depending on whether someone is a firstborn or a laterborn. These and other interaction effects, together with the three main effects, are described in Table 5.

The model makes predictions for specific subgroups, such as males, laterborn males, laterborn males who are shy, laterborn males who are shy and come from large sibships, and so forth. More than five hundred

TABLE 5

A Family Dynamics Model of Radical Behavior

Predictors	*Behavioral Consequences*
MAIN EFFECTS	
1. Birth order	Compared with firstborns, laterborns are more rebellious and open to experience. The operative variable is *relative birth rank* (from first to last)
2. Parent-offspring conflict	High conflict increases rebellion; conflict interacts with birth order (firstborns are significantly more affected than laterborns)
3. Sibship size	Larger sibships are less radical than smaller ones; sibship size also interacts with birth rank
INTERACTION EFFECTS	
4. Gender	Gender interacts with birth order, as well as with parent-offspring conflict
5. Age gaps	Moderate gaps polarize siblings, in interaction with birth order
6. Age at parental loss loss	Parental loss interacts with birth order and social class via the practice of surrogate parenting by older offspring. By disrupting attachment behavior, parental loss also affects personality (particularly shyness)
7. Social class	Social class interacts with birth order and age at parental loss, influencing available family niches and parental investment by the surviving parent
8. Temperament	Shyness interacts with birth order; shyness is itself influenced by parental loss, as well as by birth order, sibship size, and surrogate parenting

Summary of significant effects included in the model: There are three main effects (*birth order, parent-offspring conflict,* and *sibship size*). The model also includes six 2-way interaction effects (*birth order by sibship size, birth order by age gaps, birth order by parental conflict, birth order by temperament, birth order by gender,* and *parental conflict by gender*), as well as one 3-way effect (*birth order by social class by parental loss*). For this ten-variable model, the adjusted R=.33 (df= 10/1,152 [the harmonic mean], F=15.49, $p < .0001$). Alternative models are possible. The most powerful alternative models include variables for social attitudes (Chapter 9) and for social and intellectual context (Chapter 14).

subpopulations can be distinguished in this sample based on shared biographical experiences. The model differentiates its predictions for each subpopulation. For instance, one subgroup consists of lower-class males who are firstborns, extraverted, two to four years older than their closest sibling, and from sibships of two to four children. Individuals within this subgroup are further distinguishable by having lost a parent before the age of eight and by having had a reasonably good relationship with the surviving parent. Among firstborns, surrogate parenting tends to reinforce alpha male behavior. So does extraversion. The eight-variable formula I have just given is therefore an effective recipe for social conservatism.

A typical member of this highly conservative subpopulation is Hugh Miller, a nineteenth-century Scottish naturalist who campaigned zealously against the theory of evolution. In 1847 he published his *Footprints of the Creator* in rebuttal to laterborn Robert Chambers's *Vestiges of Creation* (1844). Miller's godly view of nature involved "distinct creative steps, each initiating a new and higher form of organization, culminating in man."[2] His *Footprints* became a best-seller, going through twenty-two printings, the last of which appeared in 1883. Miller is one of 12 individuals in my study who shared all eight of the biographical traits I have listed: 10 of these 12 individuals, or 83 percent, opposed liberal innovations. The model predicts that 71 percent of them should have done so.[3]

At the other end of the spectrum from reactionaries like Hugh Miller lie extreme radicals. Such fanatics for revolution tend to make mild-mannered innovators like Copernicus and Darwin seem temperate by comparison. Revolutionary extremists tend to be the extraverted lastborns of science. These zealots for radical change tend to come from family backgrounds similar to that of Hugh Miller, with one exception: *they are laterborns.* Thirteen people in my study grew up sharing the laterborn analogue to Hugh Miller's biographical profile. Eleven of these 13 individuals, or 85 percent, endorsed liberal innovations. A family dynamics model is not far off, predicting that 83 percent of them should do so. What made firstborns like Hugh Miller archconservatives made younger siblings from the same family background into consistent radicals.

One noteworthy example of this radical trend among younger siblings from families like Hugh Miller's involves Thomas Hobbes. Hobbes's father, an impoverished vicar, struck a fellow parson when his son was seven and was forced to flee, never to be seen again by his son.

Hugh Miller, in his late thirties. Originally a stonemason, Miller became interested in geology and paleontology owing to the fossils he found in the rocks that he carved. Later in life he developed stonemason's disease and eventually became deranged from its complications. In 1856, three years before publication of the *Origin of Species,* Miller committed suicide. He was only fifty-four.

Hobbes, who was a second son in a family of three children, grew up to be one of the most radical thinkers of his times.[4] He is best known for his *Leviathan* (1651), a work of political philosophy in which he argued that moral goodness was not innate in man, as theologians believed, and that strong government was required to keep human self-interest in check. For Hobbes, natural law was entirely secular, not rooted in divine guidance.[5] Contemporary reactions to Hobbes's *Leviathan* confirmed its radical nature and embroiled him in controversy "more . . . than any English thinker before or since."[6] His shocking ideas about the nature of morality were cited in the House of Commons as "a probable cause of the Great Fire of 1666," and about the same time a committee of bishops within the House of Lords urged that he be burned for heresy.[7] Based on a model of family dynamics, Hobbes's predicted likelihood of supporting radical causes was 77 percent (Fig. 8.1).[8]

Another effective route to extreme radicalism among laterborns involves conflict with parents. A good example of this biographical scenario involves that famous *enfant terrible* of the Enlightenment—Voltaire. As an extraverted lastborn who lost his mother when he was seven, and who also experienced significant conflict with his father and his Jansenist elder brother, Voltaire was truly born to rebel. Based on his family background and his temperament, his probability of supporting radical causes was 88 percent.

Other extraverted lastborns in my study include Thomas Henry Huxley and Darwin's German supporter Ernst Haeckel.[9] If Huxley is appropriately nicknamed "Darwin's Bulldog," Haeckel deserves to be called "Darwin's German Shepherd." Darwin considered both of these followers too combative for his own tastes, and he repeatedly tried to temper their zealousness. When Haeckel visited Darwin at Down House in 1866, his boisterous manners were almost more than Darwin and his wife could take.[10] The following year Darwin admonished Haeckel for his tendency to excite anger. "Anger so completely blinds every one," he warned his German advocate, "that your arguments would have no chance of influencing those who are already opposed to our views."[11] Haeckel's countryman Ernst Krause later observed that Haeckel succeeded in concentrating on himself "all the hatred and bitterness" toward Darwin's ideas. "In a surprisingly short time it became fashionable in Germany that Haeckel alone should be abused, while Darwin was held up as the ideal of forethought and moderation."[12] Such differences among radical thinkers suggest that, in extreme form, revolutionary personality can be too much of a good thing. Darwin is a prime instance of someone who succeeded by patience and moderation rather than by militant aggression. According to a family dynamics model, Darwin's predicted propensity toward radicalism was 73 percent, well above the population mean, but well below the scores of more militant scientists. For example, the model gives Haeckel a score of 85

Receptivity to Scientific Innovation Compared with Multivariate Predictions

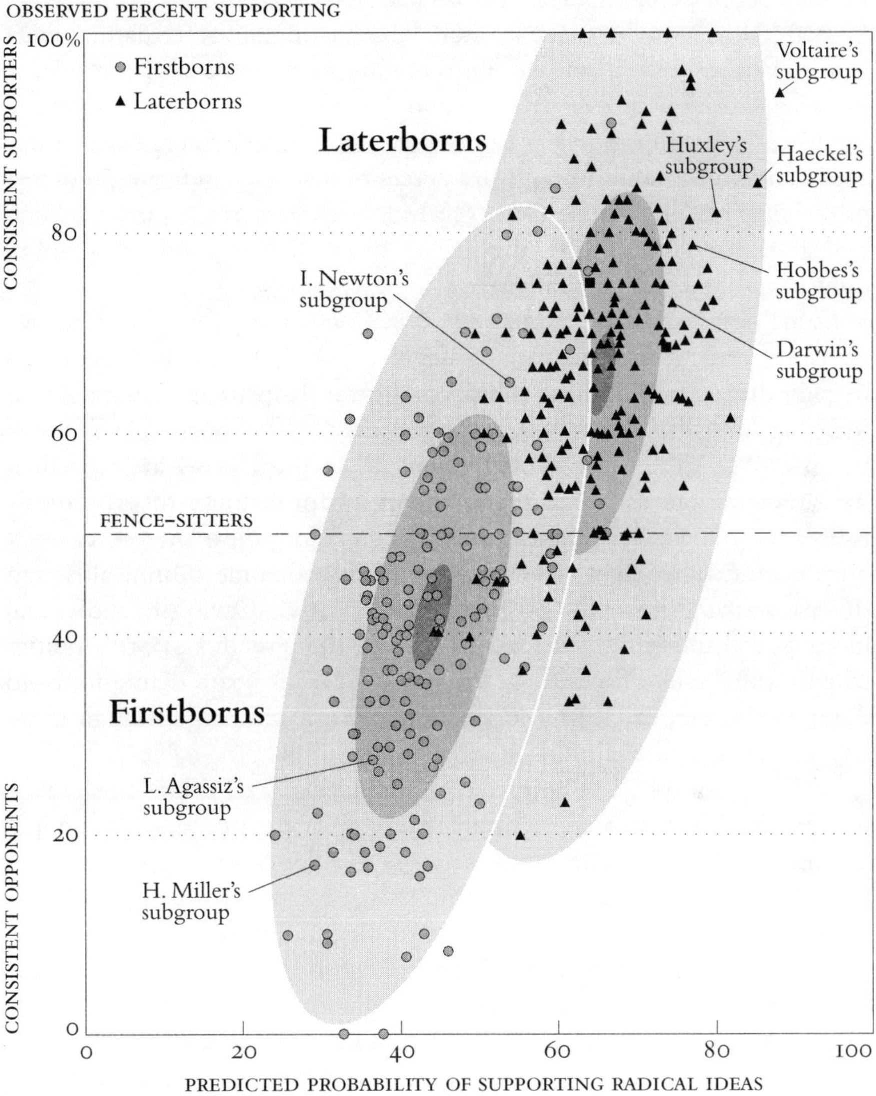

FIGURE 8.1. Predictions made by an eight-variable "family dynamics" model of scientific radicalism. The model is based on 3,111 individuals who participated in 28 scientific debates. Predictions are plotted against the observed outcomes for subgroups containing 10 or more participants. The outer ellipses indicate the 95 percent confidence limits for the two main subgroups (firstborns and laterborns). The innermost ellipses provide the 99.9 percent confidence limits for the two population centers. The model is reasonably good at identifying fence-sitters, and even better at identifying people likely to espouse extreme views.

percent, making him more similar to Voltaire (at 88 percent) and to Huxley (at 80 percent) than to mild-mannered Darwin.[13]

Overall, an eight-variable model based on family dynamics correctly classifies two-thirds of the scientists in my study. The model is especially useful in identifying people who have voiced extreme opinions. When an individual's predicted probability for radicalism exceeds 80 percent, the model is 83 percent correct. When the predicted probability exceeds 85 percent, the model is 89 percent correct. Such radical individuals are particularly likely to have taken a militant stand in their support of conceptual change.

One decided virtue of a family dynamics model for radical behavior is its predictive superiority to single variables. Like other predictors of radicalism, birth order is a *fallible* indicator. Its principal virtue lies in its being *less* fallible than any other predictor I have been able to identify. Many of the predictive shortcomings of birth order are remedied by a multivariate model. The most typical route to firstborn radicalism—epitomized, for example, by Kepler and Newton—is conflict with parents. Shyness is another route to firstborn radicalism, although this particular influence tends to be less effective. Owing to individual biographical differences among firstborns, their predicted probabilities of radicalism range from 16 to 67 percent. This is more than a fourfold difference! There is clearly no firstborn *type* in science, although there are "firstborn tendencies."

Among laterborns, one group of predictable exceptions to the rule involves people who are extremely shy. A second group involves people having an early birth rank within a large sibship. A third group involves laterborns who are particularly close in age to their next-older sibling. Darwin's colleague Joseph Hooker partook of all three biographical influences, and his scientific temperament was reasonably consistent with their consequences. Privy to all of Darwin's evolutionary speculations for fifteen years, he long resisted Darwin's heterodox ideas and was converted to evolution only after reading the *Origin of Species* in manuscript. A fence-sitter, Hooker was too cautious to be a rebel. His predicted probability of endorsing radical innovations was only 62 percent, lower even than for some firstborns. In science, fence-sitters tend to make up their minds based on a combination of public opinion and evidence. They are cautious rationalists, not scientific conquistadors.

Although a family dynamics model of radicalism is correct more often than not, it still makes errors. The best way of trying to improve on this model is to examine the model's mistakes on an individual-by-individual basis. The more an individual is misclassified, the more the error serves to pinpoint the model's greatest weaknesses.

ERRONEOUS PREDICTIONS

A family dynamics model makes mistaken predictions for two main reasons. The first reason is *erroneous data.* Biographical sources sometimes provide incorrect facts, including information about birth order, sibship size, parents' social status, and so forth. Although I have occasionally detected such errors and corrected them, other errors in reporting doubtless remain. Incorrect information is not a major source of misclassifications in a family dynamics model, but such inaccuracies probably contribute around 5 percent to the total error rate.[14]

The second and more important source of modeling error is *insufficient biographical information.* For example, age, personal friendships, and social attitudes are powerful influences that are not represented in a family dynamics model. Ethnic and religious identity, as well as disciplinary allegiances, can also affect the outcome of scientific debates. There is also the matter of scientific evidence! New research findings, and individual scientists' familiarity with them, often make a difference. The remainder of this book will demonstrate how these and other influences promote radical allegiances. The special importance of sibling differences lies in the manner in which they constantly interact with these other causes of radicalism. Given the same influences—both within and beyond the family—siblings often react very differently.

One particularly glaring error by a family dynamics model involves Galileo. As the first of four children, Galileo's predicted probability of supporting radical causes is only 30 percent. Yet he was an energetic opponent of scholastic truth based on authority—so much so that he was tried and convicted of heresy by the papal Inquisition. Of the 3,111 predictions made by a family dynamics model, Galileo represents the model's biggest mistake.

The renowned Galileo scholar Stillman Drake has suggested a plausible explanation for Galileo's radicalism.[15] This explanation involves Galileo's relationship with his father, Vincenzio, who was a professional musician and occupies an important place in the history of music theory. According to the prevailing theory of harmony, consonances and dissonances were explained in terms of Pythagorean ratios, which were thought to possess divine properties. For example, the ratios 2:1, 3:2, and 4:3 were taken to represent the musical intervals of the octave, the fifth, and the fourth. A serious problem with this theory was that sound follows a continuum, whereas numbers are discrete. In addition, what is pleasing to the ear sometimes violates Pythagorean ratios. From this clash between numbers and actual sounds arose a whole new understanding of musical harmony, an endeavor in which Galileo's father was a pioneer.

Vincenzio, it seems, was "outspokenly against the acceptance of authority in matters that can be investigated directly."[16] He grew dissatisfied with the discrepancy between what he had been taught by his teachers and what he could hear with his own highly trained musical ear. By assessing the properties of harmony based on tuned strings of varying lengths and tensions, Vincenzio demonstrated conclusively that harmony violates Pythagorean rules. In 1581, when his eldest son was seventeen, Vincenzio published these experimental findings in his *Dialogue on Ancient and Modern Music.* Based on manuscript evidence, Galileo appears to have participated in his father's experiments. A gifted amateur musician, Galileo also learned musical theory and practice from his father. According to historians of science, what was most revolutionary about Galileo's contributions to modern science was his insistence on the experimental verification of mathematical laws in physics.[17] This heterodox contribution, Drake argues, was "directly inspired" by Vincenzio Galilei's researches in music.[18]

Stillman Drake's biographical detective work suggests a compelling explanation for why Galileo was so radical: *he was the son of a radical.* His father taught him to question authority and to do so, moreover, by *experimental* means. "Like father, like son"—a hypothesis that proves, on testing, to be especially true of firstborns.[19]

The case of Galileo helps to pinpoint another shortcoming of a family dynamics model. Galileo was nine years older than his closest sibling, a sister. He therefore grew up functionally as an only child. Only children are the least predictable subgroup in my family dynamics model, precisely because they had no siblings! The absence of siblings makes only children more responsive to influences that my present family dynamics model fails to include, such as the role of parental social values. Because the niche of being the "family radical" is not already preempted by younger siblings, only children are freer to become radicals themselves.[20]

I could cite numerous biographical instances of individuals like Galileo whose radicalism appears to have been influenced by their par-

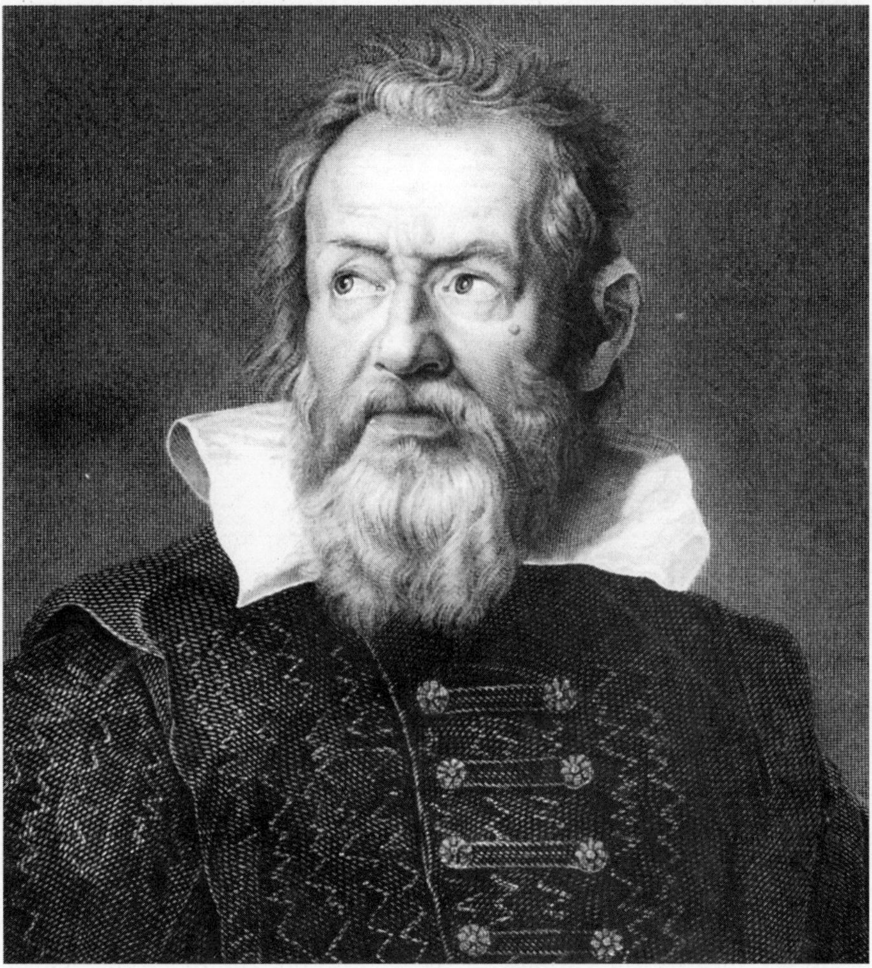

Galileo, in his late sixties, about the time of his trial for heresy (1633). According to his biographers he possessed a distinctly pugnacious disposition, which played an important role in his troubles with the Catholic Church. As a result of his conviction for heresy, he spent the last decade of his life under house arrest.

ents. Unlike personality, which shows little similarity among family members, social attitudes exhibit considerable overlap. I test this assertion in the next chapter and raise it here merely as a *hypothesis* worthy of further investigation.

A few more biographical examples will suffice to make my point about parental social attitudes and their influence on offspring. Captain

Robert FitzRoy, after his promotion to vice admiral in 1863 (age fifty-eight). In the 1860s FitzRoy's mind began to decay. Depressed by repeated criticisms of his system of storm warnings, he entered his dressing room one Sunday morning in 1865 and slit his throat with a razor.

Robert FitzRoy, a lastborn, strenuously opposed the idea of evolution. How could a man who for five years shared his *Beagle* cabin with Charles Darwin have later opposed Darwin's theories? Based on a family dynamics model, FitzRoy should indeed have accepted Darwinism (his predicted probability is 66 percent). When FitzRoy was young, he did accept phrenology—one of the five Radical Ideological Revolutions in my study, so the model classifies him correctly in at least one other scientific debate. As Darwin observed in this connection, FitzRoy "was convinced that he could judge a man's character by the outline of his features, and he doubted whether anyone with my nose could possess sufficient energy and determination for the [*Beagle*] voyage. But I think he was afterwards well-satisfied that my nose had spoken falsely."[21]

A fifth-generation descendant of Charles II, FitzRoy was from the upper aristocracy. During the *Beagle* voyage, his High Tory political opinions caused difficulties for Darwin, who was a Whig. After the voyage FitzRoy married a particularly religious woman and underwent a religious conversion. Having been a theological moderate during the *Beagle* voyage, he became a biblical literalist who strenuously defended the reality of the Deluge.[22] Years later, FitzRoy bitterly opposed Darwin's theory of evolution on religious grounds. In 1860 he showed up at the Oxford meetings, where Huxley debated Bishop Wilberforce.[23] During the arguments over Darwin's theories, FitzRoy paced about the lecture hall holding a Bible over his head and exclaiming "the Book, the Book."[24] His religious fanaticism accords with his conservative political views and was an obvious factor in his opposition to Darwinism.[25] On scientific matters that were *independent* of religion, FitzRoy was relatively open-minded. In the 1850s he became head of the newly created Meteorological Office and pioneered a system of weather forecasting, a term that he popularized. He endured considerable abuse from critics who thought that the weather would never be reduced to a science.

The question of whether FitzRoy should have supported Darwin is similar to whether the pope ought to have backed Galileo. Maffeo Barberini (Urban VIII) has the dubious honor of having ordered Galileo's trial for heresy. Urban was the fifth of six children, and a family dynamics model classifies him incorrectly during the Copernican debate. Even so, Urban's actions were predictable, given the curious chain of events that elicited them.

As popes go, Urban was rather open-minded. For more than two decades he had been an admirer of Galileo's, and he also considered himself a personal friend. In 1630, three years before Galileo's trial, Tommaso Campanella told Urban about some Germans who were undergoing conversion to Catholicism. These Germans claimed they had been scandalized by the church's edict of 1616, which officially banned Copernican theory. On hearing this, Urban replied: "That was never our intention, and if it had been up to me that decree would never have been issued."[26] This same year Urban personally gave Galileo permission to write his book about the Copernican doctrine, stipulating only that he treat the theory as a "hypothesis."

So what went wrong? Galileo's ambition got the better of him, and he openly flaunted the pope's instructions. On publication, it was obvious to everyone that Galileo's *Dialogue on the Two Chief World Systems* (1632) was not a balanced discussion of the subject. Worse yet, Galileo managed to insult the pope. In giving Galileo permission to write his heterodox book, Urban had instructed him to let Ptolemaic theory have the last word. Galileo placed this concluding discussion in the mouth of his fictional character "Simplicio," a dim-witted Aristotelian. Adding insult to injury, Galileo let Simplicio deliver one of the pope's favorite arguments on the subject. The parallel between Simplicio and the pope was not lost on Galileo's Italian readers, and a furious pope exacted his historic revenge.[27] The trial of Galileo was not just about heresy. It was also about firstborn ambition overstepping laterborn forbearance.

Religious doctrine is not the only serious source of trouble for a family dynamics model. John Lubbock, an eminent entomologist and anthropologist, illustrates two other lacunae in the model. A zealous Darwinian, Lubbock was an unlikely convert based on his family niche. He was the first of eleven children of a baronet. In addition, he got on well with his parents, neither of whom set a revolutionary example for their son. Based on a family dynamics model, Lubbock's predicted probability of accepting radical innovations was only 41 percent, clearly too low for this loyal defender of the Darwinian cause.

What my model does not know about Lubbock is that he grew up in Down as Charles Darwin's next-door neighbor. When Darwin settled in this village in 1841, Lubbock was seven. Owing to the youngster's interest in natural history, Darwin became "almost a second father."[28] Darwin arranged for Lubbock to procure his first microscope, and his protégé's earliest scientific papers dealt with some of Darwin's *Beagle* specimens. While still a teenager, Lubbock drew some of the illustrations for Darwin's monographs on barnacles, a subject that provided important evidence for the theory of evolution. Darwin nurtured Lubbock's subsequent career in crucial ways. In 1856 he sponsored a paper by Lubbock before the Royal Society, which led to Lubbock's election as a fellow. Lubbock was just twenty-four when he attained this rare honor, and he soon returned the favor by providing Darwin with important statistical advice as he was drafting the *Origin of Species.* Even before publication of this work, Lubbock had become an enthusiastic convert to Darwin's heterodox ideas.

In Lubbock's case, my model is missing three crucial biographical facts: (1) his intimate personal relationship with Charles Darwin; (2) his

John Lubbock (Lord Avebury), with his microscope. On the desk is a plant he is examining. A polymath, Lubbock did important research in botany, entomology, geology, and anthropology.

relative youth in 1859 (he was twenty-five); and his liberal social attitudes (he was later elected to Parliament as a Liberal Party candidate). Based on a family dynamics model that includes these additional predictors, Lubbock's likelihood of accepting natural selection was 80 percent.[29]

John Lubbock illuminates another otherwise puzzling feature about radical thought. Although a loyal Darwinian, he was relatively restrained about his liberal Darwinian views. "As an exponent of Darwinism," remarks one biographer, "he was as active as Huxley, without his truculence."[30] Regarding Lubbock's books on cultural evolution, this same biographer has noted that their popularity "led to their reissue in new editions for over a generation, even after their simplistic evolutionism had become outmoded. But Lubbock never modified these first conclusions."[31] Knowing his personal history, I would not have expected him to do so. Firstborns—even when liberal—are still firstborns. A liberal family background may make firstborns progressive in their social attitudes, but this influence does not usually make them rebellious or unduly open to experience. On the contrary, the most rigid radicals are usually firstborns who have been radicalized by their parents.

I could tell many additional stories about aberrant individuals, suggesting compelling reasons for why they are misclassified by a family dynamics model. No matter how compelling, such stories are ad hoc and do not constitute scientific proof. Anecdotal evidence does suggest hypotheses. But for these hypotheses to be validated, they need to be tested *for everyone in my database.* In addition, it is important to control these tests for other predictors that might bias the outcome. Let me illustrate these testing procedures with an example.

My illustration involves a variant of the question "Is the pope Catholic?" Let us suppose Urban VIII had been a Protestant. Would this factor have made any difference in his decision to have Galileo tried for heresy? A straightforward way of answering this question is to determine whether Catholics, as a whole, were more hostile to Copernican theory than Protestants. I have systematically coded participants in this debate for religious denomination. As it turns out, being Catholic does not have a measurable influence on the outcome.[32]

How about the fact that the pope was a theologian? Did this occupational factor influence his opposition to Copernican theory? To answer this question, I have systematically coded each participant in the Copernican debate for theological training. As with religious denomination, this factor turns out to have no influence.[33] However, a related occupational variable *is* significant—*status as a scientist.* People involved in the production of scientific knowledge were more open to Copernican theory than those who were not.[34] (Status as a scientist is a good proxy for familiarity with the astronomical evidence supporting this theory.) Another good predictor of support for Copernicanism is age. Older individuals were significantly less likely to adopt this theory than were younger individuals.[35]

Urban VIII's age and occupational status allow us to provide a more informed prediction about his response to Copernican theory. When Galileo's *Dialogue* appeared in 1632, Urban was sixty-four. As an elderly nonscientist, his probability of supporting Copernican theory was rather low—29 percent, give or take a small margin for statistical error. Given this expected level of support, a family dynamics model tells us

The trial of Galileo before the papal Inquisition (1633). Although evidence for outright heresy was dubious, Galileo was persuaded to admit, in an extrajudicial proceeding, to guilt through "vain ambition, ignorance, and inadvertence." A good Catholic, he then got down on his knees and recanted his Copernican views before cardinals and other witnesses (Drake 1972:245; 1978:350).

how much *higher* or *lower* the pope's radical propensities ought to have been, compared with other sixty-four-year-old nonscientists. The answer to this question places Urban's likelihood of supporting Copernican theory at 45 percent, a value that seems about right. I have not systematically analyzed the role of insults in history, but we do not need a computer model to know that Galileo's ill-chosen comparison between Simplicio and the pope caused a previously fence-sitting pope to turn against Galileo. Even then, Urban hesitated to hand his friend over to the papal Inquisition. As Stillman Drake has noted, Urban created a special commission, "thus treating Galileo better than the latter had treated him."[36]

The example of Urban VIII clarifies the limitations of a family dynamics model of radicalism. This model can only tell how likely a person is to support a radical theory, *relative to the best prediction that can be made based on other pertinent information.* Sibling differences nudge people up or down the scale of radicalism, doing so in combination with many other biographical influences. Based on scrutiny of a family dynamics model's errors, I have identified more than a dozen factors that might explain some of these exceptions. The most important of these hypothetical influences involve age, social attitudes, personal influences, and national differences. For convenience I list these hypotheses in Table 6 and also indicate which ones I have been able to test.

Adding new variables to models in order to explain individual exceptions raises the issue of refutability. Are such models falsifiable? Indeed they are. To begin with, no variable may be added to an existing model unless it provides a significant improvement over chance, after controlling for variables already included in the model.[37] This is an increasingly difficult test to pass. Even when new variables succeed in passing this test, some individuals continue to defy the model's predictions and thereby "refute" its claims to comprehensiveness.

My hypotheses about family influences are easy to refute for another reason: I have made these claims *very specific.* My family dynamics model would be seriously challenged, for example, by evidence indicating that firstborns systematically ally themselves with conservative doctrines whenever they have experienced high conflict with a parent. Similarly, evidence that shy people differ significantly by birth order, whereas extraverts do not, would refute my claims on this subject. There are more than a dozen ways to falsify a family dynamics model of radical behavior.

One additional feature of my approach makes my claims about human behavior especially vulnerable to refutation. Throughout this book I have formulated my arguments in ways that give recognition to the role of historical context. In dealing with scientific innovation, for example, I have sought to assess ideas in terms of their ideological implications, using criteria that are independent of sibling differences. As a consequence, my assertions about sibling differences can be refuted in several further ways. For example, my claims would be disproved by documentation that "conservative" innovations, such as eugenics or vitalism, have been systematically championed by laterborns and opposed by firstborns. Similarly, my claims would be seriously contradicted by the opposite historical scenario. Firstborns do not generally support radical revolutions, and systematic evidence that they do so would contradict my arguments. These arguments would also be refuted by docu-

TABLE 6
Hypotheses about Radicalism Suggested by Classification Errors in a Family Dynamics Model

Variable	*Hypothesis*	*Tested?*	*Confirmed?*
SOCIAL ATTITUDES	Controlled for sibling differences, people who are socially liberal are more open to radical change	YES	YES[a]
PARENTAL SOCIAL ATTITUDES	Controlled for sibling differences, people having liberal parents tend to be liberal and hence to support radical change	YES	YES[a]
PARENTAL BIRTH ORDERS	Controlled for sibling differences, people having laterborn parents are more likely to support radical change	YES	YES[b]
AGE	Radical change is more acceptable to young people	YES	YES[c]
PERSONAL INFLUENCES	Mentoring and friendship influence the adoption of radical ideas	YES	YES[d]
NATIONAL STYLES	National as well as geographic differences affect the outcome of revolutionary controversies	YES	YES[e]
SOCIAL CLASS	Lower-class individuals show more support for radical change than do upper-class individuals	YES	REJECTED[c]
INTERPERSONAL RIVALRY	Scientists who propose theoretical innovations tend to reject rival innovations on the topic	NO	—
SCIENTIFIC EVIDENCE	Scientists adopt radical innovations in response to disciplinary allegiances, as well as to new and compelling evidence	YES	YES[f]

a. Chapter 9
b. Chapters 9, 11
c. Chapters 2, 10–14
d. Chapters 10–11, 14
e. Chapters 10–14
f. Chapters 2, 14

mentation of innovations having marked ideological implications if sibling differences proved *irrelevant* to the outcome. I invite scholars to search for such cases. Potentially, thousands of them exist; but if I am right about the influence that family dynamics exert during personality development, few of these potential refutations will be forthcoming. There will always be individual exceptions, but the explanatory principles documented in this book should hold as a general rule.

CONCLUSION

In Part Two of this book I have tried to show how differences in family niches create differences in the family experience. Although this story line involves many individual twists and turns, it rarely departs from a timeworn Darwinian scenario: Siblings employ strategies aimed at maximizing parental investment.

From a detailed knowledge of the family experience, it would be a mistake to think that we know everything that is needed to explain revolutionary personality. Thus far we have considered only a portion of the influences that are responsible for radical thought. I have said little so far about social attitudes, empirical and cognitive considerations, and historical context—topics addressed in the remainder of this book. Chance also plays an important role. Still, none of these additional factors can be adequately understood without considering their intimate interplay with the individual dispositions that are forged by family dynamics. Like social class, which exerts no direct effects on radical thought, many "sociological" causes of radical thinking only express themselves indirectly, via sibling differences. The same conclusion is true about rationality and helps to explain why jurors, when confronted by the same evidence, often draw different conclusions from it. In reacting to the world around them, siblings do so dissimilarly. Given the same family background and historical circumstances, some siblings conform to the status quo, whereas others decide to rebel.

PART THREE

SOCIAL AND POLITICAL THOUGHT

9

SOCIAL ATTITUDES

The next five chapters probe the relationship between political and religious attitudes and support for revolutionary causes. Of numerous social influences that I have studied—including nationality, ethnic identity, and professional networks—political and religious beliefs deserve special attention because they are typically more important. In social revolutions, evidence for the intimate relationship between these beliefs and revolutionary thinking is commonplace. Social conservatives tend to resist revolutionary changes, whereas social liberals tend to support them. This much is generally known.[1] What has not been sufficiently appreciated, either by historians or psychologists, is the manner in which liberalism differs from openness to social change. Political and religious attitudes are just that—*attitudes*, which include ideas and beliefs. Openness to change is a *personality characteristic* that reflects the flexibility to modify preestablished beliefs, regardless of their specific nature. Surprisingly, some liberals are close-minded, whereas some conservatives are open to new ways of thinking.

In dealing with social attitudes, we are dealing with a hybrid construct—part social, part psychological. To understand how siblings think and behave, it is necessary to distinguish these sources of belief and to trace their origins within the family. Initially, political and religious beliefs are learned from parents and tend to be shared by siblings. Many social radicals are heirs to a radical worldview handed down by parents.

Even when they share the same core of beliefs, siblings often differ in their *styles* of social thought. Because laterborns are more open to experience, they are more willing to revise what they have been taught by their parents. In religious matters, Charles Darwin was not brought up to be an agnostic. His father was happy to see him become a clergy-

Sibling differences in social attitudes need to be understood within the broader context of parental social attitudes. Among the four patients in this cartoon, predictions about birth order would be as follows: for the openly Gay Republican, laterborn from a Republican family or firstborn from a Democratic family (but not the other way around); for the Black Conservative, firstborn; for the Feminist for Freud, firstborn, especially if the daughter of a psychoanalyst; and for the Vegetarian Vampire, laterborn, especially if from long-established vampire stock.

man, and his elder sisters did their best to fan his religious ardor while he was circumnavigating the globe on the *Beagle.* But for his voyage, Darwin would probably have taken holy orders and become a country clergyman. Because he was unusually open to experience, he continually reexamined his religious convictions as he went through life. By the time he had reached his sixties, little of these convictions remained. "My theology is a simple muddle," he told Joseph Hooker in 1870. Contrary to his youthful delight in Paley's *Natural Theology,* Darwin could no longer see "evidence of beneficent design [in the world], or indeed of design of any kind, in the details."[2]

Like the social attitudes of offspring, those of parents have their origins in family environments and the diversifying influence of family niches. To understand an individual's social attitudes, biographers must often extend their analysis back through several previous generations of family history. When this is done in a systematic fashion, a surprising conclusion emerges. Factors such as socioeconomic class explain little about radical thought. *In the domain of social attitudes, most individual differences are, or once were, sibling differences.* This chapter puts this assertion to the test.

METHODOLOGICAL CONSIDERATIONS

The social convictions of many historical figures are reasonably well known. In attempting to document social attitudes, a variety of sources are available. I have employed three different types of information. First, I have collected self-report data (from letters, autobiographies, and other documentary sources). Second, I have drawn on contemporary observations by family, friends, and colleagues. Darwin's wife and children, for instance, commented on his political and religious views, and Darwin made similar observations about his closest friends. Third, I have procured ratings by expert historians. By combining these three sources of information, I have been able to obtain reasonably reliable ratings for the social attitudes of 2,766 scientists.

Expert Raters

The bulk of my information on social attitudes is derived from expert historians, who have contributed more than 19,000 individual ratings to this study.[3] To determine the social attitudes of scientists in my sample, I asked 94 historians to make ratings using a 5-point scale: 1.0 was defined as "archconservative"; 3.0 was labeled "liberal"; and 5.0 was designated as "extremely radical." By using half points on the scale, raters could avail themselves of up to nine rank-ordered categories. Judges were asked to assess only those historical figures falling within their area of expertise. I conducted all interviews in person.

The goal of this rating process was to place individuals on a conservative-radical spectrum *relative to their contemporaries.* Before commencing the rating task, individual judges were encouraged to "customize" the rating instrument within their own minds to fit their period of historical and national expertise. In England during the 1640s, for example, a political conservative would be termed a "royalist." Two centuries later, a person holding similar political views would be called a "High Tory." Despite differing labels, both types of conservatives have typically been rated between 1.0 and 2.0 on the 5-point scale.

Because people's social views change over time, I also asked expert judges to make their assessments in terms of the year when each scientist took a specific stance on a controversial innovation. Charles Darwin, for instance, has been rated at ten different ages between 20 and 69, during which his religious convictions evolved from "Broad Church" (2.75) to "agnostic" (4.5). During this same period Darwin's political views changed only minimally within the "liberal" range (from 3.25 to 3.5).

When I initially undertook this experiment in "historical sociometrics," I wondered whether social attitudes could be reliably assessed by these methods. Fortunately, there is a high level of agreement between ratings derived from self-report information, from published descriptions by contemporaries, and from retrospective assessments by expert historians. The effective reliability by these three methods is .92[4]

SOCIAL ATTITUDES AND SCIENTIFIC CHANGE

Political and religious attitudes play a major role in how individuals respond to scientific change. *The degree to which this is true depends on the nature of the innovation.* Relative to social conservatives, scientists who hold socially liberal convictions have been more sympathetic to most scientific innovations, especially those entailing radical ideological implications. Confronted with a materialistic theory such as evolution, Darwin was 6 times more likely than his old friend FitzRoy, a High Tory and religious fanatic, to endorse a heterodox viewpoint. As a socialist, Alfred Russel Wallace was 11 times more likely than FitzRoy to accept such a theory (Fig. 9.1).[5]

Conservative scientific innovations have consistently appealed to social conservatives. The French mathematician Augustin-Louis Cauchy provides a particularly good illustration of this predilection. When Charles X was deposed by the July Revolution of 1830, Cauchy followed his depraved king into exile. "In the political sphere," comments one Cauchy biographer, "his adherence to the Bourbon cause was, for better or worse, absolute and unyielding."[6] A colleague in mathematics has confirmed this portrait of Cauchy, describing him as "infinitely Catholic, and bigoted," and Stendhal proclaimed him "a veritable Jesuit in short frock."[7] Consistent with his conservative worldview, Cauchy strongly supported vitalistic doctrines in physiology and medicine. Dur-

Receptivity to Liberal Scientific Innovations by Social Attitudes and Birth Order

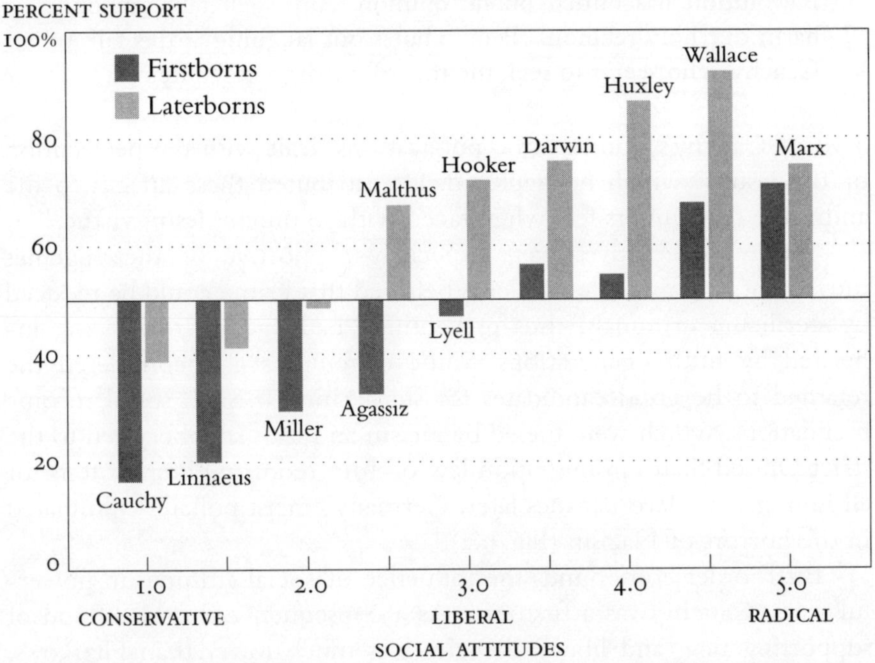

FIGURE 9.1. Mean levels of support for 23 liberal theories in science, stratified by social attitudes and birth order. Prominent scientists are indicated next to their biographical subgroup.

Compared with scientists who were extreme social conservatives (<1.5 on the scale, $N=35$), extreme social radicals (>4.5, $N=60$) have been 12.5 times more likely to support liberal innovations. The strong relationship between social attitudes and advocacy holds for firstborns and laterborns, considered separately. Controlled for social attitudes, laterborns are significantly more likely to support new theories.

ing the 1820s he attacked the phrenological theories of Franz Joseph Gall because he thought they endangered "the peace and well being of society."[8] In 1826 Stendhal reported the following incident at the Académie des Sciences:

> After the lecture of a naturalist, Cauchy rose and protested the applause. "Even if these things would be as true as I think, they are wrong"—he said—"it would not be convenient to disclose them

> to the public, given the devilish state into which our misbegotten Revolution has hurled public opinion. Any such talk can only harm our holy religion." People burst out laughing at this talk of Cauchy, who seems to seek the role of a martyr to contempt.[9]

Two of Cauchy's nonscientific publications dealt with the persecution of the Jesuits, which he deplored. He attributed these attacks to the animosity that sinners feel when faced with so much "Jesuit virtue."[10]

Social conservatives were especially supportive of the eugenics movement.[11] Mainline eugenicists believed that crime could be reduced by sterilizing criminals, thus preventing "bad" genes from being inherited by future generations. Some eugenicists also considered the retarded to be good candidates for sterilization.[12] Such social recommendations, which were fueled by racism and class snobbery, led to the strict United States immigration law of 1917 requiring literacy tests for all immigrants. Two decades later, Germany's racist policies culminated in the horrors of Nazism (Fig. 9.2).[13]

Birth order compounds the influence of social attitudes in powerful ways. Cauchy was a firstborn. As a consequence, his likelihood of supporting new and liberal theories was much lower than FitzRoy's, even though FitzRoy shared Cauchy's conservative social convictions. Taking into account FitzRoy's status as a lastborn, his probability of supporting a theory such as phrenology was 3.3 times higher than Cauchy's. Although FitzRoy strongly opposed the theory of evolution, he did support phrenology, a system that Cauchy abhorred.

Given Charles Darwin's birth order and liberal social views, his likelihood of supporting materialist doctrines was 4.4 times higher than FitzRoy's and 15 times higher than Cauchy's. One is reminded of a famous passage in Darwin's transmutation notebooks, written four months before his discovery of natural selection: "Thought (or desires more properly) being hereditary, it is difficult to image it [being] anything but structure of brain. . . . Love of the deity [is] effect of organization, oh you materialist!"[14]

If we now contrast Cauchy with a laterborn socialist such as Wallace, the difference in relative likelihood of support for liberal innovations reaches 58 to 1 in favor of Wallace! True to form, Wallace dedicated his defiant career to the kinds of radical causes that incensed Cauchy. According to one biographer, Wallace was the kind of person who "made things happen. . . . While others refrained from the lists,

Receptivity to Conservative Scientific Theories by Social Attitudes and Birth Order

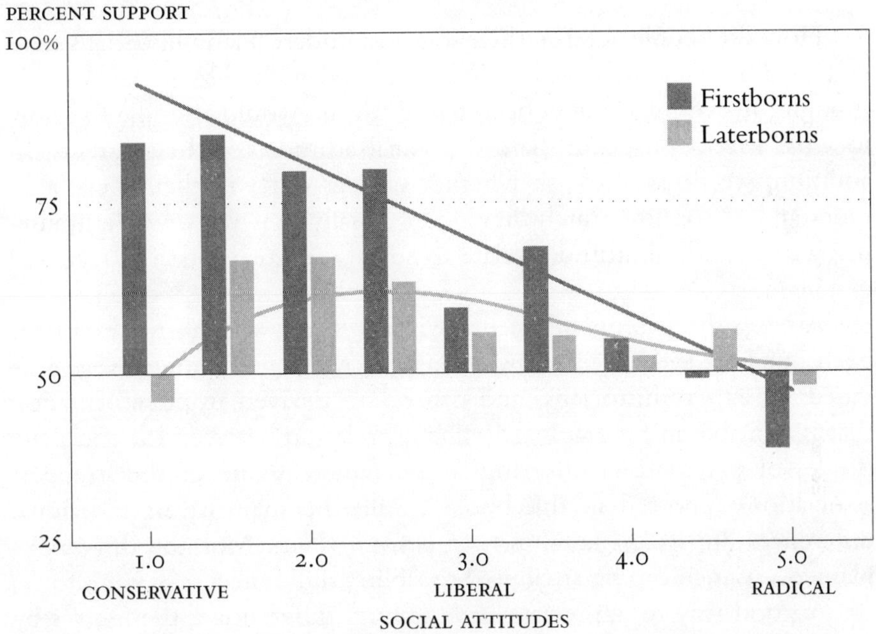

FIGURE 9.2. Mean levels of support for five conservative theories in science, stratified by social attitudes and birth order. The five theories are vitalism, idealist approaches to taxonomy, germ theory, spiritualism, and eugenics. Compared with social radicals (>4.5 on the scale, N=31), social conservatives (<1.5, N=16) have been 2.5 times more likely to support this class of innovations. The relationship between social attitudes and advocacy holds for firstborns and laterborns, considered separately. Controlled for social attitudes, firstborns are significantly more likely to support conservative innovations.

In mediating the reception of conservative scientific innovations, birth order interacts with social attitudes. Compared with laterborn conservatives, firstborn conservatives were more attracted by the reactionary ideological implications of these theories.

Wallace charged into battle."[15] He backed a variety of unorthodox causes including land nationalization, women's rights, socialism, and evolution by natural selection. Wallace's support for phrenology, a subject that he eagerly studied during his twenties, was almost a foregone conclusion.

THE ORIGINS OF SOCIAL ATTITUDES

How do people acquire their social attitudes? Many historians have endorsed the view that these attitudes are determined by social class, although the claim has rarely been tested.[16] One would also like to know to what extent offspring share the social attitudes of their parents. In addition, we do well to ask whether siblings differ in their social attitudes and, if so, how much they differ. Finally, it is worthwhile inquiring whether social attitudes relate to social categories such as race and gender.

Among the parents of scientists in my study, several hundred have been rated for their social convictions. Many of these ratings were provided by expert historians, and others are derived from information that is available in biographies.[17] The correlation between the social attitudes of parents and offspring is .47, which is one of the strongest associations reported in this book.[18] Still, the majority of individual differences are *within* families, not *between* them. Most of this unexplained variance can be attributed to sibling differences.[19]

A good way to appreciate how siblings differentiate themselves by social attitudes is to follow this process according to birth rank. Among the scientists in my study, firstborns are the most conservative siblings—significantly more so than only children.[20] Firstborns appear to become more socially conservative in response to the presence of younger siblings. Middle children tend to occupy the middle of the family spectrum in social attitudes, whereas lastborns are typically the most liberal family members (Fig. 9.3 and Fig. 9.4).[21]

Just how extensive are these sibling differences in social attitudes? The typical firstborn in my sample achieves a mean score of 2.95 for social attitudes. This score corresponds with the 43rd percentile of the sample, somewhat below the median. The typical lastborn achieves a score of 3.35, which corresponds with the 68th percentile (or 25 percentiles higher). When political elections are decided by such a margin, they are considered landslides.

Another way to evaluate birth-order effects in social attitudes is to consider changes in these attitudes across the decades. With the Scientific Revolution in the seventeenth century, and particularly with the Enlightenment during the next century, intellectuals began to adopt more liberal social attitudes. Natural philosophers became increasingly willing to allow that the universe runs by itself, without the interven-

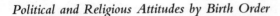

Political and Religious Attitudes by Birth Order

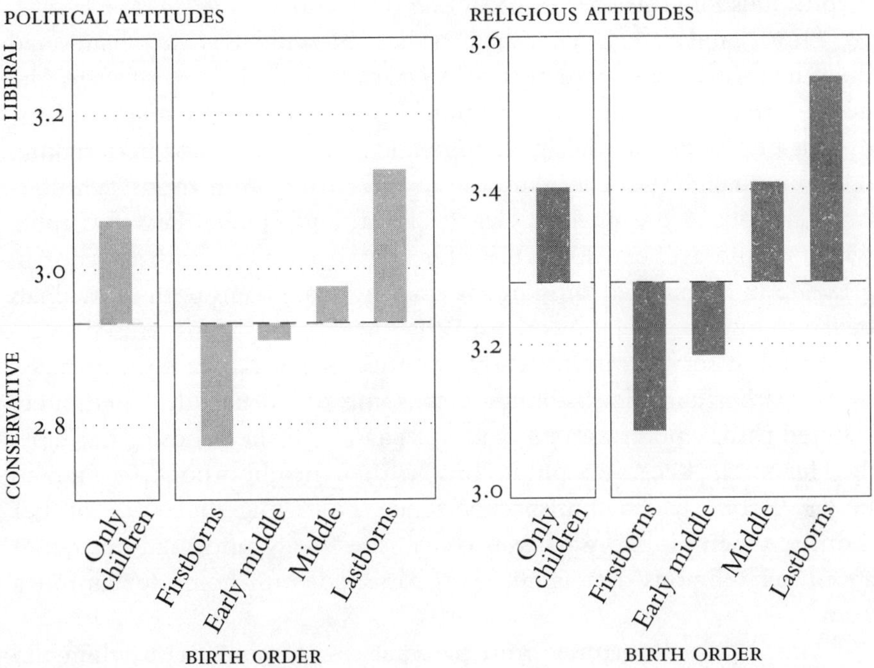

FIGURES 9.3 and 9.4. Social attitudes by birth order. The presence of younger siblings pushes firstborns in a conservative direction. Among laterborns, social radicalism is directly proportional to relative birth rank. The most radical siblings are lastborns. Compared with individuals having siblings, only children are intermediate in their social attitudes. The mean rating for each sample is indicated by the horizontal line.

When analyzed by birth rank, social attitudes exhibit a modest *zigzag* pattern. The typical increase in liberalism with birth rank is most pronounced among even-numbered offspring, providing strong evidence of niche partitioning in social attitudes.

tion of miracles. The typical lastborn in my study achieved a rating of 3.0 (or "liberal") in 1690. The typical firstborn did not achieve this same rating until 1860, 170 years later! In terms of "social enlightenment," lastborns were nearly two centuries ahead of firstborns.

Another strong indication of how siblings differ in their social attitudes comes from parent-offspring correlations, contrasted by birth order. For firstborns, the correlation is almost twice as large as it is for laterborns.[22] This finding indicates that firstborns share their parents' social values more than laterborns do. A few biographical examples will help to illustrate this process of sibling differentiation.

Historian Frank Turner has studied individuals who abandoned their religious beliefs during the Victorian period. Loss of faith, he notes, "inevitably disrupted the family." The desire to provoke the family was often "one of the inner psychological reasons" for undertaking religious change.[23] Turner cites the cases of Mary Ann Evans, who became famous as the novelist George Eliot; and Frances Power Cobbe, who became a liberal journalist. These two women, both laterborns, grew up in evangelical families. During their late teens both individuals began to lose their religious faith. When Mary Ann Evans refused to attend church services in her early twenties, she was severely ostracized by her father and older siblings. According to Turner, she "genuinely suffered pain, embarrassment, and humiliation at the hands of her family. Her plight became a public one in their neighborhood."[24] Frances Power Cobbe had a similar experience. Following the death of her mother, when Cobbe was twenty-five, she finally informed her father about her religious doubts. She was banished from home for almost a year.

The largest departures from parental social values arise when the birth orders of parents and offspring differ.[25] A dramatic example involves William, the eldest child of Benjamin Franklin. In 1763 William Franklin became the last royal governor of New Jersey. During the American Revolution he sided with the Loyalists! This political stance hardly endeared him to his radical father who at the advanced age of seventy was actively supporting the Declaration of Independence. As a defender of the Loyalist cause, William was thrown out of the country and suffered confiscation of his property. He lived out the remainder of his life in England. This political difference of opinion caused a "complete estrangement" between father and son.[26]

Birth order is just one of many factors that cause siblings to differ in their social attitudes. By using multiple predictors—including age gaps between siblings, parent-offspring conflict, gender, and parental loss—social attitudes can be predicted even more accurately. In fact, the kind of multivariate models that I employed in the preceding chapter do an excellent job of predicting social attitudes. An eight-variable model based on family dynamics is 9.8 times more powerful than birth order by itself. For all practical purposes, the causes of sibling differences in social radicalism are the same as those that polarize siblings in science. The eight predictors in this family dynamics model are (1) relative birth

George Eliot (Mary Ann Evans) in 1865, age forty-five. The youngest of five children, she scandalized her family by becoming a freethinker and, later, by taking up residence with a married man (philosopher George Henry Lewes, who was separated from his wife).

As a novelist, Eliot revolutionized the genre with what critics have called her "terrible realism." Her *Middlemarch* (1872) is considered one of the greatest novels of the nineteenth century. *Middlemarch* morality is represented in the form of Celia, sister of the main character, Dorothea. Described as a "dutiful" young woman who never did anything naughty in her entire life, Celia was modeled after Eliot's elder sister, Christiana. In the novel, Dorothea decides on an unconventional marriage and suffers the consequences.

rank, which interacts with (2) age gaps between siblings, (3) sibship size, (4) shyness, (5) parent-offspring conflict, and (6) parental loss. Relative birth rank also interacts with (7) socioeconomic class and parental loss as part of a three-way effect. The final variable is (8) gender, which enters the model as a main effect and also interacts with parent-offspring conflict. This family dynamics model is 138 times more predictive of social attitudes than is social class. Most individual differences in social attitudes are *within the family*.[27]

Daguerreotype of Charles Darwin and his eldest child, William (1842), the only offspring with whom Darwin was photographed. William lived out his rather staid life as a Southampton banker. A friend once said that he "set an example of a wholesome life." In his obituary notice of his brother, Frank Darwin emphasized William's "modest and respective manner" toward his superiors (F. Darwin 1914:19).

Once when William was with his father and uncle, he criticized an antislavery committee. This committee had recently been organized to protest the massacre of 400 Jamaican blacks. William joked that the members were raiding their donations to pay for their dinners. Darwin was so incensed by his son's remark that he curtly told him he "had better go back to Southampton." The next morning Darwin, who had not slept a wink, apologized for his uncharacteristic outburst (Darwin 1887, 3:53). William's identification with authority did not allow him to empathize, like his father, with the plight of the underdog. He is the only Darwin offspring known to have provoked his mild-mannered father to strong anger.

Disruptive Selection

Political and religious attitudes do vary between families. These between-family differences can be seen as the outcome of sibling differences that have accumulated over the generations. Parents, who do so much to shape their children's social attitudes, were once siblings themselves. As a result of assortative mating, social differences between siblings tend to be perpetuated as family worldviews.

The process by which sibling differences accrue over time involves a well-known evolutionary principle called "disruptive selection." This phenomenon is a variant of Darwin's greatest discovery—natural selection.[28] Unlike stabilizing selection, which causes deviant individuals to be eliminated from the population, disruptive selection favors individual differences, thereby preserving them. As siblings create their own individual family niches, they differentiate themselves from each other in terms of social attitudes. In adulthood, these differing worldviews become important in mate selection. Although mates are not generally concordant for personality traits, they do tend to be similar in IQ, social attitudes, and socioeconomic status.[29] In choosing spouses with ideological criteria in mind, mates increase the likelihood that offspring will share their social values.

Recent evidence indicates that social attitudes, like many features of personality, have moderate heritability. Based on studies of twins, about half of the variance in answers to certain specific questions regarding social attitudes appears to be genetic.[30] To be sure, there are no genes for being a British Tory or a member of the German Green Party. But there are heritable dispositions to accept or reject authority, just as there are inherited dispositions to be shy.[31] Twin studies have also demonstrated that some social beliefs are mostly *nongenetic.* Answers to the following question can be attributed almost entirely to the nonshared environment: "The so-called underdog deserves little sympathy or help from other people."[32] In these studies, the kinds of attitudes that have the lowest heritability are precisely those that would be expected to divide siblings based on differences in age and status. Such attitudes tend to involve racial discrimination, the merits of unfettered competition, the importance of family loyalties, and the acceptability of strong military force.[33]

Regardless of their origins in genetic dispositions or environmental influences, differences in social attitudes are often perpetuated across the generations by assortative mating. To the extent that social attitudes

Benjamin Franklin, around the time of the American Revolution. At the age of twelve Franklin was indentured to his elder brother James, a printer. The two had many disputes. As Franklin later recounted: "My brother was passionate, and had often beaten me, which I took extremely amiss" (Franklin 1916:36). When he was seventeen, Franklin broke his indentureship by fleeing to Philadelphia. There he continued what became a famous career as a printer, publisher, scientist, and statesman.

have both genetic and environmental components, siblings will tend to select mates who increase the likelihood that offspring will agree with their worldview. As this process is repeated generation after generation, the differences between siblings become established as differences between families. This is the essence of disruptive selection, a process that perpetuates individual differences rather than selecting against them.

Benjamin Franklin's radicalism can be attributed, in part, to the operation of the multigenerational process of mate selection I have been describing. A deist and political radical, Franklin was a youngest son.[34] It has been said that the only reason he was not entrusted to draft the Declaration of Independence was "for fear he might conceal a joke in the middle of it."[35] What is less well known about Franklin is that he was also the youngest son of the youngest son for five generations, dating back to the Protestant Reformation.[36] In his *Autobiography* Franklin commented on this genealogical fact and also noted his family's strong tradition of "dissenting" social convictions:

> This obscure family of ours was early in [support of] the Reformation, and continued Protestants through the reign of Queen Mary, when they were sometimes in danger of trouble on account of their zeal against popery. They had got an [outlawed] English Bible, and to conceal and secure it, it was fastened open with tapes under and within the cover of a joint-stool. When my great-great grandfather read it to his family, he turned up the joint-stool upon his knees. . . . One of the children stood at the door to give notice if he saw the apparitor coming, who was an officer of the spiritual court. In that case the stool was turned down again upon its feet, when the Bible remained concealed under it as before.[37]

The Protestant Reformation represents one of the most radical revolutions in Western thought. Tens of thousands of individuals went to their death for defying the authority of Church and State. In Reformation England, Bloody Mary persecuted Protestants with a special zeal.[38] As England turned toward middle-of-the-road Protestantism, Franklin's laterborn ancestors were forced to hold their dissenting form of religious worship in secret. In 1680 such private services were outlawed. Two years later, Franklin's parents emigrated to New England in an effort to "enjoy their mode of religion with freedom."[39] By allowing Franklin's ancestors to sail for America, the British government was nurturing a revolution that would ultimately deprive it of its American colony. *When a youngest son like Benjamin Franklin is descended from four previous generations of youngest sons, he is usually a rebel.*

The opposite side of the coin from Benjamin Franklin's story is found among the titled nobility. Inherited aristocracy is an effective system for compounding the psychological effects of firstborn status. Each generation of eldest sons tends to become more conservative than the one before it. Primogeniture, not aristocratic origins, is what causes most monarchs to be conservatives. Louis XV, Voltaire's king, is a good example. A religious conservative, he took his Catholic faith very seriously. When his conscience was troubled by a *ménage à trois* involving two of his mistresses (who were sisters), Louis refused to take the Eucharist for a time. He was alarmed by stories about people said to have died after consuming a wafer in a state of sin.[40] Louis was so offended by Voltaire's repeated attacks on the Catholic Church that he eventually banished the philosopher from France. Going back five generations, Louis was an eldest child of an eldest child. That's not all. Following the Capet family back another fifteen generations, the majority of Louis's ancestors were either firstborns or eldest sons.[41]

Another example of multigenerational sibling differences comes from the landed gentry. Charles Darwin grew up in Shrewsbury with Thomas Campbell Eyton, a childhood friend who became an ornithologist.[42] During their teens, Darwin and Eyton often hunted birds together. A firstborn, Eyton provided taxonomic descriptions for some of Darwin's Galápagos birds, and he ended up owning four of the type specimens of Darwin's famous Galápagos finches.[43] Even though Eyton was one of Darwin's oldest friends and possessed some of the best evidence for evolution in action, he was "a firm opponent of the Darwinian theory." Indeed, he was "much chagrinned" that Darwin used some of his observations on pigeons to bolster the theory of natural selection.[44]

How did Eyton, a staunch Tory, become so conservative? Quite simple: he was the direct heir of the Eyton family estates for 22 of the previous 23 generations.[45] Darwin, in contrast, was the youngest son of the youngest son for 4 generations. A combined 27 generations of birth-order differences, reinforced by assortative mating, lay behind Eyton's inability to accept his friend's radical ideas (Fig. 9.5).[46] Given Darwin's birth order and social attitudes, he was 30 times more likely than Eyton to support evolutionary theory![47] Although surrounded by nineteenth-century friends and colleagues, Darwin was ahead of his time, and his worldview was that of a twentieth-century liberal. In contrast, although he lived in the nineteenth century, Thomas Eyton's worldview harks back to the sixteenth century, when they still burned heretics and witches. Consistent with the disparate family heritages experienced by these two childhood friends, their marriages continued the trend. Darwin settled down with his liberal Wedgwood cousin, a lastborn. Thomas Eyton married a firstborn.[48]

In human populations, disruptive selection for social attitudes helps

Social Attitudes Compounded over the Generations

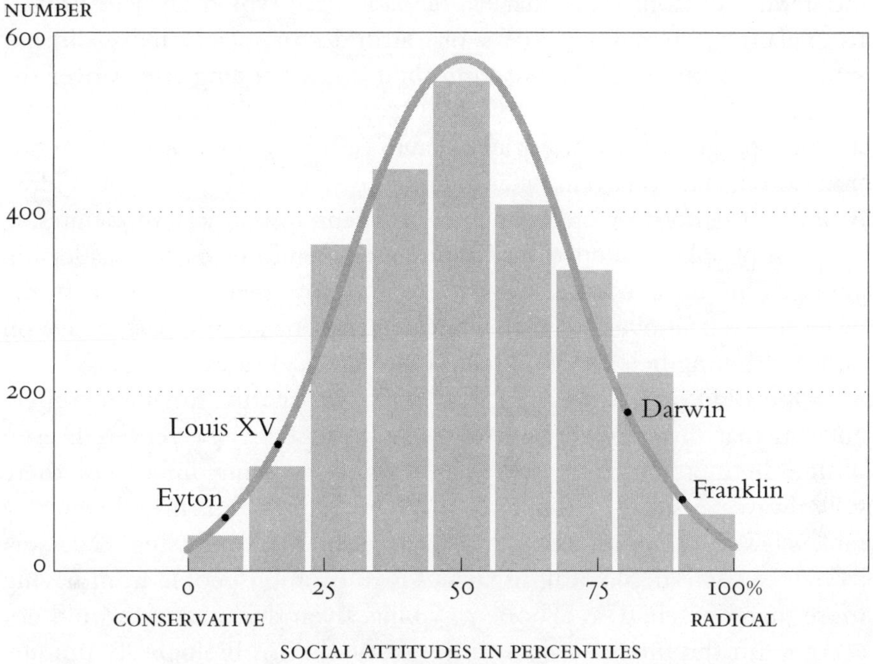

FIGURE 9.5. Differences in social attitudes, compounded over the generations. In any given population, some individuals will be descended from lineages of predominantly conservative or radical ancestors. The figure illustrates four individuals who came from such highly divergent lineages and indicates where they *should* have stood in terms of their social attitudes, based on the multigenerational effects of birth order. For the four individuals, the average deviation between observed and expected outcomes is a negligible 3 percentiles. Darwin, for example, is predicted to be in the 80th percentile. He was actually in the 84th. Eyton is predicted to be in the 9th percentile. He was actually in the 8th. Franklin is predicted to be in the 88th percentile and was actually in the 90th. Finally, Louis XV is predicted to be in the 17th percentile. He was actually in the 21st.

to explain what would otherwise be a considerable enigma. Social attitudes exhibit almost no correlation with social class.[49] Nor does social class exert much influence on the acceptance of scientific innovation. In my own study, birth order is 680 times more effective than social class in predicting scientific stance. Sibling differences as a whole are at least 1,000 times more predictive.[50] The typical differences between siblings also dwarf other group differences in radicalism, including gender and being a member of a racial or religious minority.[51] History is first biography, and only secondarily sociology. We would be hard pressed to explain the broad array of social attitudes in society if we did not know about sibling differences and their compounding effects over the centuries.[52]

Few people are like Charles Darwin or Thomas Eyton—descended from a long line of exclusively firstborn or laterborn parents. Children of mixed firstborn or laterborn ancestors tend to be social moderates, as are most people. Leaders of revolutions are therefore a rarity. Leadership generally requires a series of propitious factors that compound birth-order differences over several generations. A genealogical perspective on radical thinking helps to illuminate these unusual cases.

One additional consequence of assortative mating for sibling differences is that diversity in worldviews will constantly be renewed, even within the most egalitarian societies. Owing to sibling differences, there will always be social conservatives yearning for a return to hereditary rank, class distinctions, and other markers of social standing. One way to reduce such ideological disparities is to prohibit people from having more than one child, as is done in China. Even this measure would not accomplish the intended goal, since every child is biologically unique. In addition, singletons tend to be more variable than individuals with siblings. Because singletons are freer to occupy a variety of family niches, they embody much of individual variability that is associated with niche partitioning in larger sibships.

CONCLUSIONS

Because siblings differ from one another in systematic ways, *it is possible to predict the social attitudes of family members.* Birth order, age gaps between siblings, parent-offspring conflict, temperament, and other attributes of family niches all help to shape social attitudes. When this same biographical information is available for an individual's parents and grandparents, the predictability of social attitudes increases dramatically. Owing to the propensity for people to choose spouses with similar social attitudes, sibling differences tend to become compounded over time. These cross-generational trends are responsible for much of the diversity in social attitudes that is observed in the world around us.

Over a period of four generations, assortative mating among radically minded ancestors facilitated Darwin's own revolutionary discoveries. He was the receptive heir to a radical worldview. As he sat absorbed in his reading of Malthus's *Essay on the Principle of Population,* Darwin was led to reflect on the relentless struggle for existence that arises owing to overpopulation. This struggle begins, and sometimes ends, within the family, and is largely carried out through the agency of sibling competition. Like Malthus, Darwin got the message. God had not designed the world as a particularly happy place. In fact, God had not designed the world at all. The appearance of Design, Darwin realized, was a product of the continuous competition among rivals for scarce resources. He called this process natural selection.

Thomas Robert Malthus owed his own unconventional attack on the theory of Design to a similarly liberal family heritage. He was the youngest son of a middleborn and a lastborn, both of whom nurtured his liberal inclinations. Malthus's father, Daniel, was a friend and admirer of Rousseau, whose liberal philosophy of education the father adopted for his own children. The goal of education, Rousseau had argued, was to teach children how to think for themselves. Daniel Malthus taught his youngest son well, and when his son was ten, the father assigned him a series of tutors who were brimming with radical tendencies.[53] It has been said of the younger Malthus that he "hammered out the *Essay* [*on Population*] in discussions with his father."[54] And so it is that sibling differences, compounded across the generations, build relentlessly toward radical change.

10

THE DARWINIAN REVOLUTION AS SOCIAL HISTORY

RETHINKING SOCIAL HISTORY

Extensive research has sought to give the Darwinian revolution a Marxist interpretation. Evolution, it has been argued, "appealed to the insurrectionary working classes" and became closely allied with "working-class" science.[1] No one has labored harder in developing this thesis than British historian of science Adrian Desmond.[2] According to Desmond, evolutionary ideas were cultivated by the radical underworld of "marginal" scientific institutions.[3] Members of these organizations were intent on attacking natural theology, the cherished dogma of Oxbridge Anglicans. In his award-winning *Politics of Evolution,* Desmond provides a lively portrait of medical reformers gravitating toward materialist theories, including spontaneous generation and evolution, in their struggle against privileges enjoyed by their upper-class rivals.[4]

From a Marxist viewpoint, Darwin's own radicalism becomes a considerable puzzle. An upper-class gentleman from a landed-gentry family, Darwin was educated at Cambridge, a stronghold of the pious natural theology that Desmond's lower-class radicals were intent on undermining. As Stephen Jay Gould has reflected, after reading Desmond and Moore's biography of Darwin:

> But what made Darwin tick? Why him? For all Desmond and Moore have helped me to understand, their social approach leaves me with an immensely heightened sense of paradox. For I now grasp why Darwin was absolutely the wrong person for the job. He was exactly what Huxley yearned to sweep out—an amateur upper-class naturalist of inherited wealth, an Oxbridge product who had collected beetles and hoped for a parsonage.[5]

Receptivity to Evolutionary Theory by Social Class and Birth Order

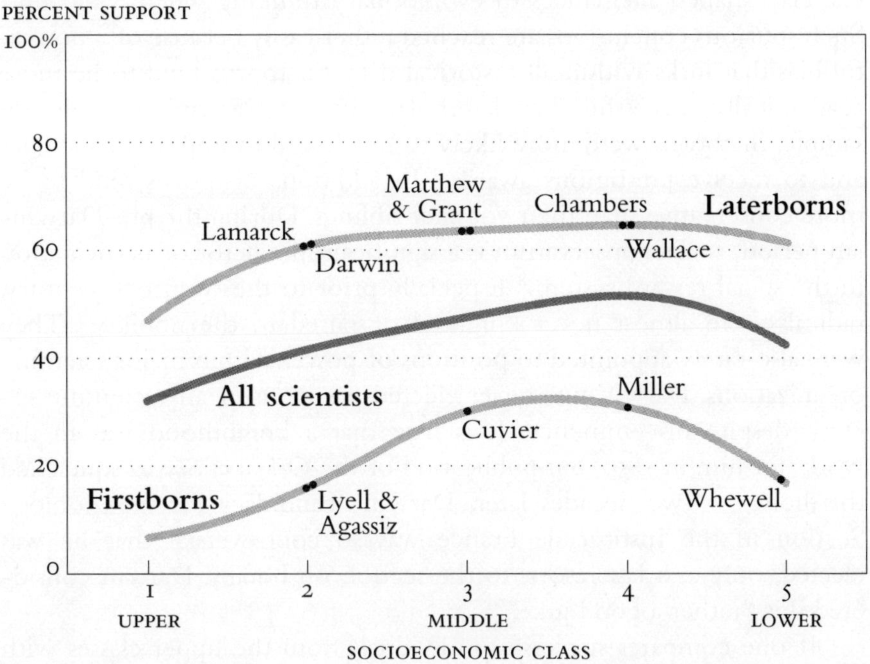

FIGURE 10.1. Mean levels of support for evolutionary theory, stratified by social class and birth order. Computed as the linear trend, the correlation between social class and support for evolution is almost zero. The correlation between birth order and support for evolution is substantial and explains more than 1,000 times the statistical variance associated with receptivity by social class.

There is a small *curvilinear* relationship between social class and support for evolution, but this nonlinear trend is not statistically significant.

The apparent paradox created by the radicalism of a gentleman scientist such as Darwin is really no paradox. During the debates over evolutionary theory, differences of opinion by social class were small and insignificant. Scientists from lower-class backgrounds were no more likely to support evolution than were members of the privileged classes. By contrast, within-class differences were enormous in the reception of evolution. Most within-class differences owe themselves to birth order and other aspects of family niches. As a consequence, the focus of the battle over the theory of evolution was *within* the family, not *between* families (Fig. 10.1).[6]

How have award-winning historians persuaded themselves that social class shaped allegiances to evolutionary thinking when it did not? Such spurious conclusions are reached rather easily because of a powerful bias that lurks within all historical data. Firstborns tend to be more academically successful than laterborns. In my Darwinian revolution sample, firstborns were more likely to be elected to important societies and to receive prestigious awards.[7] In addition, firstborns tend to be more conservative than their younger siblings. During the pre-Darwinian period, social conservatism is a significant predictor of participation in the social reward system.[8] Especially prior to the twentieth century, radicals were almost never knighted or raised to the nobility.[9] They were also rarely appointed to positions of power within major scientific organizations. Darwin was never elected president of any scientific society, despite his eminence. It is true that a knighthood was in the works for him in 1859, but publication of the *Origin of Species* squelched this honor.[10] Two decades later, Darwin's candidacy for the Zoology Section in the Institut de France was so controversial that he was elected, only as a last resort, to the section on botany. Darwin considered this "rather a good joke."[11]

If one compares successful individuals from the upper classes with less eminent radicals from the lower classes, one inevitably confounds class with differences by birth order. These differences between siblings reinforce the impression that social class lies behind radical thinking when birth order is in fact the causal variable. Firstborns will tend to be successful-but-conservative "insiders" and laterborns will tend to be radical "outsiders."

Adrian Desmond's choice of examples to illustrate his argument reveals a substantial conflation of birth-order differences with class differences. Desmond's personal hero among the radical evolutionists is Robert Edmond Grant, whose middle-class father was a writer for the Scottish courts.[12] Grant was also his father's seventh son, which is the operative variable in his radicalism. Desmond's favorite working-class agitator was Charles Southwell, who founded and edited the *Oracle of Reason* (1841–43). Southwell used this newsweekly to promote the causes of evolution and atheism.[13] Of Southwell and his fellow *Oracle* editors, Desmond observes that they "sought respectability in martyrdom. They were systematically jailed for blasphemy."[14] Southwell holds the record in my sample for having the highest absolute birth rank.[15] He was the youngest of thirty-three children.

A reanalysis of Desmond's biographical survey shows that his evi-

Desmond's Sample of Participants in the Debates over Evolution

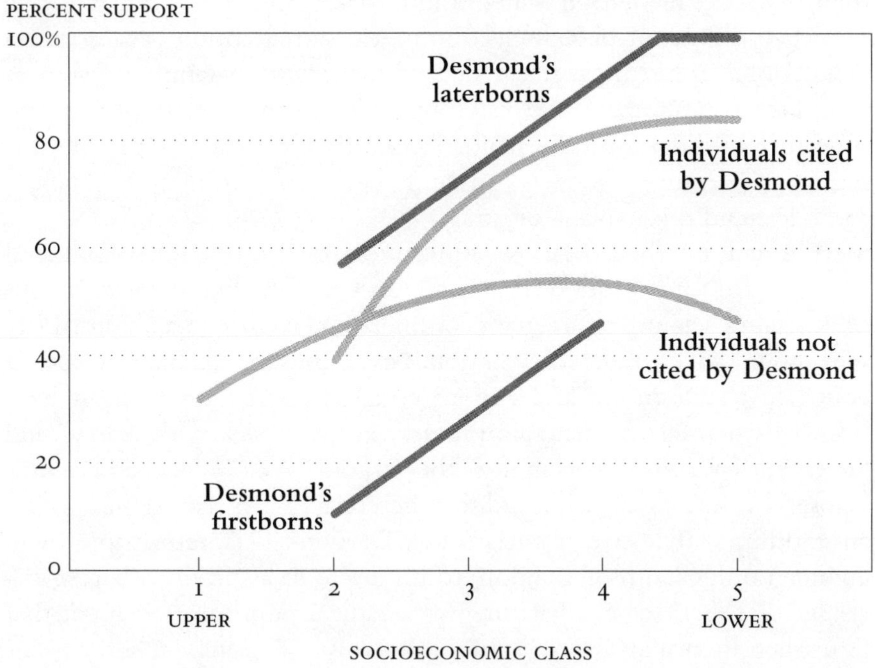

FIGURE 10.2. Adrian Desmond's sample of participants in the debates over evolution and other contemporaneous radical issues.

Compared with the larger population represented here as a control sample, Desmond's sample includes a significantly higher proportion of scientists who were both laterborns and social radicals. To support his claim that evolution was a "working-class" theory, Desmond drew especially heavily on these radical laterborns from the lower classes. In contrast, Desmond's upper-class conservatives tended to be firstborns. Correction for these sampling biases indicates that social class has nothing to do with support for radical ideas.

dence for the role of social class is the product of biased sampling that confirmed his working hypothesis. He took unwitting advantage of the enormous differences that exist between siblings raised in the same family. To make his case for upper-class conservatism, Desmond drew on establishment firstborns such as Charles Lyell and Peter Mark Roget (a physician now better known for his *Thesaurus of English Words and Phrases*). Desmond's middle- and lower-class radicals, by contrast, are overwhelmingly younger sons (Fig. 10.2).[16] On radical issues, firstborns will inevitably disagree with laterborns. Class has nothing to do with this tendency. The idea that social class explains something about the Darwinian revolution is an illusion.

The problem of biased selection merits our attention because it is a general one in historical research. Systematic within-family differences introduce a trap for unwary historians who assume that social class and other group differences are major forces of historical change. The integrity of narrative history is constantly being compromised by a failure to understand this explanatory trap.

Limited by their Marxist conception of history, Desmond and Moore were forced into a series of Don Quixote–like reconstructions of Darwin's scientific career. According to Marxist expectations, Darwin should have abhorred evolution. Given the undeniable fact that he endorsed it, Desmond and Moore conclude that Darwin must have been "tormented" by his radical ideas.[17] He was "sick with worry" and "frightened for his respectability," they argue.[18] As a result, he became a "closet evolutionist" who hid his heretical views from the people around him.[19] The two historians link Darwin's 1842 retreat to Down, eighteen miles south of London, to his desire to avoid the Chartist uprisings of the 1840s.[20] Chartism was a radical political movement that flourished in Britain from 1838 to about 1850. The movement took its name from the People's Charter, a six-point document that, among other things, demanded universal male suffrage and an abolition of property requirements for membership in Parliament.[21] There is no evidence that Darwin opposed the goals of the Chartist movement. On the contrary, there is good evidence that he sympathized with these goals.

During the spring of 1848 a revolution broke out in Europe. In Paris a new National Assembly was established. The *Globe,* a leading London newspaper, became increasingly cynical about the aims of the revolutionaries. The paper condemned the National Assembly for failing to suppress riots, as the British government had done a month earlier during widespread Chartist demonstrations. In a letter to his wife, Emma, written while Darwin was visiting his dying father in Shrewsbury, he described the *Globe*'s point of view as "simply damnable." He was so annoyed by the newspaper's reactionary views that he told his wife to stop forwarding the paper to him while he was away.[22]

Desmond and Moore tie Darwin's intellectual torment to fears of offending his "Anglican friends" and "betraying his privileged class."[23] From among Darwin's friends, it is relatively easy to find a handful of individuals who are consistent with such a thesis. But Desmond and

Moore's argument presupposes something more, namely, that *most* of Darwin's friends were social conservatives.

To test this proposition, I have constructed a measure of personal association with Darwin, based on indicators such as the number of letters exchanged with him between 1826 and 1859. Within this sample of Darwin's contemporaries, the social attitudes of more than three hundred friends and associates are documented in my database. Compared with the rest of the scientific population, Darwin's closest friends were distinctly liberal.[24] In his *Autobiography,* he later reproached his more conservative acquaintances for their "ludicrous" concern with social status and orthodoxy.[25]

Darwin's Codiscoverers

Just as Charles Darwin's social outlook fails to accord with a socioeconomic interpretation, so do the achievements of the two other individuals who anticipated his most seminal scientific insight—natural selection. Patrick Matthew, who published a brief account of this theory in 1831, was an ardent Chartist. A younger son from a middle-class family of timber growers, Matthew wrote several vitriolic tracts against the nobility. In 1839 he was a Scottish delegate to the Chartist General Convention in London. Matthew resigned when he was labeled a "middle-class traitor" by Feargus O'Connor, who had called for the use of physical violence.[26] On the Chartist scale, this political disparity marked the difference between a decided radical and an outright anarchist. Back in Perth, Matthew's constituents supported his resignation. Soon after, O'Connor was sent to prison and became hopelessly insane.[27]

Although he was only sixteen years old in 1839, Alfred Russel Wallace—inspired by Welsh reformer Robert Owen's political views—had already become a socialist. Owen influenced him, Wallace later recalled, "more than I then knew, and now that I have read his life and most of his works, I am fully convinced that he was the greatest of social reformers and the real founder of modern Socialism."[28]

In spite of being raised in disparate classes, the three codiscoverers of the theory of natural selection shared similar social attitudes.[29] Matthew, Darwin, and Wallace were particularly united in their opposition to privilege at the expense of talent. This issue is just as much a preoccupation among siblings as it is a socioeconomic concern. In particular, primogeniture has always stood in the way of upward mobility through open competition. In Matthew's book *Naval Timber,* in which he anticipated the theory of natural selection, he described primogeniture as "an outrage on this law of nature [natural selection] which she will not pass unavenged."[30] Darwin was no less animated on "the evil consequences" of primogeniture, which he discussed in the *Descent of Man*.[31] There he lamented that "worthless eldest sons" were often able to marry at the expense of younger sons with "superior" abilities.[32] Darwin's son Francis later recalled on this topic: "My father had a strong feeling as to the injustice of primogeniture, and in a similar spirit was often indignant over the unfair wills that appear from time to time."[33]

Darwin's evolutionary theories celebrate the endless biological achievements that derive from unfettered competition. In the eyes of its three originators, the theory of natural selection was the ultimate scientific justification for the abolition of primogeniture. Is it any wonder that laterborns took warmly to this Darwinian idea and that firstborns, regardless of social class, generally recoiled from it?

A COMPREHENSIVE MODEL

A comprehensive computer model of the Darwinian revolution helps to highlight the importance of within-family differences compared with sociological influences such as nationality and class. This model incorporates information on birth order, parent-offspring conflict, parental loss, age and eminence in 1859, personal ties with Darwin, social attitudes, parents' social attitudes, national differences, and social class. The model correctly classifies 84 percent of the Darwinian revolution participants as evolutionists or antievolutionists. The kinds of influences that differentiate siblings account for more than half of the model's explanatory power. Other important predictors of scientific support, such as age, nationality, and social attitudes, also make significant contributions to the model's success. By contrast, socioeconomic status does not enter the model because it explains virtually nothing. In predicting support for Darwinism, birth-order differences are 1,000 times more powerful than socioeconomic differences. Compared with national differences, which *do* enter the model, birth-order differences are 10 times more predictive. Sibling differences as a whole are 37 times more predictive than are national differences. Only one other variable in the model challenges the predictive power of sibling differences: social attitudes. Still, sibling differences are more important than social at-

Predicted Probabilities of Supporting Evolutionary Theory by Social Attitudes and Birth Order

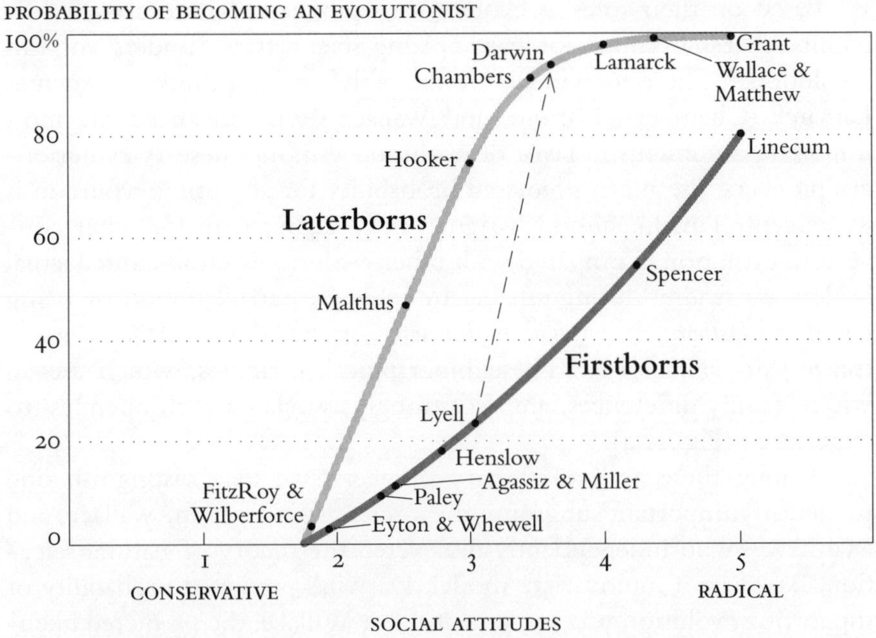

FIGURE 10.3. Predicted probabilities of supporting evolutionary theory, stratified by social attitudes and birth order (*N*=407). All individuals whose predicted probabilities are indicated as being above 50 percent endorsed evolution; individuals whose probabilities are shown as being below 50 percent opposed this theory.

Birth order and social attitudes are the two best predictors of responses to evolution, and the data are plotted in terms of these two variables. The highest predicted probabilities of support for evolution are found among social liberals, especially laterborn liberals such as Lamarck, Grant, Darwin, and Wallace. Firstborns were unlikely to support evolution, unless they were social radicals such as Herbert Spencer and Gideon Lincecum.

During the Darwinian revolution, the typical difference between firstborns and laterborns is indicated by the dashed arrow. This difference is the same as that separating Charles Darwin from his friend Charles Lyell—a disparity of 71 percent. Owing to its direct as well as indirect effects (via social attitudes), birth order is a better predictor of scientific stance than social attitudes.

titudes, principally because they explain individual differences in this variable.[34] Once again, we are led to conclude that radicalism arises largely *within* families, not *between* them (Fig. 10.3).[35]

Leaders versus Followers

Based on their roles as evolutionary pioneers, I have classified 15 members of my sample of participating scientists as "leaders" of this revolution.[36] These individuals are the path-breaking thinkers—such as Lamarck, Chambers, Darwin, and Wallace—who advanced the most important arguments in favor of evolution. Among these 15 evolutionary pioneers, the mean predicted probability for accepting evolution is 83 percent. This likelihood is significantly higher than for other converts to evolution. Compared with other evolutionists, these intellectual leaders are readily distinguishable by their greater likelihood of being *liberal* and *lastborn, having had conflict with a parent,* and *having journeyed to remote parts of the globe.* These biographical attributes, which are all within-family differences, are also strongly associated with openness to experience (Fig. 10.4).[37]

Among these 15 evolutionary pioneers, we may distinguish one particularly important subgroup: the 3 scientists—Darwin, Wallace, and Matthew—who independently discovered the theory of natural selection. Based on a multivariate model, Darwin's predicted probability of supporting evolution was 94 percent.[38] For Wallace, the predicted likelihood is even higher—96 percent. Patrick Matthew, who anticipated both Darwin and Wallace, receives a predicted probability of 97 percent. In short, the 3 scientists who discovered the theory of natural selection were significantly more predisposed to reject creationism, and to accept evolution, than other leaders of this scientific revolution.[39]

DARWIN'S GENIUS

The fact that Darwin, Wallace, and Matthew reached the same fundamental scientific insight—natural selection—highlights an important problem: How do we account for Darwin's own particular success as a scientist? A single idea, even a brilliant one, does not make someone a genius. A computer model of the Darwinian revolution may account for Darwin's receptivity toward evolutionary theory, but it does not explain his success at working out this idea. Certain features of Darwin's scientific style are relevant to this issue.

As all of Darwin's biographers have recognized, he was a worrier. There is an important distinction between being a worrier and being a

Predicted Probabilities of Supporting Evolution

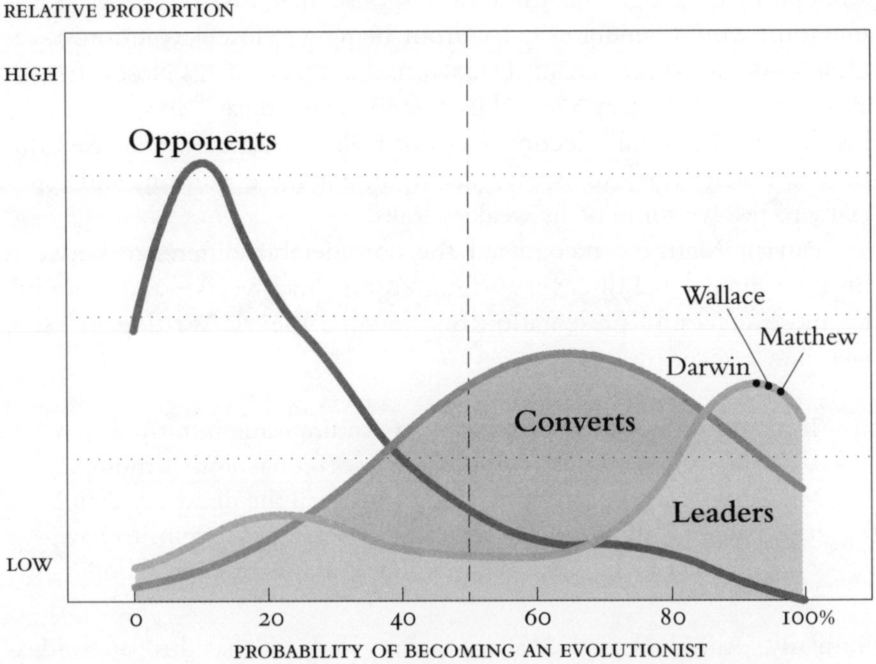

FIGURE 10.4. Predicted probabilities of supporting evolution, based on a ten-variable model (N=644). The model does a good job of separating the various factions within this debate.

In addition to the predicted probabilities for opponents and converts, probabilities are also displayed for the 15 principal leaders of the Darwinian revolution. Compared with converts to evolution, these 15 leaders were significantly more likely to endorse this radical innovation.

Among the 15 leaders of evolutionary theory, 3 younger sons independently hit on the theory of natural selection. These 3 individuals—Darwin, Wallace, and Matthew—had significantly higher probabilities of endorsing evolution than the other 12 leaders.

person who is tormented by the fear of betraying family and friends. The principal interests that Darwin sought to protect were reputational, not socioeconomic. Based on his familiarity with the voluminous correspondence in which Darwin solicited evidence for and against his controversial views, Frederick Burkhardt concludes that Darwin was "a cautious strategist." He was "sometimes confident," Burkhardt elaborates, but he was just as often "uneasy about his work, and always attempting to gauge the kind of response that his theory of transmutation would generate."[40] Far from being a "closet evolutionist," as Desmond and Moore claim, Darwin told a dozen of his closest friends about his evolutionary ideas. His twenty-year "delay" in announcing his theory of natural selection was not really a delay. Darwin used this time advantageously to bolster his argument for evolution, and especially to resolve some of its weakest links.

Patrick Matthew recognized the considerable difference between his own intellectual discovery—ignored for thirty years—and Darwin's far more successful presentation of the same theory. Writing in 1860, Matthew conceded:

> To me the conception of this law of Nature came intuitively as a self-evident fact, almost without effort of concentrated thought. Mr. Darwin here seems to have more merit in the discovery than I have had—to me it did not appear a discovery. He seems to have worked it out by inductive reason, slowly and with due caution.[41]

Similarly, Alfred Russel Wallace acknowledged that his own ideas on natural selection had been "a hasty first sketch." Compared with Darwin, Wallace described himself as "the young man in a hurry." Cursory announcements of revolutionary ideas rarely exert much influence, and the Darwin-Wallace papers of 1858 were no exception. In 1864, Wallace acknowledged as much to Darwin: "As to the theory of Natural Selection itself, I shall always maintain it to be yours and yours only. . . . My paper would never have convinced anybody or been noticed as more than an ingenious speculation, whereas your book has revolutionised the study of natural history, and carried away captive the best men of the present age." [42]

Cautious perseverance, then, was Darwin's way of accomplishing what no previous evolutionist had been able to do. He persistently believed in persistence.[43] Such personal traits transcend most group differences, including social class. In Darwin's case, stalwart determination was clearly a sibling strategy, as he himself intimated in his *Autobiography.* Faced with the overzealous efforts of his elder sister Caroline, who tried to be a surrogate mother to him after their own mother's death, Darwin developed a dogged indifference toward her authority.[44] Of course, there is more to genius than persistence (or as Thomas Edison

Alfred Russel Wallace in 1869 (age forty-six). By temperament, he was neither as cautious nor as persistent as Darwin, but he was just as radical. "My great fault," he once confessed to Darwin, "is haste. An idea strikes me, I think it over over for a few days, and then write away with such illustrations as occur to me. . . . " Reflecting back on their contributions to the theory of natural selection, Wallace contrasted their respective approaches to the problem, modestly concluding that his own share in the discovery had been "as twenty years is to one week" (quoted in Marchant 1916:92-93, 129).

once said, perspiration); but persistence, when combined with a radical outlook, goes a long way toward explaining Darwin's revolutionary achievements.

THE PHRENOLOGY MOVEMENT

Even more clearly than the Darwinian revolution, the reception of phrenology illustrates the subtle manner in which sibling differences can confound the proper telling of history. This theory was developed in the late 1790s by Franz Joseph Gall, a German-born physician living in Vienna. He was the sixth of ten children of a modest merchant who rose to become the mayor of his village. Gall's parents were both "devout Roman Catholics," but Gall himself was at best only "nominally religious"—a typical nineteenth-century deist.[45] A skilled anatomist, Gall correctly deduced that functions of the brain are localized. Incorrectly, however, Gall believed that the shape of the cranium reflected individual differences in brain functioning. He argued that one could "read" the inside of the brain—and hence character—by analyzing its outward expressions as cranial "bumps."[46] Gall's flamboyant lectures on phrenology were well attended until 1801, when Emperor Francis I proscribed them for being too materialistic.

In 1807 Gall left Vienna for Paris, where he lived the remainder of his life. Napoleon Bonaparte quickly took steps to reduce his influence. Later, in exile on St. Helena, Napoleon boasted: "I contributed greatly to Gall's ruin."[47] He engineered this feat by appointing a commission, in 1808, which he packed with antimaterialists such as Georges Cuvier. This commission—dominated by firstborns—spurned Gall's phrenological claims.[48] As a result of this official dismissal of his theories, Gall always remained a scientific outsider. In 1821 he was rejected for membership in the French Academy of Sciences. Gall "never held an academic post; and his relations with authority and orthodoxy were almost uniformly bad."[49]

Because phrenology was generally supported by laterborns, and opposed by firstborns, the theory polarized the scientific community in much the same manner that evolution did. Many of the strongest supporters of phrenology, such as Robert Chambers and Alfred Russel Wallace, were dedicated supporters of evolution. Nearly 90 percent of my sample either accepted or rejected both theories.[50] The story of phrenology is not, however, a repeat of the Darwinian revolution. Indeed, the reception of phrenology followed a distinctly different course.

Gall's theories were widely promoted by his first disciple, Johann Spurzheim, who, like Gall, was a younger son. Through well-attended

Franz Joseph Gall, who sought to bridge the gap between psychology and biology with his controversial theory of phrenology. His bold claim that cerebral function could be discerned from the shape of the skull has proved erroneous, but his associated conviction that mental functioning is localized within the brain has been amply confirmed. His adherents included Balzac, Bismarck, the Brontë sisters, George Eliot, Hegel, President James Garfield, and Queen Victoria.

lectures during the 1810s and 1820s, Spurzheim introduced these ideas in Britain and America, where they became a "popular science." In Britain, phrenology was actively proselytized by George Combe, whose *Constitution of Man* (1828) sold more than 100,000 copies during the next three decades.[51] It has been said that Combe's *Constitution of Man* was one of the three books that one could count on finding in most

British homes during the early nineteenth century. The other two books were the Bible and Bunyan's *Pilgrim's Progress.*[52] The middle son of a beer brewer, Combe was assisted by his younger brother Andrew, who was the next-to-youngest of the thirteen Combe siblings.[53]

As activists for educational reform, many phrenologists sought to make talent, not privilege, the main criterion of social advancement.[54] They believed that latent abilities could be encouraged, and disabilities overcome, by an early phrenological reading of the skull. Gall's ideas inspired one of the first "Head Start" programs! Social historians of science have generally seen this controversy as being class driven. Steven Shapin, who has studied the reception of phrenology in Edinburgh, concludes:

> The local controversies [over phrenology] . . . tended to array disaffected and iconoclastic bourgeois groups against traditional elites and their intellectual spokesmen; it is no exaggeration therefore to see the Edinburgh phrenology disputes in terms of the macrosociological category of social class.[55]

One must become wary of such claims, however, when one learns of the supporting evidence. Roger Cooter, for example, has identified "the phrenologists' lower socioeconomic and intellectual status . . . by noting who among the sample were fellows of the Royal Societies of London and Edinburgh."[56] Differences in eminence are not the same as class differences. In addition, eminence is typically correlated with status as a firstborn! More than a century ago, Darwin's cousin Francis Galton showed that firstborns were overrepresented as members of the Royal Society.[57] Such differences in status provide as much evidence for differences between siblings as they do for class differences. Only empirical testing can tell us which hypothesis is correct.

In my own sample of 177 participants in the phrenology controversy, there is a moderately strong association between support for phrenology and coming from the lower classes.[58] Superficially, this finding corroborates the historical claims of Cooter and Shapin. Much of this "socioeconomic" effect is due to the conflation of birth-order differences with class differences. Laterborn reformers tended to be recruited from the lower classes.[59] Once we control for the main effect of birth order, as well as for the tendency for phrenologists to be nonscientists, the main effect for social class turns out to be negligible (Fig. 10.5).[60]

Receptivity to Phrenology by Social Class and Birth Order

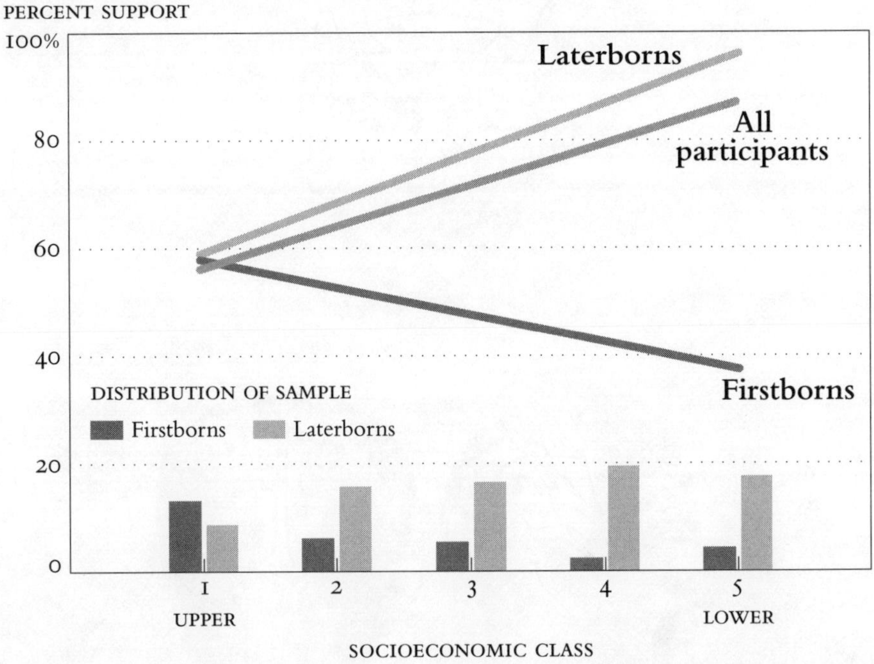

FIGURE 10.5. The reception of phrenology, stratified by social class and birth order. The influence of birth order is substantial. The influence of social class, which is superficially impressive, is due largely to its cross correlation with birth order.

At the bottom of the graph, participation rates by birth order and social class are plotted using a relativistic scale that sums to 100 percent within each class. Note the steadily increasing proportion of laterborns among participants in the middle and lower classes. Phrenology was a laterborn movement, especially among the lower classes.

As a result of recruitment bias by birth order, social class does not exert a significant effect on acceptance of phrenology. In large part, the association between radicalism and social class owes itself to the tendency for radical phrenologists to be younger sons.

Properly understood, socioeconomic considerations play a part in the reception of phrenology, but not in the way that is generally supposed. Much of the opposition to phrenology came from scientists—firstborns and laterborns alike. Darwin, for example, rejected this theory on *scientific* grounds, not because the doctrine was too radical for his upper-class tastes.[61] The same consideration influenced another

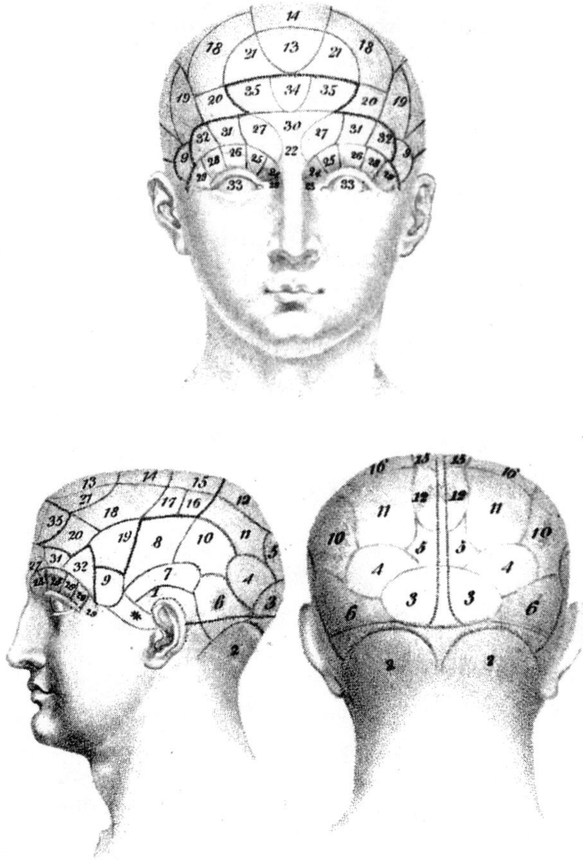

A phrenological map of the head, showing the regions where various faculties were supposed to be localized.

upper-class laterborn in my study, Hewett Cottrell Watson. A pre-Darwinian evolutionist and a strong supporter of Darwin's evolutionary ideas, Watson edited the *Phrenological Journal* for three years. In 1840 he returned to the study of botany, having concluded that phrenology would never become a critical science.[62]

Scientists have different standards of proof from nonscientists. For this reason, the most devoted phrenologists tended to be laterborn nonscientists. As educational reformers and itinerant lecturers, these nonscientific recruits were interested in employing Gall's ideas to achieve radical social reforms rather than to further the science of human behavior. Although these nonscientists were not significantly different in their class origins from scientists in my sample, they were not likely to end up as members of the Royal Society. The minute that class is confounded with scientific eminence (a firstborn tendency), it appears to be an important player in the reception of phrenology. This relationship is a pseudoeffect, based on a failure to control for confounding factors. When a correction is made for these factors, individual differences in birth order and social attitudes are 24 times more influential in explaining support for phrenology than is the nonsignificant influence of social class.[63]

CONCLUSIONS

Because individual differences are rampant, so is their role in explaining human behavior, including how it plays itself out in history. The explanation for this phenomenon is the story of this book: Extensive individual differences have been preprogrammed by Darwinian evolution and are constantly being augmented by family experience. Millions of years of biological evolution have seen to it that siblings turn out to be very different from one another. Whenever family members do not think alike, neither do the members of larger social groups who live through the same radical upheaval.[64]

When historians seek to explain radical thinking, they often call upon social class. Most scholars who do so are already convinced of a causal relationship, so they rarely bother to test their claims.[65] The moral urgency of Marxist thought, which bolsters such beliefs, tends to render them "emotionally resistant to disconfirmation."[66] The problem is a general one: the more emotionally charged a claim is, the less likely it will be given critical scrutiny. It is precisely these kinds of claims that need to be tested.

Social class is relevant to *participation* in science: peasants rarely become scientists. But the causes of intellectual radicalism are another matter entirely, as the Darwinian revolution and the phrenology movement illustrate. Of the 28 scientific controversies I have studied, phrenology exhibits the largest social-class effect in receptivity. The bulk of this relationship is a pseudoeffect, stemming from recruitment differences between firstborns and laterborns, as well as scientists and nonscientists. Compared with laterborns, firstborns are generally better educated and hence more likely to become scientists. Firstborns are especially overrepresented among the members of *establishment* science. Such tendencies toward intellectual primogeniture create a trap for the unwary historian who, without adequate hypothesis testing, opts for a Marxist explanation of radical thought.

Once we consider the enormous role of individual differences, the evidence regarding the origins of radical inclinations points to a different conclusion: the diversity of siblings raised in the same family. Marx's theory of class struggle sheds almost no light on individual differences in personality, including openness to radical ideas. In conjunction with Darwin's principle of divergence, the influence of sibling competition tells us most of what we need to know.

11

THE PROTESTANT REFORMATION

Few social movements have been more disruptive than the Protestant Reformation, which created a "titanic struggle for the hearts and minds of people."[1] Between 1517 and the end of the sixteenth century, nearly a million people died as a result of massacres, persecution, and religious wars set in motion by the Protestant revolt.[2] Along with the Italian Renaissance, the Reformation has generally been considered "the first of the great revolutions that created the modern world."[3] The Renaissance, which witnessed the revival of interest in classical learning, was in many ways a conservative revolution. The Reformation was a radical event. Throughout Europe, this bold defiance of established authority achieved a major break with the past. Indeed, this schism has been called a "Copernican revolution" in religious thought, one that turned accepted theological beliefs "upside down."[4]

The birth of the Protestant Reformation is intimately associated with the theological ideas of an Augustinian monk named Martin Luther (1483–1546). On 31 October 1517 Luther posted his famous 95 theses on the door of the castle church in Wittenberg, a university town in northern Germany. Entitled *Ninety-Five Theses or Disputation on the Power and Efficacy of Indulgences,* Luther's criticisms were aimed at a long-standing ecclesiastic abuse. Through official "letters of indulgence," the Catholic church invited sinners to make financial offerings, in return for which they received a remission of sins. Such indulgences promised substantial reductions of time in purgatory, generally commensurate with the amount of the offering. Luther's *Ninety-Five Theses* advanced a variety of arguments against this practice.[5] The pope, he argued, had no real power to reduce the penalties of purgatory, which were imposed by God, not by popes. If popes did possess such powers, why, Luther asked, did they not exercise them out of Christian compassion, rather than employing them for ecclesiastic profit? Even more important, the practice of indulgences endangered people's souls. By purchasing letters of indulgence, sinners received the false impression that they had earned forgiveness, diminishing the likelihood of true contrition. Only the genuinely contrite, Luther argued, were likely to earn God's forgiveness.

Indulgences were just the tip of an extensive iceberg of fiscal abuses. Church offices, for instance, were routinely sold to the highest bidder, rather than being awarded to the most competent candidate. By paying a "reservation fee," it was possible for someone to purchase a lucrative church office even before the incumbent had vacated it through retirement or death. At the Diet of Worms in 1521, the German princes submitted a list of 102 "oppressive burdens and abuses imposed on and committed against the German empire by the Holy See of Rome."[6] Luther's protest was the timely culmination of more than two centuries of growing complaints against church abuses.

Luther's 95 theses struck a widespread chord of discontent that he had not anticipated. Copies of these theses, translated from Latin into German, were quickly distributed throughout the German territories. Within a fortnight, Luther's cause had become a national one, and a much-surprised Luther found himself at the head of a popular revolt. During the next three years his various books and pamphlets sold some 300,000 copies, a phenomenal achievement for the sixteenth century.[7] In 1521 a papal representative in Germany complained that nine-tenths of the German people were behind Luther. Writing two years later to Charles V—the Holy Roman Emperor—his brother Ferdinand asserted: "Luther's teaching is so firmly embedded in the Empire that among a thousand persons not a single one is completely untouched; it could hardly be worse."[8]

After posting his 95 theses, Luther was ordered by Pope Leo X to recant his opinions on indulgences. Luther refused to do so unless he could be shown to have erred based on Scripture. In August 1518 the pope commanded Luther to appear in Rome to be tried for heresy. Frederick the Wise of Saxony, Luther's powerful protector throughout the affair, agreed to Luther's request that he be permitted to defend his views on German soil. A good Catholic, Frederick was probably troubled by some of Luther's progressive views. But he was also a tolerant ruler who greatly respected his most famous professor at the University of Wittenberg.

The hawking of indulgences. This sixteenth-century woodcut shows a successful vendor of indulgences, on the left. So much money is going into the vendor's coffer, under his table, that the man in the center is having to mint new coins on the spot. A contemporary jingle sums up this ecclesiastic practice: "As soon as the coin in the coffer rings,/The soul from purgatory springs."

Between 1518 and 1521, Luther participated in a series of public debates during which he gradually came to terms with the issue of papal authority.[9] In the process he reached a number of key theological views that defined the incipient "Protestant" position.* The core of Luther's liberating theology was his notion of "justification by faith." Salvation, he argued, was not gained by "good works," such as those achieved by financial offerings to the church. Rather, salvation derived from faith in Christ and His power of forgiving sins. A gift from Christ, salvation was not for sale. Indulgences, Luther insisted, were a "cruel hoax" promoted by a corrupt church in need of extensive doctrinal reform.[10]

---

*The term "Protestant" dates from 1529, when, at the Diet of Speyer, various Lutheran princes protested the decrees of the Catholic majority and thus became known as the "Protesting Estates."

Martin Luther in 1545 (age sixty-one). Luther was noted for his earthy sense of humor. "My enemies examine all that I do," he once complained. "If I break wind in Wittenberg they smell it in Rome" (Smith 1911:355).

Luther's notion of justification by faith contained the seeds of a radical theological revolution. If salvation was only possible through faith in Christ, there was no reason for the church to subordinate the laity to the powerful bishops and priests who dispensed forgiveness.[11] Forgiveness was a personal matter between the sinner and God. Most of the Catholic Church's superstructure, including its various sacramental practices, had grown up around the twin principles of assessing "good works" and dispensing forgiveness. By contrast, Luther's theology involved a return to the purity and simplicity of the Gospels.[12] His teachings celebrated "inward commitment" over "man-made rules" and legitimated what he called a "priesthood of all believers."[13]

Ultimately, the Protestant Reformation became a radical revolt against ossified church authority. Luther's teachings offered a spiritual choice between two distinct authorities: the pope, and Christ as revealed to all through the Gospels. "In the end," observes one historian of this period, "the reformers failed to obey; in the moment of truth, they rejected the notion that the church was infallible."[14]

Not surprisingly, the Protestant revolt attracted individuals who felt "bullied" by authority.[15] In addition, Luther's message appealed to "the bold risk takers," and it nurtured "a frenzy of freedom" among his early followers.[16] These attributes of Luther's theology are those that, throughout history, have typically appealed to laterborns.

SPREAD OF THE REFORMATION

No single factor determined acceptance of the Reformed faith. As one Reformation scholar has asserted:

> It would be splendid if the matter of becoming (or not becoming) a supporter of Luther followed a discernable pattern, so that all people in the cities (or in the country), in the north (or in the south), with education (or without), with wealth (or without), became Lutherans. No such pattern exists, or, if it does, it is obscure.[17]

Still, Reformation scholars have identified a variety of trends that characterize the spread of Protestant convictions.

In explaining the dissemination of the Protestant faith, we must distinguish between long-term historical forces that led up to the Reformation, such as abuses within the Catholic Church, and reasons that inclined some individuals, but not others, to adopt Protestant ideas. One may characterize these two historical problems in terms of *macrohistory* and *microhistory,* respectively. Macrohistory entails the interplay of historical forces over relatively long periods of time. In contrast, microhistory takes up the problem of individual lives and is the principal focus of biographers. The distinction between "macro-" and "micro-" historical processes allows us to break them down into more manageable subproblems. For example, macrohistorical contexts can often be employed as predictors of everyday (microhistorical) behavior. It is not necessary to solve the larger problems associated with macrohistory to make such historical inferences. The role of family dynamics, including its expression in the form of sibling differences in personality, elucidates questions about microhistory rather than macrohistory.

The spread of the Reformation is largely a problem in microhistory. In analyzing this problem, scholars have called attention to at least eight factors that appear to have played facilitating roles.[18] Most of these influences reflect individual differences in social status. People who possessed the least power and status were generally the most sympathetic to Luther's reformist message. Briefly stated, here are the eight correlates of acceptance that have been identified by Reformation scholars:

1. *Age:* Young people favored the Reformation.

2. *Social status:* The lower clergy (monks and parish priests) were among the Reformation's most dedicated "foot soldiers," whereas the higher clergy were hostile to change.[19] University professors were also antagonistic to Luther's teachings.

3. *The princes:* Political rulers, even those who supported the Reformed faith, were initially cautious about permitting its introduction into their territories.

4. *Urbanization:* Of the 65 free imperial cities of Europe, most were receptive to the Reformation. This positive attitude contrasts with the resistance to Protestant reforms encountered within princely territories, where "the ruler made all the difference."[20]

5. *Local political power and status:* Even within the free cities, governing councils (and the patricians and magistrates that ran them)

were rarely the driving force behind the introduction of the Reformation. Such councils were generally pressured by the townspeople into accepting change.

6. Humanistic training: At least initially, Erasmian humanists were sympathetic to the Reformation. Even before Luther, Erasmus himself had fully endorsed the need for church reform. His book *The Praise of Folly* (1511) had savagely satirized monks, cardinals, and even popes. To repeat the well-known adage: "Erasmus laid the egg that Luther hatched."[21]

7. Social class: The lower classes were more open to the Reformation than the upper classes.

8. Regional differences: Political regions in which power was decentralized, such as the principalities of Germany and the federated cantons of Switzerland, were more favorable to the Reformed faith than regions where power was centralized. In centralized states (France, Spain, and England), church abuses were under tighter curbs, so these states had been more successful in retaining a share of church revenues.

The substantial number of factors that may have shaped individual attitudes toward the Reformation underscores a serious methodological problem. How can we evaluate the relative importance of so many different influences, especially given the fact that these influences often overlapped in individual lives? Within imperial cities, city councils may indeed have been slower to accept the Reformation compared with the general populace. But the members of such governing bodies were probably older, on average, than the rest of the population, and probably more economically successful as well. Three different hypotheses are potentially involved in this behavioral relationship. Controlled for age and class, were council members really less receptive toward Protestantism than their imperial city contemporaries? Maybe, maybe not.

To overcome these kinds of interpretive problems, I have assembled a representative sample of 718 individuals who played prominent roles in the Reformation.[22] My survey draws on every social stratum within sixteenth-century society, from royalty to peasants, and includes individuals from 16 countries. These participants are classified as Catholics, Lutherans, Calvinists, and so forth according to the published designations of Reformation scholars. In terms of occupational status, the sample includes three major subgroups: 144 members of Europe's royalty, who generally decided the religion of their subjects; 322 prominent theologians who fought for and against the Reformed faith; and 252 laypersons who were actively involved in the Reformation as magistrates, humanists, and university professors. Among members of the overall sample, 22 percent were executed for their religious beliefs, and another 10 percent were imprisoned or were forced to flee to another political region.

MODELING REFORMATION LOYALTIES

Multivariate models allow us to assess the influence of each potential predictor of Reformation loyalties while controlling for the influence of other variables. (Technical details about such models are provided in Appendix 7.) Regardless of the statistical approach that we take, birth order emerges as the best predictor of confessional choice. Firstborns typically defended the Catholic faith. Laterborns generally endorsed Protestantism.[23]

These findings are confirmed by the acid test of birth-order differences, namely, their presence among siblings who have grown up together in the same family. Especially among European royalty, a high proportion of the sample were siblings of one another. Of these siblings—103 individuals—three-quarters are correctly classified by birth order in terms of how they responded to the Protestant rebellion.[24]

Only one other predictor—age—comes close to matching the explanatory power of birth order. Young people were particularly likely to support the Reformed faith.[25] It is illuminating to compare the influence of age with that of birth order. In 1520, a typical 70-year-old laterborn was as open to the Reformed faith as a typical eldest sibling who was 30, a 40-year difference. Among participants in the Reformation who were over the age of 40, laterborns were 17 times more likely than firstborns to support the new faith.[26]

The predictive power of birth order may be compared with another influence on confessional choice, namely, social class. As Reformation scholars have long maintained, lower-class individuals were significantly more open to the Reformation than were upper-class individuals. Still, this relationship is inflated by the fact that lower-class people were more likely to be laterborns than were prominent members of

Support for the Protestant Reformation by Social Class and Birth Order

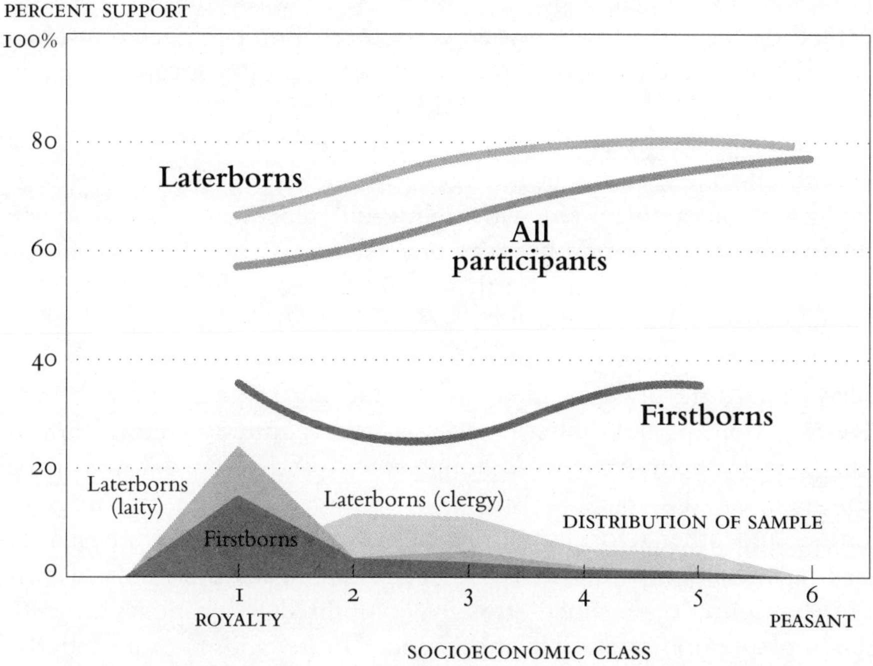

FIGURE 11.1. Adoption of the Protestant Reformation, stratified by social class and birth order. The influence of birth order is substantial, and it is also consistent within each social class. In addition, there is a modest tendency for individuals in the lower classes to express greater support for the Reformation relative to upper-class individuals. Much of this socioeconomic trend is owing to birth-order differences. Rulers and other members of the titled nobility tended to be firstborns, as can be seen from the sample distributions plotted at the base of the chart. Relative to these elites, people from the lower classes were more likely to be laterborns. This bias toward greater laterborn participation is especially true among the lower clergy, a group that strongly supported the call for church reform.

the titled nobility. Lower-class status is also moderately correlated with being a clergyman, especially being a member of the *lower* clergy, which was particularly supportive of church reform. Lower-class status and clericalism are in turn moderately correlated with being laterborn, so the causal relationship between class and religious stance is by no means straightforward. When we control for these recruitment biases, the division of opinion by birth order proves to be *15 times greater* than divisions by social class (Fig. 11.1).[27]

The spread of the Reformation is a clear confirmation of the powerful role that geography plays in history. As a rule, northern Europe accepted the Protestant faith, whereas southern Europe rejected it. How can sibling differences have been as important as I claim if geography played such a decisive role in the final outcome?

Although geography played an undeniable role in the spread of church reform, what has been largely overlooked is the fact that geography was often correlated with sibling differences in political power. The key to this relationship is the practice of "partible" inheritance, a form of territorial inheritance that occurs whenever rulers divide their lands so that each son receives a piece of the political pie.

This form of inheritance contrasts with primogeniture, which preserves territories in undivided form.[28] During the early years of the Reformation, partible inheritance was more common among Protestant than Catholic princes. Although the Reformation did not create this political difference, it strongly reinforced it. The teachings of Luther and other reformers specifically advocated partible inheritance as a manifestation of brotherly equality.[29] The leading Catholic dynasties, by contrast, remained strongly committed to primogeniture. In lending support to partible inheritance, Protestantism protected the interests of its laterborn backers, just as Catholicism tended to protect the interests of firstborns.

At the Peace of Augsburg in 1555, Protestant and Catholic rulers formally agreed on the principle *cuius regio eius religio* (whose realm, his the religion). Each ruler decided for his subjects what the official religion would be (Fig. 11.2). It follows logically that if a ruling house's territories were undivided, as was the Hapsburg empire, these territories were much more likely to be governed by a firstborn or eldest son. Such centralized powers included France, Spain, and Portugal—countries that remained loyal to the Church of Rome. Had it not been for the death of Henry VIII's older brother Arthur at the age of fifteen (and the complications that ensued when Henry failed to achieve a surviving male heir), England might have remained Catholic, as Ireland did. Owing to its many principalities and their frequent practice of partible inheritance, German soil presented an ideal region for the triumph of Protestantism. In short, owing to local disparities in territorial inheritance practices, sibling differences were crucial agents in the geographic spread of the Reformation. The more that principalities were subdivided, and hence available for political control by younger sons, the more these territories tended to adopt the Protestant cause. As a

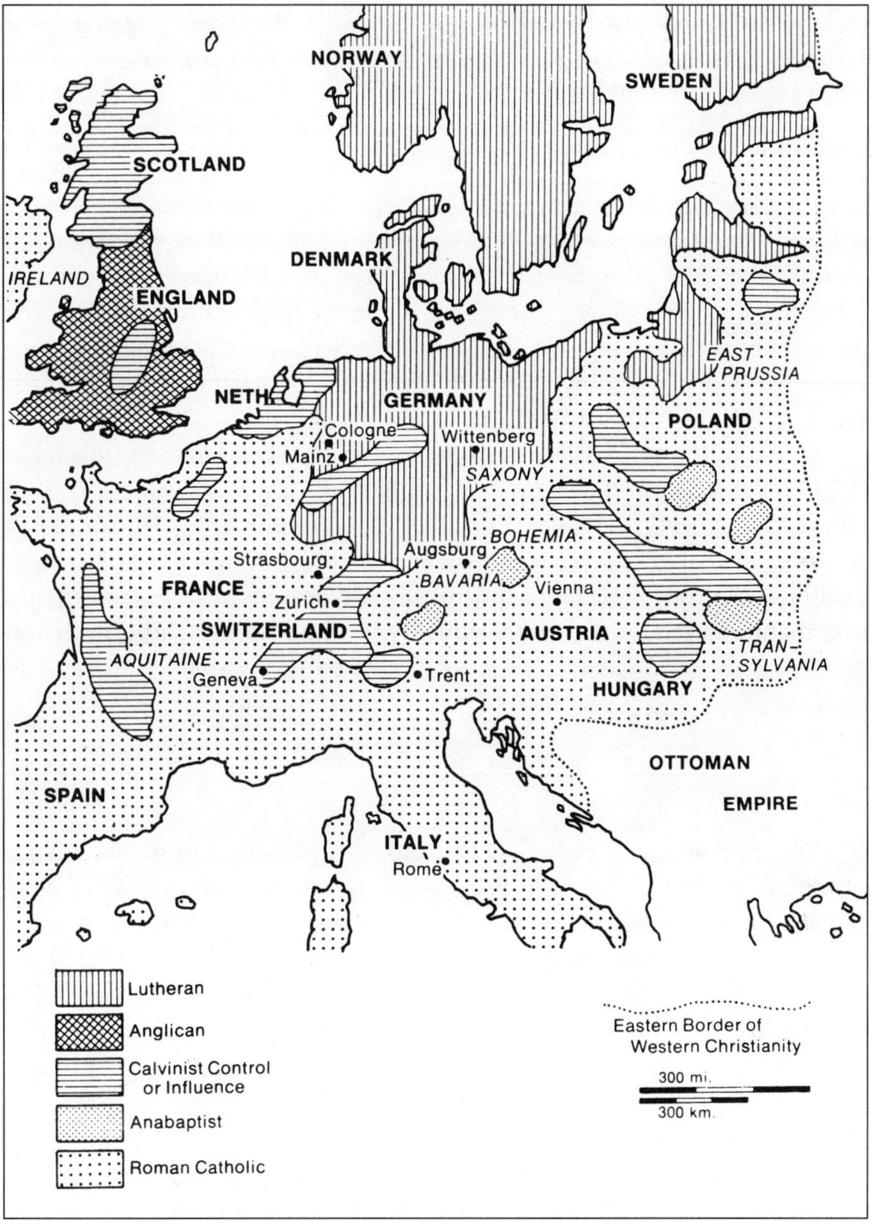

FIGURE 11.2. The religious map of Europe at the time of the Peace of Augsburg (1555). This peace agreement allowed each ruler to decide the religion of his territory. Although the distribution of Protestant territories appears to be heavily determined by geography (especially distance from Rome), many local geographic disparities resulted from birth-order differences among the ruling princes.

result, today's religious map of Europe still reflects the psychological influence of the birth order of rulers more than four centuries ago.

Reformation Theologians

Like the laterborn princes of Europe, laterborn theologians were strongly attracted to the Protestant cause.[30] Martin Luther, a firstborn, is a prominent exception to this general trend, as is Philipp Melanchthon, who was Luther's close friend and his most important disciple. Still, most of the other major Reformation leaders were younger sons, including Huldrych Zwingli, John Calvin, Guillaume Farel, John Knox, Heinrich Bullinger, and William Tyndale.

Cases like Melanchthon suggest that my Reformation model is lacking one or more predictors that might account for such exceptions to the rule. One obvious predictor that is missing from the model is close personal association with a Reformation leader. When this variable is added to the model, it significantly increases the model's predictive success and also anticipates Melanchthon's support for the Lutheran cause. When judging the merits of controversial arguments, people are often swayed by personal ties.[31]

Reformation Martyrs

The role of birth order is even more impressive among Reformation martyrs than it is among princes and theologians. People who were willing to lay down their lives for their religious convictions were generally extremists. Among people in my sample who were executed for their Protestant convictions, 23 out of 24 (96 percent) were laterborns —a much larger proportion than is expected by chance.

Catholic martyrs present a different story. Given their greater adherence to tradition, firstborns generally found it difficult to flow with the Protestant tide. In countries that adopted the Protestant faith, firstborns sometimes suffered martyrdom rather than give up their religious beliefs. In England, Henry VIII's desire for a divorce from Catherine of Aragon put many elite firstborns in a difficult situation. In addition to being a matter of religious disobedience, opposition to Henry's break with the papacy became a *treasonable* offense. Firstborns such as Cardinal Thomas Wolsey, who as lord chancellor failed to give his full support to the king's divorce, paid the usual price. Arrested in 1530 on charges of high treason, Wolsey died before he could be executed.

The martyrdom of Luther's Dutch follower Henry of Zutphen, in 1524. The man on horseback overseeing the execution, in the top left corner, is Christopher, duke of Braunschweig-Wolfenbüttel and archbishop of Bremen. The eldest of eight children (and a staunch Catholic), Duke Christopher ordered Henry's execution. The victim's birth order is not known. After Duke Christopher's death in 1558, his younger brother George replaced him as archbishop of Bremen. A third son, George welcomed the Reformed faith.

Throughout Europe, most Catholic martyrs were firstborns, the opposite trend to that observed among Protestants. Compared with firstborns, laterborns were 46 times more likely to suffer martyrdom for the Protestant faith! These findings highlight the crucial importance of historical context. Taking into account the local religious context, birth order correctly predicts the religious cause for which 86 percent of martyrs gave their lives. Laterborns were martyred for their religious radicalism, whereas firstborns were martyred for their continued adherence to the old faith.[32]

Martin Luther and Other "Exceptional" Individuals

Martin Luther, a firstborn, reminds us once again that there are always individual exceptions to aggregate generalizations. Still, we can ask which factors help to explain these exceptions. In Luther's case, there is no shortage of candidates. His openness to change is explained, in part, by his being a member of the lower clergy, as well as by his residence in a territory that was generally favorable to the Reformation. Based on these and other influences, Luther was more likely than not to be a reformer.

Not only is Luther correctly predicted to be a reformer, but he is also predicted to ally himself with the *moderate* faction for church reform.[33] Historians of the Reformation have divided the various Protestant sects into two major subgroups.[34] The "Magisterial Reformation" is associated with moderate reformers such as Luther, Zwingli, and Calvin. This historical label comes from the working alliance that existed between the local magistrates and the leading reformers. Backers of the Magisterial Reformation may have prodded their princes into ecclesiastic reform, but they rarely defied their secular authority. By contrast, the "Radical Reformation" was led by a variety of religious extremists, including Anabaptists, Spiritualists, and Rationalists. The members of these sects consistently challenged local political authority and extended the process of theological reform in directions that Luther and other Magisterial Reformers had never intended.

Assessed in terms of the multiple predictors of confessional choice included in the Reformation model in Appendix 7, Luther, Zwingli, Calvin, and Knox are all correctly classified as proponents of the Magisterial Reformation. Of these religious leaders, Luther has generally been considered "the least socially progressive" of the lot.[35] My multivariate model concurs, giving the three laterborn reformers (Zwingli, Calvin, and Knox) considerably higher probabilities of supporting radical social change. Luther's own conservatism in secular matters is reflected by his behavior during the Peasants' Revolt in the mid-1520s. He urged the German princes to "strike, kill, and burn" all the "mad dogs" associated with this movement. Luther also characterized Andreas Carlstadt and Thomas Müntzer, prominent leaders of the Radical Reformation, as "dangerous fanatics."[36] Compared with the leading Mag-

Predicted Probabilities of Adhering to the Protestant Reformation

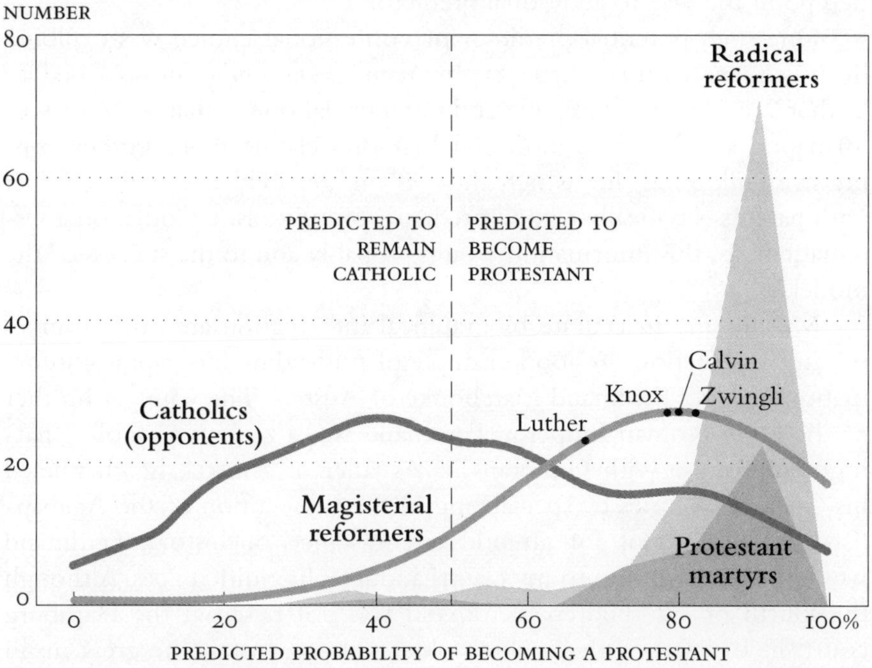

FIGURE 11.3. Predicted probabilities of adhering to the Protestant Reformation, based on a seven-variable model (N=718). Birth order is the best predictor of support for the Protestant revolt.

A seven-variable model does a good job distinguishing Catholics from moderate reformers who endorsed the Magisterial Reformation. Among the Magisterial Reformers, the model distinguishes Luther—the least progressive of the four major reformers—from Zwingli, Calvin, and Knox. The model assigns to Radical Reformers, such as Anabaptists, the highest predicted probabilities of endorsing the Protestant cause. The model also distinguishes Protestant martyrs, most of whom were Radical Reformers, from Protestants who died natural deaths.

isterial Reformers, champions of the Radical Reformation were more likely to be young, laterborn, lower class, and low in professional status. They were also more likely to be executed for their religious beliefs (Fig. 11.3).[37]

Like Martin Luther, most Reformation activists are exceptions on one or more significant predictors of confessional choice. Matters are different, however, when we consider *all* relevant predictors within the model. Using a multivariate model, 85 percent of the Reformation sample is correctly classified. Those individuals who remain misclassified point the way to additional predictors.

One such potential predictor of confessional choice was explored by psychoanalyst Erik Erikson. In *Young Man Luther* he ascribed to Luther "an Oedipus complex, and not a trivial one at that."[38] Most Reformation scholars have dismissed Erikson's claims about Luther's oppressive childhood, for which there is meager evidence. Still, conflict with parents is typically a good predictor of radicalism. Coded on a systematic basis, this information would probably add to the success of the model.[39]

Missing and inaccurate biographical information are other sources of faulty predictions. A good example of misleading biographical information involves Ferdinand I, archduke of Austria. The younger brother of the Holy Roman Emperor, Ferdinand was a zealous Catholic "hating compromise with Lutherans."[40] As ruler of Austria, he channeled his "devout energies by specializing in the persecution of the Anabaptists."[41] Were it not for an odd circumstance of history, Ferdinand would be an exception to my claims about sibling differences. Although the fourth of six children, Ferdinand was not raised at the Hapsburg court, in Brussels, with his three older siblings. Instead he grew up in Spain with his younger sister Katherine. He did not meet his older siblings until he was fourteen. Functionally he was raised as a firstborn, not as a laterborn. When Ferdinand's birth order is coded in functional terms, the multivariate model correctly predicts his harsh attitude toward heretics. His likelihood of remaining Catholic is predicted to be 76 percent, and his chances of becoming a Radical Reformer were just 1 percent. Ferdinand is one exception who appears to prove the rule.

FAMILY CONFLICTS

A multivariate model of the Protestant Reformation demonstrates that within-family conflict was widespread during the Reformation. In addition, family conflicts were far more important than differences associated with socioeconomic status, urbanization, or nationality. The family is the principal source of individual differences in radicalism, which is why its dynamics mirror the deepest schisms of society. It is this powerful psychological dimension to the Reformation that explains why so many people became Protestants "against their own economic and social best interests."[42] As most Reformation scholars have

Ferdinand I, archduke of Austria and brother of Charles V. Of Ferdinand's five siblings, one became a Lutheran and another was widely suspected of Lutheran sympathies. A functional firstborn, Ferdinand subjected his siblings to constant religious scrutiny. When the proposed marriage between Ferdinand's younger sister Katherine and Crown Prince John Frederick of Saxony, a Lutheran, was called off in 1524, Ferdinand remarked that he would have preferred to see his sister drowned than have her set foot in Lutheran territory (Ozment 1975:145).

argued, a Marxist approach sheds surprisingly little light on religious loyalties during the Reformation.

Historians have long acknowledged that Reformation families were sometimes divided, especially along generational lines. The Reformation, comments one scholar, entailed a "massive defection of sons and daughters."[43] Religious conflicts, observes another historian, set "neighbour against neighbour, father against son."[44] Indeed, the Reformation exhibited wrenching personal clashes that drove parents to inform on their own offspring, and offspring to betray their parents.[45] Although Reformation scholars have often noted such biographical facts, they have failed to appreciate the powerful intrafamily dynamics that explain them. For example, such disloyal behaviors were by no means confined to oedipal revolt along generational lines.[46]

The religious loyalties of spouses often conflicted, usually along birth-order lines.[47] An equally sharp split by birth order is true among parents and their offspring.[48] Firstborn parents found their religious authority being challenged by their laterborn offspring. In contrast, laterborn parents found their reformist inclinations being resisted by their firstborn offspring (and heirs apparent). The two forms of conflict often occurred within the same family. In northern Germany, the Hohenzollerns of Brandenburg provide a good example. In 1502 Electoress Elisabeth, second of the three children of King John of Denmark, married Joachim I, elector of Brandenburg. A firstborn, Joachim subsequently approved the sale of indulgences within his own dominions. It was Joachim's support for this practice that precipitated Luther's historic protest against such sales in 1517.

In 1527 Elisabeth of Brandenburg secretly received Communion from a Lutheran priest. She escaped imprisonment by her outraged husband by fleeing, in the middle of the night, to the safety of nearby Lutheran territory. Elisabeth was unusually knowledgeable about the writings of Reformation theologians, and it was said that she put "many a learned Doctor to shame."[49] Elisabeth corresponded frequently with Luther and played an important role in the spread of the Reformed faith.

Elisabeth's eldest child, Joachim II, was wary of reform like his father. He especially loved the pomp and ceremony of the Catholic service. Joachim II's younger sister Elisabeth became a Lutheran in 1538, as did their younger brother John II, but Joachim continued to resist the religious changes going on all around him. After his father's death in 1535, Joachim II entreated his mother to return to Berlin and the Brandenburg court. She repeatedly refused his appeals because of his conservative religious policies. Increasingly pressured by the religious arguments of his mother and younger siblings, and frustrated by the rising tide of Lutheranism in his own territories, Joachim II finally agreed to receive the Lord's Supper in its Lutheran form. Even so, his subsequent church reforms constituted "the least departure from the Roman Catholic position" in all of Germany.[50]

In 1545 Joachim II convinced his mother to return to the Brandenburg court. She spent the last decade of her life guiding her son's religious policies in a more enlightened direction. This example illustrates an important historical principle: Because of differences by birth order, parents are often more open to revolution than their own children.

There are many dramatic stories about family strife during the Reformation. The only approach to human behavior that makes sense out of the majority of these stories is one that encompasses a role for sibling rivalry and sibling contrast effects. Mismatches by birth order repeatedly help to elucidate why close relatives turned on one another, including why some people willingly sent siblings to their deaths. A good example of sibling dissension that turned lethal involves the Díaz brothers of Spain. While in Geneva during the mid 1540s, Juan Díaz converted to Calvinism. His brother Alfonso, a lawyer at the papal court in Rome, was shocked. He immediately traveled to Geneva in an effort to bring his brother back to the Catholic fold. As the better established of the two brothers, Alfonso offered Juan a handsome pension from the papal court if he would renounce his Protestant faith. Juan rejected the offer. Fearing that Juan would bring unbearable shame on their family back in Spain, Alfonso hired an assassin, who smashed in Juan's brains with an axe. Charles V refused to proceed legally against the murderers, causing outrage in Protestant countries.[51]

Another case of fratricidal behavior involves two of the brothers of Jane Seymour, the third wife of Henry VIII. After Henry VIII's death in 1547, Edward Seymour became lord protector of Jane's son, Edward VI. The king's death had created a golden opportunity for Protestants like the Seymours, who were gradually wresting political control from the older, and mostly Catholic, aristocracy. When Edward's younger brother Thomas began to intrigue for a share in the power, the lord protector allowed his brother to be arrested, tried, and executed.[52] Thomas Seymour's execution created "much popular odium" toward his brother and was a "fatal blow" to his authority.[53]

Yet another case of sibling conflict involved the most powerful Catholic family in England. Henry Howard, an arrogant earl (but a talented poet), was the eldest child of the third duke of Norfolk. The Howards, especially Henry, had long harbored a claim to the English throne. Henry went so far as to alter his coat of arms to strengthen his claim. The young earl also tried to persuade his younger sister Mary, the duchess of Richmond, to become Henry VIII's mistress in an effort to increase the family's influence over the king. Unlike her Catholic brother, Mary was an ardent Protestant who had offered her protection to the English martyrologist John Foxe. Mary indignantly rejected her older brother's sordid plan. Her "fratricidal hatred" toward her brother contributed to his subsequent arrest and trial for high treason.[54] Henry Howard was beheaded in January 1547.

Cases like the Díaz brothers, the Seymour brothers, and the Howards indicate that fratricide was the end result of some bitter Reformation antagonisms. From a Darwinian point of view, fratricide is a tactic of last resort because it eliminates a substantial portion of the killer's genes from the population. Still, the occurrence of fratricide during high-stakes conflicts, or when valuable resources are particularly scarce, poses no real puzzle based on the arguments of this book. During the Reformation, killing a sibling was merely an *extreme* manifestation of the most prevalent cause of social conflict: sibling strife.

The Wives of Henry VIII

Just as acts of fratricide can be understood as excessive expressions of a general Darwinian trend, so can many other lethal conflicts among Reformation family members. Perhaps the most famous of these dissensions involves Henry VIII and his six wives. Contrary to popular impression, not all of Henry's wives were unhappy with their marital choice. Indeed, several of Henry's wives got along rather well with him, and two of them outlived him. This variability in marital success provides a test case for my claims about sibling differences and marital discord.

Henry's wives differed from one another in telltale ways, such as their attitudes toward the Reformation, their social and sexual proclivities, and their obedience to their husband and king. At some point in their marriages, each of Henry's wives faced the crucial decision of whether to defy his authority. Their dilemmas were heightened by their gender. In this period of history, women were raised to "obey their parents without question."[55] Once married, they were expected to give absolute obedience to their husband. If their husband happened to be king of England, the decision to defy him could have lethal consequences.

Henry VIII's three least successful marriages were to laterborns who were each from the latter half of their sibship. None of these three spouses were particularly reserved in their personalities. As a result, they

Henry VIII (1491–1547). A second son and middle child, Henry was initially opposed to Lutheran reforms. For his efforts, he earned the papal title Defender of the Faith. His desire for a divorce opened his eyes to the advantages of religious reform. On Henry's capricious theology there is no better guide than Scarisbrick: "Alongside stubborn conservatism lay an often startling radicalism" (1968:409).

behaved like typical laterborns and resisted Henry's authority in perilous ways. Two of these wives ended their lives on the executioner's block, and the third (Catherine of Aragon) might also have done so had she not had the good fortune to be the aunt of the Holy Roman Emperor.

Catherine of Aragon. Only one of Henry VIII's wives was a lastborn—namely, his first wife, Catherine of Aragon. The fifth of five children, she was first married in 1501, at the age of sixteen, to Henry's older brother Arthur. Her fifteen-year-old husband died five months later, before the marriage had been consummated. Erasmus, who lived for six years in England, praised Catherine as "a rare and fine advocate" of the new Renaissance learning.[56] Tolerant of Henry's occasional infidelities, Catherine was uncompromising about her status as queen. After she had ceased to bear Henry children, she steadfastly declined to grant him a divorce, which would have undermined their daughter Mary's claim to the throne. This stubborn refusal eventually drove Henry, who was a theological conservative, to introduce the Reformation into England. By making himself supreme head of the Church in England, Henry circumvented papal authority and was able to secure a church-sanctioned divorce from the archbishop of Canterbury.

A brave and strong-willed woman, Catherine fought tooth and nail to maintain her status as Henry's lawful wife. For the last few years of her life she was repeatedly threatened with death. "Nature wronged the Queen," said Lord Chancellor Thomas Cromwell, "in not making her a man. But for her sex she would have surpassed all the heroes of history."[57] Catherine's last letter to Henry, professing her unabated love for him, brought tears to his eyes. Her death, at age fifty-one, was caused by cancer of the heart.[58]

Anne Boleyn. Henry's second wife, Anne Boleyn, was the second of three children and descended from royal blood.[59] In 1526, while Henry was still married to Catherine of Aragon, he fell madly in love with Anne. For the next six years he ardently courted Anne while he sought to obtain his divorce from Catherine. After four years of chaste courtship, Anne finally became Henry's mistress. Her first pregnancy required a secret marriage to the king in the spring of 1533 to ensure the legitimacy of any male offspring. A few months later, after Henry had finally obtained his divorce from Catherine of Aragon, the marriage to Anne was made official.

Soon after this second marriage, Henry VIII's relationship with Anne began to sour. She was demanding and difficult, and her status as

Catherine of Aragon in 1530 (age forty-five). Henry VIII's first and most courageous wife, she was known for her kindness and much beloved by the English people. After Henry divorced her, Catherine was commanded to call herself "Princess Dowager." She refused to acknowledge this title or to say that their daughter Mary was a bastard. In retaliation, Catherine was moved from place to place and forbidden to see her daughter. Gradually, Catherine's household and servants were whittled away until she was living in one room only, where she ate, prayed, and slept. To guard against poisoning, she had all of her meals prepared in her presence.

Anne Boleyn as queen. Owing to her liberal religious attitudes, Anne was widely suspected of heresy. This circumstance added to the belief that she had somehow bewitched the king.

queen only heightened her boldness. As one contemporary observer remarked about her: "When the Lady wants anything, there is no one who dares contradict her, not even the King himself."[60] Anne took "appalling risks," notes one historian, and she was "provocative and imprudent in the extreme."[61] She did not bother to disguise her strong Lutheran sympathies, which her husband did not share, and she even used her influence to save a heretic from being burned at the stake.[62]

After giving birth to a daughter (the future Queen Elizabeth I), Anne Boleyn had several miscarriages. The last of these miscarriages sealed her fate. Thomas Cromwell was charged with the dirty job of extricating Henry from this unhappy marriage. Following a well-orchestrated trial on trumped-up charges of adultery, Anne was found guilty and executed in May 1536.

Catherine Howard. The fourth of five surviving children, Catherine Howard was Henry VIII's fifth wife.[63] She has been described by historians as "vivacious" but "reckless."[64] Like her cousin Anne Boleyn, she met with the executioner's blade. Before marrying Henry, Catherine had become secretly engaged to a man with whom she subsequently had sexual relations. Under English law, her engagement was the legal equivalent of marriage, and to marry again was to commit bigamy and adultery. To make matters worse, Catherine fell in love with another admirer after her marriage to the king. A real risk taker, Catherine secretly engaged in sexual relations with this lover. Her perilous behavior finally caught up with her, and she was tried and beheaded in February 1542. Catherine's two former lovers were also executed. One, an aristocrat, was mercifully beheaded. The other, a commoner, was tortured, partially hanged, disemboweled and castrated, beheaded, and finally quartered.

Henry's three remaining marriages worked out reasonably well. Two of them can even be considered success stories. One marriage was to a firstborn. The other two unions were with laterborns, both of whom were born in the first half of their sibship. More important, these two laterborns were unusually shy, which modified the effects of their birth order, decreasing their likelihood of divorce by execution.

Jane Seymour. Henry's third wife, Jane Seymour, was an eldest daughter and the fourth of nine surviving children.[65] By all accounts, she was Henry's most beloved wife. According to Henry himself, she was endowed with "a kind and amiable disposition."[66] Others have described Jane as "timid" and "placid."[67] After her marriage to the king, she chose as her royal motto "Bound to obey and serve."[68] Jane wisely refrained from trying to exert political influence on Henry.[69] For a year and a half her marriage was happy. She died in October 1537, after giving birth to Edward VI.

Anne of Cleves. In contrast to Jane Seymour, Henry's fourth wife—Anne of Cleves—did not have a successful marriage. But Anne did live to tell about it. Henry had arranged to marry Anne, who was the second of four children, sight unseen. Upon meeting her, he discovered that she was plain, ungraceful, and barely able to speak English. He also found her physically repugnant, but it was too late for him to back out. After six months of marriage to this "rather dull, shy girl," Henry asked for an annulment on the grounds that the marriage had not been consummated.[70] To everyone's surprise, the "utterly docile" Anne readily granted Henry an annulment.[71] She received a handsome gift of lands, and lived out the rest of her life in England as the "king's sister." As Anne's English improved, she became a favorite at court, dancing merrily at parties with Henry's next wife, Catherine Parr. Anne of Cleves, concludes one historian, was "the wisest of Henry VIII's wives."[72]

Catherine Parr. The only firstborn among Henry's wives was the "motherly" Catherine Parr.[73] It is a pity that Henry waited until his last marriage to wed a firstborn, because this selection was one of his best. "A sober, godly spouse," Catherine managed Henry and his children better than any other wife.[74] In matters relating to the king's authority, she was generally heedful, as the following story illustrates. One time Catherine and Henry disagreed about a theological issue, and the mercurial Henry became irritated. "A good thing it is," he blurted out to Bishop Gardiner, "when . . . [I am] to be taught by my wife!"[75] After this argument, Henry went so far as to sign an article of heresy against Catherine, but he purposely allowed the papers to fall into her hands before having her arrested.

Upon seeing the document for her arrest, Catherine became hysterical and then physically ill. Henry sent his personal physician to her and even tried to comfort her himself. When Catherine finally regained her composure, Henry turned the topic of conversation to religion. Catherine immediately interrupted him, declaring that "it would be highly unbecoming of her to assert opinions of her own, especially in opposition to the king's wisdom." She had only meant, she added, to wile away the time with idle conversation. "Is it so, sweetheart?" replied the king. "Then we are perfect friends."[76] For firstborn Catherine Parr, matters of religious reform were distinctly subservient to the mindful obedience she paid to her volatile husband and king. As a result, she outlived him.

To sum up, the varied outcomes of Henry VIII's six marriages are directly related to the obedience that each wife showed to his authority. Obedience to authority is strongly influenced by sibling differences in birth order and temperament, particularly shyness; and so it was for Henry's wives. Controlled for differences in shyness, birth order is a significant predictor of the fates of the six wives.[77] The best marriages were to spouses of early birth rank or, failing that, to shy and cautious

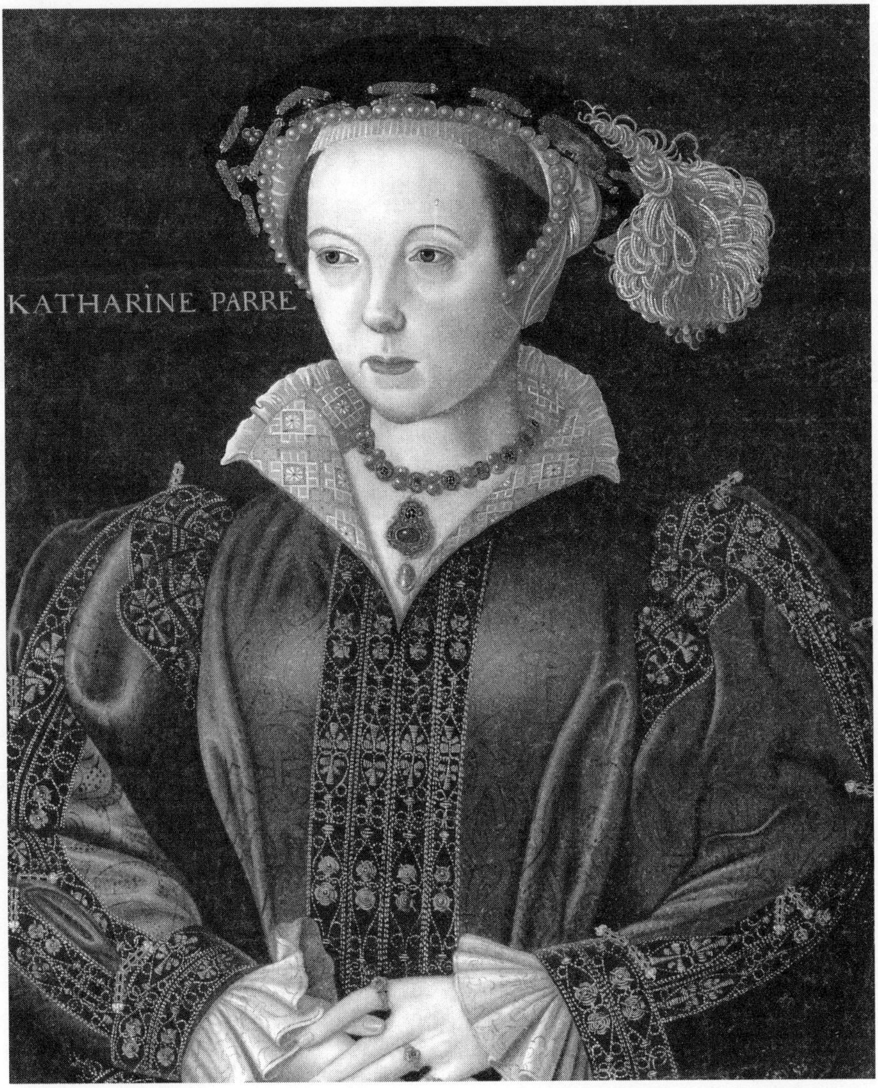

Catherine Parr, the sixth and last wife of Henry VIII. A royal chaplain said about her: "Her rare goodness made every day like Sunday, a thing hitherto unheard of in royal palaces" (quoted in Fraser 1992:377).

laterborns. Those wives who lost their heads tended to be late in birth rank and outspoken in their opinions.

It is noteworthy that Henry VIII, who began by marrying a last-born, subsequently married women who were earlier in relative birth rank, until he finally ended up with a firstborn.[78] Henry seems to have learned a lesson from his various matrimonial experiences: As far as opinionated kings are concerned, laterborns might be fun to court, but they tend to make rebellious wives.[79]

CONCLUSIONS

The Protestant Reformation constitutes a classic revolt against authority. Such revolutions typically transcend geographic and national subdivisions, as well as differences by class. Because siblings raised in the same family are nearly as diverse as unrelated individuals, revolutions typically polarize family members. These psychological considerations help to explain why the Reformation expressed itself "at all social levels."[80]

The fundamental role of sibling differences clarifies what must otherwise remain a paradox about events like the Reformation. Time and time again, the Protestant cause was adopted by people who "seemed to derive no obvious political advantage from any change."[81] The principal motivation for confessional choice was *personal*—an expression of "revolutionary personality"—and only secondarily a matter of socioeconomic gain. Such findings support the growing view among Reformation scholars that the core of this conflict was spiritual. Marxist claims about the Reformation as an "early bourgeois revolution" contribute little to an understanding of this event.[82] "Reformation history," concludes one historian, "cannot be converted into a mere shadow of economic and social history."[83]

Whether we consider heretics who became martyrs, conservatives who failed to change with the times, or rebellious wives who ended their lives on the executioner's block, differences between siblings were crucial to people's Reformation destinies. Reformation siblings were sometimes the instrument of each other's executions. Even when they were not, siblings never lacked for zealous allies who were willing to do the job for them. In a bitter contest to determine the true Christian faith, the Reformation witnessed the renunciation of brotherly love in favor of fratricidal feuding. As one Reformation historian has mused about the clashing Christian sects: "The quarrel was within the family."[84]

One final observation about Reformation history is relevant to the topic of sibling differences. The Reformation involved a radical change in worldviews. Protestant ideology promoted the values of *individualism* in a society long dominated by codes of *collectivism*. Collectivist cultures emphasize the family, community-based values, and traditional role relations.[85] Such cultures typically sanction inequities based on prerogatives of status and birth. By contrast, individualist cultures place greater value on equal opportunity and personal freedom.

Owing to its support for individualism, Protestant culture was more open than its Catholic predecessor to the many novel developments then confronting the Western world. These new developments included free enterprise, modern science, and a wide variety of increasingly egalitarian reforms.[86] Throughout the seventeenth century, Protestant scientists were significantly more open than their Catholic counterparts to controversial innovations.[87] Even Protestant firstborns reflected this cultural trend. During the past five centuries, the highest proportion of firstborn revolutionaries—including such creative scientists as Johannes Kepler, William Harvey, and Isaac Newton—occurred in the immediate wake of the Protestant Reformation.[88] To a substantial degree, this cultural trend was the legacy of sibling differences that had taken hold during the previous century.

Once the laterborn challenge to medieval authority had found fertile soil, it laid down roots that grew deeper still as each new generation compounded the radical gains of previous generations through sibling differences in assortative mating. Manifested as well in patterns of mass emigration to avoid religious persecution, differences between siblings gradually transformed the cultural face of Europe. By 1600, sibling differences had achieved full-fledged expression as ideological disparities between political states. With the birth of modern society, numerous local cultures have owed their liberating social values, and their respect for individualism, to Reformation laterborns who successfully rebelled.

12

POLITICAL TRENDS

In general, laterborns are more politically liberal than firstborns. But even when firstborns and laterborns share identical political goals, they often differ about how to attain them. In politics, tactical disagreements tend to reflect differences in sibling strategies. In addition to creating ideological disagreements, family niches promote variations in "political style." Compared with laterborn radicals, firstborn radicals tend to be more militant and moralistic. Their radicalism is usually inspired by idealism rather than by compassion for the underdog.

British psychologist Hans Eysenck has advocated a two-dimensional model of political thought. In addition to a *Conservative/Liberal* dimension, he has proposed a *Tender-minded/Tough-minded* dimension for assessing political attitudes.[1] Eysenck's model underscores the distinction between political goals and tactics. Tough-minded individuals tend to favor assertive political action. If they adhere to conservative political views, tough-minded individuals generally support the need for law and order, a strong military, and the death penalty. Liberals who are tough-minded tend to eschew these conservative political positions. But their tough-mindedness finds expression in their support for issues such as a woman's right to an abortion. If they become dedicated revolutionaries, tough-minded individuals are capable of sanctioning violence, including terrorism. Whether conservative or liberal, tough-minded individuals are inclined to agree that "the end justifies the means."[2]

On personality tests, tough-mindedness is correlated with two of the Big Five personality dimensions: Extraversion and, even more strongly, Agreeableness/Antagonism.[3] Tough-minded individuals tend to be leaders rather than followers, stubborn rather than flexible, and moralistic rather than empathetic. Such individuals are used to getting their own way. Not surprisingly, men are more tough-minded than women.[4]

In addition to being a male propensity, tough-mindedness is a firstborn characteristic. To get what they want, eldest children tend to engage in aggressive behavior. In her pioneering studies of birth order, Helen Koch found that firstborns were rated higher by teachers on anger, quarrelsomeness, cruelty, blaming others, faultfinding, and insistence on rights.[5] These psychological differences were more pronounced among males than females. Relative to their younger brothers, firstborn males seem to be budding "terrorists."[6] In their families of origin, these terrorist inclinations tend to be of small consequence (except to younger siblings). During radical revolutions, firstborn predilections for tough-minded policies can result in large-scale terrorism.

FOUR POLITICAL STYLES

Eysenck's model posits the existence of at least four styles of political thought. In world history, most political movements correspond reasonably well with one of these four styles, which also reflect four differing personality profiles. An awareness of these distinctions helps to dispel considerable confusion about what makes a given political upheaval "radical."

1. Tough-minded support for the status quo. Tough-minded conservatism is exemplified by absolute monarchy. This style of government often takes the form of despotism. Overthrowing such regimes has been the goal of most political revolutionaries.

For most of history, absolute monarchy has been the birthright of firstborns and eldest sons. In a world of tough-minded support for the status quo, social standing has usually been based on prerogatives of birth, including birth order. The practice of primogeniture reinforced the socioeconomic advantages of a favorable birthright, and also tended to promote their association with a conservative worldview. In medieval Europe, landless younger sons were widely recognized as a threat to political stability. To avoid rebellion at home, tough-minded rulers—who were usually either firstborns or eldest sons—sent these younger sons to fight in wars on foreign soil.[7]

In more recent times, tough-minded styles of conservative thought have manifested themselves in a variety of right-wing movements. Such

Political Attitudes by Birth Order

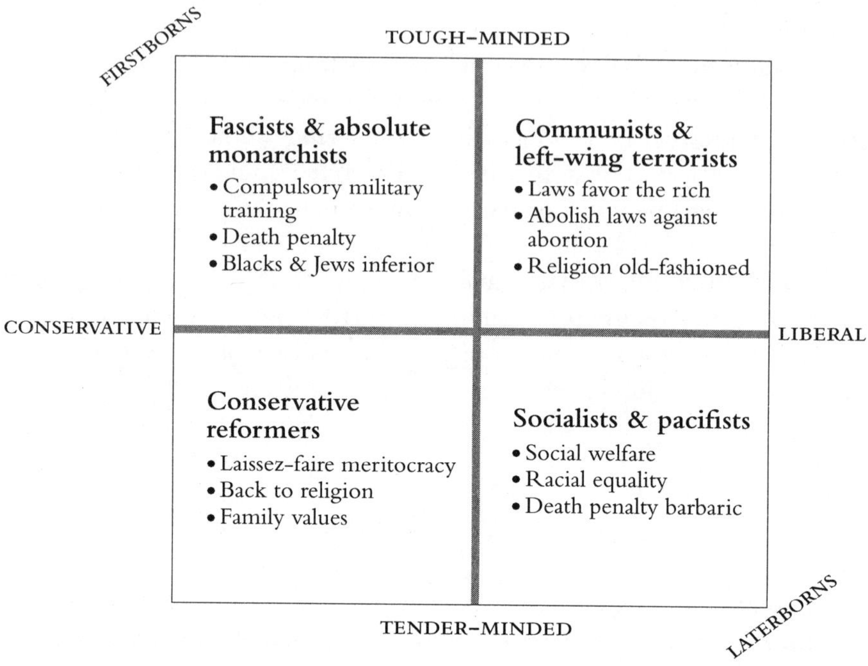

FIGURE 12.1 A two-dimensional schematic of political attitudes (after Eysenck and Wilson 1978). The figure specifies four political styles associated with four contrasting psychological profiles. In terms of birth order, conservative ideologies will typically attract firstborns. Among conservatives, firstborns will gravitate toward those ideologies, such as fascism, that are tough-minded. Among liberals, laterborns will gravitate toward tender-minded ideologies, such as socialism and pacifism. Both firstborns and laterborns will be attracted to the other two political philosophies (libertarianism and Communism), but for different reasons. The most likely reason for laterborns becoming Communists is their being unusually tough-minded. The most likely reason for firstborns doing so is their having been raised in a radical family.

movements include neo-Nazi organizations, fascism, and fundamentalist religious sects. Tough-minded conservatives tend to devalue people who are not like themselves. They are particularly inclined toward racism, as are firstborns (Fig. 12.1).[8]

2. Tender-minded support for the status quo. Not all conservatives are militant about their political beliefs, or seek to force them on others. Libertarian and laissez-faire political philosophies are both examples of conservative thinking that incline toward tender-mindedness. In practice, this second political category allows for limited reforms, such as improved systems of social welfare.

For reasons of heredity as well as upbringing, some younger siblings endorse conservative social values.[9] No matter how conservative their political views are, laterborns still tend to exhibit compassion for people who are less fortunate than themselves, and for this reason, they are generally open to moderate reforms. A good example of this political philosophy is enlightened despotism, a term that was applied to the most reform-oriented monarchs of the eighteenth century. As benevolent rulers, the enlightened despots sought to promote the welfare and individual freedom of their subjects. They brought moderate reforms to a previously conservative world order, abolishing torture, restricting capital punishment, and extending toleration to Jews.[10] The most famous of these reformist monarchs were Catherine the Great of Russia, Charles III of Spain, Frederick the Great of Prussia, Joseph II of Austria (and his younger brother Leopold II of Tuscany), Stanislaw II Augustus of Poland, and Napoleon Bonaparte.[11] Six of these seven rulers were laterborns, and—more unusual still—four of them were younger sons.[12] A firstborn, Catherine the Great defies the general trend. Still, on average, women are more tender-minded than men.

3. Tender-minded support for liberal social change. With this third political category, the trend toward social reform is even more developed than it is in the previous category. Eysenck has explicitly identified this third political philosophy with "reformist conscience."[13] Prominent examples of liberal reformers include antislavery advocates, free thinkers, socialists, and utopian dreamers. I have already reviewed a variety of these liberal reform movements in earlier chapters and have shown that, as a general rule, such movements have been consistently backed by laterborns and opposed by firstborns. Prominent laterborn reformers include Voltaire, Rousseau, Jefferson, and Marx. The most famous women reformers have also tended to be laterborns, including Mary Wollstonecraft, George Eliot, Florence Nightingale, Susan B. Anthony, Elizabeth Cady Stanton, Margaret Sanger, and Virginia Woolf.

Reform movements that advocate pacifism represent a particularly pronounced form of tender-minded liberalism. During the sixteenth century, Anabaptism was a prominent instance of this social philosophy. Like the Quakers a century later, members of this sect renounced all forms of aggressive behavior. Among the rulers of Europe, a refusal to fight was considered seditious, and Anabaptists were heavily persecuted by Protestant and Catholic authorities alike. Of the early Protestant sects, Anabaptism attracted a particularly high proportion of laterborn converts.[14] Mahatma Gandhi and Martin Luther King, Jr., are recent examples of tender-minded liberals who have successfully promoted the philosophy of passive resistance. King was the second of three children. Gandhi, who strongly influenced King, was the youngest of four. As a child, Gandhi was unusually shy.[15]

4. Tough-minded support for radical change. This last category of political movements includes Communist regimes, as well as terrorist groups that seek radical social change. Social radicals tend to be laterborn, but birth order further subdivides radicals in terms of their tough-mindedness. Owing to their characteristic inflexibility and penchant for aggressive action, firstborns are inclined toward *militancy.*

The biographical circumstances that nurture tough-minded radicalism are somewhat restricted. Tough-minded radicals tend to have liberal parents, or to have grown up within political systems in which revolution is already entrenched as the status quo. A case in point is Ernesto "Ché" Guevara, who fought alongside Castro during the Cuban revolution and later gave his life fomenting revolution in Bolivia. "It is no accident," comments one biographer, "that the future Ché Guevara hated the upper classes, hated the bourgeoisie, hated in general the whole existing social, economic, and political system: he had grown up doing so, taught from infancy by his dominating mother." Ché, the same biographer concludes, was "essentially his mother's creation."[16]

As a revolutionary leader, Guevara's tough-minded firstborn style is readily identifiable. Throughout his political career he displayed "a deep capacity for hate, and a healthy respect—even a taste—for violence."[17] In 1959, he personally supervised the liquidation of thousands of Batista supporters. These summary trials and executions became "Cuba's version of the Reign of Terror—and Ché Guevara's name became synonymous with it."[18]

After coming to power, Communist regimes often turn to firstborn leaders in an effort to maintain power. In the former Soviet Union, the revolutionary achievements of Vladimir Lenin and Leon Trotsky—both younger sons—gave way to the dictatorial leadership of two functional firstborns: Stalin and Khrushchev.[19] Another tough-minded firstborn, Mao Tse-tung, carried out a lifelong campaign of radical revolution in China.

There is an important difference between appealing to tough-mindedness as an ad hoc construct so as to dismiss inconvenient exceptions, and using this idea as a legitimate scientific hypothesis. The difference lies in the process of hypothesis testing. To merit explanatory acceptance, the construct of tough-mindedness must be applied to everyone, not just to those individuals whose behavior fails to accord with a cherished hypothesis. The two-dimension model that I have just reviewed has the virtue of being readily testable. For example, evidence showing that fascists are predominantly laterborns would constitute a convincing refutation of this model, as would evidence that pacifists are typically firstborns. Because the model specifies four distinct classes of political events, it is refutable in at least four distinct ways.

Left-Wing Militants

The political careers of three particularly tough-minded radicals are instructive because they demonstrate that the same family background that made one sibling a left-wing militant failed to have a similar effect on other siblings. In general, the eleven siblings who grew up in these three families all shared liberal social and political convictions. They differed substantially, however, in their proclivities for tough-minded implementation of these convictions.

Carlos the Jackal. A good example of a left-wing militant is Ilich Ramírez Sánchez, better known as Carlos the Jackal. Finally arrested in 1994 after a long career in international terrorism, Carlos has boasted of killing 83 people.[20] His father, a prominent Venezuelan lawyer, was a fanatical Marxist who named each of his three sons—Ilich, Lenin, and Vladimir—after the famous Russian revolutionary Vladimir Ilich Lenin. As the eldest of the three Ramírez children, Ilich took eagerly to his father's Marxist message and later implemented it under his code name Carlos. His two younger brothers, who were exposed to the same message, adopted conventional careers as an engineer and a businessman. One might say that they rebelled against what, within their own family, was the establishment viewpoint.

In 1966, when the brothers were seventeen, fifteen, and seven, their father sent them to England to practice their English and to learn more about the Old World. A close acquaintance in London has remarked about Ilich: "He was overwhelming in some ways. . . . All conversation with him would sooner or later turn into a kind of debate. He was hardheaded about getting his own way."[21] In London, the two elder brothers were taught Russian by an émigré nun. She recalled that Ilich was more keen than Lenin, "as if learning the language was the most

Carlos, with his mother and an unknown women, at a Venezuelan embassy cocktail party in London in the late 1960s. Carlos was his mother's favorite son and he had, as she noted, "the same temperament as her own—the hedonistic extrovert, the unquenchable *joie de vivre.* But behind this facade she often caught glimpses of his father's stubbornness, his brooding uncertainty and something else—strength she called it; others might have felt that viciousness was a better word" (Smith 1976:85). During this period in his life Carlos was always elegantly attired, and a real charmer with the ladies. "There was this aura of affluence around him," a London friend recalled, "that he was slightly more high-class, better situated than the rest of us" (Demaris 1977:43).

important thing in his life."[22] About this same time Ilich was fond of saying: "Bullets are the only thing that makes sense."[23]

During the 1970s Ilich became Carlos and carried out a series of bombings and assassinations in Europe. His biggest failing as a terrorist was his ego. "He could hardly bear to keep a secret," notes one biographer, "even when his liberty and perhaps his life were at risk."[24] Only a few weeks after he had organized a rocket attack at Paris's Orly airport,

Carlos got into an argument over airport security with a British friend. "Given the right element of surprise," Carlos maintained, "it would be easy to get through security at Orly and onto an aircraft."[25] Carlos's friend, who was unaware of his terrorist activities, disagreed. Carlos then described, in intricate detail, how to outwit the security systems at the Orly airport. The friend recalls: "He wasn't giving it as a hypothetical situation. He was saying, 'I've been there lots of times and I know what can be done.' "[26] After this discussion, Carlos's friend became suspicious. The next day he opened a suitcase that Carlos had left at his apartment for safekeeping. Inside were three pistols, a silencer, three M26 grenades, two pounds of gelignite explosive, and several false passports! Fortunately for Carlos, the friend hesitated before going to the police, and Carlos eluded capture.

Carlos's most famous exploit was in Vienna, in 1975, when he and four accomplices kidnapped several dozen OPEC ministers. This act of terrorism was designed to punish Iran and Saudi Arabia for their moderation toward Israel. During the kidnapping, three people were killed—one of them by Carlos, who pumped five bullets into his victim. "My son has turned out to be a general," his father proudly exclaimed when he heard news of the OPEC kidnappings.[27]

Carlos negotiated an airplane from the Austrian government, and the five terrorists flew their hostages to Algiers. The Venezuelan oil minister recalls that Carlos "acted like a movie star" during the flight. "He boasted of his deeds, handed out autographs, and told us the OPEC attack was a completely new operation developed by himself to secure the existence of a Palestinian state."[28] Eventually the oil ministers were ransomed back to their governments. The price is rumored to have been $50 million.[29]

Despite paternal efforts to radicalize the three sons, only Carlos became a terrorist. The second brother, Lenin, also attended KGB spy school, but he was never as belligerent as Ilich and took a much more scholarly approach to the spy business. Eventually Lenin returned to Caracas, where he has lived quietly as an engineer. He has described himself as "left wing" but is no longer active in politics.

In 1976 the youngest brother, Vladimir, gave an interview to a reporter from the *London Observer.* "Of course I'm with my brother," he asserted, "we're a very united family. But me, I'm about as politically neutral as you can get. I once got attracted to the Liberal Party in London. You can't go more neutral than that, now can you?"[30] About this time, an old school chum wrote to him: "Vlad, mate, if MI5 have been

Carlos and four other terrorists, with their OPEC hostages, boarding the DC-9 aircraft that flew them from Vienna to Algeria. Wearing a white trench coat and a Basque beret, Carlos is standing on the left, closest to the bus. During the flight to Algiers the pilot asked Carlos why he was a terrorist. Carlos replied: "Because violence is the one language the Western democracies can understand" (Smith 1976:276).

checking up on you, they'll have got dead bored. All you used to do was go to football, have a pint or two at the Windsor Arms and go out with your girl friend."[31] Unlike his eldest brother, Vladimir could not bring himself to hate Jews. He was so well liked by the Jewish kids with whom he played football in London that they nicknamed him Isaac.

Mussolini. Another instructive career in left-wing militancy is that of Benito Mussolini, founder of the Italian Fascist movement. Mussolini's father, a blacksmith, raised his son to worship Karl Marx.[32] Like Carlos the Jackal, Mussolini was named in accordance with his father's political predilections. Mussolini's three given names—Benito, Amilcare, and Andrea—were picked to honor three left-wing revolutionaries (Juárez, Cipriani, and Costa).

As a young man, Mussolini joined the Italian Socialist Party and gradually moved up through the ranks. With the advent of World War

I, Mussolini favored intervention, but most socialists strongly opposed this policy. A man of violent passions, Mussolini decried the antiwar sentiments of his fellow socialists and instead sought to promote nationalist and imperialist aims within his party. Owing to his repeated calls for political violence, Mussolini was finally thrown out of the Socialist Party in 1914. Thereupon he founded the Italian Fascist Party. What began political life as a liberal Marxist organization was gradually transformed, under "Il Duce," into a military alliance with Adolf Hitler. It is largely owing to this accident of history that fascism is now a "conservative" rather than a "liberal" movement. What has remained constant about this movement is its tough-minded nature.[33]

Mussolini's younger brother Arnaldo revered Benito and even wrote a biography of him. Arnaldo was outspoken, however, about his brother's "deplorable streak of delinquency," and he considered some of his brother's political actions as bordering on "criminal."[34] Excessive violence and a penchant for cruelty are firstborn traits, which even Mussolini's admiring younger brother found uncongenial in a fellow socialist.

Mao Tse-tung. For firstborns, another route to militant radicalism is through conflict with parents.[35] Mao Tse-tung, the eldest of four children, provides a good example. His father was a severe taskmaster. "He was a hot-tempered man," Mao told an American visitor in the 1930s, "and frequently beat both me and my brothers. He gave us no money whatsoever, and the most meagre food."[36] Mao identified with his father's ill-treated workers. Once a month the workers were given eggs to go with their rice, but never any meat. Charged with political tension, Mao's family evolved its own party system. Mao later described these family factions for his American visitor:

> There were two "parties" in the family. One was my father, the Ruling Power. The Opposition was made up of myself, my mother, my brother and sometimes even the labourer. In the "United Front" of the Oppression, however, there was a difference of opinion. My mother advocated a policy of indirect attack. She criticized my overt display of emotion and attempts at open rebellion against the Ruling Power. She said it was not the Chinese way.[37]

In the end, Mao's tough-minded opposition prevailed. "I learned to hate him," Mao asserted, "and we created a real United Front against him."[38]

TESTS OF THE MODEL

Supreme Court Voting

For the conservative/liberal dimension of political thought there is already considerable empirical evidence pointing to the existence of sibling differences, especially in terms of birth order.[39] A review of U.S. Supreme Court appointments, as well as the voting records of these justices, corroborates this evidence.

Since its creation in 1789, the Supreme Court has had 108 justices. Several significant trends emerge from an analysis of these data. Among the appointees, firstborns are moderately overrepresented relative to expectation, based on sibship size.[40] This finding reflects a well-documented tendency for firstborns to excel at academic achievement.

Of greater interest is the even stronger relationship between birth order and judicial style. One striking manifestation of this relationship involves the appointment choices of American presidents. Over the last two centuries, Democratic presidents have shown a consistent tendency to nominate laterborns to the Court. Republican presidents have manifested the opposite trend.[41] John F. Kennedy and Lyndon Johnson together made four appointments to the Court. All four were lastborns. As a result, the Warren Court eventually boasted 9 laterborn justices and no firstborns. With Richard Nixon's election to the presidency in 1968, Republicans held the power of Supreme Court appointments for the next fourteen years (Jimmy Carter had no opportunity to fill a vacancy). It is no secret that Nixon, Ford, Reagan, and Bush all sought to reverse the liberal bent of the Warren Court. These four Republican presidents added 6 firstborns to the Court, out of their 10 available appointments.[42]

The reason for this strong relationship becomes apparent when we consider how the justices have actually voted. Since 1946, the voting records of the justices have been rated by various legal experts on a conservative/liberal dimension. Relative to firstborn justices, laterborn justices have been significantly more likely to vote in a liberal direction.[43] With 0 as the most conservative and 100 as the most liberal rating, the 12 firstborn justices have received an average rating of 33, compared with a rating of 43 for the 11 middleborn justices. The 9 lastborns on the Court boast the highest mean rating (61). In sum, family niches are strongly reflected in concepts of justice. At the level of the

"Well, heck! If all you smart cookies agree, who am I to dissent?"

Sibling differences are typically a good predictor of dissent from the majority. On the Supreme Court laterborn justices have issued significantly more dissenting opinions than their firstborn colleagues. One firstborn justice—Horace Gray—boasted that, in 20 years on the bench, he only once dissented from the majority!

United States Supreme Court, sibling differences determine the laws of the land.

Although American presidents, in their Court appointments, have systematically tapped the connection between birth order and liberalism, this relationship has never been an explicit part of the appointment process. There is good reason why it should in fact be so, from the perspective of the appointing president. If a president wishes to push the Supreme Court in either a conservative or a liberal direction, this individual must rely entirely on a nominee's *past* judicial opinions. Family niches, however, predict openness to experience. Birth order, in particular, is a reliable predictor of openness to *future* social change. Let us suppose that a Republican president happens to nominate a conservative lastborn to the Court. This president runs the risk that his appointee may become more liberal after joining the Court, something that happened to President Eisenhower. In 1953 he nominated Earl Warren, the younger of two children, to the Supreme Court. As a previous Republican governor of California, Warren seemed like a safe bet. After taking his seat on the Court, however, Warren had a judicial change of heart. Later, as chief justice, he presided for sixteen terms over the Court's support for wide-ranging social reforms. One historian has described the Warren Court as "a revolution made by judges."[44] During the 1960s, disgruntled conservatives adopted bumper stickers with the message "Impeach Earl Warren." Eisenhower later acknowledged that his choice of Warren had been the "biggest damn fool thing I ever did."[45]

World Revolutionary Leaders

Mostafa Rejai and Kay Phillips (a political scientist and a sociologist) have sought to identify the most important characteristics of "revolutionary elites." They have documented the lives of 135 political leaders drawn from 31 rebellions.[46] Their historical survey begins with the English Civil War in the 1640s and culminates with political disturbances during the 1970s in countries such as Guatemala, Israel, Northern Ireland, South Africa, and South Vietnam.

Along with other information about family background, Rejai and Phillips considered birth order. They found meager evidence for sibling differences in radicalism and concluded that the formative years are "relatively unimportant" in the development of revolutionary personality.[47] Instead, these two investigators emphasized the importance of situational factors, such as being faced with a political crisis or growing up in a developing country.

Based on their own data, Rejai and Phillips's 135 political leaders can be readily classified into three groups: *conservative, moderate,* and *radical* revolutionaries. Conservative revolutionaries include a small number of figures whose goal has been the return to a former way of life. Religious considerations have often played an important part in this class of events. Catholic opposition to British rule in Northern Ireland is a good example of this kind of political protest, as are most anticolonial movements. Rejai and Phillips call this class of conservative leaders "defenders of the faith."[48]

At the other end of the political spectrum are radical revolutionaries. These individuals are readily identifiable by their efforts to overthrow existing governments in favor of new and generally less autocratic ones. Rejai and Phillips have characterized these political leaders as "agitators" and "professional" revolutionaries, categories they also acknowledge as mirroring the "popular stereotype of the revolutionary."[49] Well-known examples of radical revolutionaries include lifelong, dedicated rebels such as Lenin, Mao Tse-tung, Ho Chi Minh, and Chou En-lai.

In between these two political extremes fall the numerous moderates in Rejai and Phillips's study. These two researchers have further subdivided this middle group into subgroups such as "founding fathers," "moralists," "scholars," and "members of the establishment in good standing."[50] Examples of moderate revolutionaries include George Washington, Thomas Jefferson, Gabriel Mirabeau, and Abbé Emmanuel-Joseph Sieyès. The last of these figures supported the progressive reforms associated with the early stages of the French Revolution. In 1799, however, he engineered the coup d'état that brought Napoleon to power. Moderate revolutionaries have tended to be associated with populist revolutions, like those occurring in America and France during the eighteenth century. By comparison, professional revolutionaries have sought to change the system long before the populace is fully prepared for change. Ché Guevara, who died while trying to export the Cuban revolution to Bolivia, was a "radical" revolutionary.

When assessed according to this progressive scale of radicalism, political activism is strongly correlated with birth order. Compared with defenders of the faith, professional revolutionaries are 18 times more likely to be laterborns than firstborns! Moderate revolutionaries are evenly balanced between these two political groups.[51] George Washington and John Adams represent typical firstborn revolutionaries or "founding fathers" who fall into the moderate rather than the radical camp.[52] Georges-Jacques Danton, Leon Trotsky, Fidel Castro, and Yasir Arafat are all examples of radical (and laterborn) revolutionaries.

Situational Considerations: Crises and Wars

Another important predictor of revolutionary leadership is the nature of the revolutionary situation. Moderate revolutionaries, including firstborns, have typically led protests that were precipitated by a political or economic "crisis."[53] By turning minority protests into popular causes, crises make revolutionary change acceptable to the majority of the population. As Lenin once remarked: "It is not difficult to be a revolutionary when the revolution has already flared up and is at its height."[54] By sanctioning the need for change, crises open the door to firstborn leadership. In addition, crises generally call for tough-minded measures to resolve the situation.

Laterborns are truly "professional revolutionaries" and tend to seek political change through thick and thin. They include figures such as Russia's Vladimir Lenin, China's Liu Shao-chi, and Stephen Biko, the dedicated civil rights activist who was beaten to death in 1977 by the South African police. These patterns are consistent with those I have already documented for scientific revolutions. Firstborns eventually adopt new ways of thinking, but they are most likely to do so in a state of conceptual crisis, or during the later stages of the revolutionary process. Laterborns rarely wait this long to rebel.[55] Although situational factors do play important roles in revolutionary leadership, most of the explained variance can be traced to sibling differences.[56]

Wartime affects political leadership in much the same way as crises do. Wars enhance the appeal of tough-minded leadership, increasing the likelihood that firstborns will rise to power. Among American presidents elected during wartime, firstborns are significantly overrepresented. This same finding holds true of British prime ministers over the last two centuries.[57] Laterborn political leaders, who seem to be more flexible than firstborns, have also done a better job of keeping their countries out of war.[58]

During World War II, most major political leaders were firstborns or only children, including Roosevelt, Churchill, Mussolini, and Stalin. Adolf Hitler is an exception, but only a partial one. He was his mother's first surviving child, and she strongly favored him over two older stepchildren from her husband's previous marriage.[59] Hitler's closest half-sibling was six years his senior, a larger-than-average gap. An older brother left home when Hitler was seven, so he became the eldest son at home. Hitler had three younger siblings, two of whom survived childhood. Owing to his violent temper even as a child, Hitler was an expert at getting his own way.

Birth Order and Militancy

The movement to end slavery in America presents another test case for the relationship between birth order and tough-mindedness. During the decades prior to the Civil War, abolitionists were divided as to whether slavery was best combated by militant action or nonviolent methods.[60] William Lloyd Garrison, the middle of three children, advocated passive resistance, including the shunning of all political action. Slavery, he argued, should be opposed through moral arguments alone.

Of the sixty-one reform movements I have surveyed in American history, abolition attracted the largest proportion of laterborns. *Militant* abolitionists, however, included a disproportionate number of firstborns. The most famous slave revolt in America was led by firstborn

Nat Turner. In 1831, Turner and his followers "butchered horribly and mangled the bodies" of more than sixty white persons, including several dozen children. "With the blood of his victims Nat sprinkled his followers."[61] More than two hundred slaves also perished in this violent uprising.[62]

Turner was raised by his parents to believe that he was "intended for some great purpose." A fiery preacher, he considered himself to be divinely inspired. As he told his lawyer during his trial: "Having soon discovered [myself] to be great, I must appear so, and therefore studiously avoided mixing with society, and wrapped myself in mystery."[63] Like tough-minded characteristics, messianic beliefs are a firstborn trait.[64] Messianic leaders expect to be followed unquestioningly, not to negotiate with their followers.

Like Turner, abolition leader Henry Highland Garnet was born into slavery. His father, Joseph, was "an angry, brooding militant" who impressed upon his eldest child his direct descent from a Mandigo prince.[65] The Mandigo people, the father taught Henry, were a great warrior race and could never be enslaved for long. In 1824 Joseph fled to the North with his family, which included nine-year-old Henry and his younger sister.

Inspired by his father's example, Henry Garnet became a leading figure in the abolition movement. In 1843 he delivered a militant speech at a national black convention, calling for nationwide insurrection by slaves against their "blood-sucking" owners. "You had far better all die," he urged his fellow blacks, "die immediately, than live as slaves."[66] Garnet's speech "electrified the nation."[67] Many fellow abolitionists were horrified by Garnet's call for insurrection, and he quickly became known as "the most dangerous black man in the North."[68] Still, Garnet's demands for militant action began to attract a following, and his views reinforced resistance to the Fugitive Slave Act of 1850. Another committed militant, John Brown, had Garnet's address of 1843 reprinted and distributed at his own expense. By the late 1840s even lastborn Frederick Douglass, who had earlier opposed black rebellion, had come around to Garnet's point of view. Committed to establishing a national homeland for blacks, Garnet was a forerunner of twentieth-century black nationalists such as Marcus Garvey and Malcolm X.[69]

In order to test the hypothesis that birth rank is related to militant reform, I have used four independent judges to classify abolitionists according to a five-step scale of violent action.[70] Among militant abolitionists, firstborns are significantly overrepresented. So are youngest

Militancy in Racial Reform Efforts and Birth Rank

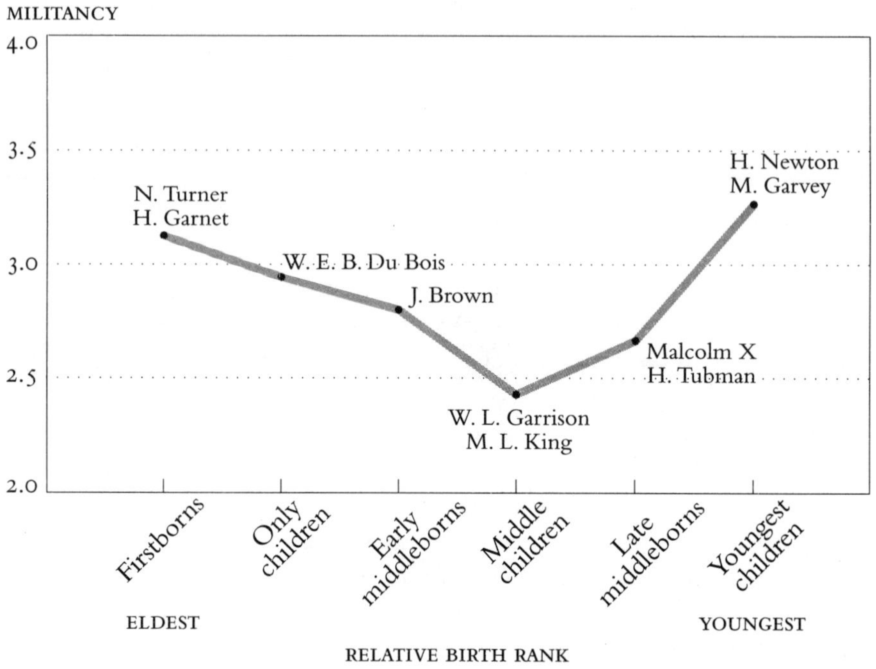

FIGURE 12.2. Militancy in racial reform efforts as a function of relative birth rank (N=94). The most militant reformers have tended to be firstborns (such as Nat Turner and Henry Highland Garnet) or lastborns (such as Huey Newton and Marcus Garvey, a prominent black nationalist). Individuals advocating nonviolent approaches to racial reform have tended to be middle children. For example, William Lloyd Garrison and Martin Luther King, Jr., were both the second of three children. Another middle child of three, Booker T. Washington, was often criticized for his "accommodation" to white society. The curvilinear relationship between relative birth rank and militancy is statistically significant. The linear relationship is essentially nil.

children. The most nonviolent group comprises middle children, such as William Lloyd Garrison.[71]

A similar relationship between birth rank and militancy is present among activists in the black rights movement. Once again, middleborns were the most strongly inclined to adopt nonviolent methods.[72] As a source of militant tendencies in racial reform, birth order is *twice* as predictive as gender or race.[73] The relationship between birth order and militant advocacy of racial equality is shown in Figure 12.2.[74]

During the 1960s, youngest children typically joined with radical firstborns in supporting militant action. The Black Panther Party was founded in 1966 by Bobby Seale, the first of three children. His co-founder and minister of defense was Huey Newton, the youngest of seven. Newton and his next older brother, Melvin, illustrate the contrast that often separates lastborns from middle children, who are typically less "radical" in the sense of being less militant. "Baby Huey" was pampered by his parents, and Melvin lost out on the attention. Comments one biographer:

> Four years separated Huey from Melvin, his brother next in line. Four years and a welter of personality differences. They looked at the same world through very different eyes; they reacted to the same world with very different sensibilities.[75]

Melvin was a loner. He was also studious and was ridiculed by the other kids for being "a square." Unlike Melvin, who was peaceable, Huey overcame an early fear of fighting. As they grew older, Huey and Melvin increasingly went their separate ways, as the same biographer has noted:

> [Huey] learned how to fight—how to kick ass. He learned how to walk that black walk and talk that black talk. You walked so that it looks to a foreigner like something's wrong with your leg but ain't nothin' wrong with your leg—you walk that way 'cause you bad—you a *bad* motherfucker.[76]

Huey eventually took to cruising around Oakland, California, carrying a loaded shotgun to intimidate the police. Melvin concentrated his childhood ambitions on getting an education. He eventually obtained a master's degree in social welfare and teaches for a living. When Huey set forth the Black Panther Party's "Ten-Point Program," Melvin corrected the text for grammatical mistakes. Huey ended up serving time in prison, convicted of killing a police officer.

Martin Luther King, Jr., the second of three children, is a particularly good example of the tendency for middle children to favor nonviolent methods of political protest. Even as a young boy, King's "preferred mode of self-defense was verbal rather than physical."[77] King's younger brother Arthur regularly teased their sister to the point of tears, and Martin often intervened on her behalf. Arthur was

Martin Luther King, Jr., addressing the March on Washington from the steps of the Lincoln Memorial (28 August 1963). "I have a dream," he told the crowd of nearly a quarter of a million people, "that one day on the red hills of Georgia sons of former slaves and the sons of former slave-owners will be able to sit down together at the table of brotherhood" (Davis 1969:263). Three and one-half years later this dedicated exponent of nonviolence was gunned down in Memphis, Tennessee, by an assassin. King was only thirty-eight.

"downright contemptuous" of Martin's verbal defenses when faced with aggression, and, for his own part, Arthur did not hesitate to retaliate when attacked by other boys.[78]

Middle Children

For many years I believed that middleborns were little different from lastborns, except in being somewhat less liberal. The biographical facts I have just related have changed my mind. Variations in family niches induce adaptive responses in personality, including the propensity for aggression. The most tough-minded individuals are firstborns. Lastborns are militant, too, but for different reasons. Their militancy arises because they are daring, zealous, and liberal, not because they are particularly dominant or punitive (firstborn traits). Compared with other siblings, middle children are more flexible and favor compromise. When they rebel, they do so largely out of frustration, or compassion for others, rather than from hatred or ideological fanaticism. Middle children make the most "romantic" revolutionaries.[79]

The key to the psyche of middle children is their unique family niche. Being a middle child appears to foster a considerable willingness to compromise, apparently because the occupation of this niche embodies a minimum of personal power. Unlike their older siblings, middle children are not in the best position to employ brute force, especially when acting alone. In addition, middle children are usually hampered in their expression of aggression toward their youngest sibling, who is typically protected as the "baby" of the family. In altercations with their siblings, youngest children can better afford to hold their ground because parents, and sometimes other siblings, intervene on their behalf. As a result of such tactical constraints, middle children do well to develop diplomatic skills and to cultivate coalitions with other siblings. One researcher has reported that middle children exhibit the lowest scores on a measure of "Fear of Power" in other people.[80] Expressed another way, middle children are more willing to *share* power with others.

The family of one famous political revolutionary illustrates the effectiveness of sibling coalitions instigated by middle children. Ernesto "Ché" Guevara had four younger siblings. In part because Ché suffered from asthma, his mother "went to extremes in the care and affection she lavished on the boy," favoring her eldest child over the others.[81] Resentful at the extra attention Ché received, his younger siblings sometimes retaliated en masse:

> They would torment him and sometimes attack him physically. Ernestito, however, was not the kind to take such treatment lying down. One day, in a fury, he hurled himself at his younger brother and two sisters all together and fought them tooth and nail. But three are stronger than one, and they overcame him. To crown their victory, they doused his head in ice-cold water and gleefully watched as Ernestito went into a violent asthma attack.[82]

None of Ché's siblings became involved in politics. Three of them chose artistic professions (architecture and design) that involved working with other people. The fourth, Ché's immediately younger brother, became a lawyer. It is relevant that Ché's fall from power in Cuba was

Fidel Castro and Ché Guevara (*right*), reviewing a peasant militia parade in August 1960. Castro became increasingly alienated by Guevara's orthodox Marxism, which led Ché to criticize Castro's Soviet backers. In 1965 Castro finally forced Guevara out of the government. Ché went to the Congo, where he fought against white mercenaries, and then to Bolivia, where he tried to start a peasant revolution. Surrounded by Bolivian rangers on 8 October 1967, Ché was captured and later executed.

due to his inability to compromise. Fidel Castro, a middle child, regarded Ché as "too dogmatic, arrogant, and upstartish."[83] Fidel was particularly annoyed by Ché's Marxist intransigence and eventually forced him to step down as minister of industries. Different niches, different political styles.

Especially in small sibships, the personality differences among siblings are reinforced by sibling contrast effects. Just as a second child seeks to be different from the first, a third child seeks to be different from the second. As a result, "jump pairs" tend to end up being more similar than adjacent pairs.[84] Because they are not usually adjacent to firstborns in the family hierarchy, lastborns are freer to emulate firstborn characteristics, including tough-mindedness.

Evolutionary psychology sheds light on some of these sibling differences, especially the tendency for parents to favor firstborns and lastborns over middle children. Normally, parents nurture their children based on the relative merits of investing in additional children. Because firstborns are older than their siblings, and hence more likely to survive and to reproduce, they have an edge in courting parental investment. When parents are no longer able to have additional children, it is sensible for them to concentrate investment in those children who are most vulnerable to death and disease.[85] The losers in this Darwinian calculus are often middle children.[86] Lastborns fare better because they are the only member of the family to receive parental investment undiluted by the needs of a younger rival.

CONCLUSIONS

Political attitudes involve two psychological dimensions, both of which are intimately related to the subject of sibling differences. Laterborns tend to be more liberal than firstborns, but firstborns tend to be more tough-minded than their younger siblings. A two-dimensional model of political styles alerts us to the fact that "radical" acts are not necessarily the work of "extreme liberals." In the psychology of political revolutions, the key to understanding individual behavior is to disentangle these disparate forms of radicalism and to appreciate their substantial sources within the family.

Armed with a two-dimensional model of political behavior, we are now in a position to understand one of the most violent revolutions in Western political history. The French Revolution, and especially its culmination in the Reign of Terror, is largely a story of sibling strife. This fraternal schism was fought at two equally lethal levels: conflicting ideological goals and bitter disputes over how to attain them.

13

THE FRENCH REVOLUTION

In the spring of 1789 a state of national bankruptcy forced Louis XVI to summon the Estates General for the first time in 175 years. A desire for fundamental changes on the part of the bourgeoisie (or Third Estate) soon created a political impasse within this parliamentary body. Simultaneously, crop failures and famine created widespread frustration, followed by numerous local insurrections. Patriotic clubs rapidly sprang up all over France, creating a "spider's web" of revolutionary agitation directed by the Jacobin Club of Paris.[1]

On 12 July, Parisians learned that the king was seeking to curtail the voting power of the Third Estate, which represented the common people. Fearful of what royal troops might do to enforce the king's position, Parisians decided to arm themselves. On the morning of 14 July 1789, a mob took 32,000 guns from the Invalides. In search of more weapons and gunpowder, the mob proceeded to the Bastille. The nervous governor, Bernard de Launey, ordered his small garrison to open fire, killing 83 citizens. After several hours of battle, the fortress capitulated. The angry mob then murdered three of the captured officers as well as the governor, and their heads were paraded on pikes through the streets.[2] The French Revolution had begun.

The day after the Bastille fell, Louis XVI dismissed the event as a "riot." The duke of La Rochefoucauld-Liancourt corrected his king: "Sire, this is not a riot, it is a revolution."[3] As the violence of the French Revolution gathered momentum, tens of thousands of lives would ultimately be sacrificed to the "national razor," as the newly invented guillotine came to be called. The height of this wanton carnage is known as the Reign of Terror, a period that lasted roughly a year (1793–94) and witnessed the execution of 40,000 people. Citizens increasingly turned on neighbors and friends. Some 300,000 people were

The fall of the Bastille (14 July 1789). Long a symbol of Bourbon despotism, the Bastille had previously housed some of the most famous exponents of Enlightenment thinking, including Voltaire.

denounced as "suspects." Many of these suspects were imprisoned and some were massacred by vengeance-seeking mobs. Mutual suspicion was so pervasive that people found themselves being denounced for trivialities. As one eyewitness recorded: "The most intimate friends no longer dared to stop or speak to each other. One trembled in one's apartment. If one laughed, one was accused of rejoicing over some bad news for the Republic; if one wept, one was accused of regretting its successes."[4]

The Constituent Assembly, which emerged from the Estates General in the late summer of 1789, gave way in October 1791 to the Legislative Assembly. Owing to Maximilien Robespierre's successful motion that no deputy from the Constituent Assembly should stand for reelection, the Legislative Assembly was much more sympathetic to the revolution than its predecessor. Still, the Legislative Assembly continued to work with an increasingly suspect king, who had lost most of his credibility after an abortive attempt to flee the country. In April 1792 the Assembly declared war on those foreign powers who were supporting the king's émigré brothers. Throughout the spring and summer, antagonism increased between the court and the Assembly, which nonetheless could not bring itself to dethrone the king.

On 10 August 1792 the people of Paris decided the king's fate. During the previous night a revolutionary "Commune" had been formed to replace the existing local government. To protect the king, the commander of the National Guard had deployed his troops around the Tuileries, where the royal family was residing. Summoned for talks with the Commune, the commander was arrested and then murdered, and his orders to the National Guard were countermanded. The Commune then directed an armed assault on the Tuileries. A massacre ensued in which six hundred of the king's loyal Swiss Guards were either shot or hacked to death by the mob. Robespierre proudly described this uprising as "the most beautiful revolution that has ever honored humanity."[5] With the fall of the monarchy, the Legislative Assembly dissolved itself to enable new elections to a National Convention, which convened the following October.

Meanwhile, the prisons in Paris were overflowing with royalists, "refractory" priests who opposed the revolution, and those of the Swiss Guards who had escaped massacre on 10 August. Nothing had been done to bring these people to justice, so the Commune took matters into its own hands. Between 2 and 6 September, roaming bands of paid assassins moved from prison to prison. After summary trials, more than a thousand people were put to death. Blood literally flowed through the gutters near the prisons.

The newly elected deputies of the National Convention took their seats in the wake of the prison massacres. Not surprisingly, the Convention was even more liberal than the previous Assembly. Anyone protesting the fall of the monarchy had been declared ineligible for election, and few royalist sympathizers dared run for office. The Left was finally in control.*

---

*The political terms "left" and "right" owe their current political connotations to the French Revolution. Within the Legislative Assembly, the deputies of these two contrasting persuasions had sat on opposite sides of the hall, with conservatives occupying the benches to the right. When the National Convention convened in a new building, the new deputies were reluctant to sit on the right side, lest they be accused of royalist sympathies. As a result, the deputies stratified themselves vertically, with the most radical deputies occupying benches at the top of the hall (Ozouf 1989d:380).

CAUSES OF THE TERROR

Two loosely defined parties emerged within the Convention. The party that ascended to power first was called the "Gironde," a label reflecting the fact that its leaders came from Bordeaux, in a geographic region called the Gironde. The party that eventually wrested power from the Gironde was called the "Mountain," named for its occupation of the uppermost benches of the National Convention. Positioning themselves between these two rival factions—both ideologically and physically—were the cautious and reticent deputies of the "Plain," who sat nearest the floor of the Convention. The ideological struggle between Girondins and Montagnards (deputies of the Mountain) lies at the heart of the Terror.[6]

The Gironde wanted the September murderers brought to justice. The Mountain sought to condone the murders in order to protect the Commune, the local Parisian government that had perpetrated the massacres. This feud is all the more puzzling in the light of the relative harmony with which these patriots had previously supported the revolution. "Newly elected provincial deputies," comments one historian, "looked on incredulously as those who had battled side by side against despotism and aristocracy now ripped one another apart."[7]

During the spring of 1793 the Mountain successfully contested for power with the Gironde, which was trying to curb the growing violence of the revolution. With the approval of radical Montagnards, the National Guard surrounded the Convention on 2 June 1793. The exits were blocked so that no one could leave the building, and more than a hundred loaded cannon were aimed at the door. An angry mob, estimated at 80,000, demanded the arrest of the Girondin leaders, 29 of whom were reluctantly handed over to the Guard. Five months later these Girondins were summarily tried and guillotined. Another 75 deputies who dared to protest these illegal arrests were themselves arrested and played no further role in the Convention.

Marxist Explanations

In conformity with Marxist theory, the French Revolution has been seen as a classic bourgeois revolution.[8] Albert Mathiez, writing in the early part of this century, was confident that the revolution was "in reality, a class struggle." Other French historians have reiterated this

The insurrection of 2 June 1793. It was a Sunday, and many workers were free to join the large crowd that gathered that day around the National Convention. The principal demand was the arrest of the Girondin leaders. When Girondin deputy Jean-Denis Lanjuinais (*at the podium*) called for something to be done, various Montagnard deputies tried to drag him down. Meanwhile the mob, which had invaded the Convention hall, threatened with pitchforks and pikes. Reluctantly, the captive Convention handed over the Girondin leaders. In the words of one deputy, terror had finally become "the order of the day."

conclusion, albeit in qualified terms.[9] Recent studies of a quantitative nature have shown that such socioeconomic differences, if they exist at all, are difficult to detect. Members of both political groups were solidly middle class—lawyers, businessmen, doctors, and clergymen. Only about 1 percent of the National Convention consisted of working-class deputies.[10] Contrary to common opinion, the chief victims of the Terror were not aristocrats. Eighty-four percent of the executions involved bourgeois merchants, artisans, and peasants.[11] Patrice Higonnet sums up the evidence on this score:

> The efforts . . . to distinguish Girondins and Montagnards either in terms of [political] principles or social class have not yielded much systematic evidence, and the paucity of the returns is all the more striking for the intensity of the search. . . . In the main, right and left were drawn from a single class and shared a common world-view.[12]

In short, whatever divided the Gironde from the Mountain was not social class or any other obvious *social* difference. Some participants of the French Revolution were acutely aware that the conflicts did not fall along class lines. Instead, the revolution resembled a contagion, sowing discord among friends and family.[13] The great Girondin orator Pierre Vergniaud called attention to this insidious feature of the Terror during the spring of 1793. The revolution had become, he somberly observed, "like Saturn, devouring successively all of her children."[14]

Among the Convention deputies, one can cite numerous anecdotal examples of such within-family clashes. Barère's republicanism cost him his marriage.[15] Le Bon's pious mother is said to have gone insane as a result of his radical persuasions.[16] Joseph Lacanal came from a large family "more royalist than the king."[17] In order to distinguish himself from the other members of his family, including four older royalist brothers, he changed the spelling of his last name to "Lakanal." Numerous other deputies found themselves having to explain awkward connections with royalist parents, offspring, or siblings.[18]

As the horrors of the revolution mounted, some deputies became mortal enemies of their own siblings. Deputy Jean Duprat fell out with his older brother Louis in 1791. The latter had been implicated in the massacre of royalist prisoners in Avignon, whereas Jean, as a Girondin, was attempting to halt the growing violence. The elder Duprat subsequently claimed that his brother's friends had tried to assassinate him, and he displayed his bruises at the Jacobin Club. Jean Duprat was forced to defend himself on the floor of the National Convention, revealing a sordid tale of sibling strife. In response, in April 1793, the elder brother denounced the younger for his "moderation." As a result of this public denunciation at the Jacobin Club, Jean Duprat was arrested three months later and guillotined with the rest of the Girondin leaders.[19]

Another deputy, Joseph Chénier, carried on a vehement political controversy with his royalist older brother, the famous poet André Chénier. When André was finally arrested during the Terror, Joseph did not try to intervene. Just two days before the fall of Robespierre, André Chénier was executed. In newspapers, and even scrawled on the door of his home, Joseph was long taunted with the accusation: "Cain, what have you done to your brother?" In actual fact, Joseph Chénier was not in a position to help his older brother, whom he had previously hidden from the authorities. As an ally of Danton, who had recently been executed by order of Robespierre and the Committee of Public Safety, the younger Chénier was himself under suspicion for his opposition to the Terror. When his parents urged him to intervene on behalf of his brother, he counseled that his brother was better "forgotten" in prison than brought to anyone's attention. The parents failed to heed this advice and wrote a letter pleading André's case to the Committee of Public Safety. This desperate act sealed André's fate on the eve of Robespierre's fall from power.[20]

Historians have been slow to treat within-family schisms on a par with socioeconomic interpretations of the Terror.[21] Still, some historians have begun to emphasize the "fratricidal" nature of this conflict.[22] Jacqueline Chaumié has described the Terror as a "rupture between enemy brothers" who stood for "two families of thought."[23] Patrice Higonnet concurs, remarking that the social similarity between Gironde and Mountain is precisely what made the struggle "fratricidal and merciless."[24] Among French historians, such allusions to "fratricide" are metaphorical and reflect the senseless fury of the Terror. This lethal feuding was not, however, metaphorical fratricide. Within the National Convention, it was deputy turning on deputy in ways that involved *systematic differences among siblings.* Foremost among these systematic differences are those that can be ascribed to the influence of birth order.

There are two straightforward ways to demonstrate the powerful role of birth order during the French Revolution. The first way involves analyzing the major political parties as they vied for power over time. A second and even more robust measure of birth-order differences makes use of voting patterns within the National Convention. Owing to a propitious accident of history—the fact that key votes within the Convention were recorded by name—we can actually perform this second test.

As the revolution gathered momentum, each newly elected body brought a higher proportion of liberals (and laterborns) to power (Fig. 13.1).[25] Staunch royalists, who had generally held power before 1789 and who vigorously opposed the revolution, were largely firstborns. Delegates to the Estates General, which precipitated the revolution in

Percentage of Firstborns within Major Political Parties as the French Revolution Took its Course (1789–94)

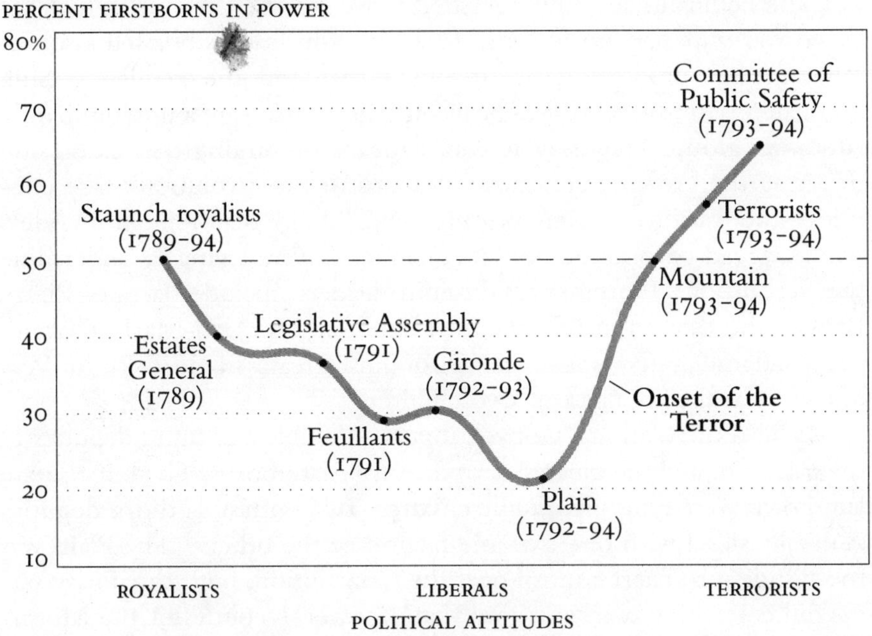

FIGURE 13.1. The mean percentage of firstborns within each major political party as the French Revolution took its course (1789–94). The relationship is strongly curvilinear. Firstborns dominate the most conservative as well as the most radical factions.

The break between the Gironde and the Mountain took place in early 1793. This rupture, which occurred as a result of the king's trial, gave rise to the repressive policies of the Terror. Directed by Robespierre and the Committee of Public Safety, the Terror was a distinctly firstborn political directive.

The curvilinear effect shown here is explained by the fact that, during the Terror, the "radical" position was not the "liberal" position. Firstborns sought to prove their revolutionary loyalties by their predilection for violence, not by their devotion to liberalism.

July 1789 and carried it through its first phase, included a somewhat larger proportion of laterborns. These delegates were replaced with an even greater proportion of laterborns as a result of elections to the Legislative Assembly. This trend toward increasing laterborn participation reached a maximum during the third year of the revolution. The Feuillants briefly held power during this period, taking their name from the convent of Feuillants in whose church they met.[26] This particularly laterborn group consisted of those "moderates" who had broken away from the militant Jacobin Club during the summer of 1791.

The Feuillants soon relinquished power to the Gironde, which favored war with foreign powers. The Girondin leaders boasted a somewhat greater proportion of firstborns than did the Feuillants. Still, compared with the royalist opposition, Girondins were a predominantly laterborn group. They saw war as a means of uniting the nation and directing the growing civil hostilities against the revolution's true enemies—the various foreign powers who, afraid that republican ideas would spread beyond the borders of France, were trying to undermine the revolution. Prominent Girondin leaders include Jacques-Pierre Brissot, the thirteenth of seventeen children, and Jean-Marie Roland, the youngest of five sons. The Girondins' greatest orator, Pierre Vergniaud, was the youngest of two children.

Within the National Convention, the flexible and timid deputies of the Plain boasted the greatest proportion of laterborns. These moderate laterborns were typically middle children. By contrast, lastborn deputies generally sided with one extreme faction or the other.[27] The Plain was too diffident to exert control over the Convention, but its majority status did determine who else could hold power. Deputies of the Mountain contemptuously disparaged these cautious souls as the "Toads of the Marsh." When members of this faction did dare to speak at the Convention, they were said by Montagnards to have "croaked." The Plain initially sided with the Gironde, which is why this party came to power before the Mountain.

The Mountain's triumph marked the beginning of a return to firstborn rule. As finally manifested in the "revolutionary dictatorship" of Robespierre and the Terror, France once again experienced political domination by firstborns.[28] Under the Terror, the degree of firstborn rule exceeded even that of the royalist opposition! Leading terrorists, such as the bloodthirsty Jean-Paul Marat, had much more in common with their firstborn tyrant, Louis XVI, than they ever dreamed.[29]

What Girondins and Montagnards clashed over was tactics, not ideology. As the French Revolution veered toward the Terror it became more "radical" by becoming more tough-minded and militant, not by becoming more liberal. Robespierre and other terrorists made a mockery of trial by jury and created a powerful dictatorship based on fear. The downfall and guillotining of the Girondin leaders lay in their doomed efforts to oppose this process. The political schism was fueled by sibling differences, not by class conflict.

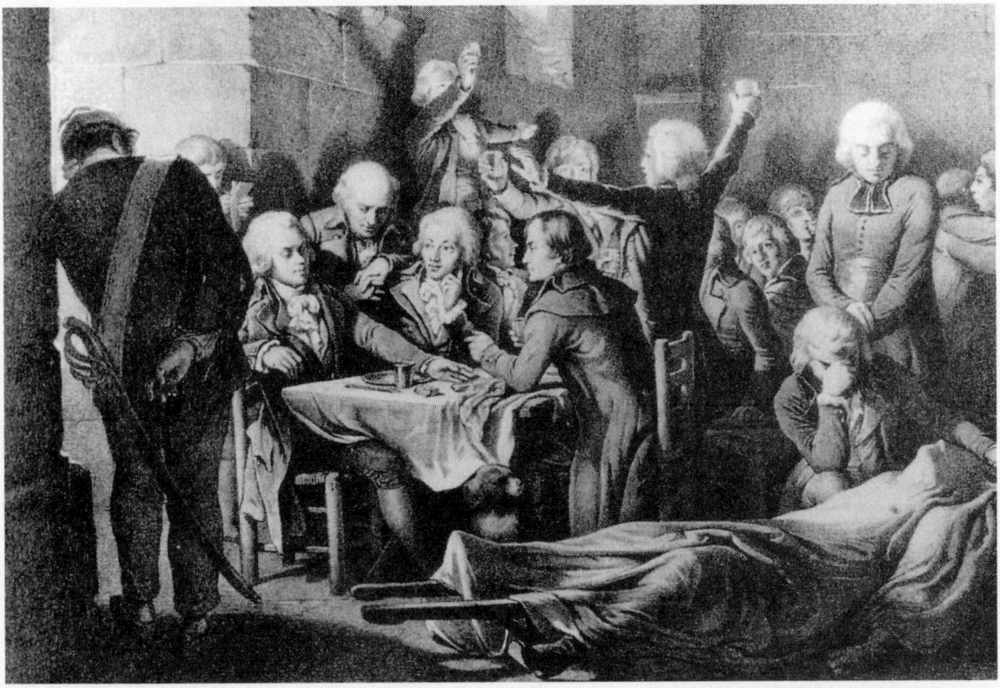

The last night of the Girondins (30 October 1793). The Girondins' greatest orator, Vergniaud, is seated at the end of the table (*facing forward, with his left arm outstretched*). In the right foreground is the body of Valazé, who had fatally stabbed himself after hearing the Revolutionary Tribunal's sentence of death. A priest and a distraught comrade look down at the body. Throughout the night, the deputies sang songs and talked quietly among themselves. The next morning, five tumbrels conveyed these 21 Girondins to their place of execution. Along the way, they sang the "Marseillaise." The last Girondin to be guillotined, Vergniaud, sang to the very end. With the silencing of Vergniaud's "holy voice," wrote French historian Jules Michelet, "one seemed to hear the dying voice of the Republic and of law" (quoted in Bowers 1950:496).

The Committee of Public Safety

Orchestrating the Reign of Terror were the twelve permanent members of the Committee of Public Safety. Seven of these twelve individuals were firstborns, the highest proportion in any major political faction during the revolution. Robert R. Palmer wrote a collective biography of these "Twelve Who Ruled" and noted that they "were almost all autocratic, jealous and short-tempered"—typical firstborn traits.[30]

Firstborns on the committee included Barère, Billaud-Varenne, Collot d'Herbois, Hérault de Séchelles, Prieur of the Côte d'Or, Saint-Just, and Robespierre. Originally a leader of the Plain, Barère was the ultimate conformist of the revolution. "It was his weakness," writes Palmer, "to agree with whichever group was successful. He was a liberal, even in his vacillation."[31] When the time was ripe, Barère finally turned on Robespierre and other terrorists in a desperate effort to save his own neck. "Testing the wind as always," notes another historian, Barère "made up his mind only at the last moment."[32] In contrast to Barère, who became a terrorist as a result of the revolution, Billaud-Varenne's personality gave clear "intimations of the terrorist he was to become."[33] Saint-Just represents "the *enfant terrible* of the Revolution."[34] Hot-tempered, selfish, and conceited, he ran away to Paris when he was nineteen, financing his trip with his mother's silver. Like Billaud-Varenne, he made the perfect terrorist because the predilection was instinctive. One biographer describes him as "cold and suspicious. . . . He saw conspiracies, traitors and corruptionists everywhere."[35] Collot d'Herbois was more unsavory still. A political fanatic, he was described by an acquaintance as "ill-natured, haughty, and vindictive."[36] During the Terror, Collot d'Herbois personally arranged for the execution of more than two thousand people in Lyons, after a Girondist rebellion there had been put down. He had two hundred people put to death in one day, carrying out mass executions by using cannon loaded with grapeshot. Because of Collot d'Herbois's zeal for vengeance in Lyons, he was nicknamed the Tiger.

Next to Billaud-Varenne, Collot d'Herbois, and Saint-Just, Maximilien Robespierre is a moderately sympathetic figure—an idealist whose adverse family background and consequent personality defects got the better of him. Robespierre's mother died when he was six, and his father abandoned his four children to the care of relatives. Robespierre's sister testified to the "total change" that came over her brother after their mother's death. From a carefree boy, he was transformed into a somber lad who "saw himself, so to speak, head of the family."[37]

Robespierre's father left behind a bad reputation and various debts, which deeply shamed his eldest child. When Robespierre, at the age of twenty-six, was elected to the Academy of Arras, he delivered a moving speech on "the harmfulness of the prejudice which caused the infamy of wrongdoers to cling to their family and relations."[38] Robespierre is a good example of the tendency for firstborn radicals to have experienced substantial conflict with a parent.

Maximilien Robespierre, sketched during a session of the National Convention. Under the portrait the artist has noted: "Eyes green, complexion pale, green striped nankeen jacket, waistcoat blue with stripes, cravat white striped with red."

Robespierre was gifted with an "oratory of the ego" that called attention to his uprighteous personal life. His speeches were "invariably punctuated by professions of martyrdom, of invitations to death" (Schama 1989:579). Having been abandoned as a child, Robespierre was hypersensitive to disloyalty and quick to take punitive action against those he suspected of it.

Although Robespierre's adverse childhood helped to make him liberal, these experiences did not make him tender-minded. Because of his unwillingness to compromise, he was nicknamed the Incorruptible.[39] One historian has observed about him that he "did not forgive easily," adding that he was "cold and distant" and "unable to smile."[40] Another historian offers a similar appraisal: "He had the virtues and the faults of an inquisitor. A lover of mankind, he could not enter with sympathy into the minds of his own neighbors."[41] Such qualities are typical of firstborns who, for whatever reason, espouse radical political views.

To understand the dramatic return of firstborns to political power during the Terror it is necessary to appreciate that "liberalism" was no longer the key to leadership after September 1792. With the prison massacres, and especially with the trial of the king later that year, the revolution entered a far more ruthless phase. This stage of mounting violence has generally been described as a period of "radicalization," a term that is somewhat misleading. For it was not "radicalism" of any simple sort that epitomized the Terror. On average, firstborn deputies are unlikely to have been more radical than their laterborn colleagues, as long as "radical" is taken to mean "extremely liberal." In any large population selected for liberal political views, laterborns will always predominate. This trend has been true in Western history for the last five centuries.[42]

On a number of key social issues, the Gironde was manifestly *more* liberal than the Mountain.[43] In contrast to the Montagnards, the Girondins expressed a positive attitude toward women and their involvement in politics. They also took a leading role in abolishing primogeniture, an initiative closely associated with support for women's rights.[44] Thus Mona Ozouf concludes: "The Montagnard charge of Girondin royalism is a red herring."[45]

Brother Deputies

Of the 893 deputies elected to the National Convention, 16 were brothers who grew up together, such as Maximilien and Augustin Robespierre. Class differences cannot explain the political differences that existed between these 16 deputies. In 12 out of the 16 instances, these brothers made their political alliances based on birth order. Younger brothers sat with the Gironde or the Plain, and elder brothers sat with the Mountain. More impressive still, no younger brother sat to the "left" of an older brother. Even in such a small sample, this trend is statistically significant and matches the broader trend within the Convention as a whole.[46]

In two of the three instances in which brothers sat together, the younger of the pair was more moderate. Robespierre's younger brother Augustin is a good example. As one biographer remarks about him: "It would have been hard to find someone more different from Maximilien."[47] Unlike the Incorruptible, who was rigid and intolerant of the people around him, Augustin was a true bon vivant—nicknamed Bon Bon by his friends. As a Montagnard, he was highly critical of terrorists such as Fréron, whose cruel excesses he sought to curb. Compared with Maximilien, Augustin showed far more tolerance toward factions within the Mountain. He even defended some of his brother's enemies on the floor of the Convention, earning himself a public rebuke from his elder sibling.[48]

Within-Party Factions

The influence of birth order is so pervasive that it even created schisms *within* parties. As the revolution progressed, faction after faction fragmented along birth-order lines. In 1791, firstborn Feuillants defected to become Jacobins. Out of the Jacobins emerged the leadership of the Girondins, who were again deserted by their most militant colleagues, the firstborns of the Mountain. Even when political figures remained formally allied under the same party label, they continually bickered among themselves along lines defined by birth order.[49] Among the Girondins, firstborns were typically more militant than their laterborn peers, who sought reconciliation with the Mountain. Of the amiable Girondin orator Pierre Vergniaud—a lastborn—one commentator asserts that he "perished as a victim of the hatred, passions, and the ambitions of the Buzots, the Guadets, and Barbarouxs [within his own party]."[50] Like other particularly militant Girondins, these three individuals were firstborns.

No faction illustrates the role of birth order more vividly than the Independents of the Mountain.[51] This group includes the most brutal extremists of the Convention. Within this generally bloodthirsty group, there was a sharp division between its most militant members, such as Billaud-Varenne and Marat, and the soft-hearted "Indulgents" who sought to moderate the Terror. The most famous of these Indulgents was Georges-Jacques Danton, whom Robespierre had guillotined in

Georges-Jacques Danton, with his hands tied behind his back, on his way to the guillotine. Warned by a friend about his impending arrest, Danton replied that "he would rather be guillotined than guillotine" (Matrat 1971:247). Just before he was executed, Danton asked the executioner if he might sing some verses that he had composed for the occasion. Having been given permission, he "sang loudly a verse of the fall of Robespierre, and then laughed as though he had been at the old café with his friends." His final words were: "Show my head to the people; it is well worth the while" (Belloc 1928:280).

April 1794. A revolutionary firebrand whose moving spirit was audacity, Danton was a flexible politician "incapable of viewing 'factions' and 'conspiracies' as indiscriminately as Marat and Robespierre."[52] Danton also felt no need to exact revenge on people with whom he disagreed.

Unlike Robespierre and other terrorists, he understood that most people are not born to rebel. As he tirelessly asserted in opposition to the Terror, the majority of individuals "are not born with revolutionary blood in their veins" and should not "be treated as criminals" for shunning militant measures.[53] Although the Independents of the Mountain were the most firstborn faction within the National Convention, the Indulgents were predominantly younger sons.[54]

THE KING'S TRIAL: A CASE HISTORY OF TOUGH-MINDEDNESS

Like any personality trait, tough-mindedness can be measured for most prominent historical figures. Fortunately, two centuries of French Revolution historians have collected an impressive pool of biographical information about the major players in this event. Based on a variety of indicators, I have created a measure of political tough-mindedness. My scale includes 19 readily documentable manifestations of militant, intolerant, vengeful, and otherwise antagonistic behaviors.[55] Using standard biographical sources for the deputies of the National Convention, I have been able to assess all 893 members on this measure.

Tough-mindedness is moderately correlated with birth order, even after controlling for party affiliations: firstborn deputies were more tough-minded than laterborn deputies.[56] The most tender-minded deputies were middle children, a finding that corroborates my claims in the previous chapter. These personality differences by birth order also help us to understand the ceaseless political schisms that turned these committed liberals against one another.[57]

How important were individual psychological differences in tough-mindedness compared with other considerations (mostly sociological) that historians have used to explain schisms within the National Convention? The trial of Louis XVI offers a convenient forum for answering this question. In December 1792, Louis was charged with treason before the Convention. A total of 721 deputies decided the king's fate, and their individual votes were recorded by name. For nearly two centuries, historians have studied these voting patterns in an effort to unravel the enigma of the Terror. As the deputies themselves fully recognized, these votes were a formal referendum on whether to accelerate or restrain the political violence.[58]

During the voting, no deputy dared to deny Louis's guilt, although a handful of deputies abstained from voting. Three additional verdicts were all closely divided. The first of these three votes focused on whether to appeal a death sentence to the people of France. This motion, sponsored by the Gironde, was defeated. The second vote involved the form of punishment: should the king suffer death for his treasonable activities? This vote was affirmed. The third and most crucial vote was over clemency. The Girondin leaders wanted to spare the king's life in order to arrest the radicalization of the revolution that was sure to follow. When the issue of mercy had been considered, the verdict was 361 deputies opting for death, 360 opposed. After all the counting, the king was guillotined because of a single vote![59] That single vote forever divided deputies into regicides and nonregicides and led to the purges that followed.

Laterborn deputies—especially middleborns—voted *for* the appeal to the people, *against* death, and *for* mercy.[60] Independently of birth order, tender-minded deputies also voted to spare the king's life.[61] The likelihood of a typical laterborn voting to execute the king is only 38 percent. The corresponding likelihood for a firstborn deputy is 73 percent—almost twice as high.

In addition to birth order and tough-mindedness, I have tested six other predictors of voting during the king's trial. These additional predictors encompass variables such as age, party affiliations, and social class that have been widely discussed by previous historians. Consistent with these previous historical claims, regicides were typically Montagnards, previously involved in revolutionary politics, and comparatively young.[62] Given the role of multiple predictors, some deputies were unusually predisposed against the king. Maximilien Robespierre's likelihood of voting for death was 97 percent, and Jean-Paul Marat's was 98 percent. Had Louis XVI's defense lawyer been able to use peremptory challenges to eliminate hostile jurors, he would have done well to dismiss young firstborn deputies, particularly those with Montagnard sympathies. Almost certainly, the dismissal of just two such jurors out of the 721 would have saved the king's life.

After controlling for other predictors, neither social class, geography, nor urban ties are significant factors in the voting.[63] These are remarkable findings given that French historians have long considered these between-family influences to be major contributors to the Terror. Within the National Convention, Montagnards repeatedly disparaged

Voting during the Trial of Louis XVI, by Social Class and Birth Order

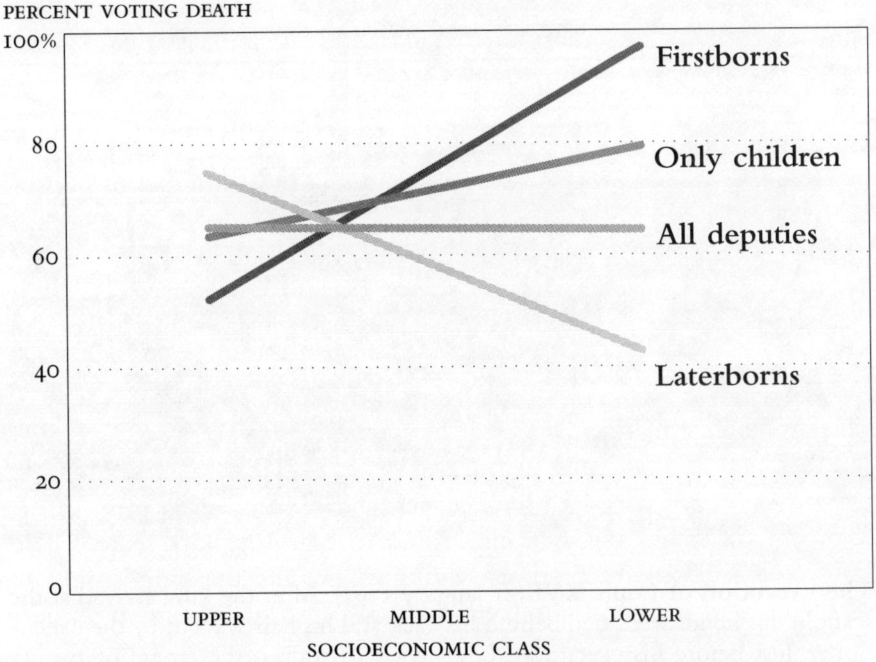

FIGURE 13.2. Voting during Louis XVI's trial, stratified by social class and birth order. Firstborn deputies conformed to the expectations of their class. Upper-class firstborns voted to save the king's life, whereas middle- and lower-class firstborns voted for death. In voting to spare the king, lower-class laterborns defied class expectations. Among the deputies, conflict was largely within the family, not between families.

As a main effect, birth order exerts a significant influence on voting patterns, but social class does not. Controlled for these two main effects, the interaction between birth order and social class is statistically significant.

Girondins as aristocratic provincials, and Girondins retaliated by attacking Montagnards for their unsavory alliance with ruffians within the Paris Commune.[64]

Although social class exerts no main effect on voting patterns, it does interact with birth order. Among firstborns, deputies from the lower classes were more likely than those from the upper classes to vote for the king's death. Firstborns behaved in a Marxist fashion! Alas for Marxist theory, laterborns followed the opposite trend (Fig. 13.2).[65] A

The execution of Louis XVI (21 January 1793). After the king arrived at the scaffold, his hands were tied behind his back and his hair was cut by the executioner. Just before his execution, Louis tried to address the crowd of twenty thousand who had gathered to watch him die. "I die innocent of all the crimes of which I have been charged," he began, "and I pray that the blood you are about to shed may never be required of France . . ." The king's speech was ignominiously drowned out in mid-sentence by a drum roll. Louis was then strapped to a plank and pushed under the waiting blade. After the guillotining, the executioner displayed the dripping head to the people. As a memento of the occasion, some bystanders dipped their handkerchiefs in the king's blood (Schama 1989:669).

reasonable explanation for this finding is that firstborns tended to conform to class expectations, just as their younger siblings tended to rebel against these expectations. The problem with a Marxist interpretation of the French Revolution is its failure to recognize the diversity among siblings.

When we have given due consideration to all of the relevant predictors of political behavior during the Terror, one firm conclusion emerges. The bulk of what we can explain about individual behavior during this event faithfully reflects sibling differences and sibling strategies. Superficially, party affiliations are the best predictor of voting during Louis's trial, but *causally,* party affiliations must be seen as playing second fiddle to the sibling differences that largely explain them. When causal models are employed to trace all of these overlapping influences, differences between siblings are almost twice as important as all other predictors of political behavior combined. Two centuries of explanations by French historians are largely a footnote to the unrecognized power of sibling differences.[66]

CONCLUSIONS

A social history of the French Revolution contains fundamental limitations, which reflect the tragedy of the revolution itself. Radical revolutions consistently transcend most sociological predictors of behavior because they polarize people who have grown up together. Sibling strife, not class conflict, lay at the heart of the Terror. The ultimate failure of the French Revolution resided in the participants' inability to grasp this fact.

During the early years of the revolution, political power passed from firstborn conservatives to laterborn liberals, who constituted a comparatively *tender-minded* group. Laterborns were zealous supporters of the revolutionary cause, but they were uneasy about the use of indiscriminate violence to attain their political goals. This dislike of brutality was particularly true of the deputies of the Plain, a largely middleborn group that eschewed the militant tactics of the other two parties. As the revolution became increasingly turbulent, power was seized by tough-minded firstborns—the leading Montagnards—whereas laterborns, in Michelet's phrase, "no longer possessed the genius of the Revolution."[67] In response to increasingly violent threats by Paris and the Commune, firstborns such as Marat, Robespierre, and Saint-Just created the ruthless apparatus of the Terror. Those individuals who dared to resist the Reign of Terror—the true "nonconformists" of the day—were proclaimed enemies of the people and sent to the guillotine.[68]

The French Revolution sought to refashion society according to republican ideals of "liberty, equality, and fraternity." Liberty and equality proved relatively easy to attain; fraternity was more elusive. The deputy Lanthénas glimpsed the depths of this problem when he insisted: "I see only brothers tearing themselves apart and doing so all the more ruthlessly because, at heart, they are agreed on the same thing—the most perfect Liberty and the Republic one and indivisible."[69] Having turned political brother against brother, the Terror swallowed up the founders of the First Republic and, in place of the despotism it had sought to overthrow, created a new and equally unfortunate tyranny. What for historians of the French Revolution has been a persistent puzzle—the "fratricidal" nature of this conflict—is actually the unpalatable solution.

PART FOUR

SYNTHESIS

14

SOCIAL AND INTELLECTUAL CONTEXT

HISTORICAL CONTEXT

No matter how comprehensive the study of a single historical event may be, the findings will always provide an imperfect and potentially misleading guide to human behavior. Even with the detailed study of numerous events, the diversity of behavioral outcomes seems to defy any prospect of reaching reliable generalizations.

The influence of birth order on revolutionary behavior exemplifies this problem. During some revolutions, birth order is a strong predictor of individual allegiances, with laterborns typically leading the crusade for change. In other revolutions, birth order's explanatory power is nil. In still others, the influence of birth order runs counter to the general trend, with firstborns directing the campaign for change. In spite of these diverse outcomes, a *consistent historical pattern* can be documented in these findings. The key to this pattern is the role of historical context. By historical context, I mean the social, political, religious, and intellectual conditions that prevail at any given moment in time within local cultures. Birth-order effects are reliably associated with *specific* situational contexts. I have spent more than two decades amassing sufficient biographical evidence to attempt this kind of context-sensitive explanation of human behavior. My approach gives equal weight to the nature of historical events and to the specific characteristics of individual participants. In this chapter I review my findings for 28 revolutions in science.

To understand behavior during periods of historical change, we need to identify the most prominent attributes of revolutionary change. Another way of posing this question is to ask "What makes revolutions 'revolutionary'?" For example, some revolutions in science have had controversial ideological implications. Other revolutions have been relatively devoid of such concerns. The invention of electric light was neither a "conservative" nor a "radical" act. Edison's light bulbs did not undermine the existence of God or challenge respect for political authority. In contrast, the invention of reliable contraceptive devices has had divisive social consequences. So have biological advances permitting fetal tissue transplants and in vitro fertilization. Because of ideological implications, the reception of in vitro fertilization has been different from the reception of Edison's light bulbs.

Some scientific discoveries are upsetting in cognitive ways. The cognitive features of innovations—how unbelievable they initially seem—help to explain why some discoveries take years to be accepted, whereas others are adopted without much ado.[1] One need only compare the fate of Alfred Wegener's theory of continental drift, a bold conjecture that took half a century to gain acceptance, with the discovery of the structure of DNA. Announced in 1953, Watson and Crick's model of the double helix was accepted with only a minimum of dispute. After reading a description of Watson and Crick's molecular structure, Linus Pauling, who had proposed a rival theory on the subject, required only *five minutes* to be convinced.[2] Crick has commented that the basic ideas necessary to understand the structure of DNA are "ridiculously easy, since they do not violate common sense, as quantum mechanics and relativity do."[3]

From Conservative Innovations to Radical Revolutions

In science, birth-order effects are driven by the ideological implications inherent in new ideas. Theories that have socially radical implications tend to be championed by laterborns and rejected by firstborns. Theories that have socially conservative implications display the opposite trend: firstborns tend to back conservative innovations, whereas laterborns are among the most vocal opponents of this class of ideas.

The biographical data that I have collected on scientists allow a formal test of my claims about birth-order effects and their relationship to ideology in science. Based on more than 19,000 ratings by expert historians, I have assessed the degree to which political and religious attitudes influence the reception of new theories. During some scientific revolutions, such as Darwinism, religious and political radicals have been dedicated supporters of conceptual change. During other controversies,

James Watson and Francis Crick (*right*) demonstrating their proposed model of DNA (1953). This discovery is a good example of creative puzzle solving in science, not of radical innovation. Although Watson and Crick's research on DNA did lead to a revolution in molecular biology, this subsequent advance represents a technical rather than a radical revolution. Firstborns are much more likely to make scientific breakthroughs of a technical nature than they are to pioneer radical revolutions. Consistent with this trend, Watson and Crick are both firstborns, as was Linus Pauling, their closest rival in the race for the structure of DNA.

such as those over the introduction of glaciation theory, social attitudes have had no detectable relationship with scientific stance. In still other scientific disputes, such as that over eugenics, religious and political conservatives have been strong champions of the new point of view. When we consider these trends in social attitudes across different scientific controversies and compare them with the trends that are observed

Birth-Order Trends in Science as Related to the Ideological Implications of Innovations

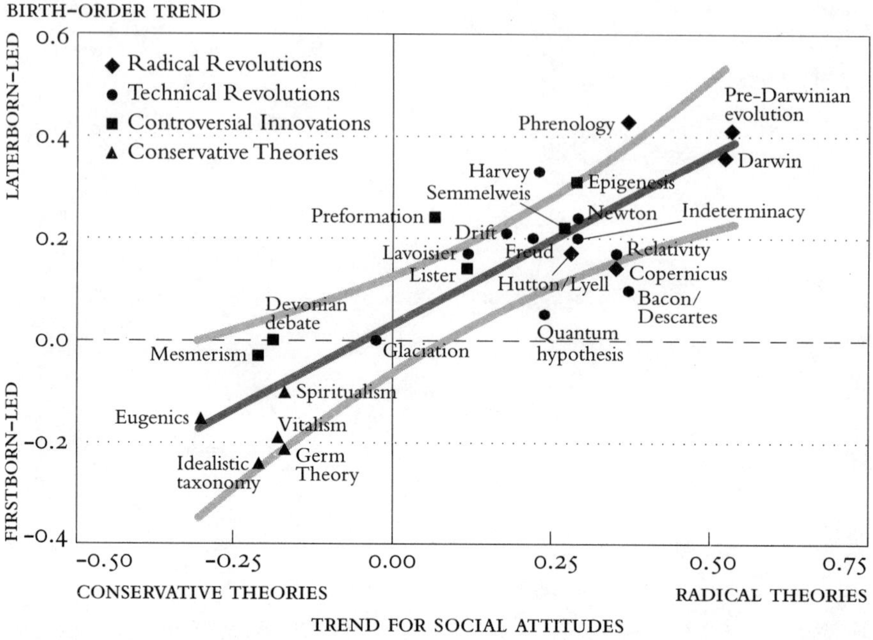

FIGURE 14.1. Birth-order effects in science, as they relate to the religious and political implications of innovations. The vertical axis depicts the correlation of *birth order* with support for scientific innovation. All events above the dividing line (0.0) were endorsed by laterborns and opposed by firstborns, whereas all events below the line reflect greater support by firstborns. The horizontal axis indicates the correlation of *social attitudes* with support for each innovation. All events to the left of the dividing line (0.00) were endorsed by social conservatives and rejected by social liberals. All events to the right of the same line reflect support by social liberals and opposition by conservatives. Determinations of social attitudes involve more than 19,000 ratings, made by expert historians who judged the religious and political attitudes of participants in each debate.

This analysis establishes a simple generalization: *The more socially radical the innovation, the more it was supported by laterborns and opposed by firstborns.* The two most radical revolutions in the history of science are early theories of evolution and Darwinism, both strongly supported by laterborns. The most conservative innovation I have surveyed is eugenics, a theory preferred by firstborns. Missing from the history of science are two classes of potential events. There are no Radical Revolutions backed by firstborns. There are also no Conservative Theories backed by laterborns.

in birth-order effects, a striking pattern emerges: the nature of each debate, depicted in terms of social attitudes, dictates the direction of birth-order effects (Fig. 14.1).[4]

The linear relationship between birth-order trends and ideological tendencies makes my argument about birth order testable in a variety of ways.[5] For example, socially conservative innovations that are championed by laterborns should never occur in history. The discovery of even *one* such episode with a significant trend would constitute a formidable challenge to my claims. Similarly, evidence of radical revolutions favored by firstborns is also not to be expected. When firstborns have "rebelled" in history, it has been to bring God back into the scientific picture or to reaffirm the social status quo. Firstborns favored eugenics because this reform movement seemed to rationalize socioeconomic disparities in terms of genetics. (The word *eugenics* comes from the Greek, meaning "well born.") Historically, firstborns have tended to support the notion that biology is destiny. Minority races, women, and laterborns have all typically resisted such deterministic notions.

Ideological factors are not the only way of defining revolutionary contexts. There are more, *lots more.* To elucidate some of these other features defining scientific innovations, I have assembled a database of 30 variables that delineate prominent attributes of these controversies.[6] Taken together, these 30 variables provide a unique "fingerprint" for each controversy. Roughly half of these 30 variables involve *biographical attributes,* including birth order, parent-offspring conflict, temperament, parental loss, and political and religious attitudes. In earlier chapters of this book, I have discussed all of these biographical predictors, as well as their relationship to radicalism.

My database also includes a variety of *structural attributes* associated with scientific change. For example, some controversies have lasted more than a century, whereas others have been resolved within a decade. Some innovations were debated almost exclusively by scientists, whereas others attracted a significant number of nonscientists. Some controversies involved national differences; others did not. Some breakthroughs occurred in the physical sciences, whereas others occurred in the life sciences. No scientific innovation displays the same values for each of the 30 variables. Each pattern is unique and reflects an equally unique historical context. What needs to be determined is whether differences in these historical fingerprints are meaningful or random.

The magnitude and direction of birth-order effects in science are typically predicted by other variables of a biographical nature. World travel, for example, is a good indicator of risk taking and openness to experience. For this reason, new scientific theories tend to appeal to people who have traveled extensively. For the same reason, new theories also appeal to laterborns, even after we control for the significant cross correlation between birth order and a proclivity for world travel. Travel and birth order are both effective proxies for the same behavioral predilection: openness to experience. In addition, the act of travel generally makes people more open to different perspectives about the world.

Similarly, birth-order effects tend to arise whenever another key aspect of family dynamics—parent-offspring conflict—is relevant to the outcome. Both variables predict attitudes toward authority, even though each variable reflects a different biographical scenario for acquiring these attitudes. In general, whenever birth order is relevant to attitudes toward change, so are other variables that mirror the dynamics of family politics. These other variables typically include age gaps between siblings, parental loss, gender, and temperament. Birth order provides a kind of psychological litmus test for the involvement of all these other behavioral predictors, which hang together causally as an interlocking cluster.[7]

The best predictors of birth-order effects are listed in Table 7. These predictors share something in common: *they are all good indicators of controversy.* For example, substantial birth-order effects are typically present in debates that involve large numbers of participants. Similarly, substantial birth-order effects are observed in debates that are widely cited as "scientific revolutions."[8] In fact, most good predictors of support for scientific innovation, such as age and friendship, are also significant predictors of birth-order effects in the same controversies. Each of these predictors helps to explain individual differences in decision making under conditions of uncertainty. Like a thermometer, birth order sums up these other indicators of controversy, expressing them as a single measure of "revolutionary temperature."

How effective are the dozen variables in Table 7 in actually predicting birth-order effects? The answer can be expressed as the multiple correlation—.90. Like a correlation, a multiple correlation varies from 0 to 1.0, but it differs in that it pools the predictive abilities of two or more variables. Correlations as large as .90 are normally found only in fields such as physiology and physics, not history or psychology. In history, the key to large correlations is to include the pivotal role of the historical context.[9] When this methodological step is implemented in the case of birth-order effects, we arrive at a simple but far-reaching

TABLE 7
Predictors of Birth-Order Effects in 28 Scientific Controversies

Predictors of Laterborn Support	*Correlation of Predictor with Laterborn Support*	*Likelihood of Trend Occurring by Chance*
BIOGRAPHICAL PREDICTORS		
Religious attitudes (supported by atheists)	.58	*Less than 1 in 1,000*
Travel (extensive)	.53	*Less than 1 in 100*
Political attitudes (supported by liberals)	.52	*Less than 1 in 100*
Conflict with parents (high)	.45	*Less than 1 in 100*
Age (supported by young people)	.39	*Less than 1 in 33*
Personal contact (supported by friends)	.39	*Less than 1 in 33*
STRUCTURAL PREDICTORS		
Phase of the debate (early)	.54	*Less than 1 in 100*
Years consumed by the controversy	.45	*Less than 1 in 100*[a]
National differences (substantial)	.40	*Less than 1 in 33*
Number of participants	.38	*Less than 1 in 33*
Controversiality (unpopular theories)	.38	*Less than 1 in 33*
Widely cited as a "revolution"	.37	*Less than 1 in 20*
NONSIGNIFICANT PREDICTORS		
Failed theory	.29	*Less than 1 in 10*
Religious denomination	.12	*Likely*
Social class	.00	*Extremely likely*

NOTE: *The unit of analysis is the effect size for each predictor in 28 different scientific controversies.* The correlations in the table reflect the degree to which each predictor of scientific stance, such as religious attitudes, is tapped during controversies that exhibit large birth-order effects. Owing to the role of temporal considerations, I have subdivided 4 of the 28 scientific controversies into "early" and "late" phases, yielding a total of 32 events. These four controversies are Copernican theory, psychoanalysis, quantum theory, and eugenics.

a. This correlation is based on the *absolute* value of birth-order effects—in other words, on the degree to which scientific controversies were polarized by birth-order, regardless of the *direction* of the effect. Theories that have taken many years to resolve have tended to divide siblings.

historical conclusion: The greater the level of controversy associated with a new idea, the larger is the observed birth-order effect. As a proxy for individual differences in openness to experience, birth-order trends reflect the pulse beat of historical change.[10]

Receptivity to Scientific Theories over Time by Birth Order

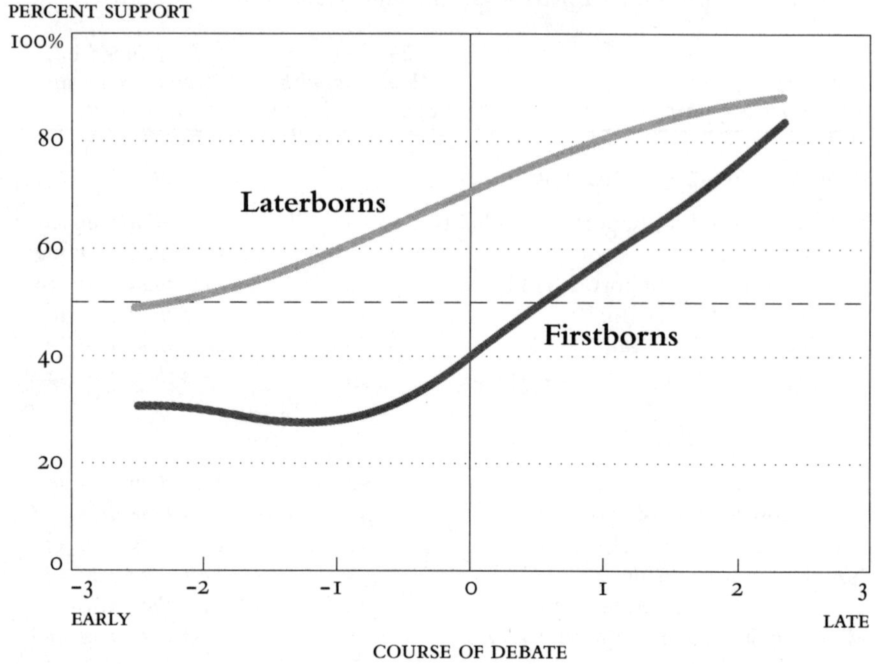

FIGURE 14.2. The "life history" of scientific controversies. The reception of 21 successful theories is depicted by birth order, which reflects individual differences in openness to experience. The horizontal axis indicates elapsed time, standardized for each debate (using *z*-scores). The mean length of these 21 controversies was 75 years. Thus each unit on the horizontal axis represents 15 years.

Although scientists differ significantly by birth order in their openness to innovation, these differences typically diminish as theories gain increasing empirical support.

The Life Cycle of Theories

After social attitudes, the phase of scientific debate (early versus late) is the next best predictor of birth-order influence. Birth-order effects typically fade over time. We may conveniently analyze this temporal relationship by considering the "life cycle" of theories. My analysis of such life cycles is limited to 21 successful theories so that we may follow their status from heterodoxy to orthodoxy.

Initially, firstborns and laterborns disagree about most scientific innovations. As empirical evidence accumulates, and as new experiments are carried out to test working hypotheses, birth-order differences begin to diminish. Subjective considerations weaken before the weight of empirical arguments. Eventually birth-order differences disappear altogether, as does opposition to the new way of thinking (Fig. 14.2).[11]

Of the 21 successful theories I have analyzed, birth order exerts 9 times more influence on the adoption of innovation than does new evidence. Most of the variance in adoption tendencies is associated with preexisting differences in attitudes toward innovation, not conversions over time. Another way of expressing this point is to note that some people (young scientists, social liberals, and laterborns) tend to be preadapted to change and hence do not really need to be converted.

These striking findings suggest that scientific rationality may be less important to the advancement of science than are subjective considerations. In practice, matters are not so cut and dried. Birth order promotes different strategies for understanding the world. Just as Darwinian evolution has promoted extensive diversity within most species so that they may live successfully in varied and unpredictable environments, relationships within human families continue this process in ontogeny. As a result, people are often preadapted in distinctly different ways to surmounting life's problems. The situation is much the same in science. There is no one way of reaching correct answers to unsolved scientific puzzles.[12]

Why Galileo Won

Copernicus's hypothesis that the earth circles the sun was based on astronomical data that had been available for centuries. During Copernicus's lifetime no direct evidence was capable of proving his theory, and only a few astronomers took his physical claims seriously.

During the half century after Copernicus's death, a series of important astronomical discoveries transformed debate over his daring hypothesis.[13] The first of these discoveries involved a new star, which appeared in 1572. This finding contradicted Aristotelian theory, which held that the heavens were immutable. Even more problematic for traditional astronomers were a series of six comets they observed between 1577 and 1596. By demonstrating parallax against the background of fixed stars, Danish astronomer Tycho Brahe proved that these comets were traveling freely through space, above the moon.[14] Traditional

Receptivity to Copernican Theory by Year and Birth Order

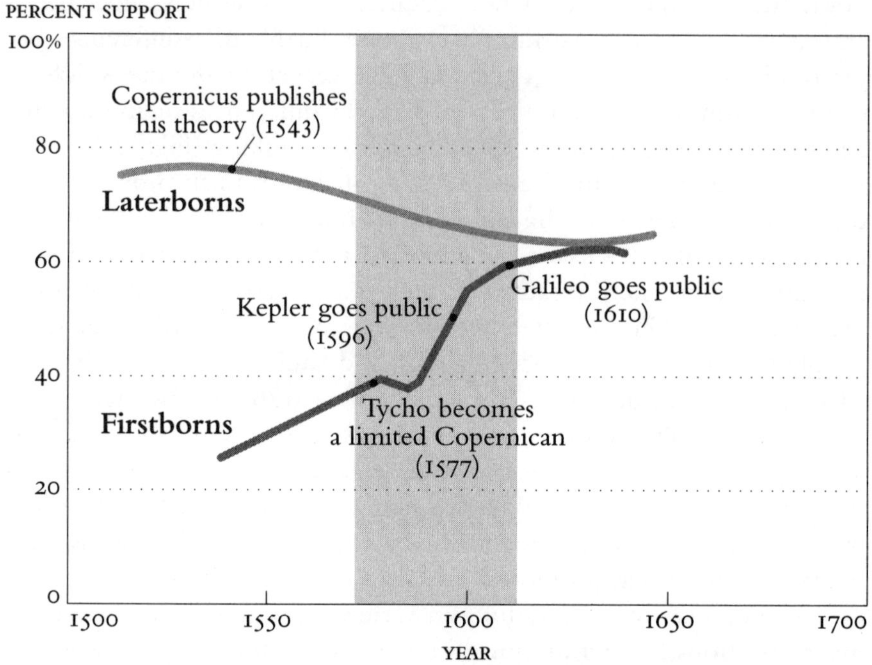

FIGURE 14.3. The reception of Copernican theory by birth order over time. Between 1572 and 1610 (*shaded in the figure*), a series of important astronomical discoveries bolstered Copernican theory, culminating in Galileo's telescopic discoveries. Before 1610, laterborns were significantly more likely than firstborns to accept Copernican theory. After 1609, birth order is no longer a significant predictor of acceptance.

cosmologists believed that the planets were carried around an immobile earth on great crystalline spheres. The study of cometary orbits demolished this scheme.[15] By 1600, even Tycho, a feisty firstborn who was known for his conservative worldview, was compelled to adopt a cosmology that admitted every Copernican innovation save a moving earth (Fig. 14.3).[16]

In March 1610 Galileo's *Starry Messenger* appeared. Backed up by the discoveries he had made with the newly invented telescope, Galileo's book came like a bombshell. The reception of this publication can only be compared to the news, three hundred years later, that man had walked on the moon. As seen through the telescope, the heavens were far from perfect, as Aristotelian theory had long insisted. The moon was pockmarked with craters, and the sun was studded with dark blemishes. Jupiter turned out to have four moons, and when this "wandering star" moved in its orbit, its moons moved with it. This unexpected finding overcame a long-standing argument against a moving earth.

Tycho's findings about comets had involved ephemeral phenomena that other astronomers could dispute after the fact. By contrast, Galileo's telescopic discoveries refused to go away. To promote his Copernican views, Galileo diligently manufactured telescopes and sent them to people in influential places.[17] When the Catholic Church banned Copernican theory in 1616, it badly missed the point—the ban should have been on telescopes.

The influx of new astronomical evidence after 1572 offers a good test case for the various factors that determine which theory a scientist endorses. When evidence in support of new theories is meager, people often make decisions about this information based on gut instinct. Birth order is typically a good predictor of such decisions, but it ceases to be predictive when evidence finally points, in a decisive fashion, toward one theory or the other. Galileo's scientific career witnessed just such a transformation in astronomical evidence and credibility. Between 1572 and 1610, the influence of birth order steadily diminishes. Too much astronomical evidence had begun to point in one direction. Firstborns, worn down by the empirical avalanche, softened their opposition to Copernican theory and finally abandoned the previously dominant system altogether.

As a particularly eminent firstborn, Galileo reflects this trend. Although privately a Copernican since the 1590s, he had refused to endorse this theory in public until the telescope finally supplied him with compelling evidence.[18] Once he had built his first telescope during the fall of 1609, Galileo became worried that a scientific rival might do the same and steal his Copernican thunder. So he transformed himself from a private Copernican into this theory's most celebrated public defender.[19]

Especially after 1609, the rapid influx of new astronomical evidence separated what had previously been intermingled components of scientific judgment. Some of these components were ideological—the product of deep-seated religious convictions. Others were empirical, and still others reflected individual differences in openness to experience. Although birth order ceases to predict attitudes toward Copernican

Although Galileo was not born to rebel, he was strongly inclined to question authority, especially when armed with compelling evidence in support of a new scientific theory. His numerous telescopic discoveries were "the first step down the path that would lead him, two decades later, to the dungeon of the Inquisition" (Westfall 1985: 28). Soon after his trial by the Inquisition, which convicted him of heresy in 1633, Galilio is reputed to have declared "*Eppur si muove*" (But still the earth moves).

theory after 1609, social attitudes continue to correlate with scientific stance for another half century. Social attitudes reflect long-established values and beliefs, mostly learned during youth. It is much easier for people to change their views about factual issues than it is for them to change their political and religious convictions.[20] Although both influences—factual and ideological—shaped decision making during the Copernican revolution, neither influence can be reduced to the other.

Being a student of a Copernican advocate is another variable that continues to explain support for this theory after 1609.[21] Especially for scientists, personal networks provided a crucial means of learning about Copernican theory. This "networking" explains additional features of the spread of beliefs that birth order and other individual differences do not. It is hardly a surprising conclusion that science is influenced by many diverse factors. What is more noteworthy is that these influences are faithfully reflected in the magnitude of birth-order effects (and hence of within-family differences).[22]

In sum, allegiances to Copernican theory were shaped by many considerations—ideological, social, psychological, and empirical. Even Copernican theory played a part, directing astronomers to make new observations that were relevant to resolving this question. Owing to new evidence, subjective considerations gradually gave way to rational ones. When the merits of endorsing new theories can be settled by rational criteria, scientists are quick to take advantage of them.[23] Allow a Galileo to peer through a telescope, and he will win in the end.

Even in science, where rational criteria of theory assessment tend to prevail in the long run, rationality is typically subject to a *threshold* effect. The point at which this threshold is surpassed varies from one individual to another, and from one social group to another. During the Copernican debates, laterborns made the transition sooner than did firstborns, and scientists made it sooner than nonscientists. Still, most people eventually made the transition, and even the Catholic Church, after a lapse of 350 years, has finally admitted its error on the matter of Galileo and Copernican theory.[24]

The decision-making process in seventeenth-century astronomy contrasts with the bitter theological debates during this same period. To this day, no one has settled the controversy over whether Christ's body is literally present in the bread and wine of the Communion. This is unfortunate, since many people were executed for their divergent opinions on this issue. It would be nice to know which ones got burned by mistake.

Albert Einstein, out walking in Berlin. After the London *Times* broke the news story of the eclipse results of 1919, Einstein became a celebrity. Just two weeks after the startling announcement, the *New York Times* described him as "the suddenly famous Dr. Einstein" (Pais 1982:309). This chance photograph was taken in 1932 by a passerby, who recognized Einstein from his pictures in the newspapers.

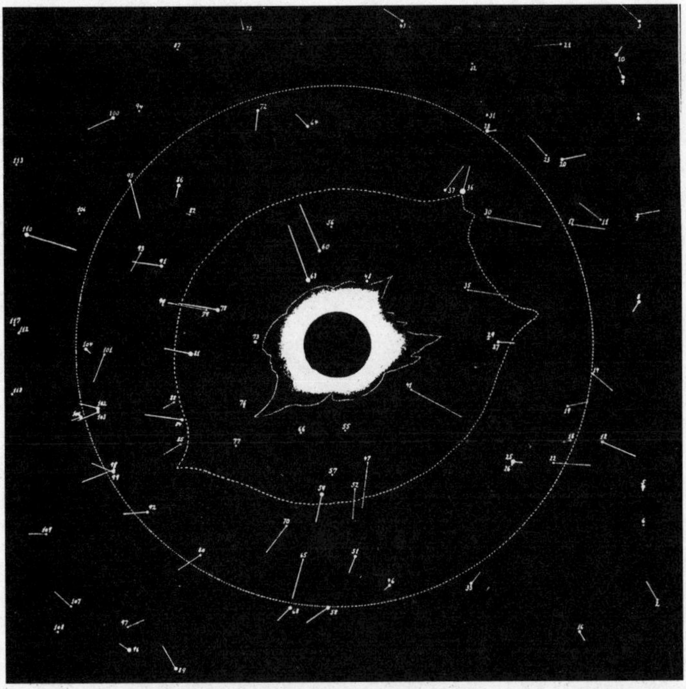

During the total eclipse of the sun on 21 September 1922, Einstein's theory of general relativity was again tested, this time by astronomical expeditions sent to Tahiti and Western Australia. This diagram is based on the photographic plates and exhibits the marked outward displacement of stars near the sun, recorded at the moment of totality. So great is the visual displacement that stars hidden behind the sun's disk appear as if they are located beyond the sun's corona.

The Man Who Bent Starlight

Firstborn Albert Einstein's rise to world fame provides an instructive parallel to the reception of Copernican theory. In November 1915 Einstein read his paper on general relativity before the Prussian Academy of Sciences. In arguing for his radical reconceptualization of space and time, Einstein made a prediction. As starlight passes near the sun, he claimed, it should bend 1.7 seconds of arc—twice the amount expected by Newtonian theory. The first good opportunity to test this prediction was in 1919, when a solar eclipse took place in the Southern Hemisphere. During the brief period of totality, photographic plates

Receptivity to Relativity Theory by Year and Birth Order

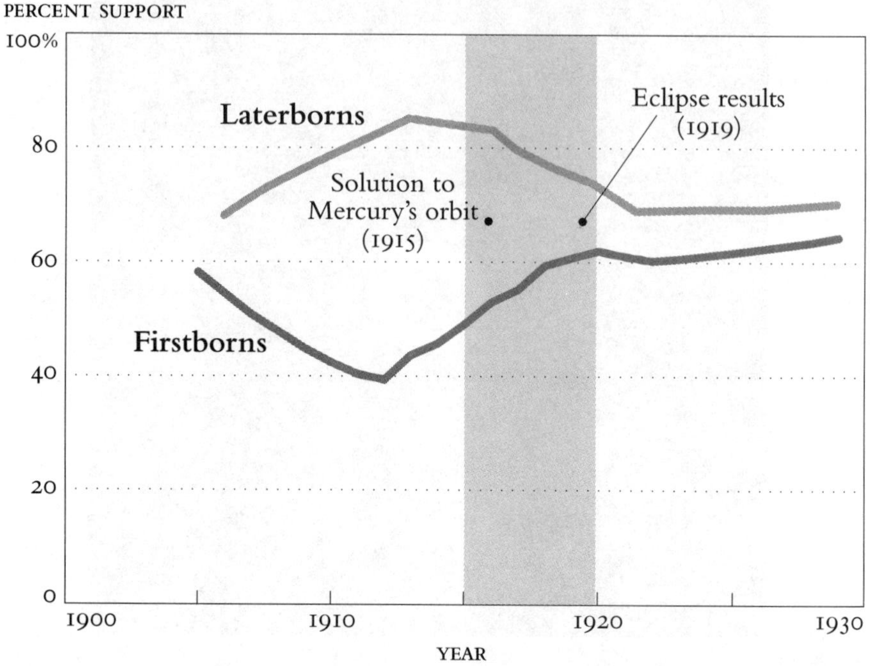

FIGURE 14.4. The reception of relativity theory by year and birth order. Prior to 1920, laterborns were more likely than firstborns to support Einstein's radical reconceptualizations of space and time. Between 1915 and 1920 (*shaded in the figure*), the theory of general relativity achieved two important empirical triumphs. In 1915, Einstein explained an anomaly in the orbit of Mercury that had puzzled astronomers for half a century. The solar eclipse of 1919 provided another stunning confirmation of his views. After 1920, birth order no longer predicts attitudes toward Einstein's theories.

were able to record faint stellar images, which confirmed the predicted deflection.

When these astronomical results were announced at the Royal Society in London, Einstein and his theory became the subject of newspaper headlines around the world. J. J. Thomson, president of the Royal Society, acclaimed Einstein's theory as "one of the greatest achievements in the history of human thought."[25] This was saying a lot, coming from a firstborn who had previously doubted Einstein's theories. Even Sir Oliver Lodge, the most zealous British defender of the Newtonian ether (and another firstborn), acknowledged Einstein's "dramatic triumph." After 1920, birth order ceases to predict attitudes toward relativity theory (Fig. 14.4).[26]

Unlike birth order, social attitudes continue to be a good predictor of support or opposition to Einstein's theories after 1919.[27] ("Relativism" appealed to liberals.) Like Galileo's telescopic evidence, the eclipse results of 1919 caused empirical arguments to uncouple from ideological ones. This kind of historical uncoupling occurs regularly during scientific controversies and reveals the insufficiency of explanations that reduce science to a social activity. Rational considerations play a substantial part in scientific deliberations, although in most cases the power of rationality changes over the course of debate.

Not every scientist needs to behave rationally for science to succeed. As long as the majority abide by the consequences of hypothesis testing, science works reasonably well. Take away this method, or the right to defend its results, and scientific controversy becomes just like any other form of social debate.[28]

The Rise and Fall of Preformation Theory

Time and changing ideological considerations sometimes act jointly to turn laterborn-led innovations into firstborn dogmas. A good example of such a transformation involves the rise and fall of preformation theory in embryology. This doctrine posited that embryos are miniature adults. Development, it was thought, mechanically inflated these miniatures like a balloon. The doctrine of preformation gained prominence during the seventeenth century, as part of the mechanical philosophy that flourished during the Scientific Revolution. This theory was also part of the general reaction against Aristotelian thinking, which argued that organs are formed gradually out of unorganized matter—a process called epigenesis.

Prior to 1700, preformation was more popular among laterborns than firstborns, as befits its iconoclastic status. Once firstborns had finally become accustomed to the new approach, they found a special comfort in this embryological dogma. Preformationists posited that embryos had all been created by God—fully formed in miniature—to await their enlargement during gestation. By offering a convincing alternative to epigenetic development, which had materialistic implications, preformation attracted the allegiance of religious conservatives.[29]

When epigenetic doctrines began to make a comeback during the middle of the eighteenth century, firstborn naturalists such as Charles

Receptivity to Preformation and Epigenesis by Year and Birth Order

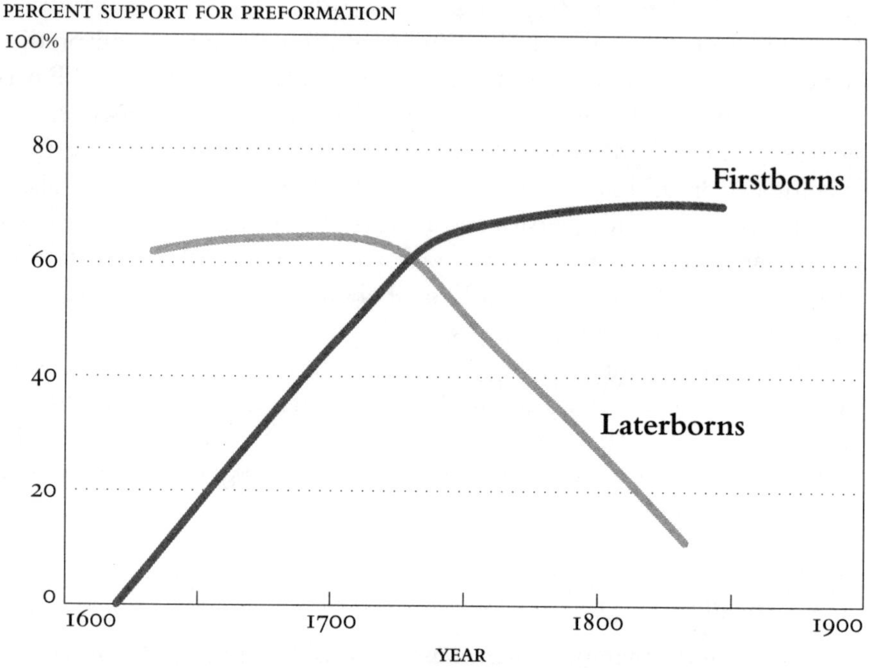

FIGURE 14.5. The reception of preformation, and later epigenesis, by birth order. Owing to the crisscrossing pattern, the overall trend by birth order is not significant. The tendency for laterborns to adopt whichever theory was out of favor is significant.

Bonnet and Lazzaro Spallanzani zealously led the attack against the materialistic intruder. In their contrasting responses to preformation theory, firstborns and laterborns were like ships passing in the historical night. When their anti-Aristotelian brainchild had finally become an orthodoxy, laterborns eagerly embraced its radical rival. Because the birth-order effect is context-sensitive, there is no significant birth-order trend as a main effect. Laterborns, however, behaved consistently throughout the debates over these two theories: they generally preferred whichever theory was out of favor (Fig. 14.5).[30]

Do Crises Precipitate Revolutions?

To what degree are scientific revolutions precipitated by a crisis? The role of crisis was central to Thomas Kuhn's influential analysis of scientific revolutions.[31] Most revolutions, he argued, are preceded by a gradual buildup in anomalies that conflict with the established paradigm. This feature of scientific revolutions is relevant to birth-order effects. The relationship is a reciprocal one. Crisis determines the magnitude of birth-order effects, and birth-order effects influence whether or not a stage of crisis is ever reached.

Radical revolutions in science are rarely preceded by a crisis.[32] From Kuhn's point of view, this is a major inconsistency: the more radical the revolution, the less it seems to accord with Kuhn's formula. The problem is that laterborns do not think or behave like good Kuhnians.[33] When a radical idea such as evolution is available for exploration, laterborns do not wait for a crisis to jettison the dominant alternative. In my survey of 28 scientific innovations, *laterborns have typically been half a century ahead of firstborns in their willingness to endorse radical innovations.* Only when faced with the toughest of technical puzzles, like the ones that preoccupied Darwin for twenty years, do some highly conscientious laterborns hesitate before jumping headlong into revolution. Still, for every Darwin who was willing to risk being scooped owing to scrupulously high standards of proof, there is usually someone like Alfred Russel Wallace who has been bold enough to risk publishing on the same topic after a week's reflection. But even Wallace was not driven by a sense of crisis, having been converted to evolution fourteen years earlier by Robert Chambers's *Vestiges of Creation*. Chambers, Darwin, and Wallace jointly *created a crisis where none had been before.*[34] In sum, the most radical revolutions rarely emerge from a state of crisis. This is why they are so radical.

Although useful in many ways, Kuhn's account of scientific advancement suffers from trying to squeeze too many disparate types of change into one structural formula. His model makes crisis into an *essential* feature of revolutions when it is not.[35] Still, crises play a greater role in some scientific transformations than in others. In particular, crises are more commonly observed in technical revolutions than they are during radical revolutions. In the most technical sciences, the esoteric nature of the issues being considered often forestalls a successful paradigm shift long after the signs of theoretical breakdown have begun to emerge. It is one matter for scientists to recognize a growing problem. It is another matter entirely for them to come up with a successful solution.

During technical revolutions, crises tend to increase the size of birth-order effects. This relationship is opposite to that observed during radical revolutions. Once again, the culprit is the role of context. In science, revolutionary thinkers do not generally rebel without some good reason. During the early stages of radical revolutions, liberal ideological goals supply this motivation. During technical revolutions, the analogous motivation is supplied by growing signs of breakdown in the established theory. In each case, laterborns are the first to rebel. In different historical contexts, however, they do so for different reasons.[36]

Individual testimony about the nature of historical change is strongly influenced by the personalities of the people who supply it. For example, radicals will tend to see political or conceptual crises at times when conservatives do not. As the first to accept radical innovations, laterborns tend to stress how problematic the old theory has become. It is not difficult to build a historical case for crisis by citing what Copernicus said about Ptolemaic theory, what Bacon said about Scholasticism, or what Darwin said about creationism. Such testimony, coming from radicals, will not be typical of the scientific community as a whole.

Similarly, firstborns cannot always be trusted when they insist that an ailing theory is in good health. As the old physics was being revolutionized by the discovery of the quantum, Henri Poincaré asked his readers whether the general principles of dynamics, which had seemed immutable since the time of Newton, were "on the point of being abandoned or at least profoundly modified." His own answer, expressed in 1908, was typical of a firstborn. After completing his review of the experimental results that were challenging the old order, he wrote: "Perhaps one is too hasty in considering these novelties as finally established, and breaking the idols of yesterday; perhaps it would be proper, before taking sides, to await experiments more numerous and more convincing."[37] Poincaré and many other scientists—mostly firstborns and elderly individuals—needed *more of a crisis* to change their thinking. Albert Einstein, Paul Ehrenfest, Max Laue, and Max Planck did not.[38] Which ones should be trusted in assessing competing historical claims about the nature of scientific change?

The extraordinary difference in sibling worldviews is relevant to another aspect of Kuhn's claims about science. Along with the notion of crisis, Kuhn made "incommensurability" an essential feature of his model of scientific revolutions. He argued that scientists holding opposing theories, such as Ptolemaic and Copernican astronomy, live in distinct conceptual worlds, and he likened this process to a gestalt shift. People on different sides of the theoretical divide, Kuhn insisted, cannot effectively communicate with one another. Once again, the problem of judging the merits of these philosophical views depends in large part on whose testimony is allowed to count.

Once they have made the transition to a new and radical point of view, laterborns find it relatively easy to think in terms of *both* theories as they plan a revolution. They often become remarkably adept at translating back and forth between old and new ways of thinking. This circumstance suggests that, on an individual basis, laterborns do not experience much "incommensurability" during theory change. Psychologically speaking, incommensurability is a problem for inflexible people, not for those who are open to experience.[39] If anyone had asked a group of newly convinced Darwinists in 1860 whether Darwinian theory was incommensurable with creationism, few would have replied that it was. Incompatible "yes," superior "yes," incommensurable "hardly."

Darwin himself seems to have considered evolution as *fully commensurable* with creationism. His *Origin of Species* was "one long argument" comparing how well the available biological evidence could be interpreted by creationism and evolution.[40] He sought to demonstrate, point by point, that rational criteria consistently favored the evolutionary alternative. Why, for example, do embryos of terrestrial vertebrates exhibit slits for gills? This vestigial organ reveals that land vertebrates have evolved from aquatic ancestors. Similarly, why do oceanic islands lack frogs and other amphibians, even though such localities possess reptiles in abundance? Frogs and their eggs, Darwin pointed out, are quickly killed by salt water, and ocean currents are the principal means of transport for such colonists. By contrast, snakes and lizards might occasionally survive oceanic transport, especially by rafting. Creationism possesses no adequate explanation for these and numerous other difficulties raised by Darwin, except to say that "it has so pleased the Creator."[41] A creationist might argue that frogs are poorly adapted for living on oceanic islands. Darwin knew better, presenting evidence that frogs, once introduced to tropical islands, have often thrived so well as to become a nuisance.[42] God's plan of creation, if there was one, was neither perfect nor based on any obvious rational considerations.

Darwin was so successful in showing how commensurable evolution and creationism were that he forced his readers to make a direct choice between the two theories. Most reasonable people had to admit that evolution was the superior theory. After Darwin's careful dissection of the Creator's handiwork, the Creator began to look so mindless that

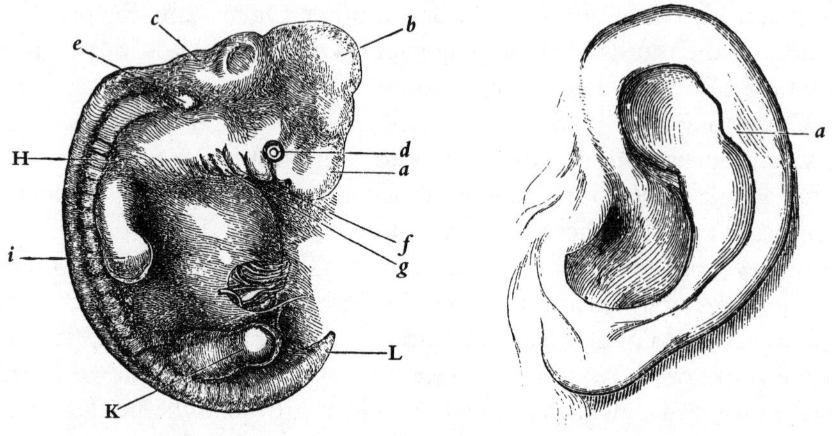

Examples of rudimentary organs in man (from Darwin's *Descent of Man,* 1871, 1:15, 22). *Left:* A human embryo, about seven weeks old. The gill slits, indicated by the letters ***f*** and ***g,*** are clearly visible just below the eye. Also visible is the rudimentary tail (***L***). *Right:* The human ear, with its rudimentary tip (***a***). In the course of primate evolution, the outer portion of the ear has been folded inward, rounded, and reduced in size. The tip still remains in vestigial form. This curious anatomical feature is sometimes called "Darwin's point," owing to Darwin's explanation of it.

many creationists wisely sought to move Him into the biological background as a "first cause": better a distant than a dim-witted god. Those few souls who were not convinced by Darwin would doubtless have sworn on a stack of Bibles that the two theories were incommensurable. Such testimony, coming mostly from firstborns, social conservatives, elderly scientists, and uninformed bishops, would be highly suspect. Lastborns such as Thomas Henry Huxley tended to make mincemeat out of them in public debates—which is how he got to be known as Darwin's Bulldog.

It is problematic, then, to accept testimony about the epistemological status of a theory without knowing something about the spokesperson's likelihood of supporting innovation.[43] As long as scientific communities typically exhibit a 100 to 1 difference in attitudes toward innovation, these communities will exhibit a similar disparity in their justifications for innovation. This is why problems relating to the advancement of science must be studied in terms of large populations, which are composed of diverse individuals. Selected individuals will always supply potentially "biased" evidence that can easily be made to support any cherished historical or philosophical argument.

CONCLUSIONS

A knowledge of human behavior, including its roots in early family experiences, is insufficient to explain how people react during major historical revolutions. Context—with all of its rich social, political, religious, and intellectual features—is the key to how personality ultimately expresses itself. Whether we are concerned with political revolutions, social reform movements, or controversies in science, the *kinds* of innovations that siblings typically support are not the same. As soon as we place these diverse episodes within their historical contexts, a consistent pattern emerges.

Firstborns lead fashionable reforms, populist revolutions, and orthodox science. Laterborns forge very different kinds of innovations. In politics they tend to be radical revolutionaries, fostering protest long before it is stylish to do so. As social reformers they support the most unpopular causes, such as abolition, socialism, anarchism, and atheism. In science, laterborns typically champion those innovations that are heterodox within the epistemological and social context of the day. They do not wait for a crisis to support radical change. Instead, they work hard to precipitate crises on their complacent elder siblings, who generally see little reason to abandon the status quo.

Throughout history, sibling conflict has been closely tied to differing worldviews. During major revolutions, choices between the old and the new order can almost always be traced to differences in family niches. Many factors contribute to the emergence of these sibling conflicts, and also moderate their expression. Within science, the influence of family niches can usually be detected during the early stages of revolutionary controversy, when there is less empirical support for new theories. Similarly, whenever national loyalties polarize the scientific community, sibling differences are likely to influence the outcome in those countries that are most opposed to the new theory.[44] As a general rule, the more heterodox the innovation, the more siblings are likely to disagree over its merits.

15

CONCLUSION

A NEW VIEW OF THE FAMILY

Psychologists have repeatedly documented that siblings who grow up together are almost as different in their personalities as people plucked randomly from the general population. Siblings differ for two fundamental reasons: first, they share, on average, only half of their genes; second, and less obviously, most of the environmental influences affecting siblings are not shared. This is true not only of the experiences children have outside the family, but also of those occurring within the home. The family does not provide a monolithic experience that automatically immerses its offspring in a single environmental bath. What psychologists once thought to be the "shared family environment" is not really shared. Many environmental factors that are extremely important—age, size, and power, as well as status and privilege within the family—are dissimilar for siblings. Families are best seen as containing an array of diverse niches, each occupied by a different individual and each presenting differing vantage points on life. From these differing perspectives, family members experience the same events differently. Families do share interests and social values. But siblings differ even in their interests and values, and these differences are caused, in substantial part, by differences in niches within the family.

The heterogeneity of family niches does not mean that these niches are randomly created. Analyzing niches *across* families reveals that these microenvironments share surprisingly predictable attributes that correspond highly with sibling status. What is similar across families is an orderly array of sibling strategies. These strategies are in turn linked to birth order, gender, and other systematic sibling differences. Birth order merits our special attention because it encapsulates disparities in age, size, power, and privilege. The typical firstborn strategy is to align his or her interests with those of the parents, adopting the parents' perspective on family life. The family status of firstborns is primary, and they seek to maintain this primacy by defending their niche against encroachments by younger brothers and sisters.

Laterborn offspring face a different developmental challenge. Their most pressing problem is to find a valued family niche that avoids duplicating the one already staked out by the parent-identified firstborn. Instead, they seek to excel in those domains where older siblings have not already established superiority. Laterborns typically cultivate openness to experience—a useful strategy for anyone who wishes to find a novel and successful niche in life. Consistent with these exploratory tendencies, laterborns take greater risks, endeavoring to achieve through openness and diversity what firstborns gain through territoriality and conformity to parental expectations. For each family niche, there are different rules of the sibling road.

There are, of course, substantial social differences *between* families, including those associated with socioeconomic status, race, and nationality. Children, however, are much less concerned about the differences that exist between families than they are about the differences that exist within their own family. Over the millennia, children have evolved motivational systems that help them to maximize nurturance from people around them, especially parents. The family has long provided the primary behavioral context for these motivational tendencies. Seen in evolutionary terms, the diverse features of personality represent different strategies for maximizing parental investment and getting out of childhood alive.

Marx was mistaken when he located the primary engine of historical change between families. Freud was considerably closer to the truth when he recognized the importance of interpersonal conflict in family life. But Freud also erred significantly when he gave primacy to libidinal urges and hence to oedipal conflict. Parent-offspring conflict is largely derivative—a product of *sibling* conflict over parental resources. Nor are these conflicts driven by sexual urges, and hence sex linked, as Freud insisted. Rather, siblings compete with one another for parental investment *in all of its typical forms,* and they seek to maximize these benefits *from both parents.* This is why, in the various revolutions I have surveyed in this book, parent-offspring conflict is a significant source of rebellious behavior independent of the parent's gender. The importance of sibling conflict over parental investment is also why birth order typically explains two to three times the variance in attitudes toward radical change that is associated with parental conflict. Both Freud and Marx seriously erred by ignoring the profound theoretical advances that Charles Darwin achieved in their own lifetimes.

Darwinian Guidance

Along with gender, birth order occupies center stage in the drama of sibling differences. No other environmental influences appear to be as important in creating the family's panoply of microenvironments. But birth order and even gender occupy supporting roles in a more extensive family drama. Parent-offspring conflict, parental loss, temperament, and the numerous contingencies of individual experience are all part of this dynamic and Darwinian account of human development.

As long as organisms have nurtured their young, competition between offspring has influenced which ones survived and reproduced. In many ways, competition among siblings is more fundamental even than competition for mates. To reproduce, organisms must first survive infancy and childhood. Individual differences in personality reflect the Darwinian strategies that we all employ toward this end. Millions of years of winners in this competitive process have destined us all to draw on the tactics that have allowed our genes to get this far. Some of these tactics are not nice. Prior to Darwin, even the most zealous disciples of natural theology were hard pressed to explain why baby cuckoos eject their foster siblings from the nest. In some species, siblicide is a necessary act of self-preservation. Among our animal ancestors, the mark of Cain is widespread and unmistakable. The counterstrategies of Abel are equally prevalent.

Even today, a simple Darwinian formula continues to drive sibling rivalry: If there is the slightest hint of favoritism by parents, *make sure that you are the favored one.* This is why siblings worry that "Mom loves you best" and vie intently for parental attention. It also explains why siblings can debate, with surprising gravity, who got the bigger piece of anything edible! Parents are sometimes astonished by the extent and pettiness of these childish rivalries. From an evolutionary perspective, such competition is natural. It is hard wired because it is adaptive. Paradoxically, so is altruism among siblings. The choice between fratricide and sacrificing one's life for a sibling is dictated by *environmental contingencies,* and only secondarily by the repertoire of Darwinian strategies that have proved adaptive in the past. When it comes to Darwinism and human affairs, the story must be told as biography and social history, not as genetic determinism. Little in life is strictly predetermined, even though human behavior is surprisingly predictable once relevant constraints have been identified.

Competition for parental investment fosters sibling "contrast effects." This relentless process of sibling differentiation is a form of Darwin's principle of divergence. During the brief period of childhood, siblings accomplish what species such as Darwin's Galápagos finches have achieved over millions of years. Like the diverse beaks of Darwin's finches, the human mind becomes adapted to the environmental niches that shape its development.[1] Unlike a finch's beak, the human mind is capable of varied and highly complex behavioral adaptations through learning. Together, the twin processes of "character displacement" and "competitive exclusion" facilitate these diverse adaptations, dictating each sibling's choice of interests and activities and supplementing biological differences in personality. As a rule, these contrast effects are greatest for siblings who are adjacent in birth order.[2]

Other aspects of the family experience (age differences between siblings, gender, and temperament) complement the effects of birth order. Many of these variables also interact with birth order, as well as with each other. For instance, firstborn sisters may be socially dominant, but they tend to express this trait differently from firstborn brothers. Whereas brothers typically avail themselves of physical aggression, sisters tend to assert their dominance through verbal means. Conflict with parents is another critical factor in personality development, although its influence is greater for firstborns than for laterborns. Birth-order effects are rooted in competition for parental favor. Absence of parental favor causes most offspring to adopt "laterborn" strategies.

Darwinian theory underscores another important guideline for understanding human behavior. Darwin introduced what has been called "population thinking."[3] The hallmark of this form of thinking is the appreciation of *individual differences.* Population thinking contrasts with "typological thinking," which considers entities as belonging to fixed categories. Creationism was inherently typological because it minimized the enormous variation within species. As a result of Darwin's insights, biologists have finally recognized that endless variation is the rule in nature. Species are highly variable populations, a generalization that applies to human beings. We are all very different from one another, even from our siblings—a circumstance that confounds most sociological claims about group differences. Our minds, in particular, embody an astonishing diversity of abilities that facilitate intelligent behavior. There are no simple "types" of intelligence, just as no single specimen of Darwin's finches can be said to represent the "type" of the species.[4]

RETELLING HISTORY

The Advancement of Science

For the past five centuries, the most consistent predictor of revolutionary allegiances turns out to be *birth order.* Compared with firstborns, laterborns are more likely to identify with the underdog and to challenge the established order. Because they identify with parents and authority, firstborns are more likely to defend the status quo. The effects of birth order transcend gender, social class, race, nationality, and—for the last five centuries—time.

To place these unexpected findings on a firm empirical foundation I have undertaken research in two broad domains, the history of science and general history. During the earliest stages of radical revolutions in science, laterborns have been *17* times more likely than firstborns to adopt a revolutionary point of view.[5] When Charles Darwin converted to the theory of evolution in 1837, his birth order made him *a hundred times* more likely to accept this theory than to champion a new plank in the prevailing doctrine of Design.[6] Firstborns such as Darwin's hero, Charles Lyell, faced equally long odds when they attempted to shift their allegiances from creationism to Darwinism. Try as he might to accept Darwin's ideas after 1859, Lyell continually felt "the old trains of thought, the old ruts, interfering with the new course."[7] Other firstborn scientists in Darwin's generation shared Lyell's psychological propensity to defend the status quo. They were just not born to rebel.

The scientific originality of firstborns, which is indisputable, lies in clever puzzle solving, pushing established theories into new but socially acceptable territory.* Firstborn Jonas Salk, who developed a vaccine against polio, and most Nobel Prize winners provide good examples. Their intense concern with personal achievement also drives firstborns to defend their scientific turf against all comers. During the last five centuries, firstborns have typically been three times more likely than laterborns to contest priority for their scientific ideas.[8] It is rare for a firstborn to act as magnanimously as Darwin and Wallace did in sharing credit for the theory of natural selection. But Darwin and Wallace were united in a more important cause: overthrowing a worldview in which privilege and status were closely linked to the fortunes of birth.

The magnitude of birth-order differences is easier to appreciate when they are translated into other familiar terms. What outspoken lastborns were willing to accept and defend in 1690, firstborns only acceded to around 1860, 170 years later.[9] In science, temporal disparities in the acceptance of change tend to be reduced by the accumulation of hard evidence. Still, laterborn scientists have typically been half a century ahead of firstborns in their willingness to back heterodox innovations.[10]

The effects of age tend to inhibit the acceptance of new ideas and typically supplement the consequences of birth order. This additional influence provides another yardstick for comparing birth-order effects. By their early thirties, the majority of firstborns have already aligned themselves with the scientific status quo. Thereafter, they tend to oppose heterodox innovations with their usual degree of erudite zeal. Among laterborns, the majority remain open to radical innovations until their early sixties, a 30-year difference compared with firstborns.[11] This greater openness to innovation translates into continuing scientific creativity at later ages.[12]

Darwin's achievements exemplify this tendency for laterborns to sustain creative discovery over a longer portion of their scientific ca-

*It is worth reiterating that the influence of birth order on personality is typically 5 to 10 times greater than it is on IQ and academic achievement (see pages 74–75). In addition, academic achievement, which is associated with firstborn status, is not the only kind of intellectual achievement. Firstborns and laterborns tend to become eminent in different ways, which in turn relate to differing features of personality and to the differing family niches that shape them (see Chapter 4, especially pages 109–10). Even within science, IQ is only weakly related to achievement among people who are smart enough to become scientists. Research has shown, for example, that a scientist who has an IQ of 130 is just as likely to win a Nobel Prize as a scientist whose IQ is 180 (Hudson 1966:104).

Charles Darwin, about 1874, photographed by his fourth son, Leonard. Two years later, in his *Autobiography,* Darwin was at a loss to explain his remarkable influence on scientific thought: "My success as a man of science, whatever this may have amounted to, has been determined, as far as I can judge, by complex and diversified mental qualities and conditions. Of these the most important have been—the love of science—unbounded patience in long reflecting over any subject—industry in observing and collecting facts—and a fair share of invention as well as of common-sense. With such moderate abilities as I possess, it is truly surprising that I should have influenced to a considerable extent the belief of scientific men on some important points" (1958 [1876]:144–45).

reers. During his twenties and early thirties, Darwin did his most original work in geology and natural history. During his forties he became a world-class invertebrate zoologist, writing three definitive monographs on barnacles. Having finally published the *Origin of Species* at the age of fifty, Darwin turned his attentions to botany, a field in which he was a self-proclaimed "Ignoramus."[13] Over the next two decades he produced six pioneering books dealing successively with orchids, climbing plants, insectivorous plants, plant reproduction, and the power of movement in plants. Professional botanists such as Joseph Hooker and Asa Gray were dumbfounded by Darwin's ability to make important discoveries that the experts had overlooked. As Gray himself noted, Darwin's findings about the power of movement in plants stemmed from an accidental observation by a botanist "in whose hands it was sterile." But the same botanical observation, when it was "touched by Darwin's genius," became "wonderfully fertile."[14]

Not one to linger over his newly acquired reputation as a world-class botanist, Darwin turned to writing the *Descent of Man* (1871) and the *Expression of the Emotions in Man and Animals* (1872), published when he was in his early sixties. With these two pathbreaking works, the study of human behavior acquired its indispensable foundations in evolutionary theory. It has taken psychologists more than a century to appreciate, and to begin to mine in earnest, the rich vein of conceptual gold that Darwin mapped out in these two books.

Darwin's last work was published in the autumn of 1881, six months before his death at the age of seventy-three. This publication chronicled the little-known habits of earthworms. Once again Darwin astonished the scientific world with his original discoveries. Worms, he demonstrated, were surprisingly intelligent creatures. Additionally, through their beneficial effects on the soil, worms were tireless friends to humankind. Darwin's charming tribute to the lowly earthworm outsold all of his other scientific publications.[15] From geology to zoology, from orchids to Venus flytraps, and from earthworms to man, Darwin's lifelong record of research exemplifies one continuous revolution in human thought. Throughout his illustrious career, Darwin's most abiding scientific hallmark was his penchant for elevating the inferior and the insignificant into the superior and the significant. "It has always pleased me, " he remarked in his *Autobiography,* "to exalt plants in the scale of organised beings."[16] With his theory of natural selection Darwin went even further, making a blind process of trial and error into a substitute for God.

Like his radical theories, Darwin's methodological style reflects his own particular personality and revolutionary genius. He valued questions over answers, curiosity over conviction, and perseverance over prerogative. He loved to perform what he termed "fool's experiments," tests of ideas that were so implausible that other people never thought to take them seriously.[17] What Darwin once said about success in science could just as easily be applied to himself: "It's dogged as does it."[18]

The same assertion sums up his greatest scientific insight, the principle of natural selection. By the selection of random variations over millions of years, this relentless biological process has produced the astonishing diversity of life on earth, including its extraordinary expression in human intelligence. Although Darwin never wrote about sibling relationships, he is a textbook example of how strategies for dealing with sibling competition, particularly openness to experience and dogged perseverance, inspire revolutionary genius.

Darwin's mechanism of natural selection was a particularly dangerous and shocking idea because it replaced the genius of God with the heretical genius of trial and error.[19] What firstborns such as Louis Agassiz and Charles Lyell feared most was not that biological change was possible, but rather that it proceeds with no evidence of intelligent foresight. Darwin's views on the evolution of man, in particular, affronted their sense of moral and intellectual superiority. In a notebook that Lyell kept during the 1860s, he confessed to feeling a distinct "Repugnance to [a] Quadrumanous Genealogy." Lyell also believed that "each race of Man has its [proper] place, like the inferior animals."[20] The Darwinian revolution was all about relationships in the family tree of life on earth. This revolution was also about the kind of creative mechanisms that, if evolution was true, could account for it. The most subversive aspect of Darwin's theories was their utter repudiation of the Creative Genius that Agassiz and Lyell, and firstborns more generally, believed to be characteristic of life.

Darwin's mechanism of evolution embodies his own kind of humble creativity: gradual improvement through unfettered competition. As Darwin himself once pointed out about science, the smartest people do not tend to make the most important discoveries.[21] Darwin was particularly puzzled by this empirical observation because, like most of his contemporaries, he tended to identify genius with supreme intelligence, especially the kind of intellectual ability that is typical of achievement in the physical sciences. Darwin knew perfectly well that he lacked these kinds of abilities. As he emphasized in his *Autobiography:* "I have no great quickness of apprehension or wit which is so remarkable in some clever men, for instance Huxley. I am therefore a poor critic: a paper or book, when first read, generally excites my admiration, and it is only after considerable reflection that I perceive the weak points."[22]

Fortunately for Darwin, creative intelligence is as diverse as the family niches that foster it. Intelligence can be mathematical, artistic, social, and even plodding, like that of the lowly worm. Darwin's own creativity—and the foundations of his particular genius—lay in a fortuitous mixture of highly diversified interests, personality attributes, and abilities. He is a prime example of *divergent genius*—the most revolutionary form that genius can take.

Political and Religious Revolutions

Compared with science, political change presents a contrasting context for observing the formative influence of family niches. In addition to openness to experience, tough-mindedness is integral to political thought. Tough-mindedness determines the manner in which conservative or liberal views are put into political practice. What makes this idea scientific, rather than ad hoc, is the fact that it can be tested. Controlled for differences in open-mindedness, differences in tough-mindedness contribute significantly to political behavior.

A willingness to employ violence in the service of the status quo combines two distinctly firstborn tendencies. Firstborns are accordingly overrepresented among tough-minded conservatives. Prior to the advent of democracy, firstborns and eldest sons, who controlled the reins of political power through the practice of primogeniture, were in a particularly favorable position to defend the status quo. For every laterborn dissenter who suffered death in an effort to challenge despotism, there were usually firstborn rulers and magistrates who signed the death warrants.

In contrast to eldest siblings, who have typically supported the established social order, laterborns have consistently backed liberal reforms. In Western history, laterborns have been 18 times more likely than firstborns to champion radical political revolutions.[23] During the Protestant Reformation, laterborns were 48 times more likely than firstborns to suffer martyrdom for this reform effort.[24] In their efforts to promote egalitarian social reforms, laterborns have fought for freedom of speech, freedom of worship, the abolition of slavery, and equality by race and by gender.

The construct of tough-mindedness sheds considerable light on *political tactics,* an issue that sometimes turns ideological allies into bitter enemies. The most moralistic and inflexible political leaders tend to be firstborns, followed by only children, lastborns, and then middleborns. Firstborn radicals (who are often the offspring of laterborn radicals) generally favor aggressive strategies. Such militant figures have included

Mussolini, Stalin, Ché Guevara, and Carlos the Jackal. Carlos spoke for all of them when he remarked: "Bullets are the only thing that makes sense."[25] In contrast, laterborns are less likely to believe that the end justifies the means. More than any other sibling group, middle children are likely to espouse peaceful methods of reform. It is rare in history to find an advocate of nonviolent resistance, such as Gandhi or Martin Luther King, Jr., who is a firstborn.[26] Compromise is a special talent of middle children. Owing to their family niche, they understand the virtues of coalitions, parliamentary procedures, and government by consensus.[27]

The split within the American abolition movement—to support or oppose armed insurrection against slavery—provides a good example of these kinds of sibling differences. If they happened to be abolitionists, firstborns called for violent action, and in some cases resorted to it themselves, whereas laterborns—particularly middle children—preached moral persuasion. During the French Revolution, a similar disparity led to the tragic clash between the Gironde and the Mountain. Militant firstborns, including Robespierre and other architects of the Terror, turned on their laterborn colleagues—the Girondins—and sent them to the guillotine. During the Reign of Terror, these tough-minded radicals mistook Girondin compassion—a laterborn tendency—for allegiance to the royalist cause. The inappropriateness of this charge of royalism has finally been recognized by French historians, but the fratricidal nature of the underlying conflict has not. Such episodes of mass fratricide are probably endemic to revolutionary politics, but the phenomenon tends to go unrecognized because people rarely kill their *own* siblings. Still, people willingly kill their siblings' political allies, thereby committing fratricide by proxy.

Although between-family differences are not particularly relevant to personality development, they do play important roles in human behavior and leave their considerable mark on history. In writing about history, it is often difficult to know which group differences are truly causal, and which ones represent pseudoeffects that are traceable to differences between siblings. Statistical methods help us to resolve these methodological problems. These methods repeatedly confirm the explanatory superiority of birth order (and family dynamics as a whole) over most sociological predictors of human behavior.

Just as the causes of historical change tend to lead back to family history, so they also tend to lead forward in time to the founding of new families. Social liberals tend to marry other liberals, and to have liberal offspring. By 1600 the European division between Catholics and

Protestants, which had begun as a within-family conflict, had become a difference between local geographic regions and even entire nations. Once these geographical subdivisions were in place, children growing up in Protestant countries were more susceptible to the liberalizing gains of the immediately preceding generation. In the wake of the Reformation, Protestants who became scientists—even firstborns—were "honorary laterborns" in their openness to experience. Protestant scientists, as a consequence, were more favorably disposed toward radical scientific change than were their Catholic counterparts. Spurred on by the liberalizing influences of the Reformation, one laterborn rebellion followed another. The rise of modern science during the seventeenth century presaged the Enlightenment during the next century. The Enlightenment in turn spawned a greater yearning for freedom of thought, causing figures such as Thomas Paine, Jean-Jacques Rousseau, and Voltaire to set in motion a plethora of new revolutions in social thought. As a result of this revolutionary cascade, sibling differences in radicalism were compounded over the generations.

The family trees of most social liberals are overflowing with laterborns who fought radical battles during prior generations. Rebels such as Charles Darwin and Benjamin Franklin—youngest sons of youngest sons going back four and five generations—exemplify the compounding power that sibling differences acquire over time. Darwin was a radical revolutionary in significant part because he grew up in a *liberal* family. His father, a lastborn, was the atheist son of another lastborn, a deist. When Darwin's father selected a mate, he picked the daughter of his father's *most radical friend,* Josiah Wedgwood. As the youngest of thirteen children, Josiah was one of the most ardent abolitionists in all of Britain. He vocally supported both the American and the French revolutions, in bold defiance of the royal family that had adopted his fine Wedgwood dinnerware.[28]

Exceptions to the Rule

Individual exceptions exist for every one of the generalizations I have set forth in this book. All human behavior is contingent and overdetermined. In the world around us, a multitude of crisscrossing influences limits our ability to predict individual action. Still, *multiple* predictors—far more effectively than *single* ones—provide an effective means of explaining individual behavior. Exceptions to one statistical generalization are often explained by another even more important generalization. What makes the treatment of these exceptions scientific is the formal testing of rival hypotheses.

Given the relationship between the social attitudes of parents and their offspring, no one should expect the eldest son of Karl Marx or Mao Tse-tung to be a social conservative. In terms of their social attitudes, most offspring take after their parents, although firstborns do so more faithfully than their younger siblings. Similarly, the fact that Martin Luther, a firstborn, became a Protestant may be attributed, in part, to his coming from Germany, where church abuses were particularly widespread. Luther's openness to religious reform also reflects his position within the lower clergy, a group that had much to gain from church reforms. These predisposing factors *apply across the board to all theologians living during the Reformation,* not just to Martin Luther.[29] This criterion is what makes such explanations scientific. A judicious account of individual behavior is one that encompasses, and tests, all important influences.

The use of multiple predictors sometimes allows us to make surprisingly strong claims about individuals. For example, young laterborns who are socially liberal are roughly 95 percent likely to adopt a radical innovation such as evolution. In other words, 95 out of 100 people with Charles Darwin's biographical attributes accepted the theory that he so ardently championed. The 5 who did not can in some cases be explained by the influence of other intervening variables, such as age, friendships, and scientific training. Conversely, older firstborns who are socially conservative are only 5 percent likely to adopt the same radical idea. With just three variables (birth order, social attitudes, and age), we can demonstrate a 20 to 1 disparity in individual probabilities of accepting radical innovation. The people who have contributed the most to radical change, along with those who have protested most strenuously against it, tend to exemplify these behavioral extremes.*

Individuals who are exceptions to statistical generalizations often

---

*For the reception of evolution (1700–1875) I have made the relevant statistical test mentioned in the text. This test compares firstborns who were over the age of fifty and who were socially conservative (rated below 2.0 on a 5-point scale) with laterborns who were under the age of thirty-five and who were socially liberal (rated 3.0 or higher). In this sample of 43 scientists, 10 were firstborns and all of them opposed evolution. In contrast, 34 of the 35 laterborns (or 97 percent) supported evolution ($r=.94$, [*phi*], $df=1/43$, $t=4.97$, $p<.0001$ [Fisher's exact test]). Appendix 11 ("How to Test Your Own Propensity to Rebel") presents a list of predicted probabilities, stratified by age, social attitudes, and birth order. The reader may employ this information to determine his or her own likelihood of supporting a radical revolution.

point the way to other causes of behavior that have been overlooked. Properly identified, statistical error is the route to even better behavioral explanations. The historian who feels uncomfortable with statistical generalizations is uncomfortable with the nature of history. Most historical claims are inherently statistical, like the nature of life experience. These claims embody hypotheses that can, and should, be tested.

HISTORY AS A SCIENCE

The Person versus the Situation

Historical claims about family dynamics exemplify the vexing problem of whether history entails general principles about human behavior. It is true that laterborns tend to rebel, but the act of rebellion implies specific goals and also takes place within specific social and intellectual contexts. Given the right circumstances, even firstborns will reject the status quo. It is hardly surprising that some firstborn slaves rebelled against this odious practice, slaughtering their masters in the process.

The single most important moderator of how individuals respond to historical change is *the nature of the change.* Innovations can be conservative, technical, tough-minded, tender-minded, radical, and so forth. Within science, firstborns are quick to endorse conceptual innovations that are either technical or conservative. If technical, such innovations tend to bring relatively prompt acclaim. If conservative, such advances represent "revolutions" in the original sense of the term: "to return again, to go through a cyclical succession, as in the seasons of the year."[30] In spite of their predilection for novelty and change, laterborns have generally resisted conservative innovations. Their hearts and souls are most thoroughly identified with radical changes that defy the status quo.

Among the more than one hundred different kinds of historical movements I have surveyed, the direction and magnitude of birth-order effects are systematically related to the degree of *controversy.* Whenever new theories are controversial—owing to social, conceptual, or ideological reasons—significant birth-order differences occur in how people react to them. And whenever there is a significant birth-order difference, there is a substantial role for other attributes of family niches.

Hypothesis Testing

For more than two decades I have tested my claims against an extensive list of rival hypotheses. Some of these rival hypotheses have survived formal testing and belong among the arsenal of accepted principles for explaining human behavior. For example, rebellious inclinations are strongly associated with being socially liberal, which is in turn associated with having liberal parents and grandparents. Temperament is another relevant factor: the most zealous revolutionaries tend to be laterborns, who are also usually extraverted. In addition, advocates of revolution are sometimes influenced by teachers and other people within their social milieu.

I have tested these rival claims to avoid error, not because I believe that history is like physics or chemistry. Still, history is remarkably similar to other sciences that deal with change, especially geology, paleontology, and evolutionary biology. In addition, history is fundamentally dependent on a scientific understanding of human behavior. Methods from the behavioral sciences can be gainfully employed to test historical hypotheses that have previously been accepted largely on faith. Historians have tended to resist the use of scientific methods, generally on the grounds that they are "inappropriate" to historical understanding.[31] However, a good case can be made for considering Charles Darwin the greatest historian of all time. Many of his methods were those employed by historians, including the careful description of the objects he studied, together with an abiding concern for context. What made Darwin's career so successful was not these descriptive methods per se, but rather his dedication to hypothesis testing.

When the mind is confronted with more information than it can absorb, it looks for meaningful (and usually *confirmatory*) patterns. As a consequence, we tend to minimize evidence that is incongruous with our expectations, causing the dominant worldview to bring about its own reaffirmation.[32] Charles Darwin understood this human predilection for reaffirming the status quo. In his *Autobiography* he noted how quickly he tended to forget any fact that seemed to contradict his theories. He therefore made it a "golden rule" to write this information down so that he would not overlook it.[33] Like Darwin's golden rule, hypothesis testing overcomes certain limitations in how the human mind processes information.

As with the study of history today, natural history was once forced to settle for multiple interpretations. Evolutionary biology passed through a long phase of debate over Darwinian versus non-Darwinian explanations. Like natural selection, which adapts species to their environments, hypothesis testing sooner or later eliminates unsuccessful theories. Empirical success, predictability, simplicity, and the independent verification of results all improve the chances that research will reach reliable conclusions.[34] Just like successful species in nature, creative scientists occupy the most favorable niches. They employ hypothesis testing to evolve conceptually and hence to avoid intellectual extinction.[35]

Hypothesis testing possesses another distinct virtue. It reduces the siren-like lure of those interpretive fads that pass for progress within the humanities. This is why so many recent humanistic approaches are now labeled as being "post" some other once-popular approach. There is no post-physics, post-biology, or post-chemistry. Over and over again, hypothesis testing has proved that it is *not a passing fad*. During the Scientific Revolution of the seventeenth century, this radical method was actively promoted by seventeenth-century lastborns such as Francis Bacon and René Descartes. Younger siblings campaigned strenuously for these methods because they constituted a powerful intellectual weapon against the status quo. In the days of the Scientific Revolution, to test was to rebel, a principle that remains equally true in our own day.[36]

The extraordinary impact of Bacon and Descartes resided in their success at convincing their colleagues to accept, and then to institutionalize, the radical principles of hypothesis testing. Henceforth Scholastic authority and the church were no longer the final arbiters of truth about the natural world. With the birth of modern science, a more democratic concept of knowledge became the norm. Its democratic nature would give rise to the Enlightenment and would also lay the foundations for further revolutions in human thought. The American Declaration of Independence, with its stress on multiple checks and balances within government, reflects these liberalizing principles, which were absorbed by Thomas Jefferson and other Founding Fathers from their study of Newtonian theory.[37] The fruition of the Scientific Revolution is the greatest of the laterborn triumphs I have discussed in this book. By winning this battle over the rules of knowledge, younger siblings successfully transformed this creative domain of human inquiry into a process of perpetual rebellion.

More than a felicitous method is needed for the advancement of human understanding. Individuals who launch radical revolutions typically require strong determination, courage, and independence of mind.

Unfortunately, their divergent ways of thinking have tended to condemn these bold thinkers to rejection, ridicule, and torment. Like Charles Darwin, who compared his belief in evolution to "confessing a murder," heterodox individuals have typically suffered for their revolutionary aspirations.[38] Not every unorthodox thinker has succeeded, and not all of them have been right. But a surprising number of them have shared a deep and powerful bond. More often than not, they were born to rebel.

APPENDICES

APPENDIX 1

A BRIEF INTRODUCTION TO STATISTICS (OR CORRELATIONS MADE EASY)

Correlations. Statistics are reasonably easy to understand, especially when they are reduced to "correlations." This particular statistic is a measure of association. We compute correlations in our heads all the time, using informal methods. A child's height, for example, gives us a good idea of a child's age, whereas a child's last name does not. When correlations (abbreviated as *r*) are computed in a formal manner, they vary from .0 to ±1.0. A correlation of .0 means that there is no relationship between two variables, such as the number of your street address and the first digit of your telephone number. A correlation of 1.0 means that there is a perfect linear relationship between two variables, such as the number of bricks in a pile and their total weight. It is not necessary for data to involve continuous metrics, such as height or weight, to be rendered as correlations. Even dichotomous data can be compared in this manner. When correlations are based on a variable with only two possible outcomes, such as gender, the resulting statistic is called *phi* rather than *r*. For example, the correlation (*phi*) between being French and being Catholic (as opposed to being non-Catholic) is roughly .8.

For most influences on human behavior, correlations range between .0 and .5. Only in fields such as physiology and the physical sciences do correlations typically exceed .5. Based on a wide variety of personality tests, the correlation between gender and assertiveness is about .25.[1] During radical scientific revolutions, the correlation between birth order and support for innovation is roughly .40. Among identical twins raised together, the correlation for most personality traits is .5.[2] To give some further idea of the magnitude of correlations—that is, their real-world import—I present here a table of equivalents. These equivalent effects involve the likelihood that a person will survive a disease, treated with or without a beneficial medication (Table 8).

From Table 8 it can be seen that even small correlations have meaningful effects. A correlation of .10, for example, is equivalent to improving your chances of surviving a potentially fatal disease, assuming that you take an effective medication, from 45 percent to 55 percent. This improvement represents an increase in survival of 22 percent over the base rate (55/45=1.22). If your life were threatened by a potentially fatal disease, you would probably be grateful to have access to drugs known to produce even such a moderate benefit. By comparison, a correlation of .30 is equivalent to nearly doubling your chances of survival, improving your likelihood of recovery from 35 percent to 65 percent. A correlation of .50 yields an

[1] Feingold 1994:443.
[2] Dunn and Plomin 1990:49.

TABLE 8

Real-World Statistical Equivalents

Correlation (r)	*Chances of Survival, without Medication (Percentage)*	*Chances of Survival, with Medication (Percentage)*	*Improvement on Initial Odds (Percentage)*	*r^2 ("Variance Explained") (Percentage)*	*Qualitative Description of the Effect*
.01	49.5	50.5	1	MUCH LESS THAN 1	VERY SMALL
.05	47.5	52.5	11	LESS THAN 1	SMALL
.10	45	55	22	1	SMALL[a]
.20	40	60	50	4	MODERATE
.30	35	65	86	9	LARGE
.40	30	70	133	16	LARGE
.50	25	75	300	25	VERY LARGE
.80	10	90	900	64	VERY LARGE

NOTE: Table adapted from Rosenthal and Rubin 1982.

a. Assigning qualitative descriptions to effect sizes is dependent on the context. Many people would consider a 22 percent increase in likelihood of surviving a potentially fatal disease—representing a correlation of .10—to be a *moderate* rather than a *small* benefit.

even more dramatic difference in recovery rates, from 25 percent to 75 percent—triple the recovery rate of the untreated group.

Table 8 also indicates the variance explained by the illustrative correlations. "Variance explained" is a technical term denoting the square of the correlation. This concept, although useful in some statistical contexts, tends to be misleading in most applications. Squaring numbers may have theoretical meaning in statistics, but this practice makes little sense in the context of ordinary reasoning about cause and effect. When we square a number less than 1.0, we always get a smaller number, sometimes a *much* smaller number. A correlation of .10, which represents a 22 percent increase in survival in our hypothetical medical scenario, translates to just 1 percent of the variance explained. Thus, relatively small correlations constitute surprisingly large effects, despite modest amounts of "variance explained," and should not be dismissed as unimportant.

Correlation versus causation. There is an old maxim that "correlation is not causation." Although this is certainly true, it is also true that, under some circumstances, correlations provide a reasonably reliable guide to causation. For example, the correlation between winning a million dollars in the lottery and having more money to spend is very high, and these two outcomes are obviously related in a causal manner. We must employ common sense in deciding whether, and to what extent, correlations suggest a causal relationship. Even when correlations do not warrant the assumption of causality, they generally suggest that *some other variable, itself associated with the two correlated variables,* is causally involved in the observed relationship. As we introduce additional variables into a statistical analysis, we can often pinpoint the most likely source of "causation." For example, birth order is not the *real* cause of radical thinking, even though it is strongly correlated with it. But birth order can be seen as a proxy for differences in age, size, power, and status within the family. Common sense tells us that causation probably lies in these other variables, not in birth order per se. We can test this claim by showing that *functional* birth order, not *biological* birth order, is what actually correlates most strongly with radical thought. Controlled for functional birth order, biological birth order is not appreciably correlated with support for radical thought.

Statistical significance. This term denotes whether a result is likely to happen simply "by chance." By convention, statistical significance is accorded to results whenever they would happen by chance less than 1 time in 20 (denoted as $p<.05$). Statistical significance reflects two different aspects about a given finding: (1) *the strength of the effect*—the so-called effect size, which can always be represented as a correlation; and (2) *sample size.* Sample size tells us nothing about the strength of an effect, but it does tell us how confident we can be that a reported effect size is representative of the true effect size. Large samples can lead to statistically significant results involving very small effects. For example, the relationship between birth order and intellectual eminence is well documented—firstborns tend to be more eminent. But the effect is typically "small" ($r<.10$), and it becomes smaller still when it is controlled for confounding influences, such as social class and sibship size.

Especially if a result is statistically significant, and often even when it is not, it is a good idea to focus on the *effect size* rather than the *level of statistical significance.* Because my own samples in this book are generally large, and, more important, because many of the effects I have documented are moderate to large, the levels of statistical significance associated with these findings are sometimes very impressive. In Chapter 2, I report levels of statistical significance that exceed $p<1\times10^{-20}$ (or less than one in a billion billion). In subsequent chapters I drop this tiresome convention of giving exact probabilities for such improbable outcomes. Instead I report all results that would occur by chance less than 1 time in 10,000 as $p<.0001$.

One-tailed versus two-tailed statistical tests. Throughout this book I generally employ "two-tailed" tests of statistical significance, but occasionally I report the results of "one-tailed" tests. The distinction between one-tailed and two-tailed tests of significance relates to the nature of the hypothesis that is being tested. When researchers confidently know the direction of an expected effect, they may legitimately increase the statistical significance of the finding compared with that indicated by a two-tailed test. The logic behind this convention is straightforward. If researchers strongly believe that two elephants weigh more than one, they do not need to guard against the possibility that two elephants might weigh less than one. With many relationships, the researcher cannot be confident about the direction of an effect. In these cases it is appropriate to apply the more stringent two-tailed test. In this book I have almost always employed two-tailed tests, but I occasionally report one-tailed tests when they are appropriate and especially when the findings seem to merit reporting. Researchers who have a preference for two-tailed tests, no matter what the hypothesis, may simply double the reported one-tailed *p*-value.

Synergistic effects and interaction effects. Another statistical concept—*synergistic effects*—is fundamental, and I frequently refer to it in this book. Imagine that you are suffering from a disease that can usually be cured by taking two drugs, but only if they are administered *simultaneously*. One drug might selectively locate cancer cells in your body, thus serving as a reliable "marker" for diseased cells. The second drug—a kind of magic bullet—might destroy all cells marked by the first drug. Let us imagine that your chances of surviving cancer are nil without the two drugs, nil with either drug administered without the other, and 95 percent after taking both drugs together. The effect of the two drugs is synergistic, not additive. Synergistic effects include what are known as "interaction effects," which represent that component of a synergism that is not attributable to a main effect. Although the two concepts are technically different, they overlap in practice, and social scientists tend to use the terms interchangeably.

Multiple regression. When more than one variable is a significant predictor of another, it is useful to employ *multiple regression*. With this statistical procedure, we seek to predict an outcome variable (the *dependent* variable) using multiple *independent* variables. This technique has two major advantages. First, independent variables are usually correlated among themselves, which can confuse the issue of cause and effect. For example, laterborns are overrepresented in lower-class families because these families tend to be larger than upper-class families. As a result, social class correlates with birth order. Without further analysis, we cannot be sure which variable—birth order or social class—is more fundamentally related to a third variable such as radicalism. Using multiple regression, we are likely to find that social class is no longer correlated with radicalism after we include sibship size in the regression analysis. In other words, the apparent association with social class disappears once we control for the spurious relationship between class and birth order.

The second advantage of multiple regression is that it allows us to assign *relative weights* to predictors. Suppose two medicines are both significantly correlated with a patient's chances of recovering from an illness. It would be useful to know that one of the two medicines is 3 times more effective than the other. It would also be useful to know that the two medicines, when administered together, act synergistically. It would be even more useful to know that this synergism yields a treatment benefit that is 5 times greater than the benefit derived from either medicine administered by itself. Typically, effect sizes in multiple regression equations are reported as *beta weights,* which are similar to correlations. Such statistics can be difficult to interpret, whereas *partial correlations* provide a much more straightforward measure of effect size. A partial correlation is the correlation of each independent variable, controlled for all other independent variables in the model. I have provided statistical information on partial correlations, not beta weights, throughout this book.

Meta-analysis. When numerous studies have already been done on a subject, and especially when many of these studies conflict, researchers often resort to meta-analytic techniques. By pooling the results of different studies, researchers gain statistical reliability and power, allowing a more accurate determination of effect sizes. Meta-analysis also permits the search for moderator variables and for significantly differing levels of effect sizes. In Chapter 3 (Table 4), I show that, among 196 birth-order studies controlled for social class and sibship size, far too many significant results have been reported for these to be chance findings. In addition, the collective findings on some aspects of personality—such as openness to experience—are significantly more likely to be positive than for other aspects of personality—such as extraversion—even though both domains of research yield more positive studies than would be expected by chance.

This discussion is all that the reader needs to know in order to understand the statistical information reported in the footnotes and appendices to this book. Where possible, I have sought to express every result in terms of a correlation. For the benefit of researchers familiar with statistical methods, I have supplied additional statistical paraphernalia, such as *t*-, *F*-, and *p*-values, in footnotes. The average reader may safely ignore these statistical details and focus only on *the size of correlations and on whether interaction effects are involved.*[3]

---

[3] For useful introductions to statistical methods, see Rosenthal and Rosnow 1991; Rosenthal 1987. On the topic of statistical effect sizes, and what they mean, see Cohen 1988; Rosenthal and Rubin 1982; Rosenthal 1994. For introductions to meta-analytic methods, see Glass, McGaw, and Smith 1981; Hunter, Schmidt, and Jackson 1982; Light and Pillemer 1984; Hunter and Schmidt 1990; Rosenthal 1991.

APPENDIX 2
CODING PROCEDURES FOR VARIABLES IN THE STUDY

OVERVIEW

In the course of this book I analyze 121 historical events, which encompass biographical data on 6,566 participants. These 121 events include 28 revolutions in science, 61 reform movements in American history, 31 political revolutions, and the Protestant Reformation. I have also assembled a database on U.S. Supreme Court voting behavior, which includes biographical information on the 108 justices to date.

In some instances, these databases include up to 256 variables—the maximum number possible in my database program. Some of these 256 variables represent dummy-coded information (that is, information coded as 0 or 1). In my database for scientific controversies, I allocate ten dummy-coded fields for nationality. These nationalities include eight of the major European countries, together with the United States. The tenth field codes information for participants from countries "other" than the first nine. Depending on how one counts such dummy-coded variables (is nationality *one* variable or *ten*?), the amount of information in these 122 databases is somewhere between a half million and a million biographical data points.

Some of this biographical information is missing in individual instances, a fact that I have systematically coded with the number 99. (My statistical programs all recognize 99 as missing information.) Each database also includes a variable for the number of missing data points for each individual. Missing information is itself information and often correlates with other predictors of behavior (see Appendix 5). The fact that a person is difficult to document in history means that he or she was probably from a lower-class background, from a large family, and a middle child.

VARIABLES IN THE DATABASES

In this appendix I describe my database for scientific controversies. These variables fall into five general classes, namely, information about (1) the family background of the participant, (2) the social attitudes of the participant, (3) the social attitudes of the parents, (4) the career characteristics of the participant, and (5) the specific historical event in which each scientist participated. Variables included in my databases for the Protestant Reformation and the French Revolution are described in appendices 7 and 8.

Family Background of the Participant

1. **Name.**
2. **Year of birth.**

3. Year of death.

4–14. Nationality. In addition to being recorded as a character field, this information is also dummy coded for the nine most common nationalities, together with a category for "other" nationalities.

15. Gender.

16. Father's occupation.

17. Father's socioeconomic status. Coded on a 5-point scale: aristocracy, professional, mercantile or middle class, lower-middle class, and working class.

18–19. Religious denomination. Dummy coded as Protestant, Catholic, and Jewish.

20. Birth order. Dummy coded in *functional* rather than *biological* terms, as firstborn or laterborn. Siblings who are reported as dying in infancy or early childhood are not counted in assessing birth order. A small number of individuals who failed to establish a stable birth order within the first seven years of their lives, and who did not maintain this birth order until the age of sixteen, have been excluded from statistical analysis (see Chapter 2). An alternative approach to the construct of functional birth order is to employ a 3-step scale and to assign an intermediate score to individuals whose birth orders have changed significantly during childhood. Although there are relatively few individuals to whom this coding scheme would apply, I have sometimes employed it in my analyses of small samples. In no instance do these two alternative methods change the statistical significance of any of the results reported in this book. Controlled for functional birth order, biological birth order is not a significant predictor of radicalism (see page 465, n. 81).

21. Birth rank. Coded in *functional* terms, as first child, second child, third child, and so forth.

22. Son rank. Coded in *functional* terms, as first son, second son, third son, and so forth. Daughters are coded in terms of the number of their older brothers (plus 1), so as to be coded analogously to sons.

23. Sibship size. Coded in *functional* terms.

24–25. Relative birth rank. This variable is coded in two ways. First, I code relative birth rank as (birth rank –1)/(sibship size –1). According to this measure, relative birth rank ranges from 0, for firstborns, to 1, for lastborns. I also code relative birth rank on a 7-point scale: (1) firstborns with younger siblings; (2) only children; (3) "eldest sons" and "only sons" (in cases where the exact birth order is unknown); (4) laterborns whose birth rank places them in the first half of their sibship; (5) laterborns whose birth rank places them in the second half of their sibship, but not in the last third; (6) laterborns whose birth rank places them in the last third of their sibship, but who are not lastborns; and (7) lastborns. Most of the statistics cited in this book employ this second measure. The correlation between the two measures is .97. The second measure allows the inclusion of substantially more cases (1,823 versus 1,451), owing to the inclusion of "eldest sons." In terms of their support for scientific innovations, "eldest sons" fall between firstborns and laterborns.

26. Age gap from next younger sibling. When available in months, recorded as such; otherwise recorded in years.

27. Age gap from next older sibling. When available in months, recorded as such; otherwise recorded in years.

28. Presence of a sibling in the sample. Dummy coded as 0 or 1.

29. Presence of a parent or an offspring in the sample. Dummy coded as 0 or 1.

30. Shyness versus extraversion. Textual information from biographical sources, transcribed and recorded as a memo field.

31–33. Independent ratings on shyness versus extraversion. Coded on a 7-point scale.

34. Shyness versus extraversion. Mean rating of independent judges.

35. Parent-offspring conflict. Textual information from biographical sources, transcribed and recorded as a memo field.

36–38. Independent ratings on conflict with the father. Coded on a 7-point scale.

39. Conflict with the father. Mean rating of independent judges.

40–42. Independent ratings on conflict with the mother. Coded on a 7-point scale.

43. Conflict with the mother. Mean rating of independent judges.

44. Parent-offspring conflict. Mean score of variables 39 and 43.

45. Father's birth order. Coded as relative birth rank.

46. Mother's birth order. Coded as relative birth rank.

47. Parents' birth orders. The mean of the two preceding variables.

48. Mother's age at participant's birth. This information is useful in estimating missing birth-order data.

49. Father's age at participant's birth. This information is useful in estimating missing birth-order data.

50. Years of marriage by parents, before the participant's birth. This information is useful for estimating missing birth-order data.

51. Age of participant at mother's death (or mother's removal from the household).

52. When information on the preceding variable is missing, highest known age of participant when the mother was still living.

53. Age of participant at father's death (or father's removal from the household).

54. When information on the preceding variable is missing, highest known age of participant when the father was still living.

55. Age of participant at earliest date of parental loss. The lower of variables 51 and 53.

56. Being named after a parent. Coded on a 3-point scale: 0 for not being named after a parent; 1 for receiving one of a parent's first two given names; 2 for receiving both of a parent's first two given names. This information is useful for estimating missing birth-order data.

Social Attitudes of the Participant

57. Social attitudes. Textual information from autobiographical and biographical sources, transcribed and recorded as a memo field.

58. Self-reported political attitudes. Coded from conservative to liberal, using a 5-point scale (see Chapter 9 and Appendix 6).

59. Observer-reported political attitudes. Coded from conservative to liberal, using a 5-point scale (see Chapter 9 and Appendix 6).

60–89. Up to thirty ratings on the participant's political attitudes by expert historians. Coded from conservative to liberal, using a 5-point scale (see Chapter 9 and Appendix 6).

90. Number of experts rating the political views of each participant.

91. Political attitudes. The mean of variables 60–89.

92. Self-reported religious attitudes. Coded from conservative to atheist, using a 5-point scale (see Chapter 9 and Appendix 6).

93. Observer-reported religious attitudes. Coded from conservative to atheist, using a 5-point scale (see Chapter 9 and Appendix 6).

94–123. Up to thirty ratings on the participant's religious attitudes by expert historians. Coded from conservative to atheist, using a 5-point scale (see Chapter 9 and Appendix 6).

124. Number of experts rating the religious views of each participant.

125. Religious attitudes. The mean of variables 94–123.

Social Attitudes of the Parents

126. Social attitudes of the parents. Textual information from biographical sources, transcribed and recorded as a memo field.

127. Father's political attitudes. Coded from conservative to radical, using a 5-step scale.

128. Father's religious attitudes. Coded from conservative to atheist, using a 5-step scale.

129. Father's social attitudes. The mean of the two preceding variables.

130. Mother's political attitudes. Coded from conservative to radical, using a 5-step scale.

131. Mother's religious attitudes. Coded from conservative to atheist, using a 5-step scale.

132. Mother's social attitudes. The mean of the two preceding variables.

133. Parents' social attitudes. The mean of variables 127–28 and 130–31.

Career Characteristics of the Participant

134. Years of formal education.

135. Highest degree received, not including honorary degrees.

136. Highest age attained by the end of formal education.

137–53. Principal fields of expertise. Recorded in text format. Involvement in different areas of research is also dummy coded in sixteen fields: mathematics, physics, astronomy, chemistry, geology, anatomy and physiology, medicine, natural history, the behavioral sciences, philosophy, the social sciences, the humanities, politics, theology, "other," and science versus nonscience.

154. Places visited outside the participant's country of origin.

155. Total number of countries visited.

156. World travel. Coded on a 5-point scale (see Chapter 4).

157. Scientific eminence. Judged by the editors of the 18-volume *Dictionary of Scientific Biography* for most of the 6,700 scientists included in this work. The editors employed a 12-point scale as a means of determining the article length assigned to each contributor.

158–60. General eminence. As determined by the number of citations in three different editions of *Biography and Genealogy Master Index* (Herbert and McNeil 1981; McNeil 1985, 1990).

161. Scientific eminence. As determined by Simonton (1984c, and personal communication), based on 15 different measures, such as the number of lines accorded to individuals in various biographical dictionaries and encyclopedias. Simonton's list of 2,026 scientists was increased in my own sample to 3,294 by giving Simonton's lowest score (zero) to all those scientists in my sample born before 1850 who were sufficiently undistinguished to be omitted from Simonton's list. The correlation between Simonton's composite scale and my own four indicators of eminence is .66 (and ranges from .56 to .74). Simonton's 15 indicators correlated with each other at the .60 level, producing a coefficient alpha of .94.

162. Overall eminence. The mean of variables 157–61, combined by means of *z*-scores. The effective reliability of this measure is .96.

163. Eminence in 1859. For participants in the Darwinian revolution only; based on the number, and general prestige, of honors and awards.

164. Lifetime eminence after 1859. For participants in the Darwinian revolution only; based on the number, and general prestige, of honors and awards.

165. Missing data. The number of missing data points for each participant on important biographical items, such as date of birth, parents' social class, birth order, parent-offspring conflict, shyness, religious denomination, and social attitudes.

166. Biographical sources. A record of the participant's inclusion in major biographical sources, including the *Dictionary of Scientific Biography* and the national biography of each participant's country of origin.

Event-Related Variables

167. The specific scientific controversy in which the participant spoke out.

168. Beginning year of the controversy.

169. Ending year of the controversy.

170. Length of the controversy.

171. Year in which the participant first spoke out.

172. Participant's age at the time of his or her scientific stance.

173. Scientific stance. Coded in binary terms, based on published designations in the secondary literature.

174. Bibliographic sources for scientific stance (See Appendix 3).

175–84. Scientific stance. Assessed by expert historians, using a 7-point scale. Up to ten experts rated each participant.

185. Number of expert raters for the scientific stance of each participant.

186. Scientific stance. The mean score of variables 175–84.

187. Scientific militancy. The tendency for individual scientists, coded on a 7-point scale of scientific stance, to depart from the mean response for each controversy.

188. Status as a creator. Whether or not the participant was a major "creator" of the scientific innovation about which he or she expressed an opinion; coded on a 3-point scale.

189. Status as a disciplinary insider. Whether or not the participant was an active member of the discipline to which the innovation was most relevant (dummy coded).

190. Chauvinism and the national origins of the innovation. Dummy coded in terms of whether or not the participant was a citizen of the country where the innovation originated.

191. National differences. Coded as –1, 0, or 1, depending on whether or not the participant's own country of origin responded to the innovation in a manner that was significantly different from that of other countries.

192. Personal influence. Information on how well the participant knew the principal originator(s) of the new theory. Coded on a 3-step scale.

193. Number of letters exchanged with Darwin before publication of the *Origin of Species* (1859). Coded only for participants in the Darwinian revolution.

194. Number of times the participant is cited in Darwin's *Origin of Species* (1859). Coded only for participants in the Darwinian revolution.

195. Citation count of the event as a major "revolution" in science. Based on the total number of citations in Kuhn (1962), Hacking (1981), Cohen (1985), and the *Dictionary of Scientific Biography.*

196. Number of participants in the controversy. Based on the total number included in the database.

197. Popularity of the innovation. Based on the mean level of support by the participants included in the database.

198. Ideological implications of the innovation. Based on the correlation between scientific stance and social attitudes (politics and religiosity) for the participants in each specific debate. These correlations are based on more than 19,000 ratings by expert historians (see Appendix 6).

199. Success or failure of the innovation. Coded on a 5-step scale.

200. Presence of a crisis prior to the initial announcement of the innovation. Coded on a 5-point scale.

Other Variables in the Database

Most of the remaining 56 variables in the database represent alternative ways of recording and coding the information already described. For example, some fields in the database delineate quadratic trends, as when firstborns and lastborns are both coded 1 and middleborns are coded −1. Still other variables have been employed for record-keeping purposes. For example, every participant is assigned a case number as well as an indicator variable for appearing more than once in the database.

APPENDIX 3
CRITERIA FOR SELECTION OF PARTICIPANTS IN SCIENTIFIC CONTROVERSIES

The process of selecting a representative sample of participants in scientific controversies can involve bias, and I have made a substantial effort to minimize this problem. For each of the 28 scientific debates I have analyzed, samples were gathered in two stages. The first stage involved assembling a list of participants based on published statements by historians of science. This appendix provides information on my principal bibliographic sources. For each individual included in the database I have recorded one or more citations from the secondary literature that validate this inclusion. The second stage in the selection process involved having more than a hundred expert historians review my selections. Twenty-six of these historians were specifically requested to assess the participants in terms of scientific stance. These experts are listed in Appendix 4. Based on the suggestions of expert raters, several hundred individuals were added to the samples, but only if their scientific stance could be documented in a published source.

My bibliographic sources include autobiographies and biographies of leading figures in these controversies, as well as secondary sources on each innovation's reception. Under the heading of each specific controversy, I list my principal secondary sources later in this appendix. As an added precaution, I have also surveyed the biographies of more than 6,700 scientists who were alive at the time of each debate and who were sufficiently noteworthy to be included in the 18-volume *Dictionary of Scientific Biography.* Those scientists recorded as having had an opinion on any of the 28 scientific controversies in the study are included in the samples.

My policy has been to include anyone in the samples who is known to have made a clear stand on the issues, regardless of his or her field of specialization. I have followed this policy on the premise that arbitrary exclusion of participants, for whatever reasons, might introduce sampling bias. Thus anthropologists, sociologists, philosophers, and even theologians are included, as long as they addressed the issues that were being debated by scientists. Twelve percent of my participants are people who were not primarily scientists, although they generally possessed considerable expertise on scientific matters. Because I have recorded the fields of specialization for each participant, I have been able to address the issue of whether such a broad sampling of participants is unrepresentative of the debate that occurred among scientists. Although nonscientists have sometimes reacted differently than scientists to scientific innovations, these differences are relatively modest and do not alter any of my principal findings.

PRINCIPAL BIBLIOGRAPHICAL SOURCES

For each scientific debate, I list here the principal secondary sources that I have employed in assembling preliminary lists of participants. The 28 debates are reviewed in chronological order, beginning with the Copernican revolution.

1. **The Copernican revolution:** Dreyer (1906), Stimson (1917), Zinner (1943), Koyré (1957, 1973), Kuhn (1957), Dobrzycki (1972), Gingerich (1975), Westman (1975a, 1975b), Rosen (1984), Baumgartner (1986), Gingerich and Westman (1988), and Biagioli (1993).

2. **Francis Bacon, René Descartes, and the new methods of experimental science:** Mouy (1934), Jones (1936, 1961), Merton (1938, 1970), Cohen (1960, 1985, 1990), Hall (1966), Westfall (1971b), and Webster (1976, 1986).

3. **William Harvey and the circulation of the blood:** Keynes (1966), Pagel (1967), Whitteridge (1971), and Frank (1980).

4. **Preformation in embryology:** Cole (1930), Roger (1963), Bodemer (1964), Gasking (1967), Hall (1969), Bowler (1971), Roe (1981), and Farley (1982).

5. **Spontaneous generation:** Ackerknecht (1948), Roger (1963), Gasking (1967), Geison (1969), Hall (1969), Farley (1977), and Roe (1981).

6. **The Newtonian revolution in celestial mechanics:** Jacob (1976), Heilbron (1979), Cohen (1980), Westfall (1971b, 1980), and Guerlac (1981).

7. **Epigenesis in embryology:** Cole (1930), Roger (1963), Bodemer (1964), Gasking (1967), Hall (1969), Bowler (1971), Roe (1981), and Farley (1982).

8. **Franz Anton Mesmer and mesmerism:** Darnton (1968) and Ellenberger (1970).

9. **Lavoisier and the chemical revolution:** McKie (1935), Ihde (1964), McCann (1978), Hufbauer (1982), and Schneider (1992).

10. **Franz Joseph Gall and phrenology:** Gibbon (1878), Tempkin (1947), Young (1970), Parssinen (1970, 1974), Cantor (1975), Shapin (1975, 1979a, b), and Cooter (1984, 1989).

11. **James Hutton's theory of the earth:** Hooykaas (1963, 1970), Davies (1969), Rudwick (1972), Porter (1975), Greene (1982), and Laudan (1987).

12. **Charles Lyell and uniformitarianism in geology:** Lyell (1881), Cannon (1960), Hooykaas (1963, 1970), Davies (1969), Rudwick (1972), Porter (1975), Greene (1982), and Laudan (1987).

13. **The Devonian controversy:** Rudwick (1985) and Secord (1986).

14. **Glaciation theory:** Agassiz (1885), Marcou (1896), Carozzi (1966, 1967, 1973, 1984), Rudwick (1970), and Imbrie and Imbrie (1986).

15. **Idealist theories of taxonomy:** Strickland (1840, 1844), Stresemann (1975), and Duffin (1976).

16–17. **Pre-Darwinian theories of evolution and Darwinism:** Darwin (1887, 1903, 1985–), Glass, Temkin, and Strauss (1959), Millhauser (1959), de Beer (1964), Glick (1972), Rudwick (1972), Hull (1973), Hull, Tessner, and Diamond (1978), Gillespie (1979), Moore (1979), Ruse (1979), Desmond (1982, 1984a, b, 1985, 1987, 1989), Harvey (1983a, b), Bowler

(1984, 1988), Corsi (1988), Junker (1989), Ellegård (1990 [1958]), and Desmond and Moore (1992).

18. Ignaz Semmelweis and puerperal fever: Sinclair (1909), Gortvay and Zoltan (1968), and Busby and Rodin (1976).

19. Spiritualism: Gauld (1968), Turner (1974), and Oppenheim (1985).

20. Louis Pasteur and germ theory: Richmond (1954a, b), Crellin (1966a, b, 1968), Farley and Geison (1974), and Farley (1977).

21. Joseph Lister and surgical antisepsis: Wrench (1913), Godlee (1917), Landis (1932), Ackerknecht (1948), and Fisher (1977).

22. Eugenics: Haller (1963), Graham (1977), Kevles (1985), Weiss (1987), Proctor (1988), Weingart, Kroll, and Bayertz (1988).

23. Sigmund Freud and psychoanalysis: Jones (1953–57), Nunberg and Federn (1962–75), Shakow and Rapaport (1964), Alexander et al. (1966), Ellenberger (1970), Hale (1971), Freud and Jung (1974), Roazen (1975), Mühlleitner (1992).

24. Max Planck's quantum hypothesis: Klein (1965), McCormmach (1967), Hermann (1971), Holton (1973), Feuer (1974), Hund (1974), and Kuhn (1978).

25–26. Einstein and relativity theory (special and general): Frank (1947), Goldberg (1968, 1984), Clark (1971), Hoffmann (1972), Feuer (1974), Miller (1981), Pais (1982), and Glick (1987).

27. Indeterminacy in quantum mechanics: Feuer (1974) and Forman (1971, 1978).

28. Alfred Wegener and continental drift (plate tectonics): Wegener (1929), Hallam (1973), Marvin (1973), Sullivan (1974), Glen (1982), Leviton and Aldrich (1985), Stewart (1986, 1987, 1990), and Le Grand (1988).

APPENDIX 4
EXPERT RATERS AND OTHER COLLABORATORS

Ninety-four of the following 110 individuals served as raters in assessing the political and religious attitudes of scientists in my study. Twenty-six of these collaborators also rated scientists on their degree of acceptance of new theories. In addition, three individuals served as raters for militancy among abolitionists and participants in the black rights movement. I am extremely grateful to all of these scholars for their time and expertise. Without their help, a number of important aspects of this study could not have been accomplished.

LIST OF COLLABORATORS

Aldrich, Michele L., AAAS, Washington, D.C.
Allen, Garland Edward, Washington University, St. Louis
Appel, Toby A., American Physiological Society, Bethesda, Maryland
Ash, Mitchell G., University of Iowa
Ashworth, William B., Jr., University of Missouri
Barkan, Eleazar, Claremont College
Bensaude-Vincent, Bernadette, Paris
Biagioli, Mario, Harvard University
Bowler, Peter, University of Belfast
Brieger, Gert H., Johns Hopkins University
Burchfield, Joe D., Northern Illinois University
Bylebyl, Jerome J., Johns Hopkins University
Bynum, William F., Wellcome Institute for the History of Medicine, London
Cantor, Geoffrey N., University of Leeds
Carrozi, Albert V., University of Illinois, Urbana
Churchill, Frederick B., Indiana University
Cohen, I. Bernard, Harvard University (professor emeritus)
Cook, Harold J., University of Wisconsin
Cooter, Roger J., Wellcome Institute for the History of Medicine, University of Manchester
Corsi, Pietro, University of Cassino, Italy
Debus, Allen G., University of Chicago
DeLacy, Margaret, Portland, Oregon
Desmond, Adrian, University College, London
Dupree, Hunter, Brown University (professor emeritus)
Durant, John, London Science Museum Library
Feingold, Mordechai, Virginia Polytechnic Institute
Finkelstein, Jonathan, Cambridge, Massachusetts
Foner, Eric, Columbia University

Forman, Paul, Smithsonian Institution
Forrester, John, Cambridge University
Frank, Robert G., Jr., UCLA Medical School
Frankel, Henry, University of Missouri
Galison, Peter, Harvard University
Gay, Peter, Yale University
Geison, Gerald, Princeton University
Gillispie, Charles Coulston, Princeton University (professor emeritus)
Goldberg, Stanley, Smithsonian Institution
Gorelik, Gennady, Institute for the History of Science and Technology, Russian Academy of Science, Moscow
Grandshaw, Lindsay, Wellcome Institute for the History of Medicine, London
Greene, Mott T., University of Puget Sound, Tacoma
Gregory, Frederick, University of Florida, Gainesville
Grosskurth, Phyllis, University of Toronto
Hahn, Roger, University of California at Berkeley
Hale, Nathan G., Oakland, California
Hankins, Thomas L., University of Washington, Seattle
Harvey, Joy, Darwin Correspondence Project, Cambridge, England; and Cambridge, Massachusetts
Harwood, Jonathan, Wellcome Institute for the History of Medicine, University of Manchester
Hatch, Robert A., University of Florida, Gainesville
Hauser, Renate, Wellcome Institute for the History of Medicine, London
Heilbron, John L., University of California at Berkeley (professor emeritus)
Hodge, M. J. S., University of Leeds
Holmes, Frederic Lawrence, Yale University
Hufbauer, Karl, University of California at Irvine
Hull, David L., Northwestern University
Hunter, Michael, Berkbeck College, London
Jacob, James, City University of New York
Jacob, Margaret C., New York School for Social Research
Junker, Thomas, Darwin Correspondence Project, Cambridge University
Kevles, Daniel J., California Institute of Technology
Klein, Martin J., Yale University
Latour, Bruno, École des Mines, Paris; and University of San Diego
Laudan, Rachel, University of Hawaii, Manoa Campus
Lawrence, Christopher, Wellcome Institute for the History of Medicine, London
Leviton, Alan E., California Academy of Sciences, San Francisco
Lindberg, David C., University of Wisconsin
Ludmerer, Kenneth M., Washington University, St. Louis
Lurie, Edward, University of Delaware
Marvin, Ursula, Harvard University
Miller, Arthur I., University College, London
Montgomery, William, North Adams State College, North Adams, Massachusetts
Moore, James, Open University, Milton Keynes, England
Morrell, Jack Bowes, University of Bradford, Bradford, England

Moulin, Anne Marie, Paris
Neve, Michael R., Wellcome Institute for the History of Medicine, London
Newman, Richard, W. E. B. Du Bois Institute for Afro-American Research, Harvard University
Numbers, Ronald L., University of Wisconsin
Pastore, Nicholas (ratings taken from Pastore [1949])
Pelling, Margaret, University of Oxford
Pickstone, John V., Wellcome Institute for the History of Medicine, University of Manchester
Porter, Roy, Wellcome Institute for the History of Medicine, London
Proctor, Robert, Penn State University
Rainger, Ronald, Texas Tech University
Richards, Robert J., University of Chicago
Roazen, Paul, York University, Toronto
Roe, Shirley A., University of Connecticut
Rose, Lawrence, Princeton University
Rosenkrantz, Barbara, Harvard University (professor emerita)
Rudwick, Martin J. S., University of California at San Diego
Rupke, Nicholaas, Oxford University
Salomon-Bayet, Claire, Paris
Schaffer, Simon, Cambridge University
Schneider, Hans Georg, Oxford University
Schofield, Robert E., Iowa State University
Schorske, Carl, Princeton University
Secord, James, Imperial College, London
Steuwer, Roger H., University of Minnesota
Stocking, George W., Jr., University of Chicago
Swales, Peter, New York
Todes, Daniel, Johns Hopkins University
Turner, Frank M., Yale University
Warner, John Harley, Yale University
Webster, Charles, All Souls College, Oxford
Weindling, Paul, Wellcome Unit for the History of Medicine, Oxford
Weingart, Peter, University of Bielefeld, Germany
Westfall, Richard S., Indiana University (professor emeritus)
Westman, Robert S., University of California at San Diego

I would also like to express my gratitude to the following scholars, now deceased, who also served as expert raters: William Coleman, University of Wisconsin; Betty Joe Teeter Dobbs, University of California at Davis; Jacques Roger, Sorbonne, Paris; Victor E. Thoren, Indiana University.

APPENDIX 5
TECHNIQUES FOR ESTIMATING MISSING DATA

DEALING WITH MISSING DATA

Missing historical data pose a serious obstacle to understanding the past. For historians who wish to *test* their hypotheses by means of statistical methods, missing data present an even greater dilemma. In order to engage in the kind of hypothesis testing that lies at the heart of this book, I have been forced to confront this problem. This appendix explains some of the technical procedures I have employed toward this end and also provides an explanation for why the estimation of missing data is usually superior to the most common alternative, namely, dropping cases for which data are not completely observed.

The problem of missing data tends to be compounded whenever one engages in multivariate analysis. When we look at *many* variables simultaneously, including such elusive ones as parent-offspring conflict and temperament, there tends to be an increasingly larger percentage of individuals for whom we have incomplete information on at least one variable. Normally, these cases would have to be dropped from the analysis. My database for scientific debates includes 3,890 individuals. For the eight variables reviewed in chapters 2–8 (and summarized in the family dynamics model presented in Chapter 8, Table 5), I have been able to find information on 41 percent of the total. But the number of cases that have complete data *for all eight variables* is only 4 percent! Thus most multivariate modeling techniques would force me to throw away 96 percent of my data in order to undertake a multivariate analysis. Obviously, there would not be much biographical information left to analyze! To overcome this problem I have availed myself of recently developed techniques for estimating missing data.[1] I provide here a brief overview of what is involved.

From a statistical point of view, dropping cases in order to solve the problem of missing data tends to be an unsatisfactory procedure. Not only do we lose much of our data, but we are likely to bias our results. Here is an example: Firstborns and lastborns tend to be more eminent than middleborns in my sample. As a result, more biographies tend to be written about them.[2] Psychologically, firstborns

---

[1] See Rubin 1978, 1987; Little and Rubin 1987; Rubin 1987; Rubin and Schafer 1990; Schafer 1991.

[2] For the relationship between eminence and relative birth rank, coded as a quadratic trend, $r=.13$ ($df=1/1{,}504$, $t=5.22$, $p<.0001$). This partial correlation is controlled for year of birth and sibship size, which are themselves both good predictors of eminence (partial $r=-.34$, $df=1{,}504$, $t=-14.07$, $p<.0001$; and partial $r=-.09$, $df=1/1{,}504$, $t=-3.48$, $p<.001$, respectively). Controlled for sibship size, social class, and the quadratic trend in birth order, rela-

and lastborns are different from middleborns—for example, they are more militant. We would not want to generalize about an entire population based on this nonrepresentative subpopulation. Owing to missing data, the study of most historical revolutions is distinctly biased in favor of the most militant participants.

These kinds of sampling biases can create discrepancies between *observed* statistical correlations and the *true* correlation. During the French Revolution, firstborn and lastborn deputies to the French National Convention were significantly more likely than middleborns to support terrorist measures. I am most likely to lack biographical information on these middleborn deputies, who tend to have been members of the Plain and to have voted against executing the king. Because this political group is underrepresented in terms of birth-order information, and because this group stands out from the rest of the sample in its voting behavior, the missing biographical data on the French Revolution appear to be as good as the data that are actually observed (Appendix 8). Fortunately, computer algorithms are able to estimate missing data and to correct for biases associated with them. When I estimate the missing data for birth order in the French Revolution, the correlations between birth order and voting behavior tends to increase slightly relative to the observed data. This result is methodologically comforting.

Discrepancies between correlations involving observed and estimated data are typically small. I have calculated both sets of correlations, to be sure that sampling bias is minimal in my study, but I usually report correlations only for the observed data. For example, the observed data suggest a correlation of –.29 between birth order and voting for radical measures during the Reign of Terror. The estimation of missing data suggests that the true correlation is –.30. This discrepancy is too small to be of serious concern.

My main purpose for estimating missing data in this book has been to facilitate references to individual behavior in cases where one or more variables are missing. A warning is appropriate on this subject. In estimating missing data, it is not the purpose to guess at data that cannot possibly be known. Rather, the estimation process helps us to ascertain the *degree of error* that is involved in making predictions that we are already capable of making, based on *known data*. When pollsters announce that their surveys have a margin of error of ±3 percent, they are making a similar estimation of error. The statistical procedures that I have employed in this book are a much more sophisticated way of arriving at the same information for individual cases.

Donald Rubin has developed a useful statistical technique for handling miss-

tive birth rank (from first to last) is also a significant predictor of eminence (partial r=.08, df=1/1,504, t=5.22, p<.005): lastborns are more eminent than firstborns, who are in turn more eminent than middle children. It should be kept in mind that eminence is context sensitive (see Chapter 4). Because my own historical samples are biased for revolutionary achievements, this circumstance probably enhances the eminence of laterborns in the sample.

My measure of eminence is based on a composite measure of 19 different historical indices, including retrospective ratings, number of published biographies, and amount of space given to figures in standard reference works. The average intercorrelation of these various indices of eminence is .61. The effective reliability of my composite scale is .96.

ing data.[3] Rubin's approach begins with the recognition that some "missing" data are not entirely missing. For example, lastborns are much more likely than firstborns to lose a parent early in life. By the time lastborns come into the world, their parents are significantly older than they were when they had their first child. Even if we lack information on age at parental loss for a given individual, we may possess some indication of this information if we know something about birth order, or birth rank, or how old the parents were when an individual was born. I often possess this kind of biographical information about people in my sample. Even though I lack information on the year of a parent's death, I may possess this missing information in an indirect and *probabilistic* way.[4]

To start to estimate the distribution of missing data, one employs a special "Estimation-Maximization" (or EM) algorithm, which is especially critical when data are not "missing completely at random." (They almost never are.) The EM algorithm analyzes the entire pattern of observed data to see in what ways, and to what extent, the pattern of observed data is biased. The greater the bias, the more important it is to take into account information about missing variables. When significant bias is involved, the missing information tends to be systematically related to other information that is already observed in the database.

To cite an example, suppose I encounter an obscure eighty-year-old scientist who turns out to be an avid supporter of Darwinism, and suppose I lack information on this person's birth order. In fact, I already possess a pretty good idea of this person's birth order. At age eighty, a laterborn is 3 times more likely to have supported Darwinism than a firstborn at the same age (Chapter 2, Fig. 2.2).[5] If I also possess information that this person was born ten years after the marriage of his parents, the probability that he or she is laterborn rises substantially. Given the data that I have collected on this last variable, the likelihood of this individual being a functional laterborn would be more than 100 to 1. Of course, without specific information on this person's birth order, I would not cite them in this book as actually being a laterborn. But I would be able to include information on this individual's age, gender, and social attitudes in any analyses to determine the relative contributions of these other variables to revolutionary personality. In other words, I would not have to throw away this biographical information just because birth order is missing in this particular instance.

One serious problem threatens to foil any attempts to impute missing data. The so-called EM algorithm is very good at estimating what missing data should be like *in theory*. By itself, however, this algorithm is not particularly good at generating these missing data. The problem is that the EM algorithm, like Maxwell's famous demon, "knows the answer" to the statistical relationships among the observed data. Left to itself, this algorithm will tend to impute data that are "too

---

[3] See Rubin 1987; Little and Rubin 1987, section 12.4.

[4] I collected information on certain variables in my study with the technique in mind of imputing missing data. Thus I have procured information on how old parents were when an individual was born. I also have collected information on whether individuals were named after a parent, as well as how many years elapsed between the parents' marriage and the subject's birth.

[5] See also Chapter 15, p. 357.

good." At least one major statistics package uses the EM algorithm to impute data that are indeed too good.[6]

Donald Rubin's method of multiple imputation solves this problem. The ingenious solution involves imputing the missing data in a manner that introduces just the kind of error variance (or random "noise") that is typical of real data. Using this technique, missing data must be imputed several times, which involves creating different datasets. Each of these datasets provides an equally reasonable estimate of what the real world, with its normal range of error, would have been like if we had been able to obtain complete data. These multiple datasets can then be separately analyzed. The individual results must then be combined statistically, usually by averaging answers and adding variabilities.

Joseph Schafer, a statistician who completed his doctoral dissertation on this problem at Harvard University under the direction of Donald Rubin, has implemented this idea into a workable computer program.[7] He has also significantly improved the method of imputing missing data by taking into account possible interaction effects among variables. Schafer's program, and the sophisticated algorithm on which it is based, are described elsewhere.[8] I could not have written chapters 8, 10–11, or 13 in their present form without the help of Schafer's program. This program has allowed me to supply predicted probabilities of support for radical change among participants in various revolutions, both in science and in social thought, even in cases where individuals are missing some biographical data. Usually the missing data involve predictors such as parent-offspring conflict, temperament, and age gaps between siblings, which are particularly difficult to document for everyone in the sample.

An example will illustrate my use of this program. Suppose I possess nearly complete biographical information on a given individual, who is known to be a lastborn from an intact family. But suppose I lack data on the age gap between this individual and his or her next older sibling. It would be a shame to have to drop this case from further analysis, when the information that is missing would only add a small amount to a computer model's ability to make a prediction for this individual. It would be much better to have a computer model inform us that this individual's predicted probability for accepting new ideas is, say, 80 percent but with a larger than usual margin of error—perhaps ±15 percent—that is directly at-

[6] I am referring to BMDP's AM program for estimating missing data (Dixon 1992, 2:959–76). If one takes a completely filled-in database, randomly deletes *known* information on certain variables, and then imputes these missing data, the resulting correlations among variables go up compared with correlations based on the observed data. The estimates are therefore too good. This program, as well as program 8D, can be used quite safely to generate *correlation matrices* from incomplete data, since actual missing data points do not need to be imputed to create a correlation matrix. The fault in BMDP's AM program lies in the imputation process, not in the EM algorithm. The practice of substituting the mean for missing variables leads to the opposite problem: correlations become lower than they should be.

[7] Schafer 1991. I was able to help fund Schafer's development of this program using part of my stipend as a Fellow from the MacArthur Foundation.

[8] See Rubin and Schafer 1990, and especially Schafer 1991.

tributable to missing information. Given this error range, we could be 95 percent confident that this individual's true predicted probability of support for revolution is no lower than 65 percent and no higher than 95 percent. Even though the model lacks complete information, its probabilistic prediction would definitely be contradicted if the individual failed to support the revolution in which he or she participated. In short, missing data do not prohibit us from making a prediction about individual behavior. Instead, missing data increase the range of error that we must build into each prediction. For researchers working with historical data, this approach represents an enormous asset in hypothesis testing. The same principles for dealing with missing data are employed by the United States Census Bureau.[9]

We can easily discover what the appropriate range of error is for each and every prediction made by the model. To do so we need to impute various possible outcomes for such cases, based on the known data. Using multiple imputation, each individual biographical instance will have its own distinct margin of error, depending on how much biographical information is missing. Finally, because the estimation process is not employed when data are fully observed, predictions for prominent individuals such as Galileo, Newton, and Darwin will not be affected. In practice, calculating separate error terms for each of several thousand individuals may seem rather complicated, but this kind of statistical exercise is what computers are good at.

In my database of 3,890 scientists, the 95 percent confidence limits for predicted probabilities are as follows (assuming that the specified probability, based on the observed data, is about 50 percent). For cases with no missing data, the 95 percent confidence limits for the error term are 1.96 times the standard deviation in the imputed predicted probabilities (or 1.96 times 4.8 percent, which equals ±9.4 percent). For cases with one missing variable, the 95 percent confidence limits become ±22 percent. And for cases with two missing variables, the confidence limits are ±30 percent. In practice, these confidence limits are dependent on the *actual variables that are missing* as well as on the *specific predicted probability* that is generated by the observed variables. For example, when there are two missing variables, the error rate for a predicted probability of support of 10 percent, based on the observed variables, is only ±8. The fact that the predicted probability is so low indicates that birth order, age, and social attitudes are almost certainly not among the missing variables. If the information that is missing is social class and age spacing between siblings, its presence in the model would have only minimal influence on the outcome. It would be nice to know this information, but it is not essential to know it in order to make a prediction for most of the individuals in my study.

---

[9] An up-to-date review article, which discusses many other applications of multiple imputation, is Rubin 1996.

APPENDIX 6
DATA AND EXPERT RATINGS ON SOCIAL ATTITUDES

ASCERTAINING SOCIAL ATTITUDES

In Chapter 9 I have described the method I used for procuring ratings from expert historians, 94 of whom assessed the social attitudes of scientists in my study. In this appendix I provide some additional details on these rating procedures and also explain how I assessed individuals in terms of self-report and observer data.

Self-Report and Observer Data

Historical figures sometimes comment about their own social attitudes. Charles Darwin, for example, answered a questionnaire for Francis Galton in which he remarked on his social attitudes as well as those of his father. He described his father as politically "Liberal" and himself as "Liberal or Radical."[1] Other members of my sample, such as Robert FitzRoy and John Lubbock, ran for political office, and as a consequence were members of official parties. FitzRoy was elected to Parliament as a Tory, whereas Lubbock was elected as a Liberal. I have coded all such political descriptions on a 5-point scale. On this scale, 1.0 corresponds to arch-conservative, 2.0 is a moderate, 3.0 is a liberal, 4.0 is a progressive or advanced liberal, 4.5 is a socialist, and 5.0 is an extreme radical. For religiosity, the corresponding codings are 1.0 for religious fanatics, 2.0 for religious moderates (High Church in England), 3.0 for liberals (Broad Church in England), 3.5 for adherence to dissenting religious sects such as Unitarianism, 4.0 for deists, 4.5 for agnostics, and 5.0 for atheists. These are merely rules of thumb and have been applied within the context of other available information, including the specific historical period in which a person lived. I have generally allotted a half point to comments that qualify descriptions. For example, an "ardent deist" would be rated 3.5 rather than 4.0, and a "conservative Whig" would be rated 2.5. Such qualifying phrases are common in descriptions of people's social attitudes.

In assigning ratings based on self-report and observer data, I have allowed myself a half point range for possible error on either side of my assigned rating. If I could not reduce the probable error to one point or less, I did not attempt to rate an individual. Hugh Miller, for example, was a biblical fundamentalist, whose best-selling *Footprints of the Creator* (1847) led the pre-Darwinian defense of creationism. It is reasonably safe to rate him at 1.5 for his religious beliefs, on the assumption that he cannot be any lower than 1.0 nor any higher than 2.0 (a religious

[1] Darwin 1887, 3:178.

moderate). Sixteen expert raters have agreed closely with this judgment, giving Miller an average rating of 1.35 for religiosity. Politically, Miller was somewhat more liberal. In an autobiographical work he described his support for several liberal causes, such as the abolition of slavery and the Reform Bill, but he also remarked that he was "thoroughly an Establishment Man" and never lost "an hour's sleep" over the need for political change.[2] On the basis of these comments, Miller cannot be rated 1.0 or even 1.5. He was certainly not a liberal (3.0), so he falls somewhere between 2.0 and 3.0. I rated him at 2.5, splitting the difference, knowing that my probable error was no more than half a point on either side. Nine expert raters have assigned Miller an average political rating of 2.4, not far from my own rating based on self-report information.

My second measure of social attitudes is derived from observer data—reports by contemporaries, including friends, spouses, children, and biographers. Darwin's description of himself as "Liberal or Radical" is reasonably accurate, but it is still vague and could be coded anywhere from 3.0 to 5.0. His son William described him as "an ardent Liberal," and most other contemporary observers have placed Darwin somewhere between a "liberal" and an "advanced liberal" (that is, between 3.0 and 4.0 on the scale).[3] Darwin was certainly not a political radical like his grandfather, Erasmus Darwin. Based on observer data, I have assigned Darwin a rating of 3.5. By comparison, 21 expert historians have placed Darwin between 3.3 and 3.45, depending upon the year in which he is rated. The mean rating for Darwin is 3.4.

The use of self-report and observer data on social attitudes is largely dependent on the employment of specific phrases, such as "arch-conservative," "royalist," "High Tory," "moderate," "liberal," "radical," and so forth. For this reason, I have been able to obtain far less data from these two sources than I have from expert raters. Overall, I have managed to obtain 670 assessments by self-report and another 1,214 by contemporary observers.

Retrospective Ratings

I have asked 94 historians of science to assess the religious and political persuasions of all 3,890 scientists in my study. A minimum of 6 historians (and as many as 27) rated the participants in each scientific controversy, generating more than 19,000 ratings. A total of 2,587 individuals have been assessed by expert historians.

Historical experts on each scientific debate were asked to rate only those individuals who they knew well enough to place confidently within ±0.5 points on the 5-step scales. If raters appeared to be in any way doubtful about an individual, I encouraged them to skip the individual rather than offer a rating. To discourage experts from guessing, I often asked them to justify their ratings and took notes on their remarks. Each historian rated an average of 81 scientists on the religiosity scale and 51 on the politics scale. Overall, 2,488 scientists were rated at least once

---

[2] Miller 1871 [1854]:521, 523.

[3] E. Darwin 1915, 2:169.

on the religiosity scale, and 2,426 scientists were rated at least once on the politics scale. The mean number of ratings is 3.4 for politics and 4.4 for religiosity.

I am extremely grateful for the assistance given me by these learned colleagues. A small number of individuals (three out of more than one hundred) refused to assist me in this process. In addition, a few scholars who agreed to help nevertheless felt uncomfortable in making ratings, which they perceived as being alien to their own way of doing history. (Interestingly, the ratings of such "reluctant raters" are just as reliable as ratings by other raters.) Doubting raters were not poor raters but simply cautious people who hesitated to generalize. For them, there seemed to be an exception to every rule.

Expert ratings were gathered in two different ways, using "blind" and "partially blind" methods. With the method of partially blind ratings, experts were allowed to see where a broad selection of individuals stood, based on previous ratings. This method, although it did not involve strictly independent assessment, had the advantage of anchoring the scales with reference to specific individuals, allowing successive raters to fine-tune their ratings around groups of similarly rated participants. It was much easier for most raters to think of scientists as being politically "more radical than Darwin," or "less radical than Karl Marx," than to assign a specific number on a scale. Using this partially blind method, raters would often say that someone "belonged with Charles Lyell," or "with Darwin," or "with Thomas Henry Huxley." Even with the use of a partially blind approach, many ratings were made without reference to previous ratings, inasmuch as the reference group was considerably smaller than the pool of individuals being rated.

With the use of blind ratings, experts were allowed to set up their own scale, using major figures as anchor points, but they were not allowed to see how previous historians had rated any of the participants. Although expert raters clearly felt more comfortable with the procedure of partially blind ratings, I eventually dispensed with this approach, after satisfying myself that experts were able to perform the task without guidance from previous raters. Seventy-three experts made their ratings using the partially blind method, and another 21 experts made their ratings using the blind method. All ratings for social attitudes were made completely blind of information collected about birth order and other biographical variables in the study.

Interrater Reliability

With three separate forms of information about people's social attitudes (self-report, contemporary "observer" assessments, and retrospective ratings by historians), we have the means to assess the reliability of these three methods. These results are reassuring. The correlation between self-report data and observer data is .89 for politics and .93 for religiosity. The correlation between self-report data and expert ratings is .90 for religious attitudes and .93 for political attitudes. The correlation between contemporary observer data and expert ratings is .91 for religious attitudes and .90 for political attitudes. The mean correlation between ratings by various experts is .76, for totally blind ratings, and .85 for ratings made on a partially blind basis. The agreement of expert raters with one another is about as high as the level of agreement between the same rater at two different points in time

(.81).[4] When these three forms of assessment are combined, the effective reliability of ratings is .91 for politics and .93 for religiosity.

There is no reason to believe that any one of these three methods of assessing social attitudes is significantly more reliable than the others. Each method has its virtues, and the combined information is probably more accurate than the separate scales. I have therefore averaged all sources of information in the social attitudes measures that I have used for modeling purposes.[5] The total number of individuals rated by at least one of the three methods is 2,768 (or 71 percent of the sample). Whether they are based on self-report data, observer data, or expert ratings, the findings presented in this book are virtually indistinguishable.

Tough-mindedness

Hans Eysenck has shown that social attitudes involve at least two independent dimensions.[6] The first is a dimension of conservatism-radicalism, which I have tried to capture with my two scales for politics and religiosity. The second dimension is described as "tough-minded–tender-minded" or "authoritarian-democratic." Eysenck's conservatism-radicalism scale typically accounts for twice the variance in political attitudes as does his tough-minded–tender-minded scale.[7]

For certain debates in science, such as those involving modern spiritualism and eugenics, Eysenck's second scale would probably provide significant insight into the reasons for individual support. It took "tough-minded" individuals to advocate the drastic measures of compulsory sterilization associated with so-called negative eugenics. Conversely, modern spiritualism was a tender-minded doctrine, and a belief in life after death is a defining feature of tender-minded attitudes.[8]

In my treatments of the abolition and black rights movements (Chapter 12), as well as in my treatment of the French Revolution (Chapter 13), I have attempted to assess participants along a tough-minded–tender-minded dimension. In these specific historical contexts, tough-mindedness is an excellent predictor of sibling differences as well as attitudes toward revolutionary change. My scales for tough-mindedness are described in Chapter 12, note 70, and in Appendix 8.

---

[4] I thank Pietro Corsi, of the University of Cassino in Italy, for his willingness to be subjected to this particular test.

[5] My scores for political and religious attitudes are based on the trimmed mean, with the highest and lowest ratings being omitted and the remainder being averaged.

[6] Eysenck 1954; Eysenck and Wilson 1978.

[7] Robinson, Rusk, and Head 1972:113.

[8] For a test of this assertion about tough-mindedness and attitudes toward modern spiritualism, see page 524, note 74.

APPENDIX 7
MODELING THE PROTESTANT REFORMATION

REFORMATION VARIABLES

In Chapter 11 I have described eight hypotheses that have been advanced by historians in order to explain the spread of the Reformation. I relate here how I collected data to test each of these eight hypotheses and coded the resulting information.

1. **Religious stance during the Reformation (the dependent variable).** I have coded religious allegiances in two different ways. First, I have recorded confessional choice as Protestant or Catholic for all 718 individuals in my Reformation sample, based on the information provided in standard secondary sources.[1] Individuals who endorsed more than one religious position—for example, by converting back to Catholicism—are multiply entered in the database. My sample encompasses most major political rulers, religious leaders, magistrates, humanists, and martyrs. Participation is limited to people active prior to 1570.

My second manner of coding religious allegiances takes into account support for the Magisterial Reformation versus the Radical Reformation. Lutherans, Zwinglians, Calvinists, Huguenots, and Anglicans belong to the Magisterial Reformation. Anabaptists, Spiritualists, Anti-Trinitarians, and Rationalists belong to the Radical Reformation. In identifying Radical Reformers, I have used George Hunston Williams's *The Radical Reformation* (1962) as my principal guide. The distinction between Magisterial and Radical Reformers justifies the use of a 3-step scale for religious allegiances. Catholics receive the lowest score and Radical Reformers receive the highest. My multivariate model of the Reformation uses this 3-step scale as the dependent variable. When making other statistical comparisons between Catholics and Protestants, I have sometimes employed the binary measure. Odds ratios, for example, have been calculated based on a binary outcome.

2. **Age.** My variable for age is based on date of birth. In cases where date of birth is approximate, but known to within a few years, I have employed the estimate. (In standard biographical sources, approximate birth dates are indicated by a "circa" before the date. Such birth dates have generally been estimated

---

[1] These secondary sources include Durant 1957; Williams 1962; Elton 1963; Léonard 1965; Hillerbrand 1971, 1973; Moeller 1972; Ozment 1975, 1980, 1992; Spitz 1985; Dickens 1989; and various national biographies. These secondary works are also the source of my Reformation sample, as described in Chapter 11.

based on age of matriculation at universities, which tends to be accurate within two or three years.)

3. Status within the clergy or within universities. I have rated individuals whose ecclesiastic status was archbishop or higher at 2 on this scale. Ordinary clergymen and monks are rated 1. Individuals with no status within the church are rated 0. I have employed an analogous ranking system for status within academic institutions. A 2 is reserved for heads of universities. Ordinary professors receive a 1. Nonacademics are rated 0.

4. Royal status (the princes). Dummy coded as 0 or 1.

5. Residence within imperial cities. Dummy coded as 0 or 1.[2]

6. Status as a government official or magistrate. Dummy coded as 0 or 1.

7. Humanistic sympathies. I have employed a 3-point scale to assess this variable. Individuals who exhibited no apparent humanistic sympathies have been rated 0 on the scale. Individuals reported to have received a humanistic education, or who were patrons of humanistic research, are rated 1. A rating of 2 is reserved for those individuals, such as Erasmus, who made important contributions to humanist thinking and scholarship. I have coded these three categories based on a three-volume biographical dictionary, *Contemporaries of Erasmus,* which documents most prominent humanists active during this period.[3]

8. Social class. I have coded this variable on a linear scale from 1 (royalty) to 6 (peasant), based on father's occupation. In cases where father's occupation is not known, I have coded social class based on the occupation of the participant in my sample. There is not much difference between the socioeconomic status of fathers and their offspring. The status of fathers, however, exhibits greater variance and is marginally better as a predictor of religious stance.

9. Regional differences. I have dummy coded regional differences, employing separate variables for Austria, Czechoslovakia, England, France, Germany, Italy, the Netherlands, Poland, Scandinavia, Scotland, Spain, Switzerland, and "all other" nationalities. These dummy codings facilitate the creation of an indicator variable for national differences. Individuals living in countries that *significantly opposed* the Reformation (such as Austria, Italy, and Spain) receive a −1 on this indicator variable. Receiving a +1 are individuals from countries that were *significantly supportive* of the Reformation (Germany, Switzerland, the Netherlands, and Czechoslovakia). All other individuals receive a 0 on this variable.

---

[2] For information on imperial cities, see Moeller (1972:41) and the various sources cited by him.

[3] Bietenholz 1985–87.

REFORMATION MODELS

My model for the Protestant Reformation is derived from BMDP's programs 8D (Correlations with Missing Data) and 9R (All Possible Subsets Regression).[4] BMDP program 8D uses the Estimation Maximization algorithm to create a correlation matrix that corrects for biases inherent in the pattern of missing information.[5] For example, obscure people in my Reformation sample are more likely to be radical reformers than are prominent people. Obscure people are also more likely to be from the lower classes. When information on social class is missing for an individual (usually because he or she is obscure), the Estimation Maximization algorithm makes a projection that is consonant with the known correlation between biographical obscurity and social class.

To aid in this estimation process, I have included an indicator variable for missing information in my database. This indicator variable sums up the number of missing biographical data points for each individual. This measure is significantly correlated with support for the Reformation, as well as with other predictors of religious stance. For this reason, the absence of biographical information is itself useful "information."[6]

Even though missing information is one of the best predictors of support for the Reformation, my indicator variable for "missingness" does not enter a comprehensive computer model: its relationship with confessional choice is adequately reflected by the other predictors, especially after correction for informational bias using the Estimation Maximization algorithm. Individual predicted probabilities for supporting the Reformation are based on logistic regression, using a model analogous to that selected by BMDP's Program 9R. In cases where data are missing, the data have been multiply imputed to derive the most likely predicted probability (and its error term).

An Alternative Reformation Model

In Chapter 11 I have presented a seven-variable model for the Protestant Reformation. There is a significantly better model that includes an eighth predictor. *Personal contact* with a leader of the Reformation (Luther, Calvin, Zwingli, Knox, and the principal Anabaptist leaders) is an excellent predictor of support for the Reformation. The role of personal contact in conversion to Protestantism is often cited by biographers. Whenever such information has been mentioned I have

---

[4] Dixon 1992.

[5] Unlike BMDP's Program AM, 8D may be safely employed to generate a correlation matrix corrected for biases arising as a consequence of missing data. See Appendix 5 for further discussion of the principles involved in the estimation of missing data.

[6] The correlation between obscurity and support for the Reformation is .26, based on the number of missing data points for each individual (df=1/716, t=7.06, p<.0001). The correlation between the number of missing data points for each individual and social class is .22 (df=1/587, t=5.35, p<.0001). Other variables that correlate significantly with data being observed rather than missing are: being a government official (.32), being a humanist (.31), being a member of the royalty (.29), being a firstborn or a lastborn (.18), and having high status within the church or universities (.11).

recorded it, using a 3-step scale. It is admittedly difficult to assess this kind of information for the Reformation because so many different people were active in proselytizing the Reformed faith. For this reason, my variables for personal contact probably underestimate its real influence. Still, I have tried to establish a lower bound for the influence of personal contact by evaluating this predictor in the same way I have assessed personal contact with the leaders of scientific revolutions. Measured in this manner, the influence of personal contact is significantly greater than zero. During the Protestant Reformation, the influence of personal contact is also substantially greater than it is during scientific revolutions.[7]

The Role of Humanism

It is worth commenting on the fact that humanistic sympathies appear to be *negatively* related to support for the Reformation. Bernd Moeller, among others, has reached the opposite conclusion: "No humanism, no Reformation" was his verdict.[8] "Humanists," he argues, "were both the real pioneers and ultimately the real supporters of the Reformation movement."[9]

Support for the Reformation, especially the Radical Reformation, is positively correlated with being a commoner, belonging to the lower clergy, being German or Swiss, and living in an imperial city. Each of these three variables also correlates with being a humanist.[10] As a result, humanists should have been enthusiastic about the Reformation. Indeed, they should have been much more enthusiastic about the Reformation than nonhumanists in my sample, owing to the significant cross correlations between being a humanist and other significant predictors of Reformation loyalties. Yet humanists, including Erasmus himself, were often ambivalent about the Reformation, and some were decidedly hostile. It is true that humanists had long been critical of church abuses. But their overall program of reform, as Spitz notes, was "superficial compared with the radical thrust of the Protestant Reformation."[11]

---

[7] The correlation between personal contact with a Reformation leader and support for Protestantism is .31 (df=1/365, t=6.18, p<.0001). For revolutions in science, the correlation between personal contact with the relevant scientific innovator and support for new theories is .18 (df=1/3,806, t=11.30, p<.0001). The difference between the correlations for personal contact during the Reformation (.31), and in science (.18), is itself significant (z=2.53, p<.01). In the eight-variable model of the Reformation, the *partial* correlation between personal contact and support becomes .22 (df=1/509, t=5.09, p<.0001).

[8] Moeller 1972:36.

[9] Moeller 1972:14.

[10] The correlations between being a humanist and other variables mentioned in the text are as follows: for status as a commoner (.11); for residency in an imperial city (.23); for being German (.16); for being Swiss (.10). Being a humanist is also negatively correlated with date of birth: humanists were older, on average, than most participants (.33). All of these correlations are significant at p<.02. Scott Hendrix has noted the tendency for humanists to be clerics and has argued that clericism, not humanism, was the main source of receptivity toward the Reformation (personal communication). For the relationship between being a clergyman and being a humanist, r=.09 (df=1/636, t=2.25, p<.05).

[11] Spitz 1985:58.

When we control for the various considerations that made it easier for humanists to support the Reformed faith, they exhibit significantly *less* support than we might expect. As a result, being a humanist enters my Reformation model as a *negative* predictor of support for Protestantism. Potential loss of patronage was probably one reason why humanists adopted a cautious attitude toward the Reformation. Eminent humanists were also significantly older than the average participant in my sample.

These findings about the role of humanism show how difficult it is to know, by casual inspection, whether a given variable exerts a significant influence on the reception of a new way of thinking, *after being controlled for other relevant predictors.* Proper judgment on such issues requires that we hold statistically constant many relevant variables, and then statistically vary the influence that we wish to assess. Given the complexity of such assessments of cause and effect, it is not surprising that historians have reached different conclusions about the influence of humanism. Especially when effect sizes are small, as is the case with humanistic sympathies, the question of influence is best addressed with the help of formal statistical techniques. It is easy—indeed almost inevitable—for scholars to be misled using a purely narrative approach to such problems.

APPENDIX 8
MODELING THE FRENCH REVOLUTION

THE SAMPLE

My sample for the French Revolution encompasses 1,097 individuals, 893 of whom were deputies of the National Convention (1792–95).[1] Another 186 members of this sample were either staunch opponents of the revolution or early supporters who were left behind as the revolution progressed. My selection of opponents includes all of the great orators who represented the political "right" within the Constituent and Legislative Assemblies. I have gathered this sample from a variety of sources.[2] The remainder of the sample comprises 18 "ultraradicals" such as René-Jacques Hébert, Charles-Philippe-Henri Ronsin, François-Nicholas Vincent, and Jacques Roux.

A study of major participants in the French Revolution could easily encompass several thousands of individuals, but this has not been my intent. Because I have devoted Chapter 13 to an analysis of the rupture between Girondins and Montagnards within the National Convention, I have assembled biographical information on counterrevolutionaries and ultraradicals solely in order to place this clash within its broader behavioral context (Chapter 13, Fig. 13.1).

VARIABLES ENCOMPASSED IN THE STUDY

My database for the National Convention includes more than a hundred variables. It encompasses such information as the department from which each deputy was elected, the population size of this department in 1789, deputies' membership in various political clubs, biographical details about parents, and many other facts that I have not employed in modeling.[3] I have condensed some of these variables

---

[1] Kuscinski 1917–19.

[2] Foremost among these sources are Aulard 1882, 1885–86; Beik 1970; Godeschot 1971; and Lemay 1991, 2:996–97. I have included every individual whose opposition to the revolution was clearly indicated in these four sources. I have also drawn on Lefebvre 1962–64 and Furet and Richet 1970 for additional participants who played prominent roles from 1789 to 1792. I have found Challamel 1895 useful in understanding the general political spectrum of the revolution up to 1792. The far greater availability of biographical information (particularly birth order) for opponents of the revolution makes this sample equivalent to nearly 600 deputies to the National Convention.

[3] In the French Revolution database, I have recorded information on the number of years a deputy's parents were married before the deputy was born. I have also collected information on parents' ages at the time the deputy was born. In many instances this is the only in-

into other "indicator" variables. For example, I have classified all deputies according to their political affiliations. This important information is derived from six variables that record classifications made by previous historians.[4] I have coded these political affiliations on a 10-step scale, from counterrevolutionaries to ultraradicals, and employ this scale to derive the statistics that accompany Figure 13.1.[5] I have also dummy coded party affiliations (0 or 1) for each political group. This form of coding avoids the problem of specifying where a deputy stood on a "conservative/radical" dimension. As I have shown in Chapter 13, political radicalism is a multidimensional construct that, during the French Revolution, requires flexible methods of coding. One reason why my database is so large is that many variables must be coded in alternative ways to accommodate the complexities of the subject.

I employ both multiple regression models and logistic regression models in analyzing voting patterns during the king's trial. These models include eight variables. Because these are the most important variables in my database, I describe them here:

1. **Voting during the king's trial (the dependent variable).** In this analysis I have included all deputies who voted at least once (N=732).[6] A "radical" vote is defined as being *against* the appeal to the people, *for* death, and *against* mercy. Deputies generally voted consistently, with 334 of them voting mostly

formation I possess about the deputy's family constellation. I have not actually utilized such information, but if more of it were available it would become useful in estimating missing data. For example, the correlation between a deputy's relative birth rank and the number of years elapsed between his parents' date of marriage and the deputy's date of birth is a whopping .65 (df=1/41, t=5.42, p <.0001).

I have determined membership in the Jacobin Club and the Feuillant Club from lists published in Aulard (1889, 1:xxxiii–xxvi) and Challamel (1895:286–323).

[4] In classifying deputies' political affiliations I have drawn on Kuscinski 1917–19; Sydenham 1961; Patrick 1972; Jordan 1979; Chaumié 1980; Brunel 1980; Pertué 1981a, b; and Higonnet 1985.

[5] These 10 steps comprise (1) staunch royalists and counterrevolutionaries, (2) constitutional monarchists, (3) Feuillants, (4) Girondins, (5) Girondin sympathizers, (6) the Plain, (7) Montagnard sympathizers, (8) Montagnards, (9) the far left (Higonnet's [1985] "other left"), and (10) ultraradicals.

[6] I have corrected a small number of errors in Patrick's (1972) reporting of votes, based on information provided by Jordan (1979) and Lewis-Beck, Hildreth, and Spitzer (1988). I have also included the "votes" of 7 deputies who were on mission during the trial and who made their opinions known in advance by letter (Kuscinski 1917–19:309, 327). Another 4 deputies voted at least once, although not on the issue of death. Hence my total of 732 voters corresponds with the official total of 721, plus 7 unofficial voters on mission, plus 4 voters on issues other than the king's death. Following Patrick (1972:95, 103–4), I have counted all votes for the ambiguous Mailhe amendment as votes against executing the king only if the deputy subsequently voted for mercy.

in a conservative direction and 398 voting mostly in a radical direction. A second and even broader measure of political allegiances includes voting on the reinstatement of the pro-Girondin Commission of Twelve, voting on the impeachment of Marat, and whether or not a deputy subsequently protested the arrest of the Girondin leaders.

2. Relative birth rank. I have coded this information on a 7-point scale but actually employ eight categories. The codings are: (1.0) firstborns with younger siblings; (2.0) only children; (3.0) "eldest sons"; (4.0) laterborns who fall below .51 in relative birth rank (determined by the ratio of birth rank to sibship size); (5.0) laterborns who fall between .51 and .69 in relative birth rank; (5.5) laterborns (predominantly younger sons) whose exact birth rank and sibship size are unknown;[7] (6.0) laterborns who fall between .70 and .99 in relative birth rank; and (7.0) youngest children. The logic for this linear classification is implicit in the overall findings of this book.[8] The most effective multiple regression models contrast middleborns (those in categories 5.0 through 6.0) with all other individuals. This contrast captures the significant linear and curvilinear trends within the data.[9]

3. Tough-mindedness. This variable is a composite of measures of (1) extraversion and (2) antagonism. I provide further details about these two measures later in this appendix. Because antagonism is a somewhat better predictor of voting, my measure of tough-mindedness is a weighted average.[10] An alternative to using a weighted average is to allow both extraversion and antagonism to enter the regression model. I have combined the two variables in order to simplify the model. The logistic regression model employs three categories of tough-mindedness, which divide the sample evenly.

4. Region of France. This variable represents the geographic region in which a deputy was elected to office. I have coded this information in binary form, following Alison Patrick's division of the 82 departments of France

---

[7] Of the 47 individuals in this category, at least 41 (or 87 percent) possessed one or more older brothers. The mean relative birth rank for laterborns of *known* birth rank and sibship size is .73 (the equivalent of 5.6 on the 7-point scale).

[8] On the linear relationship between relative birth rank and openness to experience, see Chapter 4, especially Figure 4.1.

[9] On the use of focused contrasts in statistical analysis, see Rosenthal and Rosnow 1985.

[10] The weights are .3 for extraversion and .5 for antagonism, which correspond to the correlations these two variables exhibit with voting for death during the king's trial. Some psychologists might prefer restricting the term "tough-minded" to a measure of Agreeableness/Antagonism on the Big Five personality dimensions (Feingold 1994). Eysenck (1954:178) initially considered tough-mindedness to be strongly correlated with extraversion, and he still considers this association to be an important part of the construct, although less so than formerly (Eysenck and Wilson 1978:309). See also McCrae and Costa (1987:85), who present evidence that adjective pairs such as "ruthless/soft-hearted" correlate with *both* Big Five dimensions. Tough-minded political acts are not usually the work of shy people.

into two equal groups.[11] It is important not to employ too many geographic subdivisions, which increasingly take advantage of chance differences. Patrick's two categories separate northeastern and central France from the rest of the country. Coded in this manner, "region" is a reasonably good proxy for distance from Paris. "Region" is also a good proxy for closeness to the war-torn frontiers of northeastern France. A three-way subdivision, separating off most of southern France, offers little improvement on Patrick's two-way division.

5. **Age.** In multiple regression models I employ an interval measure, based on date of birth. Logistic regression models include three categories, which divide the sample evenly.

6. **Previous political experience in the Legislative Assembly.** Dummy coded as 0 or 1. Alison Patrick's research has demonstrated the relevance of this predictor, which was the most important one reported in her study.[12]

7. **Urban versus rural.** This variable incorporates information on place of birth as well as place of residence in 1789.[13] I have recorded these data on a continuous scale and then recoded them categorically for use in logistic regression models. My categorical codings include four levels. I give the highest score to deputies who were born in Paris (which had a population of 524,000) or who lived there in 1789. The next category is for deputies who were born in towns of 15,000 or more individuals, or who lived in such towns as of 1789. The third category is for deputies who were born in towns of 4,000 to 15,000 individuals, or who lived in them in 1789. All other deputies fall into the fourth category. A variable that incorporates both place of birth and place of residence in 1789 is marginally better as a predictor of voting than either variable separately.

8. **Socioeconomic status.** I have coded this variable on a 6-point scale (from upper nobility to working class). The first two steps on the scale are for members of the upper and lower aristocracy. The remaining four steps correspond with the scale I employ for scientists (Appendix 2). My classifications follow the ordinal scale and socioeconomic information published by Chaumié.[14] I have assessed father's and deputy's socioeconomic status separately and employ an average of the two measures. In models using logistic regression I include only three subdivisions in socioeconomic status: (1) nobility and upper bourgeoisie; (2) middle bourgeoisie (for example, doctors and lawyers); and (3) lower bourgeoisie (merchants) and below. Further subdivisions are not particularly helpful.

Although the majority of the eight predictors of voting patterns are either continuous or interval variables, the bulk of explanatory power can be captured by

---

[11] Patrick 1972:189.

[12] Patrick 1972:297–98.

[13] In coding urban versus rural residence, I have followed both the methods and primary sources of Higonnet (1985).

[14] Chaumié 1980. I have also benefited from the socioeconomic information published by Patrick (1972).

just two or three subdivisions in each variable. Allowing more than three categories generally adds little to most logistic regression models and makes the results substantially harder to interpret. With logistic regression, the primary goal is to follow subgroups of identical individuals and to determine their predicted probabilities of belonging to the dichotomous outcome variable. Such models are well suited to the needs of historians. For example, I may wish to know a deputy's likelihood of voting for the king's death if this deputy happened to be young, urban, and from northern France, and if he was also tough-minded and an eldest son. This group includes Maximilien Robespierre, and the group's predicted probability of voting for death was 97 percent. There are ten deputies in this group, and all ten voted for death. To subdivide my sample much finer than this would not be historically useful.

RELIABILITY AND VALIDITY OF PERSONALITY MEASURES

Subjective Scales

I have assessed Extraversion and Agreeableness/Antagonism in two different ways. The first two scales are based on content analysis and hence are partly subjective. These two scales help to determine validity for the two objective scales that I actually employ in modeling voting patterns. I describe the two subjective scales first.

Assessing Extraversion. My subjective measure of extraversion involves my own ratings, using a 7-point scale, based on the biographical descriptions of deputies provided in Auguste Kuscinski's *Dictionnaire des conventionnels.*[15] A Polish historian who was exiled for his revolutionary activities, Kuscinski resettled in France and spent the next fifty years documenting the lives of the 893 National Convention deputies. Kuscinski tells us who among the 893 deputies were the great orators, who fought for which political proposals, and how deputies aligned themselves within the Convention. We learn which deputies committed atrocities on missions, who denounced their colleagues, who voted for the king's death, and numerous other details. Kuscinski also provides considerable information on the deputies' personalities, often citing the recollections of other deputies.

In general, Kuscinski's biographical descriptions leave little doubt about people who belong to the two extremes on an extraversion scale. For example, he describes Jean-Marie Collot d'Herbois, a member of the Committee of Public Safety, as a "fiery" Jacobin who often "harangued" his fellow club members. According to Kuscinski, Collot d'Herbois was also "hot-headed," "haughty," and "passionate."[16] Other deputies are said to be "charming," "eloquent," and "affable" (Barère), "ardent and enthusiastic" (Basire), "irascible," "eloquent," "bold," and "critical" (Guadet), and so forth. Deputies such as Collot d'Herbois, Barère, Basire, and Guadet define the positive end of the extraversion scale. By contrast,

[15] Kuscinski 1917–19.

[16] Kuscinski 1917–19:57, 146–49.

Kuscinski portrays other deputies as being "timid" and afraid even to speak out on the floor of the Convention. For example, Jacques-Antoine Boudin had a speech printed rather than deliver it himself, and he is also said to have buried himself in the obscurity of committee work. Other deputies are described as "frightened" by the violence around them (Claude Bernard), as having never appeared at the tribune (Charles-Robert Hecquet), as having rarely attended the Convention (Jean-Jacques Fiquet), or as having resigned their office out of fear (Jacques-Baptiste-Augustin-Prosper Mennesson).

In making ratings for extraversion I followed a formal set of rules based on a systematic content analysis of the text. If a deputy was described as either "outgoing" or "bold," he received +1 point on the extraversion scale. If a deputy was described as "affable, outgoing, and ardent," he received +3 points on the scale (the maximum). Similarly, if a deputy was described as "timid," he received –1 point; "shy and retiring" merits –2 points, and so forth, until a maximum of –3 was reached on the scale. My extraversion scale is therefore closely tied to Kuscinski's use of adjectives and adverbs to describe personality. Based on such descriptions, I was able to rate 669 deputies on extraversion.

Assessing Antagonism/Agreeableness. As with signs of extraversion, Kuscinski often noted this aspect of the deputies' temperaments. For example, he describes Jean-Louis Albitte, the younger brother of deputy Antoine-Louis, as "not at all made for political agitation. Of a peaceable character, he hardly appeared at the Convention."[17] No one would confuse such a gentle deputy with Fréron, whom Kuscinski reports as being "ferocious by character, violent by temperament, and destructive by instinct"; or with Marat, whom Kuscinski portrays as "bilious, peevish, opinionated, ferocious, and bloodthirsty."[18] Based on such descriptions, I was able to rate 470 deputies on antagonism.

Like my subjective measure of extraversion, my subjective measure of antagonism incorporates Kuscinski's use of adjectives and adverbs in a formal manner. Thus a deputy who is described as "violent" received +1 point on the antagonism scale. Someone characterized as both "violent" and "heedless" received +2 points on the antagonism scale.[19] Similarly, a deputy described as "friendly and kind," but also as "arrogant," received a *net* score of –1 points on antagonism. Like my scale for extraversion, the antagonism scale varies from –3 to +3.

Objective Scales

Assessing Extraversion. My second set of scales is composed of objective indicators. As I read through Kuscinski's dictionary I made a systematic record of the kinds of information that were guiding my judgments. I then constructed scales for these indicators and coded them in a purely mechanical manner for each

---

[17] Kuscinski 1917–19:4.

[18] Kuscinski 1917–19:274, 430–31.

[19] I have treated descriptions of many actions by deputies (for example, those involving "kindness" or "leniency") as if they were adjectival equivalents (that is, "kind" or "lenient" acts). This research approach is an adaptation of Buss and Craik's (1980, 1983a) "act psychology" approach to behavior.

deputy. In general order of their importance, I list here those measures that are highly correlated with extraversion, as measured by the subjective index described earlier. Each of these indicator variables has an objective data source documented in the database. Extraverted deputies tended (1) to have spoken out frequently on the floor of the National Convention;[20] (2) to be known as famous "orators";[21] (3) to have had active political careers (as measured by article length in Kuscinski's dictionary); (4) to be well documented in my database (that is, to exhibit very few missing data points); (5) to have gone on one or more missions outside of Paris; (6) to have met with a violent death during the revolution; (7) to have been members of one of the two great executive committees under the Terror; (8) to have published an opinion on the king's trial in contemporary pamphlets; (9) to be labeled a "terrorist";[22] (10) to have been proscribed from the Convention during the Terror;[23] (11) to have held previous political office; (12) to be classified as political "agitators"; and (13) to have abstained rarely during voting. In contrast, timid deputies tended (14) to "lay low" during the Terror and (15) to ensconce themselves in the anonymity of committee work. These last two attributes have been tabulated by Patrick, whose systematic researches have allowed me to construct indicator variables for these and several other measures.[24] Some of these indicator variables, such as being labeled a "terrorist," also correlate highly with the scale for antagonism.

The correlations between these indirect measures of extraversion and my subjective ratings vary from a high of .53 (for degree of activity recorded in the official minutes of the Convention), to .35 for going on missions, to a low of .13 for not abstaining during voting. The *mean* correlation is a respectable .31. The first of these objective measures (namely, each deputy's record of activity in the official minutes of the National Convention) is itself so highly correlated with extraversion that it could be employed in my computer models with almost the same results as those obtained using a more detailed measure.

---

[20] In coding this indicator, I have counted the number of lines taken up by each deputy in the three-volume index that summarizes the minutes of daily sessions (Lefebvre, Reinhard, and Bouloiseau 1959–63). The range among deputies is from a low of 2 lines to a high of 161 lines (for Marat). Although much of the discussion in the entry for Marat is about his death and various memorials in his honor, Marat was ahead of all deputies on this measure at the time of his assassination.

[21] Aulard 1882, 1885–86; Lemay 1991, 2:995–97. I have coded this variable on a 3-step scale: "very frequent" parliamentary speakers, "frequent" speakers, and all others.

[22] My list of terrorists (N=39) is compiled from Kuscinski (1917–19), Lefebvre (1962–64), Furet and Richet (1970), and Furet and Ozouf (1989), among other sources. Even after being controlled for the seven overlapping variables in my own two measurement scales, antagonism and extraversion are moderately correlated dimensions of personality (r=.44). Terrorists were rarely shy people.

[23] A variable recording "proscription" from the National Convention helps to correct for the fact that proscribed deputies tend to have fewer lines in the index of the official minutes of the Convention (Lefebvre, Reinhard, and Bouloiseau 1959–63). Still, deputies who were under arrest did receive mention for this and other facts relating to their arrest, trial, or execution. This circumstance tends to make up for the lesser number of lines these deputies received because of their proscription.

[24] Patrick 1972.

By pooling these 15 measures, I have sought to document extraversion across a variety of political domains, thus increasing reliability. For these 15 indicator variables, the *effective* reliability is .86.[25] This objective measure of extraversion correlates .74 with the subjective index, based on content analysis.

Assessing Antagonism. I have found it more difficult to construct an objective measure for "antagonism" owing to the smaller number of surrogate indicators of this behavior in my database. Still, my subjective measure of antagonism exhibits a respectable multiple correlation of .58 with 11 objective predictors. This objective index of antagonism includes, in order of importance: (1) being described as a "terrorist"; (2) being a member of the Far Left; (3) speaking out frequently in the National Convention; (4) being actively involved in political life; (5) voting against the impeachment of Marat;[26] (6) voting against the Commission of Twelve (which was supposed to investigate the Commune's plans to assassinate the Girondin leaders); (7) not protesting the arrest of the Girondin leaders; (8) being labeled a political "agitator"; (9) being a member of one of the two great executive committees under the Terror; (10) going on one or more missions; and (11) not "laying low" under the Terror. The *effective* reliability of this mechanical index is .77. Because I combine my measures of extraversion and antagonism into a single scale of tough-mindedness, I have not been concerned to keep these two indices distinct from one another, and 7 of the 26 scales overlap.

Tough-mindedness. In my model of voting during the king's trial, I have combined the 11 indicator scales for antagonism with the 15 indicator scales for extraversion. Because 7 of the scales are common to both measures, my variable for tough-mindedness is a composite of 19 rather than 26 measures. All told, these 19 measures reflect more than 16,000 individual personality attributes and publicly documented political behaviors.

Reliability

Although each of these indicators, taken alone, is only moderately predictive of tough-mindedness, the effective reliability of all 19 measures is .89—more than adequate for the task at hand.[27]

---

[25] Rosenthal 1987:10.

[26] Because voting on Marat's impeachment and two of my other indicators of antagonism are also included in my comprehensive six-issue measure of voting within the National Convention, I do not attempt to correlate this comprehensive measure of political behavior with tough-mindedness.

[27] This determination of effective reliability takes into account the fact that seven predictors overlap between the two scales and do not therefore contribute to increased reliability. I have not employed expert historians as independent raters of tough-mindedness for a practical reason. It took me several months to assemble biographical information on tough-mindedness for all 893 deputies, and expert historians would not have been able to provide this kind of detailed assessment without several weeks of work on their part. Owing to the large number of indicator variables that I have employed, independent ratings from five expert historians would raise reliability by only .05 (to .94), assuming that these five experts exhibited an interrater reliability of at least .60.

Validity

Measurement scales should be both reliable and valid. A scale is *valid* if it measures what it claims to measure. My subjective measures of extraversion and antagonism are reasonably good guides to validity, since they are based directly on Kuscinski's use of adjectives, like "outgoing" and "ferocious," that define these two measures.[28] It is comforting to observe that the correlations between my two personality scales, derived from content analysis, and other objective measures are roughly what they ought to be. For example, the correlation between my subjective measure of extraversion and being cited as a "frequent speaker" or famous "orator" in revolutionary politics is .45.[29] Being a deputy of the Plain, whose members have typically been described as "timid," has a negative correlation of .51 with extraversion. The correlation between being labeled as a "terrorist" correlates .44 with my subjective measure of antagonism, based on content analysis. These correlations are about what one would expect. Almost nothing in personality psychology correlates with anything else at a level much higher than .5 (unless one pools multiple measures).[30]

For birth order, the correlation with extraversion is −.17 (firstborns are more extraverted).[31] The correlation between antagonism and birth order is −.26 (firstborns are more antagonistic).[32] In Helen Koch's studies of six-year-olds, the correlations between birth order and various measures of extraversion and antagonism are about the same magnitude.[33]

MISSING DATA

Using path-analytic methods, which control for cross correlations, birth order is the most important predictor of voting during the king's trial. It is also the least observed predictor in my study. Alas, there seems to be a strong relationship in historical research between the importance of information and its unavailability. History is therefore a massive "missing data" problem, which is why I am concerned about this issue.[34]

Although I have had access to extensive biographical resources, including the personal library of French historian Alphonse Aulard, I have been able to docu-

---

[28] McCrae and Costa 1987.

[29] Aulard 1882, 1885–86; Lemay 1991, 2:996–97.

[30] Cohen 1977:78.

[31] For relative birth rank and extraversion among the deputies of the National Convention, r=–.17 (df=1/199, t=–2.40, p<.02). This correlation is based on the objective measure. For the subjective measure based on content analysis of Kuscinski's (1917–19) biographical entries, r=–.14 (df=1/94, t=–1.93, p<.06).

[32] For relative birth rank and antagonism among the deputies of the National Convention, r=–.26 (df=1/199, t=–3.79, p<.001). This correlation is based on the objective measure. For the subjective measure based on content analysis, r=–.19 (df=1/183, t=–2.60, p<.01).

[33] Koch 1955a.

[34] For the problem of missing data, and techniques to deal with it, see Appendix 5.

ment birth order for only 206 Convention deputies.[35] This total, after many years of research, represents just 23 percent of the National Convention. For my sample of opponents (N=186) I have been more successful. I have ascertained birth order in 120 instances (or 65 percent). The lives of the opposition are far better documented than those of the deputies, who often emerged from obscurity in 1792 and then returned to obscurity after their term in office.

The point of conducting statistical tests is to be sure that any trend found within a limited sample is not a chance effect that would disappear if one had access to larger samples. The probability that birth order played *no* role in the king's trial is very small (less than 1 in 10,000). Still, birth order may have been somewhat more, or somewhat less, important than I have been able to document based on *known* biographical data. In order to assess the degree of error inherent in my findings, I have created an extensive database that encompasses information that correlates with birth order. For example, firstborns are more likely to be named after their father, as are eldest sons. Similarly, firstborns and eldest sons are more likely to follow in their father's profession and are especially likely to inherit any office he might have purchased. Firstborns are also more likely to become eminent. For this reason, a simple arithmetic total of the number of missing data points for each deputy correlates significantly (and negatively) with being firstborn.[36] Odd as it may seem, missing information itself is useful information. Obscure deputies, who were generally laterborns, were also significantly more likely to vote to spare the king's life during his trial.[37] Based on these two correlations, it is likely that the missing birth-order data for deputies of the National Convention is just as good as the data that are actually observed. The EM algorithm, described in Appendix 5, agrees. The correlation between birth order and voting in a "radical" direction during the king's trial is .29 for the *fully observed* data and .30 for the *estimated* data.[38]

Birth records exist in France that would provide additional birth-order information on the deputies of the National Convention. Kuscinski located baptismal certificates for almost all of the deputies, but it did not occur to him to look for similar information about siblings. I am hopeful that French historians will consider pursuing this line of research and will cooperate to create a communal data-

---

[35] Aulard's collection was acquired by Harvard University after his death in 1923. In seeking information on birth order I have examined hundreds of biographies, inspected the principal journals of French revolutionary history issue by issue, and hunted down individual deputies in countless dusty genealogical tomes. I have also consulted most of the standard biographical sources listed in Lemay 1991, 2:1014–19.

[36] For the correlation between relative birth rank and missing biographical information, r=.21 (df=1/199, t=3.04, p<.01). Controlled for relative birth rank, a quadratic trend in birth order (contrasting middleborns with firstborns and laterborns) is also significant (partial r=.19, df=1/198, t=2.67, p<.01): middleborns are most likely to exhibit missing biographical information.

[37] For missing biographical information and voting for death during the king's trial, r=–.18 (df=1/730, t=–4.95, p<.0001).

[38] These two birth-order correlations both include the significant curvilinear component.

base available to future historians. Such data, collected on a systematic basis, would go a long way toward solving a number of interesting historical problems. For example, some deputies, such as Carnot, Fouché, and Jeanbon Saint-André, served under Bonaparte. Others refused to have anything to do with him. The analysis of political behavior that I have provided in Chapter 13 is probably relevant to this problem. Tough-minded individuals of early birth rank should have been at home with a tyrant like Napoleon. After all, they largely invented the strategy of "saving the revolution" through tyranny.

Another significant benefit from additional birth-order data would be the ability to detect interaction effects. To do so requires relatively large samples, since the "interaction" is what is left over after the "main" effects have been partialed out. It is likely that many of the predictors of voting during the king's trial interact significantly with birth order, just as does social class (Chapter 13, Fig. 13.2). To the extent that historians are able to increase the amount of documented biographical information on this topic, we will have a much better idea of how sibling differences interact with between-family differences in historical change.

The history of France from 1789 to the July Revolution of 1830 offers an unusual opportunity to test a number of hypotheses about changing political behavior during a remarkably turbulent period. A study of "career paths" during these four decades would be well worth undertaking on a systematic basis (see Appendix 10, Section 11).

CONCLUSION

The history of political radicalism is largely entwined with sibling differences and their relationship to the Big Five personality dimensions. We therefore need ways of measuring within-family differences in history if we are to test the power of these influences against between-family predictors such as regional differences, social class, and religious denomination. Content analysis of biographical sources, which makes possible the use of indicator variables, is one useful approach to the problem.[39] The use of independent raters, which I have frequently called upon in other historical contexts in this book, supplies another valuable means of hypothesis testing. The future of research on political change will benefit from these and other techniques to measure individual differences and their relationship to family dynamics, as well as to the broader social context.

---

[39] For a similar approach to U.S. Supreme Court voting, based on content analysis of newspaper editorials about the nominee's standing on a conservative/liberal spectrum, see Segal and Spaeth 1993:226–28.

APPENDIX 9
MISCELLANEOUS TECHNICAL DISCUSSIONS

Technical Discussion 1 (Chapter 2, note 8): Seasonality of birth and revolutionary temperament. According to Michael Holmes, a British psychologist at the University of Edinburgh, the stance taken toward revolutionary scientific ideas is related to seasonality of birth.[1] Holmes's study, published in the prestigious journal *Nature,* contains a number of methodological flaws that led him to endorse a spurious result.

Holmes obtained information on month of birth for 28 participants in the pre-Darwinian debates over evolution and another 19 individuals who spoke out on Einstein's theory of relativity. Holmes does not explain how he selected his historical samples, and he did not employ independent raters to verify his classifications. In both samples, Holmes found that revolutionaries were significantly more likely to be born during winter months (October through April) compared with opponents of these theories. He attributed this finding to the fact that infants born in winter months would have been swaddled at first, but would then have enjoyed more freedom during the summer, when they were ready to begin exploring the world.

I have duplicated and extended Holmes's analysis for the 636 individuals who are recorded in my own databases as being involved in these two scientific debates.[2] As a bivariate correlation, seasonality of birth is indeed significantly related to support for revolutionary ideas. The correlation is small, however, and it is also in the *opposite direction* to that reported by Holmes.[3] When this modest correlation is analyzed more closely and corrected for methodological biases, it ceases to be significant.

Several methodological flaws confound the temporal association that Holmes has reported. First, the decision as to how to subdivide a sample by seasonality of birth can be arbitrary when the subdivision is made on a dichotomous basis. If birth patterns for scientists born in April happen to be favorable to the hypothesis, then April is easily considered a "winter" month. If April's data happen to go the other way, then April can just as easily become a "summer" month. The data for October can be manipulated in the same way. A proper analysis of the influence of

---

[1] Holmes 1995.

[2] In this analysis of seasonality of birth, I have included participants in the debates over Darwinism, in addition to participants in the pre-Darwinian debates over evolution.

[3] For birth during winter months and support for revolutionary theories, $r=-.08$ ($df=1/553$, $t=-1.92$, $p<.06$). For individuals whose birth orders are known (and who are more eminent than the rest of the sample), the correlation is statistically significant ($r=-.12$, $df=1/405$, $t=-2.52$, $p<.02$).

seasonality requires a more rigorous statistical approach than that employed by Holmes. Ideally, each month of the year should be rank ordered by seasonality, based on an objective criterion such as temperature. When this precaution is taken, the correlation I have reported between seasonality and revolutionary temperament for my own data ceases to be statistically significant.[4] My preliminary result was therefore a statistical fluke, based on an arbitrary subdivision of the year into two temporal categories.

Holmes was not just statistically lucky (or unlucky) in his approach to the problem. Such spurious results will tend to arise much more frequently than chance given the methods that he employed.[5] To begin with, Holmes stopped counting participants at 47 individuals, an exceedingly small sample for this kind of study. The readily available data on participants in these two scientific controversies is more than 10 times the size of Holmes's published sample.[6] Whenever a researcher assembles a small sample from a much larger sample that is *readily accessible,* there is an inevitable temptation to stop counting participants as soon as a working hypothesis happens to reach statistical significance. If not decided in advance, the decision when to stop counting tends to create a bias in the testing procedures, which cease to obey the usual rules of statistical probability. Had Holmes employed expert historians to check his assessments of scientific stance, these experts would surely have asked him about the many prominent scientists who were *missing* from his samples. Adding these scientists to Holmes's samples would have rendered his initial findings nonsignificant.

Seasonality of birth is related to other confounding variables that Holmes did not consider. Foremost among these confounding variables is seasonality of marriage. There is a considerable literature on seasonality of marriage, a temporal pattern that has been well documented in European countries over the last five centuries.[7] Seasonality of marriage is in turn related to seasonality differences in birth, by birth order. Historically, births have tended to peak in February and to reach a low in July.[8] The pattern for firstborn children tends to deviate from this

---

[4] For this test, I have coded seasonality of birth on a 12-step scale, with January being assigned a score of 6 and July being assigned a score of −6. For the resulting correlation between seasonality of birth and scientific stance, r=–.06 (df=1/553, t=–1.42, p<.16). Shifting the temporal scoring system by one month in either direction makes little difference in the results.

[5] Given that the true effect size for seasonality of birth and revolutionary temperament is probably zero (or very close to it), Holmes's finding is significantly better than chance and would arise only once in a thousand times. What is particularly striking about Holmes's finding is the effect size (r [*phi*] =.59, χ^2=16.13, p<.001). This finding explains 9 times the variance associated with receptivity to scientific innovation by nationality, 19 times the variance associated with friendship, and 35 times the variance associated with field of specialization—all of which are significant predictors of scientific stance in their own right. In short, the *effect size* that Holmes has published is way out of proportion to anything that one might plausibly expect for an influence of this kind.

[6] See particularly Glick 1972, 1987.

[7] See, for example, Wrigley and Schofield 1981:298–99.

[8] Wrigley and Schofield 1981:288.

general trend because this pattern is directly linked to seasonality of marriages. Marriages have been the least frequent during March, reflecting ancient church prohibitions against marriage during Lent and Rogation. These temporal patterns tend to be more pronounced in Catholic countries. People who do not engage in sexual intercourse during Lent tend not to have winter-born offspring.[9] To the extent that national differences exist in science, they can introduce seasonality of birth effects owing to the cross correlation with religious denomination. Holmes did not consider this issue in his analysis, although he was aware of the possible confounding effects of these variables.[10] As covariates for religious denomination and nationality are introduced into my own sample, the correlation between seasonality of birth and support for revolutionary theories increasingly approaches zero.[11]

Another test of Holmes's thesis involves the role of climate. If infants who are no longer tightly swaddled at six months of age tend to become revolutionaries, then children raised in equatorial regions around the world should be significantly more rebellious than children who are raised in temperate climates. This does not appear to be the case. In my own sample, the correlation between the mean latitude of the country of origin and support for radical ideas is exactly zero.[12]

When expected effect sizes are small in the behavioral sciences, as they ought to be for variables such as seasonality of birth and its effects on personality, large samples are needed to test properly for an association. In addition, such samples need to be controlled for obvious covariates that might lead to spurious conclusions. Holmes failed to observe either of these two basic precautions. Yet he had ample time and reason to do so. Initially conducted in 1974, his study sat unpublished in a file drawer for twenty years before he finally submitted it to *Nature.* What is particularly remarkable about the publication of Holmes's findings is that peer review at *Nature* did not question his methods.

Technical Discussion 2 (Chapter 2, note 78): Radical thinking and primogeniture. It is possible to test for the role of primogeniture as a spur to

---

[9] For seasonality of birth (coded on a 12-step scale) and being Protestant, $r=.11$ ($df=1/535$, $t=2.49$, $p<.02$). Catholics tended to be born during the summer months more often than Protestants. For being French and being born in the summer months, $r=.09$ ($df=1/553$, $t=2.21$, $p<.03$; based on the 12-step seasonality measure). Because the French were significantly more likely to oppose Darwinian evolution than any other national group in Europe, a spurious cross correlation arises between seasonality of birth and attitudes toward Darwinism.

[10] In 1974 I gave a talk on birth order and receptivity to scientific revolutions at the University of Edinburgh. Holmes attended this presentation. His study of seasonality of birth was conducted at this time and was partly inspired by my own unpublished research.

[11] For seasonality of birth and support for revolutionary theories, controlled for religious denomination and national differences, $r=-.05$ ($df=1/534$, $t=-1.27$, $p<.20$).

[12] For mean latitude of country of birth and support for revolutions, $r=.00$ ($df=1/634$, $t=0.06$, $p<.96$). An even better test would be to contrast scientists born in the Southern Hemisphere with those born in the Northern Hemisphere. Unfortunately, my database does not include enough scientists from the Southern Hemisphere to permit such a test.

radical thinking among younger siblings. In 1700 primogeniture was still a widespread practice throughout Europe.[13] Matters changed toward the end of the century. In the wake of the French Revolution, primogeniture was made illegal in many countries.[14] To the extent that birth-order effects are caused by the practice of primogeniture, any reduction in this practice should be reflected over time by a reduction in birth-order effects.

Testing for this possibility involves comparing the efficacy of birth order as a predictor of radical thinking from 1517 to 1967, a period of 450 years. Because birth-order effects are strongly correlated with the ideological radicalism of revolutions, I have included this variable as a covariate in the test.[15] What we seek to know, then, is whether birth-order effects, controlled for their known relationship with ideological radicalism, have become smaller over time.

This test involves an analysis of variance, in which support for radical revolutions becomes the dependent variable and (1) birth order, (2) year of participation, and (3) the ideological radicalism of the controversy are entered in the model as covariates.[16] What we are looking for is whether a model saturated with birth order, year of participation, and ideological context also accepts a significant two-way interaction between birth order and year of participation.

The partial correlation for the influence of birth order since 1517 is .22.[17] Controlled for both main effects, the partial correlation for the two-way interaction between birth order and year of participation is a tiny .03, which is not significant. Omission of the variable for ideological context does not alter the statistical outcome. Still, the inclusion of what proves to be an unnecessary control variable is preferable to its omission. These null findings are supported by another finding: birth-order effects for every social class are nearly identical over the last 450 years, even though inheritance practices often varied between the upper and lower classes.[18]

The test conducted here is also an indirect test of the influence of changing child-rearing practices. Along with the family as a social institution, child-rearing practices have undergone significant changes over time.[19] Still, the influence of these changes on openness to new ideas is so small as to be undetectable. It is worth noting that differences in age gaps between adjacent siblings are significantly more important in explaining scientific radicalism than four centuries of changes

---

[13] Stone 1979:412; Mitterauer and Sieder 1983:68.

[14] Lefebvre 1962–64, 1:148; Mitterauer and Sieder 1983:99.

[15] For the relationship between birth-order effect sizes and the ideological implications of scientific innovations, see Chapter 14, especially Figure 14.1.

[16] In this statistical test, the ideological radicalism of controversies is indicated by the event-specific effect size for political and religious factors in predicting the outcome of the debate. See Chapter 14, Figure 14.1.

[17] For birth order and scientific stance, controlled for year of participation and ideological context, r=.22 (df=1/2,083, t=10.41, p<.0001). For the interaction between birth order and year of participation, r=.03 (df=1/2,083, t=1.21, p<.28).

[18] Wedgwood 1929:148; Mitterauer and Sieder 1983:34, 68; Hrdy and Judge 1993.

[19] Ariès 1962.

in child-rearing practices.[20] Changes in child-rearing practices may well affect some aspects of human behavior, but they appear to have had no influence on openness to experience.

Such results make considerable sense in the light of the general argument of this book. Independently of child-rearing practices, siblings experience strong and enduring rivalries with one another. Siblings do not need socioeconomic discrimination by parents to become as different as they typically are. In a Darwinian world in which siblings compete for parental investment, sibling differences arise automatically, even when parents do their best to treat all of their offspring equitably.

Technical Discussion 3 (Chapter 5, note 5): Validity of "parental relationship" evidence. Some readers may be skeptical that an issue as complex as parent-offspring conflict can be reliably assessed from historical data. I therefore provide several biographical examples to illustrate how this information has been assembled and coded. Three independent judges were employed to rate this biographical information using a 7-point scale.[21]

Louis Agassiz. Darwin's opponent Louis Agassiz had a secure relationship with his parents. He was devoted to his father, Rodolphe, who inspired in him a love of teaching. "I wish it may be said of Louis Agassiz," he wrote to his father when he was twenty-one, "that he was the first naturalist of his time, a good citizen, and a good son."[22] A strong-willed Protestant minister, Rodolphe wanted his son to be a businessman, and he initially opposed his son's going to the university. When Louis's maternal uncle agreed to pay for his educational expenses, the father relented.

Concerned that Louis might not be able to make a living as a natural scientist, Rodolphe wanted him to obtain a medical degree first. He became upset after learning that Louis was writing a book about the fish of Brazil instead of pursuing his medical studies, but was delighted when the book was published and highly praised. Agassiz perceived his father in a somewhat idealized light, for no amount of conflict between the two seems to have diminished his filial respect. Rodolphe's death "brought great sorrow to his son."[23] Using a 7-point scale on which 7.0 represents a close and harmonious relationship, three independent raters give Agassiz 5.8 points. This rating puts him well above the sample mean (5.1).

Agassiz's relationship with his mother was even closer.[24] According to one biographer, Louis was "clearly her favorite child, the source of her highest hopes and aspirations."[25] Rose Agassiz lavished on him "a profound maternal love, com-

---

[20] See Chapter 5, Figure 5.2.

[21] The interrater reliability for assessments of parent-offspring conflict is .78. Based on the use of three raters, the effective reliability is .90.

[22] Marcou 1896, 1:30; Lurie 1960:31.

[23] Lurie 1960:92.

[24] Lurie 1960:5; Marcou 1896, 1:26.

[25] Lurie 1960:5.

forting him in all his trouble, giving gentle counsel."[26] Occasionally she chided him for being "fickle" in his studies and hence "inconsiderate" of his parents' wishes.[27] After Louis became world famous, she cherished his scientific writings and collected them together, even those in English, which she was unable to read. Her death was "the heaviest sorrow of his life."[28] Independent raters assign this positive relationship a score of 6.5, putting Agassiz in the 92nd percentile.

Charles Darwin. Compared with Agassiz's, Darwin's relationship with his parents was rather different, being complicated by his mother's early death. In his *Autobiography* Darwin devoted considerable space to his father, Robert, whom he greatly admired. He described his father as "in many ways a remarkable man" and "the kindest man I ever knew."[29] He goes on to relate how Dr. Darwin became a highly successful physician on account of his talent at winning his patients' confidence. The doctor had an uncanny ability to sense people's true motives and appeared, at times, to read his patients' minds. Darwin never tired of telling his children stories about his father. One of Darwin's favorite expressions was "My father used to say . . ." Darwin's reverence for his father, Darwin's son Francis recalled, "was boundless and most touching."[30]

In spite of Darwin's warm regard for his father, as a child his relationship with him was somewhat troubled. Darwin himself believed his father had been "a little unjust to me when I was young, but afterwards I am thankful to think I became a prime favourite with him."[31] John Bowlby, who spent a lifetime studying attachment behavior, has commented on Darwin's "difficult, though far from bad, relationship with his father during boyhood and adolescence."[32] Three independent judges agree with Bowlby. Darwin's relationship with his father is rated 4.5, somewhat below the mean. If Darwin were being rated separately for this relationship in childhood and adulthood, he might receive 3.5 for the early period and 6.5 as an adult. Overall, a rating of 4.5 seems reasonable.

Samuel Butler. Different raters might quibble over whether Darwin should be rated exactly as he has been, but few judges would have much doubt about Samuel Butler. He was the celebrated author of *Erewhon* (1872), a best-selling satire about a world turned topsy-turvy. In the strange land of Erewhon, illness was punishable by imprisonment or death, and criminals were sent to hospitals to be cured. The second of four children, Samuel Butler wrote of his father:

> He never liked me, nor I him; from my earliest recollections I can recall to mind no time when I did not fear him and dislike him. . . . For years and years I have never passed a day without thinking of him many times

---

[26] Marcou 1896, 2:161.
[27] E. Agassiz 1885, 1:61.
[28] Marcou 1896, 2:161.
[29] Darwin 1958 [1876]:28.
[30] Darwin 1887, 1:10–11.
[31] Darwin 1887, 1:11.
[32] Bowlby 1990:13.

> over as the man who was sure to be against me, who would see the bad side rather than the good side of everything I said and did. He used to say to his [childhood] nurse . . . "I'll keep you: you shan't leave: I'll keep you on purpose to torment you."
>
> And I have felt that he has always looked upon me as something which he could badger with impunity, or very like it, as he badgered his nurse. . . . An unkind fate never threw two men together who were more naturally uncongenial than my father and myself.[33]

Butler once quipped that if anyone was interested in writing his biography, he should begin with the opening line: "The subject of this Memoir was born of rich and dishonest parents."[34] Judges have assigned this relationship a 1.0, the lowest possible score. Needless to say, Butler's satire about a land where suffering elicits cruelty appears to reflect his relationship with his father.

The kind of biographical information I have just reviewed is not always available in such detail. This raises an important question. Suppose Charles Darwin, who is one of the most documented figures in history, had left behind only the statement that he once made as an adult: "I do not think any one could love a father much more than I did mine."[35] Judges would doubtless have assigned Darwin a different rating on parent-offspring conflict compared with the one that they actually gave him.

Two considerations mitigate the consequences of this problem. First, I have derived most of my data on parent-offspring conflict from eminent figures whose attitudes toward their parents are known throughout the course of their lives.[36] More important, the influence of parental conflict is such that even a *crude* scale suffices to capture the bulk of the relationship with radical thinking. For example, a 2-step scale, which distinguishes highly conflicted relationships (like that experienced by Samuel Butler) from all others, is almost as good a predictor of revolutionary personality as is a 7-point scale. This circumstance is inherent in the causal relationship. Most of the explanatory power of parent-offspring conflict is found among firstborns who have experienced high conflict with their parents (Chapter 5, Fig. 5.1). Such cases are hard to miss, even with retrospective evidence.

Although some degree of error is inevitable in attempting to rate parent-offspring relationships, the important point is that no one would confuse an Agassiz with a Butler. Each of these two individuals experienced significantly different relationships with their parents. These conspicuous contrasts, not minor differences, are what foster radical thinking.

Technical Discussion 4 (Chapter 10, notes 7 and 8): Birth order, conservatism, and eminence during the Darwinian revolution. To document my assertion that firstborns and social conservatives were more eminent than laterborns

---

[33] Jones 1919, 1:20–21.

[34] Jones 1919, l:viii.

[35] Darwin 1887, 3:39.

[36] The correlation between being eminent in my sample and the availability of information on parent-offspring conflict is .39 ($df=1/3{,}790$, $t=25.82$, $p<.0001$).

and social liberals, I have constructed an index of eminence as of 1859, the year that Darwin's *Origin of Species* was published. This issue sheds light on Adrian Desmond's biographical sample, and the conclusions he drew from it in his *Politics of Evolution*.[37]

My index of eminence is based on a point system that counts awards, honors, and memberships in prestigious societies, as well as elected offices in such societies. The correlation between eminence and being firstborn in the Darwinian revolution sample is statistically significant. Controlled for sibship size, firstborns were 1.7 times more likely than laterborns to be in the top half of the eminence distribution.[38]

The correlation between social attitudes and eminence is also statistically significant in my Darwinian revolution sample. Distinguished individuals tended to be social conservatives.[39] A multiple regression model predicting eminence in 1859 accepts social attitudes and birth order as significant predictors. Combining these two trends, socially conservative firstborns were 4.0 times more likely than socially liberal laterborns to be in the top half of the eminence distribution.[40] When Adrian Desmond assembled a list of establishment scientists to compare with his lower-class radicals, he was selecting from a population that was significantly overrepresented by conservative firstborns.[41] As a result, Desmond found a "class" difference in radicalism that owes itself to sibling differences, not class.

After 1859 the criteria for scientific eminence changed significantly as a result of the triumph of Darwin's theories. Those scientists who backed the Darwinian revolution were more likely to accrue honors, such as international prizes and membership in distinguished foreign scientific societies. Comparing participants in the Darwinian revolution for eminence in 1859 versus eminence by the end of their lifetimes, laterborns were significantly more likely than firstborns to rise in stature.[42]

Technical Discussion 5 (Chapter 10, note 16): Adrian Desmond's (1989) sample. In Appendix B of his *Politics of Evolution* (1989), Adrian Desmond lists 75 individuals who were relevant to his analysis. Not every one of these 75 individuals spoke out on the four radical theories (evolution, phrenology, spontaneous generation, and opposition to idealistic theories of classification) that form the

---

[37] Desmond 1989.

[38] For birth order and eminence among scientists in 1859, the partial correlation is −.14 (df=1/309, t=−2.48, p<.02; controlled for sibship size and social class). Both covariates are significant predictors of eminence in their own right. The most eminent scientists came from small, upper-class families: for sibship size, the partial correlation is −.18 (df=1/309, t=−3.29, p<.001); for social class, the partial correlation is −.15 (df=1/309, t=−2.58, p<.02).

[39] For eminence and social conservatism, r=−.27 (df=1/375, t=−4.80, p<.0001).

[40] For the focused contrast between conservative firstborns and liberal laterborns, as it relates to eminence in 1859, r=−.33 (df=1/248, t=−5.56, p<.0001). For the multiple correlation with both predictors, R=.31 (df=2/374, F=20.00, p<.0001).

[41] See Chapter 10, Figure 10.2.

[42] For the *relative change* in eminence by birth order after 1859, r=.16 (df=1/174, t=2.15, p<.05; a relationship that favors laterborns).

basis for my test of Desmond's claims. Some of the individuals included in Desmond's appendix are background figures to his general narrative. Thirty-six members of Desmond's sample spoke out on one or more of the four theories I have surveyed in my study. Collectively, these individuals took 75 "positions." These are the individuals included in Figure 10.2.

Technical Discussion 6 (Chapter 10, note 24): Social class, friendship, and support for Darwinism. In their biography of Darwin, Desmond and Moore claim that friendships among upper-class individuals may have inhibited these scientists' evolutionary zeal.[43] During the debates over evolutionary theory (1700–1875), the correlation between personal contact with leading evolutionists and support for this theory is essentially nil, undermining this claim.[44]

This empirical finding is corroborated by two related results. The correlation between the number of letters an individual exchanged with Darwin prior to 24 November 1859, when the *Origin of Species* was published, and this individual's subsequent response to evolution is nil.[45] Finally, the correlation between support for Darwin's theories and the number of times a scientist was cited in the *Origin* is also essentially nil.[46]

I have calculated the multiple correlation between these same three measures of personal association with Darwin (that is, personal contact with Darwin, letters exchanged with him, and citations in the *Origin*) and the social views of Darwin's contemporaries. This association is also statistically nonsignificant.[47] Barely significant is the fact that Darwin tended to have friendships with, and to correspond with, upper-class individuals like himself.[48] As an upper-class gentleman, Darwin slightly favored such individuals in his personal contacts and correspondence. This is hardly surprising: scientists tend to correspond with one another.

In addition, I have tested the possibility that Darwin's friendships before 1859 were predominantly with people who shared his social values. I have divided Darwin's contemporaries into four groups (conservatives, moderates, liberals, and rad-

---

[43] Desmond and Moore 1992:295–96, 317, 353, 354.

[44] For personal influence and acceptance of Darwinian evolution, $r=.00$ ($df=1/348$, $t=-0.08$, $p<.94$). For the pre-Darwinian period, the correlation is .07 ($df=1/294$, $t=1.12$, $p<.27$). There is no significant interaction with social class. My variable for personal influence employs three steps that differentiate "good friends" from "acquaintances" and "strangers." In the case of the Darwinian revolution sample, I have supplemented this information with a measure of the number of letters exchanged with Darwin as of 1859. The correlation between the two scales is .67 ($df=1/333$, $t=16.50$, $p<.0001$).

[45] For letters exchanged with Darwin by 1859 and subsequent support for Darwin's theories, $r=.00$ ($df=1/359$, $t=-0.02$, $p<.99$).

[46] For being cited by Darwin in the *Origin,* as it relates to subsequent acceptance of his theories, $r=-.03$ ($df=1/360$, $t=-0.49$, $p<.63$).

[47] For acceptance of Darwinian theory, as it relates to (1) being cited by Darwin in the *Origin,* (2) the number of letters exchanged with him by 1859, and (3) degree of personal contact with Darwin, $R=.06$ ($df=3/268$, $F=0.37$, $p<.78$).

[48] For personal contact with Darwin, as it relates to social class, $r=-.10$ ($df=1/297$, $t=-1.73$, $p<.09$). For the relationship between the social class of Darwin's correspondents and letters exchanged with him as of 1859, $r=-.11$ ($df=1/285$, $t=-1.89$, $p<.06$).

icals). The focused contrast compares social liberals (such as Darwin) against the other three groups.[49] This test indicates that Darwin's closest friends tended to be liberal like himself. Darwin was 1.8 times as likely to have friends who were social liberals as he was to have friends who were either conservatives or radicals.[50] If Darwin was at all worried about alienating his friends with his evolutionary ideas, he need not have been—these friends were predominantly social liberals who generally supported his theories after 1859.

Technical Discussion 7 (Chapter 10, notes 35 and 38): Multivariate models of the Darwinian revolution. A family dynamics model for the Darwinian revolution includes four significant predictors: (1) birth order, (2) parental loss (which interacts with birth order), (3) parent-offspring conflict (which interacts with birth order), and (4) individual differences in travel. For this model, the multiple correlation with acceptance of evolution is .47. The bulk of the explanatory power in this family dynamics model derives from birth order.[51]

A more comprehensive model for the Darwinian revolution includes the four variables in my family dynamics model, together with six additional predictors: age, eminence in 1859, social attitudes, parents' social attitudes, national differences, and personal contact with Darwin as of 1859. This model correctly classifies 84 percent of the participants in this scientific debate. Table 9 indicates the partial correlation of each predictor in the comprehensive model, controlled for the other nine predictors. The most successful predictor is birth order, followed by social attitudes, eminence in 1859, and parent-offspring conflict. Age would be statistically significant as a predictor were it not so highly correlated with eminence in 1859. What apparently motivated older scientists to oppose Darwinism was not so much age per se but rather the greater status that went with it.

Other multivariate models of the Darwinian revolution are possible. For example, birth order enters the model as part of a three-way interaction effect with social class and parental loss, as discussed in Chapter 5 (see Fig. 5.3). In order to minimize multicollinearity among variables, I have included only two-way interaction effects as candidate predictors in the model outlined in Table 9.

The addition of social class to the ten-variable model in Table 9 raises the multiple *R* from .6668 to .6674, a minuscule and nonsignificant difference. Like socioeconomic status, field of specialization adds almost nothing to the model.

---

[49] The "cutpoints" for this focused contrast are 2.0, 3.0, and 4.0 on my two 5-point scales for social attitudes.

[50] For Darwin's friendships with other scientists, as they relate to social attitudes, $r=.11$ ($df=1/166$, $t=1.47$, $p<.15$). This test contrasts scientists whose social attitudes resembled Darwin's (that is, scientists rated between 3.0 and 4.0 on a 5-point scale) with all other scientists.

[51] For a four-variable family dynamics model and acceptance of evolution, $R=.47$ ([adjusted $R=.46$], $df=4/373$ [the harmonic mean], $F=25.89$, $p<.0001$). For birth order—the best predictor in the model—the partial correlation is .38 ($df=1/373$, $t=8.05$, $p<.0001$). Social attitudes also reflect the influence of family dynamics (Chapter 9). If social attitudes are added to this four-variable model, the multiple correlation increases from .47 to .63 ([adjusted $R=.63$], $df=5/392$, $F=52.51$, $p<.0001$).

TABLE 9

Predictors of Support for Darwinism (1859–75)

Variable	*Partial Correlation*	T-*Value*	*Degrees of Freedom*	*Likelihood of Trend Occurring by Chance*
SIGNIFICANT PREDICTORS				
Birth order *(being laterborn)*	.37	7.57	1/363	*Less than 1 in a billion*
Social attitudes *(being liberal)*	.36	7.29	1/363	*Less than 1 in a billion*
Eminence in 1859 *(being eminent)*	–.22	-4.38	1/363	*Less than 1 in 10,000*[a]
Conflict with parents *(being substantial)*	.15	2.87	1/363	*Less than 1 in 200*[b]
Age at parental loss *(being older)*	.15	2.87	1/363	*Less than 1 in 200*[b]
Travel *(being extensive)*	.12	2.25	1/363	*Less than 1 in 33*
National differences	.12	2.22	1/363	*Less than 1 in 33*
Parents' social attitudes *(being liberal)*	.11	2.03	1/363	*Less than 1 in 20*
NONSIGNIFICANT PREDICTORS				
Personal contact with Darwin before 1860	.10	1.82	1/363	*Less than 1 in 15*
Age in 1859	–.08	-1.50	1/363	*Less than 1 in 7*[a]

NOTE: This ten-variable model was selected from among various alternative models, using BMDP's Program 9R (All Possible Subsets Regression) and Mallows' C_p as the selection criterion. For the ten-variable model, R=.68 ([adjusted R=.66], df=10/363 [harmonic mean], F=30.49, p<1 in a billion). Using Mallows' C_p as a guide, the second-best model omits age; the third-best model omits personal contact with Darwin. For both alternative models, the adjusted R remains .66.

a. If eminence in 1859 is omitted from the model, the partial correlation for age becomes –.15 (df=1/364, t=–2.78, p<.01).

b. Variable interacts with birth order, affecting firstborns more than laterborns.

Technical Discussion 8 (Chapter 12, note 43): Supreme court voting. For data on Supreme Court justices' voting records, I have drawn on Friedman and Israel (1969), Schubert (1974, 1983), Ryan and Tate (1980), Tate (1981), Ulmer (1986), and Epstein et al. (1994). For the two justices appointed since 1991, I have supplemented these data with conservative/liberal rankings obtained from the files of the *Wall Street Journal*.[52]

Schubert (1974, 1983) has published ratings on liberalism for 59 recent justices, based on a 2-step scale. Pooling these data with the more sophisticated measures published by other scholars, the voting records of 66 justices are available for analysis. The relationship between birth order and voting in a liberal direction is statistically significant in this sample.[53]

Based on analyses of the early justices' legal careers, available in Friedman and Israel (1969), together with other available biographical information on their lives, I have been able to assign a liberalism score to all 108 justices. I have rated 26 early justices on a 3-step scale (conservative, moderate, or liberal), based on published judgments by contributors to Friedman and Israel (1969). Because judicial assessments are lacking for the remaining 16 justices, I have rated them in terms of their social attitudes. Based on two independent raters, the interrater reliability for social attitudes is .85 in this sample.[54] All scores for "liberalism" (that is, ratings on social attitudes, together with five different measures of judicial opinions) have been z-scored and averaged for the 108 justices.

For the Supreme Court as a whole, the correlation between relative birth rank and liberalism, as determined by the six-variable measure, is significant and similar to that observed for the 66 most recent justices.[55] Using BMDP's Program 9R (All Possible Subsets Regression) together with the selection criterion of Mallows' C_p, only the first two variables in the following list of six are selected for inclusion: (1) relative birth rank, (2) party affiliation, (3) social class, (4) religious denomination, (5) year of appointment, and (6) sibship size. In path-analytic models, relative birth rank accounts for 61 percent of the explained variance because this variable also predicts party affiliations.[56] In short, most of what can be said about Supreme Court voting appears to represent within-family differences.

---

[52] I thank David Stipp for providing me with this information.

[53] For relative birth rank and voting in a liberal direction on the Court, r=.35 (df=1/64, t=3.00, p<.01). The contrast between middleborn and lastborn justices is also significant (r=.41, df=1/31, t=2.51, p<.02). Controlled for sibship size and social class (neither of which are significant predictors of voting), the partial correlation between relative birth rank and voting is statistically significant (r=.41, df=1/47 [the harmonic mean], t=3.07, p<.005; based on the estimation of some missing data for sibship size, using BMDP's program 8D).

[54] The correlation between social attitudes and judicial liberalism is .60. The two different methods of assessing liberalism yield a mean reliability of .80. The *effective* reliability is .90, based on the two measurement scales (judicial and social) and two independent raters.

[55] For the entire history of the Supreme Court, the correlation between relative birth rank and liberalism is .26 (df=1/106, t=2.73, p<.01). For birth order coded dichotomously, the correlation is .23 (df=1/106, t=2.41, p<.02).

[56] For relative birth rank and party affiliations, r=.27 (df=1/106, t=2.91, p<.005).

Other models of Supreme Court voting behavior have been proposed, based on the assessment of fewer justices and employing a larger number of variables.[57] These more complex models tend to involve "overfitting" and are rejected by BMDP's Program 9R (All Possible Subsets Regression), based on the criterion of Mallows' C_p. To prevent against overfitting, this criterion penalizes models for adding new variables. Two scholars, Segal and Spaeth, have recognized this methodological problem. They also offer a valuable discussion of the distinction between *predictive* and *causal* models.[58] Being a Democrat, for example, predicts liberal voting on the Court, but liberalism and being a Democrat are both proxies for the same *causal* influence. These causal influences generally arise within the family, simultaneously motivating both party affiliations and trends in voting. Predictive models often take advantage of variables, such as party affiliation, that owe their predictive power to other variables that the models are trying to explain. Causal models attempt to avoid such redundancies.

Several other researchers have reported nonsignificant findings for birth order's relationship to Supreme Court voting.[59] These negative findings are readily explained by one or more of the following methodological shortcomings: (1) inaccurate biographical data, (2) the coding of *biological* rather than *functional* birth order, (3) modest sample sizes, (4) inappropriate outcome measures, and (5) the failure to test for the role of relative birth rank as opposed to birth order. For example, Somit, Arwine, and Peterson report a nonsignificant relationship between birth order and voting trends on the Court.[60] In their own analysis (N=57), they employ birth order—coded dichotomously—rather than relative birth rank. The use of a dichotomous variable, especially in such a small sample, entails a moderate loss of statistical power. Somit et al. also code some of their birth orders biologically, rather than functionally.[61] For example, Ruth Bader Ginsburg had an elder

---

[57] See, for example, Tate and Handberg 1991; Segal and Spaeth 1993.

[58] Segal and Spaeth 1993:231–34.

[59] In addition to Somit et al. 1996, see also Weber 1984 and Ulmer 1986. Ulmer's two outcome measures—support for state and local government and support for the federal government—are not particularly good measures of conservatism, although the first measure is moderately correlated with this variable. Many social liberals have advocated federal intervention to achieve liberal goals, as the history of civil rights legislation testifies. For this reason I employ Ulmer's first scale, but not his second, in the six pooled z-score measures that define my own liberalism scale for the 108 justices.

[60] Somit et al. 1996:46.

[61] Somit et al. (1996:50–52) provide a table of birth-order information for all 108 justices. Forty of these birth orders are incorrect. After bringing this fact to the authors' attention, I was informed that the errors occur only in the table and do not affect the statistical results reported in their book (personal communication, Alan Arwine, 13 May 1996). Although Somit et al. generally code birth order in biological terms, they are not consistent in this respect. I have made a special effort, in my own sample of Supreme Court justices, to double-check every birth order that is not identical with those reported by Weber (1984) and by Somit et al. (1996). My own biographical information represents an accurate assessment of *functional* birth order for all 108 Supreme Court justices.

sister who died of meningitis when Ruth was one. Ginsburg was raised as an only child. I have recorded her as a firstborn (and only child). Somit et al. record her as a laterborn, which makes no sense based on my own book's psychological thesis.[62]

Weber (1984) reports a nonsignificant association between relative birth rank and liberalism among the justices. The lack of statistical significance in his sample is explained by its limited size (N=25) as well as by three errors in the birth-order information he employed. Three of his "firstborns" were laterborns: Felix Frankfurter and Potter Stewart were middle children, and Earl Warren was a lastborn. Corrected for these three errors, Weber's own findings are statistically significant.

Technical Discussion 9 (Chapter 14, note 6): Kuhnian revolutions in science. My measure of how well Thomas Kuhn's model of scientific change fits each of my 28 controversies is based on six different measures that are relevant to Kuhn's argument.[63] These measures are: (1) the number of times Kuhn cited each event in *The Structure of Scientific Revolutions;* (2) being a controversy in the physical sciences; (3) frequency of citation of the controversy in the secondary literature on scientific revolutions; (4) proportion of participants who were exclusively scientists; (5) being a successful rather than a failed revolution; and (6) the presence of a preceding crisis. The last two measures are based on my own ratings, which draw on the published opinions of historians of science. Each of the six variables for "Kuhn-like" features has been converted to a z-score and averaged in the composite measure. The correlation between an event having Kuhnian features and its being cited by Kuhn in the *Structure of Scientific Revolutions* is .51, with the citation count having been removed from the dependent variable. The correlation between an event having Kuhnian features and its being in the physical sciences is .73, with status as a physical science having been removed from the dependent variable.[64]

Technical Discussion 10 (Chapter 14, note 30): Time and national differences as moderator variables of scientific radicalism. The reception of eugenics exhibits a reversal in the relationship between birth order and acceptance over time. Relative to firstborns, laterborns were more likely to turn against eugenics during the course of the controversy, although the trend misses being statistically significant.[65] A more detailed subdivision of eugenicists into adherents of "positive" and "negative" social policies would probably yield a significant temporal trend by birth order, as would the use of a larger sample. The interactive relationship between support for eugenics and elapsed time becomes clearer when we

---

[62] See also page 465 (n. 81) for a test of the distinction between functional and biological birth order, as they relate to openness to new ideas.

[63] Kuhn 1962.

[64] The use of independent raters for Kuhnian features such as "incommensurability" or "crisis" would make a useful addition to my measure of Kuhnian events. This approach, which is quite feasible, would also permit the testing of many interesting issues in the philosophy of science that are otherwise largely intractable. For a list of such issues, see Donovan, Laudan, and Laudan 1988.

[65] Controlled for the main effects of birth order and year of participation, as they relate to support for eugenics, the partial correlation for the interaction effect is –.11 (df=1/150, t=–1.30, p<.20).

consider participants' social attitudes and their relationship to support for eugenics. Early supporters of eugenics tended to be social liberals, whereas late supporters tended to be conservatives. This difference *is* statistically significant.[66]

Chauvinistic considerations sometimes moderate the reception of scientific theories. Newtonian theory offers a good instance of this tendency. What was acceptable to a member of the Royal Society of London in 1700 was highly contentious for a French Cartesian such as Bernard Fontenelle. Although Fontenelle balked at accepting Newton's theory of universal gravitation, he was hardly a conservative thinker. A younger son, Fontenelle had become a radical Cartesian in his twenties, thereby committing himself to a physics based on swirling vortices. When Newton's *Principia* appeared in 1687, Fontenelle was confronted by a far-reaching British assault on his heterodox worldview. If Descartes's vortices truly existed, then the friction they generated should have been detectable as a deviation from Newton's inverse square law regarding gravitational effects: No deviation, no vortices. Alas for the French, there was no detectable deviation. "When the new revolutionary science of Isaac Newton was set forth in 1687," I. Bernard Cohen asserts, "it was obvious that the real enemies to be routed were not the Aristotelians and scholastics but the Cartesians and their physical cosmology based on vortices."[67]

The fact that Isaac Newton was British, and that his primary opponents were French, blunted opposition to Newton's theories within Britain. Although there was a strong birth-order effect during the Continental reception of Newton's theories, there was none at all in Britain.[68] Had Isaac Newton been a Frenchman, or had René Descartes been British, the reception of Newton's theories would probably have been different by birth order and nationality. As it is, birth-order differences reflect the national rivalry between Cartesian and Newtonian physics.

The chemical revolution reveals a similar story about national differences. We can divide the relevant scientific population into two groups—French scientists, many of whom were personal friends of Lavoisier's, and the rest. Non-French scientists were significantly slower to accept the new chemistry than were French scientists. Among non-French scientists, being laterborn is an excellent predictor of support for Lavoisier's ideas. Within France, birth order is not a significant predictor.[69]

These kinds of interaction effects reveal another distinctive feature about

---

[66] For the two-way interaction between social attitudes and elapsed time, as they relate to support for eugenics, the partial correlation is $-.23$ ($df=1/121$, $t=-2.64$, $p<.01$). On the changing ideological background of the eugenics controversy, see Graham 1977; Kevles 1985:76–95; Weiss 1987; Weingart, Kroll, and Bayertz 1988.

[67] Cohen 1985:12.

[68] The correlation between birth order and acceptance of Newton's theories is .28 on the Continent ($df=1/38$, $t=1.80$, $p<.05$ [one-tailed test]). Within Britain, the correlation is $-.08$ ($df=1/23$, $t=-0.39$, $p<.70$).

[69] For birth order and acceptance of Lavoisier's theories outside France, $r=.42$ ($df=1/60$, $t=3.54$, $p<.01$). For birth order and acceptance of Lavoisier's theories within France, $r=-.12$ ($df=1/34$, $t=-0.70$, $p<.49$).

birth-order effects. Such effects reflect *the degree of scientific controversy* far more than they do adherence to any particular way of viewing the world. Laterborns do not automatically support specific worldviews or scientific "themata," such as those that are associated with realism, skepticism, or discontinuity. When it was radical to do so, seventeenth-century laterborns supported the doctrine of atomism, which envisioned the world as being composed of discontinuous particles. By contrast, evolution emphasized the *continuity* between man and lower animals. Because evolution was a radical theory, laterborns found its emphasis on biological continuity just as congenial as atomism's emphasis on discontinuity.[70]

[70] The notion that birth order dictates certain philosophical preferences has been put forth by Harris (1964). See also Sutton-Smith and Rosenberg (1970:9). The related concept of "thematic" preferences in science has been discussed by Holton (1973). Birth-order effects may mediate *some* preference for differing themata. Evidence suggests that firstborns are more likely to view the world as hierarchical, ordered, and predictable (Kagan 1971: 148–49; see also Stein, Stein, and Kagan 1970). These thematic preferences are modest in size compared with the *contextual* considerations that make new theories controversial or not. This is why laterborns enthusiastically endorse, and then abandon, the same "themata" when they are no longer controversial.

APPENDIX 10
SUGGESTIONS FOR FUTURE RESEARCH

This appendix consists of suggestions for future studies on topics integral to this book. Some of these topics entail research projects I have been tempted to do myself and, in some cases, have begun work on. Other topics involve questions for which I wish answers existed. I group these research topics under four general headings: (1) personality development; (2) mate selection; (3) social and political behavior; and (4) intellectual achievement.

PERSONALITY DEVELOPMENT

1. Sibling attachment. Does the degree of attachment among siblings affect personality development? Research on sibling deidentification strongly suggests this should be the case, as does the influence of age spacing between siblings.[1] According to this hypothesis, siblings who are closely attached to one another, for whatever reasons, ought to exhibit greater cooperation and hence less pronounced sibling contrast effects. The strategy of sibling cooperation is particularly likely to occur in lower-class families, where extensive parental investment cannot be counted on.[2]

2. The family as a system. More research needs to be done on siblings who have grown up together within the same family. Of the more than two thousand studies involving birth order, only a handful involve individuals who were siblings of one another. Because sibling strategies are tailored to other members of the family environment, a critical step in future research is to study the family as an interactive system. Such studies would allow a much better understanding of how siblings occupy and defend family niches. For example, a secondborn whose older sibling is particularly shy has a better chance of achieving social dominance over this sibling, something that would rarely occur under other circumstances. Ability is another relevant consideration. If younger siblings happen to be more skillful than their elder siblings in the same activity, such as a sport, they need not go out of their way to specialize in a different activity. In sum, niches are determined not just by birth order, gender, and the gender of siblings, but also by the specifics of the niches *actually occupied* by other family members.

3. Birth order by gender interaction effects. The relatively small number of women included in this study (N=324) has limited my ability to document in-

[1] Schachter et al. 1976; Schachter et al. 1978; Schachter 1982. On age spacing between siblings, see Chapter 5, especially Figure 5.2. On patterns of sibling attachment, see the valuable studies by Dunn and Kendrick (1982), Dunn (1985, 1993), and Segal (1993).

[2] See page 128.

teraction effects between birth order and gender. In Helen Koch's pioneering studies of birth order, birth order by gender interaction effects were far more numerous than expected by chance.[3] In the context of openness to experience, more research is needed on this topic, including the manner in which the gender of siblings affects personality development. From a Darwinian point of view, gender and birth order appear to be the two most important determinants of family niches. Sibling strategies should therefore be influenced by birth order and gender, operating not only as *main effects* but also as *interaction effects* with other aspects of the family system.

4. Radicalism and the Trivers-Willard hypothesis. According to Robert Trivers and Dan Willard, Darwinian theory leads to the following prediction about gender biases in parental investment: Organisms that are in good physiological condition benefit from having male offspring, who are better able to compete successfully for mates.[4] Organisms in poor physiological condition benefit from having female offspring, who can usually reproduce successfully without competing for a mate. Considerable research, in animal as well as human populations, has corroborated this hypothesis.[5] In the context of humans living in agrarian societies, where land is a limiting resource, upper-class parents tend to favor male offspring, who can sire more offspring than one female can give birth to. Lower-class parents tend to favor female offspring. Landless males may not be able to marry, but females often succeed in marrying, sometimes upward in class.

The Trivers-Willard hypothesis may be applied to the problem of radical thinking. To the extent that upper-class females are discriminated against, and lower-class females are favored, radicalism should entail two interaction effects: (1) a two-way *gender by social class effect;* and (2) a three-way *birth order by gender by social class effect.* Among women, lower-class firstborns should be particularly conservative, whereas upper-class laterborns should be particularly radical.[6]

5. Birth order and physical differences. Physical attributes, such as height and weight, should interact with birth order in much the same manner as does shyness (Chapter 7). It is much easier for firstborns to be socially dominant if physical size is in their favor. Similarly, resistance to domination by older siblings is

---

[3] See page 76.

[4] Trivers and Willard 1973.

[5] See, for example, Trivers and Willard 1973; Voland 1984; Boone 1986; Hrdy 1987.

[6] A preliminary analysis of my own data do not support either of these two hypotheses. For example, lower-class women have been more radical than lower-class men, contradicting the Trivers-Willard hypothesis (partial $r=.05$, $df=1/2{,}320$, $t=2.28$, $p<.05$). There is also a gender-by-birth-order interaction effect: controlled for the gender difference, firstborn women have been significantly more radical than firstborn men (partial $r=.05$, $df=1/2{,}320$, $t=2.41$, $p<.05$). These findings involve the pooling of my samples for 28 scientific controversies, 61 American reform movements, and the Protestant Reformation. Because these data are drawn from 90 different historical events, and because the effect size for the results is small, it is possible that unexamined moderator variables are confounding the results. In the reception of scientific innovations, for example, gender interacts with social class in the manner expected on the basis of the Trivers-Willard hypothesis (partial $r=-.04$, $df=1/2{,}759$, $t=-1.79$, $p<.04$ [one-tailed test]).

also favored among younger siblings whenever the latter possess an advantage in physical size. If findings on the subject of shyness are a reasonable guide, the largest contrast effects between siblings should occur when both siblings possess imposing physical attributes.

6. Birth order and hormonal differences. The more that is learned about personality development, the more this process appears to involve a continuous feedback loop between genetic dispositions, proximate-causal physiological mechanisms, and environmental influences. It seems likely that family niches may trigger physiological switches. In this connection, someone might consider doing a study to see if firstborns and laterborns differ in their hormone levels. Among both men and women, levels of testosterone, androstenedione, and estradiol are known to vary positively with status. In addition, individuals with high testosterone tend to have more sexual partners.[7] Because birth order is correlated with social dominance, it may also be correlated with hormone levels.

This hypothesis is consistent with research on social primates. When scientists give low-ranking primates an injection of testosterone, these animals tend to rise to the top of the dominance hierarchy.[8] As a result of being displaced, the alpha male suffers a reduction in his testosterone level. Antidepressant drugs such as Prozac have a similar effect. After being put on Prozac, beta males become alpha males.[9]

7. Gene-environment interaction effects. Even when genes play a role in personality development, they usually interact with environmental influences. I have discussed one relevant example in Chapter 7: shyness is known to be heritable, and it is also associated with half a dozen physiological markers. In moderating openness to experience, shyness interacts significantly with birth order.[10] Family niches therefore determine how genetic potentials express themselves in connection with this personality attribute.

It is difficult to study gene-environment interaction effects, in part because large sample sizes are need to detect these effects. In addition, behavioral geneticists have not found a reliable means of assessing the nonshared environment. One promising approach to this problem would be to study identical twins reared apart and to control for differences in their adoptive family niches. Thus identical twins reared apart as functional firstborns and functional laterborns ought to exhibit personality traits differing from those of twins who have been reared apart with the same functional birth order. By controlling for the most important aspects of family niches (birth order, gender, the gender of siblings, and levels of parent-offspring conflict), it should be possible to test for interaction effects between genetic dispositions and environmental influences.

8. People who outgrow childhood shyness. Among individuals who have outgrown childhood shyness, one would expect to observe an interaction effect with birth order. Compared with shy firstborn children, shy laterborn children should tend to become significantly more extraverted over time. The reason for

---

[7] Cashdan 1995.

[8] Maccoby and Jacklin 1974:243–46.

[9] McDonald 1994.

[10] See Chapter 7, Figure 7.1.

this expectation is that laterborns tend to be more sociable than firstborns. Once they are no longer physically and socially dominated by older siblings, laterborns are freer to cultivate greater sociability in interactions with their peers.

9. Risk taking. Laterborns are more likely than firstborns to engage in dangerous sports and other risk-oriented activities.[11] It would be interesting to study the degree to which athletes and their coaches engage in high-risk behavior as a function of their family niches. In a sport such as American football, plays could be assessed in terms of their risk-to-gain ratio. One would expect laterborn athletes to be more likely than firstborns to attempt high-risk plays. Such studies would need to be controlled for the *context* of athletic behavior. Early in an athletic contest, the risk associated with a daring strategy is different from that during the last few minutes of the contest, when a significant gamble may decide victory or loss. In assessing risk-oriented athletic behavior, researchers should look for interaction effects between birth order, the stage of the match, the stage of the athletic season, and even the stage of the athlete's career.

MATE SELECTION

10. Sibling strategies as sexual strategies. A recent study has shown that individual differences in romantic love styles owe themselves predominantly to the nonshared environment.[12] This finding came as a considerable surprise to the researchers who documented it. Most personality traits have a substantial genetic component, but not love styles. These results suggest that love styles are particularly responsive to the family environment in which an individual has been raised. This conclusion strongly implicates birth order and other sibling differences in strategies of mate selection.

From a Darwinian point of view, it makes considerable sense that decisions about mating should be under substantial environmental control. Research has shown, for example, that offspring who grow up in homes with inconsistent or rejecting child-rearing practices tend to reach puberty earlier, to engage in intercourse earlier, and to have more sexual partners than children who have grown up in stable and loving homes. Having learned that they cannot count on parental investment, offspring from unstable homes seem to opt for short-term mating strategies.[13]

Someone might want to do a study to see if firstborns and laterborns differ in their sexual strategies. I would expect laterborns to be more likely to engage in high-risk strategies, such as mate poaching and infidelity.[14] Throughout history, laterborns were less likely to reproduce, at least in a socially accepted manner. In societies where primogeniture has been practiced, laterborns tended to leave more illegitimate children than their elder siblings.[15] In addition, laterborns are more

---

[11] See pages 112–17.

[12] Waller and Shaver 1994.

[13] Belsky, Steinberg, and Draper 1991; see also Buss 1994:217.

[14] For mate poaching and other mating strategies, see Buss 1994. Firstborns are more conscientious than laterborns, which leads to the prediction that they will be more faithful to their mates. Still, laterborns are more empathetic than firstborns, so birth order might relate more strongly to the *reasons* for infidelity than it does to infidelity per se.

[15] Boone 1986:870.

likely to experiment sexually, which may help to explain the higher rate of homosexuality that is reported among laterborn males.[16]

According to Toman's "complementarity hypothesis," a firstborn brother having a younger sister should get along best with a younger sister who grew up with an elder brother.[17] Empirical support for Toman's hypothesis is conflicting and, even when statistically significant, has involved small effect sizes.[18] During radical social revolutions, conflict between spouses is significantly increased by mismatches in birth order, a finding that is inconsistent with Toman's hypothesis (Chapter 11).

Another hypothesis that is worth exploring is that siblings are most attracted to individuals who resemble their second-closest sibling rather than their immediately adjacent sibling. To the extent that siblings cooperate more with each other when they are not in direct competition, they may also be freer to express affectionate feelings toward their next closest siblings in age.

SOCIAL AND POLITICAL BEHAVIOR

11. Political revolutions and radical social movements. The receptions of a wide variety of political and social revolutions remain to be examined for within-family differences. Among those events whose study would probably be particularly fruitful are the English Civil War, the Chartist movement in Britain, the Russian Revolution, and right-wing movements such as Fascism and Nazism.[19] Most civil wars probably entail significant birth-order effects. A particularly intriguing study would involve the loyalties of siblings from border states during the American Civil War. Other relevant studies might involve the proliferation of various religious movements, especially those of the dissenting sects.

Anonymous authorship is an iconoclastic strategy that probably reflects within-family differences.[20] Another closely related topic involves authors whose books have been listed on the Catholic *Index* of prohibited books. Virtually any kind of protest movement against the establishment ought to manifest within-family differences, including those related to birth order. For the results of such studies to be

---

[16] See Blanchard et al. 1995; Blanchard and Bogaert 1996.

[17] See Toman 1992.

[18] See Ernst and Angst 1983:177–81. See also Toman and Preiser 1973.

[19] For family schisms during the English Civil War (1640–60), see Durston (1989), who notes many cases of family members who fought on opposite sides of this conflict. Durston emphasizes the fact that families often sought reconciliation after the war was over and argues that family loyalty tends to triumph over temporary political and religious disagreements. The American Revolution, which was not a particularly radical revolution, is not likely to produce substantial birth-order effects, at least as *main* effects (see Chapter 12, pages 296–97). Still, one would expect native-born Americans who sided with the British to be firstborns and native-born British who sided with the Americans to be laterborns.

[20] Anonymous authorship should be most common among laterborns, who tend to have reason to protect themselves against charges of heresy or sedition. In addition, this strategy is most likely to be employed by *shy* laterborns.

properly interpretable, they need to be controlled for sibship size, social class, and the role of ideological context (see Chapter 14, especially Fig. 14.1).

Attitudes toward the Dreyfus affair, which deeply divided French society at the end of the nineteenth century, probably entail significant within-family differences. As one scholar has commented: "The anti-Dreyfusards, true to a conservative tradition with deep roots in French history, affirmed that the claims of the state and its major institutions, above all of the army and the judiciary, were superior to the claims made in the name of such abstract ideals as justice and individual rights."[21] If this historical verdict is correct, then sibling differences were virtually inevitable in the course of this famous controversy.

Tracing the lives and political careers of the deputies to the French National Convention under the Empire would be well worth undertaking. One might expect firstborns to have been more willing to work with Bonaparte, who replaced a fledgling democracy with a dictatorship.

The ideal approach to political and social revolutions is to study large populations in *many different historical events,* and to include a large number of *within-* and *between-family variables* in the analyses. If researchers also incorporate situational variables into their analyses, then the cumulative results will eventually allow a meta-analytic approach to the problem. As I have shown in Chapter 14, within-family differences vary significantly from one scientific controversy to another. The main reason for these significant variations is the differing ideological nature of the events.

12. Heads of state. Research on election results for the American presidency, and for the office of prime minister in Britain, suggest that firstborns are elected preferentially during "crisis" periods. Unfortunately, previous researchers have failed to provide an adequate measure as to what constitutes a "crisis."[22] Historians who are interested in this problem might consider using expert judges to obtain interrater reliabilities for such situational classifications. In addition, the role of political ideology along a conservative-liberal spectrum needs to be assessed simultaneously with the role of tough-mindedness. Controlled for differences in the relative appeal of conservative versus liberal candidates, tough-minded firstborns should be overrepresented as elected officials during times of crisis.

13. Jury selection. As with voting by Supreme Court Justices (Chapter 12), the opinions of jurors are likely to be influenced by within-family differences. Firstborns are more likely to accept the authority of science and the state, and hence to agree with arguments advanced by the prosecution. If the role of tough-mindedness during the French Revolution is a reliable guide, firstborns are more likely to support the death penalty. Firstborns have a higher moral conscience than laterborns, and they also tend to be more vindictive. Accordingly, firstborns are more likely to conclude that a convicted criminal should be severely punished. Because laterborns are more tender-minded, they are more likely to oppose the death penalty and to give greater weight to extenuating circumstances in deciding appropriate punishments.

---

[21] Coser 1965:215.

[22] Stewart 1977, 1992.

The principles that are already being used by jury consultants in connection with gender will be similar to those that are applicable by birth order. In general, defense lawyers should prefer jurors who are female and laterborn (particularly middleborns). Prosecuting attorneys should prefer jurors who are male and firstborn.

Can differences by birth order really make a difference in jury deliberations? The trial of Louis XVI (1792–93) provides a good test. Judged by the deputies of the National Convention, Louis lost his life based on a single vote, 361 to 360. Elder sons were 1.8 times more likely to vote for death than younger sons (Chapter 13). The king's lawyers were not permitted to challenge jurors in this trial. If they had been able to do so, even a slight change in the composition of jurors selected from the National Convention, especially by birth order, would have saved his life. So would an appeal to the people, which the Gironde supported. The population of France was substantially more middleborn than the membership of the National Convention, and, within the Convention, middleborns voted most consistently to spare the king's life.

14. Risk taking and elevation to the nobility. Were noble titles, which have often been given for military success or battlefield bravery, generally acquired by laterborns and then passed on to firstborn descendants through primogeniture? This hypothesis could be readily checked by means of genealogical sources such as Burke's *Peerage* (1970).

15. Terrorist movements. Psychologists know little about the psychology of terrorist movements. Based on a study of the French Revolution, I would expect firstborns to show greater support than laterborns for movements that employ terrorist tactics. The highest proportion of firstborns ought to be found in right-wing movements that advocate violence, including neo-Nazi organizations, white supremacist groups such as the Ku Klux Klan, and militant religious fundamentalist groups.

The alleged Unabomber, Theodore J. Kaczynski, is the elder of two children. For two decades he apparently waged a campaign of deadly terror by sending bombs through the U.S. mail. His goal was to return life to the technologically free past, a conservative ideological aim that motivated his killing of 3 people and the maiming of 22 more. Kaczinski's younger brother, David, a typically tender-minded laterborn, is a vegetarian and a poet. He earns his living by counseling runaway youth. After beginning to suspect that his elder brother might be the Unabomber, David Kaczynski undertook his own discreet investigation of the matter and eventually turned incriminating evidence over to the FBI. This particular sibling contrast is a replay of the deadly feud between the deputies of the National Convention during the French Revolution. Theodore is the analogue of Robespierre—superior, aloof, and vindictive. David is the analogue of the shy and peace-minded deputies of the Plain.

16. Fratricide. In their pioneering study *Homicide,* Martin Daly and Margo Wilson have shown that patterns of murder among family members concur strongly with Darwinian principles.[23] Parents are 70 times more likely to kill a

---

[23] Daly and Wilson 1988a.

stepchild than they are to kill one of their own children. When parents do kill their own biological children, they are much more likely to do so in a relatively painless way and then take their own life.[24]

Fratricide has yet to be studied in the kind of systematic manner that Daly and Wilson have employed in their studies of homicide involving parents and offspring. These two researchers report that, in agricultural societies, about 10 percent of homicides involve fratricide.[25] In feudal societies, the history of royal families provides "a seemingly endless tale of fraternal bloodletting."[26] In sixteenth-century Denmark, fratricidal disputes had become so widespread that a law was finally passed decreeing that no nobleman who had killed his brother could inherit his property.[27]

From a Darwinian point of view, predictions can be made about the most likely targets of fratricide. Because firstborns tend to reproduce first, laterborns have more to lose by committing homicide against an older sibling. A younger sibling's inclusive fitness will be enhanced by any offspring produced by older siblings. If a younger sibling kills an older sibling, this act may endanger the survival prospects of nieces and nephews already born to the older sibling. If there is a difference in fratricide rates by birth order, the prediction must be that firstborns are more fratricidal—a conclusion that is also suggested by the Bible. A study of Old Testament accounts shows that firstborns have been typically portrayed as immoral, whereas laterborns tend to be depicted as heroes.[28]

I have collected a variety of newspaper reports on the subject of fratricide. Although my informal survey is relatively small, every instance I have encountered involves an elder sibling killing a younger sibling. For example, a ten-year-old Florida girl recently shot her three-year-old brother after "an argument over a video game."[29] The same day, newspapers reported that a five-year-old Harlem boy "accidentally" shot his baby sister with a derringer.[30] Three months later a ten-year-old Oregon boy was convicted, in a nonjury trial, of murdering his five-year-old sister. He shot her with a rifle because, he claimed, "she was annoying him."[31] One final instance of fratricide involves a love triangle among two sisters—both young adults—and the boyfriend of the elder sister. Out of jealousy, the elder sister asked her boyfriend to strangle the younger sister, which he did as the elder sister watched.[32]

---

[24] Daly and Wilson 1994.
[25] Daly and Wilson 1988a:30–31.
[26] Daly and Wilson 1988a:31.
[27] Thoren 1990.
[28] Antman 1993.
[29] *Boston Globe,* 21 August 1995, p. 4.
[30] *Boston Globe,* 21 August 1995, p. 4.
[31] *USA Today,* 28 November 1995, p. 3A.
[32] *Boston Globe,* 18 April 1996, p. 73.

INTELLECTUAL ACHIEVEMENT

17. Scientific innovation. Patterns of reception in many important scientific innovations have not yet been studied. Some of these controversies include (1) Paracelsus's iconoclastic medical theories; (2) eighteenth-century theories of electricity; (3) Malthus's theory of population pressure and its associated economic implications; (4) medical theories of contagion, especially from 1780 to 1830;[33] (5) debates over mechanism and vitalism in the history of biology; (6) Maxwell's electromagnetic theories, beginning with Faraday and ending with Hertz; (7) non-Euclidian geometry; (8) atomic theory in the nineteenth century; (9) the discovery of X rays and other evidence associated with the new view of the atom; (10) Mendel's laws; (11) evolutionary theory from 1875 to the Modern Synthesis in the 1940s; and (12) Keynesian economic theory. This list could be greatly-expanded upon and is limited, in practice, only by the availability of sufficiently large numbers of participants to derive meaningful statistical results. Even relatively small samples, however, can be usefully employed in subsequent meta-analyses. To provide meaningful tests of the claims made throughout this book, such studies need to be controlled for social class, sibship size, and especially the ideological implications of the innovation.

18. Rapid conceptual change. Most of the revolutions I have studied in this book took decades and sometimes centuries to resolve. In general, the role of within-family differences, including birth order, in the reception of revolutionary ideas is directly proportional to the length of the controversy. The longer a revolution takes to run its course, the more likely it is to be led by laterborns and to involve substantial birth-order effects.

What is not adequately known is whether sizable birth-order effects are also present, more fleetingly, during rapid conceptual change. From experimental research on conformity behavior, we know that birth-order effects can be impressive. It is possible that birth-order effects are much more pervasive than my own study of *brief* scientific controversies would suggest. The phase during which such effects are substantial may be so transient that they are unlikely to be detected based on historical samples. We know little, for example, about reactions to a theory such as Planck's quantum principle during the days or weeks following scientists' first exposure to this idea. Many technical scientific innovations that exhibit no birth-order effects on a long-term basis may exhibit substantial short-term effects. Further research needs to be done to resolve this issue. In such studies, any significant birth-order effects are likely to be proxies for other within-family differences, which also deserve study.

Another scientific activity in which one would expect to find substantial within-family differences is peer review. Articles that are rejected for being too radical or too speculative are probably the work of laterborns whose unconventional ideas are being questioned by firstborns. Firstborns are the police of science. Laterborns are the outlaws.

19. Fraud in science. Birth order does not seem to correlate directly with fraud in science. Fraud can be motivated by many considerations, especially flaws

---

[33] Ackerknecht 1948.

of character that are unrelated to birth order. Still, scientific frauds sometimes promote ideological predilections, and this circumstance leads to a more subtle prediction. Frauds that have tended to perpetrate conservative political or social views, such as Cyril Burt's concocted IQ data, will tend to involve firstborns. (Burt himself was the first of two children.) In contrast, scientists whose doctored results support a liberal point of view should tend to be laterborns. The key to understanding who commits a fraud in science will probably involve interaction effects between birth order, the Big Five personality dimension of Conscientiousness, and the ideological implications of the fraud. In other words, the study of scientific fraud—like that of human behavior more generally—will benefit from the careful search for person-by-situation interaction effects.

20. Age and creative achievement. In most intellectual fields, laterborns ought to make important discoveries at a later age than firstborns. Becoming an expert involves a gradual process of enculturation, which tends to make people more close-minded. Younger siblings should resist this process longer than firstborns, allowing laterborns to make important breakthroughs at later stages in their careers.

A study of Nobel Prize winners would be worth undertaking to test this hypothesis. An existing study on the subject has brought to light several related trends. Compared with the earliest winners of Nobel Prizes, recent winners are more likely to have been laterborns. This finding probably relates to changes in the criteria by which Nobel Prizes have been awarded.[34] Alfred Nobel's will specified that prizes be awarded for important "discoveries," which tend to be ideologically neutral. The earliest Nobel awards tended to honor Nobel's wishes. Albert Einstein won the Nobel Prize in 1921 for his work on the photoelectric effect, not for his development of relativity theory.

To the extent that Nobel Prizes have been increasingly awarded for conceptual innovations, which tend to involve bold theoretical leaps and, in many instances, to be ideologically laden, the criteria of awards may have begun to favor laterborns over firstborns. The best way to study this issue is to assess the most salient features of the innovations for which awards have been given. *How controversial* was the innovation? Did the innovation possess any *ideological implications*? *How long* did it take for the Nobel committee to decide to make an award for the research? These are some of the indicators that distinguish radical (laterborn) from technical (firstborn) innovations.

A shift in award winners by birth order may also have occurred in economic science. When the Nobel Memorial Prize was created for this field in 1968, there was a backlog of potential winners who had established the foundations of modern economic theory. Once this potential pool of winners was exhausted, the Nobel Prize committee began to broaden the scope of the awards to include more subjective areas, such as history, sociology, and philosophy.[35] This shift from abstract mathematical theory to research areas with practical applications has probably been more favorable to laterborns than firstborns.

---

[34] Clark and Rice 1982. On age and scientific creativity, see Simonton 1994.

[35] Bennett 1994.

APPENDIX 11
HOW TO TEST YOUR OWN PROPENSITY TO REBEL

This final appendix outlines a formula that can be used to predict any individual's likelihood of supporting radical innovations. The formula builds on the base-rate probabilities given in Table 10. These predicted probabilities are derived from a logistic regression model for the 28 scientific debates in my study. The table specifies the likelihood that an individual will support a radical revolution such as Copernican theory or Darwinism. These probabilities are stratified by age, social attitudes, and birth order.[1]

To determine an individual's base-rate probability, find the applicable category in Table 10. For example, a firstborn who is over the age of sixty and socially conservative has a 3 percent likelihood of endorsing a radical innovation such as Darwinism. A lastborn who is under the age of thirty and who is socially liberal, has a likelihood of acceptance of 96 percent.

These base-rate probabilities may be adjusted to take into account seven additional biographical influences. To the appropriate predicted probability in Table 10, add or subtract the following percentages, depending on an individual's attributes:

1. Pronounced parent-offspring conflict. In the case of firstborns who have experienced pronounced conflict with a parent, add 30 percent to the relevant base-rate probability in Table 10. "Pronounced parent-offspring conflict" may be defined as more conflict than is found in four-fifths of the

[1] The predicted probabilities listed in Table 10 are based on a logistic regression model that includes complete biographical data on 1,436 participants in 28 scientific controversies (1543–1967). The model includes four significant main effects: age, social attitudes, relative birth rank, and ideological implications of the innovation. The model also includes three significant two-way interaction effects: ideological implications by age; ideological implications by social attitudes; and ideological implications by relative birth rank. All main effects are statistically significant at $p<.0001$, and the interaction effects are statistically significant at $p<.005$. The two-way interaction effects reflect the fact that age, social attitudes, and relative birth rank are all significantly better predictors of receptivity in proportion to the radicalism of the innovation.

Predicted probabilities in Table 10 are listed only for those scientific controversies that involved radical ideological implications. For this class of controversies, the model's predictors yield a multiple correlation with observed radicalism of .50 ($df=1/582$, $t=13.46$, $p<1$ in a billion; 75.2 percent correct classifications, based on the 2×2 table of observed versus predicted outcomes). For participants in Technical Revolutions and Controversial Innovations, the multiple correlation is .31 ($df=1/482$, $t=6.38$, $p<1$ in a billion; 69.0 percent correct classifications). For scientists who debated Conservative Theories, the multiple correlation is: .10 ($df=1/366$, $t=1.88$, $p<.06$; 59.2 percent correct classifications). The chance rate for correct classifications is 50.4 percent.

general population. For laterborns who have experienced pronounced parent-offspring conflict, add 10 percent to appropriate base-rate probability in Table 10. For cases in which parent-offspring conflict (or deidentification) is less extreme, but exceeds that observed in two-thirds of the general population, these two adjustments may be halved.

2. **Pronounced shyness.** For firstborns who are shyer than four-fifths of the general population, add 20 percent to the relevant probability in Table 10. For shy lastborns, subtract 15 percent from the appropriate probability in Table 10. Make no adjustment for middle children.

3. **Age gaps between adjacent siblings.** For firstborns whose age gap with their closest sibling is less than 2.0 years or more than 5.0 years, add 5 percent to the base rate probability in Table 10. Only children may consider themselves to be large-age-gap firstborns. For laterborns who are less than 2.0 years younger than their next older sibling, or more than 5.0 years younger, subtract 5 percent from the base-rate probability.

4. **Parental loss and surrogate parenting by older siblings.** If a firstborn has lost a parent before the age of ten and has acted as a surrogate parent toward younger siblings, subtract 15 percent from the base-rate probability in Table 10. If a laterborn has lost a parent before the age of ten and has experienced surrogate parenting by older siblings, add 10 percent to the base-rate probability in Table 10.

5. **Gender.** For females born prior to 1900, add 10 percent to the base-rate probability in Table 10. Recent studies do not show consistent gender differences on openness to ideas.[2] Still, women are more politically liberal than men, and a modest upward adjustment—perhaps 5 percent—seems warranted for women in contemporary populations.

6. **Race.** For individuals from minority races—especially those subject to discrimination (for example, blacks and Jews)—add 10 percent to the base-rate probability in Table 10.

7. **Friendship.** If an individual is particularly good friends with the leader of a radical revolution, add 10 percent to the predicted probability in Table 10.

This ten-variable formula for openness to radical innovation mimics the results of a multivariate logistic regression model. One should use common sense in applying this model within any particular behavioral context. For example, during pre-Darwinian debates over evolution, less than a third of the scientific community endorsed this controversial idea. For the scientific population as a whole, the mean rate of acceptance for pre-Darwinian theories of evolution was 30 percent, not 50 percent, as Table 10 assumes.

Applied to the participants of a radical controversy, the formula presented in this appendix will do a good job of rank ordering participants according to their likelihood of acceptance. On average, the base-rate formula in Table 10, Section A, should be 75 percent correct in classifying individuals as supporters or opponents of innovation, as long as the innovation is truly a Radical Ideological

---

[2] On studies of gender and openness to ideas, see Feingold 1994.

TABLE 10

Predicted Probabilities of Supporting Radical Conceptual Innovations

A. BASE-RATE PROBABILITIES

	Firstborns (including only children)	*Middle children*	*Lastborns*
Individuals under the age of 30			
Social conservatives[a]	14	40	49
Social moderates[a]	48	77	84
Social liberals[a]	75	92	96
Individuals aged 30 to 59			
Social conservatives	6	22	26
Social moderates	25	58	66
Social liberals	52	82	86
Individuals aged 60 and over			
Social conservatives	3	12	15
Social moderates	15	44	50
Social liberals	36	72	76

Enter relevant base rate (A) here: ______ %

B. ADJUSTMENTS TO BASE-RATE PROBABILITIES

1. **Pronounced parent-offspring conflict** + ______ %
(add 30 percent for firstborns and 10 percent for laterborns)

2. **Pronounced shyness** ± ______ %
(add 20 percent for firstborns; subtract 15 percent for lastborns)

3. **Age spacing** ± ______ %
(add 5 percent for firstborns, for close [0–2.0 years] or distant [more than 5.0 years] spacing; subtract 5 percent for laterborns, for close or distant spacing)

4. **Early parental loss and surrogate parenting** ± ______ %
(subtract 15 percent for firstborns; add 10 percent for laterborns)

5. **Gender** + ______ %
(for women born before 1900, add 10 percent; for women born after 1900, add 5 percent)

6. **Race** + ______ %
(add 10 percent for minorities)

7. **Friendship** + ______ %
(add 10 percent for being a close personal friend of a radical innovator)

8. . . . . *Total adjustments from Section B (preliminary)* ______ %[b]

C. Calculate the absolute difference between 50 percent and the applicable base-rate percentage (from Section A) ______ %

D. Subtract line C from 50 and divide the result by 50 ______ %

E. Multiply line B.8 by the fraction on line D ______ %

F. If line E is positive, add line E to Line A
If line E is negative, subtract line E from line A

This is the applicable predicted probability ______ %

---

a. For the purposes of this table, social *conservatives* rank in the first quartile of the general population; social *moderates* are in the middle half of the population; and social *liberals* are in the last quartile of the population.
b. No predicted probability can be lower than 0 or higher than 100, so adjustments in Section B need to be modified as Section A base-rate probabilities depart from 50 percent. Suppose that the base-rate probability in Section A is 92 percent, as it is for a young and socially liberal middle child. Suppose also that the total adjustments in Section B sum to +10 percent. The formula for determining the *corrected* adjustment would be line C (92–50=42), modified by line D, which is (50–42)/50, or 8/50, or .16. When the line B.8 adjustment (+10 percent) is multiplied by .16, the corrected adjustment becomes 1.6 percent rather than 10 percent. When this modified adjustment is added to line A (92 percent), the correct predicted probability becomes 93.6 percent.

Revolution.[3] After making appropriate adjustments to this base-rate prediction in sections B–F, the formula's accuracy should approach 85 percent. Fudging on details will decrease the formula's accuracy.

---

[3] For Technical Revolutions and Controversial Innovations, approximate probabilities derived from the model may be calculated as follows. For conservative firstborns, multiply the base-rate probability in Table 10 by 5.0. For socially moderate firstborns, multiply the base-rate probability by 1.8. For radical firstborns, multiply the base-rate probability by 1.2. For middleborns and lastborns who are social conservatives, multiply the base-rate probability by 1.8. For middleborns and lastborns who are social moderates or liberals, multiply the base-rate probability by 1.1. In debates over Conservative Theories, firstborns and social conservatives are more likely than their counterparts to endorse new ideas. Although young people are more likely to endorse Conservative Theories, the role of age is significantly less predictive than it is during liberal innovations.

If you, or someone else, is a clear-cut exception to the formula's prediction, ask yourself *why.* The most likely causes of exceptions will involve some of the influences, especially *situational factors,* that are discussed throughout this book. No formula can do complete justice to all of the contingencies that affect human behavior, although formulas can include appropriate adjustments for some of these contingencies.

ILLUSTRATIONS

FIGURES

TABLES

ACKNOWLEDGMENTS

This book has been twenty-six years in the making. Along the way, my intellectual debts have been numerous. Without the unstinting support of mentors, family, and friends, I would never have been able to complete the kind of large-scale biographical research that represents the heart of this study.

I am grateful to the John D. and Catherine T. MacArthur Foundation for five years of uninterrupted support as a Fellow. The foundation's generous assistance was essential to the completion of this study in its present form. I am also grateful for fellowship support from the Harvard Society of Fellows, the Miller Institute for Basic Research in Science (University of California, Berkeley), the John Simon Guggenheim Foundation, the National Endowment for the Humanities, and the Dibner Institute for the History of Science and Technology. Additional research was facilitated by grants from the National Science Foundation.

History provides an unparalleled source of data about human behavior. As a discipline, however, history is weak in theory and weaker still in its commitment to hypothesis testing. Numerous colleagues in the behavioral sciences have helped me to place my own historical claims within a theoretically informed framework and, more importantly, to test these claims using statistical methods. For their guidance on many theoretical issues that are fundamental to this book, I wish to thank the members of the Human Behavior and Evolution Society (especially Richard Alexander, Michael Bailey, Laura Betzig, David M. Buss, Martin Daly, Jennifer Davis-Walton, Sarah Blaffer Hrdy, Kevin MacDonald, John K. Pearce, Catherine Salmon, Donald Symons, and Margo Wilson). David M. Buss, Harmon R. Holcomb III, and Sarah Blaffer Hrdy provided many insightful comments on the manuscript, especially those portions dealing with Darwinian theory and its relevance for human behavior. For much of my understanding of evolutionary biology I am indebted to my former teachers Stephen Jay

Gould, Ernst Mayr, and Edward O. Wilson. In particular, Ernst Mayr has been a tremendous source of inspiration to me, and his contributions to this book have been innumerable.

I also thank Robert Rosenthal, Donald Rubin, Hal Stern, Douwe Yntema, Alan Zaslavsky, and other members of the Brown Bag Statistics Seminar in the Department of Psychology at Harvard University. For nearly a decade I attended this seminar, off and on, and absorbed a variety of valuable statistical insights from the gurus who run it. On a number of methodological issues, David Pillemer also provided valuable counsel, as did David Faust and Bruce H. Jones. I owe a special debt of gratitude to Donald Rubin and to Joseph Schafer for their expertise concerning the problem of missing data. The technique of imputing missing data, which I have occasionally drawn upon in this book, was made possible by a computer program written by Joseph Schafer (and described in Appendix 5).

Some of the hypotheses developed in this book could not have been tested without the help of the 110 historians who have assisted as expert judges. These historians have collectively supplied more than 20,000 ratings involving more than 4,000 historical figures. Their assessments have included judgments about religious and political attitudes, as well as individual stances taken during revolutionary debates. I am indebted to these experts for their willingness to share their historical knowledge with me.

Over the years I have benefited from the help of several energetic research assistants, one of whom, Joseph Eros, developed a computerized floor plan of Harvard's Widener Library so that he could track down hundreds of biographies according to the most efficient route. Other research assistants have included Tim Alborn, Husam Ansari, Shari Bassik, Bari Kuhl, Dominique Marchand, Anne-Marie Moulin, Kevin Nabe, Fran O'Connell, Irina Sirotkina, Karine Tran-Minh, and Gail Weingart. I am indebted to them all. A personal interest in the topic inspired Jonathan Finkelstein to do some of the biographical legwork in connection with U.S. Supreme Court voting patterns (Chapter 12), and he also assisted me in other ways.

Over the years, various science writers—some of them respected scholars in their own right—have taken an interest in my research. Their stories about my developing ideas and findings have stimulated me to think about my topic in new ways. I am indebted to these writers, particularly to Daniel Goleman and Matt Ridley. I owe special thanks to Olivia Judson, Michael Shermer, David Stipp, and Robert Wright, who read the manuscript in its entirety and offered numerous suggestions that have improved it.

I. Bernard Cohen gave the manuscript the kind of thoughtful critique that only a doyen in the history of science could provide. Phillip Kitcher also made numerous constructive suggestions, as did Donald Fleming, John Kerr, Paul-André Rosental, Richard Sens, and Miriam Solomon. Dean Keith Simonton shared with me some of his data on scientific eminence. Elizabeth Knoll provided a number of astute recommendations about the organization of the book.

Other scholars have assisted me with individual chapters. On matters related to Darwin and the Darwinian revolution, I have benefited over the years from the judicious advice of Frederick Burkhardt, Pietro Corsi, Peter Gautrey, Malcolm Kottler, Duncan Porter, and Sam Schweber. Loren R. Graham assisted me on issues relating to the eugenics movement, as did David B. Ralston on questions about European history. Patrice Higonnet critiqued the chapter on the French Revolution, as did Phillip Converse, who provided technical advice on my statistical analysis of voting during Louis XVI's trial. Steven Harris, Scott H. Hendrix, and Steven Ozment made constructive suggestions concerning the chapter on the Protestant Reformation.

Frederick Crews, whose valiant efforts to debunk pseudoscience have earned him the hostility of many people (and the gratitude of still many more), provided advice and inspiration on a variety of issues, particularly the shortcomings of Marxism and psychoanalysis. Over the years I have also benefited from the critical researches on psychoanalysis by Morris Eagle, Adolf Grünbaum, J. Allan Hobson, John Kerr, Malcolm Macmillan, and Peter Swales.

Both as a friend and a colleague, Shirley Roe rendered special assistance to the completion of this project. My father, Alvah W. Sulloway, read through the entire manuscript, which he peppered with pertinent comments like "get this mind-numbing detail out of the text." The merits of this sound advice are reflected in the appendices. John Lupo did most of the photographic work for the book, with his usual flare for making copies look better than the original. I am also grateful to the team at AlphaGraphics, which assisted me with reproductions and in many other ways. Edward Tenner, Harvey Shoolman, and especially Frank Curtis ably advised me in the domain of literary rights. My good friend and indefatigable advisor Jeanne O'Connell provided valuable suggestions about every aspect of this project. As the work took form, she patiently listened to, and critiqued, my developing ideas, and the book has been much improved by her judicious advice.

Dan Frank, my editor at Pantheon, has played a major role in sharpening the argument of this book, and his contribution has been editing at its best. He read some chapters so many times that he sometimes seemed to know my argument better than I did. His astute advice, invariably delivered in the most tactful manner, made the final stages of manuscript revisions a real pleasure. Claudine O'Hearn helped me to track down some of the most elusive illustrations in the book and also assisted me in a variety of other ways, including the onerous task of obtaining permissions. Fearn Cutler, who designed the book, also provided numerous suggestions about the format of tables, charts, and illustrations. I am grateful to Nancy Gilbert, my copy editor, who made many improvements in the text. In addition, Jeanne Morton, senior production editor at Pantheon, provided repeated advice on matters of style.

The charts for this book were initially produced using SYSTAT, a statistics program with unusually versatile graphics capabilities.* As I was researching and writing this book, this program allowed me to explore my data visually and to understand better the complex relationships among many of the variables I have studied. When presented in visual form, statistical results that are noteworthy tend to *look* noteworthy. My SYSTAT charts were redesigned in their present form by Bonnie Scranton, a graphics designer at *Newsweek* magazine, using Adobe Illustrator. David Ershun at NK Graphics provided essential technical expertise for converting SYSTAT files into Adobe format.

I have been privileged to have two especially valuable colleagues and critics in John K. Pearce and Carolyn Phinney. Over the last eight years, John read every chapter of this book, draft after draft, and advised me on content and style. My discussions with him about Darwinian theory and family dynamics have greatly enriched my understanding of these topics. Carolyn Phinney provided a comprehensive critique of the book. Her ability to detect subtle (and not-so-subtle) gaps in logic allowed her to make repeated and creative contributions to the book, both in its overall organization and in the final form of the text. In addition, her demanding standards of empirical demonstration were a constant source of inspiration to my own understanding of my research results.

---

* Wilkinson and Hill 1994.

From 1989 to the present, my academic home has been the Program in Science, Technology, and Society at the Massachusetts Institute of Technology. I am grateful to this program, and to its two most recent directors, Kenneth Keniston and Merritt Roe Smith, for providing an independent scholar with a lively intellectual environment.

My greatest debt is to Jerome Kagan, to whom I have dedicated this book. Jerry's enthusiastic backing for my original project (conceived in 1970, during my first year as a graduate student), and his unflagging endorsement of this project's endless reincarnations, have exerted a major influence on my career. Young at heart, Jerry is ever excited by new ideas. His eclectic scientific interests have stood me in particularly good stead and are reflected in the interdisciplinary thrust of this book.

I owe one final debt to someone I know only through the printed word. I first became interested in the life of Charles Darwin as an undergraduate and spent one summer retracing his footsteps in South America. Intrigued by the problem of scientific creativity, I began to investigate Darwin's intellectual development. In the spirit of Darwin's own empirical tenacity, I have ended up studying more than 6,000 lives in the hopes of understanding just one—that of Darwin—well. If anyone was ever "born to rebel," and also excelled at doing it, it was Darwin. What I have learned from my study of Darwin's life and thought can be summed up in a sentence: The best way of understanding creative genius is through the remarkable insights that Darwin's own theories provide about the human mind.

NOTES

Introduction

1. On age and scientific innovation, see, for example, Hull, Tessner, and Diamond 1978; Blackmore 1978.
2. On oedipal conflict and radicalism, see Erikson 1958; Wolfenstein 1967; Rejai and Phillips 1979:175–78; Rejai and Phillips 1983:151–52.
3. For claims about socioeconomic factors in political change, see Lefebvre 1962–64, 1:214, 266; Martin 1973:95; Rejai and Phillips 1979:97–99; Rejai and Phillips 1983:75; Soboul 1980:8. On the Protestant Reformation, see Hillerbrand 1973:38; Spitz 1985:184; Ozment 1992:20. For social class and revolutionary tendencies in science, see Shapin 1979b; Cooter 1984:43–44; Desmond 1989; Desmond and Moore 1992.
4. Quoted in Loomis 1964:55.
5. Dickens 1989:51, 220. See also Scarisbrick 1968:508; Kelley 1981:78.
6. For useful reviews of the research on sibling differences, see Plomin and Daniels 1987; Dunn and Plomin 1990.
7. On birth order and reproductive success, see Duby 1978; Boone 1986:869; MacDonald 1991. On birth order and infanticide, see Scrimshaw 1978, 1984; Hrdy 1987. On sibling conflict in history, see Daly and Wilson 1988a:30, who note that feudal royalty supplies "a seemingly endless tale of fraternal bloodletting."
8. One reason why historians have been able to dispense with formal hypothesis testing is that no one has ever died as a result of bad history. In the medical sciences, untested assertions about the benefits of a new drug, leading to its premature use on patients, would constitute malpractice. Still, it does not take a loss of life to demonstrate that, as a method of testing hypotheses, objective procedures are preferable to narrative modes of evaluation (Faust 1984).

1. Openness to Scientific Innovation

1. Darwin 1985– , 3:2.
2. Darwin 1985– , 1:134; Josiah Wedgwood to Robert Waring Darwin, letter of 31 August 1831.
3. Darwin 1958 [1876]:85.
4. The Galápagos Islands are the symbolic equivalent of the famous "falling apple" that is supposed to have inspired Isaac Newton's ideas on universal gravitation. Like the story of Newton's discoveries, the story of Darwin and the Galápagos has become the subject of a considerable legend (Sulloway 1982a, 1983a).
5. On the age of the Galápagos Islands, see Hickman and Lipps 1985; Christie et al. 1992.
6. Darwin 1933:334.
7. I am quoting from the second and revised edition of Darwin's *Journal* (1845:377–78), in which he expanded his remarks on the Galápagos Islands. The first edition appeared in 1839.

8. Darwin 1933:383; entry of 18 January 1836.
9. Darwin 1845:380. For modern studies of Darwin's finches, see Lack 1947 and Grant 1986.
10. Darwin 1933:334.
11. Darwin 1845:390.
12. Darwin 1845:393.
13. Herbert 1974; also Sulloway 1982a, 1982b, 1983b, 1984.
14. On John Gould's life, see Sauer 1982 and Sharpe 1893.
15. Owen 1894, 2:250–51; Sharpe 1893:xxiv (from whom I quote).
16. Sulloway 1982c:358.
17. Sulloway 1982c:357.
18. Sulloway 1982c:362–86.
19. Darwin 1959:7.
20. Darwin 1985– , 2:32; letter of 30 July 1837.
21. Darwin 1958 [1876]:120.
22. Darwin 1985– , 3:43–44.
23. Publication of Darwin's "Big Book" on species had to wait more than a century (Darwin 1975). Darwin expanded some of the chapters of this big book, which he called *Natural Selection,* into *The Variation of Animals and Plants under Domestication* (1868).
24. Darwin and Wallace 1958 [1858]. The American naturalist was Asa Gray.
25. Bell 1860 [1859]:viii.
26. Mayr 1964:vii.
27. Agassiz 1860:154.
28. Darwin 1887, 2:248.
29. Clark and Hughes 1890, 2:360; letter of 2 January 1860.
30. Flourens 1864:65.
31. FitzRoy 1839:503.
32. Lurie 1960:373. Here I draw on Stephen Jay Gould's (1983) account of Agassiz's trip.
33. Mayr 1988:185–95.
34. Kuhn 1962.
35. Kuhn 1962:24.
36. Kuhn 1962:66–91; see also Cohen 1985:28–29. Kuhn's influential view of science has spawned a large literature on the "social construction" of scientific thought. The most important advocates of the social construction of science include Fleck (1979 [1935]), Latour and Woolgar (1986 [1979]), Latour (1987), Shapin (1982, 1993), Shapin and Schaffer (1985), Collins and Pinch (1982), Collins (1985), and Pickering (1984). For a review of the recent literature on science as a practice, embedded in social activities that reflect traditions of experimentation and instrumentation, see Lenoir 1988 and Golinski 1990.
37. Lightman and Gingerich 1992.
38. See, for example, the classic article by Barber (1961); see also Merton 1973: 497–559; Mahoney 1976:116; Cohen 1985:17–18, 321.
39. Mayr 1982:311–12, 328–29; Bowler 1984:65–67. See also Lovejoy 1959:356, 380.
40. Darwin 1903, 1:305; letter to Joseph Hooker, 28 July 1868.

41. See Greene 1971:17, 25 n. 9, and Ghiselin 1972:123.
42. Darwin 1958 [1876]:124.
43. Quoted in Millhauser 1959:122.
44. Darwin 1985– , 3:2; letter to Joseph Hooker, 11 January 1844.
45. Mitroff 1983:264. See also Giere (1988, 1989:8), who remarks that "the most promising approach to a general theory of science is one that takes individuals as the basic unit of analysis." Kitcher (1993) provides an elaboration of this general argument, showing that rationality is the outcome of a competitive process among scientists who occupy different conceptual niches.
46. Lovejoy 1959:360. Appeals to Darwin's genius are undermined by the sizable number of scientists who became evolutionists before 1859. By my own count, at least 30 persons endorsed evolution by 1837, when Darwin himself was converted to this theory, and 85 people had done so by 1859 (Chapter 2).
47. Huxley 1887:197.
48. Darwin 1887, 2:226–27.

2. Birth Order and Scientific Revolutions

1. Ernst Mayr has called attention to this striking point: "Those who were best informed about biology, especially about classification and morphology, upheld most strongly the dogma of creation and the constancy of species" (1964:ix).
2. McCrae and Costa 1987, 1990:41, 44; Loehlin 1992:64–66.
3. Eaves, Eysenck, and Martin 1989:360–65, 385; Bouchard et al. 1990; Dunn and Plomin 1990:50; Loehlin 1992:66–67, 91.
4. In addition to the works in behavioral genetics already cited in this chapter, see Plomin and Daniels 1987; Dunn and Plomin 1991.
5. I review the literature on birth order and personality in Chapter 3.
6. See, for example, Palmer 1966; Harris and Howard 1968; Price 1969; Sutton-Smith and Rosenberg 1970:113–14; Singer 1971; Smith 1971; Kagan 1971:148, 1977.
7. It is typical of a great deal of experimental research in psychology that no one knows whether this research has much relevance to behavior in the real world. In her meta-analytic review of gender differences in persuasion and conformity, Becker (1986:206) calls attention to this problem.
8. Hormonal and antigen differences have been reported by birth order, but there is no compelling evidence that these physiological differences are responsible for birth-order differences in personality. Following the birth of a child, hormonal changes associated with pregnancy return to normal after four years, whereas birth-order effects are heightened when the age gap is three to four years (see chapters 3 and 5). Still, the issue of possible differences in fetal environments is worth further research. See, further, Foster and Archer 1979; Miller 1994; Blanchard et al. 1995.

That birth-order effects are largely environmental can be shown by comparing biological laterborns who were raised as firstborns with those who were not. I mention several examples in the text. Later in this chapter (n. 81) I present formal statistical evidence on this issue.

Holmes (1995) has argued that stance during scientific revolutions is significantly related to seasonality of birth, an association that could have either biological or environmental causes. Birth order covaries with seasonality, but this modest association is not responsible for the substantial birth-order effects discussed in this book. On further analysis using a larger and more representative sample, Holmes's claims about seasonality of birth prove to be spurious (see Appendix 9, Technical Discussion 1).

9. Each individual included in my study has been coded for a wide variety of biographical factors. Besides birth order and sibship size, these other variables include gender, social class, nationality, religious denomination, field of specialization, age at the time of participation, and more than thirty other variables. In coding birth order I have taken into account sibling mortality, adoptions, and the presence of step-siblings during childhood. A birth-order status established before an individual's seventh birthday must have remained stable until his sixteenth birthday for this information to be used as evidence. Cases not fulfilling these criteria were excluded from any statistical tabulations. Coding procedures for these variables are described in Appendix 2.

10. See, however, chapters 4–6, and 8–9, where findings for only children are presented separately.

11. Lurie 1960:4.

12. Coleman 1964:6.

13. Winsor 1979:112.

14. Lurie 1970:72.

15. Coleman 1964:14, 15, 175.

16. Bourdier 1971b:527.

17. Bourdier 1971b:524.

18. Bourdier 1971b:527.

19. Bourdier 1971b:524, 523.

20. Bourdier 1971a:521.

21. Bourdier 1971a:521.

22. Williams-Ellis 1966.

23. Wallace 1905, 1:15.

24. Thoren 1990:5.

25. Thoren 1990:4; see also Koestler 1959:283.

26. Hellman 1973:410; Thoren 1990:426.

27. Thoren 1990:337.

28. Thoren 1990:250.

29. Thoren 1990:468–69.

30. Cohen 1985:42.

31. In identifying a representative population for each scientific debate, I have followed an important rule: Any individual who is reported as having spoken out during a particular controversy, no matter what his or her occupation, is included in my samples. Theologians and philosophers, many of whom were also scientists, are therefore represented in my survey.

The boundaries between science and other disciplines were less sharply drawn in past centuries than they are today, and many theologians were well informed about scientific issues. Copernicus, Priestley, and Mendel all occupied official church posts. Even Darwin contemplated a career in the ministry before sailing on the *Beagle,* and professors at major British universities were required to take holy orders until the middle of the nineteenth century. Because 12 percent of my sample of disputants can be classified as nonscientists, I have recorded this information in my database, together with the specific fields in which participants achieved notable expertise.

32. For every participant whom I have classified as a supporter or opponent of a particular innovation, I have entered a *published citation* in my database, along with the date at which this particular individual spoke out. The bulk of my sources on scientific stance, which include more than a hundred publications, are listed in Appendix 3. The 18-volume *Dictionary of Scientific Biography* also reports information on scientific stance for many of the individuals included in this study. Articles on more than 1,700 members of my sample appear in this dictionary, a point of information that is also coded in my database.

33. The 110 experts who have served as raters in this study are listed in Appendix 4. I am grateful to these scholars for their generous assistance. Many aspects of this research project would have been impossible without their help.

34. During the pre-Darwinian period, the criterion of support for evolution is belief in evolution as a *physical* process. Some *Naturphilosphen* believed that species evolve as "ideas" in the mind of God. These individuals are not considered evolutionists because they did not endorse the physical reality of this process. Such metaphysical ideas were fully consistent with creationism.

35. The use of multiple judges permits the determination of "interrater reliabilities." The mean interrater reliability for my 10 raters of evolutionary controversies (including Darwinism) is .89, which is respectably high. Owing to the use of multiple ratings, which attenuate the effects of error, the "effective reliability" of ratings is .93. Reliabilities of this magnitude are more than sufficient to justify the statistical analyses presented in this book.

I have employed independent raters to assess scientific stance for all 28 scientific innovations surveyed in this chapter. The mean interrater reliability for my study as a whole, based on 26 judges, is .90. For further details on interrater reliabilities, see Appendix 3.

36. Darwin 1887, 2:326.

37. Lyell 1881, 2:364; see also Wilson 1970.

38. Darwin 1887, 3:10.

39. Colp 1977:141–44; Bowlby 1990:372.

40. Darwin 1985– , 7:397.

41. Agassiz 1860:154.

42. Hull 1978:200–207.

43. Crocker 1959:123; Carozzi 1974:27; Mayr 1982:311–12; Bowler 1984: 65–67.

44. Carozzi 1974:26.

45. *Technical information for Figure 2.1:* For the entire period from 1700 to 1875, the correlation between birth order and scientific stance is .39 ($r=phi$, $df=1/446$, $t=9.07$, $p<1\times10^{-15}$). Using a 7-point measure of scientific stance, the point-biserial correlation with birth order is .36 ($df=1/431$, $t=8.07$, $p<1\times10^{-13}$). The use of a 7-step scale makes little difference in the outcome of most statistical tests and also necessitates dropping cases. (Firstborns here include only children, who are similar to other firstborns in their attitudes toward evolution.)

These statistics merge two separate samples. For the pre-Darwinian period, the correlation between birth order and support for evolution is .43 (*r*=*phi*, *df*=1/218, *t*=6.99, $p<1\times10^{-11}$). The partial correlation for birth order and scientific stance, controlled for sibship size and social class, is .40. Controlled for birth order, neither sibship size nor social class is a significant predictor of support for evolution.

For the reception of Darwinism, the correlation between birth order and scientific stance is .35 (*r*=*phi*, *df*=1/226, *t*=5.58, $p<1\times10^{-8}$). The partial correlation of birth order with scientific stance, controlled for sibship size and social class, is .32. Controlled for birth order, neither sibship size nor social class is a significant predictor of support for Darwinism.

46. Darwin 1987 [1838]:250.

47. For the period before 1850, *r*=.50 (*df*=1/143, *t*=6.87, $p<1\times10^{-10}$).The 95 percent confidence limits for this odds ratio (17.5 to 1) are 5.6 and 53.5.

48. Significantly more scientists were converted by Darwinian theory than by previous evolutionary theories (*r*=.23, *df*=1/644, *t*=6.00, $p<1\times10^{-9}$). The increase in support from firstborns was greater than the increase in support from laterborns, who were already favorably disposed toward evolution.

49. Eiseley 1961.

50. The mean sibship size for my Darwinian revolution sample (1700–1875) is 3.55 (*N*=381), calculated by the Greenwood-Yule (1914) rule. Because 47 percent of this sample is actually firstborn (compared with the expected proportion of 28 percent), this ordinal position is significantly overrepresented, a phenomenon that is consistent with other evidence for firstborn intellectual achievement (Altus 1966, Belmont and Marolla 1973).

51. Darwin 1887, 2:72.

52. The mean sibship size for countries other than France is 3.8 rather than 3.6 because France lowers the mean. Mean sibship size among French scientists was significantly smaller than among scientists from other countries (2.10 versus 3.76, calculated by the Greenwood-Yule rule [1914]); *r*=–.28, *df*=1/190, *t*=–3.96, *p*<.001). Owing to its earlier passage through the demographic shift, France became more hostile to evolution over time, relative to other countries (*r*=–.08, *df*=1/642, *t*=–2.03, *p*<.05). For the reception of Darwinism in France (versus elsewhere), *r*=–.13 (*df*=1/349, *t*=–2.48, *p*<.02). Controlled for birth order, this significant nationality effect is reduced to *r*=–.08 (*df*=1/225, *t*=1.21, *p*<.23).

53. Mayr 1982:536.

54. The role of Cuvier, whose opposition to evolution "cast a long and pervasive shadow over the question," has been discussed by Stebbins (1972:118–19).

55. Evidence regarding age and openness to innovation in science is largely anecdotal, but the generalization is overwhelmingly true. On the role of age in the Darwinian revolution, see Hull, Tessner, and Diamond 1978, who have surveyed the British reception of Darwin's theories. See also Kuhn 1962:90, 150–52; Blackmore 1978; Sulloway (in preparation).

56. *Technical information for Figure 2.2:* The partial correlation of age with support for evolution, controlled for birth order, is –.20 (*df*=1/403, *t*=–4.08, *p*<.0001; based on the pre-Darwinian and Darwinian debates combined). Age interacts significantly with birth order. Controlled for the main effects of birth order and age,

the partial correlation for the interaction effect is –.09 (df=1/403, t=–1.82, p<.05).

57. The classic work on innovation diffusion is by Rogers (1962). See also Rogers (1971, 1983) and Mahajan and Peterson (1985) for overviews of some of the methods and general findings of this research. Meta-analytic methods are essential to the study of innovation diffusion and have shaped every aspect of the research in this book, from the collection of data to analysis and presentation of results. On meta-analytic methods, see Glass, McGaw, and Smith 1981; Hunter, Schmidt, and Jackson 1982; Rosenthal 1987.

58. In compiling this citation count for "revolutionary" innovations, I have relied on the number of pages devoted to each theory in Kuhn 1962/1970, 1977; Cohen 1985; Hacking 1981; and the 18-volume *Dictionary of Scientific Biography.* These page counts are formalized as a variable in my database.

In this secondary literature, the most cited "revolution" is Newtonian theory (with 978 page references), followed by the Darwinian revolution (525), Einstein's theories of special and general relativity (374); the Copernican revolution (323); and the chemical revolution led by Lavoisier (321). Sixteen of the 17 most cited "revolutions" are included in my historical survey. I have not collected data on the development of electromagnetic theory by Faraday, Maxwell, Hertz, and others (which received 273 page references). I was unable to find a sufficiently detailed account of the reception of these ideas to justify a formal statistical survey.

59. Four of the 12 Technical Revolutions in my survey have frequently been mentioned for their ideological implications. These four events are Newtonian theory, psychoanalysis, relativity theory, and quantum mechanics (Popper 1980:103; Cohen 1985:379). Following Hacking (1983:493) and Cohen (1985:95), we may subdivide these 12 technical events into the 4 "big revolutions" I have just mentioned and 8 "smaller" ones. I provide a test of these distinctions, using a continuous measure of ideological radicalism, in Chapter 14.

60. Popper (1981:81, 98–106) has proposed a similar distinction between "ideological" and "scientific" revolutions. He includes Copernicanism and Darwinism in the first category. Cohen (1985:284, 377), who endorses Popper's distinction, agrees on the radical ideological status of Copernican and Darwinian theory.

61. In addition to the guidelines mentioned in the text, I have considered two other indicators of radicalism: (1) published statements by historians of science that an innovation contradicted the literal truth of the Bible; and (2) evidence that the teaching of a theory was banned by religious or political institutions.

62. Hutton 1788:304.

63. The assumption that the world was only 6,000 years old was based on the calculations of Archbishop James Ussher (1650), who concluded that the world was created on Sunday the 23rd of October in the year 4004 B.C. Ussher was not the first person to claim this particular date for the creation of the world, but he succeeded in popularizing it (Davies 1969:13–14; Rudwick 1972:70).

64. Each of the five innovations that I classify as a Conservative Theory is explicitly described as such by historians of science. On vitalistic doctrines (including opposition to spontaneous generation), see Gasking 1967; Farley 1977, 1982; Roe 1981. On idealistic systems of classification, see Stresemann 1975; Desmond 1989. On germ theory, see Farley and Geison 1974. On modern spiritualism (which is generally considered a form of religion), see J. Oppenheim 1985. On eugenics, see Kevles 1985; Proctor 1988; Weingart, Kroll, and Bayertz 1988.

Preformation theory in embryology is usually portrayed as a conservative theory, owing to its strong links with creationism and vitalism. This biological idea, which was inspired by the mechanical philosophy during the seventeenth century, was not a conservative theory to begin with, and it superseded the conservative alternative (Aristotle's theory of epigenesis). Preformation did become the conservative alternative to epigenesis during the eighteenth century (Roe 1981:3–9). Epigenesis, one of my seven Controversial Innovations, was grounded in liberal assumptions friendly to the notion of biological change. See Chapter 14, where I deal in more detail with this problem of historical context.

65. Quoted in Roe 1981:98.

66. Roe 1981:119.

67. Stresemann 1975:170–91.

68. Desmond 1989:22.

69. For the odds ratio (2.0 to 1 in favor of laterborns), $\chi^2(1)=55.15$ [r=.17], N=2,015, $p<1\times10^{-13}$. The odds ratio is computed across events using the Mantel-Haenszel statistic, which adjusts for differences in cell frequencies and sample size. The 95 percent confidence intervals for this odds ratio are 1.7 and 2.6. Because these results are significantly heterogeneous among themselves, they underestimate the extent of the influence of birth order in radical innovations.

For the entire sample of 28 innovations, the mean weighted correlation of birth order with scientific stance is .24 (r=*phi*, df=1/2,013, t=11.08, $p<1\times10^{-20}$).

70. I have designated 78 individuals in my study as major "initiators" of scientific innovation. Laterborns are overrepresented by a factor of 4.5 among the initiators of Radical Ideological Revolutions (r=.32, $\chi^2[1]=6.88$, N=66, $p<.01$). Laterborns are not overrepresented among the initiators of Technical Revolutions or Controversial Innovations, although they were significantly more likely to support these theories than firstborns were.

71. For the test of homogeneity among the 28 scientific disputes, $\chi^2(29)=84.69$, N=2,015, $p<1\times10^{-7}$, which means that the effect sizes for birth order vary significantly across events. (I have analyzed two of the 28 controversies in terms of early and late stages of the same debate, causing the degrees of freedom to sum to 30.)

72. On the materialist implications of phrenology, see Young 1970, 1972, and Cooter 1984.

73. To deal with this problem, I present a multidimensional classification of scientific debates in Chapter 14 (especially Figure 14.1). Cohen (1985) has emphasized the importance of contemporary indications of revolutionary status.

74. Owing to the manifestly radical nature of phrenology, I include this theory with other Radical Ideological Revolutions when presenting further statistical findings. If phrenology is reclassified as a Radical Ideological Revolution, and if the later debates over Copernican theory are considered a Technical Revolution, the birth-order effects for all four classes of scientific controversies pass the test for homogeneity of effect sizes. In Chapter 14 I present evidence to show that, among scientists after 1609, the adoption of Copernican theory was largely determined by technical considerations, not by ideological commitments.

75. Laterborns are significantly overrepresented as supporters of scientific innova-

tion during the early as well as the later stages of debate. During later stages of debate, however, the odds ratio in favor of laterborn support is typically half that observed during earlier stages in the same debates. The difference in birth-order effects is significant ($z=1.98$, $p<.05$).

76. *Technical information for Figure 2.4:* The ellipses represent Gaussian bivariate confidence intervals on the centroid of each class of innovations. The confidence intervals have been set at 95 percent. The orientation of each ellipse is determined by the slope of the Pearson correlation between the birth-order effect and elapsed time (Wilkinson and Hill 1994:373)

Controlled for (1) status as a Radical Ideological Revolution and (2) phase of debate, the interaction between these two variables is significant (partial $r=-.47$, $df=1/26$, $t=-2.79$, $p<.01$).

77. Controlled for type of scientific innovation, the partial correlation between the odds ratio for each innovation and its year of commencement is .02 ($df=1/27$, $t=0.13$, $p=.90$).

78. I provide a more detailed test of this assertion about primogeniture in Appendix 9, Technical Discussion 2.

79. See Wedgwood 1929:70; Stone 1979:167; and Segaleû 1985:63.

80. For laterborn eldest sons versus younger sons in all but Conservative Theories, $r=.00$ ($\chi^2[1]=0.02$, $N=678$, $p<.89$); for Conservative Theories, the results are similar ($r=.00$, $\chi^2[1]=0.00$, $N=181$, $p<.97$).

81. A formal test of birth order as a functional construct is provided by scientists who were biological laterborns (such as Louis Agassiz and Tycho Brahe), but who were raised as firstborns. I know of 29 such instances in my sample. In their responses to scientific innovation, these individuals are statistically indistinguishable from other firstborns. In addition, these functional firstborns were significantly less likely to support liberal innovations than were functional laterborns ($r=.11$, $\chi^2[1]=14.82$, $N=1{,}265$, $p<.001$). Relative to laterborns raised as firstborns, those who were not were 4.4 times more likely to support liberal scientific breakthroughs.

82. For the odds ratio of 3.1 laterborn adopters for every firstborn adopter in 23 liberal innovations, $r=.26$, $\chi^2[1]=112.77$, $N=1{,}618$, $p<1\times10^{-15}$ (using the Mantel-Haenszel test). The 95 percent confidence limits for this odds ratio are 2.5 and 3.8. For these same 23 controversies, the correlation between birth order and scientific stance is .27 ($r=phi$, $df=1/1{,}616$, $t=11.12$, $p<1\times10^{-22}$). The mean-weighted correlation is .31. For scientific stance coded on a 7-point scale, the mean-weighted correlation with birth order is almost the same ($r=.29$, $N=1{,}089$).

83. These statistics follow from the fact that the odds ratio for liberal theories is 3.1 to 1 in favor of laterborns, compared with an odds ratio of 0.54 to 1 in favor of firstborns during Conservative Theories: 3.1/0.54 =5.7 to 1. For Radical Ideological Revolutions versus Conservative Innovations, the analogous odds ratios are 4.8÷0.54, or 8.9 to 1.

84. I expand on these observations in Chapter 14, especially Figure 14.1 and Table 7. There I show that the magnitude of birth-order effects during scientific innovations is dependent on a dozen moderator variables.

85. If we dichotomize the 28 debates in my survey into two groups, based on the mean for each moderator variable, the resulting differences in birth-order effects

are statistically significant. For degree of support, r=.08, $\chi^2(1)$=11.41, N=2,001, p<.001; for number of participants, r=.10, $\chi^2(1)$=10.31, N=2,001, p<.005; and for length of the debate, r=.07, $\chi^2(1)$=21.05, N=2,001, p<.0001.

86. See Ernst and Angst 1983.

87. *Technical information for Figure 2.5:* For the 23 controversies representing liberal debates in my survey, birth-order effects are statistically significant within each sibship size from 2 to 7 and above. The test for heterogeneity across sibship size is not significant ($\chi^2[5]$=3.47, p=.63).

88. *Technical information for Figure 2.6:* For the 23 liberal controversies in my survey, birth-order effects are significant within each socioeconomic level, except the aristocracy. The point-biserial correlation of scientific stance with socioeconomic status (computed as a linear trend) is .04 (df=1/1,499, t=1.47, p<.15).

89. Aristocrats are more likely than other participants in my sample to be nonscientists. Laterborn aristocrats are more likely than firstborn aristocrats to be theologians (a birth-order trend that is not present within other socioeconomic groups). Finally, aristocrats are more likely to be personal friends or students of the originator of a new theory. Each of these confounding factors (which are statistically significant) tends to diminish the role of birth order within this socioeconomic group.

If we consider those aristocrats who were scientists (and, at the same time, neither theologians nor friends of the architect of a new theory), the difference in adoption by birth order becomes statistically significant (r=.28, $\chi^2[1]$=6.32, N=78, p<.02). For this control group, the odds ratio is 3.6 in favor of laterborns, similar to the odds ratio for the comparable population of nonaristocrats (3.7 to 1).

90. *Technical information for Figure 2.7:* For siblings involved in liberal scientific disputes, r=.41 ($\chi^2[1]$=13.76, N=83, p<.001). This birth-order effect is significantly larger than for the rest of the sample. For the contrast between r=.26 (for 1,521 nonsiblings) and r=.41 (for 83 siblings), z=1.48, p<.15. Basing the contrast on scientific stance, scored on a 7-point scale, the difference in effect sizes is significant (z=2.35, p<.02; contrasting r=.25 [N=1,028] and r=.49 [N=70]). Similarly, if we include 74 parents and their offspring in a contrast between family members and unrelated individuals, the difference is also significant (z=3.20, p<.005).

Another 22 siblings in my study spoke out on Conservative Theories such as vitalism and eugenics. The correlation between birth order and scientific stance is .01, which is significantly lower than the correlation for liberal innovations (z=1.67, p<.05, one-tailed test).

91. This difference of 1.92 points among sibling-scientists is twice that for unrelated scientists in my sample (0.98 points): N=1,098, z=2.35, p<.02.

92. Bourdier 1971a:521. Controlled for family size and social class, laterborn scientists in my sample were more likely than firstborns to undertake research in the behavioral sciences (r=.07, df=1/885, t=2.02, p<.05; contrasting research done in animal biology, psychology, and psychiatry with work done in other fields). For laterborns, being good interpreters of human behavior is a useful strategy in dealing with more powerful elder siblings. Within the family context, psychological sophistication is a form of power. In influencing the choice of specialization in this scientific domain, birth order interacts with the age gap between siblings. Laterborns were most likely to specialize in the behavioral sciences if they were sepa-

rated from their next older sibling by a large age gap—defined as four or more years (r=.11, df=1/440, t=2.34, p<.02; the odds ratio under these circumstances is an impressive 2.76 laterborns for every firstborn behavioral scientist). It is worth noting that Frédéric Cuvier was 49 months younger than Georges. Another nineteenth-century pioneer in psychology, Francis Galton, was the youngest of seven children and six years apart from his next older sibling. A large age gap between siblings heightens the inequality associated with birth order. Scarce family resources also seem to cause siblings to take an interest in psychology. Lower-class scientists from large families were especially likely to pursue this science (for this two-way interaction effect, the partial correlation is r=.10 [df=2/885, F=4.20, p<.02]).

93. Richards 1987:69.

94. Richards 1987:65.

95. Richards 1987:65.

96. The likelihood of such a disparity in theory choice arising by chance is less than one in a thousand billion ($p<1\times10^{-12}$). This comparison is based on the contrast between responses to pre-Darwinian evolution and idealist theories of taxonomy. The laterborn preference for the radical alternative—124 to 1—is also the odds ratio of the two relevant odds ratios in Table 2 (9.7 to 1 versus .078 to 1). For the contrast in theory choice among firstborns, r=.75 (df=1/120, t=8.00, $p<1\times10^{-13}$). For the same contrast among laterborns, r=.08 (df=1/139, t=0.95, p=.78). For the difference between the two contrasts, z=7.14, $p<1\times10^{-12}$.

97. Darwin 1887, 3:91.

98. Darwin 1887, 2:385.

3. Birth Order and Personality

1. See, for example, Steelman and Powell 1985.

2. Adler 1927, 1928, 1956:376–83; see also Ernst and Angst 1983:85–87. Freud and other early psychoanalysts mostly ignored the subject of birth order. Freud himself (1916–17:334) made only one brief reference to the topic.

3. Adler 1956:377.

4. Adler 1956:379; Ernst and Angst 1983:85.

5. Adler 1956:378–79.

6. Adler 1956:379.

7. Adler 1956:380.

8. Adler 1956:381.

9. On the numerous shortcomings of psychoanalytic theory, see Grünbaum 1984, 1993; Eysenck 1985; Crews 1986, 1995; Sulloway 1979b, 1991a. Psychoanalytic hypotheses cannot be tested in the clinical setting because therapist and patient are both contaminated by psychoanalytic expectations (Grünbaum 1984). It is worth noting that Adlerians, through their *Journal of Individual Psychology,* have done considerably more than Freudians to promote hypothesis testing, a method that they have sometimes brought to bear in birth-order research (Miley 1969; Vockell, Felker, and Miley 1973).

10. Adler's hypotheses have been expanded upon and refined by other psychologists. For a summary of other such extensions, see Sutton-Smith and Rosenberg 1970:4–10; Ernst and Angst 1983:86–87. One intriguing psychoanalytic account employs birth order to explain various historical tendencies, such as being holistic or atomistic, romantic or realistic, connected or disconnected, and so forth (Harris 1964). Although Harris's claims are largely impressionistic and based on small samples, many of his hypotheses are consistent with the general thrust of the empirical literature.

11. Hamilton 1963, 1964a,b.

12. Dawkins (1982:185–86), whose definition of inclusive fitness I have paraphrased, explains why this notion is properly defined in terms of an individual's *effects* on the reproductive success of relatives, rather than as an absolute property of the individual. Were inclusive fitness an absolute property, individual organisms would possess inclusive fitness even though deceased or not yet born.

13. For the Haldane anecdote, see Richards 1987:541. Writing in the 1950s, Haldane failed to grasp the full implications of this idea, so the honor for the insight fell to Hamilton a decade later. Building on Hamilton's ideas about inclusive fitness, Edward O. Wilson (1975) proposed the broad outlines of an evolutionary theory of social behavior under the term "sociobiology." During the two decades since Wilson's treatment of this subject, it has become a burgeoning research domain. Owing to the heated controversies that greeted Wilson's 1975 book, many researchers have abandoned Wilson's "sociobiology" label for other designations. Today's sociobiologists call themselves behavioral biologists, Darwinian anthropologists, and evolutionary psychologists. This tactic has tended to diminish intellectual credit where credit is due. The term "evolutionary psychology" is appropriate for use by psychologists, but the approach remains a subfield of the broader project that Wilson originally sketched under the term "sociobiology." Although he did not use the term, Darwin was a sociobiologist, which is why all sociobiologists are Darwinians. For additional publications on sociobiology, see Wilson 1978; Alexander 1979; Symons 1979; Trivers 1985; Buss 1994; Ridley 1994; Wright 1994. For a thoughtful critique of sociobiology, see Kitcher 1985.

14. Trivers 1985:47.

15. Trivers 1985:47.

16. Trivers 1974. The notion of parent-offspring conflict, like that of sibling conflict, is implicit in Hamilton's ideas about kin selection, and these two conflicts were fully appreciated by Hamilton himself (1964a,b). By using a cost-benefit approach to individual development (and to the parent-offspring relationship), Trivers extended these two principles in new and important ways.

17. Trivers 1985:145–55.

18. Genetic considerations also predict that siblings will share scarce resources whenever the benefits of doing so are more than twice the costs (Trivers 1985:148).

19. Based on Darwinian theory, identical twins ought to be angelic altruists, free of sibling rivalry. Twinning is too rare a phenomenon in our own species for behaviors to have evolved for such a special case (Alexander 1979:157; Daly and Wilson 1988a:11). Unlimited altruism prevails in many asexual organisms because siblings are usually twins (Wilson 1975). Some species of aphids give birth to two different forms of offspring, which are in fact twins. One form, a soldier caste, remains in the first larval stage and defends the lives of the second form. The second form, which is adapted to feeding on plant sap, grows to adulthood and reproduces. Soldier aphids are altruists because their siblings reproduce on their behalf (Trivers 1985:42).

A remarkable tendency toward cooperation has evolved among the social insects—ants, bees, and wasps. As William Hamilton grasped in 1963, the social insects owe their altruistic propensities to an unusual genetic arrangement called haplodiploidy (Hamilton 1964a,b; Wilson 1971). Females have two sets of chromosomes, whereas males, who develop from an unfertilized egg, have only one set of chromosomes derived from their mother. On average, sisters share ¾ of their genes, but they are related to their brothers by only ¼. As a result, social insects have evolved female-based societies in which sisters perform most of the work. In some species, sisters actively limit the queen's production of male offspring (Trivers 1985:178, 279–80). After all, who needs brothers who mostly loaf around and who are genetically like nephews.

20. Mock 1984; see also Mock, Drummond, and Stinson 1990.
21. Mock, Drummond, and Stinson 1990:445.
22. Mock 1984:17. Given the complementary nature of siblicide and parental infanticide, one would predict that primary control for the process will generally lie with one or the other member of the parent-offspring pair. In other words, a species ought not to be simultaneously siblicidal and infanticidal, with no coordination between the two behaviors. One might also expect parental control of infanticide to be most common in those species in which the physiological costs of producing an offspring are particularly high. The cost of a bird's egg is relatively small compared with the cost of a nine-month pregnancy in humans.
23. Hayssen 1984:114. Other cases of mammalian siblicide are discussed by Trivers (1985:23) and Frank, Glickman, and Licht (1991).
24. Angier 1994 (who reports the researches of Hubert Schwabl).
25. On the complementary nature of siblicide, parental infanticide, nutritional neglect, and contraception, see Hrdy and Hausfater 1984:xv. I am grateful to Sarah Hrdy (personal communication) for information on the physiological issues discussed in this paragraph. See also Hrdy 1992.
26. Hrdy and Hausfater 1984:xix.
27. Hrdy 1987:98. On infanticide in animals as well as humans, see the useful volumes by Hausfater and Hrdy (1984) and Parmigiano and von Saal (1994).
28. Daly and Wilson 1988a:41–42, 46, 61.
29. Scrimshaw 1984:459 (quoting A. Aguirre).
30. Scrimshaw 1984:458.
31. Scheper-Hughes 1992:310.
32. Scheper-Hughes 1992:365.
33. Scrimshaw 1984:458–59 (quoting A. Aguirre).
34. Alexander (1979:158) has fully appreciated the relationship between age differences among siblings and Darwinian fitness. The topic of parental discrimination is treated by Daly and Wilson (1988a:41–42, 46–48, 72–73, 75; 1988b). My point about parental favoritism and birth order is subtle because parents typically provide more care for younger offspring, who would generally die without it. As fitness maximizers, parents will tend to invest in each child according to its age-related needs, but with a bias toward nurturing offspring who are the most likely to survive and reproduce. Prevailing conditions will also sometimes play a role. For

example, when conditions are poor, parents might well prefer the unborn over a firstborn (Hrdy 1992). The attempt to nurse a child during a famine might cost the lives of both mother and child, terminating further reproductive opportunities for the mother.

35. For this 39-country survey on firstborn social status, see Rosenblatt and Skoogberg 1974. The ancient Japanese dining custom also involved a sex bias (Kay 1972:117). Eldest males were privileged over eldest females, a bias that also has Darwinian implications, as I discuss later in this chapter.

36. For a critique of Alexander's (1979:158) suggestions about the Darwinian logic for primogeniture, see Kitcher 1985:294–98.

37. Hrdy and Judge (1993) have masterfully treated this topic. See also Segaleû 1985.

38. Herlihy 1973.

39. This hypothesis was first set forth by Trivers and Willard (1973) and has inspired a great deal of research, mostly confirmatory. Considerable biological evidence, judiciously reviewed by Hrdy (1987), indicates that females of certain species regulate the sex ratio of offspring to enhance inclusive fitness. Among deer, for example, a male offspring must be in good condition to compete successfully for mates. When in good biological condition, females give birth to a higher proportion of male offspring. Females in poor condition give birth to a higher proportion of female offspring.

40. Boone 1986. See also Voland 1984, 1990; Hrdy 1987; Hrdy and Judge 1993.

41. Results from Voland's (1984, 1990) genealogical study of a German farming community during the eighteenth and nineteenth centuries closely mirror Boone's (1986) Portuguese case. Voland's research shows that parental discrimination by birth order and gender is not limited to the elite classes. Discrimination tends to prevail in any saturated environment in which wealth is stratified and tied to land.

42. Boone 1986:869.

43. Compared with eldest males, younger sons were significantly more likely to father illegitimate offspring (r=.16, $\chi^2[1]$=87.21, N=3,285, p<.0001; calculated from Boone's Table 5 [1986:870]). Someone should do a study to determine whether laterborns are more likely to engage in mate poaching and other sexual strategies (see Appendix 10, section 10). I would predict birth-order differences in mating strategies based on theoretical considerations, as well as owing to the birth-order differences in personality reported later in this chapter.

44. Betzig 1986.

45. Mitterauer and Sieder 1983:56; Vogel 1992.

46. Dunn and Plomin 1990:73.

47. I have discussed this topic elsewhere (Sulloway 1995).

48. McCrae and Costa 1987, 1990; see also Goldberg 1981, 1982; Digman 1990; John 1990.

49. The Big Five personality dimensions represent a folk taxonomy and need to be employed judiciously (Kagan 1994:42–46). Buss (1991) argues that these five dimensions have been shaped by evolutionary considerations to provide, in shorthand form, maximally useful information about people. This same logic applies to Osgood, Suci, and Tannenbaum's (1957) semantic differential (good–bad, strong–weak, and active–passive). These three dimensions, which overlap with

the Big Five personality dimensions, convey a maximum of information about friend or foe with a minimum of mental activity. Among lower animals, protective mimicry makes frequent use of these three dimensions of biological "judgment." See also D. S. Wilson 1996.

50. See, for example, Koch 1956e:408; Brim 1958; Sutton-Smith and Rosenberg 1970:114–16; Ernst and Angst 1983:148.

51. Forbes 1971; Stewart 1977, 1992.

52. Sutton-Smith and Rosenberg 1970:59.

53. Sutton-Smith and Rosenberg 1970:39–68. Similar strategies by status are observed in primate dominance hierarchies (de Waal 1989).

54. Sutton-Smith and Rosenberg 1970:118–19; see also Batson 1991 on birth order and altruism. Especially in ancestral times, it would often have been in the interests of younger siblings to cooperate with older siblings, since older siblings were more likely to survive and reproduce. With high levels of childhood mortality in previous centuries, many younger siblings' genes were propagated only via older siblings. Among some species of birds, younger siblings help to raise the offspring of older siblings (Trivers 1985:184–85; Emlen, Wrege, and Demong 1995).

55. See Altus 1966, Belmont and Marolla 1973, and Zajonc 1976. Properly interpreted, birth-order differences in achievement reflect Conscientiousness rather than Openness on the Big Five personality dimensions. IQ is not a personality dimension and represents a sixth factor (McCrae 1994).

56. The quotation is noteworthy because it comes from Ernst and Angst (1983: 240), who are critical of most other claims about birth order. See also MacArthur 1956; Altus 1963; Palmer 1966; Harris and Howard 1968; Price 1969; Sutton-Smith and Rosenberg 1970:113–14; MacDonald 1969a,b, 1971a,b; Singer 1971; Smith 1971; Kagan 1971:148; 1977; Baskett 1984.

57. Ernst and Angst 1983:159. Firstborns may be more anxious about status than laterborns, but they are also more self-confident (Koch 1955a). These behavioral differences are strongly dependent on context.

58. Adjective pairs that define Neuroticism include "not envious–envious," "even-tempered–temperamental," and "unemotional–emotional" (McCrae and Costa 1987:85). On the psychological functions of jealousy, see DeKay and Buss 1992:187–88.

59. Koch 1955a:36.

60. Koch 1955a:24; 1956e:397–98, 406.

61. See, for example, Koch 1955a:26, 28, 36; Koch 1956a:17; Koch 1956e:407.

62. Relevant to my claim about laterborns being "champions of the underdog" is a curious finding in behavioral genetics (Eaves, Eysenck, and Martin 1989:323). In a 60-item questionnaire involving social attitudes, in which many items exhibit moderate heritability, the following item had almost no heritability: "The so-called underdog deserves little sympathy or help from other people." Most differences in answers to this item are attributable to the nonshared environment (and hence to sibling differences). Although the issue has not been investigated in behavioral genetic research, it is not hard to predict the direction of any birth-order difference.

63. On birth order and conformity, see Bragg and Allen 1970; Sampson and Hancock 1967; Sutton-Smith and Rosenberg 1970:83–84, 140–42. For birth order and conventional morality, see MacDonald 1969b; Sutton-Smith and Rosen-

berg 1970:110; Ernst and Angst 1983:124–26. On birth order and dangerous activities, see Sutton-Smith and Rosenberg 1970:82; Nisbett 1968.

64. Schooler 1972.

65. Ernst and Angst 1983. Researchers owe a considerable intellectual debt to Ernst and Angst for their systematic analysis of the birth-order literature. Their book convinced me of the need for controlling my own historical samples for important background factors such as social class and sibship size. For other useful compilations and reviews of the birth-order literature, see Miley 1969; Vockell, Felker, and Miley 1973; Schubert, Wagner, and Schubert 1976; Schubert, Wagner, and Schubert 1984.

66. Ernst and Angst 1983:242 (their emphasis).

67. Dunn and Plomin 1990:85. Similar critical conclusions about birth-order research have been reached by other researchers. See, for example, Scarr and Grajek 1982; Plomin and Daniels 1987; Blake 1989a,b; Somit, Arwine, and Peterson 1996.

68. In the preface to their 1983 book, Ernst and Angst remarked that meta-analytic methods, which were just coming into usage at this time, would have provided their analysis with "a much firmer footing" (1983:xi). When applied to Ernst and Angst's own data, these methods do just this, revealing surprisingly consistent trends in birth-order research.

69. For an introduction to meta-analytic procedures, see Glass, McGaw, and Smith 1981; Hunter, Schmidt, and Jackson 1982; Hunter and Schmidt 1990; Rosenthal 1984/1991, 1987; Wolf 1986. On the use and abuses of meta-analysis, especially in medicine, see Mann 1990.

70. Hunter, Schmidt, and Jackson 1982:132.

71. The vote-counting method that I employ here tends to underestimate significant trends, causing a Type II statistical error (Mann 1994). Because the findings on birth order and personality in Table 4 are so consistent, this limitation of the vote-counting method is irrelevant.

72. The overrepresentation of significant birth-order studies is so extreme that it is independent of my designations of results as "confirming" or "refuting" the hypotheses. If we ignore the direction of reported effects, 86 studies exhibit significant findings, far too many to be a chance result (z=15.81, $p<10^{-8}$). These birth-order findings also pass the File Drawer Test. This test takes into account the tendency for nonsignificant studies to end up in file drawers, rather than being published (Sulloway 1995).

73. As I have already mentioned, the Big Five personality dimensions represent a folk taxonomy, not a natural classification of personality differences (Kagan 1994: 42–46). McCrae and Costa (1990:43, 47) identify six facets of Extraversion, of which social dominance is one. It does not follow that firstborns should also be more sociable and fun-loving than laterborns, which represent two other facets of Extraversion. These traits are correlated with being laterborn (MacArthur 1956; Hall and Barger 1964).

74. For the test of heterogeneity among studies, $\chi^2[4]$=44.96, $p<.001$; the findings are not homogeneous.

75. I base this comparison of relative effect sizes on the typical "variance explained." Steelman and Powell (1985) found significant birth-order differences for

social skills (laterborns scored higher), but not for academic performance. In this study, which draws on a sample of more than 3,000 individuals, the effect sizes for personality variables are typically 2 to 10 times larger than for academic variables (the mean factor being 7).

A great deal of needless controversy in birth-order studies would be eliminated if researchers were more cognizant of the *expected* effect sizes for birth order, given its significantly heterogeneous influence on different classes of behavior (Table 4). For example, Somit et al. (1996) rightly question the relevance of birth order to many aspects of political leadership, documenting its meager and inconsistent influence in a variety of political contexts. Finding little support for such eminence relationships, Somit et al. proceed to dismiss *all* birth-order claims as baseless, confounding findings about eminence with findings about openness to experience. This unfortuanate logic leads them to reject as a "statistical quirk" their own significant finding that laterborn Supreme Court justices have been more likely than firstborns to dissent from the majority (1996:48). Their documented finding would happen by chance less than once in 50,000 times. That's some statistical quirk!

76. Ernst and Angst (1983:43–45, 48) list 33 studies on birth order and IQ that have been controlled for sibship size and/or social class. Sixteen studies confirm the hypothesis that firstborns have higher IQs. Only one study reveals a significant difference in favor of laterborns. The remaining 16 studies report inconclusive results. Meta-analytically, this outcome is impressive ($z=5.34$, $p<10^{-8}$). Still, birth rank typically explains only 1 percent of the variance in IQ scores. The consistent meta-analytic showing for the relationship between birth order and IQ is due to *large samples,* not *large effects.*

For birth order and scholastic achievement, the trend in favor of firstborns is equally impressive, based on 35 controlled studies reported by Ernst and Angst ($z=4.35$, $p<10^{-6}$). The effect sizes reported in these studies are typically small ($r \leq .10$), like those documented for IQ.

77. The method of meta-analysis that I have employed (namely, counting studies with significant findings) does not allow us to estimate effect sizes, at least directly. (See Hunter, Schmidt, and Jackson 1982:130–32; Hedges and Olkin 1980.) A more elaborate meta-analysis is necessary to calculate effect sizes directly and would be worth undertaking. My own estimates of effect sizes are based on an informal survey of studies reporting this information. For openness, see Chapter 2, Table 2, where the largest effect sizes are just above $r=.40$. Meta-analysis of these effect sizes shows that they agree closely with *expected* effect sizes, based on the heterodoxy of each theory (Chapter 14, Figure 14.1). Extrapolating from the effect sizes observed for openness to experience and from Table 4, we may expect the following *maximum* correlations for other Big Five personality dimensions: Conscientiousness ($r \approx .35$), Agreeableness ($r \approx .30$), and Neuroticism ($r \approx .20$). Effect sizes for Extraversion rarely exceed $r=.10$ (see Chapter 7, Figure 7.2). *Mean* correlations, which typically confound disparate behavioral contexts and modes of assessment, will generally be half the size of the maximum correlations I have specified here. By the term "maximum correlation" I mean an effect size that consistently replicates in large samples and that owes its consistency to a match between birth order, the specific outcome variable, and the behavioral context.

78. On gender and the Big Five personality dimensions, see Feingold 1994:443. Two additional conclusions emerge from my meta-analytic overview of the birth-order literature. Ernst and Angst have argued that birth-order effects dissipate with age and are rarely found among adults. For the 196 studies analyzed in Table 4, there is no relationship between age and outcome, contradicting Ernst and Angst's assertion (1983:184, 284; for age of subjects and study outcome, $r=-.04$—not significant). Ernst and Angst (1983:187) have also questioned the reliability of paper-and-pencil tests. This criticism is justified. Both "experimental" studies and "observer" data are more likely to exhibit birth-order effects than "self-report" data ($r=.22$, $\chi^2[1]=9.60$, $N=196$, $p<.0001$; contrasting study outcome using paper-and-pencil tests, and all other results). The superiority of experimental studies over self-report data has sometimes been demonstrated using the same subjects. Stewart (1967), for example, found differences in dependency as tested by the Embedded Figures Test, but not when measured by adjective checklists. How many firstborns are willing to describe themselves as "callous" or "unadventurous"? Self-report measures of empathy and risk taking yield generally meager birth-order findings (Ernst and Angst 1983:103–5, 161–62). In *experimental* studies, people are more likely to reveal their true colors. Consider a study involving painful electrical shocks. Laterborns were significantly more likely than firstborns to volunteer to take the place of experimental subjects expressing visible distress (Batson 1991).

79. See Koch 1954, 1955a,b, 1956a,b,c,d,e, 1957, 1960. A former pupil has described Koch as being "of the old school, a very proper, formal lady, noted for her kindness to students. She always lectured with her hat on, and gloves" (personal communication, Bruce Cushna, 20 July 1992).

80. Koch 1955a:36; 1956c:325; 1956e:397–98, 403, 406, 408.

81. Koch 1955a:36.

82. For birth order, sibling's sex, and age spacing, the expected number of significant effects by chance is 40.6 (including interactions). This total, based on Koch's use of two-tailed tests, compares with the reported number of 72 significant effects ($\chi^2[1]=25.96$, $z=5.06$, $p<1$ in one million). For birth order, the likelihood of obtaining 36 significant effects (including interactions) by chance is also small ($\chi^2[1]=7.43$, $z=2.73$, $p<.01$).

All told, there are 96 significant effects in Koch's study, including interactions. The expected number by chance is 43.5 ($\chi^2[1]=66.69$, $z=8.17$, $p<1\times10^{-16}$). Gender accounts for 24 main effects. The other 72 effects involve birth order, age gaps between siblings, and sex of sibling, sometimes interacting with gender. Relative to gender, the other three variables are more likely to express themselves as interaction effects, which makes their influence more difficult to appreciate at the "trait" level ($\chi^2[1]=4.44$, $p<.05$).

83. Koch 1955a:15, 26–27. For boys, these birth-order trends in anger, vengefulness, and cruelty were especially pronounced at the middle age spacing (2 to 4 years). Hence some of these effects involve three-way interactions (birth order × age spacing × gender).

84. Koch 1956a:8, 17. This significant difference in "quarrelsomeness" by birth order emerges as a "gender × birth order" interaction effect. Laterborn boys are

actually more quarrelsome than firstborn boys, which reflects their tendency to employ low-power tactics.

85. Koch herself was surprised by the frequency of these birth-order interactions and warned readers against drawing any "simple" conclusions on the topic (1956a:37). In fact, simple conclusions are fully warranted, but not about specific traits. Ernst and Angst (1983:125, 167) echo Koch's own conservative verdict, which treats significant interaction effects as "inconsistencies" rather than as significant effects in their own right. This approach to human behavior, which equates complexity with spurious findings, is fundamentally mistaken.

86. Birth-order differences do not map perfectly onto those associated with sex. Firstborns and women, for example, are more conscientious than laterborns and males.

87. Brim 1958.

88. Parsons and Bales 1955.

89. These two contrasting classes of behavior are only slightly modified ways of describing Extraversion and Agreeableness. McCrae and Costa 1990:27; see also Wiggins 1979.

90. The partial correlation between birth order and instrumental behavior, controlled for gender and sex of sibling, is −.91 (df=1/20 [cells], t=9.85, p<.0001). The partial correlation for sibling's sex, controlled for the other two predictors, is .87 (df=1/20, t=8.00, p<.0001). The partial correlation between gender and instrumental traits is −.83 (df=1/20, t=6.65, p<.0001). This last correlation favors girls, who were perceived by their teachers as being more planful and assertive than boys in a school environment. These correlations are unusually large because they are derived from group differences.

In attempting to replicate Brim's (1958) method of analyzing Koch's data, I encountered a number of minor inconsistencies that I found impossible to resolve. I therefore repeated Brim's reanalysis of Koch's data, and the statistics provided here are derived from my reanalysis rather than from Brim.

91. For birth order, the partial correlation with expressive behavior is .66 (df=1/20, t=3.89, p<.001, controlled for the other two predictors, namely, sex and sibling's sex). For gender the partial correlation for expressive traits is .91 (df=1/20, t=9.64, p<.001).

92. Koch 1955a:34; 1956a:12, 15, 21, 26. For effeminate tendencies, the main effect by birth order held only for the middle age spacing (2 to 4 years apart), see Koch 1956d:238. On masculine versus feminine attitudes and birth order, see Ernst and Angst 1983:259–60.

93. A note of caution is warranted on the topic of gender differences in Koch's study. Brim (1958:13) believed that teachers were rating boys and girls differently on some of the scales. In particular, Brim thought that girls received higher ratings than boys on "instrumental" traits whenever they displayed these traits to the same absolute degree. An equally plausible explanation is that teachers made their ratings in the context of the school environment. Girls were rated as more "planful," "self-confident," and "responsible" in this context. This possible source of bias is small and affects only a few of the scales. In any event, this problem does not affect the significant within-gender differences that consistently emerge by birth order.

94. On dominance versus cooperation in primate groups, see de Waal 1982 and Trivers 1985:363, 381.

4. Family Niches

1. Plomin and Daniels (1987) review the research on sibling differences in personality. See also Scarr and Grajek 1982; Loehlin et al. 1990; Loehlin 1992; Dunn and Plomin 1991; Plomin et al. 1991. The distinction between the "shared" and "nonshared" family environment is problematic in practice because it is not possible to measure the nonshared family environment directly. For this reason, the nonshared environment is judged to be whatever remains after genetic factors, the shared environment, and errors in measurement have been assessed. On this methodological issue, see the 31 critiques that follow Plomin and Daniels's (1987) review of the relevant literature, especially those by Bock and Zimowski, Eysenck, Hartung, Hay, and Jensen. Despite problems of measurement, the nonshared environment has far more influence on personality than was previously suspected, as most researchers now agree.

For evidence that sibling differences increase with time, see Loehlin et al. 1990:227–29; Loehlin 1992:83, 100–101; McCartney, Harris, and Bernieri 1990.

2. Darwin 1958 [1976]:42–42. In their book *Separate Lives,* Judy Dunn and Robert Plomin (1990) have noted many cases of writers and other intellectuals who differed strikingly from their siblings.

3. Bruhns 1873, 1:46.

4. Humboldt and Bonpland 1814–1829; Bruhns 1873, 1:351.

5. Parton, 1881, 1:236.

6. Darwin 1858 [1876]:121.

7. Darwin 1985– ,7:102.

8. Mayr 1963:33. The term "sibling species" was coined by Mayr (1942).

9. Grant 1986:314–47.

10. Mayr 1963:68. Following Darwin's evolutionary logic, Gause (1934) tested and confirmed the principle of competitive exclusion experimentally with microorganisms. His findings exerted a major influence on David Lack (1947), to whom we owe much of the modern understanding of Darwin's Galápagos finches.

11. The term "character displacement" was coined by Brown and Wilson (1956), who drew on Lack's (1947) evidence regarding Darwin's finches.

12. A Darwinian perspective on the family is consistent with family-systems theory, which has long emphasized the uniqueness of individuals, conflicting interests, and the importance of family "subsystems" (Bossard and Boll 1956; Hoffman 1981; Minuchiun 1985). What is missing from a family-systems approach, however, is the evolutionary logic that underlies the interlocking pattern of adaptive responses.

13. Siblings share much more than half of their genes with one another (as well as with other members of the species). On average, relatively *novel* genes will reside in half of all siblings. In dealing with the evolution of new behaviors or traits, these novel genes are the ones that generally matter (Wright 1994:158).

14. Buss and Plomin 1984; Thomas and Chess 1977; Chess and Thomas 1986; Kagan 1984, 1994.

15. Zuckerman 1987.

16. Lykken 1982; Lykken et al. 1992.
17. See Hartung 1987 and Lykken 1987.
18. Lykken et al. 1992:1572.
19. Lykken et al. 1992:1565.
20. See, for example, Tooby and Cosmides 1990a; Buss 1991; MacDonald 1991, 1995.
21. MacDonald 1991, 1995.
22. Zuckerman 1990.
23. Pinker 1994.
24. Maccoby and Jacklin 1974:243–46; McDonald 1994. Some of the personality differences distinguishing firstborns and laterborns may be linked to analogous physiological mechanisms that are context dependent and also reflect gene-environment interactions. Among women, individual differences in social dominance are associated with differing levels of sex hormones (Cashdan 1994).
25. Alexander 1995.
26. The importance of "open" genetic programs, and the role of extended parental care, have been duly emphasized for humans by Mayr (1976:23).
27. Owing to what may be termed "sib selection," personality traits in the human gene pool are likely to have evolved at different rates in firstborns and laterborns. Our species probably owes more of its capacity for Conscientiousness to firstborns than to laterborns. Openness to Experience is a laterborn attribute, and selection for this trait was probably more intense within this sibling group. In the course of evolution, the genetic results of "sib selection" would have been continuously pooled through mating, making new behavioral strategies available to future generations.
28. Darwin 1958 [1876]:76–77.
29. On the role of chance events in life, see Dunn and Plomin 1990:135–50, who cite Darwin's voyage as an example. Many seemingly "chance" events are not as accidental as they seem, including Darwin's voyage (Chapter 4, Figure 4.3).
30. In ancestral environments, the "family unit" was more extended than it is in modern societies. This circumstance has made certain features of modern family life, including perhaps birth-order differences, more important than they once were. Still, the basic story of personality development, viewed psychodynamically, is probably much the same. Sibling rivalry involves the effort to maximize investment from any parentlike individual. Similarly, behavioral strategies for dealing with status hierarchies are just as useful within peer groups as they are within the family.
31. Daniels 1986.
32. Koch 1960; Dunn and Plomin 1990:63–64, 74–75.
33. Daly and Wilson 1988a. There is compelling evidence that humans discriminate very finely about matters of social justice and reciprocity (Cosmides 1989; Glantz and Pearce 1989).
34. Stephen 1888:20.
35. Stephen 1888:20–21.
36. Forster 1874:23; also quoted in Dunn and Plomin 1990:80, who cite the example of Charles Dickens as evidence for the importance of parental discrimination.

37. Forster 1874:24. See also MacKenzie 1979:11, 80.
38. Forster 1874:16.
39. Forster 1874:17.
40. Johnson 1977:349.
41. Ackroyd 1990:5.
42. Plomin and Daniels 1987:7; Dunn and Plomin 1990:79.
43. The work of Tooby and Cosmides (1990a,b, 1992), who have emphasized the "domain-specific" nature of many cognitive mechanisms, provides an important Darwinian framework for conceptualizing many aspects of family life.
44. Dunn and Munn 1985.
45. Dunn and Plomin 1990:88.
46. Parton 1881, 1:29.
47. Brandes 1930, 1:27.
48. Brandes 1930, 1:27.
49. Besterman 1969:31.
50. Parton 1881, 1:51, 28.
51. Parton 1881, 1:51.
52. Schachter et al. 1976.
53. A follow-up study, using judgments by mothers of 325 siblings, confirmed these results about sibling deidentification (Schachter 1982). It must be cautioned that Schachter and her colleagues studied perceived dissimilarities between siblings, not actual dissimilarities (Scarr and Grajek 1982:371).
54. Schachter 1982:148.
55. Freud 1900, 4:250–56; 1916/1917, 15:204–7; 16:333–34.
56. Mayr (1963:66–88, 248) reviews this evidence, including cases of ecological diversification *within* species (polymorphism and sexual differences); see also Gause 1934; Brown and Wilson 1956; Schluter, Price, and Grant 1985; Grant 1986.
57. An intriguing finding supports this conclusion about sibling strategies to exploit differences between parents. A study of the three oldest siblings in 70 families found that first and second children were the most disparate in their interests *when the parents also differed strongly in their interests.* Under such circumstances, the jump pair (the first and third siblings) were more similar, in accordance with the typical even-odd trend in sibling differences (Verger 1968).
58. *Technical information for Figure 4.1:* For birth rank and scientific radicalism during liberal debates, $r=.19$ ($df=1/1,133$, $t=6.38$, $p<.0001$). For sibship size and scientific radicalism, $r=-.11$ ($df=1/1,133$, $t=-3.56$, $p<.001$). For the interaction between birth rank and sibship size, $r=-.09$ ($df=1/1,133$, $t=-3.05$, $p<.005$). This interaction effect suggests that laterborn radicalism is largely in response to firstborn conservatism. As family size increases, younger siblings become further removed in age from the most conservative member of their sibship. This circumstance reduces the motives for extreme radicalism. There is significant heterogeneity in these findings, expressed in the interaction between birth order and sibship size. In large sibships, lastborns exhibit increased heterogeneity relative to middleborns and especially relative to firstborns (partial $r=.14$, $df=6/1,130$, $F=3.95$, $p<.01$; based on the two-way interaction effect, as determined by Levine's test for the equality of variances). In other words, the lastborn niche is the least predictable (especially in large lower-class families).

59. The Trivers-Willard hypothesis that lower-class parents will favor daughters over sons is a good example of an evolutionary hypothesis that is *not* self-evident. This hypothesis has received considerable empirical support (Trivers and Willard 1973; see also Voland 1984; Boone 1986; Hrdy 1987, 1992; Gaulin and Robbins 1991; Wright 1994:173). Darwinian theory has led to a number of findings about cognition that were not previously known. For example, humans make certain logical errors when thinking in abstract terms, but they do not make such errors when it comes to concrete matters of social reciprocity (Cosmides 1987).

60. Gould and Lewontin (1979) have pointed out the dangers of "Panglossian" thinking in evolutionary biology. Just because something exists does not mean that it is adaptive. Although it is ironic to see orthodox Darwinian theory being compared with the philosophy of Dr. Pangloss (which Darwinism overturned), Gould and Lewontin make an important point.

61. Birembaut 1971:350.

62. Huxley 1887:185 (on Élie de Beaumont and evolution); Marcou 1896, 1:110–11 (on Élie de Beaumont and glaciation theory).

63. Greene 1982:94.

64. Butts 1976:292.

65. Darwin 1887, 2:261 n.

66. In addition to 38 scientists cited by Robert Merton (1973:286–324) in his classic article on priority disputes, I have analyzed another 162 individuals indexed in the *Dictionary of Scientific Biography* under the heading "priority disputes."

67. For birth order and involvement in priority disputes, r=–.22 (χ^2[1] =6.06, N=120, p<.01). This test contrasts individuals who were deeply concerned about priorities, and aggressively involved in disputes about them, with individuals reported to be "unconcerned" with priority or "ambivalent" about claiming them. I have based these categories on Merton's (1973:288, 305, 318) useful distinctions.

68. Cohen 1974:84.

69. Merton 1973:314–25.

70. Cohen 1974:84.

71. Shapin and Schaffer 1985:128–39.

72. Moore 1944:92.

73. Moore 1944:134. Shapin and Schaffer's (1985) intriguing thesis about "civility" and the emergence of the scientific method illustrates the problem of basing broad claims about history on modest biographical examples selected without adequate controls for sibling differences. Biagioli (1992) makes the same methodological error when he argues that differences in the national political styles of England and Italy during this same period shaped the scientific styles of Boyle and Galileo. He asserts: "The striking difference between Galileo's aggressive style and Boyle's polite one is a result of the different [social] contexts framing the 'civilizing process'" (1992:37). Really? Galileo, a firstborn, has been described as "pugnacious" and "quick to anger" (Drake 1970:66; 1972:247–48), personality traits that are typical of individuals having this birth order. Convincing proof that Italian scientists were less civil as a whole than British scientists can only be established by comparing Italian firstborns, like Galileo, with British firstborns like Newton; or alternatively, by comparing Italian laterborns like Robert Bellarmine with British laterborns like Boyle. For the record, Bellarmine, who receives an entry in the *Dic-*

tionary of Scientific Biography, has been described as a person whose "temperament was at once gentle and gay" and who found dealing with controversy to be "uncongenial" (McMullin 1970: 587). The kinds of sociocultural claims made by Shapin and Schaffer (1985) and Biagioli (1992, 1993) might well have something to them, but the evidence they offer does not prove their case and also has a much simpler explanation in terms of within-family differences.

74. Bartlett 1955:266.
75. Williams 1965:160.
76. Williams 1971:527; see also Merton 1973:288.
77. Williams 1965:160.
78. Gillispie 1978:347.
79. Gillispie 1978:347.
80. Wallace 1905, 1:363.
81. Darwin 1985– , 7:107; letter of 18 June 1858.
82. Darwin 1985– , 7:117–18.
83. Darwin and Wallace 1859 [1858].
84. For the phrase "delicate situation," see Leonard Huxley 1901, 1:500. For Wallace's response, see Darwin 1985– , 7:166; Alfred Russel Wallace to Joseph Hooker, letter of 6 October 1858. It is worth noting that Darwin's friends were quick to protect his interests without bothering to consult Wallace in the matter. (See also Brackman 1980.) Given this fact, Wallace's amiable response is all the more remarkable.
85. Darwin 1887, 2:309; letter of 18 May 1860.
86. Darwin 1887, 3:121.
87. Merton 1973:289.
88. On multiple interests and openness to experience, see McCrae and Costa 1985:163–66.
89. Weiner 1994:287.
90. On convergent and divergent thinking, see Guilford 1957, 1959; Getzels and Jackson 1962; Hudson 1966.

Considerable research has been conducted on the topic of birth order and divergent thinking, with conflicting results (Ernst and Angst 1983:150–53). As the discussion in the text tries to make clear, the relationship is complex because it is mediated by birth order, sibship size, age gaps between siblings, and social class. That laterborns are "divergent thinkers"—in the sense of being unconventional—is overwhelmingly substantiated by the evidence I have presented in chapters 2 and 3. Divergent thinking is best conceptualized as a facet of openness to experience on the Big Five personality dimensions (McCrae 1994:256).

91. These data are based on the fields of expertise listed for each scientist in the *Dictionary of Scientific Biography,* Marquis's *World Who's Who in Science,* and various national biographies.
92. Because most scientific fields have subfields, assessing the number of fields in which scientists have done significant work depends on the level of analysis. I have coded scientific careers in a *consistent* manner in terms of contributions to 15 general fields, such as mathematics, physics, medicine, and physiology. I count research in uncommon fields, such as oceanography and meteorology, in a separate category for "other" research.

93. For the relationship between eminence and number of fields in which scientists made significant contributions, r=.24 (df=1/2,258, t=11.53, p<.0001). Conditioned on this linear trend, there is also a significant quadratic trend. Eminence was achieved most *efficaciously* by specialization or by extreme diversification. In the middle of the distribution, people received relatively less distinction for their efforts at diversification (r=.06, df=1/2,258, t=2.83, p<.005).

94. For number of scientific interests and birth rank, r=.09 (df=1/780, t=2.42, p<.02). When sibship size is also considered, this relationship includes a quadratic trend: Middle children have fewer scientific interests than firstborns or lastborns (r=.07, df=1/780, t=2.08, p<.05). For the linear and quadratic trends combined, r=.13 (df=2/780, F=6.36, p<.005).

These and other effect sizes relating to scientific interests are small, but collectively they add up. In addition to being tailored to the exigencies of family niches, career strategies are obviously influenced by many other considerations, foremost among which are cognitive abilities.

95. For social class and number of scientific interests, r=.08 (df=1/742, t=2.32, p<.05).

96. For scientific interests and sibship size, r=.10 (df=1/688, t=2.67, p<.01).

97. For the three-way interaction between birth order, social class, and family size, as they relate to number of scientific interests, the partial r=.08 (df=1/742, t=2.29, p<.05). The two-way interaction between birth order and family size is also significant (partial r=.07, df=1/742, t=1.99, p<.05). These findings are related to the concept of resource dilution, which has sometimes been used to explain birth-order effects in eminence and achievement (Powell and Steelman 1990; Travis and Kohli 1995).

98. [Anna Freud] Bernays 1940:337.

99. [Anna Freud] Bernays 1940:337.

100. One intriguing manifestation of Rule 4 ("*Whenever expedient, disregard Rules 1–3 and specialize*") involves a three-way interaction effect between birth order, social class, and general research domain (the physical versus the biological sciences). When firstborns sought to *generalize* in a particular science (as upper-class firstborns did in physics), laterborn scientists from the same social class opted to *specialize* in that science. In this maze of crisscrossing career strategies, there is one invariant: Whatever firstborns did, laterborns did the opposite (partial r=.11, df=1/697, t=2.88, p<.005).

101. *Technical information for Figure 4.2:* For the quadratic trend in number of scientific fields by birth order, controlled for sibship size, r=.07 (df=1/780, t=2.08, p<.05). The quadratic trends in Figure 4.2 are similar to those reported by Runco (1987) in a study of divergent thinking. To the extent that broad interests in science reflect divergent thinking, Figure 4.2 illustrates why studies on this subject often conflict. In two-child families, the secondborn is divergent. In three-child families, the secondborn is convergent (and surrounded by two divergent siblings). Because the merits of divergence are keyed to family size (and resources), studies of divergent thinking need to control for birth rank, sibship size, and social class. Such controls are almost totally lacking in the extant research literature.

Age gaps between siblings affect divergent thinking, mostly in interaction with birth order and sibship size. When firstborns do not have a closely spaced sibling (defined here as less than four years apart), they cease their modest efforts to diversify and retreat into specialization. Under the same circumstance, laterborns diversify strongly (for the two-way interaction effect between birth order and age gaps, the partial r=.20 [df=2/441, F=9.36, p<.001]).

Differences in family size modify the last pattern. In small families, a small age gap is conducive to diversification. In large families, the opposite is true: closely spaced siblings specialize and distantly spaced siblings are the most diversified (partial r=.10, df=1/441, t=2.17, p<.05). This last tendency is especially pronounced among laterborns (for this three-way interaction effect, the partial r=.15, df=2/441, t=2.32, p<.005).

To sum up: Age gaps function in much the same manner that social class does. An individual without a sibling close in age can generally count on greater parental investment, so the attractiveness of diversification is greater under these circumstances. In general, laterborns diversify whenever it is both *expedient and practical.*

102. On birth order and intellectual achievement, see Ernst and Angst 1983: 29–69. In my own sample of scientists, the correlation between birth order and eminence is –.08 (df=1/1,993, t=–3.69, p<.001). The trend is significantly curvilinear, with firstborns and lastborns being the most eminent (r=.12, df=2/1,588, F=10.80, p<.0001). Controlled for social class and family size, the linear correlation is –.04 (df=1/719, t=–0.97, p<.34). Although firstborns are not overrepresented among *eminent* scientists, they are overrepresented among *scientists as a whole* (controlled for family size, based on the Greenwood-Yule [1914] rule). Thus birth order influences who becomes a scientist, but not how eminent scientists become.

103. For the two-way interaction effect between birth order and field of specialization (the physical versus the life sciences), as they relate to scientific eminence, the partial r=.09 (df=1/697, t=2.41, p<.02).

104. Based on the measure of eminence I have employed, which includes 19 biographical indicators (15 of which are based on the work of Simonton [1984c]), Darwin was the fifth most eminent scientist in my sample—and the most eminent biologist. Other individuals among the top ten, in order of eminence, are (1) Newton, (2) Galileo, (3) Descartes, (4) Copernicus, (6) Kepler, (7) Lavoisier, (8) Pascal, (9) Huygens, and (10) Leibniz. Among biologists, Cuvier ranks 12, Lamarck 15, Harvey 17, and Linnaeus 20. Other figures discussed in this chapter include Laplace (ranked 13), Faraday (14), Davy (16), Freud (21), Franklin (27), Humboldt (29), Voltaire (31), and Mendel (52). At the level of individuals, attempts to assess eminence involve a subjective element. These rankings should therefore be taken with a grain of salt. Personally, I would rate Darwin higher than Descartes. I would also put Darwin ahead of Copernicus, whose originality was confined to a single field. With a ranking of 21, Freud seems overrated by these measures, which largely reflect space accorded scientists in biographical dictionaries.

105. For the two-way interaction effect between birth order and social class, as they relate to scientific eminence, the partial r=.07 (df=1/1,162, t=2.46, p<.02). Birth order is also significantly related to eminence: firstborns are more eminent than laterborns (partial r=–.10, df=1/1,162, t=–3.46, p<.001). For social class, the trend is not statistically significant. In addition to these effects, there is a four-way interaction effect between birth order, social class, field of specialization (physics

versus biology), and number of research fields, as they relate to scientific eminence. In general, firstborns and laterborns became eminent through different career strategies, which were in turn significantly different by social class (partial r=.09, df=1/723, t=2.44. p<.02; controlled for sibship size, all main effects, and all lower-order interaction effects). One of the three-way effects is also significant: relative to firstborns, laterborns were more likely to become eminent through specialization in physics or through diversification in biology (partial r=.13, df=1/723, t=3.50, p<.001).

106. Expressed in terms of eminence per unit of "family resources" (represented as a ratio between social class and sibship size), eminence involves a two-way interaction effect between ordinal position and number of fields pursued. Middle children were unusually adept at becoming eminent by pursuing only one scientific field. By comparison, firstborns and youngest children excelled in the pursuit of multiple fields (partial r=.12, df=4/686, F=2.56, p<.05). In addition, there is a three-way interaction effect between ordinal position, number of fields pursued, and type of science—physical versus life sciences (partial r=.14, df=4/686, F=3.62, p<.01). Middle children were most likely to become eminent if they pursued one field in the *physical sciences.* Firstborns were adept at becoming eminent by pursuing two fields, also in the *physical sciences.* Lastborns excelled at becoming eminent in three or more fields, especially in the *life sciences.*

The ability to become eminent via specialization involves a curious "odd-even" effect by birth rank. In addition to secondborns, scientists in birth ranks four, six, eight, and ten were significantly better at achieving eminence through specialization than scientists whose birth ranks were first, third, fifth, seventh, or ninth. For this odd-even effect, r=.09 (df=1/750, t=2.35, p<.02; computed as a focused contrast, and conditioned on the linear trend for number of fields pursued). I would not have looked for these zigzagging patterns without the impetus of G. William Skinner (1992), who found similar patterns in political attitudes within Chinese families.

107. Iltis 1932:40.

108. Iltis 1932:95.

109. McCrae and Costa 1985:166. On risk taking, social status, and reproductive success, see Buss 1994:201.

110. Longstreth 1970.

111. For boxing and parachute jumping, see Sutton-Smith and Rosenberg 1970: 20–22. For other sports, see Nisbett 1968. Nisbett's findings have been replicated in another, smaller sample, controlled for social class and sibship size (Casher 1977).

112. In his survey of a thousand eminent figures, Harris (1964:17–18) found that younger sons were overrepresented in only two fields: military leaders and explorers.

113. Bruhns 1873, 1:400–401.

114. My assessment of travel is based on a 5-point scale. People received a score of zero if they failed to travel outside of their own country. Travel to a neighboring country (from England to France, for example) earned an individual 1 point. I assigned 2 points for moderate oceanic or land travel (such as from western Europe to North America). Individuals traveling to faraway places (from England to

Malaysia, for example) received 3 points, as did individuals making more than two transatlantic trips. Finally, those individuals who engaged in particularly extensive travel, including circumnavigation of the globe, earned 4 points.

115. *Technical information for Figure 4.3:* The following tests are all controlled for social class and family size. For ordinal position and world travel, partial r=.11 (df=1/664, t=2.76, p<.01). Travel was more common in large sibships, but the trend is not significant. Social class interacts significantly with sibship size: travel was most common in large lower-class families and least common in large upper-class families (partial r=.11, df=2/664, F=3.92, p<.05).

In addition to the linear trend in world travel by birth order, there is a quadratic trend by birth rank (r=.13, df=1/642, t=3.36, p<.001). Travel peaks among thirdborns.

Contrasted with firstborns, only children and laterborn eldest sons were together more likely to engage in world travel (r=.08, df=1/441, t=1.71, p<.05 [one-tailed test]).

Age gaps between siblings affect the likelihood of world travel, but only in conjunction with birth order. A large age gap (more than four years) causes firstborns to travel less but laterborns to travel more (r=.11, df=1/349, t=2.14, p<.05). Family size modifies this relationship, which is especially true in large families. In small families, travel increases moderately with a large age gap (for this three-way effect, the partial r=.13, df=1/349, t=2.54, p<.05). These interaction effects involving age gaps and world travel parallel those associated with scientific diversity, discussed earlier in this chapter.

Controlled for ordinal position, social class, and family size, the partial correlation of world travel with date of birth is .38 (df=1/664, t=10.62, p<.0001). The influence of ordinal position on world travel is just as great among twentieth-century scientists as it is among scientists in previous centuries.

116. Darwin 1958 [1876]:44.
117. Bruhns 1873, 1:27
118. Darwin 1958 [1876]:68.
119. Darwin 1985– , 1:126.
120. Blunt 1971:102; see also p. 117.
121. Bourdier 1972a:356.
122. E. Agassiz 1885, 2:635.
123. Wallace 1905, 1:282.
124. Wallace 1905, 1:361–63; McKinney 1972:131.

125. The correlation between world travel and support for Darwinism is .15 (df=1/413, t=2.99, p<.005). The partial correlation, controlled for birth order, is .07 (df=1/413, t=1.55, p<.13). In the reception of 23 liberal theories in science, world travel *is* a significant predictor of acceptance of new theories, controlled for birth order (r=.08, df=1/787, t=2.20, p<.03).

126. For this "cubic" trend in world travel by relative birth rank, r=.13 (df=1/664, t=3.47, p<.001). There is also a significant "odd-even" effect in world travel by son rank. Among laterborns, odd-numbered sons were more likely to travel than even-numbered sons. It would appear that travel by the first laterborn son made this option less attractive to the next son, which in turn made the same option more attractive to the third son, and so on (r=.07, df=1/864, t=1.98, p<.05).

127. In support of the intimate relationship between world travel and the goal of finding a family niche, travel is significantly related to number of scientific interests, even when travel itself is not counted as an interest (r=.14, df=1/663, t=3.72, p<.001).

Travel (or rather the psychological inclination that underlies it) interacts with birth order and sibship size in determining number of scientific interests. Younger siblings who engaged in any form of transoceanic travel had more interests than those who did not travel extensively (for the two-way effect, the partial r=.17, df=2/663, F=9.76, p<.001). The same trend is found among people from large families who traveled extensively (for the two-way effect, the partial r=.12, df=1/663, t=3.01, p<.005). The three-way interaction is also significant: scientific diversity was greatest among younger siblings from large families, especially if they traveled (partial r=.15, df=2/663, F=7.74, p<.001). Darwin and Wallace are good examples of this last trend.

Odds ratios provide a good way of summing up the evidence on travel and diverse interests, interpreted as openness to experience. Contrasting scientists whose combined scores on both variables place them above the median with those whose scores place them below the median, lastborns were 4.4 times more likely than firstborns to score above the median. Other odds ratios, with firstborns as the comparison group (1.0), are 2.9 for only children, 1.3 for middleborns in the first half of their sibship, 1.8 for middleborns in the second half of their sibship (but not in the last third), and 3.8 for middleborns in the last third of their sibship (but not lastborn).

128. Sulloway 1991b.

129. Darwin 1879, 1958 [1876], and 1877.

130. Darwin 1958 [1876]:28.

5. Developmental Glitches

1. See Bowlby 1958, 1960, 1969–1980, 1988; Ainsworth 1967; Main 1977; Rutter 1977, 1979, 1981. For a useful review of the literature, including an overview of Bowlby's career, see Karen 1994.

2. Bowlby began his psychoanalytic training at a time when the profession had become an established movement dominated by firstborns (see Chapter 2, Table 2). A younger son, he rebelled against the prevailing orthodoxy. Bowlby was rewarded by the movement's indifference to his ideas, which soon turned to hostility. It is worth noting that Bowlby (1969) fully appreciated the non-Darwinian assumptions of psychoanalysis, a topic that I have elaborated on elsewhere (1979b, 1991b).

3. See Hrdy 1977; Hausfater and Hrdy 1984.

4. Harlow 1958.

5. In assessing parent-offspring conflict, raters employed a 7-point scale. The mean correlation between three independent judges is .78. The *effective* reliability of multiple ratings is .90. I deal with the *validity* of the evidence regarding parent-offspring relationships in Appendix 9, Technical Discussion 3. Parent-offspring conflict, as measured in this study, is not synonymous with standard measures of attachment. Still, the two constructs are closely related.

6. *Technical information for Figure 5.1:* Controlled for birth order, conflict with parents exerts a significant influence on scientific radicalism (r=–.16, df=1/675, t=–4.21, p<.001, for liberal scientific controversies; the sign of the correlation is negative because high parent-offspring conflict is denoted by a low score on the parental relationship scale). Controlled for birth order and parent-offspring conflict, the interaction effect is also significant (r=.08, df=1/675, t=2.07, p<.05). For birth order as a main effect, the partial correlation is .22 (df=1/675, t=5.90, p<.0001).

My findings about birth order and parent-offspring conflict agree with an intriguing study of philosophical attitudes. Researchers examined 27 pairs of brothers (all Harvard undergraduates from two-child sibships). Differences by birth order were found only when individuals identified strongly with the father. Non-identifiers were similar in their world views (Stein, Stein, and Kagan 1970). These researchers did not assess identification with mothers.

7. In 1975 I informed Freud's daughter Anna about the relationship between birth order and scientific radicalism, including its role in the early reception of psychoanalysis. She played down these findings with the remark: "It's not a person's birth order that counts but how much they are loved" (conversation at 20 Maresfield Gardens, London, in June 1975). Both considerations are important, but, even in Freud's own movement, birth order is a better predictor of revolutionary personality than is oedipal conflict.

8. A good example is Erikson's *Young Man Luther* (1958). For other instances, see the useful review by Stannard (1980).

9. On the psychoanalytic confusion between parent-offspring conflict, which is consistent with Darwinian theory, and oedipal conflict, which is not, see Trivers (1985:146–47), and especially the insightful treatment by Daly and Wilson (1990).

10. In liberal scientific controversies, the correlation between openness to innovation and parent-offspring conflict is similar for paternal and maternal conflict. For paternal conflict, r=–.14 (df=1/649, t=–3.67, p<.001). For maternal conflict, r=–.13 (df=1/538, t=–3.12, p<.005). It is also worth noting that the relationship between father-son conflict and mother-son conflict is positive, not negative (r=.38, df=1/575, t=9.74, p<.0001). Freudians might counter that conflict with parents is largely unconscious and not therefore accessible using nonclinical evidence. This logic, to continue the psychoanalytic argument, would explain why parent-offspring conflict appears to be less influential than birth order. This argument is refuted by the data I have already presented. The high level of support that laterborns typically manifest toward scientific innovation makes it virtually impossible for parental conflict, *in any psychic form,* to explain more "variance" than birth order.

11. For the interaction between birth order and openness to experience, as they relate to parent-offspring conflict (partial r=.11, df=1/418, t=2.22, p<.05). Openness has been assessed in terms of openness to scientific innovation, travel, and broad interests (z-scored and averaged together). This measure of openness is significantly correlated with parent-offspring conflict (partial r=–.15, df=1/418, t=–3.04, p<.005). These findings are controlled for sibship size. Larger sibships ex-

perience less parent-offspring conflict (partial r=.10, df=1/418, t=2.03, p<.05). Controlled for these main effects and the interaction effect between birth order and openness, laterborns experience more conflict with parents than do firstborns (partial r=.11, df=1/418, t=2.19, p<.05).

12. For relevant evidence, see the studies by Singer (1971) and Smith (1971).
13. See Burkhalter 1965:17–27, 105–6.
14. Darwin 1985– , 8:542; see also 9:45–48.
15. Burkhalter 1965:18.
16. Burkhalter 1965:18.
17. Cohen 1985:144–45.
18. Koestler 1959:229.
19. Koestler 1959:229; see also Gingerich (1973:289) and Caspar (1962:36–38, 252) for these details.
20. Koestler 1959:230.
21. Koestler 1959:236.
22. Based on the "family dynamics model" of radicalism that I present in Chapter 8, Kepler's predicted probability of supporting radical causes is 65 percent. Compared with other firstborns, this predicted probability places him in the 97th percentile.
23. Based on the "family dynamics model" of radicalism presented in Chapter 8, Newton's probability of supporting innovation is 60 percent, which places him in the 89th percentile for all firstborns.
24. Westfall 1980:53–55.
25. Westfall 1980:53.
26. In his psychoanalytic *Portrait of Isaac Newton* (1968), Frank Manuel has argued that Newton spent the rest of his life expressing his rage over the loss of his mother by targeting various surrogates, such as Robert Hooke and Gottfried Leibniz. Westfall asks about this provocative thesis: "Is it . . . true? It appears to me that we lack entirely any means of knowing. It is plausible; it is equally plausible that it is misguided. I am unable to see how empirical evidence can be used to decide on it, one way or the other" (1980:53n.). I agree. Manuel's hypothesis *is* testable using population data, but this is another matter entirely.
27. Millhauser 1959:16.
28. Chambers 1872:216.
29. In general, laterborn eldest sons are similar to other laterborns in their radicalism. The principal exception to this rule involves secondborns, but only in large families. Under these conditions, being an eldest son promotes conservatism. This finding involves a three-way interaction effect between birth rank, son rank, and sibship size (partial r=.11, df=1/435, t=2.31, p<.03; for laterborns involved in liberal scientific controversies). None of the main effects or the two-way interaction effects are significant.
30. Durant and Durant 1965:448.
31. Simon 1963:46.
32. Asprey 1986:47.
33. Durant and Durant 1965:441.
34. Asprey 1986:47; Durant and Durant 1965:441.

35. Reported by Frederick the Great's elder sister, Wilhelmina, margravine of Bayreuth, and quoted by Durant and Durant (1965:441).
36. A number of studies have shown that homosexuality is associated with being laterborn, at least among males (Blanchard and Sheridan 1992; Zucker and Blanchard 1994; Blanchard et al. 1995; Blanchard and Bogaert 1996). The effect size in these studies is generally small ($r<.10$). One important psychological reason why laterborns might tend to become homosexuals is that they are more open to experience and hence willing to act on their unconventional sexual inclinations. For particularly radical behaviors, the effect size for birth order's influence on openness to experience is substantial ($r\approx.40$). An effect size of .40, applied to 10 percent of the population, would produce a net effect size of $r=.04$, which is about half the *observed* correlation between birth order and homosexuality. The fact that homosexuality appears to be correlated with number of older brothers, but not with number of older sisters, is consistent with an immunological explanation of homosexuality, based on maternal antigens to previous male fetuses (Blanchard and Bogaert 1996). Still, these findings are also consistent with the influence of birth order and sex of siblings on gender-related personality traits (Chapter 3, Fig. 3.2). More research is needed to decide between these alternative explanations, which may both have merit.
37. Durant and Durant 1965:448.
38. Asprey 1986:404.
39. Asprey 1986:1.
40. Koestler 1971:19.
41. Scrimshaw 1984:458; Daly and Wilson 1988a:46.
42. *Technical information for Figure 5.2:* For the quadratic trend, computed as two inverted contrasts to reflect the interaction effect, the partial $r=.08$ ($df=1/734$, $t=2.15$, $p<.05$; for liberal scientific debates only). For birth order, the partial $r=.24$ ($df=1/734$, $t=6.56$, $p<.0001$).

Helen Koch (1955a, 1956a) found the greatest personality differences to be associated with an age difference of 24 to 48 months. Harris and Howard (1968) and Hayden (1973) have also documented the quadratic relationship between age spacing and personality differences.
43. For birth order and a composite measure of openness to experience (openness to scientific innovation, broad interests, and travel), $r=.30$ ($df=1/756$, $t=8.61$, $p<.0001$). For the quadratic trend by birth interval, computed as two inverted contrasts to reflect the interaction effect, $r=.23$ ($df=1/756$, $t=6.55$, $p<.0001$). For the difference between this quadratic trend in openness to experience and the quadratic trend for scientific stance, $z=4.36$, $p<.0001$. There is also a linear trend, by birth interval, in the relationship with openness to experience ($r=.12$, $df=1/756$, $t=3.39$, $p<.001$). Social attitudes are also a good indicator of openness. In my sample of scientists, social attitudes are correlated with birth order and age gaps between siblings in the expected manner (see Chapter 9).
44. In terms of this composite measure of openness to experience, the top ten ranking scientists are (1) Athanasius Kircher; (2) Francis Galton; (3) Charles Darwin, who is tied with Alfred Russel Wallace and Alexander von Humboldt; (6) Benjamin Franklin; (7) Robert Hooke; (8) Reginald Daly (a geophysicist whose devotion to field work took him all over the world); (9) geologist Frank Deben-

ham, who accompanied Robert Scott to the South Pole; and (10) philosopher-psychologist John Dewey. All ten of these individuals are laterborns. Alfred Wegener is ranked 11th. The youngest of four children, he pioneered the theory of continental drift and lost his life on the Greenland ice cap trying to resupply a scientific expedition.

On openness to experience, the median ranking for firstborns places them in the 37th percentile. The median ranking for laterborns places them in the 60th percentile, a substantial difference (r=.25, df=1/1,617, t=10.44, p<.0001). Even after birth order is employed to predict openness, the partial correlation for relative birth rank (from first to last) is also significant (r=.11, df=1/1,312, t=4.02, p<.001). The most open individuals have typically been lastborns, like Galton, Humboldt and Wegener, or near the tail end of their sibship, like Darwin and Wallace. The median ranking for lastborns with a four-year age gap puts them in the 73rd percentile.

Besides birth order and age spacing, sibship size and social class predict broad scientific interests (see Chapter 4, Figure 4.2, and the accompanying text). Firstborns like Freud who score high on this measure (Freud ranks 13th) tend to have grown up in large families in the middle or lower classes.

45. This logic about age gaps between siblings and sibling conflict leads to another conclusion: Younger siblings should be more altruistic toward their older siblings than vice versa, since the older sibling is a better genetic insurance policy. Evidence relating to the Big Five dimension of agreeableness is consistent with this hypothesis (Chapter 3, Table 4).

46. For data on reproductive value with age, see Daly and Wilson 1988a:74. This likelihood function rises steeply until age five. Thereafter the increase in reproductive value is progressively less and peaks at age fifteen. Whether the adjusted costs of having a younger sibling reach a maximum between three and five years of age is something that I have not been able to determine. These adjusted costs will be influenced by the level of family resources, so there is no fixed answer to this question at the purely individual level. Still, almost any crude estimate as to what these adjusted costs would be indicates a maximization of the costs with an age gap between two and six years.

47. The tendency for firstborns to experience greater conflict with parents at three-to-four-year age spacings represents a two-way interaction (r=.18, df=1/269, t=2.95, p<.005). Parent-offspring conflict as a whole follows a quadratic trend, being lowest at middle age spacings (three to four years) (r=.18, df=1/269, t=1.97, p<.05). At close age spacings (less than four years), laterborns experience elevated levels of conflict. This is the interval at which parents in traditional societies are most likely to consider infanticide. When the birth interval is greater than five years, parent-offspring conflict is again elevated. Only children, in particular, manifest greater conflict with parents than do offspring who have siblings. Several explanations are possible for this finding, and I lack the means to decide between them. For example, siblings may direct conflict toward one another rather than toward parents. Conflict with a parent is also more costly as a strategy when there are other siblings in the family. Parent-offspring conflict is significantly lower in large sibships than it is in small ones (r=.17, df=1/406, t=3.41, p<.001).

48. I have calculated these correlations from the data summarized in Plomin

1986:71–74; Plomin, DeFries, and McClearn 1990:383–84; Loehlin 1992:15, 32, 37, 47–68. For fraternal twins, the N is greater than 15,000. For biological siblings, the N is greater than 3,500. For the difference between the two correlations, $z=2.68$ ($p<.005$).

This argument about age gaps between siblings and sibling contrast effects has important methodological implications for research in behavioral genetics. Because sibling contrast effects are different for twins and nontwins, standard estimates of heritability may be affected by the methods typically used to calculate them. Behavioral geneticists have generally ignored this issue.

49. Plomin 1986:236.

50. *Technical information for Figure 5.3:* For birth order as a main effect, $r=.20$ ($df=1/843$, $t=6.10$, $p<.0001$). For the three-way interaction effect between birth order, social class, and age at parental loss, the partial $r=.09$ ($df=2/843$, $F=3.58$, $p<.03$). There are no other significant effects.

The interaction effect in Figure 5.3 holds for a three-way split in social class (upper, middle, and lower classes). Individuals from the middle class follow a pattern that is intermediate between those of the other two classes. The three-way interaction effect in Figure 5.3 is independent of whether the loss involves a father or mother.

Openness to experience (as measured by scientific openness, breadth of interests, and travel) exhibits a similar three-way effect ($r=.08$, $df=2/1{,}050$, $F=3.66$, $p<.03$). This dependent variable manifests a two-way effect involving birth order and age at parental loss (partial $r=.11$, $df=2/1{,}050$, $F=6.07$, $p<.005$). The most open individuals are laterborns who have lost a parent early. Firstborns having the same experience become close-minded.

51. The short-term consequences of parental loss generally include greater closeness on the part of siblings. The long-term consequences vary, depending on the nature of surrogate parenting (Ross and Milgram 1982:243).

52. Bruhns 1873, 1:15.

53. Bruhns 1873, 1:30.

54. Born 1978:7.

55. Born 1978:8.

56. In his scientific work Born was one of the earliest converts to Einstein's theory of special relativity. He was also a strong supporter of the quantum hypothesis and a leader in the development of quantum mechanics. Born's support for these novel theories would be more difficult to understand had he not lost a parent when he was young. Based on the multivariate model that I discuss in Chapter 10, Born's likelihood of supporting these three theories was 61 percent.

57. In contrast to brothers, sisters are regularly thrust into substitute parenting regardless of their social class. Hence some of the effects I am describing here may be true only for males.

58. Absolon 1979–87,1:7. Billroth was initially an opponent of Joseph Lister's new technique of antisepsis. Later, however, he came around and helped to promote the technique in Germany.

59. Ross and Milgram 1982:243. Another study corroborates my assertions about surrogate parenting. In her study of the reception of sociobiology, Flaherty (1980) compared firstborns who admitted to "acting like a domineering parent" toward

their younger siblings with younger siblings who reported "resenting" older siblings for their domineering behavior. In general, firstborns in Flaherty's survey were more supportive of sociobiology than were laterborns, but this difference was *significantly larger* in the subsample reporting conflicts over surrogate parenting (z=1.89, p<.05).

60. For early parental loss and conflict with the surviving parent, r=.15; (df=2/299, F=3.60, p<.03). Conflict is significantly greater among laterborns, independent of parental loss (r=.12, df=1/282, t=2.09, p<.03; controlled for sibship size). Social class also exerts a main effect: conflict is greater in lower-class families, largely due to laterborns.

For the interaction between birth order and parental loss, as they relate to parent-offspring conflict, the partial r=.20 (df=2/299, F=6.37, p<.005). Parental loss also interacts with social class: conflict is much greater after a loss in the lower classes (partial r=.15, df=2/299, F=3.23, p<.05). This two-way effect is most pronounced among laterborns, which is why there is also a significant three-way effect (partial r=.22, df=2/299, F=7.63, p<.001).

61. Here I draw on Bowlby 1990 and Sulloway 1991b.

62. I use the term "repressed" advisedly and in a different manner from the traditional psychoanalytic usage. Bowlby (1988:70–71) has reformulated the concept of repression as "selective exclusion." His concept is much less pretentious than Freud's and explains far less. What it does explain, it explains well.

63. See Bowlby (1990:78) and Raverat (1952:245), on whom he draws for this story. Raverat correctly predicted that "psychologists might get a great deal of fun out of this anecdote."

64. See Bowlby (1990:57, 71) for these details.

65. Darwin 1958 [1876]:28.

66. Darwin 1887, 1:11.

67. Darwin, 1958 [1876]:22.

68. Darwin 1985– , 1:502.

69. For a discussion of the epidemiology of hyperventilation syndrome, and findings that support Bowlby's hypothesis, see Brown et al. 1986. Certain of these findings have been questioned by Champion (1990). See also Guze 1992:28.

I have tested Bowlby's hypothesis that early parental loss undermines self-confidence. To do so, I have assessed his claim in terms of shyness, which tends to be associated with anxiety (Chapter 7). Early parental loss is indeed associated with shyness (partial r=.13, df=2/595, F=5.31, p<.01). In this relationship, parental loss interacts with social class. The general trend is reversed in lower-class families (partial r=.18, df=2/595, F=10.02, p<.005). Becoming the "man of the house," which is more likely to occur in lower-class families, gives firstborns more status and makes laterborns more resentful and hence rebellious. Such contrasting family niches (and associated family dynamics) are not likely to foster shy personalities. The correctness of Bowlby's explanation for Darwin's illness is therefore contingent on multiple aspects of family niches, rather than being true across the board. In particular, Bowlby's explanation would not generally be true for lower-class firstborns.

70. Darwin 1985– , 2:279.

71. Darwin 1903, 1:252; see also Bowlby 1990:6, 240, 377.

72. Darwin 1887, 2:360.
73. Darwin 1958 [1876]:139; see also Fleming 1961.
74. Bowlby 1990:12.
75. Here I offer an interpretation that is different from Bowlby's (1990). He dwelt mostly on Darwin's sensitivity to criticism. My own emphasis is on Darwin's determination to overcome such criticism, even at the expense of anxiety and overwork (Sulloway 1991b).
76. Darwin 1958 [1876]:140, 145; see also Darwin 1903, 2:41.
77. Darwin 1887, 1:149. This is a line from one of Anthony Trollope's novels.
78. Darwin 1887, 1:149.
79. Darwin 1985– , 7:388.
80. Darwin 1859:243–44.
81. Quoted in Mayr 1991b:105.
82. Social class has no influence on scientific radicalism. For liberal scientific debates, r=.01 (df=1/2,173, t=0.31, p=.76). For the sample employed in Figure 5.3, r=.04 (df=1/843, t=1.21, p=.23).

6. Gender

1. Gould 1981.
2. Becker 1986:205.
3. Linn 1986:217.
4. Recent meta-analytic reviews of gender research encompass more than a thousand publications. See Hyde and Linn 1986, and especially Feingold 1994. Still useful is Maccoby and Jacklin's (1974) pioneering survey. This study predates meta-analytic techniques and was criticized on this and other methodological grounds by Block (1976).

The largest gender difference is in physical strength (r≈.67). Substantial gender differences exist only in one cognitive domain, namely the ability to perform mental rotations (r≈.45). Among personality traits, tender-mindedness involves a substantial gender difference (r≈.53). For aggression, the average point biserial correlation is .25 (a moderate difference). Most other personality differences are small: for assertiveness, r≈.15; for conformity, r≈.12. For these statistics, see Becker 1986:199; Linn 1986:218; Feingold 1994:448. The mean correlation for the Big Five personality dimensions is .28. Although I have called some of these psychological differences "small," they are not trivial. As a therapeutic effect, a correlation of .10 is equivalent to increasing the patient's likelihood of surviving a deadly disease from 45 percent to 55 percent.
5. Buss 1994. For differences in the criteria of mate selection by gender, the mean correlation is .20 (Feingold 1994:450).
6. Linn 1986:211.
7. Linn 1986:220; see also Becker 1986.
8. Zimbardo and Leippe 1991:60. For other examples of "gender by situation" interaction effects, see Hyde and Linn 1986; Linn 1986:221.
9. Bragg and Allen (1970) review this literature.
10. *Technical information for Figure 6.1:* The figure combines seven measures of conformity. Four of these measures are derived from Koch (1955b:19–21), and are pooled into a single measure. Another two measures come from Sampson and

Hancock (1967). The final measure is provided by Bragg and Allen (1970). See also Sutton-Smith and Rosenberg (1970:141) for a similar synthesis. (Their Table 9.2 contains several transcription errors.)

The vertical scale in Figure 6.1 records the mean rank order in conformity behavior for each sibling configuration. In two-child families there are eight possible configurations based on birth order, sex, and sibling's sex. For the interaction between birth order and sex of sibling, the partial correlation is .48 (df=1/12, t=1.90, p<.05 [one-tailed test]). This statistical test is based on pooled scores rather than the original data, and the substantially larger *N*s for the original data would increase the statistical significance of these findings. Koch's (1955b) data are not easily incorporated within a comprehensive meta-analytic test, but the other studies can be readily combined by this method. For these other studies, the gender by birth-order interaction is r=.22 (df=1/248, t=3.47, p<.01). The combined correlation for birth order is an equally significant .25, whereas that for gender is only .06, which is not significant. Birth order also interacts with sex of siblings. Laterborns of both sexes are more likely to be nonconforming if their older sibling is a brother (r=.13, df=1/248, t=2.10, p<.05).

11. Bragg and Allen 1970.

12. Koch 1956d.

13. Research shows that girls are more likely than boys to conform to directives from teachers and parents (Maccoby and Jacklin 1974:272). See also Gilligan 1982.

14. On instrumental versus expressive family roles, see Parsons and Bales 1955. On patterns of parental identification among sisters, see Koch 1960:37–38, 100, 103; Sutton-Smith and Rosenberg 1970:145–46.

15. I am not satisfied with the birth-order research on conformity among women. Not enough is known about the *motives* for conforming in experimental circumstances (Sampson and Hancock 1967:406). Perhaps younger sisters of sisters conform to be agreeable (a laterborn trait). In real life, such individuals might be relatively nonconforming about important social issues, although I present historical evidence in this chapter that suggests otherwise. In any event, it is important to keep in mind that psychological experiments tap short-term behavior. In the long run, behavior may be different.

16. Edwards and Klemmack 1973:623–24; see also Hess 1971.

17. Gender differences are significantly smaller than birth-order differences for many psychological attributes, including need for achievement and need for autonomy (Sampson and Hancock 1967). Laterborn males exhibit many traits in common with stereotypical behavior for women, such as being more cooperative, agreeable, flexible, and effeminate. Laterborn females are generally more "feminine" than firstborn females, who tend to be achievement oriented and domineering (see Chapter 3, as well as Koch 1955a:38, and Ernst and Angst 1983: 259–60). See also Maccoby and Jacklin 1974:351.

18. My sample of reformers is based on the 504 individuals listed in *American Reformers,* a biographical dictionary edited by Whitman (1985).

19. For my sample of conservatives, I have drawn on the *Dictionary of American Conservatism* (Filler 1987). In the combined sample, 213 of the 614 individuals (or 35 percent) are women.

20. These five categories of reform emerge clearly from factor analysis of the 61 varieties of reform delineated by Whitman (1985:919–27). A person engaging in one subcategory of reform was likely to engage in another reform within the same subcategory, but not in other types of reforms.

My classification of reform movements is based on multiple criteria, including recruitment patterns by social class, race, religious denomination, gender, and historical period. I have excluded birth order as a criterion of classification, although this precaution makes no difference in the outcome. Factor analysis of these reform movements and their participants indicates a clear-cut conservative/radical dimension as the first factor. The second factor involves gender-related interests and issues.

21. Whitman 1985:xiv.

22. I have represented the category of "radical reformers" as individuals involved in issues dealing with politics, religion, and race relations. Radicalism is scored on a three-point basis: −1 for involvement in conservative causes, 0 for involvement in moderate reforms, and +1 for participation in radical reforms. Three variables are accepted by a multivariate model predicting participation in radical reforms: birth order, social class, and minority racial status. Radical reforms were more common in earlier centuries, so I have included year of birth in the multivariate model. These four predictors continue to be significant even after sibship size, which is not significant, is forced into the model.

I provide here the partial correlations for predictors in this model: For year of birth, $r=-.36$ ($df=1/520$ [the harmonic mean], $t=-8.94$, $p<.0001$); for minority racial status, $r=.22$ ($df=1/520$, $t=5.22$, $p<.0001$); for birth order, $r=.20$ ($df=1/520$, $t=4.58$, $p<.0001$); and for social class, $r=.15$ ($df=1/520$, $t=3.40$, $p<.005$). For the combined model, $R=.47$ (adjusted $R=.46$, $df=4/520$, $F=36.67$, $p<.0001$). For women, treated separately, the correlation of birth order with support for radical reforms is $r=.20$ ($df=1/168$, $t=2.64$, $p<.01$). For gender and radicalism, the partial $r=.04$ ($df=1/532$ [the harmonic mean], $t=1.04$, $p<.30$).

23. "Social underdogs" are here defined as blacks, Jews, people from lower-class backgrounds, and laterborns. See also Lieberman and Reynolds (1978), who employed a similar construct in their survey of anthropologists' attitudes toward the concept of race.

24. For birth order and support for abolition, $r=.16$ ($df=1/356$, $t=2.98$, $p<.001$); this test contrasts support for abolition with support for all other reform movements. The same contrast is significant for women, treated separately ($r=.17$, $df=1/175$, $t=2.28$, $p<.05$). Paralleling these birth-order findings, Sherwood and Nataupsky (1968) have found that firstborn researchers are significantly more likely than laterborns to conclude that blacks have innately inferior IQs. This finding involves the personal opinions of researchers and says nothing about whether races actually differ in intelligence.

25. Hurwitz 1985:781.

26. An "intermediate" child, Tubman's relatively late birth rank can be inferred from the age of her parents at the time of her birth. They were both about forty (Conrad 1943:5, 33, 211).

27. Wrench 1985b:817.

28. Wrench 1985b:817.

29. Conrad 1943:127.

30. For the contrast between women conservatives and reformers, by birth order, r=.18 (df=1/182, t=2.51, p<.02).

31. Filler 1987:294. Schlafly's hero, Barry Goldwater, is also included in my sample of American conservatives. Like Schlafly, Goldwater is a firstborn.

32. Filler 1987:234.

33. Krasno 1985:63.

34. For birth order among women and involvement in gender-incongruent behavior, r=.13 (df=1/175, t=2.30, p<.05). This birth-order effect is based on the contrast between female participation in male-dominated reforms versus female participation in reforms, such as child welfare and women's issues, that have typically preoccupied women. The gender bias of reforms has been assessed as the difference between each reform's sex ratio and the mean sex ratio for all reforms.

35. Reed 1985:381.

36. For birth order and type of reform effort among women, r=.14 (df=1/175, t=1.87, p<.05; one-tailed test). This contrast is based on women participating in reforms divided into two categories, based on the mean social class of the participants (upper or lower). For women specifically crossing class barriers, r=.23 (df=1/47, t=1.66, p<.06, one-tailed test). This contrast is based on an analysis of upper-class women and their support for upper-class versus lower-class reforms.

37. Minority status is here defined as being black, Hispanic, Catholic, or Jewish. Controlling for the significant main effects of minority status and birth order on support for radical causes, the partial correlation for the two-way interaction is –.10 (df=1/344, t=3.69, p<.05, for both sexes, one-tailed test). For women, the partial correlation for the same interaction is –.11 (df=1/180, t=1.52, p<.07, one-tailed test).

38. Wrench 1985a:815.

39. Wrench 1985a:815.

40. See also Chapter 5, where I present related evidence that birth-order effects are disrupted (1) by conflict with parents and (2) by the failure of offspring to identify with parents who are economically unsuccessful. In Chapter 9 I show that firstborns are more likely than laterborns to adopt the political attitudes of their parents.

41. The overrepresentation of firstborn women in the movement for women's rights is indicated by the Greenwood-Yule (1914) rule, which corrects for sibship size (r=.24, χ^2=4.80[1], N=85, p<.05).

42. In understanding firstborn support for women's rights, it must be kept in mind that firstborns possess greater need for achievement than do laterborns (Sampson and Hancock 1967).

43. For the contrast between women involved in women's rights and those who were also involved in political and racial reforms (as they relate to birth order), r=.27 (df=1/85, t=2.63, p<.01). "Personal involvement" is a significant predictor of support for reform. In this connection, I define personal involvement as being either a woman campaigning for women's rights or a black or a Jew fighting for racial rights. Personal involvement also interacts with birth order. Controlled for birth order, gender, and personal involvement as main effects, the interaction between the personal involvement and birth order generates a partial correlation of −.10 (*df*=1/363, t=−1.91, p<.03, one-tailed test). For women considered separately, the partial correlation is −.11 (*df*=1/168, t=1.41, p<.10, one-tailed test).

44. Another 28 women in my sample participated in various "conservative" debates such as eugenics and modern spiritualism. On my definition of "conservative" debates, see Chapter 2, Table 2, and Chapter 14, Figure 14.1.

45. For gender and acceptance of innovation in liberal debates, r=.09 (*df*=1/3,117, t=4.81, p<.0001). Do not be misled by the low correlations involving women in my sample. Because most scientists in my sample are men, it is difficult to obtain large correlations for *any* effect involving women. If there were as many women as men in my sample, the correlation between sex and support would be a whopping .52. Lopsided samples produce lopsided correlations. Odds ratios help to correct for this problem. Women were 1.7 times as likely as men to support liberal scientific innovations.

46. In my sample of scientists, the correlation of gender with relative birth rank (from first to last) is .06 (*df*=1/1,410, t=2.39, p<.02, for participants in liberal debates). This result is confirmed by an analysis of sibship size. Based on the Greenwood-Yule (1914) rule, 26 percent of the women in liberal scientific debates should have been lastborns (45 percent actually came from this birth rank). Another 27 percent of the sample are firstborns with younger siblings, almost exactly the expected proportion (but lower than usual for eminent individuals). Middle children are underrepresented, an outcome that is typical of eminent individuals. Firstborns and lastborns get more attention from parents, which stimulates intellectual ability and motivates them to achieve academically (Altus 1966; Zajonc 1976).

The number of women in my sample who were laterborns and who also grew up with an elder brother (16 of 16) is significantly greater than chance (χ^2=3.66[1], p<.05, for participants in liberal debates [one-tailed test]).

47. In addition, women who became particularly eminent in my sample were more likely to be laterborns than were men who became eminent. This is especially true for women involved in liberal scientific debates (z=2.76, p<.005).

48. Sonnert 1995.

49. Year of birth is correlated with social attitudes in my study (people have become more liberal with time). Comparisons between men and women must control for this fact because the men, on average, have earlier dates of birth than the women. Controlled for year of birth, the women are still more liberal than the men. The partial correlation of gender with social attitudes is .12 (*df*=1/2,125, t=4.84, p<.0001; for women involved in liberal debates). Controlled for year of birth, the partial correlation of gender with parents' social attitudes is .18 (*df*=1/374, t=3.45, p<.001, for participants in liberal debates). I treat the assessment of social attitudes in Chapter 9.

50. For gender and parent-offspring conflict, r=.13 (*df*=1/542, t=2.97, p<.005; women experienced more conflict).

51. The correlation between gender and conflict with mothers is .25 (*df*=1/373, t=4.99, p<.0001); for fathers, the analogous correlation is .02 (*df*=1/459, t=0.75, which is not significant). The difference between the two correlations is itself significant, indicating that women scientists experienced more conflict with their mothers than did men (z=3.24, p<.001). These results about parental conflict agree with Jeanne Block's (1973:524) longitudinal study of sex differences. Women experiencing high levels of parental conflict, Block found, were unconventional and less stereotypically feminine than other women.

52. For firstborn overrepresentation in support of conservative theories (among women), χ^2=4.15[1], N=27, p<.05, based on the Greenwood-Yule (1914) rule. If we combine these two classes of debates in my sample (conservative and liberal), firstborn women were significantly more likely to adopt the conservative stance available to them in each debate (χ^2=7.69 [2], N=47, p<.05, based on the Greenwood-Yule [1914] rule).
53. Grosskurth 1988:39, 73, 76–77.
54. Grosskurth 1988:76.
55. Grosskurth 1988:49.
56. Mead 1972:64.
57. Goertzel, Goertzel, and Goertzel 1978:94, 96.
58. Rensberger 1983:34; Freeman 1983:284.
59. Howard 1984:79.
60. Mead 1928:8; Freeman 1983:83.
61. Interview with Margaret Mead on the BBC (1976), quoted in Freeman 1983:77.
62. Mead 1928:151.
63. Mead 1928:213.
64. Freeman 1983:94.
65. Howard 1984:322.
66. Quoted in Freeman 1983:244.
67. Freeman 1983:244–48.
68. Howard 1984:323.
69. Freeman 1983:289; see also pp. xv and 251.
70. Freeman 1983:289–90.
71. Freeman 1983:290.
72. Bateson 1984:226.
73. Ehrman 1986:61.
74. Ehrman 1986:2.
75. See Heilbron 1979:278; see also Guerlac 1981:73.
76. Ehrman 1986:2.
77. Wade 1969:445.
78. Ehrman 1986:56.
79. Darwin 1985– , 2:81.
80. Martineau 1877, 1:355.
81. See Pichanick 1980:3–4; Martineau 1877, 1:133.
82. Stephen 1890:1194.
83. Petersen 1979:38, 46, 217.
84. Martineau 1877, 1:211, 327–29.
85. I thank Peter J. Gautrey for this detail.
86. Roazen 1975:439.
87. Rubins 1978:120; see also pp. xii and 17.
88. Freud 1933.

89. Rubins 1978:143–56; Grosskurth 1986:176–78.
90. Grosskurth 1986:176.
91. Rubins 1978:239–40.
92. Roazen 1975:486, 487.
93. Grosskurth 1986:237, 433; Karen 1994:44–45.
94. Grosskurth 1986:121.
95. Grosskurth 1986:3.
96. Karen 1994:42–44.
97. Roazen 1975:482–87.
98. Grosskurth 1986:404n.
99. Karen 1994:47.
100. Women scientists were younger, on average, than the men in my study. Because age is a good predictor of openness to experience, I have included it in the multiple regression model for scientific stance, along with relative birth rank, social attitudes, and conflict with parents. The multiple correlation for this model is .53 (df=5/581, F=45.24, p<.0001; for liberal debates). The model includes a significant two-way interaction between birth order and parental conflict, as documented in Chapter 5, Figure 5.1. The partial correlation of gender, controlled for these five predictors of radicalism, is .04 (df=1/581, t=0.99, p<.33). The outcome of multivariate modeling is unrelated to the order in which variables are entered. Gender is always rejected, and the other four variables are always accepted.
101. Keller 1983; 1985:173. Geneticist Barbara McClintock, whom Keller (1985: 173–74) sees as embodying these kinds of open-minded attributes, was the third of four children. Even as a woman, McClintock was a "maverick" in science.

7. Temperament

1. See, for example, Dunn and Plomin 1990:34, 50; Loehlin 1992:68. For personality traits, about 30–40 percent of the variance is estimated to be genetic, compared with 80 percent for physical traits such as height and weight. It is biologically adaptive for organisms to have "open" behavioral programs. In the domain of personality, evolution has selected for open programs that include a substantial role for learning (Mayr 1982:612).

A note of caution must be sounded on the issue of heritability estimates, which are subject to inflation owing to sibling contrast effects. Given the manner in which heritability is sometimes calculated, the very influences that I document in this book tend, in twin studies, to confuse the issue. For example, heritability is often calculated as twice the difference between twin correlations for personality traits among monozygotic and dizygotic twins. To the extent that dizygotic twins exhibit greater contrast effects than monozygotic twins, the heritability estimate will be inflated by twice this amount. The term "contrast effects" has also been used to denote the tendency for parents, in rating the personalities of their offspring, to exaggerate the differences they claim to observe. This bias has the same inflationary influence on heritability estimates as do contrast effects stemming from sibling competition (Saudino et al. 1995). Although these methodological problems can affect heritability estimates, the extent of the required adjustments is probably small relative to the total variance explained by genetic factors.
2. Thomas and Chess 1977; Chess and Thomas 1986; Kagan 1994.

3. Buss and Plomin 1984; Plomin, DeFries, and McClearn 1990:384–85; Loehlin 1992:4.
4. Philip Zimbardo, who has written several influential books on shyness, has remarked that "shyness is a fuzzy concept" (Zimbardo 1977:13). Since Zimbardo made this statement, considerable research has been conducted on the subject and has helped to make the concept less fuzzy. Much of this research is summarized by the contributors to Jones, Cheek, and Briggs 1986. Correlations between shyness and introversion range from .40 to .60, depending on the measure employed (Plomin and Daniels 1986:63; Crozier 1986:135–36). On the relationship between shyness and the Big Five personality dimensions, see McCrae and Costa (1987:85; 1990:3).
5. Eysenck and Rachman 1965:19.
6. Eysenck 1956; see also Geen 1986:274.
7. Kagan 1994:167–68; Plomin and Daniels 1986:65–69; Loehlin 1992:67.
8. Kagan and Reznick 1986; Kagan, Reznick, and Snidman 1988.
9. Kagan and Reznick (1986:88) review this research.
10. Kagan, Reznick, and Snidman 1988:171. There are nevertheless conflicting findings on the relationship of birth order to shyness, a point I address later in this chapter.
11. Drawing on autobiographies and biographies, I have recorded descriptive information about shyness for more than a thousand individuals in my database. I have coded these reports using a 7-point scale and have employed three independent raters to determine reliability. Among the four judges, the average correlation for ratings is .76.

In an attempt to avoid positive and negative connotations of shyness, Gough and Thorne (1986) provide a useful schematic for this trait. I have tried to implement their approach in my own ratings.
12. F. Darwin 1888:533.
13. Darwin 1887, 1:143.
14. Darwin 1958 [1876]:115.
15. Desmond and Moore 1992:307.
16. Darwin 1872:329.
17. Lurie 1960:18, 33.
18. Marcou 1896, 1:15.
19. Marcou 1896, 1:15–16.
20. Marcou 1896, 1:23, 13.
21. Walter 1990:16–17.
22. *Technical information for Figure 7.1:* Birth order exerts a significant main effect on receptivity to liberal scientific innovations (partial r=.22, df=1/745, t=6.11, p<.001). Shyness does not exert a significant main effect (partial r=–.03, df=1/745, t=–0.72, p<.48). Controlled for birth order and shyness, the two-way interaction is significant (partial r=.09, df=1/745, t=2.41, p<.02).

Shyness is also reflected in "scientific militancy." I have assessed this behavioral propensity in terms of a 7-point scale for the acceptance of scientific innovations. Militancy is defined as the absolute difference between the mean of the scale (4.0) and the scientific stance actually taken. (Twenty-six historians of science, acting as independent raters, provided these assessments of scientific stance.) Shy sci-

entists were significantly more likely than extraverted scientists to adopt a moderate rather than an extreme position, whichever viewpoint they defended (r=.09, df=1/702, t=2.35, p<.02). Shy scientists are also socially more conservative than extraverted scientists (r=.10, df=1/458, t=2.23, p<.03; controlled for birth order).
23. Arkin, Lake, and Baumgardner 1986:193–94. It seems likely that physical attributes, such as height and weight, may interact with birth order in much the same way as shyness does. It is easier to be socially dominant—a firstborn tendency—if one has the build of a heavyweight boxer. To my knowledge, no research has been conducted on this topic. But see the section "Causes of Shyness" later in this chapter for indirect support for this hypothesis based on the influence of age gaps between siblings. See also Appendix 10, section 5.
24. Quoted in de Beer 1964:166; see also Bibby 1960:69.
25. Darwin 1903, 1:158; Darwin 1887, 2:324.
26. Besterman 1969:497.
27. Gay 1966:385.
28. Hearsey 1976:18.
29. Parton 1881, 1:50.
30. Parton 1881, 2:134.
31. Voltaire 1953–1965, 81:39; Parton 1881, 1:19–20.
32. Besterman 1969:106–7; Parton 1881, 1:184–92.
33. Parton 1881, 1:284.
34. Olby 1985:236–39; Mayr 1982:729–31.
35. Kruta and Orel 1974:282; see also Olby 1985:93.
36. Mendel rates a 2.0 on my 7-point shyness scale, well below the mean rating.
37. Koestler 1959:117.
38. Rosen 1984:59.
39. Rosen 1984:187.
40. Koestler 1959:152.
41. Rosen 1884:184–85.
42. Rosen 1984:82, 161.
43. Westman 1975: 182, 184, 190.
44. Rosen 1984:167.
45. Koestler 1959:190.
46. Hermann 1971:23. Planck's recollections overemphasize his initial endorsement of discontinuity in physics (Kuhn 1978:140).
47. Kuhn 1962/1970:77; see also Kuhn 1978.
48. Heilbron 1986:33, 21. On the shyness scale, Copernicus rates a 2.5, Rheticus a 6.0, and Planck a 2.5.
49. For evidence that firstborns tend to be more shy than laterborns, see McArthur 1956:48–49; Price 1969:194; and Asendorpf 1986:100. For the opposite claim, see Kagan, Reznick, and Snidman 1988:171. Depending on whether an investigator is assessing sociability (a laterborn trait) or social dominance (a firstborn trait), measures of extraversion will tend to conflict. See my meta-analytic review of the conflicting literature in Chapter 3, Table 4.
50. *Technical information for Figure 7.2:* Overall, birth order exerts a significant main effect on shyness (partial r=–.12, df=1/370, t=–2.78, p<.05). The interaction between birth order and sibship size is also significant (partial r=–.15,

df=1/370, *t*=–2.83, $p<.005$). As a main effect, sibship size is not significant (partial *r*=.05, *df*=1/370, $p<.34$).

51. Asendorpf 1986:100. In my own study, the shyest sibling group is middle children, followed by only children, youngest children, and firstborns. Only children are not significantly less extraverted than firstborns, but the sample size for only children who have been rated on shyness is small (*N*=38).

52. Kagan, Reznick, and Snidman 1988:171. Helen Koch (1955a, 1956c, 1956e) found that, relative to laterborns, firstborns were more self-confident, competitive, emotionally intense, and insistent on their rights—all correlates of extraversion (in the sense of social dominance).

53. For shyness in a younger sibling and the age gap between them and the next older sibling, *r*=.11 (*df*=1/334, *t*=2.01, $p<.05$). For shyness in an older sibling and the age gap between them and the next younger siblings, *r*=.–08 (*df*=1/266, *t*=1.25, $p<.21$). For the two effects combined (expressed as the difference between the two age gaps), *r*=.14 (*df*=1/222, *t*=2.12, $p<.05$). According to this last statistic, an optimum formula for extraversion is having a younger sibling who is closely spaced in age—especially three to four years younger—but no immediately older sibling. An optimum formula for shyness is having an immediately older sibling and no immediately younger sibling.

54. For the interaction between age at loss of mother and social class, as they affect shyness, the partial correlation is .10 (*df*=1/464, *t*=2.27, $p<.05$; controlled for the main effects).

55. See, for example, Bowlby (1969–80, 1988), whose "anxiously attached" children agree closely with the stereotype of shy individuals; and Pilkonis (1986).

56. For the three-way interaction between birth order, social class, and age at maternal loss, as they affect shyness, partial *r*=–.12 (*df*=1/388, *t*=–2.46, $p<.02$).

57. For Bowlby's explanation of Darwin's illness (hyperventilation syndrome), see Bowlby 1990 and Chapter 5.

58. Groddeck is rated 3.5 on the shyness scale.

59. Grossmann and Grossmann 1965:18–19.

60. Martineau 1877, 1:19, 394. As an adult, Martineau is rated 4.3 on the shyness scale.

61. Mayr 1932:97.

62. Personal communication with Ernst Mayr, 4 August 1992.

8. Exceptions to the Rule

1. I have tested the claim that famous people are likely to be extremists. In doing so, I have assessed "extremism" as the absolute value of the difference between the population mean on openness to experience and the score for each individual in my study. Openness is measured here as an equally weighted index of (1) openness to scientific innovation, (2) travel, and (3) number of scientific interests. Openness is strongly correlated with eminence (*r*=.15, *df*=1/2,156, *t*=7.05, $p<.0001$). After controlling for the linear influence of openness on eminence, the partial correlation of the absolute deviation from the mean is also a significant predictor of eminence (*r*=.06, *df*=1/2,156, *t*=2.85, $p<.005$). In addition, birth order interacts with extremism. Laterborns achieved greater eminence through extremism than did firstborns (partial *r*=.07, *df*=1/917, *t*=2.01, $p<.05$; controlled for the main ef-

fects of birth order, openness, and extremism). Firstborns, however, were significantly more likely than laterborns to become eminent through *scientific militancy* (endorsing an extreme position, either in support of or in opposition to a new theory—r=–.09, df=1/592, t=–2.22, p<.05). In many ways militancy is the opposite of openness, so extremism on the two measures yields different results in relation to birth order.

2. Rudwick 1974:389.

3. Based on a more comprehensive model, which includes social attitudes, Miller's predicted probability of supporting evolution was only 11 percent. See Chapter 10, Figure 10.3.

4. Hobbes was anticlerical. Although a royalist, he was an unconventional one who believed that any form of absolute rule (monarchist or parliamentary) was necessary for a stable society. Based on ratings by expert historians, Hobbes's religious and political attitudes place him in the 96th percentile on social radicalism relative to his contemporaries. On a scale of openness to experience, assessed as openness to scientific innovation, travel, and number of scientific interests, Hobbes's ranking puts him in the 89th percentile.

5. Although Hobbes has sometimes been seen as a precursor of totalitarianism, this interpretation is a gross misreading of his intentions. His strong endorsement of the doctrine of human equality is "wholly at variance with the precepts and practices of the modern totalitarian state" (Mintz 1972:447). See also Harris 1964:37–40.

6. Mintz 1972:448.

7. Mintz 1972:449.

8. *Technical information for Figure 8.1:* This eight-variable family dynamics model is based on logistic regression, which is simply a variant of regression procedures for use with binary outcome variables. For this model, the adjusted R=.29. Data from all 28 scientific revolutions are employed in the model. (Support for the five "conservative" theories is modeled as a conservative stance.) Of the 3,890 participants in my database, 779 have been dropped owing to excessive missing data. For the remainder of the sample (N=3,111), missing data were imputed five times to create five different datasets (see Appendix 5).

The model correctly classifies 72.5 percent of the cells, based on the mean response of each cell. I have employed jackknife procedures, which prohibit a case from predicting itself. The *base rate* for success is 62.3 percent (the proportion of the sample supporting a liberal position).

Logistic regression does not fully reflect the explanatory power of a family dynamics model, owing to the necessity of multiply imputing missing data. This technique tends to dilute the results because of the difficulty of imputing interaction effects. I have employed logistic regression, together with the multiple imputation of missing data, primarily to calculate predicted probabilities for *specific historical figures.* A better indication of the explanatory power of a family dynamics is obtained using the EM algorithm in BMDP's 8D program and by analyzing the resulting correlation matrix with BMDP's 9R program (All Possible Subsets Regression). With these methods, the adjusted R=.33 (df=10/1,152 [the harmonic mean], F=15.49, p<.0001). This model's multiple R of .33 is equivalent to classifying 67 percent of the sample correctly, given a base rate of 50 percent success.

Models that include information on religious and political attitudes, which reflect within-family as well as between-family differences, improve significantly on these results (adjusted R=.49, df=12/1,221 [the harmonic mean], F=32.76, p<.0001). This model's success is equivalent to classifying 75 percent of the sample correctly in terms of support or opposition, given a base rate of 50 percent success. In particularly radical scientific innovations, such as the Darwinian revolution, a comprehensive model is even more successful, correctly classifying 84 percent of the participants. See further, Chapter 10, Figure 10.3, and Appendix 9, Technical Discussion 7.

9. For this group of extraverted lastborns, the predicted probabilities of support for liberal innovation range from 80 to 93 percent. By comparison, Darwin receives a predicted probability of only 73 percent.

10. E. Darwin 1915, 2:223.

11. Darwin 1887, 3:69.

12. Darwin 1887, 3:68.

13. Huxley's predicted probability of support for liberal innovations is 80 percent.

14. About 10 percent of information collected in behavioral research is considered "error variance." The remaining 90 percent of the information is what one tries to model. Although I have not kept formal track of biographical inconsistencies, I would estimate that they occur in 1 to 2 percent of all biographical reports. Some of these discrepancies can be resolved by taking into account the difference between functional and biological birth order. Other discrepancies include date of birth (especially for figures born prior to the seventeenth century), father's occupation, and age at parental loss. The use of expert raters also entails error, although the use of multiple independent raters tends to attenuate this source of error.

15. Drake 1970:43–62.

16. Drake 1970:58.

17. Drake 1970:58.

18. Drake 1970:58.

19. See, for example, Chapter 9, where I test this hypothesis about parent-offspring resemblances by birth order in the domain of social attitudes.

20. Only children are significantly more variable on openness to experience than either firstborns or laterborns. For the contrast, r=.10 (df=1/812, t=2.99, p<.005; using Levene's test). Openness to experience is here assessed as (1) openness to scientific innovation, (2) number of scientific interests, (3) liberal social attitudes, and (4) world travel (z-scored and combined in a single measure).

21. Darwin 1958 [1876]:72.

22. FitzRoy 1839.

23. Mellersh 1968:274.

24. De Beer 1964:167.

25. When we take into account FitzRoy's social attitudes, his likelihood of supporting evolution was only 5 percent (see Chapter 10, Figure 10.3).

26. Drake 1978:312.

27. Drake 1978:320, 338–43; Biagioli 1993:336–48.

28. Hutchinson 1914, 1:23, 56.

29. This comprehensive model, which places Lubbock's probability of supporting

Darwinian theory at 80 percent, is described in Chapter 10 (see especially Figure 10.3).
30. Somkin 1973:529.
31. Somkin 1973:528.
32. For religious denomination and support of Copernican theory, r=.00 (df=1/237, t=0.00, p<.95).
33. For status as a theologian and support for Copernican theory, r=–.06 (df=1/199, t=–0.80, p<.43).
34. For status as a scientist and support for Copernican theory, r=.13 (df=1/242, t=1.43, p<.05). I elaborate on this influence in Chapter 14 (see the section "Why Galileo Won").
35. For age and acceptance of Copernican theory, r=–.23 (df=1/242, t=–3.25, p<.005).
36. Drake 1978:339.
37. For most of the models tested in this book I have employed Mallows' C_p as the criterion of variable entry. Mallows' C_p penalizes models for each new variable that is added, thus guarding against overfitting (Dixon 1992, 2:1098).
38. What do not constitute refutations of my behavioral claims in this book are nonsignificant birth-order findings concerning vaguely defined outcome variables such as "eminence," "leadership," and "achievement" (see, for example, Ernst and Angst 1982:43–69; and Somit et al. 1996). The relationship between birth order and these kinds of behavioral outcomes is typically weak, although statistically significant trends are sometimes found in *large* samples (Chapter 3, page 74). To permit meaningful tests of the claims I make throughout this book, such outcome variables must be defined in terms of conservative/radical achievement (or other pertinent personality dimensions, such as agreeableness). In addition, the samples employed in hypothesis testing need to be controlled, at minimum, for sibship size and social class. Ideally, samples should also be controlled for a variety of other variables, including social attitudes, that are relevant to the situational context. See further, Chapter 14, especially Figure 14.1 and Table 7.

9. Social Attitudes

1. See, for example, Bailyn (1967) and Martin (1973) on the American Revolution; and Godechot (1971) and Furet and Richet (1970) on the French Revolution. Efforts to relate social attitudes to scientific thought include Merton 1938; Westfall 1958; Jacob 1976; Webster 1976; Moore 1979; Jacob and Jacob 1980; Corsi 1988; Desmond 1989; and Cohen 1990.
2. Darwin 1903, 1:321.
3. I have used self-report information and contemporary observer data mostly as a check against the reliability of expert ratings. For this reason, I do not describe my methods of collecting these data here. For further information on this topic, see Appendix 4.
4. In Appendix 6 I provide further technical information on these rating procedures. The mean correlation among 94 expert raters is .83. The correlation between these expert ratings and ratings based on self-report data is .93. The correlation between contemporaneous observer ratings and expert ratings is .90. When expert ratings are pooled, the *effective* reliability is .90 for politics and .92 for

religiosity. The effective reliability by all three methods is .91 for politics and .93 for religiosity. Political and religious attitudes are themselves strongly correlated (r=.62, df=1/2,142, t=36.87, p<.0001). The 94 judges who participated in this study are listed in Appendix 4.

5. *Technical information for Figure 9.1:* Scores for social attitudes are based on the mean of all individual assessments for politics and religion. For 23 liberal innovations in science, the partial correlation between social attitudes and support, controlled for birth order, is .30 (df=1/1,386, t=11.74, p<.0001). For political attitudes separately, r=.30 (df=1/1,977, t=14.11, p<.0001). For religious attitudes separately, r=.32 (df=1/2,074, t=15.27, p<.0001). The partial correlation between birth order and support is .26 (df=1/1,386, t=10.12, p<.0001). In assessing likelihood of support for liberal innovations, the odds ratio of 12.5 reflects the contrast between individuals rated lower than 1.5 for their social attitudes (N=35) versus those rated above 4.5 (N=60). Odds ratios adjust for the fact that cell frequencies are unequal. This statistic provides a more effective measure of individual differences than do comparisons based on percentages.

6. Belhoste 1991:viii.

7. Freudenthal 1971:133 (quoting the mathematician Niels Henrik Abel); Belhoste 1991:139.

8. Belhoste 1991:138.

9. Quoted in Freudenthal (1971:133) and Belhoste (1991:139), whose accounts I have here combined. Although Stendhal's remarks appear to be somewhat fanciful, they accurately reflect what Cauchy had said two years earlier about Franz Joseph Gall.

10. Freudenthal 1971:133.

11. For social attitudes as they relate to support for eugenics, r=–.30 (df=1/219, t=–4.60, p<.0001). On the eugenics movement, see Haller 1963; Kevles 1985; Proctor 1988; Weingart, Kroll, and Bayertz 1988.

12. Kevles 1985. Among psychologists, Sherwood and Nataupsky (1968) found that firstborns are more likely than laterborns to endorse the view that blacks have innately inferior IQs. Although this study did not assess social attitudes, the authors did find that belief in the innate inferiority of blacks was significantly correlated with upper-class status.

Two related birth-order studies bear mentioning in this context. Lieberman and Reynolds (1978) found that firstborn physical anthropologists were more likely than laterborns to believe in the biological reality of racial differences. A 1980 study of the reception of sociobiology among Harvard and Wellesley professors, most of whom were *not* biologists, found significantly greater acceptance of this theory among firstborns than laterborns (r=–.25, N=94, p<.01). Among individuals who considered this theory to be innovative, as opposed to being compatible with accepted scientific beliefs, laterborns were more supportive (Flaherty 1980; and personal communication, David Pillemer).

13. *Technical information for Figure 9.2:* For five conservative scientific innovations, the partial correlation of social attitudes with support, controlled for birth order, is –.20 (df=1/345, t=–3.71, p<.001). The partial correlation for birth order with support is –.14 (df=1/345, t=–2.70, p<.01). The interaction between birth order and social attitudes is significant. Relative to laterborns, firstborns were more sus-

ceptible to conservative ideological influences in evaluating theories ($r=-.11$, $df=1/345$, $t=-2.12$, $p<.05$).

14. Darwin 1987:291 (*Notebook C,* p. 166).

15. McKinney 1976:139–40.

16. For claims about social class and social radicalism, see Shapin 1975, 1979a, 1979b, 1982; Cooter 1984; Desmond 1989; Desmond and Moore 1992.

17. One hundred twenty-nine members of my sample were either fathers or sons of one another. In 74 instances, expert historians have rated the social attitudes of both individuals. I have been able to rate another 445 parents of individuals in my study based on published biographical descriptions, which are recorded in textual form in my database. Biographers often employ the terms "conservative," "moderate," "liberal," and "radical" in describing the social attitudes of their subjects. Whenever these terms have been employed, I have assigned a rating that corresponds directly with these descriptions. For example, 1.0 corresponds to "very conservative, " 1.5 to "conservative," 2.0 to "moderate," 3.0 to "liberal," 4.0 to "advanced liberal" or "progressive," and 5.0 to "radical."

18. For the social attitudes of parents and their offspring, $r=.47$ ($df=1/481$, $t=11.55$, $p<.0001$). Based on assortative mating and heritability, the predicted correlation for radicalism between biological parents and their offspring is nearly the same (.52). See Martin et al. 1986:4368; Eaves, Eysenck, and Martin 1989:386. Because of assortative mating, similar genetic dispositions among parents appear to explain some of the resemblance between parents and their offspring.

19. Studies in behavioral genetics suggest that about half of this unexplained variance is genetic in origin. The remaining half is due to the nonshared environment (Eaves, Eysenck, and Martin 1989:363). Either way, both sources of unexplained variation appear to be differences between siblings.

20. Other researchers have also reported that only children are more liberal than firstborns (Boshier and Walkey 1971; Farley and Farley 1974).

21. *Technical information for Figure 9.3 and Figure 9.4:* The correlation between relative birth rank and religious attitudes is .16 ($df=1/1{,}500$, $t=6.22$, $p<.0001$). For political attitudes, the correlation is .13 ($df=1/1{,}464$, $t=4.82$, $p<.0001$).

Analyzed by birth rank, social attitudes exhibit a zigzag pattern. Controlled for the linear trend, the effect size for the zigzag is $r=.09$ ($df=1/554$, $t=2.01$, $p<.05$; for laterborns). This zigzag pattern is particularly pronounced among offspring who are odd numbered among the sequence of sons. Controlled for birth rank and status as an odd- or even-numbered son, the interaction effect is $r=.21$ ($df=1/554$, $t=5.10$, $p<.0001$; for laterborns). For example, secondborns are socially conservative if they are eldest sons, but radical if they are second sons.

Skinner (1992) has drawn attention to similar sawtooth patterns in his study of Chinese families living in Jakarta. Sons tended to be "filial," in the sense of endorsing traditional values, the earlier they were in the son series. In addition, these patterns were influenced by whether a son was odd or even in the sibling sequence. Social attitudes were also affected by odd or even sibship size, and by sex of siblings. Older daughters tended to "humanize" their fathers, reducing parent-offspring conflict involving younger sons.

22. For the social attitudes of firstborns and their parents, $r=.62$ ($df=1/91$, $t=7.18$, $p<.0001$). For laterborns, the correlation is $r=.36$ ($df=1/131$, $t=4.44$,

$p<.0001$). For the difference between the two correlations, $z=2.17$ ($p<.02$). For the difference in variance explained, $.62^2/.36^2=3.0$ to 1.

23. Turner 1990:21. For scientists in my study, I have conducted a formal test of Turner's claims. Within this sample, liberal social attitudes are significantly correlated with parent-offspring conflict ($r=-.14$, $df=1/491$, $t=-3.23$, $p<.01$; the sign of the correlation is negative because a *low* score on the parental relationship scale signifies a *high* level of parent-offspring conflict).

24. Turner 1990:29.

25. Controlled for parents' social attitudes, as well as for the significant two-way interaction between parents' birth orders and parents' social attitudes, laterborn parents have tended to have more radical offspring ($r=.18$, $df=1/125$, $t=2.03$, $p<.05$). Firstborn offspring in my study were especially likely to conform to their *firstborn* parents' social values ($r=.73$), but less so to the social values of *laterborn parents* ($r=.48$; for the contrast, $z=1.34$, $p<.10$). The two-way interaction effect indicates that firstborn parents, when conservative, tended to have more radical offspring, mostly owing to increased radicalism among their laterborn children ($r=-.17$, $df=1/125$, $t=-1.98$, $p=.05$). Among conservative parents (<2.5 on the social attitudes scale), the correlation between birth order and social attitudes among offspring is .23. Among liberal parents (rated higher than 2.5), the same correlation is only .05. When both parents are liberal, and especially when the firstborn is liberal too, it is more difficult for laterborns to differentiate themselves from other siblings in terms of social attitudes. As I am writing, this conclusion suggests a testable hypothesis: In liberal families, laterborns should differentiate themselves from older siblings by other means, such as diverse interests, travel, or openness to innovation. For openness to innovation, this hypothesis is confirmed (for the contrast between the two relevant correlations, $z=2.03$, $p<.03$). For travel, the trend is in the expected direction, and nearly significant ($p<.15$). For number of scientific interests, the trend is not significant, but the relevant effect sizes are small for this variable.

26. Tanner 1931:601.

27. For social attitudes, the multiple correlation of an eight-variable family dynamics model is .47 (adjusted $R=.44$, $df=9/325$, $F=10.09$, $p<.0001$; the model also includes one significant interaction effect).

Using BMDP's program 8D (which estimates missing data) and 9R (All Possible Subsets Regression), an eight-variable model (with eleven terms, including interactions) is selected by the criterion of Mallows' C_p ($R=.45$, adjusted $R=.43$, $df=11/1{,}185$, $F=26.68$, $p<.0001$). This model includes three main effects: birth order, parent-offspring conflict, and shyness. In addition, there are seven 2-way interactions: birth rank by sibship size; birth order by age gaps; birth order by parent-offspring conflict; birth order by shyness; birth order by parental loss; birth order by social class; and social class by parental loss. The model also includes one 3-way effect: birth order by parental loss by social class.

For the variance explained by sibling differences as a whole, as opposed to birth order, $.47^2/.15^2=9.8$ to 1. For the correlation between social class and social attitudes, $r=.04$ ($df=1/2{,}211$, $t=1.93$, $p<.06$). For the variance explained by birth order as opposed to social class, $.15^2/.04^2=14.1$ to 1. For the variance explained by sibling differences, as opposed to social class, $.47^2/.04^2=138$ to 1.

28. Mayr 1963:472.

29. In my own study, the similarity in spouses' social attitudes is substantial, a fact that is consistent with other research indicating that parents are assortatively mated (r=.63, df=1/143, t=9.79, p<.0001). Larger samples have reported correlations for spousal social attitudes ranging between .35 and .68, with the mean being .50. See Eaves, Eysenck, and Martin 1989:376–78. See also Buss and Craik 1983b, 1994:36.

Assortative mating for worldviews has been treated empirically by Buss and Craik (1983b), who have shown that spouses mate according to "contemporary worldviews." One of their two scales of "worldviews" emphasized a respect for technology, rationality, and free enterprise. The second scale measured attitudes toward (1) a policy of lower economic growth in order to attain improvements in the environment and (2) a redistribution of wealth from richer to poorer countries. Spouse correlations for the first scale were .37. Spouse correlations for the second scale were .50.

30. Eaves, Eysenck, and Martin 1989:322.

31. Martin et al. 1986; Eaves, Eysenck, and Martin 1989; Dunn and Plomin 1990:37; Waller et al. 1990.

32. Eaves, Eysenck, and Martin 1989:322.

33. To my knowledge, twin studies have ignored the role of birth order and other systematic sibling differences, information that should shed considerable light on the role of the nonshared environment in behavioral genetic models. See Appendix 10, section 7.

34. Franklin 1916:11. By his first wife, Franklin's father had seven children; by his second wife he had ten more. Thirteen of these children lived to adulthood. One of Franklin's two younger siblings, a brother, was drowned as an infant in a bathtub, making Franklin the second-to-last child and youngest son.

35. Becker 1931:597. Franklin was one of five people appointed by the Continental Congress in June 1776 to draft a declaration of independence from Britain. Most of the document was the work of Thomas Jefferson. The declaration was adopted by the delegates of the Continental Congress on 4 July 1776.

36. Franklin 1916:7, 11.

37. Franklin 1916:10.

38. Ozment 1980:426–27; Kagan, Ozment, and Turner 1987:395.

39. Franklin 1916:11.

40. Michelet, n.d., 5:325.

41. Schwennicke 1980–81, 2:Tafel 30.

42. The "Eyton" and "Darwin" families are both included in Burke's *Landed Gentry* (1965–1972), a compendium of the most affluent families in England since the Middle Ages.

43. Sulloway 1982b:73.

44. Adamson 1890:971.

45. Adamson 1890:971. I would never have gone looking for such a genealogical fact, but Eyton's biographer mentions it, perhaps because Eyton himself was fond of reciting it.

46. *Technical information for Figure 9.5:* Based on his genealogy, Eyton ought to have been in the 9th percentile on social attitudes (his actual placement is in the

8th percentile). I have derived the predicted status of Eyton's social views in the following manner. First, I have assumed that Eyton's ancestor in the first generation was in the 50th percentile. Second, for each subsequent generation I have assumed a modest correlation of .12 between being an "eldest son" and adopting socially conservative views. For relative birth rank and social attitudes, the known correlation is .16 (df=1/1,608, t=6.33, p<.0001). I encountered one instance in the Eyton genealogical record in which a younger son inherited the Eyton estates, which is included in my calculations (Burke 1965–72, 3:308). The net result of these calculations is to place Eyton's predicted social attitudes at 1.83 on my 5-point scale (which is the 9th percentile). By the same logic, Darwin should have been in the 80th percentile on social attitudes. During the course of his life, Darwin's ranking on social radicalism rose from the 64th to the 84th percentile. Benjamin Franklin is predicted to be in the 88th percentile (he was actually in the 90th percentile). Louis XV is predicted to be in the 21st percentile (he was actually in the 17th percentile).

47. Darwin's probability of supporting evolutionary theory was 94 percent, based primarily on his birth order and his social attitudes. Eyton's likelihood was 3 percent. For documentation of this point, see Chapter 10, Figure 10.3.

48. In theory, there should be a small trend toward assortative mating by birth order. Although my own sample for this variable is relatively small, the parents of scientists were assortatively mated, but only in conjunction with social class. Upper-class laterborn males displayed a moderate preference for firstborn wives, who may have been heiresses. Lower-class laterborn males consistently married laterborn wives (partial r=.24, df=1/97, t=2.40, p<.02). This tendency is particularly pronounced among individuals who held extreme social views.

49. In my sample, the correlation between social attitudes and social class is .04 (df=1/2,211, t=1.93, p<.06).

50. For openness to liberal scientific innovations, the correlation with birth order is .26; for social class, the correlation is .01. Accordingly, the explained variances are .068 versus .0001, or 680 to 1. This disparity should not be taken to mean that birth order explains everything, only that social class explains very little (in this context). For sibling differences as a whole, the multiple correlation with scientific stance is .33, for an eight-variable model. The explained variance (.109) is 1,090 times greater than the explained variance associated with social class.

51. For status as a religious minority (being a Catholic in a Protestant country, and vice versa), the partial correlation for the interaction effect with nationality, controlled for religious denomination and minority status, is .10 (df=1/1,513, t=4.05, p<.001). As a main effect, the partial correlation of minority status is .01 (not significant). French Protestants, for example, were historically more open to scientific innovation than both French and British Catholics, but the two religious minorities were not more open as a whole (owing to the relative conservatism of British Catholics).

The social attitudes of Jewish scientists in my study are significantly more liberal than those of other participants (r=.29, df=1/575, t=7.28, p<.0001; compared against a generationally matched sample from the nineteenth and twentieth centuries). Still, sibling differences in social attitudes are 2.4 times larger than this group difference, and 3.5 times larger than gender differences (r=.24, df=1/356,

t=4.62, p<.0001; comparing women against a generationally matched sample of men). Much of these differences by race and gender are probably *recruitment* effects. For example, women in my study are significantly more likely to be laterborns than the men, causing an individual difference to appear as a group difference.

52. Path analysis reinforces these conclusions. For example, the contribution of parental social values to those of their offspring is r=.47; but the multiple correlation of sibling differences with social attitudes is .44. As a consequence, .47×.44 (or .21) of this influence is a sibling difference among parents. The total influence of sibling differences becomes .44+.21, or .65, versus .47 for the shared family environment. Even then, some of what appears to be attributable to the "shared family environment" is actually due to genetic similarities among assortatively mated parents (Martin et al. 1986; Eaves, Eysenck, and Martin 1989).

For openness to scientific innovation, social attitudes are only one of many relevant predictors. For this reason, sibling differences are even more important in predicting this dependent variable than they are in predicting social attitudes. By the same kind of path analysis I have just reviewed, 63 percent of the explained variance in openness to innovation is attributable to sibling differences. If we take our path analysis back more than one generation, the role of sibling differences becomes more substantial still.

53. Petersen 1979:23.

54. Simpkins 1974:68.

10. The Darwinian Revolution as Social History

1. Desmond 1989:4. Robert Young (1985:164–67) has also long advocated a Marxist approach to the history of science, especially for the Darwinian period.

2. Desmond 1975.

3. Desmond 1982, 1984a, 1984b, 1985, 1987, and especially 1989; see also Desmond and Moore 1992.

4. Desmond's *Politics of Evolution* won the Pfizer Award of the History of Science Society and has been described by the awards committee as "a paradigm of how the history of science can truly become melded with social history" (Mauskopf 1992:279). In addition, Desmond and Moore's (1992) biography of Darwin received the Watson-Davis Prize of the History of Science Society, given for books that promote the history of science among the general public.

5. Gould 1992:216. See also I. Bernard Cohen (1992:10), who wonders "how a gentleman naturalist of Darwin's social class and background could have propounded such radical notions about evolution."

6. *Technical information for Figure 10.1:* For the correlation between birth order and support for evolution, r=.40 (df=1/447, t=9.21, p<.0001). Computed as a linear trend, the correlation of social class with support is almost zero (r=.01, df=1/552, t=0.20, p=not significant). For the curvilinear relationship, r=.06 (df=1/552, t=1.31, p<.20). For the relative variance explained by the two linear relationships, $.40^2/.01^2$=1,600 to 1.

7. On firstborn "intellectual primogeniture," see Sutton-Smith and Rosenberg 1970:69–79; Zajonc 1976. For documentation of this tendency during the Darwinian revolution, see Appendix 9, Technical Discussion 4.

8. Prior to 1859, laterborns and social liberals were significantly less likely than firstborns and social conservatives to achieve scientific eminence. The Darwinian revolution significantly changed this balance of power and prestige. For documentation of this point, see Appendix 9, Technical Discussion 4.
9. Morrell and Thackray 1981:23–29.
10. Bunting 1974:88–89; Desmond and Moore 1992:488.
11. Darwin 1887, 3:224.
12. Desmond cites Grant over six hundred times in his *Politics of Evolution*—more than any other individual. Desmond (1984a, 1984b) has also devoted several articles to the predicaments that Grant's radicalism created for his checkered scientific career.
13. Southwell 1840:19.
14. Desmond 1987:85.
15. Desmond 1987:86, 97, 109. Southwell's thirty-two older siblings were the product of his father's several previous wives. Southwell was his mother's first and only child. See Southwell's *Confessions of a Free-Thinker* (ca. 1845).
16. *Technical information for Figure 10.2:* In Desmond's sample, 76 percent of the participants are laterborns, compared with only 60 percent of the control population ($r=.11$; $df=1/616$, $t=2.69$, $p<.01$). For the relationship between social class and support for radical theories, the correlation in Desmond's sample is .28 ($df=1/70$, $t=2.43$, $p<.02$). Controlled for birth order and the significant interaction between birth order and recruitment by social class, the partial correlation becomes a nonsignificant .09 ($df=1/50$, $t=0.62$, $p<.54$). Similarly, in Desmond's sample the correlation between birth order and social attitudes is a whopping .48 ($df=1/50$, $t=3.94$, $p<.001$). Controlled for birth order, the partial correlation between social class and social attitudes is not significant ($r=.12$, $df=1/49$, $t=0.82$, $p<.42$). For additional information on Desmond's sample, see Appendix 9, Technical Discussion 5.
17. I am quoting here from the catchy subtitle of the American edition of Desmond and Moore's book *Darwin: The Life of a Tormented Evolutionist* (1992).
18. Desmond and Moore 1992:286, 297.
19. Desmond and Moore 1992:354.
20. Desmond and Moore 1992:287.
21. Thompson 1984.
22. Darwin 1985– , 4:144.
23. Desmond and Moore 1992:317.
24. See Appendix 9, Technical Discussion 6. Desmond and Moore are among the nearly thirty independent raters who have helped me to assess the social attitudes of Darwin's colleagues.
25. For Darwin's critical comments on the conservative tendencies he observed among his scientific friends, see Darwin 1958 [1876]: pp. 64–65 (for Henslow); p. 76 (for FitzRoy); p. 101 (for Lyell); p. 102 (for Buckland); and p. 103 (for the "ludicrous" Murchison).
26. Desmond and Moore 1992:286; Desmond 1987:425.
27. Wells 1973:241; Wilson 1970:71–72, 75, 104; Thompson 1984:329.
28. Wallace 1905, 1:104.
29. William Charles Wells, an American-born physician who lived most of his

adult life in England, is sometimes considered a codiscoverer of the theory of natural selection. This claim is based on an 1818 essay in which Wells discusses a white woman who possessed numerous brown discolorations of her skin. In his essay, Wells outlined how natural selection might take advantage of such mutations to produce a race of blacks. Unlike Matthew, Darwin, and Wallace, Wells confined his argument to the races of man. He did not comment on the broader issue of whether species were capable of extended change (Mayr 1982:499). Wells was a second son. In his social attitudes, he is rated a liberal (3.0). See also Gould 1985:338.

30. Reprinted in Dempster 1983:98 from Matthew 1831:365.

31. Darwin 1871, 1:135.

32. Darwin 1871, 1:135. On Darwin and primogeniture, see also Hrdy and Judge 1993.

33. Darwin 1887, 2:385n.

34. The omission of birth order from the comprehensive model results in a loss in variance explained of 9 percent (the partial correlation is .37 [df=1/346, t=7.34, p<.0001]). Omission of social attitudes results in a loss of 8 percent in variance explained. The next best predictor of scientific stance—eminence in 1859—is responsible for 3 percent in variance explained. (Eminent individuals, who also tended to be older, generally *opposed* Darwinism.) No other predictor contributes more than 2 percent in variance explained to a saturated model. Estimates of the relative variance explained by birth order and other sibling differences are based on path-analytic models.

35. *Technical information for Figure 10.3:* For the ten-variable model predicting adoption of Darwinism, the multiple R=.68 (df=10/363 [the harmonic mean], F=30.49, p<.0001). Further details about this model are provided in Appendix 9, Technical Discussion 7.

36. My selection of "leaders" of the Darwinian revolution is based on citation counts in standard works on the history of evolution, including Glass, Tempkin, and Straus 1959; Gillespie 1979; Ruse 1979; Mayr 1982; and Bowler 1984.

37. *Technical information for Figure 10.4:* For the contrast in predicted probabilities between pioneers and converts to evolutionary theory, r=.16 (df=1/263, t=2.56, p<.02). For converts to evolution, the mean probability of support is 64 percent.

38. Darwin's predicted probability of accepting evolution (94 percent) is derived from a logistic regression model, which employs the same predictors included in my ten-variable multiple regression model (Appendix 9, Technical Discussion 7).

39. For the contrast between the three codiscoverers of evolution by natural selection (Matthew, Darwin, and Wallace) and the other 12 leaders of the Darwinian revolution, r=.45 (df=1/13, t=1.83, p<.05; one-tailed test).

40. Burkhardt 1987:xiv.

41. Matthew 1860b:433.

42. Wallace 1905, 1:363; Marchant 1916:92–93, 131.

43. Darwin 1887, 1:149.

44. Darwin 1958 [1876]:22.

45. Young 1972:250.

46. See Young 1970, 1972, and Cooter 1984 for excellent overviews of the phrenology movement.

47. Möbius 1907:11.
48. Three of the five members of this phrenology commission were firstborns (Georges Cuvier, Philippe Pinel, and Jacques René Tenon). A fourth member (Antoine Portal) was an "eldest son," and may have been a firstborn. I do not know the birth order of the fifth member of the commission (Raphael-Bienvenu Sabatier). I have employed a multivariate model to predict the likelihood that this commission would support phrenology. The mean predicted probability of support for the five commission members (including Sabatier), is 8 percent—significantly lower than that for the participating population as a whole. In deriving predicted probabilities for each member of the commission, I have estimated missing data by the technique of multiple imputation (see Appendix 5). Multiple imputation allows one to determine the error term for these probabilities. Based on this technique, we may be 95 percent confident that the commission's true probability for accepting phrenology was 8 percent (±6 percent).

Whenever scientific commissions are staffed by eminent experts from "establishment science," they tend to be biased for firstborns (and hence conservative conclusions). This topic has important implications for science policy.
49. Young 1972:250.
50. The correlation between accepting phrenology and accepting evolution is .59 ($\chi^2[1]=9.26$, $p<.001$, based on 27 paired stances).
51. Cooter 1984:10; Young 1985:4. By comparison with the enormous sales for Combe's *Constitution of Man* (more than 100,000 copies), Darwin's *Origin* had sold only 18,000 copies by 1876 (Freeman 1978:221).
52. Young 1972:255.
53. Gibbon 1878. A multivariate model for the reception of phrenology does a reasonably good job of identifying the leaders of this movement. Gall, Spurzheim, and the two Combe brothers are all assigned probabilities of support between 83 and 93 percent. Gall's predicted probability is 90 percent.
54. Cooter 1984:141–42, 175–80, 261.
55. Shapin 1982:193; see also Shapin 1975, 1979a, 1979b.
56. Cooter 1984:43–44.
57. Galton 1874. The tendency for firstborns to be overrepresented among eminent scientists is well documented (Visher 1947; Roe 1953; West 1960; Clarke and Rice 1982).
58. For social class and acceptance of phrenology, $r=.25$ ($df=1/86$, $t=2.38$, $p<.05$). I have drawn my sample of phrenologists and their opponents from various publications of the scholars whose views about the importance of social class I am questioning, including Shapin (1975, 1979a, 1979b) and Cooter (1984, 1989). I have also benefited from Parssinen's (1970, 1974) sample of 155 phrenologists listed either in the *Dictionary of National Biography* or *Modern English Biography.*
59. For the relationship between social class and status as a laterborn, $r=.20$ ($df=1/86$, $t=1.86$, $p<.07$).
60. *Technical information for Figure 10.5:* For birth order and acceptance of phrenology, $r=.40$ ($df=1/86$, $t=4.03$, $p<.0001$). For status as a nonscientist, $r=.26$ ($df=1/86$, $t=2.51$, $p<.02$). For social class and acceptance of phrenology, $r=.25$ ($df=1/86$, $t=2.38$, $p<.05$). These are all uncontrolled correlations. For social class and acceptance of phrenology, controlled for birth order, the partial $r=.19$

(df=1/85, t=1.77, p<.10). When controlled for status as a scientist, this partial correlation becomes .13 (df=1/84, t=1.24, p<.23). In the acceptance of phrenology, there is a significant interaction between birth order and status as a nonscientist, r=–.38 (df=1/84, t=–3.77, p<.001). Firstborns were more strongly affected by a lack of scientific training than were laterborns, who tended to support phrenology even when fully trained in scientific methods.

61. Darwin 1985– , 1:97.

62. Egerton 1976:189.

63. Based on a four-variable path-analytic model, social class is responsible for 4 percent of the explained variance (in terms of cumulative path coefficients), and just 1 percent of the actual variance. Besides birth order, this model includes social attitudes, status as a scientist, and social class (R=.65, df=4/70, F=12.76, p<.001). For the other variables, the contributions to the explained variance, broken down by path analysis, are: birth order (54 percent of the total), social attitudes (37 percent), and status as a scientist (5 percent). All predictors except social class are statistically significant. For the relative variance explained by social class versus the other three predictors, 4 percent/96 percent=1/24. Social class and status as a scientist are only weakly correlated (r=.14), so social class is not being excluded from the model because it cross correlates highly with this other variable. As soon as birth order enters the model, social class ceases to be a significant predictor.

64. Claims by historians of science, based on group differences, are generally suspect if they are not controlled for individual differences. Recognizing such errors of historical interpretation can be extremely difficult without hypothesis testing. Group differences may be present superficially, based on *recruitment effects*, but resolve themselves into individual differences once appropriate controls are instituted.

A good example of this problem is Paul Forman's thesis about the rise of indeterminacy in physics in Weimar Germany. According to Forman (1971, 1978), Germany's defeat during the First World War caused Weimar intellectuals to think differently about science. People let go of their faith in science and technology, which had failed them during the war, and instead turned to mystical and spiritual beliefs. One consequence of this intellectual trend, Forman argues, was the rejection of classical causality in physics. Because individual differences are so extensive, they seriously confound Forman's thesis. Firstborns, social conservatives, and older scientists consistently defended the causal point of view, whereas laterborns, social liberals, and younger scientists endorsed indeterminacy (R=.39, df=1/32, t=2.38, p<.03). For this reason, the First World War inspired some people to *reaffirm* their faith in rationality, not to repudiate it. Firstborn Albert Einstein, who refused to believe in a dice-playing God, is a prime example.

By assuming individual differences to be unproblematic, Forman's sociological thesis misses an important feature of this scientific debate. If we systematically weigh the most important individual differences in the reception of quantum mechanics, these differences are actually more influential than whether a scientist was German or not, or lived through the First World War. Based on a computer model that employs just five biographical variables, Einstein's predicted probability of supporting indeterminacy was 28 percent. Controlled for the individual differences that made Einstein and other physicists resist indeterminacy, being German is not a significant factor in this dispute (r=.01, df=1/31, t=0.49, p<.96). Controlled for individual and national differences, year of participation in this debate is also not a significant predictor of scientific stance (r=–.25, df=1/30, t=–1.40, p<.17).

My test of Forman's thesis does not refute his general claim that attacks on scientific rationality arose in response to the First World War. There is considerable impressionistic evidence in support of this claim (see also Harrington 1987, 1992). What is called into question is the claim that, controlled for individual differences in revolutionary personality, the Zeitgeist exerted itself as a significant "main effect" on the thinking of German mathematicians and physicists.

65. In addition to the research I have cited in this chapter, scholarship on the French Revolution illustrates the consistent failure of historians to test their claims about social class (Chapter 13, especially Figure 13.2).

66. Crews 1986:140.

11. The Protestant Reformation

1. Spitz 1985:346, 384.
2. Kelley 1981:125.
3. Ozment 1992:xiv.
4. Liermann 1941:322; Moeller 1972:72; Spitz 1985:77, 87, 380; Ozment 1992:11.
5. Bainton 1950:79–83; Spitz 1985:66–68.
6. Quoted in Ozment 1992:11–12.
7. Spitz 1985:88–89.
8. Hillerbrand 1973:38; see also Spitz 1985:74.
9. See Hendrix's (1981) valuable account of Luther's changing attitudes toward the papacy during this critical period.
10. Ozment 1992:6.
11. Moeller 1972:71.
12. Spitz 1973:67.
13. Hillerbrand 1973:187.
14. Hillerbrand 1973:187.
15. Ozment 1992:20.
16. Dickens 1989:326; Heimpel 1954:156 (quoted in Moeller 1972:114).
17. Hillerbrand 1973:40.
18. I have distilled these eight claims from the works of Swanson (1967), Moeller (1972), Hillerbrand (1973:38–41, 186, 206), Spitz (1985:181–91), Dickens (1989:325–38), and Ozment (1975; 1992:19–21, 32–37).
19. Moeller 1972:14.
20. Hillerbrand 1973:38; see also Moeller 1972, who has argued convincingly for this thesis.
21. Dickens 1989:89.
22. My principal sources for this sample include Durant 1957; Williams 1962: Elton 1963; Léonard 1965; Hillerbrand 1971, 1973; Ozment 1975, 1980, 1992; Dickens 1989; and Spitz 1985. Further technical details on my Protestant Reformation sample are provided in Appendix 7.
23. I have employed multiple regression, but other modeling approaches, such as

path analysis, are also possible. The partial correlation of birth order with support for the Reformation, controlled for the six other significant predictors in the model, is .37 (*df*=1/513, t=9.12, p<.0001).

Appendix 7 provides further technical details on the model described here, as well as on alternative models. The best model, selected by the criterion of Mallows' C_p accepts 7 of the 9 predictors discussed in the text (multiple R=.61 [adjusted R=.60], *df*=7/513 [the harmonic mean], F=42.60, p<.0001). Being a humanist is not a significant predictor, and being a member of the royalty is too highly correlated with social class to add significantly to the seven-variable model.

24. For birth order and acceptance of the Protestant Reformation among siblings, r=.33 (*df*=1/112, t=3.69, p<.001).

25. The correlation of age with support for the Reformation is −.22 (*df*=1/511, p<.0001). Birth order interacts with age. Laterborns were significantly more immune to the effects of age than were firstborns (partial r=.20, *df*=1/131, t=2.36, p<.02).

26. Two-thirds of laterborns over the age of thirty-nine accepted the Reformation (32 out of 46). Only 2 of the 17 firstborns did so (r=.52, *df*=1/61, t=4.69, p<.0001). For other comparisons between the influence of birth order and that of age, see Chapter 2, Figure 2.2 (on the Darwinian revolution); Chapter 9 (on social attitudes during the Enlightenment); and Chapter 14 (on revolutions in science).

27. *Technical information for Figure 11.1:* The partial correlation of social class with confessional choice, controlled for the other six predictors in the model, is .10 (*df*=1/513, t=2.32, p<.05). For birth order, the partial correlation is .37 (*df*=1/513, t=9.12, p<.0001). For the difference in variance explained, $.37^2/.10^2$=15.2 to 1. A recruitment bias is present in the data for social class, since members of the royalty exhibit the highest frequency of being firstborn. For the relationship between birth order and social class, r=.11 (*df*=1/349, t=2.08, p<.05). In addition, members of the clergy (especially the lower clergy) tended to be laterborn relative to nonclergy (r=.10, *df*=1/362, t=1.84, p<.05; one-tailed test).

28. In this discussion of partible inheritance I have drawn on Fichtner's (1989) valuable study.

29. Fichtner 1989:53; Ozment 1983:152.

30. For birth order and support for Protestantism among theologians, r=.29 ($\chi^2[1]$=5.34, N=64, p<.05).

31. In an eight-variable model, the partial correlation of personal influences with confessional choice is .19 (*df*=1/512, t=4.34, p<.001). On the definition and coding of "personal influence," see Appendix 7.

32. For the relationship between birth order and the religious cause for which a person was martyred, r=.68 ($\chi^2[1]$=16.67, N=36, p<.001).

33. On Luther as a religious "moderate," see Dickens 1989:87; Ozment 1992: 121, 127, 136, 141. See also Hillerbrand 1973:208; Hendrix 1981:15, 139.

34. On the distinction between the Magisterial and Radical Reformations, see Williams (1962).

35. Ozment 1980:264. See also Moeller 1972:34; Dickens 1967:72.

36. Ozment 1992:127.

37. *Technical information for Figure 11.3:* Based on a seven-variable model of the Reformation, Martin Luther's predicted probability of becoming a Protestant was 67 percent. Based on the same seven-variable model, Knox's likelihood of joining the Protestant Reformation was 78 percent. For Calvin and Zwingli, the analogous likelihoods are 80 and 82 percent, respectively. By contrast, the predicted probabilities of becoming a Protestant were generally greater than 90 percent for the leaders of the Radical Reformation. These probabilities are derived from BMDP's LR program (Logistic Regression), which assigns a specific probability to each individual outcome (Dixon 1992).
38. Erikson 1958:73.
39. For convincing rebuttals of Erikson's claims about Luther, see Bainton 1977; Spitz 1977; and Ozment 1980:225–31. The fact that Erikson exaggerated the evidence for parental conflict in Luther's case does not negate the circumstance that parental conflict is a good predictor of radicalism (Chapter 5, especially Figure 5.1). If Luther had experienced the kinds of hostile feelings toward his parents that Erikson claims, a multivariate Reformation model suggests that he should have become a Radical Reformer.
40. Armstrong 1910, 1:259.
41. Armstrong 1910, 1:259.
42. Spitz 1985:184. My interpretation of the Reformation lends support to the views of Ozment (1975) and Brady (1982:176), who have criticized socioeconomic theses about the Reformation, including the famous Weber thesis. According to these scholars, the Reformation entailed a spiritual schism.
43. Kelley 1981:78.
44. Scarisbrick 1968:508.
45. Dickens 1989:51.
46. Hendrix (1990, 1994) has sought to explain confessional choice in terms of "family loyalties." Across generations, family loyalty is indeed a significant predictor of confessional choice (r=.66, df=1/57, t=6.56, p<.0001). This circumstance follows from the strong correlation between the social attitudes of parents and their offspring (Chapter 9). A two-variable model, which includes birth order, does an even better job of predicting religious allegiances. Offspring tended to adopt their parents' religious views, except in cases involving the disruptive influence of birth order (partial r=.21, df=1/42, t=1.81, p<.05 [one-tailed test]). Many offspring were disloyal to their parents, especially when their birth orders were different.
47. For birth order and confessional choice among spouses, r=.55 ($\chi^2[1]$=12.51, N=41, p<.001).
48. For birth order and confessional choice among parents and their offspring, r=.46 ($\chi^2[1]$=16.00, N=75, p<.0001).
49. Schultze 1957:443.
50. Kawerau 1910b:183.
51. Kamen 1985:124.
52. Pollard 1897b:331, 332.
53. Pollard 1897a:305.
54. Dickens 1989:229.

55. Weir 1991:3.
56. Erickson 1980:117.
57. Routh 1964:35.
58. Fraser 1992:229–30.
59. The order of birth of Anne Boleyn and her two siblings has been much discussed. Of the three Boleyn children, Mary was definitely the eldest daughter and Anne almost certainly the second child. Anne's other sibling was a brother (Weir 1991:146–47; see also Paget 1981).
60. Weir 1991:281.
61. Dickens 1989:135, 136.
62. Warnicke 1989:111; Weir 1991:224.
63. Weir 1991:413. Various sources give Catherine Howard's birth order and sibship size differently (for example, as fifth of ten children), but all agree that she was "born low down in the family order, and formed part of a crowd from birth" (Fraser 1992:318).
64. Scarisbrick 1968:429; Fraser 1992:322.
65. An older brother died the year after Jane was born, making ten Seymour siblings in all (Fraser 1992:235).
66. Hume 1905:293.
67. Hume 1905:293, 298. See also Weir 1991:341; Fraser 1992:233.
68. Fraser 1992:262.
69. Hume 1905:293.
70. Scarisbrick 1968:375.
71. Scarisbrick 1968:373.
72. Weir 1991:429.
73. Spitz 1985:267.
74. Scarisbrick 1968:433; see also Routh 1964:41.
75. Weir 1991:519.
76. Gairdner 1887:1219.
77. Controlled for shyness, the partial correlation of relative birth rank with the fates of the marriages is .98 ($df=1/4$, $t=7.87$, $p<.01$). Given the large number of variables in my study, one might argue that this is a chance effect. Still, birth order is a significant predictor of confessional choice among Reformation spouses, which in turn predicts marital conflict during the Reformation (see n. 47). In addition, I have considered only five variables in my analysis of Henry's wives: birth order, marital order, shyness, social mores (including sexual behavior), and religious attitudes. Using the criterion of Mallows' C_p, which penalizes the model for each variable that is added, a two-variable model (birth order and shyness) is selected from among all possible models. For the two-variable model, $R=.99$ (adjusted $R=.99$, $df=2/3$, $F=98.77$, $p<.005$). Both social proclivities and religious attitudes are strongly correlated with the outcome of the marriage (liberals fared worse than conservatives). Because these two variables are already predicted by birth order and shyness, they do not enter the multivariate model.
78. Based on relative birth rank (from firstborn to lastborn), the order of Henry VIII's marriages is significant: $r=-.74$ ($df=1/4$, $t=-2.21$, $p<.05$ [one-tailed test]).
79. The question of birth order and marital satisfaction has been explored by

Toman (1992; see also Toman and Preiser 1973). The evidence in support of his theory of "complementarity" (which holds that successful marriages duplicate one's relationship with one's older or younger siblings) is conflicting (Ernst and Angst 1983:177–81). According to Toman, a firstborn male with a younger sister should tend to get along better with a laterborn female who grew up with an elder brother. Toman also applies this thesis to parent-offspring relationships. If there is a link between birth order and mate selection, it is undoubtedly more complex than posited by Toman. In the context of interpersonal behavior during radical revolutions, most of the evidence presented in this book contradicts Toman's thesis. During these upheavals, complementary birth orders *increase* conflict, not only between siblings but also between parents and their offspring, and between spouses. On the topic of sibling differences and mate selection, see further Appendix 10, section 10.

80. Dickens 1989:36.

81. Hillerbrand 1973:38.

82. Brady (1982:164) critically reviews such claims.

83. Dickens 1989:92; see also Spitz 1985:184.

84. Hillerbrand 1973:188.

85. For the literature on collectivist versus individualist cultures, see Ross and Nisbett 1991:181.

86. On Protestantism and the rise of modern science, see Stimson 1935; Jones 1936/1961; and Merton 1938. The history of research on this topic, with summaries of the literature spawned by the "Merton thesis," has been comprehensively surveyed by I. Bernard Cohen (1990) in an extremely useful volume. The Merton thesis is an extension of the Weber thesis, which argued that the Reformation was engineered by "the needs of men who were determined that the church should no longer fetter their economic lives through ethical norms" (Brady 1982: 164). See Weber (1904), Troeltsch (1913), and Tawney (1926), who developed this general argument.

87. For religious denomination and support for liberal scientific innovations before 1750, r=.21 (df=1/629, t=5.39, p<.0001). After 1750 there is no significant difference in support by religious denomination.

88. Controlled for social attitudes, which were more liberal among Protestant than Catholic scientists, *firstborn* Protestants were significantly more likely than *firstborn* Catholics to support liberal scientific innovations between 1543 and 1750 (r=.20, df=1/83, t=1.87, p<.05 [one-tailed test]). The effect size for laterborns is almost the same. Hence Protestantism exerted an independent effect, over and above birth order, on openness to scientific innovation (r=.16, df=1/180, t=2.21, p<.03; for individuals whose birth orders are known).

Controlled for birth order, religious denomination, and year of birth, these three variables exhibit a three-way interaction with scientific eminence (r=.06, df=1/1,750, t=2.36, p<.02). Relative to the rest of the population, firstborn Protestants and laterborn Catholics are significantly more eminent during the early modern period. Early modern firstborns, in particular, exhibit a particularly high frequency of being among the leaders of major scientific revolutions. This interaction effect may reflect the fact that firstborns tend to have higher IQs than laterborns (Zajonc 1976). In science, the benefits of intelligence are facilitated by open-mindedness. Intelligent conservatives tend to be formidable opponents of radical innovation, detracting from their eminence in historical retrospect.

12. Political Trends

1. Eysenck 1954; Eysenck and Wilson 1978.
2. Eysenck and Wilson 1978:5, 31, 181.
3. Eysenck 1954:178–79, 210, 226; Eysenck and Wilson 1978:309; McCrae and Costa 1987; Feingold 1994.
4. Eysenck and Wilson 1978:113; Feingold 1994.
5. Koch 1955a. For a review of Koch's findings, see Chapter 3, especially Figure 3.2.
6. Koch 1955a:15, 26. Males who kill their mates out of jealousy are likely to be firstborns, although no one, to my knowledge, has tested this hypothesis.
7. Boone 1986.
8. For the relationship between birth order and racism, see Sherwood and Nataupsky 1968:55–56; Lieberman and Reynolds 1978.
9. For research on the heritability of political and religious attitudes, see Martin et al. 1986; Eaves, Eysenck, and Martin 1989.
10. Andrews 1968:185.
11. My list of enlightened despots includes the figures most cited by Gagliardo (1967) and Andrews (1968). Some enlightened despots, such as Joseph II (and especially his younger brother Leopold II), might be considered borderline "liberals" rather than conservatives (Andrews 1968:7–8). Others, like Napoleon, were more tough-minded than the rest. As a whole, however, these seven rulers were either conservatives or moderates who leaned toward limited reforms of a tender-minded nature.
12. In addition to Leopold II of Tuscany, the other three younger sons were Charles III, Stanislaw II Augustus, and Napoleon Bonaparte.
13. Eysenck and Wilson 1978:181.
14. For birth order and support for the various Reformation sects, coded on a 3-step scale of radicalism, r=.33 (df=1/248, t=5.44, p<.0001). Anabaptists fall within the most radical category (Ozment 1992:22, 126; Williams 1962:226). Although my sample of known birth orders is small for members of this heavily persecuted sect, every Anabaptist in my survey was a laterborn.
15. Paynes 1969:25.
16. James 1969:34.
17. James 1969:44.
18. James 1969:112.
19. This birth-order information on Soviet political leaders differs from that reported by Somit et al. (1996:84), who cite biological rather than functional birth order. For example, they report Stalin as being the youngest of four children, but all of his older siblings died in infancy, making him functionally an only child (Hingley 1974). Because birth-order information on Soviet leaders is not readily available, and because it is sometimes contradictory, I list here the most trustworthy sources. For Stalin: Hingley 1974:3; for Khrushchev: Leonhard 1965:13. Other Soviet leaders whose birth orders are known include Brezhnev, who was

the second of three children and an elder son (Academy of Sciences of the USSR 1978:16; and Murphy 1981:6). Dornberg (1974:39) considers Brezhnev to have been a firstborn, which is almost certainly an error. Two other post-Stalin leaders on whom birth-order information is available—Gorbachev and Yeltsin—are both functional firstborns (Doder and Branson 1990:3–4; and Solovyov and Klepikova 1992:115). By his father's previous marriage, Gorbachev had an elder brother who died on the front during World War Two. Gorbachev does not appear to have grown up with this elder half-brother.

20. Stipp 1994.

21. Demaris 1977:43.

22. Smith 1976:32.

23. Smith 1976:29.

24. Smith 1976:154.

25. Smith 1976:154.

26. Demaris 1977:45.

27. Demaris 1977:22.

28. Demaris 1977:16.

29. Smith 1967:283.

30. Smith 1976:87.

31. Smith 1976:88.

32. Smith 1982:1.

33. Elms 1976:31.

34. Smith 1982:38, 116.

35. Oedipal conflict is not the key to revolutionary personality in politics, as Wolfenstein (1967) has proposed, even if it often provides an important influence on firstborns. For a formal test of this assertion, see n. 51 and n. 56.

36. These and other details are taken from Rejai and Phillips 1979:176–77.

37. Quoted in Rejai and Phillips 1979:177.

38. Quoted in Rejai and Phillips 1979:177.

39. See Chapter 6, especially the discussion of "Women Reformers"; Chapter 9, especially figures 9.3 and 9.4; and Chapter 11, especially Figure 11.1.

40. Weber 1984:562.

41. Weber 1984.

42. For the entire history of the Supreme Court, with its 108 appointments, the correlation between relative birth rank and the party of the nominating president is .36 (df=1/106, t=3.99, p<.001). Laterborn justices have also tended to be Democrats (r=.30, df=1/106, t=3.22, p<.005). Controlled for this fact, Democratic presidents have still tended to nominate laterborns (and particularly lastborns), whereas Republican presidents have tended to nominate firstborns (partial r=.21, df=1/106, t=2.20, p<.05).

43. For relative birth rank and Supreme Court voting in a liberal direction, r=.38 (df=1/64, t=3.29, p<.01).

Independently of birth order, party affiliations of the justices are a significant predictor of liberal voting (partial r=.27, df=1/63, t=2.22, p<.05). Using a two-variable model that includes relative birth rank and party affiliation, the multiple correlation with voting patterns is .46 ([adjusted r=.43], df=2/63, F=8.22, p<.001). There is significant tendency for laterborn justices to dissent more often from the majority. For the entire period of the court for which such evidence has been compiled, $r=.21$, ($df=1/96$, $t=2.09$, $p<.05$). See also Somit et al. (1996:48) For additional information on Supreme Court voting trends, including the sources from which these statistics are derived, see Appendix 9, Technical Discussion 8.

44. Lewis 1969:2721.

45. McInerney 1985:844.

46. Rejai and Phillips 1979, 1983, and 1988.

47. Rejai and Phillips 1983:125.

48. Rejai and Phillips 1983:111. These two investigators have provided an elaborate classification of revolutionary types, based on factor analysis of their data. My 3-step classification of revolutionaries along a conservative/radical scale is based on their own taxonomy, which includes nine subcategories. Some political leaders load highly on more than one subcategory. These individuals have been assigned to the category for which they display the highest factor score. The criteria for being a conservative revolutionary are being a member of the IRA in Northern Ireland and/or a high loading on the factor for "defenders of the faith." Radical revolutionaries comprise agitators, professional revolutionaries, and elders (former professional revolutionaries who have become elder statesmen). All other revolutionary subtypes have been assigned to the category of moderate revolutionaries.

49. Rejai and Phillips 1983:110.

50. Rejai and Phillips 1983:102–5.

51. For birth order and support for radical political revolutions, $r=.48$ ($df=1/47$, $t=3.77$, $p<.001$). Controlled for sibship size, the partial correlation between birth order and support is .39 ($df=1/45$, $t=2.84$, $p<.01$). Controlled for birth order, the partial correlation between parent-offspring conflict and support is .30 ($df=1/39$, $t=1.93$, $p<.06$). Relative to parent-offspring conflict, birth order explains 2.6 times the variance in support for radical revolutions.

52. George Washington, the eldest of five surviving children, had two older half brothers many years his senior. These two brothers were raised in England. When these brothers returned to America, about the time George turned eleven, they lived on separate estates (Flexner 1965:12). Rejai and Phillips count Washington as a firstborn. So do I.

53. For support for radical revolutions and the influence of a crisis, $r=.48$ ($df=1/47$, $t=2.48$, $p<.02$). For birth order and support for revolutionary causes during a state of crisis, $r=-.20$ ($df=1/47$, $t=-1.43$, $p<.16$). This statistic would surely be significant if more biographical data were available. Missing data are most common for political agitators in developing countries. These people tend to be laterborn and to have participated in revolutions that lacked a precipitating crisis. Based on the estimation of the missing data using BMDP's Program 8D, the correlation between birth order and being a leader in a crisis situation is $-.35$ ($df=1/56$ [the harmonic mean], $t=-2.80$, $p<.01$): firstborns are crisis leaders.

In my quantitative assessment of "crises," I have followed Rejai and Phillips (1983). Based on a variety of situational attributes, they have classified their 31 revolutions into two groups: (1) those, like the American and French Revolutions, that were triggered by an escalating series of conflicts; and (2) those that arose independently of a preexisting crisis. The noncrisis group includes most Third World revolutions, which, according to Rejai and Phillips, have been "systematically . . . planned, organized, and executed by relatively elite groups over long periods of time" (1983:132).

54. Quoted in Pistrak 1961:3.

55. I expand on this discussion of crises in Chapter 14, where I deal with their role in scientific revolutions.

56. Using BMDP's Program 8D to estimate missing data, and Program 9R (All Possible Subsets Regression), a five-variable model is chosen by the criterion of Mallows' C_p. Rank ordered in terms of the partial correlations, the most efficacious predictors of being a radical revolutionary are (1) coming from a developing country, (2) having had high parent-offspring conflict, (3) being laterborn, (4) coming from a large sibship, and (5) not being involved in a crisis situation (R=.68, adjusted R=.65, df=5/64 [the harmonic mean], F=10.94, p<.0001). In path-analytic models, sibling differences account for 59 percent of the explained variance, whereas situational variables (coming from a developing country, and the presence or absence of a crisis) account for the remaining 41 percent of the explained variance. In sum, sibling differences appear to be more important than situational factors. Path analysis also reverses the explanatory importance of parent-offspring conflict and birth order because being laterborn tends to promote greater conflict with parents.

57. See Stewart 1977, 1992. See also Simonton 1990b for a review of related evidence that reinforces Stewart's findings.

58. On political leaders, see Stewart 1977, 1992. On Nobel laureates, see Clark and Rice 1982.

59. Toland 1976:9–11.

60. Mabee 1970.

61. Hamilton 1936:69.

62. Oates 1975:126.

63. Foner 1971:1.

64. Harris 1964; Sutton-Smith and Rosenberg 1970:9.

65. Pasternak 1995:3.

66. Shute 1985:333.

67. Pasternak 1995:xii.

68. Pasternak 1995:48.

69. Pasternak 1995:xiii.

70. My sample of abolitionists is drawn from Whitman's *American Reformers* (1985) and includes 91 individuals. Another 25 individuals in Whitman's survey were involved in the later black rights movement and 10 additional individuals are recorded as having fought for Indian rights. My militancy scale encompasses the following ordinal categories, as described by Whitman's contributors: (1) strongly favored nonviolent resistance; (2) campaigned for the abolition of slavery (or racial discrimination), but rejected pacifist methods; (3) advocated some militant methods, particularly *defensive* aggression; (4) supported individuals who advocated the use of violent means to overthrow slavery (or racial discrimination), but did not adopt violent methods themselves; (5) employed violent means to achieve racial equality. With the use of four independent raters, the effective reliability of militancy ratings is .91.

These militancy classifications correlate reasonably highly with another classification based on the organizational affiliations detailed by Mabee (1970): r=.81 (df=1/30, t=7.57, p<.001).

71. For the abolition movement, the partial correlation of the quadratic (U-shaped trend) in militancy, controlled for relative birth rank and family size, is .27 (df=1/62, t=2.16, p<.04). This trend is present among women as well as men, and among blacks as well as whites.

72. For the black rights movement, the partial correlation of the quadratic (U-shaped trend) in militancy, controlled for relative birth rank and family size, is .43 (df=1/21, t=2.17, p<.05). These quadratic trends in militancy (see also note 71) match that observed in the French Revolution (Chapter 13).

73. In my sample of participants in the struggle for racial equality, blacks were more militant than whites (which is hardly surprising) and men were more militant than women. However, neither race nor gender is a *significant* predictor of militancy, whereas birth order is.

74. *Technical information for Figure 12.2:* Controlled for the linear trend, as well as for sibship size, the relationship between birth rank and militancy is strongly curvilinear (partial r=.27, df=1/91, t=2.68, p<.01).

Hypothetically, *inverted* U-shaped relationships with birth rank should manifest themselves in conservative movements displaying a tender-minded bent. Modern spiritualism, which affirmed the existence of life after death, was one such movement. Support for this belief exhibits the expected curvilinear trend. Middle children disproportionately favored this theory, controlled for the linear effect that birth order exerts on liberal thinking (partial r=–.16 [df=1/106, t=1.69, p<.05; one-tailed test]). Firstborns seem to have become spiritualists because it was a conservative doctrine, reaffirming the existence of God. Middle children appear to have adopted spiritualism because it was tender-minded. Lastborns, who tend to be liberal and tough-minded, wanted little to do with what they perceived as superstitious nonsense.

75. Moore 1971:38–39.

76. Moore 1971:39.

77. Lewis 1970:12.

78. Lewis 1970:12; Davis 1969:17.

79. In Rejai and Phillips's (1983:152, 156–57) study of revolutionary elites, middle children are rated somewhat higher on a measure of "romantic" political inclinations (r=.20, df=1/43, t=1.31, p<.10 [one-tailed test; based on the contrast]). According to these two investigators, this measure reflects the "gentler side" of revolutionary character. On middleborns more generally, see Salmon 1996.

80. Winter 1973:158.

81. James 1969:33.

82. James 1969:33–34.

83. James 1969:171–72.

84. Schachter et al. 1976; Schachter et al. 1978; Schachter 1982.

85. Alexander 1979:158; see also Daly and Wilson 1988a:52, 62, 75.

86. We still know very little about the day-to-day psychological dynamics that

promote sibling differences in militancy, and much of my discussion of this topic has been more speculative than I would prefer. More research needs to be done on the ways in which siblings stake out their family niches and develop strategies to maximize their interests. This is a topic that will require greater attention to siblings who have grown up together. See further Appendix 10, section 2.

13. The French Revolution

1. Furet and Richet 1970:105.
2. Lefebvre 1962–64, 1:124.
3. Schama 1989:8.
4. Quoted in Bowers 1950:323.
5. Schama 1989:615.
6. Higonnet 1985:538.
7. Ozouf 1989c:351.
8. Higonnet 1985:513–14, 534.
9. Soboul 1980:8 (quoting Mathiez); Lefebvre 1962–64, 1:214, 266; Bowers 1950:260.
10. Patrick 1972:216, 219, 225; Soboul 1980:11.
11. Greer 1935:97.
12. Higonnet 1985:517, 530, 538.
13. Bowers 1950:34.
14. Bowers 1950:340.
15. Palmer 1989:108.
16. Kuscinski 1917–19:382.
17. Dawson 1948:1.
18. See, for example, Kuscinski's (1917–19) articles on Bonnet de Meautry, Chénier, Crassous, Dufriche-Valaze, Dumont, Gaston, Laloy, Marey, Méjansac, Montaut, Reverchon, Second, Serveau, Valdruche, and Yzarn-Valady. A number of deputies, including Chénier, Crassous, La Revellière-Lépeaux, and Second, had brothers who were executed for their royalist views.
19. Kuscinski 1917–19:230; d'Amat 1968.
20. Robert and Gougny 1889–91, 2:86–87.
21. Ozouf 1989c:351.
22. Ozouf 1989c:351.
23. Chaumié 1980:22, 29.
24. Higonnet 1985:538.
25. *Technical information for Figure 13.1:* For the curvilinear relationship between birth order and party allegiances, r=.24 (df=1/325, t=4.53, p<.0001). Within the National Convention, the Plain includes a significantly larger proportion of middle children than other factions. Controlled for the linear influence of relative birth rank (from first to last), the quadratic trend (contrasting middleborns with other deputies) is also a significant predictor of radicalism. The most radical deputies were either firstborns or lastborns (r=.16, df=1/195, t=2.31, p<.03).
26. Lefebvre 1962–64, 1:209–10.
27. Firstborns and lastborns exhibit significantly greater heterogeneity in party affiliations than do middleborns, who generally sided with the Plain (r=.40,

df=1/193, *t*=6.03, *p*<.0001). In his memoirs, the Montagnard Choudieu disdainfully described the Plain as comprising "all the men who did not have the courage to have an opinion" (1897:219).

28. Lefebvre 1962–64, 2:121.

29. I refer to Louis XVI as a firstborn because his elder brother died when Louis was six, leaving him as the eldest of five surviving siblings (Schwennicke 1980–91, 2: Tafel 30).

30. Palmer 1989:4. The seven firstborns on the Committee of Public Safety include five individuals having younger siblings (Barère, Billaud-Varenne, Collot d'Herbois, Robespierre, and Saint-Just) and two only children (Hérault de Séchelles and Prieur of the Côte d'Or). The four younger sons on the committee were Carnot, Couthon, Robert Lindet, and Jeanbon Saint-André. Prieur of the Marne was the second of three children, but I have not been able to determine the sex of his elder sibling. Among the temporary members of the committee, three were firstborns (Cambon, Gasparin, and Treilhard) and only one was a younger son (Danton). By and large, the younger sons on the committee were less ruthless than the elder sons. Lindet, for example, refused to sign the death warrant for Danton. Only one of these younger sons (Couthon) was executed or banished for his role in the Terror, as against six of the firstborns. Even in such a small sample, this contrast is statistically significant (*r*=.61, *N*=11, *p*<.05 [exact test]). It is worth noting that the other great executive committee under the Terror, the Committee of General Security, included a majority of firstborns among its members. Among individuals for whom birth-order information is available, five out of nine were firstborns. Another three members are known only as "eldest sons" and may also have been firstborns.

31. Palmer 1989:9.

32. Lefebvre 1962–64, 2:133.

33. Palmer 1989:12.

34. Palmer 1989:9.

35. Curtis 1973:244.

36. Begis 1893:262, 279; Palmer 1989:166–71.

37. Ward 1934:18.

38. Ward 1934:19.

39. Mazlish (1976) has written about Robespierre as a "revolutionary ascetic." In terms of the Big Five personality dimensions, this feature of Robespierre's personality is probably best classified under Conscientiousness, not Antagonism (McCrae and Costa 1987:85).

40. Lefebvre 1962–64, 2:134.

41. Palmer 1989:7.

42. See Chapter 9, especially figures 9.3–9.4. For France alone, the correlation between birth order and liberal social attitudes is .15 (*df*=1/260, *t*=2.43, *p*<.02). This correlation is derived from those scientists in my study, from the Reformation to the present, who have been rated on their social attitudes. This sample includes several prominent participants in the French Revolution, such as Bailly, Fourcroy, Guillotin, Guyton de Morveau, Marat, and Monge.

43. Chaumié 1980:32, 41, 43, 49.

44. Kates 1985:112–15.

45. Ozouf 1989c:357.
46. Among these sibling deputies, the contrast between Montagnards and non-Montagnards yields a correlation with birth order of –.63 (r=*phi*, N=16, p<.05 [exact test]).
47. Matrat 1971:169. Augustin Robespierre's nickname derives from his second given name: Bon.
48. Augustin defended the ultraradical Hébert at the National Convention in January 1794, only to be rebuked by his older brother with the retort: "He [Augustin] has rendered great services [on mission] at Toulon, but in intervening in the present discussion, he is in error" (Kuscinski 1917–19:531). Maximilien Robespierre had Hébert guillotined two months later.
49. For the birth-order contrast between Feuillants and later Jacobins (who broke away from the Feuillants in 1791), r (*phi*) =.20 (χ^2=5.30, N=135, p<.05); for the contrast between Feuillants and "core" Girondins, r (*phi*) =.23 (χ^2=2.64, N=49, p<.06 [one-tailed test]). For the contrast between "core" Girondins and Girondin "sympathizers," r (*phi*) =.32 (χ^2=5.72, N=55, p<.01). For the contrast between "core" Montagnards and Montagnard "sympathizers," r (*phi*) =.28 (χ^2=6.99, N=90, p<.001).

For the overall relationship between relative birth rank and party affiliations within the National Convention, r=.20 (*df*=1/196, t=2.83, p<.005). Controlled for relative birth rank, a quadratic trend contrasting middleborns with all other birth positions is also statistically significant (partial r=.19 *df*=1/195, t=2.76, p<.01). A better measure of birth order's influence is the two trends combined: r=.27 (*df*=2/195, F=7.94, p<.001). Firstborns and lastborns were both more likely than middleborns to gravitate toward the two militant extremes of the National Convention. When party affiliations are coded as a quadratic trend, with the Plain taken as the convention's middle ground, the multiple R for a two-variable model (using relative birth rank and the significant contrast between middleborns and other birth positions) increases to .36 (*df*=2/195, F=14.14, p<.0001).

My classification of deputies is based on the pooled assessments of Patrick (1972), Higonnet (1985), and Brunel (1980). (It makes little difference in the results which historian's classification scheme one employs.) For further historiographical sources and technical details, see Appendix 8.
50. Kuscinski 1917–19:603.
51. Higonnet (1985:525) calls this bloodthirsty bunch the Other Left.
52. Ozouf 1989b:221.
53. Ozouf 1989b:221–22. A relative dearth of revenge motives among younger siblings helps to explain an otherwise puzzling fact about the French Revolution. Those Girondins who survived the Terror were not generally among the deputies who pursued former terrorists (Chaumié 1980:29–30). This act of political hypocrisy was left largely to firstborns, such as Amar, Barère, Billaud-Varenne, and Merlin of Thionville, who had themselves supported the Terror. Having learned how to be tough on "moderates," this wily group was equally adept at being tough on former "extremists." Regardless of the stage of the revolution, a tendency toward moral outrage was their strong suit.
54. Of the 29 Independents of the Mountain for whom I have birth-order information, 24 are correctly classified as being Indulgents or not, based on birth order

and the political assignments of Kuscinski and other scholars (r=.48, df=1/27, t=2.81, p<.01). Three of the 4 Indulgents whose birth orders are known were youngest sons (Basire, Joseph Chénier, and Danton himself). Basire and Danton were next-to-youngest children, whereas Chénier was a youngest child. Desmoulins, a firstborn, is generally classified with the Indulgents, but he "differed markedly" from them, as Ozouf (1989b:221) has pointed out. Whereas Danton sought reconciliation with his militant colleagues, and even freed some of the people that Desmoulins successfully campaigned to imprison, Desmoulins consistently wielded moderation "as a weapon" against his enemies.

Danton's close friend Philippeaux, whom Prieur of the Côte d'Or described as "blundering, heedless, and vain," was a firstborn. According to Kuscinski, Philippeaux perished owing to his "arrogance" and "self-conceit" rather than for any "indulgent" qualities (1917–19:493). Although a Dantonist, he was not an Indulgent.

Twenty-one of the 25 Independents of the Mountain who were not Indulgents were either firstborns or eldest sons. The most well known of these firstborns and eldest sons include (with italics indicating the names of firstborns) *Billaud-Varenne,* Carrier, *Collot d'Herbois, Fabre d'Eglantine,* Fouché, *Fréron, Hérault de Séchelles* (an only child), and *Merlin of Thionville* (all Hébertists); *Javogues* and *Marat* (Maratists); *Jullien* and *Le Bon* (Robespierrists); and *Tallien* (a terrorist). *Hébert,* the ultraradical publisher of *Le Père Duchesne,* was a functional firstborn, but he was not a member of the National Convention.

55. In addition to being a measure of aggressive and antagonistic behavior, my scale of tough-mindedness accords closely with the kinds of political attitudes described by Eysenck (1954:178–79, 210, 226) and Eysenck and Wilson (1978:309). This scale is described in more detail in Appendix 8.

56. The uncontrolled correlation between birth order and tough-mindedness is –.27 (df=1/192, t=–3.84, p<.001). Controlled for party affiliation, the partial correlation is –.19 (df=1/184, t=–2.57, p<.02). Controlling for party affiliations allows for the fact that Montagnard deputies may have engaged in tough-minded acts because of greater opportunity, creating a spurious cross correlation between party affiliation and the personality trait we wish to measure. The partial correlation indicates that this cross correlation is minimal. It also overcorrects for any bias, given that party affiliation is itself significantly related to birth order. Path-analytic models (see Appendix 8) provide perhaps the best way of analyzing these data.

57. For the contrast between middle children and other birth positions, as they related to tough-mindedness, the partial r=–.25 (df=1/192, t=–3.60, p<.001; controlled for party affiliation).

58. Higonnet 1985:516; Ozouf 1989a:102.

59. Seligman (1913) and especially Patrick (1972:104) have greatly illuminated the complexities surrounding the counting of these votes. I discuss the problem of votes for the ambiguous Mailhe amendment in Appendix 8.

60. For the three separate votes, the correlations (*phi*) comparing elder sons with younger sons are as follows: for the appeal to the people (r=–.17, df=1/172, t=–2.24, p<.03); for the king's death (r=–.15, df=1/182, t=–2.06, p<.05); and for clemency (r=–.17, df=1/177, t=–2.29, p<.03). The negative values indicate that elder sons were more likely to vote the radical line. Younger sons voted to impeach Marat for inciting violence against the Convention (r=–.16, df=1/141, t=–1.95, p<.06). In addition, younger sons voted in favor of the Commission of Twelve, which was appointed in May 1793 to investigate plots to assassinate members of the Girondin party (r=–.22, df=1/142, t=–2.74, p<.01). Finally, younger sons were more likely than elder sons to protest the arrest of the Girondin leaders (r=.22, df=1/192, t=3.17, p<.005). For all six political issues, the correlation between birth order and "radicalism" is –.20 (df=1/192, t=–2.76, p<.01). I provide these statistics as a contrast between elder and younger sons because French sources frequently report birth-order information in this form. For birth order, coded dichotomously, the sample size is smaller, but the correlation for the six political issues is nearly the same (r=–.21, df=1/161, t=–2.69, p<.01). Owing to the significant interaction between birth order and social class, these correlations underestimate the full influence of birth order. See page 323, Figure 13.2.

All six of these political tendencies exhibit quadratic (U-shaped) trends: *Lastborn* deputies were significantly more likely than middleborns to vote in a radical direction. Based on the use of quadratic contrasts, the correlations in voting behavior are as follows: for the appeal to the people (r=.20, df=1/170, t=2.59, p<.05); for the king's death (r=.21, df=1/180, t=2.92, p<.01); for clemency (r=.21, df=1/175, t=2.76, p<.01); for the impeachment of Marat (r=.27, df=1/138, t=3.33, p<.01); for reinstatement of the Commission of Twelve (r=.27, df=1/140, t=3.31, p<.01); and for protesting the arrest of the Girondin leaders (r=.28, df=1/188, t=4.04, p<.0001). For the three votes during the king's trial, a quadratic contrast yields a correlation of .29 (df=1/182, t=4.01, p<.0001). For the six different political issues, the quadratic contrast yields a correlation of .34 (df=1/192, t=4.94, p<.0001). For these six issues, the partial correlation of the quadratic trend in relative birth rank is statistically significant, controlled for the significant linear trend by relative birth rank: for the quadratic trend, the partial r=.28 (df=1/191, t=4.04, p<.0001). I have discussed such quadratic trends in militancy in Chapter 12.

61. For tough-mindedness and voting for death, r=.48 (df=1/730, t=14.62, p<.0001). Controlled for birth order, the partial correlation is .44 (df=1/173, t=6.47, p<.0001).

62. For a five-variable model, R=.69 ([adjusted R=.68], df=5/531 [the harmonic mean], F=94.02, p<.0001). This five-variable model correctly classifies 85 percent of the deputies in terms of their votes. The five variables are birth order, tough-mindedness, age, party affiliation, and previous political experience.

63. As bivariate correlations, two of these three variables are only weakly related to voting. For social class, r=.03 (df=1/725, t=0.78, p<.44; for urban versus rural, r=.10 (df=1/725, t=2.67, p<.01). The correlation with voting displayed by region of the country, subdivided as northeast versus southwest, is more substantial (r=.16, df=1/730, t=4.49, p<.0001). This geographical variable is sufficiently correlated with other predictors to be rejected by most multivariate models.

64. Higonnet 1985:526.

65. *Technical information for Figure 13.2:* Birth order exerts a significant main effect on voting, but social class does not. Controlled for these two predictors, the partial correlation for the two-way interaction effect is .17 (df=1/180, t=2.27, p<.03).

The largest correlation that social class exhibits with any of the other seven predictors of voting during the king's trial is its correlation with birth order. Lower-class deputies tended to be laterborns, in part because lower-class families tended to be larger than upper-class families (r=–.19, df=1/192, t=–2.70, p<.01). This relationship helps to explain why lower-class deputies were not particularly supportive of the Terror.

In predicting voting during the king's trial, several additional interaction effects are worth citing. Controlled for birth order and tough-mindedness, the partial correlation for the two-way interaction effect is .18 (df=1/180, t=2.41, p<.02). Firstborns were likely to vote for the king's death regardless of how tough-minded they were. By comparison, laterborns were more influenced by this aspect of temperament. Tough-mindedness also interacts with party affiliation. In general, Montagnards voted for a death (a significant main effect). Among non-Montagnards, tough-mindedness played a significantly greater role in determining who voted for death (partial r=–.16, df=1/177, t=–2.17, p<.05; controlled for all main effects—birth order, tough-mindedness, and party affiliation—and all two-way interaction effects).

Another significant interaction effect involves birth order and temperament, as they influenced the predilection for becoming a terrorist. Low birth rank predicts being cited by French historians as a "terrorist" (r=–.20, df=1/194, t=–2.77, p<.01), as does a high score on extraversion (r=–.28, df=1/194, t=–3.98, p<.0001). Controlled for these main effects, the two-way interaction is significant. Extraversion played a greater role in turning firstborns into terrorists than it did among laterborns (partial r=–.22, df=1/202, t=–3.18, p<.01).

My analysis of interaction effects involving birth order is limited by the current availability of biographical information on this variable. If future scholars are able to obtain additional birth-order information for the deputies to the National Convention, other significant interaction effects are likely to emerge, based on social context. Given any specific social context, such as living in an urban environment or coming from the south of France, firstborns and laterborns will tend to have responded differently to this influence.

66. Unlike multiple regression models, path analysis makes assumptions about cause and effect. Although party affiliation exhibits by far the largest correlation with voting patterns, this superficial association is misleading. A three-variable path-analytic model—which includes party affiliations, birth order, and tough-mindedness—makes this point clear. In this three-variable model, the total influence of party affiliations on voting is .59 (its partial correlation). The total influence of birth order is .29 (its correlation with voting), plus all of its indirect effects. These indirect effects include .29×.59 (the influence of birth order on voting via party affiliation), plus .17×.30 (the influence of birth order on voting via tough-mindedness), plus .17×.22×.59 (the influence of birth order on voting via tough-mindedness and its influence on party affiliations). For birth order, the total effects sum to .53. For tough-mindedness, which is also a sibling difference, the total effects sum to .43. Sibling differences therefore explain 0.96 units of "influence" versus 0.59 for party affiliation (or 62 percent of the explainable variance). If we include a term for party affiliations as a quadratic trend (with middleborns siding preferentially with the Plain), the explainable variance attributable to sibling differences increases to 66 percent. The addition of other predictors to a path-analytic

model makes little difference to these basic conclusions. For a useful review of issues in causal modeling, see Asher 1983 and Davis 1985.
67. Quoted in Lefebvre 1962–64, 2:52.
68. Palmer 1989:123.
69. Chaumié 1980:23.

14. Social and Intellectual Context

1. Some of the best research on cognitive strategies in science has been conducted by Dunbar (1995), who has analyzed hundreds of hours of problem-solving discussions among the scientists at three different laboratories. This kind of research is so labor intensive that one can readily understand why few people have been willing to undertake it.
2. Judson 1979:177.
3. Crick 1988:63.
4. *Technical information for Figure 14.1:* For the fourfold classification of scientific controversies, see Chapter 2, where the effect sizes for birth order are reported in Table 2. For the two controversies in which the sample size for the observed data is less than 30 (preformation theory and the Devonian debate), I have estimated the missing data (Appendix 5).

Based on social attitudes, each class of events is significantly different from the others. The mean-weighted correlations between social attitudes and support for innovation are as follows: for Radical Ideological Revolutions, r=.46 (N=946); for Technical Revolutions, r=.27 (N=1,085); for Controversial Innovations, r=.10 (N=224); and for Conservative Theories, r=–.21 (N=510). For the contrast between Radical Ideological and Technical Revolutions, z=4.98 (p<.0001). For the contrast between Technical Revolutions and Controversial Innovations, z=2.30 (p<.05). For the contrast between Controversial Innovations and Conservative Theories, z=3.76 (p<.0001). Based on the mean-weighted correlations for birth order, three of the four classes of events are significantly different. Only Technical Revolutions and Controversial Innovations are not separated by this variable, although these two classes of events *are* distinguishable statistically in terms of how social attitudes affected the participants.
5. Paul Meehl (1990:202–3) has emphasized the poverty of statistical methods that seek only to test the null hypothesis. He has also recognized that general claims about science are true only in a statistical sense and must therefore be tested using meta-analytic methods (Meehl 1984:xxii). In part, my approach in this chapter is in response to these dual problems. Here is a specific example of what I have in mind, based on the linear relationship in Figure 14.1. A scientific revolution such as Darwinism, which displays a correlation of .53 between social attitudes and scientific stance, should display a corresponding correlation between birth order and scientific stance of about .36, plus or minus .11 (the 95 percent confidence interval for the correlation). Birth-order effects that *exceed* this predicted range (.25 to .47) are anomalous and represent potential refutations of my claims.

In practice, matters are a bit more complicated than this two-variable model suggests, although these complications serve only to *increase* the riskiness of predictions. Ideological context is not the sole determinant of birth-order effects.

Also relevant are cognitive and temporal factors (such as conceptual novelty and empirical evidence). Still, my general point remains the same: convincing refutations of claims about birth order must reflect the overall relationships among *multiple* variables. As we succeed in identifying additional factors that moderate revolutionary debates, predictions about birth-order effects become potentially more precise (and hence increasingly liable to refutation).

6. My database for these structural attributes of scientific innovation includes information on 30 variables and their relationship to scientific stance. These variables fall into two general categories: *biographical variables* that predict support or opposition to innovation among the participants; and key *structural attributes* of the innovations. Biographical attributes include: (1) birth order, (2) parent-offspring conflict, (3) shyness, (4) parental loss, (5) religious attitudes, (6) political attitudes, (7) travel, (8) age, (9) social class, (10) personal ties, (11) religious denomination, (12) education, and (13) disciplinary allegiances. Among the structural attributes of innovations are (14) national differences (which is also a biographical attribute), (15) degree of controversiality, (16) years consumed by the controversy, (17) phase of debate (early or late), (18) frequency of being cited as a "revolution" by historians of science, (19) number of participants in the debate, (20) type of science (physical or life sciences), (21) being a "failed" theory, (22) proportion of disciplinary insiders involved in the debate, (23) proportion of nonscientists involved in the debate, (24) proportion of women involved in the debate, and (25) proportion of clergymen involved in the debate.

Other variables in this database reflect judgments on how well each theory accords with various historical and philosophical claims about the advancement of science. For example, the database incorporates information relevant to various Kuhnian (1962) hypotheses, including whether theories were (26) "preparadigmatic" or "paradigmatic," (27) preceded by a "crisis," and (28) involved signs of "incommensurable" debate. Although these assessments are based on my own judgments, they reflect a substantial body of published material on the subject. As a check on these judgments, I have also included a number of related and objective indicators in my database, such as (29) the number of times Kuhn and other scholars have cited each innovation, and (30) whether the innovation was announced in a book or an article (an indicator of disciplinary maturity). For further discussion of these variables, see Appendix 9, Technical Discussion 9.

7. Other risky predictions follow from my hypothesis about birth order and its relationship to various features of family niches. As a refutation of my argument, I would accept the discovery of any *positive* birth-order effect (that is, acceptance by laterborns, and rejection by firstborns) in which parent-offspring conflict predicts *opposition* to the innovation. In the case of conservative innovations, the contrary outcome would also provide compelling refutation of my claims about the importance of family niches. A variety of other potential refutations can be formulated in terms of other predictors of sibling differences. My point is that these variables are all part of a *causal network* reflecting the family system and cannot therefore vary wholly independently of one another.

8. My variable for citation as a revolution is based on total the number of times each of the 28 controversies is mentioned in Kuhn 1962; Hacking 1981; Cohen 1985; and the 18-volume *Dictionary of Scientific Biography.*

9. For the relationship between birth-order effect sizes and the 12 significant predictors in Table 7, R=.90 (adjusted R=.83, *df*=12/19, F=6.64, p<.0001). Selection of the best possible regression model, using Mallows' C_p as the selection criterion, yields a six-variable model (religious attitudes, political attitudes, phase of the debate, travel, parental conflict, and national differences). This parsimonious model has a multiple correlation of .89 (adjusted R=.85, *df*=6/25, F=15.01, p<.0001). Because some variables interact with one another in predicting birth-order effects, more powerful models are possible. I discuss some of these interaction effects in the course of this chapter.

10. Birth order provides just one effective means for taking the pulse beat of historical change. Other measures are also possible. In this connection, I have analyzed my database of structural features of scientific innovations in terms of intercorrelated "factors." Four well-defined factors emerge. The first factor involves *ideological controversy* and manifests high loadings for birth order (.80), religious attitudes (.74), and political attitudes (.71). The second factor denotes *failed revolutions* (.79) and strongly corroborates Kuhn's (1962) distinction between preparadigmatic and paradigmatic sciences. Psychoanalysis has the highest score on this factor, based largely on its tendency to recruit nonscientists (.57), as well as scientists who do not become eminent (–.28). The third factor involves *technical innovations* and is associated with adoption by insiders (.85), eminent scientists (.67), and firstborns (.20). The last factor denotes *modern scientific innovations,* which run their course more quickly than past innovations (.71) and place a greater premium on the intellectual openness that is typically associated with youth (.53).

11. *Technical information for Figure 14.2:* Elapsed time has been standardized, using *z*-scores, for each debate in the figure. This analysis excludes 7 "failed" revolutions: preformation theory, mesmerism, phrenology, idealistic systems of classification, spiritualism, eugenics, and psychoanalysis. The observed tendency toward closure during scientific debates occurs for other "subjective" influences in my study, including social attitudes and personal networks.

For the relationship between birth order and support for successful innovations, the partial correlation is .24 (*df*=1/1,344, t=8.88, p<.0001). For elapsed time, the partial correlation is .08 (*df*=1/1,344, t=3.01, p<.005). Relative to elapsed time, birth order explains 9 times the variance ($.24^2/.08^2$=9.0 to 1). Path analysis helps to reinforce this point. Elapsed time leads to new empirical discoveries, which in turn cause scientists to adjust their conceptual allegiances; but much of this new evidence is itself owing to sibling differences in research styles.

12. Sociologists tend to underestimate the rational nature of science, in part because they minimize the importance of the individual. "For most purposes," claims Harry Collins (a social constructivist), "an individual's thoughts *qua individual* are of no interest" (Collins 1985:148). To the extent that sociologists seek to explain scientific consensus, they are right: individuals are not the key. Individuals are vital, however, to the adversarial nature of science, and hence to scientific advancement. In this vein, Mitroff (1983:264) has rightly criticized Kuhn's (1962) conception of science for its undervaluation of the individual. As Giere (1988:46, 241) points out, this tendency to minimize the role of individuals is shared by most philosophers of science.

Kitcher (1993) has put forth an adversarial model of scientific rationality.

His approach combines a recognition of cognitive and social biases with an account of how scientists, by *testing* their hypotheses, reduce the need for "negotiating" about facts. Much of this chapter coincides closely with Kitcher's argument, as well as with Solomon's (1994) closely related views. My emphasis on cognitive diversity and the importance of individuals is also consonant with the views of Mayr (1976), Giere (1988), and Hull (1988).

13. Kuhn 1957:206.

14. Hellman 1973; Gingerich and Westman 1988.

15. Hellman 1973:403.

16. *Technical information for Figure 14.3:* For birth order and the reception of Copernican theory before 1610, r=.38 (df=1/28, t=2.18, p<.05). After 1609, there is no significant difference by birth order (r=.00, df=1/49, t=0.00, p<1.00).

17. Biagioli 1992.

18. Drake 1978:164; Westfall 1985.

19. Westfall 1985:28.

20. "After 1609," writes Thomas Kuhn (1957:224), "the main psychological force of the Ptolemaic system was its conservatism. Those who held to it would not be forced to learn new ways." Strictly speaking, the "conservatism" that remained relevant in this debate was more "ideological" than "cognitive." The influence of social attitudes on Copernican allegiances increases with time (for the interaction, the partial r=.15 [df=1/175, t=2.05, p<.05]). After 1609, the effect size for social attitudes is significantly larger than the effect size for birth order (z=3.50, p<.001). Before 1610 there is no significant difference between the two variables: both are good predictors, although the effect size for birth order is somewhat larger than that for social attitudes.

21. After 1609, friendship with leading Copernicans is significantly more important than birth order as a predictor of support for Copernican theory (z=2.29, p<.05). Before 1610, both variables are equally good predictors.

22. Birth order is not the only variable to exhibit interactions with various moderator variables during the Copernican revolution. *Status as a scientist* is another. Because nonscientists lacked a familiarity with astronomical fine points, they were not in a position to appreciate the technical merits of the Copernican system. Accordingly, laymen were more concerned than scientists with religious considerations and hence were slower to accept Copernican theory (for the interaction between religious attitudes and status as a scientist, the partial r=–.18 (df=1/240, t=–2.77, p<.01). Among scientists, astronomers were particularly supportive. This finding is relevant to Solomon's (1994) argument about *cognitive salience* in science. Individuals who are most familiar with empirical evidence tend to give it the greatest weight.

Theologians were particularly sensitive to religious criteria of truth. Over time they increasingly reacted to Copernican theory in terms of ideological commitments rather than evidence, the reverse of the trend observed among scientists. Their beliefs were too "socially constructed" to be changed by the discovery of new stars or mountains on the moon. (For the interaction effect between status as a theologian and religious attitudes, as they relate to scientific stance, the partial r=–.16 [df=1/176, t=–4.78, p<.05]).

Status as a theologian also interacts with *status as a scientist:* those theologians who were scientists (such as Gassendi) were significantly more likely to accept Copernican theory than those who were not (partial r=–.32, df=1/37, t=–2.12, p<.05; for the period after 1609).

23. Compared with *insiders, outsiders* are sometimes more likely to endorse scientific innovations, but only when the issues being debated are nontechnical and laden with radical ideological implications. Two relevant examples are phrenology and psychoanalysis. For the two-way interaction between the ideological trend of innovations (defined in terms of politics and religion) and support by outsiders, as they affect birth-order trends, the partial r=.38 (df=1/28, t=2.14, p<.05). Again and again, the kinds of generalizations that can be made reliably about scientific advancement are sensitive to the historical context *and do not hold across the board.*

24. Cowell 1992. In connection with the illustration of Galileo standing in an Inquisition dungeon, which I have shown on page 340, it is worth noting that Galileo was treated with considerably more respect than this portrait suggests. Given his age and the uncertain grounds on which the Inquisition was seeking to build its case, Galileo was actually lodged in an apartment within the Palace of the Holy Office (Redondi 1987:258).

25. Frank 1947:141; Hoffmann 1972:132.

26. *Technical information for Figure 14.4:* For the relationship between birth order and support for relativity theory before 1915, r=.34 (df=1/40, t=2.37, p<.05). For the period after 1914, r=.09 (df=1/67, t=0.74, p<.47).

27. For social attitudes and acceptance of relativity theory after 1919, r=.34 (df=1/42, t=2.37, p<.05). For the period after 1914, r=.39 (df=1/67, t=0.74, p<.47).

28. Social constructionists have rightly drawn attention to the role of social influences in science. See, for example, Barnes 1974, 1977, 1982; Barnes and Bloor 1982; Latour and Woolgar 1979; Latour 1987; Knorr-Centina 1981; Collins and Pinch 1982, 1993; Collins 1985; Pickering 1984; and the seminal Fleck 1979 (1935). Golinski (1990) reviews some of the recent literature on rhetoric in science and notes its links with this sociological approach. To scholars who study scientific rhetoric, it's not *what* scientists say but *how they say it* that really matters.

In spite of their informative efforts to expand the notion of what is social about science, social constructionists are dead wrong in their efforts to minimize the cognitive and empirical aspects of science. Latour (1987:247), for example, has gone so far as to call for a "moratorium" on cognitive approaches in science studies. Neither Latour nor any other social constructionist has ever bothered to *test* their claims, using formal scientific methods. Rather than calling for moratoriums on approaches that do not agree with their own, these scholars ought perhaps to recognize that, in choosing to forgo testing, their own research program already embodies a moratorium on critical inquiry. Without hypothesis testing, claims about the nature of scientific thought are likely to end up as intellectual fads. Crews (1986) offers a lucid critique of such relativistic views about knowledge, as do Gross and Levitt (1994).

29. *Technical information for Figure 14.5:* For the tendency for laterborns to adopt whichever theory (preformation or epigenesis) was out of favor, the partial correlation is .28 (df=1/56, t=2.18, p<.05). Neither main effect (birth order or elapsed time) is significant.

In Appendix 9, Technical Discussion 10, I present evidence in connection with a variety of other "birth order × situation" interaction effects. Some of these interaction effects involve the moderating role of time. For example, the eugenics movement became more conservative in its goals over time and, after 1900, appealed more strongly to firstborns and to social conservatives. Other interaction effects that I discuss in this appendix involve the role of national differences. Two particularly good examples involve the Newtonian revolution and Lavoisier's chemical revolution, which were more favorably received within the countries represented by the two principal originators. In general, given the national context of debate, laterborns were more likely to support innovations in those countries where they were most controversial.

30. Roe 1981:8.

31. Kuhn 1962; see also Kuhn 1957; and, for a convenient review of Kuhn's ideas, Hoyningen-Huene 1993.

32. Numerous historians of science, and even the participants themselves, have testified about the lack of crises during radical revolutions. On the Darwinian revolution, see Greene (1971), Ghiselin (1972), and Darwin (1958 [1876]:124). On the Copernican revolution, see Gingerich (1975), who produces much historical evidence to counter Kuhn's (1957, 1962) claims about this event. In my database for 28 scientific controversies, status as a Radical Ideological Revolution is negatively correlated with the presence of a crisis ($r=-.53$, $p<.005$). The same is true of Conservative Theories ($r=-.48$, $p<.01$). In the case of Technical Revolutions, the correlation is positive ($r=.33$, $p<.07$), making this class of events significantly different from both Radical Ideological Revolutions and Conservative Theories ($z=3.54$, $p<.001$, and $z=3.27$, $p<.005$, respectively). In *The Structure of Scientific Revolutions* (1962), revolutions having crises tend to be cited more frequently by Kuhn than those lacking a crisis ($r=.44$, $p<.05$).

33. Kuhn's (1962) model of science provides a better description of firstborn behavior than it does of laterborn behavior. Kuhn himself is a firstborn, so perhaps this is no surprise.

34. In predicting birth-order effects, crises interact strongly with ideology (partial $r=-.49$, $df=1/28$, $t=-2.95$, $p<.01$; controlled for the two main effects). The more radical the revolution, the more a crisis *dilutes* birth-order effects, as happened during the Copernican and Darwinian revolutions. In nonradical revolutions, crises tend to *increase* birth-order effects. Revolutionary thinkers do not usually rebel in science without some good cause. Liberal ideology supplies this motivation during radical revolutions. During technical revolutions, the breakdown of an established theory supplies an analogous motivation, impelling laterborns, but not firstborns, to begin the process of rebellion.

35. Kuhn (1970c:181) has relaxed somewhat the requirement of a crisis as a prelude to revolutions. See also Hoyningen-Huene 1993:232–33. Still, Kuhn believes that crises are a usual feature of revolutions. For Radical Ideological Revolutions, crisis is not a *usual* feature.

36. Crises are less likely to occur in the life sciences, even when these disciplines are paradigmatic, because ideological considerations give radicals the opportunity to jump the revolutionary gun. The correlation between a theory displaying a crisis and its occurring in the physical sciences is a whopping .75 ($df=1/30$, $t=6.12$, *p*<.0001). Kuhn (1962) largely ignored the life sciences in his account of revolutionary change. (The correlation between a theory being biological in nature and its being cited in Kuhn's *Structure of Scientific Revolutions* is –.52 [df=1/30, t=–3.30, p<.005].) Kuhn devoted just *one* page to the Darwinian revolution, an event that represents one of the most radical revolutions in the history of science and that *lacked* a crisis. On Kuhn's underrepresentation of the biological sciences, see Ruse 1970, 1971; Mayr 1976:277, 294; and Hoyningen-Huene 1993:5.

37. Poincaré 1908:199; 1913:486.

38. Kuhn 1978:143–44, 210.

39. I employ the phrase "psychologically speaking" advisedly here, since my own remarks on incommensurability are on a somewhat more pragmatic level than would perhaps concern Kuhn or strike him as philosophically problematic.

40. Gillespie 1979:19–40. See also Mayr 1982:407. Theory comparison is not precluded by Kuhn's (1962:202) notion of incommensurability; but, for Kuhn, conversion always entails incommensurability. See also Hoyningen-Huene 1993: 218–21.

41. Darwin 1859:435.

42. Darwin 1859:393.

43. My argument in the text has practical implications for the selection of scientific commissions and the evaluation of their conclusions. Because commission tend to be packed with eminent individuals (and hence firstborns), their votes should perhaps be "weighted" to adjust for individual biases in attitudes toward innovation.

44. On the relationship between birth-order effect sizes in theory adoption and those for nationality differences in science, see this chapter, Table 7, and Appendix 9, Technical Discussion 10.

15. Conclusion

1. Weiner 1994:287.

2. Schachter et al. 1976, 1978; Schachter 1982.

3. Mayr 1964; 1976:26–29.

4. The notion of intellect as a multifaceted collection of specialized "intelligences" derives from the work of Howard Gardner (1983, 1987, 1993, 1995). This psychological perspective is also consistent with the notion of the brain as composed of adaptive modules that evolved to solve specific behavioral problems (Tooby and Cosmides 1990a,b, 1992; Barkow, Cosmides, and Tooby 1992). Gould (1996) has emphasized the importance of this multifaceted approach to intelligence in connection with Darwin's own intellectual abilities, a view that I wholeheartedly endorse. According to Gould, Darwin's success as a scientist was nurtured by three different sets of influences: (1) fortuitous circumstances—for example, his upper-class family background, which allowed him to devote most of his time to scientific research; (2) an equally fortuitous combination of diverse mental abilities; and (3) the felicitous interaction of these mental abilities with a particular scientific problem. Recast in terms of the perspective of this book, Darwin was unlikely to demonstrate—as did Redi, Spallanzani, and Pasteur—that life arises only from previous life. This was a conservative achievement requiring minds "preadapted" to a conservative point of view.

5. See Chapter 2, figures 2.3 and 2.4.
6. See the Conclusions to Chapter 2.
7. Lyell 1881, 2:363.
8. See page 101.
9. See page 224.
10. See Chapter 14, Figure 14.2. Even in debates that have lasted only a decade, such as those over Lister's methods of antiseptic surgery, laterborns have adopted the novel viewpoint 7.5 years ahead of firstborns.
11. See Chapter 2, Figure 2.2, and page 262; see also pages 357 and 516 (n. 25).
12. On age and creativity, see the useful theoretical model developed by Simonton (1994:181–91). For the relationship between age at scientific discovery and birth order, $r=.18$ ($df=1/64$, $t=1.50$, $p<.07$; for the 66 leaders of revolutions in my study [one-tailed test]). My sample size for this statistical test is small, which in turn limits the test's power to attain significance. My attempt to expand the scope of this inquiry met with strong objections from my colleagues in the history of science. See footnote 31 of this chapter.
13. Darwin 1985– , 2:408.
14. Gray 1889, 2:430.
15. Freeman 1978:283.
16. Darwin 1958 [1876]:135.
17. Darwin 1887, 1:149.
18. Darwin 1887, 1:149; see also Darwin 1903, 2:41.
19. On natural selection as Darwin's "dangerous idea," see Dennett 1995.
20. L. Wilson 1970:347.
21. E. Darwin 1915, 2:207.
22. Darwin 1958 [1876]:140.
23. See page 297.
24. See Chapter 11, especially Figure 11.3.
25. Smith 1976:29.
26. A prominent exception to the rule that firstborns endorse violent methods is seen in groups like the Quakers. Quakerism originated as a dissenting religious movement whose pacifist philosophy became institutionalized as a group norm. Anabaptism was a laterborn precursor of this religious trend (Chapter 11, especially Figure 11.4). Exceptions to the rule that lastborns endorse violent political methods are encountered among individuals such as Gandhi who are particularly shy. This generalization applies even more strongly to firstborns. For a test of these claims, see Chapter 13, n. 65.
27. It is a curious footnote to history that Henry Martyn Robert, who systematized parliamentary procedures with his famous *Robert's Rules of Order* (1876), was the fourth of seven children—exactly in the middle.
28. Mackey 1979:518.
29. See pages 268–70.
30. Cohen 1985:5.
31. I recently applied to the National Science Foundation to pursue research on aging and creativity in science. My proposal outlined a series of hypotheses that I wished to test using multivariate methods. The effects of aging, for example, must be disentangled from covariates such as number of years of research in a given

field, eminence, type of achievement, and individual differences in openness to experience. The NSF panel for the History and Philosophy of Science Program is composed largely of historians. The panel issued the following judgment about my proposal:

> One of the most pervasive issues discussed by the panelists was the approach the Principal Investigator was taking toward history. Many panelists thought that applying a heavy-duty statistical analysis to history is *naive, inappropriate, and even peculiar.* Is it really the case that generalizations in history should be tested with statistics, rather than be tested through a detailed examination of the sources? Some [panelists] noted that it seemed as if the Principal Investigator was going back to 19th-century beliefs that history is a science which could uncover laws. Panelists were opposed to such a narrow view of history (Panel Recommendation on grant proposal SBR-9512062, "Testing Theories of Scientific Change," April 1995; italics added).

Needless to say, I did not receive this grant, in spite of nearly perfect scores from outside peer review.

Besides being an odd response to receive from the National *Science* Foundation, where the principal criterion of grant evaluation is supposed to be "scientific merit," this panel's criticisms confuse a method of research (hypothesis testing) with a theory of history. Testing is what makes an approach scientific, not the particular viewpoint that is endorsed. Even the claim that history can be studied scientifically can only evaluated properly through hypothesis testing. On the antiscientific attitude that has come to characterize the recent history and sociology of science, see Gross and Levitt 1994.

32. Kuhn 1962. The same insight was part of Piaget's theory of learning through assimilation and accommodation (Inhelder and Piaget 1969), which influenced Kuhn. On some of the important cognitive limitations in scientific research, see Faust 1984.

33. Darwin 1958 [1876]:123.

34. Kuhn (1962) has emphasized some of these criteria of rationality, although this circumstance has not stopped his work from being widely misinterpreted as supporting irrationality in science. See also Hoyningen-Huene 1993.

35. Campbell (1965, 1970, 1974) has developed this analogy between hypothesis testing and natural selection. See also Toulmin 1972 and Richards 1987.

36. During the seventeenth century, laterborn support for the scientific method is much stronger than might appear from the data I present in Table 2 (page 39) and in Figure 14.1 (page 332). When I originally gathered biographical information on participants in this debate, birth order quickly emerged as an impressive predictor of support. Only as I enlarged this sample did this initial effect fade. Two aspects of this debate, which entail significant interaction effects, help to explain this attenuation of the initial finding. First, the most zealous promoters of the scientific method were younger sons (such as Bacon and Descartes), and these individuals were the first to come to my attention. Here is a simple test of this assertion: I have constructed a model in which each participant is weighted for the number of times he or she is cited in two standard reference works that chronicle this scientific debate (Mouy 1934, and Jones 1961). In this model, birth order is a moderately good predictor of support (r=.28, df=1/79, t=2.59, p<.02). This weighted correlation places the "Bacon/Descartes" effect size very near the regression line for 28 scientific debates in Figure 14.1. The key to birth-order effects in this particular debate is being an "activist" in favor of the new science. It is also noteworthy that the correlation between support for the new experimental method and relative birth rank is considerably larger than the correlation for birth order, coded dichotomously: for relative birth rank, r=.27 (df=1/60, t=2.17, p<.05; this statistic compares with the bivariate correlation [*phi*] of only .08). When weighted by activism, the correlation between relative birth rank and support rises to .30.

The second interaction effect characterizing this particular debate involves birth order and status as a scientist. Among scientists, birth order is not a significant predictor of support for the new experimental method (r=.01, df=1/54, t=0.07, p<.95). Status as a scientist is itself a significant predictor of support, which is hardly surprising. The methodological issues that were being debated about knowledge production in science were clearly less controversial among scientists than they were among nonscientists. Accordingly, birth order is a significantly better predictor of support for the experimental method among nonscientists (r=.40, df=1/23, t=2.11, p<.05). For the two-way interaction effect, the partial correlation is .25 (df=1/77, t=2.29, p<.05). Documentation of this interaction effect leads me to make the following prediction. A significant birth-order effect in attitudes toward the authority of the ancients is likely to be found among *scientists from the sixteenth century*, a period that I have not surveyed.

37. Cohen 1985:175, 208–9. See also Randall 1940:276; Jacob 1976:18; Berlin 1980:44.

38. Darwin 1985– , 3:2.

BIBLIOGRAPHY

Absolon, Karel B.

1979–1987. *The Surgeon's Surgeon: Theodor Billroth, 1829–1894.* 3 vols. Lawrence, Kans.: Coronado Press.

Academy of Sciences of the USSR

1978. *Leonid I. Brezhnev: Pages from His Life.* New York: Simon and Schuster.

Ackerknecht, Erwin H.

1948. Anticontagionism between 1821 and 1867. *Bulletin of the History of Medicine* 22:562–93.

Ackroyd, Peter

1990. *Dickens.* London: Sinclair-Stevenson.

Adamson, Robert

1890. Eyton, Thomas Campbell (1809–1880). *Dictionary of National Biography* 6:971.

Adler, Alfred

1927. *Understanding Human Nature.* New York: Greenberg.

1928. Characteristics of the first, second, and third child. *Children* 3:14–52.

1956. *The Individual Psychology of Alfred Adler: A Systematic Presentation in Selections from His Writings.* Edited and annotated by Heinz L. Ansbacher and Rowena R. Ansbacher. New York: Basic Books.

Agassiz, Elizabeth Cary

1885. *Louis Agassiz: His Life and Correspondence.* 2 vols. Boston: Houghton, Mifflin.

Agassiz, Rudolphe Louis

1860. Professor Agassiz on the Origin of Species. *American Journal of Sciences,* 2d series, 30:142–55.

Ainsworth, Mary

1967. *Infancy in Uganda: Infant Care and the Growth of Attachment.* Baltimore: Johns Hopkins University Press.

Alexander, Franz, Samuel Eisenstein, and Martin Grotjahn, eds.

1966. *Psychoanalytic Pioneers.* New York: Basic Books.

Alexander, Richard D.

1979. *Darwinism and Human Affairs.* Seattle: University of Washington Press.

1987. *The Biology of Moral Systems.* Hawthorne, N.Y.: Aldine de Gruyter.

1990. Epigenetic rules and Darwinian algorithms: The adaptive study of learning and development. *Ethology and Sociobiology* 11:241–313.

1991. Social learning and kin recognition: A reply to Paul Sherman and an addendum. *Ethology and Sociobiolgy* 12:387–99.

1995. The view from the president's window: Impression from the Santa Barbara meeting. *Human Behavior and Evolution Society Newsletter* 4, no. 2 (September): 1–3.

ALTUS, WILLIAM D.

1963. The first-born as a conservative: Adler revisited. *American Psychologist* 18:356.

1966. Birth order and its sequelae. *Science* 151:44–49.

1970. Marriage and order of birth. *Proceedings of the 78th Annual Convention of the American Psychological Association* 5:361–62.

ANDREWS, STUART

1968. *Enlightened Despotism.* New York: Barnes & Noble.

ANGIER, NATALIE

1994. Canary chicks: Not all created equal. *New York Times (Science Times),* 25 January, pp. C1, C8.

ANONYMOUS

1837a. Zoological Society. *The Morning Chronicle,* 12 January, p. 3.

1837b. Zoological Society. *The Morning Herald,* 12 January, p. 5.

ANSBACHER, HEINZ L.

1959. The significance of the socio-economic status of the patients of Freud and of Adler. *American Journal of Psychotherapy* 13:376–82.

ANTMAN, A. E.

1993. Big brother. Letter to the Editor. *The Economist,* 25 December, p. 8.

APPEL, TOBY

1987. *The Cuvier–Geoffroy Debate. French Biology in the Decades before Darwin.* New York and Oxford: Oxford University Press.

APPERLY, FRANK L.

1939. A study of American Rhodes scholars. *Journal of Heredity* 30:493–95.

ARBUCKLE, ELISABETH SANDERS, ED.

1983. *Harriet Martineau's Letters to Fanny Wedgwood.* Stanford, Calif.: Stanford University Press.

ARIÈS, PHILIPPE

1962. *Centuries of Childhood: A Social History of Family Life.* Translated by Robert Baldick. New York: Alfred A. Knopf.

ARKIN, ROBERT M., ELIZABETH A. LAKE, AND ANN H. BAUMGARDNER

1986. Shyness and self-presentation. In *Shyness: Perspectives on Research and Treatment,* edited by Warren E. Jones, Jonathan M. Cheek, and Stephen R. Briggs, pp. 189–203. New York and London: Plenum.

ARMITAGE, ANGUS

1966. *John Kepler.* London: Faber and Faber.

ARMSTRONG, EDWARD

1910. *The Emperor Charles V.* 2d ed. 2 vols. London and New York: Macmillan.

ASENDORPF, JENS

1986. Shyness in middle and late childhood. In *Shyness: Perspectives on Research and Treatment,* edited by Warren H. Jones, Jonathan M. Cheek, and Stephen R. Briggs, pp. 91–103. New York and London: Plenum.

ASHER, HERBERT B.

1983. *Causal Modeling.* 2d ed. Newbury Park, Calif.: Sage Publications.

ASPREY, ROBERT B.

1986. *Frederick the Great: The Magnificent Enigma.* New York: Ticknor & Fields.

AULARD, FRANÇOIS-ALPHONSE

1882. *L'Éloquence parlementaire pendant la révolution française: Les Orateurs de l'Assemblée Constituante.* Paris: Hachette.

1885–86. *L'Éloquence parlementaire pendant la révolution française: Les Orateurs de la Législative et de la Convention.* 2 vols. Paris: Hachette.

1889. *La Société des Jacobins: Recueil de documents pour l'histoire du club des Jacobins de Paris.* Vol. 1: *1789–1790.* Paris: Jouaust.

BAER, KARL ERNST VON

1986. [1886]. *Autobiography of Dr. Karl Ernst von Baer.* Edited by Jane M. Oppenheimer. Translated by H. Schneider. Canton, Mass.: Science History Publications.

BAILLET, ADRIEN

1690. *Auteurs déguisez sous des noms étrangers, empruntez, supposez, feints à plaisir, chiffrez, renversez, retournez, ou changez d'une langue en une autre.* Paris: Antoine Dezallier.

BAILYN, BERNARD

1967. *The Ideological Origins of the American Revolution.* Cambridge: Harvard University Press.

BAINTON, ROLAND H.

1950. *Here I Stand: A Life of Martin Luther.* New York: Abingdon-Cokesbury Press.

1977. Psychiatry and history: An examination of Erikson's *Young Man Luther.* In *Psychohistory and Religion: The Case of Young Man Luther,* edited by Roger A. Johnson, pp. 19–56. Philadelphia: Fortress Press.

BARBER, BERNARD

1961. Resistance by scientists to scientific discovery. *Science* 134:596–602.

BARKOW, JEROME H., LEDA COSMIDES, AND JOHN TOOBY, EDS.

1992. *The Adapted Mind: Evolutionary Psychology and the Generation of Culture.* New York: Oxford University Press.

BARLOW, NORA

1958. The Darwin-Butler controversy. In *The Autobiography of Charles Darwin, 1809–1882: With Original Omissions Restored,* edited with Appendix and Notes by Nora Barlow, pp. 167–219. London: Collins.

BARNES, BARRY

1974. *Scientific Knowledge and Sociological Theory.* London and Boston: Routledge & Kegan Paul.

1977. *Interests and the Growth of Knowledge.* London: Routledge & Kegan Paul.

1982. *T. S. Kuhn and Social Science.* New York: Columbia University Press.

BARNES, BARRY, AND DAVID BLOOR

1982. Relativism, rationalism and the sociology of knowledge. In *Rationality and Relativism,* edited by M. Hollis and S. Lukes, pp. 21–47. Cambridge: MIT Press.

BARNES, BARRY, AND STEVEN SHAPIN, EDS.

1979. *Natural Order: Historical Studies of Scientific Culture.* Beverly Hills, Calif.: Sage Publications.

BARNETT, CORRELLI

1978. *Bonaparte.* New York: Hill and Wang.

BARTLETT, JOHN
1955. *Familiar Quotations.* Boston and Toronto: Little, Brown.
BASKETT, LINDA MUSUN
1984. Ordinal position differences in children's family interactions. *Developmental Psychology* 20:1026–31.
BATESON, MARY CATHERINE
1984. *With a Daughter's Eye: A Memoir of Margaret Mead and Gregory Bateson.* New York: William Morrow.
BATSON, C. DANIEL
1991. *The Altruism Question: Toward a Social Psychological Answer.* Hillsdale, N.J.: Lawrence Erlbaum.
BAUMGARTNER, FREDERIC J.
1986. Scepticism and French interest in Copernicanism to 1630. *Journal for the History of Astronomy* 17:77–88.
BECKER, BETSY JANE
1986. Influence again: An examination of reviews and studies of gender differences in social influence. In *The Psychology of Gender: Advances through Meta-analysis,* edited by Janet Shibley Hyde and Maria C. Linn, pp. 178–209. Baltimore and London: Johns Hopkins University Press.
BECKER, CARL L.
1931. Franklin, Benjamin (1706–1790). *Dictionary of American Biography* 6:585–98.
BECKER, SELWYN W., AND JEAN CARROLL
1962. Ordinal position and conformity. *Journal of Abnormal and Social Psychology* 65:129–31.
BECKER, SELWYN W., MELVIN J. LERNER, AND JEAN CARROLL
1964. Conformity as a function of birth order, payoff, and type of group pressure. *Journal of Abnormal and Social Psychology* 69:318–23.
BEESLY, A. H.
1899. *Life of Danton.* London: Longmans, Green.
BEGIS, ALFRED, ED.
1893. *Curiosités révolutionnaires: Billaud Varenne, membre du Comité de Salut Public. Mémoires inédits et correspondance accompagnés de notices biographiques sur Billaud Varenne et Collot-d'Herbois.* Paris: Librairie de la Nouvelle Revue.
BEIK, PAUL H.
1970. *The French Revolution Seen from the Right: Social Theories in Motion, 1789–1799.* Transactions of the American Philosophical Society, new series 46 (part 1); New York: Howard Fertig.
BELHOSTE, BRUNO
1991. *Augustin-Louis Cauchy: A Biography.* Translated by Frank Ragland. New York and Berlin: Springer-Verlag.
BELL, ERIC TEMPLE
1937. *Men of Mathematics.* New York: Simon and Schuster.
BELL, THOMAS
1860 [1859]. Presidential address to the Linnean Society on the anniversary of Linnaeus's birth, May 24, 1859. *Journal of the Proceedings of the Linnean Society: Botany* 4:vii–xx.

BELLOC, HILAIRE
1928. *Danton: A Study.* London: Nisbet.
BELMONT, LILLIAN, AND FRANCIS A. MAROLLA
1973. Birth order, family size, and intelligence. *Science* 182:1096–1101.
BELSKY, J., L. STEINBERG, AND P. DRAPER
1991. Childhood experience, interpersonal development, and reproductive strategy: An evolutionary theory of socialization. *Child Development* 62:647–70.
BENNETT, AMANDA
1994. Along with high honor, Nobel award in economics influences future research. *Wall Street Journal,* 11 October, pp. B1, B16.
BENRATH, KARL
1911. Renée of France (Renata of Ferrara) [1510–1575]. *The New Schaff-Herzog Encyclopedia of Religious Knowledge* 9:486–87. Edited by Samuel Macauley Jackson. New York and London: Funk and Wagnalls.
BERGER, PHILIP A.
1977. Antidepressant medications and the treatment of depression. In *Psychopharmacology: From Theory to Practice,* edited by Jack D. Barchas, Philip A. Berger, Roland D. Ciaranello, and Glen R. Elliot, pp. 174–207. New York: Oxford University Press.
BERLIN, ISAIAH
1980. *Personal Impressions.* Edited by Henry Hardy. London: Hogarth Press.
BERNAYS, ANNA FREUD
1940. My brother, Sigmund Freud. *The American Mercury* 51:335–42.
BESTERMAN, THEODORE
1969. *Voltaire.* London: Longmans, Green.
BETZIG, LAURA
1986. *Despotism and Differential Reproduction: A Darwinian View of History.* Hawthorne, N.Y.: Aldine de Gruyter.
BIAGIOLI, MARIO
1992. Scientific revolution, social bricolage, and etiquette. In *The Scientific Revolution in National Context,* edited by Roy Porter and Mikulás Teich, pp. 11–54. Cambridge: Cambridge University Press.
1993. *Galileo, Courtier: The Practice of Science in the Culture of Absolutism.* Chicago: University of Chicago Press.
BIBBY, CYRIL
1960. *T. H. Huxley: Scientist, Humanist, and Educator.* New York: Horizon Press.
BIERMANN, KURT R.
1972. Humboldt, Friedrich Wilhelm Heinrich Alexander von (1769–1859). *Dictionary of Scientific Biography* 6:549–55.
BIETENHOLZ, PETER G., ED.
1985–87. *Contemporaries of Erasmus: A Biographical Register of the Renaissance and Reformation.* 3 vols. Toronto: University of Toronto Press.
BIREMBAUT, ARTHUR
1971. Élie de Beaumont, Jean-Baptiste-Armand-Louis-Léonce [1798–1874]. *Dictionary of Scientific Biography* 4:347–50.

BLACKMORE, JOHN T.
1978. Is Planck's "principle" true? *British Journal for the Philosophy of Science* 29:347–49.
BLAKE, JUDITH
1989a. *Family Size and Achievement.* Berkeley and Los Angeles: University of California Press.
1989b. Number of siblings and educational attainment. *Science* 245:32–36.
BLANCHARD, RAY, AND ANTHONY F. BOGAERT
1996. Homosexuality in men and number of older brothers. *American Journal of Psychiatry* 153:27–31.
BLANCHARD, RAY, AND PETER M. SHERIDAN
1992. Sibship size, sibling sex ratio, birth order, and parental age in homosexual and nonhomosexual gender dysphorics. *Journal of Nervous and Mental Disease* 180:40–47.
BLANCHARD, RAY, AND KENNETH J. ZUCKER
1994. Reanalysis of Bell, Weinberg, and Hammersmith's data on birth order, sibling sex ratio and parental age in homosexual men. *American Journal of Psychiatry* 151:1375.
BLANCHARD, RAY, KENNETH J. ZUCKER, SUSAN J. BRADLEY, AND CAITLIN S. HUME
1995. Birth order and sibling sex ratio in homosexual male adolescents and probably prehomosexual feminine boys. *Developmental Psychology* 31:22–30.
BLANNING, T. C. W.
1987. *The French Revolution: Aristocrats versus Bourgeois?* Atlantic Highlands, N.J.: Humanities Press International.
BLOCK, JACK
1989. Critique of the act frequency approach to personality. *Journal of Personality and Social Psychology* 50:234–45.
BLOCK, JEANNE HUMPHREY
1973. Conceptions of sex role: Some cross-cultural and longitudinal perspectives. *American Psychologist* 28:512–26.
1976. Issues, problems, and pitfalls in assessing sex differences. *Merrill-Palmer Quarterly* 22:283–308.
[BLOMFIELD] JENYNS, LEONARD
1862. *Memoir of the Rev. John Stevens Henslow.* London: Van Voorst.
BLUNT, WILFRID
1971. *The Compleat Naturalist: A Life of Linnaeus.* With the assistance of William T. Stearn. New York: Viking Press.
BODEMER, CHARLES W.
1964. Regeneration and the decline of preformation in eighteenth century embryology. *Bulletin of the History of Medicine* 38:20–31.
BOEHMER, HEINRICH
1930. *Luther and the Reformation in the Light of Modern Research.* Translated by E. S. G. Potter. New York: Dial Press.
BOONE, JAMES L.
1986. Parental investment and elite family structure in preindustrial states: A case study of late medieval–early modern Portuguese genealogies. *American Anthropologist* 88:859–78.

BORING, EDWIN G.
1964. Cognitive dissonance: Its use in science. *Science* 145:680–85.
BORN, MAX
1978. *My Life: Recollections of a Nobel Laureate.* London: Taylor & Francis.
BOSHIER, ROGER, AND FRANK H. WALKEY
1971. Birth order and conservatism: An Adlerian myth? *Psychological Reports* 29:392–94.
BOSSARD, J. H. S., AND E. BOLL
1956. *The Large Family System.* Philadelphia: University of Pennsylvania.
BOUCHARD, THOMAS J., JR., DAVID T. LYKKEN, MATTHEW MCGUE, NANCY L. SEGAL, AND AUKE TELLEGEN
1990. Sources of human psychological differences: The Minnesota study of twins reared apart. *Science* 250:223–25.
BOUCHARD, THOMAS J., JR., AND MATTHEW MCGUE
1990. Genetic and rearing environmental influences on adult personality: An analysis of adopted twins reared apart. *Journal of Personality* 58:263–92.
BOURDIER, FRANCK
1971a. Cuvier, Frédéric (1773–1838). *Dictionary of Scientific Biography* 3:520–21.
1971b. Cuvier, Georges (1769–1832). *Dictionary of Scientific Biography* 3:521–28.
1972a. Geoffroy Saint-Hilaire, Étienne (1772–1844). *Dictionary of Scientific Biography* 5:355–58.
1972b. Geoffroy Saint-Hilaire, Isidore (1805–1861). *Dictionary of Scientific Biography* 5:358–60.
BOWERS, CLAUDE G.
1950. *Pierre Vergniaud: Voice of the French Revolution.* New York: Macmillan.
BOWLBY, JOHN
1958. The nature of the child's tie to his mother. *International Journal of Psycho-Analysis* 39:350–73.
1960. Grief and mourning in infancy and early childhood. *The Psychoanalytic Study of the Child* 15:9–52.
1969–1980. *Attachment and Loss.* 3 vols. New York: Basic Books; London: Hogarth Press.
1988. *A Secure Base: Parent-Child Attachment and Healthy Human Development.* New York: Basic Books.
1990. *Charles Darwin: A New Life.* London: W. W. Norton; New York: W. W. Norton, 1991.
BOWLER, PETER J.
1971. Preformation and pre-existence in the seventeenth century: A brief analysis. *Journal of the History of Biology* 4:221–44.
1984. *Evolution: The History of an Idea.* Berkeley and Los Angeles: University of California Press.
1988. *The Non-Darwinian Revolution: Reinterpreting a Historical Myth.* Baltimore and London: Johns Hopkins University Press.
BRACKMAN, ARNOLD C.
1980. *A Delicate Arrangement: The Strange Case of Charles Darwin and Alfred Russel Wallace.* New York: Times Books.

BRADFORD, SARAH H.
1869. *Scenes from the Life of Harriet Tubman.* Auburn, N.Y.: W. J. Moses.
BRADY, THOMAS A., JR.
1982. Social history. In *Reformation Europe: A Guide to Research,* edited by Steven Ozment, pp. 161–81. St. Louis: Center for Reformation Research.
BRAGG, BARRY W., AND VERNON L. ALLEN
1970. Ordinal position and conformity: A role theory analysis. *Sociometry* 33:371–81.
BRANDES, GEORG
1930. *Voltaire.* 2 vols. Translated by Otto Kruger and Pierce Butler. New York: Albert & Charles Boni.
BRANDI, KARL
1939. *The Emperor Charles V: The Growth and Destiny of a Man and of a World-Empire.* Translated from the German by C. V. Wedgwood. New York: Alfred A. Knopf.
BRANNIGAN, AUGUSTINE
1981. *The Social Basis of Scientific Discoveries.* Cambridge: Cambridge University Press.
BRAUDEL, FERNAND
1972–73. *The Mediterranean and the Mediterranean World in the Age of Philip II.* 2 vols. Translated by Sian Reynolds. New York: Harper & Row.
BRELAND, HUNTER M.
1974. Birth order, family configuration, and verbal achievement. *Child Development* 45:1011–19.
BRIM, ORVILLE G., JR.
1958. Family structure and sex role learning by children: A further analysis of Helen Koch's data. *Sociometry* 21:1–16.
BROAD, WILLIAM, AND NICHOLAS WADE
1982. *Betrayers of the Truth.* New York: Simon and Schuster.
BROCKLISS, L. W. B.
1992. The scientific revolution in France. In *The Scientific Revolution in National Context,* edited by Roy Porter and Mikulás Teich, pp. 55–89. Cambridge: Cambridge University Press.
BROME, VINCENT
1983. *Ernest Jones: Freud's Alter Ego.* New York: W. W. Norton.
BROOKE, JOHN HEADLEY
1977. Richard Owen, William Whewell and the *Vestiges. British Journal for the History of Science* 10:132–45.
BROWN, G. W., T. HARRIS, AND A. BIFULCO
1986. Long-term effects of early loss of parent. In *Depression in Young People: Developmental and Clinical Perspectives,* edited by Michael Rutter, Carroll E. Izard, and Peter B. Read, pp. 251–96. New York: Guilford.
BROWN, W. L., AND E. O. WILSON
1956. Character displacement. *Systematic Zoology* 5:49–64.
BROWNE, JANET
1995. *Charles Darwin: Voyaging.* New York: Alfred A. Knopf.

BROWNING, OSCAR

1885. Bateson, William Henry (1812–81). *Dictionary of National Biography* 1:1321.

BRUHNS, KARL, ED.

1873. *Life of Alexander von Humboldt: Compiled in Commemoration of the Centenary of His Birth by J. Löwenberg, Robert Avé-Lallemant, and Alfred Dove.* 2 vols. Translated by Jane and Caroline Lassell. London: Longmans, Green.

BRUNEL, FRANÇOIS

1980. Les députés Montagnards. In *Actes du colloque Girondins et Montagnards,* edited by Albert Soboul, pp. 343–61. Paris: Société des Études Robespierristes.

BRUSH, STEPHEN G.

1974. Should the history of science be rated X? *Science* 183:1164–72.

BUFFON, GEORGES LOUIS

1753. Discours prononcé a L'Académie Française par M. de Buffon, le jour de sa réception. In *Oeuvres complètes.* 44 vols. Paris: Verdière and Ladrange, 1824–1832. Vol. 1: cxlix–clxiii.

BUNTING, JAMES

1974. *Charles Darwin: A Biography.* Folkeston, Kent: Bailey Brothers & Swinfen.

BURKE, JOHN, AND SIR BERNARD BURKE

1965–1972. *Burke's Genealogical and Heraldic History of the Landed Gentry. Founded 1836 by John Burke and Sir Bernard Burke.* 18th ed. 3 vols. Edited by Peter Townsend. London: Burke's Peerage.

1970. *Burke's Genealogical and Heraldic History of the Peerage, Baronetage and Knightage. Founded in 1826 by John Burke and Sir Bernard Burke.* 105th ed. 3 vols. Edited by Peter Townsend. London: Burke's Peerage.

BURKHALTER, LOIS WOOD

1965. *Gideon Lincecum, 1793–1874: A Biography.* Austin and London: University of Texas Press.

BURKHARDT, FREDERICK

1986. Introduction to *The Correspondence of Charles Darwin.* Edited by Frederick Burkhardt and Sydney Smith. Vol. 2: 1837–1843. Cambridge: Cambridge University Press.

1987. Introduction to *The Correspondence of Charles Darwin.* Edited by Frederick Burkhardt and Sydney Smith. Vol. 3: 1844–1846. Cambridge: Cambridge University Press.

BURKHARDT, RICHARD W., JR.

1977. *The Spirit of System: Lamarck and Evolutionary Biology.* Cambridge and London: Harvard University Press.

BURLINGAME, LESLIE J.

1973. Lamarck, Jean-Baptiste (1744–1829). *Dictionary of Scientific Biography* 7:584–94.

BUSBY, M. J., AND A. E. RODIN

1976. Relative contributions of Holmes and Semmelweis to the understanding of the etiology of puerperal fever. *Texas Reports on Biology and Medicine* 34:221–37.

BUSS, ARNOLD H., AND ROBERT PLOMIN

1984. *Temperament: Early Developing Personality Traits.* Hillsdale, N.J.: Lawrence Erlbaum.

BUSS, DAVID M.

1989. Sex differences in human mate preferences: Evolutionary hypotheses tested in 37 cultures. *Behavioral and Brain Sciences* 12:1–14.

1991. Evolutionary personality psychology. *Annual Review of Psychology* 42:459–91.

1994. *The Evolution of Desire: Strategies of Human Mating.* New York: Basic Books.

1995. Evolutionary psychology: A new paradigm for psychological science. *Psychological Inquiry* 6:1–30.

BUSS, DAVID M., JEANNE HUMPHREY BLOCK, AND JACK BLOCK

1980. Preschool activity level: Personality correlates and developmental implications. *Child Development* 51:401–8.

BUSS, DAVID M., AND KENNETH CRAIK

1980. The act frequency concept of disposition. *Journal of Personality* 48:379–92.

1983a. The act frequency approach to personality. *Psychological Review* 90:105–26.

1983b. Contemporary worldviews: Personal and policy implications. *Journal of Applied Social Psychology* 13:259–80.

BUTLER, SAMUEL

1872. *Erewhon; or, Over the Range.* London: Trubner.

1877. *Life and Habit.* London: Trübner.

1879. *Evolution, Old and New; or the Theories of Buffon, Dr. Erasmus Darwin, and Lamarck, as Compared with that of Mr. Charles Darwin.* London: Hardwicke and Bogue.

BUTTS, ROBERT E.

1976. Whewell, William (1794–1866). *Dictionary of Scientific Biography* 14:292–95.

CAMPBELL, DONALD T.

1965. Variation and selective retention in socio-cultural revolution. In *Social Change in Developing Areas,* edited by H. R. Barringer, G. I. Blanksten, and R. W. Mack, pp. 19–49. Cambridge, Mass.: Schenkman Press.

1970. Natural selection as an epistemological model. In *A Handbook of Methods in Cultural Anthropology,* edited by Raoul Naroll and Ronald Cohen, pp. 51–85. Garden City, N.Y.: Natural History Press.

1974. Evolutionary epistemology. In *The Philosophy of Karl Popper* 1:413–63. Edited by Paul A. Schlipp. La Salle, Ill.: Open Court.

CAMPBELL, W. W., AND R. TRUMPLER

1923. Observations on the deflection of light in passing through the sun's gravitational field. *Lick Observatory Bulletin* 11:41–54.

CANNON, WALTER F.

1960. The Uniformitarian-Catastrophist debate. *Isis* 51:38–55.

CANTOR, GEOFFREY N.

1975. Phrenology in early nineteenth-century Edinburgh: An historiographical discussion. *Annals of Science* 32:195–218.

CAROZZI, ALBERT V.
1966. Agassiz's amazing geological speculation: The Ice-Age. *Studies in Romanticism* 5:57–83.
1967. Introduction to *Studies on Glaciers,* by Louis Agassiz. Preceded by the *Discourse of Neuchâtel.* Translated and edited by Albert V. Carozzi. New York: Hafner.
1973. Agassiz's influence on geological thinking in the Americas. *Archives des Sciences (Genève)* 27:5–38.
1974. Maillet, Benoît de (1656–1738). *Dictionary of Scientific Biography* 9:26–27.
1984. Glaciology and the Ice Age. *Journal of Geological Education* 32: 158–70.

CASHDAN, ELIZABETH
1995. Hormones, sex, and status in women. *Hormones and Behavior* 29:354–66.

CASHER, BONNIE BERGER
1977. Relationship between birth order and participation in dangerous sports. *The Research Quarterly* 48:33–40.

CASPAR, MAX
1962. *Kepler, 1571–1630.* Translated and edited by C. Doris Hellman. New York: Collier Books.

CASPI, A., G. H. ELDER, JR., AND D. J. BEM
1987. Moving against the world: Life-course patterns of explosive children. *Developmental Psychology* 23:308–13.

CATON, HIRAM
1958. *The Politics of Progress: The Origins and Development of the Commercial Republic, 1600–1835.* Gainesville, Fla.: University of Florida Press.

CATTELL, J. MCKEEN
1917. Families of American men of science. III. Vital statistics and the composition of families. *Scientific Monthly* 5:368–77.

CHALLAMEL, AUGUSTIN
1895. *Les Clubs contre-révolutionnaires: Cercles, comités, sociétés, salons, réunions, cafés, restaurants et libraries.* Paris: L. Cerf.

[CHAMBERS, ROBERT]
1844. *Vestiges of the Natural History of Creation.* London: Churchill.

CHAMBERS, WILLIAM
1872. *Memoir of Robert Chambers, with Autobiographical Reminiscences of William Chambers.* Edinburgh: William and Robert Chambers.

CHAMPION, L.
1990. The relationship between social vulnerability and the occurrence of severely threatening life events. *Psychological Medicine* 20:157–61.

CHÂTELET, GABRIELLE-ÉMILIE LE TONNELIER DE BRETEUIL
1738. Lettre sur les éléments de la philosophie de Newton. *Journal des sçavans,* September, pp. 534–41.

CHAUMIÉ, JACQUELINE
1980. Les Girondins. In *Actes du colloque Girondins et Montagnards,* edited by Albert Soboul, pp. 19–60. Paris: Societé des Études Robespierristes.

CHESS, STELLA, AND ALEXANDER THOMAS
1986. *Temperament in Clinical Practice.* New York and London: Guilford Press.

CHOUDIEU, PIERRE-RENÉ
1897. *Mémoires et Notes de Choudieu.* Edited by Victor Barrucand. Paris: E. Plon, Nourrit.

CHRISTIE, D. M., R. A. DUNCAN, A. R. MCBIRNEY, M. A. RICHARDS, W. M. WHITE, K.S. HARPP, AND C. G. FOX
1992. Drowned islands downstream from the Galápagos Islands imply extended speciation times. *Nature* 355:246–48.

CLARK, JOHN WILLIS, AND THOMAS MCKENNY HUGHES
1890. *The Life and Letters of the Reverend Adam Sedgwick.* 2 vols. Cambridge: Cambridge University Press.

CLARK, ROGER D., AND GLENN A. RICE
1982. Family constellations and eminence: The birth orders of Nobel Prize winners. *Journal of Psychology* 110:281–87.

CLARK, RONALD W.
1971. *Einstein: The Life and Times.* New York: World Publishing.

CLARK, WILLIAM
1992. The scientific revolution in the German nations. In *The Scientific Revolution in National Context,* edited by Roy Porter and Mikulás Teich, pp. 90–114. Cambridge: Cambridge University Press.

CLEVELAND, W. S.
1981. LOWESS: A program for smoothing scatterplots by robust locally weighted regression. *American Statistician* 35:54.

COHEN, I. BERNARD
1956. *Franklin and Newton.* Philadelphia: American Philosophical Society.
1960. *The Birth of a New Physics.* Garden City, N.Y.: Anchor Books.
1974. Newton, Isaac (1642–1727). *Dictionary of Scientific Biography* 10:42–101.
1975. *Benjamin Franklin, Scientist and Statesman.* New York: Charles Scribner's Sons.
1980. *The Newtonian Revolution: With Illustrations of the Transformation of Scientific Ideas.* Cambridge: Cambridge University Press.
1985. *Revolution in Science.* Cambridge and London: The Belknap Press of Harvard University Press.
1988. The publication of *Science, Technology and Society:* Circumstances and consequences. *Isis* 79:571-81.
1990. Editor. *Puritanism and the Rise of Modern Science: The Merton Thesis.* With the assistance of K. E. Duffin and Stuart Strickland. New Brunswick and London: Rutgers University Press.
1992. The agnostic in the abbey. Review of *Darwin,* by Adrian Desmond and James Moore. *New York Times Book Review,* 2 August, p. 10.
1993. What Galileo saw: The experience of looking through a telescope. In *From Galileo's "Occhialino" to Optoelectronics,* edited by Paolo Mazzoldi, pp. 445–72. London: World Scientific.

COHEN, JACOB
1977. *Statistical Power Analysis for the Behavioral Sciences.* Rev. ed. New York: Academic Press; 2nd ed., 1988.

COHEN, ROBERT S.
1978. Marx, Karl (1818–1883). *Dictionary of Scientific Biography* 15:403–17.

COLE, F. J.
1930. *Early Theories of Sexual Generation*. Oxford: Clarendon Press.
COLEMAN, WILLIAM
1964. *Georges Cuvier, Zoologist: A Study in the History of Evolution Theory*. Cambridge: Harvard University Press.
1970. Bateson, William (1861–1926). *Dictionary of Scientific Biography* 1:505-6.
COLLINS, HARRY M.
1985. *Changing Order: Replication and Induction in Scientific Practice*. London and Beverly Hills: Sage Publications.
COLLINS, HARRY M., AND TREVOR J. PINCH
1982. *Frames of Meaning. The Social Construction of Extraordinary Science*. London: Routledge & Kegan Paul.
1993. *The Golem: What Everyone Should Know about Science*. Cambridge and New York: Cambridge University Press.
COLP, RALPH, JR.
1977. *To Be an Invalid: The Illness of Charles Darwin*. Chicago and London: University of Chicago Press.
COMBE, GEORGE
1828. *Of the Constitution of Man and Its Relation to External Objects*. Edinburgh: Anderson; London: Longman.
CONANT, JAMES BRYANT
1942. The advancement of learning during the Puritan Commonwealth. *Proceedings of the Massachusetts Historical Society* 66:3–31.
CONDON, EDWARD UHLER
1973. Reminiscences of a life in and out of quantum mechanics. *International Journal of Quantum Chemistry Symposia* 7:7–22.
CONGDON, LEE
1983. *The Young Lukács*. Chapel Hill, N.C.: University of North Carolina Press.
CONRAD, EARL
1943. *Harriet Tubman*. Washington, D.C.: Associated Publishers.
COOK, HAROLD J.
1992. The new philosophy in the Low Countries. In *The Scientific Revolution in National Context*, edited by Roy Porter and Mikulás Teich, pp. 115-49. Cambridge: Cambridge University Press.
COOTER, ROGER
1984. *The Cultural Meaning of Popular Science: Phrenology and the Organization of Consent in Nineteenth-Century Britain*. Cambridge: Cambridge University Press.
1989. *Phrenology in the British Isles: An Annotated, Historical Biobibliography and Index*. Metuchen, N.J., and London: Scarecrow Press.
CORSI, PIETRO
1988. *The Age of Lamarck: Evolutionary Theories in France, 1790–1830*. Translated by Jonathan Mandelbaum. Berkeley and Los Angeles: University of California Press.
COSER, LEWIS A.
1965. *Men of Ideas: A Sociologist's View*. New York: Free Press.

COSMIDES, LEDA
1989. The logic of social exchange: Has natural selection shaped how humans reason? *Cognition* 31:187–276.

COSTA, PAUL T., JR., P. J. FAGAN, R. L. PIEDMONT, Y. PONITCAS, AND T. N. WISE
1992. The five-factor model of personality and sexual functioning in outpatient men and women. *Psychiatric Medicine* 10:199–215.

COSTABEL, PIERRE
1974. Malebranche, Nicolas (1638–1715). *Dictionary of Scientific Biography* 9:47–53.

COWELL, ALAN
1992. After 350 years, Vatican says Galileo was right: It moves. *New York Times,* 3 October, pp. 1, 4.
1993. Low birth rate is becoming a headache for Italy. *New York Times,* 28 August, pp. 1, 5.

CRELLIN, J. K.
1966a. The problem of heat resistance of micro-organisms in the British spontaneous generation controversies of 1860–1880. *Medical History* 10:50–59.
1966b. Airborne particles and the germ theory: 1860–1880. *Annals of Science* 22:49–60.
1968. The dawn of the germ theory: Particles, infection and biology. In *Medicine and Society in the 1860s,* edited by F. L. Paynter, pp. 57–76. London: Wellcome Institute of the History of Medicine.

CREWS, FREDERICK
1986. *Skeptical Engagements.* New York and Oxford: Oxford University Press.
1995. *The Memory Wars: Freud's Legacy in Dispute.* With responses by 18 critics. New York: New York Review of Books.

CRICK, FRANCIS
1988. *What Mad Pursuit: A Personal View of Scientific Discovery.* New York: Basic Books.

CROCKER, LESTER G.
1959. Diderot and eighteenth century French transformism. In *Forerunners of Darwin: 1745–1859,* edited by Bentley Glass, Owsei Temkin, and William L. Straus, Jr., pp. 114–43. Baltimore: Johns Hopkins University Press.

CRONIN, VINCENT
1972. *Napoleon Bonaparte: An Intimate Biography.* New York: William Morrow.

CROSS, J. W., ED.
ca. 1885. *George Eliot's Life as Related in Her Letters and Journals.* 3 vols. New York: Harper & Brothers.

CROZIER, W. RAY
1986. Individual differences in shyness. In *Shyness: Perspectives on Research and Treatment,* edited by Warren H. Jones, Jonathan M. Cheek, and Stephen R. Briggs, pp. 133–45. New York and London: Plenum.

CURTIS, EUGENE NEWTON
1973. *Saint-Just: Colleague of Robespierre.* New York: Octagon Books.

CUVIER, FRÉDÉRIC, ED.
1826. *Dictionnaire des Sciences Naturelles. Portraits.* Strasbourg: Levrault.

DAJER, TONY
1992. Divided selves. *Discover,* September, pp. 38–69.
DALY, MARTIN, AND MARGO WILSON
1988a. *Homicide.* New York: Aldine de Gruyter.
1988b. The Darwinian psychology of discriminative parental solicitude. *Nebraska Symposium on Motivation* 35:91–144.
1990. Is parent-offspring conflict sex-linked? Freudian and Darwinian models. *Journal of Personality* 58:163–89.
1994. Some differential attributes of lethal assaults on small children by stepfathers versus genetic fathers. *Ethology and Sociobiology* 15:207–17.
D'AMAT, ROMAN
1968. Duprat, Jean. *Dictionnaire biographique française* 12:508–9.
DANIELS, DENISE
1986. Differential experiences of siblings in the same family as predictors of adolescent sibling personality differences. *Journal of Personality and Social Psychology* 51:339–46.
DARNTON, ROBERT
1968. *Mesmerism and the End of the Enlightenment in France.* Cambridge: Harvard University Press.
1974. Mesmer, Franz Anton (1734–1815). *Dictionary of Scientific Biography,* 9:325–28.
DARWIN, CHARLES ROBERT
1837. Remarks upon the habits of the genus *Geospiza, Camarhynchus, Cactornis,* and *Certhidea* of Gould. *Proceedings of the Zoological Society of London* 5:49.
1839. *Journal of Researches into the Geology and Natural History of the Various Countries Visited by H.M.S. Beagle, under the Command of Captain FitzRoy, R.N. from 1832 to 1836.* London: Henry Colburn.
1841. *The Zoology of the Voyage of H.M.S. Beagle, under the Command of Captain FitzRoy, R.N., during the Years 1832–1836.* Edited and superintended by Charles Darwin. Part 3: *Birds.* London: Smith, Elder.
1845. *Journal of Researches into the Natural History and Geology of the Countries Visited during the Voyage of H.M.S. Beagle round the World, under the Command of Capt. FitzRoy, R.N.* 2d ed. London: John Murray.
1859 [1858]. On the tendency of species to form varieties. Communicated by Charles Lyell . . . and J. D. Hooker. [Read 1 July 1858.] *Journal of the Proceedings of the Linnean Society (Zoology)* 3:45–52; reprinted in Darwin and Wallace (1958:259–67).
1859. *On the Origin of Species by means of Natural Selection, or, The Preservation of Favoured Races in the Struggle for Life.* London: John Murray.
1868. *The Variation of Animals and Plants under Domestication.* 2 vols. London: John Murray.
1871. *The Descent of Man, and Selection in Relation to Sex.* 2 vols. London: John Murray.
1872a. *The Expression of the Emotions in Man and Animals.* London: John Murray.
1872b. *On the Origin of Species by means of Natural Selection, or, The Preservation of the Favoured Races in the Struggle for Life.* 6th ed. London: John Murray.

1877. A biographical sketch of an infant. *Mind* 2:285–94.

1879. Preliminary notice. In *Erasmus Darwin,* by Ernst Krause, pp. 1–127. Translated by W. S. Dallas. London: John Murray.

1887. *The Life and Letters of Charles Darwin, including an Autobiographical Chapter.* Edited by Francis Darwin. 3 vols. London: John Murray.

1890. *Journal of Researches into the Natural History and Geology of the Countries Visited during the Voyage of H.M.S. Beagle round the World, under the Command of Capt. FitzRoy, R.N.* A new edition with illustrations by R. T. Pritchett. London: John Murray; New York: D. Appleton.

1903. *More Letters of Charles Darwin: A Record of His Work in a Series of Hitherto Unpublished Letters.* Edited by Francis Darwin and A. C. Seward. 2 vols. New York: D. Appleton.

1909. *The Foundations of the Origin of Species: Two Essays Written in 1842 and 1844.* Edited by Francis Darwin. Cambridge: Cambridge University Press.

1933. *Charles Darwin's Diary of the Voyage of H.M.S. "Beagle."* Edited by Nora Barlow. Cambridge: Cambridge University Press; New York: Kraus Reprint, 1969.

1958 [1876]. *The Autobiography of Charles Darwin, 1809–1882. With the Original Omissions Restored.* Edited with Appendix and Notes by Nora Barlow. London: Collins.

1959. *Darwin's Journal.* Edited by Gavin de Beer. *Bulletin of the British Museum (Natural History) Historical Series* 2, no. 1.

1963 [1836]. *Darwin's Ornithological Notes.* Edited with Introduction, Notes, and Appendix by Nora Barlow. *Bulletin of the British Museum (Natural History) Historical Series* 2, no. 7.

1975 [1854–1858]. *Natural Selection.* Edited by Robert Stauffer. Cambridge: Cambridge University Press.

1985– . *The Correspondence of Charles Darwin.* Edited by Frederick Burkhardt and Sydney Smith. 10 vols. (to date). Cambridge: Cambridge University Press.

1987. *Charles Darwin's Notebooks, 1836–1844: Geology, Transmutation of Species, Metaphysical Enquiries.* Transcribed and edited by Paul H. Barrett, Peter J. Gautrey, Sandra Herbert, David Kohn, and Sydney Smith. Ithaca, N.Y.: British Museum (Natural History)/Cornell University Press.

DARWIN, CHARLES, AND ALFRED RUSSEL WALLACE

1859 [1858]. On the tendency of species to form varieties; and on the perpetuation of varieties and species by natural means of selection . . . Communicated by Charles Lyell . . . and J. D. Hooker. [Read 1 July 1858.] *Journal of the Proceedings of the Linnean Society (Zoology)* 3:45–62; reprinted in Darwin and Wallace (1958).

1958 [1858]. *Evolution by Natural Selection.* Foreword by Sir Gavin de Beer. Cambridge: Cambridge University Press.

DARWIN, EMMA

1915. *Emma Darwin: A Century of Family Letters, 1792–1896.* Edited by Henrietta [Darwin] Litchfield. 2 vols. Cambridge: Cambridge University Press.

DARWIN, ERASMUS
1794–96. *Zoonomia; or, the Laws of Organic Life.* 2 vols. London: J. Johnson.
DARWIN, FRANCIS
1888. Darwin, Charles Robert (1809–1882). *Dictionary of National Biography* 5:522–534.
1914. William Erasmus Darwin (1839–1914). *Christ's College Magazine* 29:16–23.
DAVIES, GORDON L.
1969. *The Earth in Decay: A History of British Geomorphology, 1578–1878.* New York: Elsevier.
DAVIES, NICHOLAS B.
1992. *Dunnock Behavior and Social Evolution.* Oxford and New York: Oxford University Press.
DAVIS, JAMES A.
1985. *The Logic of Causal Order.* Newbury Park, Calif.: Sage Publications.
DAVIS, LENWOOD G.
1969. *I Have a Dream . . . The Life and Times of Martin Luther King, Jr.* Chicago: Adams Press.
DAWKINS, RICHARD
1976. *The Selfish Gene.* Oxford: Oxford University Press.
1982. *The Extended Phenotype: The Gene as the Unit of Selection.* Oxford and San Francisco: W. H. Freeman.
DAWSON, JOHN CHARLES
1948. *Lakanal the Regicide: A Biographical and Historical Study of the Career of Joseph Lakanal.* Tuscaloosa: University of Alabama Press.
DEAK, ISTVAN
1987. The convert. *New York Review of Books,* 12 March, pp. 39–44.
DE BEER, GAVIN
1964. *Charles Darwin: Evolution by Natural Selection.* Garden City, N.Y.: Doubleday.
DEBUS, ALLEN G., ED.
1968. *World Who's Who in Science: A Biographical Dictionary of Notable Scientists from Antiquity to the Present.* Chicago: Marquis Who's Who.
DEKAY, W. TODD, AND DAVID M. BUSS
1992. Human nature, individual differences, and the importance of context: Perspectives from evolutionary psychology. *Current Directions in Psychological Science* 1:184–89.
DEMARIS, OVID
1977. *Brothers in Blood: The International Terrorist Network.* New York: Charles Scribner's Sons.
DEMSTER, W. J.
1983. *Patrick Matthew and Natural Selection.* Edinburgh: Paul Harris.
DENNETT, DANIEL C.
1995. *Darwin's Dangerous Idea: Evolution and the Meaning of Life.* New York: Simon and Schuster.
DESMOND, ADRIAN
1982. *Archetypes and Ancestors: Palaeontology in Victorian London, 1850–1875.* Chicago and London: Chicago University Press.

1984a. Robert E. Grant: The social predicament of a pre-Darwinian transmutationist. *Journal of the History of Biology* 17:189–223.

1984b. Robert E. Grant's later views on organic development: The Swiney Lectures on "palaeozoology," 1853–1857. *Archives for Natural History* 11:395–413.

1985. Richard Owen's reaction to transmutation in the 1830s. *British Journal of the History of Science* 18:25–50.

1987. Artisan resistance and evolution in Britain, 1819–1848. *Osiris* 3:77–110.

1989. *The Politics of Evolution: Morphology, Medicine, and Reform in Radical London.* Chicago and London: University of Chicago Press.

DESMOND, ADRIAN, AND JAMES MOORE

1992. *Darwin: The Life of a Tormented Evolutionist.* New York: Warner Books; London: Michael Joseph (under the title *Darwin*), 1991.

DE WAAL, FRANS

1982. *Chimpanzee Politics: Power and Sex among Apes.* New York: Harper & Row.

1989. *Peacemaking among Primates.* Cambridge and London: Harvard University Press.

DIAMOND, ARTHUR M.

1980. Age and the acceptance of cliometrics. *Journal of Economic History* 40:838–41.

DIAMOND, SOLOMON

1976. Wundt, Wilhelm (1832–1920). *Dictionary of Scientific Biography* 14:526–29.

DIBELIUS, FRANZ WILHELM

1909. George, Duke of Saxony (George the Bearded) [1471–1539]. *The New Schaff-Herzog Encyclopedia of Religious Knowledge* 4:458–59. Edited by Samuel Macauley Jackson. New York and London: Funk and Wagnalls.

DICKENS, ARTHUR GEOFFREY

1967. *Martin Luther and the Reformation.* London: English Universities Press.

1989. *The English Reformation.* 2d ed. London: B. T. Batsford.

DICKENS, CHARLES

1849–50. *The Personal History of David Copperfield.* London: Bradbury & Evans.

1861. *Great Expectations.* London: Chapman & Hall.

DIEUDONNÉ, JEAN

1975. Poincaré, Jules Henri (1854–1912). *Dictionary of Scientific Biography* 11:51–61.

DIGMAN, JOHN M.

1990. Personality structure: Emergence of the five-factor model. *Annual Review of Psychology* 41:417–40.

DIXON, W. J., ED.

1992. *BMDP Statistical Software Manual.* 2 vols. Berkeley and Los Angles: University of California Press.

DOBRZYCKI, JERZY

1972. *The Reception of Copernicus' Heliocentric Theory.* Dordrecht and Boston: D. Reidel.

DOBZHANSKY, THEODOSIUS, FRANCISCO J. AYALA, G. LEDYARD STEBBINS, AND JAMES W. VALENTINE

1977. *Evolution.* San Francisco: W. H. Freeman.

DOCK, WILLIAM
1976. Wells, William Charles (1757–1817). *Dictionary of Scientific Biography* 14:253–54.

DODER, DUSKO, AND LOUISE BRANSON
1990. *Gorbachev: Heretic in the Kremlin.* New York: Viking Press.

DOMINEY, WALLACE J., AND LAWRENCE S. BLUMER
1984. Cannibalism of early life stages in fishes. In *Infanticide: Comparative and Evolutionary Perspectives,* edited by Glenn Hausfater and Sarah Blaffer Hrdy, pp. 43–64. New York: Aldine.

DONOVAN, ARTHUR, LARRY LAUDAN, AND RACHEL LAUDAN, EDS.
1988. *Scrutinizing Science: Empirical Studies of Scientific Change.* Dordrecht and Boston: Kluwer Academic Publishers; Baltimore: Johns Hopkins University Press, 1992.

DORNBERG, JOHN
1974. *Brezhnev: The Masks of Power.* London: Andre Deutsch.

DOROZYNSKI, ALEXANDER
1991. Privacy rules blindside French glaucoma effort. *Science* 252:369–70.

DRAKE, STILLMAN
1957. Introduction to *Discoveries and Opinions of Galileo.* Translated by Stillman Drake. Garden City, N.Y.: Doubleday Anchor Books.
1970. *Galileo Studies.* Ann Arbor, Mich.: University of Michigan Press.
1971. Cesi, Federico (1585–1630). *Dictionary of Scientific Biography* 3:179–80.
1972. Galilei, Galileo (1564–1642). *Dictionary of Scientific Biography* 5:237–50.
1978. *Galileo at Work: His Scientific Biography.* Chicago and London: University of Chicago Press.

DREYER, J. L. E.
1906. *History of the Planetary Systems from Thales to Kepler.* Cambridge: Cambridge University Press. Reprinted as *A History of Astronomy from Thales to Kepler.* New York: Dover, 1953.

DUBY, GEORGES
1977. *The Chivalrous Society.* Translated by Cynthia Poston. Berkeley: University of California Press.
1978. *Medieval Marriage: Two Models from Twelfth-Century France.* Translated by Elborg Forster. Baltimore: Johns Hopkins University Press.

DUFFIN, KATHLEEN ELIZABETH
1976. The search for a natural classification: Perspectives on the quinarian episode in ornithology. Senior honors thesis, Harvard College, Committee on History and Science.

DUNBAR, KEVIN.
1995 How scientists really reason: Scientific reasoning in real-world laboratories. In *The Nature of Scientific Insight,* edited by Robert J. Sternberg and Janet E. Davidson, pp. 365–95. Cambridge: MIT Press.

DUNN, JUDY
1985. *Sisters and Brothers.* Cambridge: Harvard University Press.
1993. *Young Children's Close Relationships: Beyond Attachment.* Newbury Park, Calif.: Sage Publications.

DUNN, JUDY, AND CAROL KENDRICK
1982. *Siblings: Love, Envy, and Understanding.* Cambridge: Harvard University Press.
DUNN, JUDY, AND P. MUNN
1985. Becoming a family member: Family conflict and the development of social understanding. *Child Development* 56:480–92.
DUNN, JUDY, AND ROBERT PLOMIN
1990. *Separate Lives: Why Siblings Are So Different.* New York: Basic Books.
1991. Why are siblings so different? The significance of differences in sibling experience within the family. *Family Process* 30:271–83.
DURANT, WILL
1957. *The Reformation: A History of European Civilization from Wyclif to Calvin: 1300–1564.* The Story of Civilization, Part 6. New York: Simon and Schuster.
DURANT, WILL, AND ARIEL DURANT
1965. *The Age of Voltaire: A History of Civilization in Western Europe from 1715 to 1756, with Special Emphasis on the Conflict between Religion and Philosophy.* The Story of Civilization, Part 9. New York: Simon and Schuster.
DURSTON, CHRISTOPHER
1989. *The Family in the English Reformation.* Oxford: Blackwell.
DURUY, GEORGE, ED.
1895. *Memoirs of Barras, Member of the Directorate.* Translated by Charles E. Roche. 4 vols. Vol. 1: *The Ancien Régime—The Revolution.* London: Osgood, McIlvaine.
EAVES, J. L., H. J. EYSENCK, AND N. G. MARTIN
1989. *Genes, Culture and Personality: An Empirical Approach.* London and New York: Academic Press.
EDWARDS, JOHN N., AND DAVID L. KLEMMACK
1973. Birth order and the conservators of tradition hypothesis. *Journal of Marriage and the Family* 35:619–26.
EGERTON, FRANK N., III
1972. Forbes, Edward, Jr. (1815–1854). *Dictionary of Scientific Biography* 5:66–68.
1976. Watson, Hewett Cottrell (1804–1881). *Dictionary of Scientific Biography* 14:66–68.
EHRMAN, ESTHER
1986. *Mme du Châtelet: Scientist, Philosopher and Feminist of the Enlightenment.* Leamington Spa, UK: Berg Publishers.
EISELEY, LOREN
1961. *Darwin's Century.* New York: Doubleday.
EISENMAN, RUSSELL
1987. Creativity, birth order, and risk taking. *Bulletin of the Psychometric Society* 25:87–88.
EKMAN, PAUL, ED.
1973. *Darwin and Facial Expression: A Century of Research in Review.* New York: Academic Press.

ELLEGÅRD, ALVAR

1990 [1958]. *Darwin and the General Reader: The Reception of Darwin's Theory of Evolution in the British Periodical Press, 1859–1872.* With a new Foreword by David L. Hull. Chicago and London: University of Chicago Press.

ELLENBERGER, HENRI F.

1970. *The Discovery of the Unconscious: The History and Evolution of Dynamic Psychiatry.* New York: Basic Books.

ELMS, ALAN C.

1976. *Personality in Politics.* New York: Harcourt Brace Jovanovich.

ELTON, G. R.

1963. *Reformation Europe, 1517–1559.* London and Glasgow: Collins.

EMLEN, STEPHEN T., PETER H. WREGE, AND NATALIE J. DEMONG

1995. Making decisions in the family: An evolutionary perspective. *American Scientist* 83:148–57.

EPSTEIN, LEE, JEFFREY A. SEGAL, HAROLD J. SPAETH, AND THOMAS G. WALKER

1994. *The Supreme Court Compendium: Data, Decisions, and Developments.* Washington, D.C.: Congressional Quarterly.

ERDMANN, DAVID

1908. Albert of Prussia (1490–1568). *The New Schaff-Herzog Encyclopedia of Religious Knowledge,* 1:106–8. Edited by Samuel Macauley Jackson. New York and London: Funk and Wagnalls.

1909. George of Brandenburg (1484–1543). *The New Schaff-Herzog Encyclopedia of Religious Knowledge* 4:457–58. Edited by Samuel Macauley Jackson. New York and London: Funk and Wagnalls.

ERICKSON, CAROLLY

1980. *Great Harry.* New York: Summit Books.

ERIKSON, ERIK HOMBERGER

1958. *Young Man Luther: A Study in Psychoanalysis and History.* New York: W. W. Norton.

ERNST, CÉCILE, AND JULES ANGST

1983. *Birth Order: Its Influence on Personality.* Berlin and New York: Springer-Verlag.

EYSENCK, HANS J.

1954. *The Psychology of Politics.* London: Routledge & Kegan Paul; New York: Praeger.

1956. The questionnaire measurement of neuroticism and extraversion. *Revista de Psicologia* 50:113–40.

1985. *The Decline and Fall of the Freudian Empire.* Middlesex, England: Penguin Books; New York: Viking Press.

1990. Genetic and environmental contributions to individual differences: The three major dimensions of personality. *Journal of Personality* 58:245–61.

EYSENCK, HANS J., AND S. RACHMAN

1965. *The Causes and Cures of Neurosis: An Introduction to Modern Behavior Therapy Based on Learning Theory and the Principles of Conditioning.* London: Routledge & Kegan Paul.

EYSENCK, HANS J., AND GLEN D. WILSON

1978. *The Psychological Basis of Ideology.* Lancaster: Medical and Technical Publishing.

FAHRENBERG, J., H. SELG, AND R. HAMPEL

1973. *Das Freiburger Persönlichkeitsinventar FPI.* 2d ed. Göttingen: Verlag für Psychologie Dr. C. J. Hogrefe.

FARBER, SUSAN L.

1981. *Identical Twins Reared Apart: A Reanalysis.* New York: Basic Books.

FARLEY, FRANK, AND SONJA V. FARLEY

1974. Birth order and political orientation in college women. *Psychological Reports* 34: 1045–146.

FARLEY, JOHN

1977. *The Spontaneous Generation Controversy from Descartes to Oparin.* Baltimore and London: Johns Hopkins University Press.

1982. *Gametes and Spores: Ideas about Sexual Reproduction, 1750–1914.* Baltimore and London: Johns Hopkins University Press.

FARLEY, JOHN, AND GERALD L. GEISON

1974. Science, politics and spontaneous generation in 19th century France: The Pasteur-Pouchet debate. *Bulletin of the History of Medicine* 48:161–98.

FAUST, DAVID

1984. *The Limits of Scientific Reasoning.* Minneapolis: University of Minnesota Press.

FAUST, DAVID, AND PAUL E. MEEHL

1992. Using scientific methods to resolve questions in the history and philosophy of science: Some illustrations. *Behavior Therapy* 23:195–211.

FAVIER, JEAN, ANIKE BLAISE, SERGE COSSERON, AND JACQUES LEGRAND, EDS.

1989. *Chronicle of the French Revolution.* London: Chronicle Communications.

FEINGOLD, ALAN

1994. Gender differences in personality: A meta-analysis. *Psychological Bulletin* 116:429–56.

FELLOWS, OTIS

1989. *Diderot.* Updated Edition. Boston: Twayne Publishers.

FESHBACK, SEYMOUR, AND BERNARD WEINER

1986. *Personality.* 2d ed. Lexington, Mass.: D. C. Heath.

FESTINGER, LEON

1957. *A Theory of Cognitive Dissonance.* Stanford: Stanford University Press.

FEUER, LOUIS

1963. *The Scientific Intellectual.* New York: Basic Books.

1974. *Einstein and the Generations of Science.* New York: Basic Books.

FICHTNER, PAULA SUTTER

1989. *Protestantism and Primogeniture in Early Modern Germany.* New Haven and New York: Yale University Press.

FILLER, LOUIS

1987. *Dictionary of American Conservatism.* New York: Philosophical Library.

FISCH, R.

1977. Psychology of Science. In *Science, Technology, and Society: A Cross-Disciplinary Perspective,* edited by J. Spiegel-Rosing and D. de S. Price, pp. 277–318. Newbury Park, Calif.: Sage Publications.

FISHER, RICHARD B.
1977. *Joseph Lister, 1827–1912.* New York: Stein and Day.

FITZROY, ROBERT
1839. *Narrative of the Surveying Voyages of His Majesty's Ships Adventure and Beagle, between the Years 1826 and 1836, Describing Their Examination of the Southern Shores of South America, and the Beagle's Circumnavigation of the Globe.* Vol. 1: *Proceedings of the First Expedition, 1826–1830, under the Command of Captain P. Parker King.* Vol. 2: *Proceedings of the Second Expedition, 1831–1836, under the Command of Captain Robert Fitz-Roy, R.N.* With *Appendix.* London: Henry Colburn.

FLAHERTY, JENNY
1980. Psychological correlates of scientific attitudes. Senior honors thesis, Wellesley College, Wellesley, Mass.

FLECK, LUDWIG
1979 [1935]. *Genesis and Development of a Scientific Fact.* Edited by Thaddeus J. Trenn and Robert K. Merton. Translated by Fred Bradley and Thaddeus J. Trenn. Chicago: University of Chicago Press.

FLEMING, DONALD
1961. Charles Darwin, the anaesthetic man. *Victorian Studies* 4:219–36.

FLEXNER, JAMES THOMAS
1965. *George Washington: The Forge of Experience (1732–1775).* Boston: Little, Brown.

FLOURENS, PIERRE
1864. *Examen du livre de M. Darwin sur l'origine des espèces.* Paris: Garnier.

FONER, ERIC, ED.
1971. *Nat Turner.* Englewood Cliffs, N.J.: Prentice-Hall.

FORBES, GORDON B.
1971. Birth order and political success: A study of the 1970 Illinois general elections. *Psychological Reports* 29:1239–42.

FORMAN, PAUL
1971. Weimar culture, causality, and quantum theory, 1918–1927: Adaptation by German physicists and mathematicians to a hostile intellectual environment. *Historical Studies in the Physical Sciences* 3:1–115.
1978. The reception of an acausal quantum mechanics in Germany and Britain. In *The Reception of Unconventional Science,* edited by Seymour H. Mauskopf, pp. 11–50. Boulder, Colo.: Westview.

FORSTER, J.
1874. *Life of Charles Dickens.* London: Chapman and Hall.

FOSTER, JOHN W., AND STANLEY J. ARCHER
1979. Birth order and intelligence: An immunological interpretation. *Perceptual and Motor Skills* 48:79–93.

FRANK, LAURENCE G., STEPHEN E. GLICKMAN, AND PAUL LICHT
1991. Fatal sibling aggression, precocial development, and androgens in neonatal spotted hyenas. *Science* 252:702–704.

FRANK, PHILIPP
1947. *Einstein: His Life and Times.* Translated from the German by George Rosen. New York: Alfred A. Knopf.

FRANK, ROBERT G., JR.
1980. *Harvey and the Oxford Physiologists: A Study of Scientific Ideas.* Berkeley and Los Angeles: University of California Press.
FRANKLIN, BENJAMIN
1916. *The Autobiography of Benjamin Franklin.* Garden City, N.Y.: Garden City Publishing.
FRASER, ANTONIA
1992. *The Wives of Henry VIII.* New York: Alfred A. Knopf.
FREDERICK II
1751. Frederick the Great's eulogy on Julien Offray de La Mettrie. Reprinted and translated in *Man a Machine,* by Julien Offray de La Mettrie. La Salle, Ill.: Open Court, 1912.
FREDERICK, JEFFREY T.
1987. *The Psychology of the American Jury.* Charlottesville, Va.: Michie.
FREEMAN, DEREK
1983. *Margaret Mead and Samoa: The Making and Unmasking of an Anthropological Myth.* Cambridge and London: Harvard University Press.
FREEMAN, R. B.
1978. *Charles Darwin. A Companion.* Folkestone, England: William Dawson; Hamden, Conn.: Archon Books.
FREUD, SIGMUND
1900. *The Interpretation of Dreams.* In *The Standard Edition of the Complete Psychological Works of Sigmund Freud,* 4–5. 24 vols. Translated from the German under the general editorship of James Strachey, in collaboration with Anna Freud, assisted by Alix Strachey and Alan Tyson. London: Hogarth Press and The Institute of Psycho-Analysis, 1953–1975.
1916–17. Introductory Lectures on Psycho-Analysis. In *The Standard Edition of the Complete Psychological Works of Sigmund Freud* 15–16.
1933. *New Introductory Lectures on Psycho-Analysis.* In *The Standard Edition of the Complete Psychological Works of Sigmund Freud* 22:3–182.
1940. *An Outline of Psycho-Analysis.* In *The Standard Edition of the Complete Psychological Works of Sigmund Freud* 23:141–207.
FREUD, SIGMUND, AND CARL GUSTAV JUNG
1974. *The Freud/Jung Letters: The Correspondence between Sigmund Freud and C. G. Jung.* Edited by William McGuire. Translated by Ralph Manheim and R. F. C. Hull. Bollingen Series XCIV. Princeton: Princeton University Press; London: Routledge & Kegan Paul.
FREUDENTHAL, HANS
1971. Cauchy, Augustin-Louis (1789–1857). *Dictionary of Scientific Biography* 3:131–48.
FRIEDMAN, LEON, AND FRED L. ISRAEL, EDS.
1969. *The Justices of the United States Supreme Court, 1789–1969: Their Lives and Major Opinions.* 4 vols. New York and London: Chelsea House, in association with R. R. Bowker.
FULLER, STEVE
1989. *Philosophy of Science and Its Discontents.* Boulder, Colo.: Westview Press.

FULTON, JOHN F., AND ELIZABETH H. THOMSON

1947. *Benjamin Silliman: Pathfinder in American Science.* New York: Henry Schuman.

FURET, FRANÇOIS, AND MONA OZOUF, EDS.

1989. *A Critical Dictionary of the French Revolution.* Translated by Arthur Goldhammer. Cambridge: The Belknap Press of Harvard University Press.

1991. *La Gironde et les Girondins.* Paris: Payot.

FURET, FRANÇOIS, AND DENIS RICHET

1970. *French Revolution.* Translated from the French by Stephen Hardman. New York: Macmillan.

GAGLIARDO, JOHN G.

1967. *Enlightened Despotism.* New York: Thomas Y. Crowell.

GAIRDNER, JAMES

1885. Askew, Anne (1521–1546). *Dictionary of National Biography* 1:662–64.

1887. Parr, Catherine (1512–1548). *Dictionary of National Biography* 3:1217–21.

GALILEI, GALILEO

1957 [1610]. *The Starry Messenger.* In *Discoveries and Opinions of Galileo,* pp. 20–58. Translated with Introduction and Notes by Stillman Drake. Garden City, N.Y.: Doubleday Anchor Books.

1967 [1632]. *Dialogue Concerning the Two Chief World Systems—Ptolemaic and Copernican.* Translated by Stillman Drake. 2d ed. Berkeley and Los Angeles: University of California Press.

GALISON, PETER

1987. *How Experiments End.* Chicago: University of Chicago Press.

GALTON, FRANCIS

1874. *English Men of Science.* London: Macmillan.

GARDNER, HOWARD

1983. *Frames of Mind: The Theory of Multiple Intelligences.* New York: Basic Books.

1987. *The Mind's New Science.* New York: Basic Books.

1993. *Creating Minds: An Anatomy of Creativity Seen through the Lives of Freud, Einstein, Picasso, Stravinsky, Eliot, Graham, and Gandhi.* New York: Basic Books.

1995. *Leading Minds: An Anatomy of Leadership.* In collaboration with Emma Laskin. New York: Basic Books.

GASKING, ELIZABETH

1967. *Investigations into Generation, 1651–1828.* Baltimore: Johns Hopkins University Press.

GAULD, ALAN

1968. *The Founders of Psychical Research.* New York: Schocken Books.

GAULIN, STEVEN J. C., AND CAROLE J. ROBBINS

1991. Trivers-Willard effect in contemporary North American society. *American Journal of Physical Anthropology* 85:61–69.

GAUSE, G. F.

1934. *The Struggle for Existence.* Baltimore: Williams and Wilkins.

GAY, PETER

1959. *Voltaire's Politics: The Poet as Realist.* Princeton: Princeton University Press

1966. *The Enlightenment: An Interpretation. The Rise of Modern Paganism.* New York: Alfred A. Knopf.

GEEN, RUSSELL G.

1986. Physiological, affective, and behavioral implications of extraversion-introversion. In *Shyness: Perspectives on Research and Treatment,* edited by Warren H. Jones, Jonathan M. Cheek, and Stephen R. Briggs, pp. 265–78. New York and London: Plenum.

GEISBERG, MAX

1974. *The Single-leaf Woodcut: 1500–1550.* 4 vols. Revised and edited by Walter L. Strauss. New York: Hacker Art Books.

GEISON, GERALD L.

1969. The protoplasmic theory of life and the vitalist-mechanist debate. *Isis* 60:273–92.

GEORGE, CHARLES H., AND KATHERINE GEORGE

1961. *The Protestant Mind of the English Reformation 1570–1640.* Princeton: Princeton University Press.

GETZELS, JACOB W., AND PHILIP W. JACKSON

1962. *Creativity and Intelligence: Explorations with Gifted Students.* London and New York: John Wiley & Sons.

GHISELIN, MICHAEL T.

1969. *The Triumph of the Darwinian Method.* Berkeley and Los Angeles: University of California Press.

1972. The individual in the Darwinian revolution. *New Literary History* 3: 113–34.

GIBBON, CHARLES

1878. *The Life of George Combe, Author of "The Constitution of Man."* 2 vols. London: Macmillan.

GIBNEY, LEO

1989. *An Investigation into the Verdict Preferences of Death Qualified and Non-Death Qualified Juries.* Ann Arbor, Mich.: University Microfilms.

GIERE, RONALD N.

1988. *Explaining Science: A Cognitive Approach.* Chicago and London: University of Chicago Press.

1989. The units of analysis in science studies. In *The Cognitive Turn: Sociological and Psychological Perspectives on Science,* edited by Steve Fuller, Marc de Mey, Terry Shinn, and Steve Woolgar, pp. 3–11. Dordrecht: Kluwer Academic Publishers.

GIERYN, THOMAS F.

1988. Distancing science from religion in seventeenth-century England. *Isis* 79:582–93.

GIERYN, THOMAS F., AND RICHARD F. HIRSH

1983. Marginality and innovation in science. *Social Studies of Science* 13:87–106.

GILLESPIE, NEAL C.

1979. *Charles Darwin and the Problem of Creation.* Chicago and London: Chicago University Press.

GILLIGAN, CAROL
1982. *In a Different Voice: Psychological Theory and Woman's Development.* Cambridge and London: Harvard University Press.

GILLISPIE, CHARLES COULSTON
1951. *Genesis and Geology: A Study in the Relations of Scientific Thought, Natural Theology, and Social Opinion in Great Britain, 1790–1850.* Cambridge: Harvard University Press.
1974. Mertonian theses. *Science* 184:656–60.
1978. Laplace, Pierre-Simon, Marquis de (1749–1827). *Dictionary of Scientific Biography* 15:273–356.

GINGERICH, OWEN
1973. Kepler, Johannes (1571–1630). *Dictionary of Scientific Biography* 7:289–312.
1975. "Crisis" versus aesthetic in the Copernican revolution. In *Vistas in Astronomy,* edited by Arthur Beer and K. Aa. Strand, pp. 85–95. Oxford and New York: Pergamon.

GINGERICH, OWEN, AND ROBERT S. WESTMAN
1988. The Wittich connection: Conflict and priority in late sixteenth-century cosmology. *Transactions of the American Philosophical Society* 78, Part 7.

GINI, CORRADO
1915. Superiority of the eldest. *Journal of Heredity* 6:37–39.

GLANTZ, KALMAN, AND JOHN K. PEARCE
1989. *Exiles from Eden: Psychotherapy from an Evolutionary Perspective.* New York: W. W. Norton.

GLASS, BENTLEY
1959. Maupertuis, pioneer of genetics and evolution. In *Forerunners of Darwin, 1745–1859,* edited by Bentley Glass, Owsei Tempkin, and William L. Straus, Jr., pp. 51–83. Baltimore: Johns Hopkins University Press.

GLASS, BENTLEY, OWSEI TEMPKIN, AND WILLIAM L. STRAUS, JR., EDS.
1959. *Forerunners of Darwin, 1745–1859.* Baltimore: Johns Hopkins University Press.

GLASS, GENE V., BARRY MCGAW, AND MARY LEE SMITH
1981. *Meta-Analysis in Social Research.* Beverly Hills, Calif.: Sage Publications.

GLEN, WILLIAM
1982. *The Road to Jaramillo: Critical Years in the Revolution in Earth Sciences.* Stanford: Stanford University Press.

GLICK, THOMAS F., ED.
1972. *The Comparative Reception of Darwinism.* Austin and London: University of Texas Press.
1987. *The Comparative Reception of Relativity.* Dordrecht and Boston: D. Reidel.

GLUCK, MARY
1985. *Georg Lukács and His Generation: 1900–1918.* Cambridge: Harvard University Press.

GODECHOT, JACQUES
1971. *The Counter-Revolution: Doctrine and Action, 1789–1804.* Translated from the French by Salvator Attanasio. Princeton: Princeton University Press.

GODLEE, RICKMAN J.
1917. *Lord Lister.* London: Macmillan.

GOERTZEL, MILDRED GEORGE, VICTOR GOERTZEL, AND TED GEORGE GOERTZEL

1978. *Three Hundred Eminent Personalities.* San Francisco: Jossey-Bass Publishers.

GOLDBERG, LEWIS ROBERT

1981. Language and individual differences: The search for universals in personality lexicons. In *Review of Personality and Social Psychology,* edited by L. Wheeler, vol. 2, pp. 141–65. Beverly Hills, Calif.: Sage Publications.

1982. From ace to zombie: Some explorations in the language of personality. In *Advances in Personality Assessment,* edited by C. D. Spielberger and J. N. Butcher, vol. 1, pp. 203–34. Hillsdale, N.J.: Erlbaum.

GOLDBERG, STANLEY

1968. *The Early Responses to Einstein's Special Theory of Relativity, 1905–1911: A Case Study in National Differences.* Cambridge: Harvard University Press.

1984. *Understanding Relativity: Origin and Impact of a Scientific Revolution.* Boston, Basel, and Stuttgart: Birkhäuser.

GOLINSKI, JAN

1990. The theory of practice and the practice of theory: Sociological approaches in the story of science. *Isis* 81:492–505.

GORTVAY, GYORGY, AND I. ZOLTAN

1968. *Semmelweis: His Life and Work.* Translated by Éva Róa and R. Bonnerjea. Budapest: Akadémiai Kiadó.

GOSSE, EDMUND

1890. *The Life of Philip Henry Gosse.* London: Kegan Paul, Trench, Trübner.

GOSSE, PHILLIP HENRY

1857. *Omphalos: An Attempt to Untie the Geological Knot.* London: John Van Voorst.

GOUGH, HARRISON G., AND AVRIL THORNE

1986. Positive, negative, and balanced shyness: Self-definitions and the reactions of others. In *Shyness: Perspectives on Research and Treatment,* edited by Warren H. Jones, Jonathan M. Cheek, and Stephen R. Briggs, pp. 189–203. New York and London: Plenum.

GOULD, JOHN

1837a. Remarks on a group of ground finches in Mr. Darwin's collection, with characters of the new species. *Proceedings of the Zoological Society of London* 5:4–7.

1837b. Observations on the raptorial birds from Mr. Darwin's collection, with characters of the new species. *Proceedings of the Zoological Society of London* 5:9–11.

1837c. Exhibition of the fissirostral birds from Mr. Darwin's collection, and characters of the new species. *Proceedings of the Zoological Society of London* 5:22.

1837d. Three species of the genus *Orpheus,* from the Galapagos, in the collection of Mr. Darwin. *Proceedings of the Zoological Society of London* 5:27.

1837e. On a new rhea (*Rhea darwinii*) from Mr. Darwin's Collection. *Proceedings of the Zoological Society of London* 5:35.

1841. *The Zoology of the Voyage of H.M.S. Beagle, under the Command of Captain FitzRoy, R.N., during the Years 1832–1836.* Edited and superintended by Charles Darwin. Part 3: *Birds.* London: Smith, Elder.

1868. *A Prospectus of the Works on Ornithology, etc. by John Gould, F.R.S., with a List of Subscribers to, or Possessors of, the Works.* London: Published by the author.

GOULD, STEPHEN JAY

1981. *The mismeasure of man.* New York: W. W. Norton.

1983. Agassiz in the Galápagos. In *Hen's Teeth and Horses' Toes,* pp. 107–19. New York: W. W. Norton.

1985. *The Flamingo's Smile.* New York: W. W. Norton.

1987. *Time's Arrow, Time's Cycle: Myth and Metaphor in the Discovery of Geological Time.* Cambridge and London: Harvard University Press.

1992. The paradox of genius. Review of *Darwin,* by Adrian Desmond and James Moore (1991). *Nature* 355:215–16.

1996. Why Darwin? Review of *Charles Darwin: Voyaging,* by Janet Browne (1995). *New York Review of Books,* 4 April, pp. 10–14.

GOULD, STEPHEN JAY, AND RICHARD LEWONTIN

1979. The spandrels of San Marco and the Panglossian paradigm: A critique of the adaptationist programme. *Proceedings of the Royal Society of London (B)* 205:581–98.

GRAHAM, LOREN

1972. *Science and Philosophy in the Soviet Union.* New York: Alfred A. Knopf.

1977. Science and values: The eugenics movement in Germany and Russia in the 1920s. *American Historical Review* 82:1133–64.

GRANT, PETER R.

1986. *Ecology and Evolution of Darwin's Finches.* Princeton: Princeton University Press.

GRANT, ROSEMARY B., AND PETER R. GRANT

1989. *Evolutionary Dynamics of a Natural Population: The Large Cactus Finch of the Galápagos.* Chicago and London: University of Chicago Press.

GRAY, ASA

1889. *Scientific Papers of Asa Gray.* Selected by Charles Sprague Sargent. 2 vols. Boston and New York: Houghton, Mifflin.

GREAVES, RICHARD L.

1969. Puritanism and science: The anatomy of a controversy. *Journal of the History of Ideas* 30:345–68.

GREENE, JOHN C.

1971. The Kuhnian paradigm and the Darwinian revolution in natural history. In *Perspectives in the History of Science and Technology,* edited by H. D. Roller, pp. 3–25. Norman, Okla.: University of Oklahoma Press.

GREENE, MOTT T.

1982. *Geology in the Nineteenth Century: Changing Views of a Changing World.* Ithaca and London: Cornell University Press.

GREENSON, RALPH R.

1968. Disidentifying from mother: Its special importance for the boy. *International Journal of Psycho-Analysis* 49:370–74. Reprinted in *Explorations in Psychoanalysis,* pp. 305–12. New York: International Universities Press, 1978.

GREENWOOD, M., AND G. U. YULE

1914. On the determination of size of family and of the distribution of characteristics in order of birth from samples taken through members of the sibships. *Journal of the Royal Statistical Society* 77:179–99.

GREER, DONALD

1935. *The Incidence of the Terror during the French Revolution: A Statistical Interpretation.* Cambridge: Harvard University Press.

GROSS, PAUL R., AND NORMAN LEVITT

1994. *Higher Superstition: The Academic Left and Its Quarrels with Science.* Baltimore and London: Johns Hopkins University Press.

GROSSKURTH, PHYLLIS

1980. *Havelock Ellis: A Biography.* London: Allen Lane.

1986. *Melanie Klein: Her World and Her Work.* New York: Alfred A. Knopf.

1988. *Margaret Mead: A Life of Controversy.* London: Penguin.

1991. *The Secret Ring: Freud's Inner Circle and the Politics of Psychoanalysis.* Reading, Mass.: Addison-Wesley.

GRUBER, HOWARD

1974. *Darwin on Man: A Psychological Study of Scientific Creativity.* Together with *Darwin's Early and Unpublished Notebooks.* Transcribed and annotated by Paul H. Barrett. New York: E. P. Dutton.

GRÜNBAUM, ADOLF

1984. *The Foundations of Psychoanalysis: A Philosophical Critique.* Berkeley and Los Angeles: University of California Press.

1993. *Validation in the Clinical Theory of Psychoanalysis: A Study in the Philosophy of Psychoanalysis.* Introduction by Philip S. Holzman. *Psychological Issues,* monograph 61. Madison, Conn.: International Universities Press.

GUENIFFEY, PATRICE

1989. Robespierre. In *A Critical Dictionary of the French Revolution,* edited by François Furet and Mona Ozouf; translated by Arthur Goldhammer, pp. 298–312. Cambridge: Harvard University Press.

GUERLAC, HENRY

1981. *Newton on the Continent.* Ithaca and London: Cornell University Press.

GUILFORD, J. P.

1957. A revised structure of intellect. Reports from the Psychological Laboratory, no. 19, University of Southern California.

1959. Traits of creativity. In *Creativity and Its Cultivation,* edited by H. H. Anderson, pp. 142–61. New York: Harper & Row.

GUTTING, GARY, ED.

1980. *Paradigms and Revolutions. Appraisals and Applications of Thomas Kuhn's Philosophy of Science.* Notre Dame, Ind.: University of Notre Dame Press.

GUZE, SAMUEL B.

1992. *Why Psychiatry Is a Branch of Medicine.* New York and Oxford: Oxford University Press.

HAAG, EUGÈNE, AND ÉMILE HAAG

1852. Budé. *La France Protestante* 3:74–77. Paris: Joël Cherbuliez.

HACKETT, FRANCIS

1934. *Francis the First.* New York: The Literary Guild.

HACKING, IAN

1981. *Scientific Revolutions.* Oxford and New York: Oxford University Press.

1983. Was there a probabilistic revolution, 1800–1930? In *Probability Since 1800: Interdisciplinary Studies of Scientific Development,* edited by Michael Heidelberger, Lorenz Krüger, and Rosemarie Rheinwald, pp. 487–506. Bielefeld: B. Kleine Verlag.

HAHLWEG, KAI, AND C. A. HOOKER, EDS.

1989. *Issues in Evolutionary Epistemology.* Albany: State University of New York Press.

HAHN, ROGER

1971. *The Anatomy of a Scientific Institution: The Paris Academy of Sciences, 1666–1803.* Berkeley, Los Angeles, and London: University of California Press.

HAGSTROM, WARREN O.

1965. *The Scientific Community.* New York: Basic Books.

HALE, NATHAN G., JR.

1971. *Freud and the Americans.* Vol. 1: *The Beginnings of Psychoanalysis in the United States, 1876–1917.* New York: Oxford University Press.

HALL, A. RUPERT

1966. *The Scientific Revolution 1500–1800: The Formation of the Modern Scientific Attitude.* 2d ed. Boston: Beacon Press.

HALL, EVERETT EARL, JR.

1963. Psychological correlates of ordinal position in the two-child family. *Dissertation Abstractions* 24:2116–17.

HALL, EVERETT EARL, JR., AND BEN BARGER

1964. Attitudinal structures in older and younger siblings. *Journal of Individual Psychology* 20:59–68.

HALL, MARIE BOAS

1984. *All Scientists Now: The Royal Society in the Nineteenth Century.* Cambridge: Cambridge University Press.

HALL, THOMAS S.

1969. *Ideas of Life and Matter: Studies in the History of General Physiology, 600 B.C. to A.D. 1900.* 2 vols. Chicago and London: Chicago University Press.

HALLAM, ANTHONY

1973. *A Revolution in Earth Sciences: From Continental Drift to Plate Tectonics.* Oxford: Clarendon Press.

HALLER, JOHN S., JR.

1971. *Outcasts from Evolution: Scientific Attitudes of Racial Inferiority, 1859–1900.* Urbana, Ill.: University of Illinois Press.

HALLER, MARK H.

1963. *Eugenics: Hereditarian Attitudes in American Thought.* New Brunswick, N.J.: Rutgers University Press.

HAMILTON, J. G. DER.

1936. Nat Turner. *Dictionary of American Biography* 19:69–70.

HAMILTON, WILLIAM D.

1963. The evolution of altruistic behavior. *American Naturalist* 97:354–56.

1964a. The genetical evolution of social behavior. I. *Journal of Theoretical Biology* 7:1–16.

1964b. The genetical evolution of social behavior. II. *Journal of Theoretical Biology* 7:17–32.

HARLOW, HARRY

1958. The nature of love. *American Psychologist* 3:673–85.

HARRINGTON, ANNE

1987. *Medicine, Mind, and the Double Brain: A Study in Nineteenth-Century Thought.* Princeton: Princeton University Press.

1992. Other "ways of knowing": The politics of knowledge in interwar German brain science. In *So Human a Brain: Knowledge and Values in the Neurosciences,* edited by Anne Harrington, pp. 229–44. Boston: Birkhäuser.

HARRIS, IRVING D.

1964. *The Promised Seed: A Comparative Study of Eminent First and Later Sons.* Glencoe, Ill.: Free Press; London: Collier Macmillan.

HARRIS, IRVING D., AND KENNETH I. HOWARD

1968. Birth order and responsibility. *Journal of Marriage and the Family* 30:427–32.

HARRIS, MICHAEL

1974. *A Field Guide to the Birds of the Galapagos Islands.* London: William Collins Sons.

HARRIS, STEVEN J.

1989. Transposing the Merton thesis: Apostolic spirituality and the establishment of the Jesuit scientific tradition. *Science in Context* 3:29–65.

HART, MICHAEL H.

1978. *The 100: A Ranking of the Most Influential Persons in History.* New York: Hart Publishing Company.

HARTUNG, JOHN

1987. On nonheritable genetic differences. *Brain and Behavioral Sciences* 10:25.

HARVEY, JOY

1983a. *Races Specified, Evolution Transformed: The Social Context of Scientific Debates Originating in the Société d'Anthropologie de Paris, 1859–1902.* Ph.D dissertation, Harvard University. Ann Arbor, Mich.: University Microfilms International.

1983b. Evolutionism transformed: Positivists and materialists in the Société d'Anthropologie de Paris from Second Empire to Third Republic. In *The Wider Domain of Evolutionary Thought,* edited by David Oldroyd and I. Langhan, pp. 289–310. Dordrecht: D. Reidel.

HARWOOD, JONATHAN

1987. National styles in science: Genetics in Germany and the United States between the world wars. *Isis* 78:390–414.

HAUSFATER, GLENN, AND SARAH BLAFFER HRDY, EDS.

1984. *Infanticide: Comparative and Evolutionary Perspectives.* New York: Aldine.

HAYDEN, DELBERT JOSEPH

1973. Trait oppositeness in siblings. *Dissertation Abstracts International (B)* 33:3285.

HAYSSEN, VIRGINIA D.

1984. Mammalian reproduction: Constraints on the evolution of infanticide. In *Infanticide: Comparative and Evolutionary Perspectives,* edited by Glenn Hausfater and Sarah Blaffer Hrdy, pp. 105–23. New York: Aldine.

HEARSEY, JOHN E. N.

1976. *Voltaire.* London: Constable.

HEDGES, LARRY V., AND INGRAM OLKIN

1980. Vote-counting methods in research synthesis. *Psychological Bulletin* 88:359–69.

HEILBRON, JOHN L.

1979. *Electricity in the 17th and 18th Centuries: A Study of Early Modern Physics.* Berkeley and Los Angeles: University of California Press.

1986. *The Dilemmas of an Upright Man: Max Planck as Spokesman for German Science.* Berkeley and Los Angeles: University of California Press.

HEIMPEL, HERMANN

1954. *Der Mensch in seiner Gegenwart: Sieben historische Essais.* Göttingen: Vandenhoeck and Ruprecht.

HELLMAN, C. DORIS

1973. Brahe, Tycho (1546–1601). *Dictionary of Scientific Biography* 2:401–16.

HELMREICH, ROBERT, AND DONALD KUIKEN

1968. Effects of stress and birth order on attitude change. *Journal of Personality* 36:466–73.

HENDRIX, SCOTT H.

1981. *Luther and the Papacy: Stages in a Reformation Conflict.* Philadelphia: Fortress Press.

1990. Luther's loyalties and the Augustinian order. In *Augustine, the Harvest, and Theology (1300–1650): Essays Dedicated to Heiko Augustinus Oberman in Honor of His 60th Birthday,* edited by Kenneth Hagen, pp. 236–58. Leiden: E. J. Brill.

1994. Loyalty, piety, or opportunism: German princes and the Reformation. *Journal of Interdisciplinary History* 25:211–24.

HENDRY, JOHN

1980. Weimar culture and quantum causality. *History of Science* 18:155–80.

HENRY, JOHN

1992. The scientific revolution in England. In *The Scientific Revolution in National Context,* edited by Roy Porter and Mikulás Teich, pp. 178–209. Cambridge: Cambridge University Press.

HERBERT, MIRANDA, AND BARBARA MCNEIL, EDS.

1981. *Biography and Genealogy Master Index.* 8 vols. 2d ed. Detroit, Mich.: Gale.

HERBERT, SANDRA

1974. The place of man in the development of Darwin's theory of transmutation. Part 1. To July 1837. *Journal of the History of Biology* 7:217–58.

HERLIHY, DAVID

1973. Three patterns of social mobility in medieval history. *Journal of Interdisciplinary History* 3:622–47.

1977. Family and property in Renaissance Florence. In *The Medieval City,* edited by David Herlihy and A. L. Udovitch, pp. 3–24. New Haven: Yale University Press.

HERMANN, ARMIN

1971. *The Genesis of Quantum Theory (1899–1913).* Translated from the German by Claude W. Nash. Cambridge: MIT Press.

1973. Lenard, Philipp (1862–1947). *Dictionary of Scientific Biography* 8:180–83.

HESS, KATHRYN ELAINE

1971. Ordinal position and acceptance of conventional morality. *Dissertation Abstracts (A)* 32:1073.

HICKMAN, CAROLE S., AND JERRE H. LIPPS

1985. Geologic youth of Galápagos Islands confirmed by marine stratigraphy and paleontology. *Science* 227:1578–80.

HIGONNET, PATRICE

1985. The social and cultural antecedents of revolutionary discontinuity: Montagnards and Girondins. *English Historical Review* 100:513–44.

HILL, CHRISTOPHER

1965. *Intellectual Origins of the English Revolution.* Oxford: Clarendon Press.

1974. Puritanism, capitalism, and the scientific revolution. In *The Intellectual Revolution of the Seventeenth Century,* edited by Charles Webster, pp. 243–53. London: Routledge & Kegan Paul. Originally published in *Past and Present* 29 (1964):88–97.

HILLERBRAND, HANS J.

1971. *Christendom Divided: The Protestant Reformation.* London: Hutchison; New York: Corpus Instrumentorum.

1973. *The World of the Reformation.* New York: Charles Scribner's Sons.

HILTS, PHILIP J.

1991. Crucial research data in report biologist signed are held fake: Nobelist to ask retraction of paper he defended. *The New York Times,* 21 March, pp. A1, B10.

HINGLEY, RONALD

1974. *Joseph Stalin: Man and Legend.* London: Hutchinson.

HOBSON, J. ALLAN

1988. *The Dreaming Brain.* New York: Basic Books.

HODGE, M. J. S.

1972. The universal gestation of nature: Chamber's *Vestiges* and *Explanations. Journal of the History of Biology* 5:127–52.

HOFFMAN, LYNN

1981. *Foundations of Family Therapy: A Conceptual Framework for Systems Change.* New York: Basic Books.

HOFFMANN, BANESH

1972. *Albert Einstein: Creator and Rebel.* With the collaboration of Helen Dukas. New York: Viking Press.

HOLDEN, CONSTANCE

1993. The making of a (female) scientist. *Science* 262:1815.

HOLMES, MICHAEL

1995. Revolutionary birthdays. *Nature* 373:468.

HOLMQUIST, HJALMAR FREDRIK

1917. *Martin Luther: Mindskrift til Reformationsjubilaeet.* Copenhagen: V. Pios Boghandel.

HOLTON, GERALD

1973. *Thematic Origins of Scientific Thought: Kepler to Einstein.* Cambridge: Harvard University Press.

HOOKE, ROBERT

1989. Statistics, sports, and some other things. In *Statistics: A Guide to the Unknown.* 3d ed. Edited by Judith M. Tanur, Frederick Mosteller, William H. Kruskal, Erich L. Lehmann, Richard F. Link, Richard S. Pieters, Gerald R. Rising, pp. 188–97 Pacific Grove, Calif.: Wadsworth and Brooks.

HOOKER, JOSEPH DALTON

1846. Enumeration of the plants in the Galapagos Islands, with descriptions of the new species. *Proceedings of the Linnean Society of London* 1:276–79.

1847a. An enumeration of the plants of the Galapagos Archipelago; with descriptions of those which are new. *Transactions of the Linnean Society of London,* 20:163–233.

1847b. On the vegetation of the Galapagos Archipelago as compared with that of some other tropical islands and of the continent of America. *Transactions of the Linnean Society of London* 20:235–62.

HOOYKAAS, REIJER

1963. *Natural Law and Divine Miracle: The Principle of Uniformity in Geology, Biology and Theology.* Leiden: E. J. Brill.

1970. *Catastrophism in Geology, Its Scientific Character in Relation to Actualism and Uniformitarianism.* Amsterdam: North-Holland.

HOWARD, JANE

1984. *Margaret Mead: A Life.* New York: Simon and Schuster.

HOYNINGEN-HUENE, PAUL

1993. *Reconstructing Scientific Revolutions: Thomas S. Kuhn's Philosophy of Science.* Translated by Alexander T. Levine. With a Foreword by Thomas S. Kuhn. Chicago and London: University of Chicago Press.

HRDY, SARAH BLAFFER

1977. *The Langurs of Abu: Female and Male Strategies of Reproduction.* Cambridge: Harvard University Press.

1987. Sex-biased parental investment among primates and other mammals: A critical evaluation of the Trivers-Willard hypothesis. In *Child Abuse and Neglect,* edited by Richard Gelles and Jane Lancaster, pp. 97–147. New York: Aldine de Gruyter.

1992. Fitness tradeoffs in the history of evolution of delegated mothering with special reference to wet-nursing, abandonment, and infanticide. *Ethology and Sociobiology* 13:409–42.

HRDY, SARAH BLAFFER, AND GLENN HAUSFATER

1984. Comparative and evolutionary perspectives on infanticide: Introduction and overview. In *Infanticide: Comparative and Evolutionary Perspectives,* edited by Glenn Hausfater and Sarah Blaffer Hrdy, pp. xiii–xxxv. New York: Aldine.

HRDY, SARAH BLAFFER, AND DEBRA S. JUDGE

1993. Darwin and the puzzle of primogeniture. *Human Nature* 4:1–45.

HUDSON, LIAM

1962. Intelligence, divergence and potential originality. *Nature* 196:601.

1963. Personality and scientific aptitude. *Nature* 198:913.

1966. *Contrary Imaginations: A Psychological Study of the English Schoolboy.* London: Methuen.

HUDSON, VALERIE M.
1990. Birth order and world leaders: An exploratory analysis of effects on personality and behavior. *Political Psychology* 11:583–601.
HUFBAUER, KARL
1982. *The Formation of the German Chemical Community (1720–1795).* Berkeley and Los Angeles: University of California Press.
HULL, DAVID L.
1973. *Darwin and His Critics: The Reception of Darwin's Theory of Evolution by the Scientific Community.* Cambridge: Harvard University Press.
1988. *Science as a Process: An Evolutionary Account of the Social and Conceptual Development of Science.* Chicago and London: University of Chicago Press.
HULL, DAVID L., PETER D. TESSNER, AND ARTHUR M. DIAMOND
1978. Planck's principle. *Science* 202:717–23.
HUMBOLDT, ALEXANDER VON, AND AIMÉ BONPLAND
1814–29. *Personal Narrative of Travels to the Equinoctial Regions of the New Continent during the Years 1799–1804.* 7 vols. published in 9. Translated by H. M. Williams. London: Longmans, Hurst, Rees, Orme, and Brown.
HUME, MARTIN
1905. *The Wives of Henry the Eighth and the Parts They Played in History.* New York: McClure, Phillips & Co.
HUND, FRIEDRICH
1974. *The History of Quantum Theory.* Translated from the German by Gordon Reece. New York: Barnes & Noble.
HUNT, LYNN
1992. *The Family Romance of the French Revolution.* Berkeley and Los Angeles: University of California Press.
HUNT, ROBERT
1888. Davy, Humphry (1778–1829). *Dictionary of National Biography* 14:187–93.
HUNTER, JOHN E. AND FRANK L. SCHMIDT
1990. *Methods of Meta-analysis: Correcting Error and Bias in Research Findings.* Newbury Park, Calif.: Sage Publications.
HUNTER, JOHN E., FRANK L. SCHMIDT, AND GREGG B. JACKSON
1982. *Meta-Analysis: Culminating Research Findings Across Studies.* Beverly Hills: Sage Publications.
HUNTER, MICHAEL
1981. *Science and Society in Restoration England.* Cambridge: Cambridge University Press.
1982. *The Royal Society and Its Fellows, 1660–1700: The Morphology of an Early Institution.* Chalfont St. Giles: The British Society for the History of Science.
HURWITZ, EDITH F.
1985. Harriet Elizabeth Beecher Stowe. In *Amencan Reformers,* edited by Alden Whitman, pp. 780–83. New York: H. W. Wilson.
HUTCHINSON, HORACE G.
1914. *Life of Sir John Lubbock, Lord Avebury.* 2 vols. London: Macmillan.

HUTTON, JAMES
1788. The theory of the earth; or an investigation of the laws observable in the composition, dissolution, and restoration of land upon the globe. *Transactions of the Royal Society of Edinburgh* 1:209–304.

HUXLEY, LEONARD
1901. *Life and Letters of Thomas Henry Huxley.* 2 vols. New York: D. Appleton.

HUXLEY, THOMAS HENRY
1887. On the reception of the "Origin of Species." In *The Life and Letters of Charles Darwin,* edited by Francis Darwin, 2:179–204. London: John Murray.

HYDE, JANET SHIBLEY
1986. Introduction: Meta-analysis and the psychology of gender. In *The Psychology of Gender: Advances through Meta-analysis,* edited by Janet Shibley Hyde and Maria C. Linn, pp. 1–13. Baltimore and London: Johns Hopkins University Press.

HYDE, JANET SHIBLEY, AND MARIA C. LYNN, EDS.
1986. *The Psychology of Gender: Advances through Meta-analysis.* Baltimore and London: Johns Hopkins University Press.

IHDE, AARON J.
1964. *The Development of Modern Chemistry.* New York: Harper & Row.

ILTIS, HUGO
1932. *Life of Mendel.* Translated by Eden and Cedar Paul. New York: W. W. Norton.

IMBRIE, JOHN, AND KATHERINE PALMER IMBRIE
1986. *Ice Ages: Solving the Mystery.* Cambridge and London: Harvard University Press.

INHELDER, BÄRBEL, AND JEAN PIAGET
1969. *The Psychology of the Child.* New York: Basic Books.

JACOB, JAMES R., AND MARGARET JACOB
1980. The Anglican origins of modern science: The metaphysical foundations of the Whig constitution. *Isis* 71:251–67.

JACOB, MARGARET C.
1976. *The Newtonians and the English Revolution, 1689–1720.* Ithaca, N.Y.: Cornell University Press.

JACYNA, L. S.
1984a. Principles of general physiology: The comparative dimension to British neuroscience in the 1830s and 1840s. *Studies in the History of Biology* 7:47–92.
1984b. The Romantic programme and the reception of cell theory in Britain. *Journal of the History of Biology* 17:13–48.

JÄGER, RALF J., MARIA ANVRET, KERSTIN HALL, AND GERD SCHERER
1990. A human XY female with frame shift mutation in the candidate testis-determining gene *SRY. Nature* 348:452–54.

JAMES, DANIEL
1969. *Ché Guevara: A Biography.* New York: Stein and Day.

JENKINS, ELIZABETH
1959. *Elizabeth the Great.* New York: Coward-McCann.

JENSEN, WILLIAM A., BERND HEINRICH, DAVID B. WAKE, MARVALEE H. WAKE, AND STEPHEN L. WOLFE
1979. *Biology.* Belmont, Calif.: Wadsworth.

JENSSEN, JOHANNES
1896–1910. *History of the German People at the Close of the Middle Ages.* 16 vols. London: K. Paul, Trench, Trübner, and Co.

JOHN, OLIVER P.
1990. The "Big Five" factor taxonomy: Dimensions of personality in the natural languages and in questionnaires. In *Handbook of Personality: Theory and Research,* edited by Lawrence A. Pervin, pp. 55–100. New York: Guilford Press.

JOHNSON, EDGAR
1977. *Charles Dickens: His Tragedy and Triumph.* Revised and abridged. New York: Viking Press.

JONES, ERNEST
1953–57. *The Life and Work of Sigmund Freud.* 3 vols. New York: Basic Books; London: Hogarth Press.

JONES, HAROLD E.
1954. The environment and mental development. In *Manual of Child Psychology,* pp. 631–92. 2d ed. Edited by L. Carmichael. New York: John Wiley.

JONES, HENRY FESTING
1919. *Samuel Butler, Author of Erewhon (1835–1902): A Memoir.* 2 vols. London: Macmillan and Co.

JONES, RICHARD FOSTER
1936. *Ancients and Moderns: A Study of Background of the Battle of the Books.* Saint Louis: Washington University Studies.
1961. *Ancients and Moderns: A Study of the Rise of the Scientific Movement in Seventeenth-Century England.* 2d ed. St. Louis: Washington University, 1961; Berkeley and Los Angeles: University of California Press, 1965.

JONES, WARREN H., JONATHAN M. CHEEK, AND STEPHEN R. BRIGGS
1986. *Shyness: Perspectives on Research and Treatment.* New York and London: Plenum.

JOHNSON, JOHN A., CHRISTOPHER K. GERMER, JAY S. EFRAN, AND WILLIS F. OVERTON
1988. Personality as the basis for theoretical predilections. *Journal of Personality and Social Psychology* 55:824–35.

JORAVSKY, DAVID
1970. *The Lysenko Affair.* Cambridge: Harvard University Press.

JORDAN, DAVID P.
1979. *The King's Trial: The French Revolution vs. Louis XVI.* Berkeley: University of California Press.

JUDD, JOHN WESLEY
1909. Darwin and geology. In *Darwin and Modern Science,* edited by A. C. Seward, pp. 337–84. Cambridge: Cambridge University Press; New York: G. P. Putnam's Sons.

JUDSON, HORACE FREELAND
1979. *The Eighth Day of Creation: The Makers of the Revolution in Biology.* New York: Simon and Schuster.

JUNKER, THOMAS
1989. *Darwinismus und Botanik: Rezeption, Kritik und Theoretische Alternativen im Deutschland des 19. Jahrhunderts.* Stuttgart: Deutscher Apotheker Verlag.

KAGAN, DONALD, STEVEN OZMENT, AND FRANK M. TURNER
1987. *The Western Heritage.* 2 vols. 3rd ed. New York: Macmillan.

KAGAN, JEROME
1971. *Personality Development.* New York: Harcourt Brace Jovanovich.
1977. The child in the family. *Daedalus* 106:33–56.
1984. *The Nature of the Child.* New York: Basic Books.
1986. *The Power and Limitations of Parents.* Austin, Tex.: Hogg Foundation for Mental Health.
1994. *Galen's Dream.* New York: Basic Books.

KAGAN, JEROME, AND J. STEPHEN REZNICK
1986. Shyness and temperament. In *Shyness: Perspectives on Research and Treatment,* edited by Warren H. Jones, Jonathan M. Cheek, and Stephen R. Briggs, pp. 81–90. New York and London: Plenum.

KAGAN, JEROME, J. STEPHEN REZNICK, AND NANCY SNIDMAN
1988. Biological bases of childhood shyness. *Science* 240: 167–71.

KALA, A. K., AND N. N. WIG
1982. Delusions across cultures. *International Journal of Social Psychiatry* 28:185–93.

KAMEN, HENRY
1985. *Inquisition and Society in Spain in the Sixteenth and Seventeenth Centuries.* London: Weidenfeld and Nicolson.

KAMMEYER, KENNETH
1967. Birth order as a research variable. *Social Forces* 46:71–80.

KAREN, ROBERT
1994. *Becoming Attached: Unfolding the Mystery of the Infant-Mother Bond and Its Impact on Later Life.* New York: Warner Books.

KATES, GARY
1985. *The* Cercle Social, *the Girondins, and the French Revolution.* Princeton: Princeton University Press.

KAWERAU, PETER GUSTAV
1910a. Joachim I [1484–1535]. *The New Schaff-Herzog Encyclopedia of Religious Knowledge* 7:182–83.
1910b. Joachim II [1505–1571]. *The New Schaff-Herzog Encyclopedia of Religious Knowledge* 7:183.

KAY, GEORGE F.
1972. *The Family in Transition: Its Past, Present, and Future Patterns.* Newton Abbot, England: David and Charles.

KEARNEY, HUGH F.
1974. Puritanism, capitalism, and the Scientific Revolution. In *The Intellectual Revolution of the Seventeenth Century,* edited by Charles Webster, pp. 218–42. London: Routledge & Kegan Paul. Originally published in *Past and Present* 28(1964):81–101.

KELLER, EVELYN FOX
1983. *A Feeling for the Organism: The Life and Work of Barbara McClintock.* New York: W. H. Freeman.

1985. *Reflections on Gender and Science.* New Haven and London: Yale University Press.

KELLEY, DONALD R.

1981. *The Beginning of Ideology: Consciousness and Society in the French Reformation.* Cambridge: Cambridge University Press.

KEVLES, DANIEL J.

1985. *In the Name of Eugenics: Genetics and the Uses of Human Heredity.* New York: Alfred A. Knopf.

KEYNES, GEOFFREY

1966. *The Life of William Harvey.* Oxford: Clarendon Press.

KEYNES, RICHARD DARWIN, ED.

1979. *The Beagle Record.* Cambridge: Cambridge University Press.

KIMBLE, JOHN W.

1975. *Man and Nature: Principles of Human and Environmental Biology.* Reading, Mass.: Addison-Wesley.

1978. *Biology.* 4th ed. Reading, Mass.: Addison-Wesley.

KITCHER, PATRICIA

1992. *Freud's Dream: A Complete Interdisciplinary Science of Mind.* Cambridge: MIT Press.

KITCHER, PHILIP

1982. *Abusing Science: The Case against Creationism.* Cambridge: MIT Press.

1985. *Vaulting Ambition: Sociobiology and the Quest for Human Nature.* Cambridge and London: MIT Press.

1993. *The Advancement of Science: Science without Legend, Objectivity without Illusion.* New York: Oxford University Press.

KLEIN, MARTIN J.

1965. Einstein, specific heats, and the early quantum theory. *Science* 148: 173–80.

KNORR-CETINA, KARIN

1981. *The Manufacture of Knowledge: An Essay on the Constructivist and Contextual Nature of Science.* Oxford: Pergamon Press.

KOCH, HELEN L.

1954. The relation of "primary mental abilities" in five- and six-year-olds to sex of child and characteristics of his sibling. *Child Development* 25:209–23.

1955a. Some personality correlates of sex, sibling position, and sex of sibling among five- and six-year-old children. *Genetic Psychology Monographs* 52:3–50.

1955b. The relation of certain family constellation characteristics and the attitudes of children toward adults. *Child Development* 26:13–40.

1956a. Attitudes of young children toward their peers as related to certain characteristics of their siblings. *Psychological Monograph* 70:1–41.

1956b. Children's work attitudes and sibling characteristics. *Child Development* 27:289–310.

1956c. Sibling influence on children's speech. *Journal of Speech and Hearing Disorders,* 21:322–28.

1956d. Sissiness and tomboyishness in relation to sibling characteristics. *Journal of Genetic Psychology* 88:231–44.

1956e. Some emotional attitudes of the young child in relation to characteristics of his sibling. *Child Development* 27:393–426.

1957. The relation in young children between characteristics of their playmates and certain attributes of their siblings. *Child Development* 28: 175–202.

1960. The relation of certain formal attributes of siblings to attitudes held toward each other and toward their parents. *Monograph of the Society for Research in Child Development* 25:1–124.

KOESTLER, ARTHUR

1959. *The Sleepwalkers.* With an Introduction by Herbert Butterfield. New York: Macmillan.

1960. *The Watershed: A Biography of Johannes Kepler.* Latham, Md.: University Press of America.

1971. *The Case of the Midwife Toad.* New York: Random House.

KOHN, ALEXANDER

1986. *False Prophets.* Oxford and New York: Basil Blackwell.

KOLDE, THEODOR FRIEDRICH HERMANN

1909. Frederick III, the Wise [1486–1525]. *The New Schaff-Herzog Encyclopedia of Religious Knowledge* 4:375–77. Edited by Samuel Macauley Jackson. New York and London: Funk and Wagnalls.

KOYRÉ, ALEXANDER

1957. *From the Closed World to the Infinite Universe.* Baltimore: Johns Hopkins University Press.

1973. *The Astronomical Revolution: Copernicus, Kepler, Borelli.* Translated by R. E. W. Maddison. Ithaca, N.Y.: Cornell University Press.

KOYRÉ, ALEXANDER, AND I. BERNARD COHEN

1962. Newton & the Leibniz-Clarke correspondence, with notes on Newton, Conti, and Des Maizeaux. *Archives Internationales d'Histoire des Sciences* 15:63–126.

KRAFT, P., AND P. KROES

1984. Adaptation of scientific knowledge to an intellectual environment. Paul Forman's "Weimar Culture, Causality, and Quantum Theory, 1918–1927": Analysis and criticism. *Centarus* 27:76–99.

KRASNO, FRANCIS

1985. Catherine Esther Beecher. In *American Reformers,* edited by Alden Whitman, pp. 62–64. New York: H. W. Wilson.

KRUTA, VLADISLAV

1976. Wagner, Rudolph (1805–1864). *Dictionary of Scientific Biography* 14:113–14.

KUHN, THOMAS S.

1957. *The Copernican Revolution: Planetary Astronomy in the Development of Western Thought.* Cambridge: Harvard University Press, 1957; New York: Vintage Books, 1959.

1962. *The Structure of Scientific Revolutions.* Chicago: University of Chicago Press; 2d ed., 1970.

1963. The essential tension: Tradition and innovation in scientific research. In *Scientific Creativity: Its Recognition and Development,* edited by Calvin W.

Taylor and Frank Barron, pp. 341–54. New York and London: John Wiley & Sons; reprinted in Kuhn (1977:225–39).

1970a. Logic of discovery or psychology of research. In *Criticism and the Growth of Knowledge,* edited by Imre Lakatos and Alan Musgrave, pp. 1–20. Cambridge: Cambridge University Press; reprinted in Kuhn (1977:266–92).

1970b. Reflections on my critics. In *Criticism and the Growth of Knowledge,* edited by Imre Lakatos and Alan Musgrave, pp. 231–78. Cambridge: Cambridge University Press.

1970c. Postscript—1969. In *The Structure of Scientific Revolutions,* pp. 174–210. 2d ed. Chicago: University of Chicago Press.

1977. *The Essential Tension: Selected Studies in Scientific Tradition and Change.* Chicago and London: University of Chicago Press.

1978. *Black-Body Theory and the Quantum Discontinuity, 1894–1912.* Chicago: University of Chicago Press.

KUSCINSKI, AUGUSTE

1917–19. *Dictionnaire des conventionnels.* Paris: F. Rieder.

LACK, DAVID

1945. *The Galapagos Finches (Geospizinae): A Study in Variation. Occasional Papers of the California Academy of Sciences,* no. 31. San Francisco: Published by the Academy.

1947. *Darwin's Finches: An Essay on the General Biological Theory of Evolution.* Cambridge: Cambridge University Press.

LAKATOS, IMRE, AND ALAN MUSGRAVE, EDS.

1970. *Criticism and the Growth of Knowledge.* Cambridge: Cambridge University Press.

LA METTRIE, JULIEN OFFRAY DE

1748. *L'Homme machine.* Leyden: Élie Luzac; reprinted and translated by Gertrude Carman Bussey as *Man a Machine, Including Frederick the Great's "Eulogy" on La Mettrie* (La Salle, Ill.: Open Court, 1912); cited from the 1912 translation.

LANDIS, H. R. M.

1932. The reception of Koch's discovery in the United States. *Annals of Medical History* 4:531–37.

LANGFORD, JEROME J.

1971. *Galileo, Science and the Church.* Rev. ed. Ann Arbor: University of Michigan.

LATOUR, BRUNO

1973. Les idéologies de la competence en milieu industrial à Abidjan. *Cahier Orstrom Sciences Humaines* 9:1–174.

1987. *Science in Action: How to Follow Scientists and Engineers through Society.* Cambridge: Harvard University Press.

LATOUR, BRUNO, AND STEVE WOOLGAR

1986. [1979]. *Laboratory Life: The Construction of Scientific Facts.* Introduction by Jonas Salk. Princeton: Princeton University Press.

LAUDAN, LARRY, ARTHUR DONOVAN, RACHEL LAUDAN, PETER BARKER, HAROLD BROWN, JARRET LEPLIN, PAUL THAGARD, AND STEVE WYKSTRA

1986. Scientific change: Philosophical models and historical research. *Synthese* 69:141–223.

LAUDAN, RACHEL

1987. *From Mineralogy to Geology: The Foundations of a Science, 1650–1830.* Chicago and London: University of Chicago Press.

LAUDAN, RACHEL, LARRY LAUDAN, AND ARTHUR DONOVAN

1988. Testing theories of scientific change. In *Scrutinizing Science: Empirical Studies of Scientific Change,* edited by Arthur Donovan, Larry Laudan, and Rachel Laudan, pp. 3–44. Dordrecht and Boston: Kluwer Academic Publishers; Baltimore: Johns Hopkins University Press, 1992.

LAYMAN, C. H., ED.

1990. *Man of Letters: The Early Life and Love Letters of Robert Chambers.* Edinburgh: Edinburgh University Press.

LEARY, WARREN E.

1990. Lab notes are false, Secret Service says. *New York Times,* 15 May, C5.

LEE, SIDNEY

1892. Seymour, Jane (1509?–1537). *Dictionary of National Biography* 10:678–80.

1912. Stephen, Sir Leslie (1837–1904). *Dictionary of National Biography,* Supplement, 1901–1911:398–405.

LEFEBVRE, GEORGES

1962–64. *The French Revolution.* 2 vols. Vol. 1: *From Its Origins to 1793.* Translated by Elizabeth Moss Evanson. Vol. 2: *From 1793 to 1799.* Translated by John Hall Stewart and James Friguglietti. London: Routledge & Kegan Paul; New York: Columbia University Press.

1969. *Napoleon: From 18 Brumaire to Tilsit, 1799–1807.* Translated by Henry F. Stockhold. New York: Columbia University Press.

LEFEBVRE, GEORGES, MARCEL REINHARD, AND MARC BOULOISEAU, EDS.

1959–63. *Procès verbaux des séances de la Convention Nationale.* 3 vols. Paris: Centre National de la Recherche Scientifique.

LEGGE, FRANCIS

1900. Wilberforce, Samuel (1805–1873). *Dictionary of National Biography* 21:204–8.

LE GRAND, H. E.

1988. *Drifting Continents and Shifting Theories: The Modern Revolution in Geology and Scientific Change.* Cambridge and New York: Cambridge University Press.

LEIBNIZ, GOTTFRIED WILHELM, AND SAMUEL CLARKE

1956. *The Leibniz-Clarke Correspondence, together with Extracts from Newton's "Principia" and "Opticks."* Edited with Introduction and Notes by H. G. Alexander. Manchester: Manchester University Press.

LEMAY, EDNA HINDIE

1991 Les révélations d'un dictionnaire: Du nouveau sur la composition de l'Assemblée Nationale Constituante (1789–1791). *Annales de la Révolution Française* 284:159–89.

LEMAY, MORRIS L.

1968. Birth order and college misconduct. *Journal of Individual Psychology* 24:167–69.

LENOIR, TIMOTHY

1988. Practice, reason, context: The dialogue between theory and experiment. *Science in Context* 2:3–22.

LÉONARD, ÉMILE G.
1965. *A History of Protestantism.* 2 vols. London: Thomas Nelson and Sons.
LEONHARD, WOLFGANG
1965. *Nikita Sergejewitsch Chruschtschow: Aufsteig und Fall eines Sowjetführers.* Lucerne and Frankfurt am Main: C. J. Bucher.
LESKY, ERNA
1965. *Die Wiener medizinische Schule in 19. Jahrhundert.* Graz and Cologne: Verlag Hermann Böhlaus Nachf.
LEVITON, ALAN E., AND MICHELE L. ALDRICH, EDS.
1985. Plate tectonics: Biogeography. *Journal of the History of the Earth Sciences Society* 4, no. 2.
LEWIS, ANTHONY
1969. Earl Warren. In *The Justices of the United States Supreme Court, 1789–1969: Their Lives and Major Opinions,* 4:2721–2899. Edited by Leon Friedman and Fred L. Israel. 4 vols. New York: R. R. Bowker.
LEWIS, BOB D.
1975. Birth order and religiosity. *Psychological Reports* 37:809–10.
LEWIS, DAVID L.
1970. *King: A Critical Biography.* New York: Praeger.
LEWIS-BECK, MICHAEL S., ANNE HILDRETH, AND ALAN B. SPITZER
1988. Was there a Girondin faction in the National Convention, 1792–93. *French Historical Studies* 15:519–36.
LIEBERMAN, LEONARD, AND LARRY T. REYNOLDS
1978. The debate over race revisited: An empirical investigation. *Phylon* 39:333–43.
LIERMANN, HANS
1941. Untersuchungen zum Sakralrecht des protestantischen Herrschers. *Zeitschrift der Savigny-Stiftung für Rechtsgeschichte, Kanonistische Abteilung* 30:311–83.
LIGHT, RICHARD J., AND DAVID B. PILLEMER
1984. *Summing Up: The Science of Reviewing Research.* Cambridge and London: Harvard University Press.
LIGHTMAN, ALAN, AND OWEN GINGERICH
1992. When do anomalies begin? *Science* 255:690–95.
LILLEY, S.
1949. Social aspects of the history of science. *Archives Internationales d'Histoire des Sciences* 28:376–443.
LINDROTH, STEN
1973. Linnaeus, Carl (1707–1778). *Dictionary of Scientific Biography* 8:374–81.
LINN, MARCIA C.
1986. Meta-analysis of studies of gender differences: Implications and future directions. In *The Psychology of Gender: Advances through Meta-analysis,* edited by Janet Shibley Hyde and Maria C. Linn, pp. 210–231. Baltimore and London: Johns Hopkins University Press.
LIPSET, DAVID
1980. *Gregory Bateson: The Legacy of a Scientist.* Englewood Cliffs, N.J.: Prentice-Hall.

LITTLE, RODERICK J. A., AND DONALD B. RUBIN
1987. *Statistical Analysis with Missing Data.* New York: John Wiley & Sons.

LOEHLIN, JOHN C.
1982. Are personality traits differentially heritable? *Behavior Genetics* 12:417–28.
1987. Twin studies, evironment differences, age changes. *Behavioral and Brain Sciences* 10:30–31.
1992. *Genes and Environment in Personality Development.* Newbury Park, Calif.: Sage Publications.

LOEHLIN, JOHN C., JOSEPH M. HORN, AND LEE WILLERMAN
1990. Heredity, environment, and personality change: Evidence from the Texas Adoption Project. *Journal of Personality* 58:221–43.

LOEHLIN, JOHN C., AND ROBERT C. NICHOLS
1976. *Heredity, Environment, and Personality: A Study of 850 Sets of Twins.* Austin and London: University of Texas Press.

LONGSTRETH, LANGDON E.
1970. "Birth order and avoidance of dangerous activities. *Developmental Psychology* 2:154.

LONGSTRETH, LANGDON E., GAYLE V. LONGSTRETH, CHRISTOPHER RAMIREZ, AND GLORIA FERNANDEZ
1975. The ubiquity of big brother. *Child Development* 46:769–72.

LOOFT, WILLIAM R.
1971. Conservatives, liberals, radicals, and sensation-seekers. *Perceptual and Motor Skills* 32:98.

LOOMIS, STANLEY
1964. *Paris in the Terror: June 1793–July 1794.* Philadelphia and New York: J. B. Lippincott.

LOVEJOY, ARTHUR O.
1959. The argument for organic evolution before the *Origin of Species,* 1830–1858. In *Forerunners of Darwin, 1745–1859,* edited by Bentley Glass, Owsei Tempkin, and William L. Straus, Jr., pp. 356–414. Baltimore: Johns Hopkins University Press.

LUEPTOW, LLOYD B., LORI GAROVICH, AND MARGARET B. LUEPTOW
1995. The persistence of gender stereotypes in the face of changing sex roles: Evidence contrary to the sociocultural model. *Ethology and Sociobiology* 16:509–30.

LURIE, EDWARD
1960. *Louis Agassiz: A Life in Science.* Chicago: University of Chicago Press.
1970. Agassiz, Jean Louis Rodolphe (1807–1873). *Dictionary of Scientific Biography* 1:72–74.

LYELL, CHARLES
1830–33. *Principles of Geology, Being an Attempt to Explain the Former Changes of the Earth's Surface, by Reference to Causes Now in Operation.* 3 vols. London: John Murray.
1863. *The Geological Evidences of the Antiquity of Man.* London: John Murray.
1881. *Life, Letters and Journals of Sir Charles Lyell Bart.* Edited by Katherine M. Lyell. 2 vols. London: John Murray.

LYKKEN, DAVID T.
1982. Research with twins: The concept of emergenesis. *Society for Psychophysiological Research* 19:361–73.
1987. An alternative explanation for low or zero sib correlations. *Brain and Behavioral Sciences* 10:31.

LYKKEN, DAVID T., MATTHEW MCGUE, AUKE TELLEGEN, AND THOMAS J. BOUCHARD, JR.
1992. Emergenesis: Genetic traits that may not run in families. *American Psychologist* 47:1565–77.

MABEE, CARLETON
1970. *Black Freedom: The Nonviolent Abolitionists from 1830 Through the Civil War.* London: Macmillan.

MACALPINE, I., AND R. HUNTER
1969. *George III and the Mad Business.* New York: Pantheon Books.

MACARTHUR, CHARLES
1956. Personalities of first and second children. *Psychiatry* 19:47–54.

MCCANN, H. GILMAN
1978. *Chemistry Transformed: The Paradigmatic Shift from Phlogiston to Oxygen.* Norwood, N.J.: Ablex.

MCCARRY, CHARLES
1972. *Citizen Nader.* New York: Saturday Review Press.

MCCARTNEY, K., M. J. HARRIS, AND F. BERNIERI
1990. Growing up and growing apart: A developmental meta-analysis of twin studies. *Psychological Bulletin* 107:226–37.

MACCOBY, ELEANOR EMMONS, AND CAROL NAGY JACKLIN
1974. *The Psychology of Sex Differences.* Stanford: Stanford University Press.

MCCORMMACH, RUSSELL
1967. Henri Poincaré and the quantum theory. *Isis* 58:37–66.

MCCRAE, ROBERT R.
1887. Creativity, divergent thinking, and openness to experience. *Personality and Social Psychology* 52:1258–65.
1994. Openness to experience: Expanding the boundaries of factor V. *European Journal of Personality* 8:251–72.

MCCRAE, ROBERT R. AND PAUL T. COSTA, JR.
1985. Openness to experience. In *Perspectives in Personality,* edited by Hogan and W. H. Jones, vol. 1, pp. 145–72. Greenwich, Conn.: JAI Press.
1987. Validation of the five-factor model of personality across instruments and observers. *Journal of Personality and Social Psychology* 52:81–90.
1990. *Personality in Adulthood.* New York and London: Guilford Press.
1994. The paradox of parental influence: Understanding retrospective studies of parent-child relations and adult personality. In *Parenting and Psychopathology,* edited by C. Perris, W. A. Arrindell, and M. Eisemann, pp. 107–25. New York: John Wiley & Sons.

MACDONALD, A. P., JR.
1969a. Manifestations of differential levels of socialization by birth order. *Developmental Psychology* 1:485–92.
1969b. Birth order and religious affiliation. *Developmental Psychology* 1:628.

1971a. Birth order and personality. *Journal of Consulting and Clinical Psychology* 136:171–76.

1971b. Relation of birth order to morality types and attitudes toward the poor. *Psychological Reports* 29:732.

MACDONALD, KEVIN

1991. A perspective on Darwinian psychology: The importance of domain-general mechanisms, plasticity, and individual differences. *Ethology and Sociobiology* 12:449–80.

1995. Evolution, the five-factor model, and levels of personality. *Journal of Personality* 63:525–67.

MCDONALD, KIM A.

1994. Biology and behavior. *The Chronicle of Higher Education,* 14 September, pp. A10–11, A21.

MCINERNEY, PETER

1985. Earl Warren. In *American Reformers,* edited by Alden Whitman, pp. 844–49. New York: H. W. Wilson.

MACKENZIE, NORMAN IAN

1979. *Dickens, a Life.* Oxford and New York: Oxford University Press.

MACKEY, HOWARD

1979. Wedgwood, Josiah (1730–95). In *Biographical Dictionary of Modern British Radicals.* Vol. 1: *1770–1830,* pp. 517–18. Edited by Joseph O. Baylen and Norbert J. Gossman. Hassocks, Sussex: Harvester Press; Atlantic Highlands, N.J.: Humanities Press.

MCKIE, DOUGLAS

1935. *Antoine Lavoisier: The Father of Modern Chemistry.* Philadelphia: J. B. Lippincott.

MACKINNEY, H. LEWIS

1972. *Wallace and Natural Selection.* New Haven and London: Yale University Press.

1976. Wallace, Alfred Russel (1823–1913). *Dictionary of Scientific Biography* 14:133–40.

MACKINNON, DONALD, W.

1962. The personality correlates of creativity: A study of American architects. *Proceedings of the XIVth International Congress of Applied Psychology,* 2:11–39. Copenhagen: Munksgaard; partially reprinted in Vernon (1970:289–311).

MACLEAN, GEORGE, AND ULRICH RAPPEN

1991. *Hermine Hug-Hellmuth.* New York and London: Routledge.

MACLEAY, WILLIAM SHARPE

1819–21. *Horae entomologicae; or, Essays on the Annulose Animals.* London: S. Bagster.

MACLEOD, ROY M.

1965. Evolution and Richard Owen. *Isis* 56:259–80.

MACMILLAN, MALCOLM

1991. *Freud Evaluated: The Completed Arc.* Amsterdam: Elsevier; Cambridge: MIT Press, 1996.

McMullin, Ernan
1970. Bellarmine, Robert (1542–1621). *Dictionary of Scientific Biography* 1:587–90.
McNeil, Barbara, ed.
1985. *Biography and Genealogy Master Index, 1981–1985.* 5 vols. Detroit, Mich.: Gale.
1990. *Biography and Genealogy Master Index, 1986–1990.* 3 vols. Detroit, Mich.: Gale.
McNeill, William H.
1986. *Mythhistory and Other Essays.* Chicago: University of Chicago Press.
Mahajan, Vijay, and Robert A. Peterson
1985. *Models for Innovation Diffusion.* Newbury Park, Calif.: Sage Publications.
Mahoney, Michael J.
1976. *Scientist as Subject.* Cambridge: Ballinger.
1979. Psychology of the scientist: An evaluative review. *Social Studies of Science* 9:349–75.
Main, Mary B.
1977. Analysis of a peculiar form of reunion behavior in some day-care children: Its history and sequelae in children who are home-reared. In *Social Development in Childhood: Daycare Programs and Research,* edited by Roger A. Webb, pp. 33–78. Baltimore and London: Johns Hopkins University Press.
Malcolm, Janet
1981. *Psychoanalysis: The Impossible Profession.* New York: Alfred A. Knopf.
Malthus, Thomas Robert
1798. *An Essay on the Principle of Population, as It Affects the Future Improvement of Society. With Remarks on the Speculations of Mr. Godwin, M. Condorcet, and Other Writers.* London: J. Johnson.
Mandeville, Bernard
1732–33. *The Fable of the Bees: or, Private Vices, Public Benefits.* 6th ed. 2 vols. London: J. Tonson; 1st ed., 1714.
Mann, Charles C.
1990. Meta-analysis in the breech. *Science* 249:476–80.
1994. Can meta-analysis make policy. *Science* 266:960–62.
Manuel, Frank E.
1968. *A Portrait of Isaac Newton.* Cambridge: Harvard University Press.
Marchant, James
1916. *Alfred Russel Wallace: Letters and Reminiscences.* New York: Harper & Brothers.
Marcou, Jules
1896. *Life, Letters, and Works of Louis Agassiz.* 2 vols. New York and London: Macmillan.
Marjoribanks, Kevin
1979. Social attitudes: Social status and sibling constellation correlates. *Psychological Reports* 45:995–1000.
Martin, James Kirby
1973. *Men in Rebellion: Higher Governmental Leaders and the Coming of the American Revolution.* New Brunswick, N.J.: Rutgers University Press.

MARTIN, N. G., L. J. EAVES, A. C. HEATH, ROSEMARY JARDINE, LYNN M. FEINGOLD, AND HANS J. EYSENCK

1986. Transmission of social attitudes. *Proceedings of the National Academy of Science* 83:4364–68.

MARTINEAU, HARRIET

1877. *Harriet Martineau's Autobiography. With Memorials by Maria Weston Chapman.* 3 vols. London: Smith, Elder.

MARVIN, URSULA B.

1973. *Continental Drift: The Evolution of a Concept.* Washington, D.C.: Smithsonian Institution Press.

MATRAT, JEAN

1971. *Robespierre: Or the Tyranny of the Majority.* Translated from the French by Alan Kendall, with Felix Brenner. New York: Charles Scribner's Sons.

MATTHEW, PATRICK

1831. *On Naval Timber and Arboriculture.* Edinburgh: Adam Black.

1860a. Nature's law of selection. *The Gardener's Chronicle,* 7 April, p. 312.

1860b. Letter. *The Gardener's Chronicle,* 12 May, p. 433.

MAUSKOPF, SEYMOUR H.

1988. Molecular geometry in 19th-century France: Shifts in guiding assumptions. *In Scrutinizing Science: Empirical Studies of Scientific Change,* edited by Arthur Donovan, Larry Laudan, and Rachel Laudan, pp. 125–44. Dordrecht and Boston: Kluwer Academic Publishers.

1992. Prize Announcements. *Isis* 83:278–79.

MAYR, ERNST

1932. A tenderfoot explorer in New Guinea: Reminiscences of an expedition for birds in the primeval forests of the Arfak Mountains. *Natural History* 32:83–97.

1942. *Systematics and the Origin of Species from the Viewpoint of a Zoologist.* New York: Columbia University Press.

1961. Cause and effect in biology. *Science* 134:1501–1506.

1963. *Animal Species and Evolution.* Cambridge: The Belknap Press of Harvard University Press.

1964. Introduction to *On the Origin of Species. A Facsimile of the First Edition,* by Charles Darwin. Cambridge and London: Harvard University Press.

1976. *Evolution and the Diversity of Life: Selected Essays.* Cambridge and London: The Belknap Press of Harvard University Press.

1982. *The Growth of Biological Thought: Diversity, Evolution, and Inheritance.* Cambridge and London: The Belknap Press of Harvard University Press.

1988. *Toward a New Philosophy of Biology: Observations of an Evolutionist.* Cambridge: Harvard University Press.

1991a. The ideological resistance to Darwin's theory of natural selection. *Proceedings of the American Philosophical Society* 135:123–39.

1991b. *One Long Argument: Charles Darwin and the Genesis of Modern Evolutionary Thought.* Cambridge: Harvard University Press.

1995. Ernst Mayr: An informal chronology. Prepared for the dedication of the Ernst Mayr Library, at the Museum of Comparative Zoology, Harvard University, Cambridge, Mass.

MAZLISH, BRUCE
1976. *The Revolutionary Ascetic: Evolution of a Political Type.* New York: Basic Books.
MEAD, MARGARET
1928. *Coming of Age in Samoa: A Psychological Study of Primitive Youth for Western Civilization.* New York: William Morrow.
1969. *Social Organization of Manu'a.* Honolulu, Hawaii: Bernice P. Bishop Museum, Bulletin 76; reissue of the original, published in 1930.
1972. *Blackberry Winter: My Early Years.* New York: William Morrow.
MEEHL, PAUL E.
1954. *Clinical versus Statistical Prediction: A Theoretical Analysis and a Review of the Evidence.* Minneapolis: University of Minnesota Press.
1965. Seer over sign: The first good example. *Journal of Experimental Research in Personality* 1:27–32.
1978. Theoretical risks and tabular asterisks: Sir Karl, Sir Ronald, and the slow progress of soft psychology. *Journal of Consulting and Clinical Psychology,* 46:806–34.
1984. Foreword to *The Limits of Scientific Reasoning,* by David Faust, pp. xi–xxiv. Minneapolis: University of Minnesota Press.
1990. Why summaries of research on psychological theories are often uninterpretable. *Psychological Reports* 66:195–244.
MELLERSH, H. E. L.
1968. *FitzRoy of the Beagle.* London: Rupert Hart-Davis.
MERRIMAN, ROGER BIGELOW
1902. *Life and Letters of Thomas Cromwell.* 2 vols. Oxford: Clarendon Press.
MERTON, ROBERT K.
1938. Science, technology and society in seventeenth-century England. *Osiris* 4:360–632; reprinted in Merton (1970).
1947. *Social Theory and Social Structure.* New York: Free Press; rev. ed. 1957; enlarged ed., 1968.
1965. *On the Shoulders of Giants: A Shandean Postscript.* New York: Free Press.
1967. *On Theoretical Sociology.* New York: Free Press.
1970. *Science, Technology and Society in Seventeenth-Century England.* New York: Howard Fertig.
1973. *The Sociology of Science: Theoretical and Empirical Investigations.* Chicago and London: University of Chicago Press.
MICHELET, JULES
n.d. [ca. 1875]. *Histoire de France.* 5 vols. Paris: J. Hetzel.
MILEY, CHARLES HARVEY
1969. Birth order research 1963–1967: Bibliography and index. *Journal of Individual Psychology* 25:64–70.
MILLER, ARTHUR I.
1981. *Albert Einstein's Special Theory of Relativity: Emergence (1905) and Early Interpretation (1905–1911).* Reading, Mass.: Addison-Wesley.
MILLER, DONALD G.
1971. Duhem, Pierre-Maurice-Marie (1861–1916). *Dictionary of Scientific Biography* 4:225–33.

MILLER, EDWARD M.

1994. Prenatal sex hormone transfer: A reason to study opposite-sex twins. *Personality and Individual Differences* 17:511–29.

MILLER, HUGH

1847. *Foot-Prints of the Creator; or, the Asterolepis of Stromness.* Edinburgh; 22d ed., Edinburgh: William P. Nimmo, 1883.

1871 [1854]. My *Schools and School Masters.* Boston: Gould and Lincoln.

MILLHAUSER, MILTON

1959. *Just Before Darwin: Robert Chambers and Vestiges.* Middletown, Conn.: Wesleyan University Press.

MILNE, EDWARD ARTHUR

1952. *Sir James Jeans, a Biography.* With a Memoir by S. C. Roberts. Cambridge: Cambridge University Press.

MINTZ, SAMUEL L.

1972. Hobbes, Thomas (1588–1679). *Dictionary of Scientific Biography* 6:444–51.

MINUCHIUN, P.

1985. Families and individual development: Provocations from the field of family therapy. *Child Development* 56:289–302.

MISCHEL, WALTER

1968. *Personality and Assessment.* New York: John Wiley & Sons.

MITFORD, NANCY

1970. *Frederick the Great.* New York: Harper & Row.

MITROFF, IAN

1983. *The Subjective Side of Science: A Philosophical Inquiry into the Psychology of the Apollo Moon Scientists.* Seaside, Calif.: Intersystems Publications.

MITTERAUER, MICHAEL, AND REINHARD SIEDER

1983. *The European Family: Patriarchy to Partnership from the Middle Ages to the Present.* Translated by Karla Oosterveen and Manfred Hörzinger. Chicago: University of Chicago Press; Oxford: Basil Blackwell, 1982.

MOCK, DOUGLAS W.

1984. Infanticide, siblicide, and avian nestling mortality. In *Infanticide: Comparative and Evolutionary Perspectives,* edited by Glenn Hausfater and Sarah Blaffer Hrdy, pp. 3–30. New York: Aldine.

MOCK, DOUGLAS W., HUGH DRUMMOND, AND CHRISTOPHER H. STINSON

1990. Avian siblicide: Killing a brother or a sister may be a common adaptive strategy among nestling birds, benefiting both the surviving offspring and the parents. *American Scientists* 78:438–49.

MÖBIUS, PAUL JULIUS

1907. *Franz Joseph Gall.* In *Ausgewählte Werke.* Vol. 7. Leipzig: J. A. Barth.

MOELLER, BERND

1962. *Reichsstadt und Reformation.* Gütersloh: Gerd Mohn; translation 1972.

1972. *Imperial Cities and the Reformation: Three Essays.* Edited and translated by Erik Midelfort and Mark U. Edwards, Jr. Philadelphia: Fortress Press.

MOODY, PAUL AMOS

1970. *Introduction to Evolution.* New York: Harper & Row.

MOORE, GILBERT

1971. *A Special Rage.* New York: Harper & Row.

MOORE, JAMES R.

1979. *The Post-Darwinian Controversies: A Study of the Protestant Struggle to Come to Terms with Darwin in Great Britain and America, 1870–1900.* Cambridge: Cambridge University Press.

MOORE, RUTH

1966. *Niels Bohr: The Man, His Science, and the World They Changed.* New York: Alfred A. Knopf.

MORE, LOUIS TRENCHARD

1944. *The Life and Works of The Honourable Robert Boyle.* London: Oxford University Press.

MORNINGSTAR, LASHA

1993. Can Edmonton psychologists save the Royal marriage? *Toronto Star,* 16 July, B2.

MORRELL, JACK B.

1971. Professors Robison and Playfair, and the *Theophobia Gallica:* Natural philosophy, religion, and politics in Edinburgh, 1789–1815. *Notes and Records of the Royal Society* 26:43–63.

MORRELL, JACK B., AND ARNOLD THACKRAY

1981. *Gentlemen of Science: Early Years of the British Association for the Advancement of Science.* Oxford: Clarendon Press.

MOUY, PAUL

1934. *Le développement de la physique Cartésienne, 1646–1712.* Paris: J. Vrin.

MÜHLLEITNER, ELKE

1992. *Biographisches Lexikon der Psychoanalyse: Die Mitglieder der Psychologischen Mittwoch-Gesellschaft und der Wiener Psychoanalytischen Vereinigung 1902–1938.* Tübingen: Edition Diskord.

MULLIGAN, LOTTE

1980. Puritans and English science: A critique of Webster. *Isis* 71:456–69.

MURPHY, PAUL J.

1981. *Brezhnev: Soviet Politician.* Jefferson, N.C.: McFarland.

MURRAY, PENELOPE, ED.

1989. *Genius: The History of an Idea.* With an Introduction by Penelope Murray. Oxford: Basil Blackwell.

NEU, JOHN, ED.

1989. *Isis Cumulative Bibliography, 1976–1985.* 2 vols. Boston: G. K. Hall.

NICHOLS, ROBERT C.

1968. Heredity, environment, and school achievement. *Measurement and Evaluation in Guidance* 1:122–29.

NISBETT, RICHARD E.

1968. Birth order and participation in dangerous sports. *Journal of Personality and Social Psychology* 8:351–53.

NORMAN, W. T.

1963. Toward an adequate taxonomy of personality attributes: Replicated factor structure in peer nomination personality ratings. *Journal of Abnormal and Social Psychology* 66:574–83.

NUNBERG, HERMAN, AND ERNST FEDERN, EDS.
1962–75. *Minutes of the Vienna Psychoanalytic Society.* 4 vols. Translated by M. Nunberg in collaboration with Harold Collins. New York: International Universities Press.

OATES, STEPHEN B.
1975. *The Fires of Jubilee: Nat Turner's Fierce Rebellion.* New York: Harper & Row.

OLBY, ROBERT
1985. *Origins of Mendelism.* 2d ed. Chicago: University of Chicago Press.

OPPENHEIM, A. N.
1968. *Questionnaire Design and Attitudes Measurement.* London: Heinemann Educational Books.

OPPENHEIM, JANET
1985. *The Other World: Spiritualism and Psychical Research in England, 1850–1914.* Cambridge: Cambridge University Press.

ORIEUX, JEAN
1979. *Voltaire.* Translated from the French by Barbara Bray and Helen R. Lane. Garden City, N.Y.: Doubleday.

ORNSTEIN, MARTHA
1928. *The Rôle of Scientific Societies in the Seventeenth Century.* Chicago: University of Chicago Press.

OSGOOD, CHARLES EGERTON, GEORGE J. SUCI, AND PERCY H. TANNENBAUM
1957. *The Measurement of Meaning.* Urbana: University of Illinois Press.

OSTWALD, FRIEDRICH WILHELM
1926–27. *Lebenslinien: Eine Selbstbiographie.* 3 vols. Berlin.

OUTRAM, DORINDA
1984. *Georges Cuvier: Vocation, Science and Authority in Post-Revolutionary France.* Manchester: Manchester University Press.
1986. Uncertain legislator: Georges Cuvier's laws of nature in their intellectual context. *Journal of the History of Biology* 19:323–68.

OWEN, REV. RICHARD
1894. *The Life of Sir Richard Owen.* With the scientific portions revised by C. Davies Sherborn. 2 vols. London: John Murray.

OZMENT, STEVEN
1975. *The Reformation in the Cities.* New Haven and London: Yale University Press.
1980. *The Age of Reform, 1250–1550: An Intellectual and Religious History of Late Medieval and Reformation Europe.* New Haven and London: Yale University Press.
1982. Editor. *Reformation Europe: A Guide to Research.* St. Louis: Center for Reformation Research.
1983. *When Fathers Ruled: Family Life in Reformation Europe.* Cambridge: Harvard University Press.
1990. *Three Behaim Boys: Growing up in Early Modern Germany: A Chronicle of Their Lives.* New Haven: Yale University Press .
1992. *Protestants: The Birth of a Revolution.* New York: Doubleday.

OZOUF, MONA
1989a. King's trial. In *A Critical Dictionary of the French Revolution,* edited by François Furet and Mona Ozouf; translated by Arthur Goldhammer, pp. 95–105. Cambridge: Harvard University Press.
1989b. Danton. In *A Critical Dictionary of the French Revolution,* edited by François Furet and Mona Ozouf; translated by Arthur Goldhammer, pp. 213–22. Cambridge: Harvard University Press.
1989c. Girondins. In *A Critical Dictionary of the French Revolution,* edited by François Furet and Mona Ozouf; translated by Arthur Goldhammer, pp. 351–61. Cambridge: Harvard University Press.
1989d. Montagnards. In *A Critical Dictionary of the French Revolution,* edited by François Furet and Mona Ozouf; translated by Arthur Goldhammer, pp. 380–92. Cambridge: Harvard University Press.

PACKARD, ALPHEUS S.
1901. *Lamarck, the Founder of Evolution: His Life and Work.* New York: Longmans, Green.

PAGEL, WALTER
1967. *William Harvey's Biological Ideas: Selected Aspects and Historical Background.* Basel and New York: S. Karger.

PAGET, HUGH
1981. The youth of Anne Boleyn. *Bulletin of the Institute of Historical Research* 55:162–70.

PAIS, ABRAHAM
1982. *"Subtle is the Lord . . . ": The Science and the Life of Albert Einstein.* Oxford and New York: Oxford University Press.

PALMER, ROBERT D.
1966. Birth order and identification. *Journal of Consulting Psychology* 30:129–35.

PALMER, R. R.
1969. *Twelve Who Ruled: The Year of the Terror in the French Revolution.* Princeton: Princeton University Press.

PANNEKOEK, A.
1961. *A History of Astronomy.* New York: Interscience Publishers.

PARFAIT, NOËL
1848. *Notice biographique sur A.-F. Sergent.* Chartres: Garnier.

PARMIGIANO, STEFANO, AND FREDERICK S. VON SAAL, EDS.
1994. *Infanticide and Parental Care.* London: Harwood Academic Publishers.

PARSONS, TALCOTT, AND ROBERT F. BALES
1955. *Family, Socialization and Interaction Process.* Glencoe, Ill.: Free Press.

PARSSINEN, TERRY M.
1970. Popular science and society: The phrenology movement in early Victorian Britain: Appendix A (unpublished manuscript).
1974. Popular science and society: The phrenology movement in early Victorian Britain. *Journal of Social History* 8:1–20.

PARTON, JAMES
1881. *Life of Voltaire.* 2 vols. Boston: Houghton, Mifflin; London: S. Low, Marston, Searle & Rivington.

PASTERNAK, MARTIN B.

1995. *Rise Now and Fly to Arms. The Life of Henry Highland Garnet*. New York and London: Garland.

PASTORE, NICHOLAS

1949. *The Nature-Nurture Controversy.* New York: Columbia University Press.

PATRICK, ALISON

1972. *The Men of the First French Republic: Political Alignments in the National Convention of 1792.* Baltimore and London: Johns Hopkins University Press.

PAYNE, ROBERT.

1969. *The Life and Death of Mahatma Gandhi.* New York: E. P. Dutton.

PERTUÉ, MICHEL

1981a. Remarques sur les listes de Conventionnels. *Annales de la Révolution Française* 245:366–78.

1981b. La liste des Girondins de Jean-Paul Marat. *Annales de la Révolution Française* 245:379–89.

PETERSEN, WILLIAM

1979. *Malthus.* Cambridge: Harvard University Press.

PICHANICK, VALERIE KOSSEW

1980. *Harriet Martineau: The Woman and Her Work, 1802–76.* Ann Arbor, Mich.: University of Michigan Press.

PICKERING, ANDREW

1981. Constraints on controversy: The case of the magnetic monopole. *Social Studies of Science* 11:63–93.

1984. *Constructing Quarks: A Sociological History of Particle Physics.* Edinburgh: Edinburgh University Press.

PILKONIS, PAUL A.

1986. Short-term group psychotherapy for shyness. In *Shyness: Perspectives on Research and Treatment,* edited by Warren H. Jones, Jonathan M. Cheek, and Stephen R. Briggs, pp. 375–85. New York and London: Plenum.

PINKER, STEVEN

1994. *The Language Instinct*. New York: William Morrow.

PISTRAK, LAZAR

1961. *The Grand Tactician. Khrushchev's Rise to Power.* New York: Praeger.

PLANCK, MAX

1949. *Scientific Autobiography and Other Papers.* Translated by Frank Gaynor. New York: Philosophical Library.

PLOMIN, ROBERT

1986. *Development, Genetics, and Psychology.* Hillsdale, N.J.: Lawrence Erlbaum.

1994. *Genetics and Experience: The Interplay between Nature and Nurture.* Thousand Oaks, Calif., and London: Sage Publications.

PLOMIN, ROBERT, HILARY COON, GREGORY CAREY, J. C. DEFRIES, AND DAVID W. FULKER

1991. Parent-offspring and sibling adoption analyses of parental ratings of temperament in infancy and childhood. *Journal of Personality* 59:705–32.

PLOMIN, ROBERT, AND DENISE DANIELS
1986. Genetics and shyness. In *Shyness: Perspectives on Research and Treatment,* edited by Warren H. Jones, Jonathan M. Cheek, and Stephen R. Briggs, pp. 63–80. New York and London: Plenum.
1987. Why are children in the same family so different from one another. *Behavioral and Brain Sciences* 10:1–60.

PLOMIN, ROBERT, J. C. DEFRIES, AND JOHN C. LOEHLIN
1977. Genotype-environment interaction and correlation in analysis of human behavior. *Psychological Bulletin* 84:309–22.

PLOMIN, ROBERT, J. C. DEFRIES, AND G. E. MCCLEARN
1990. *Behavioral Genetics: A Primer.* 2d ed. New York: W. H. Freeman.

POINCARÉ, HENRI
1908. *Science et Méthode.* Paris: Ernest Flammarion.
1913. *The Foundations of Science: Science and Hypothesis, The Value of Science, and Science and Method.* Translated by George Bruce Halsted. Lancaster, Pa.: Science Press.

POLLARD, ALBERT FREDERICK.
1897a. Seymour, Edward (1506?–1552). *Dictionary of National Biography* 17:1237–48.
1897b. Seymour, Thomas (1508?–1549). *Dictionary of National Biography* 17:1268–71.

POMEAU, RENÉ HENRY
1992. Voltaire. *The Encyclopaedia Britannica* 29:524–28. 15th ed. Chicago: University of Chicago.

POPPER, KARL R.
1959. *The Logic of Scientific Discovery.* London: Hutchinson.
1962. *Conjectures and Refutations: The Growth of Scientific Knowledge.* New York: Basic Books; London: Routledge & Kegan Paul, 1963.
1981. The rationality of scientific revolutions. In *Scientific Revolutions,* edited by Ian Hacking, pp. 80–106. Oxford: Oxford University Press.

PORTER, ROY
1975. *The Making of Geology: Earth Science in Britain, 1660–1815.* New York: Cambridge University Press.
1982. The descent of genius: Charles Darwin's brilliant career. *History Today,* July, pp. 16–22.
1990. *The Enlightenment.* Atlantic Highlands, N.J.: Humanities Press International.

POWELL, BRIAN, AND LALA CARR STEELMAN
1990. Beyond sibship size: Sibling density, sex composition, and educational outcomes. *Social Forces* 69:181–206.

PRICE, JOHN
1969. Personality differences within families: Comparisons of adult brothers and sisters. *Journal of Biosocial Science* 1:177–205.

PRIOLEAU, L., M. MURDOCK, AND N. BRODY
1983. An analysis of psychotherapy versus placebo. *The Behavioral and Brain Sciences* 6:275–85.

PROCTOR, ROBERT N.
1988. *Racial Hygiene: Medicine under the Nazis.* Cambridge and London: Harvard University Press.

QUATREFAGES DE BREAU, ARMAND DE
1894. *Les Émules de Darwin.* 2 vols. Paris. F. Alcan.

RANDALL, JOHN
1940. *The Making of the Modern Mind.* Rev. ed. Boston: Houghton Mifflin; first edition, 1926.

RAVERAT, GWEN
1952. *Period Piece: A Cambridge Childhood.* London: Faber and Faber.

REDONDI, PIETRO
1987. *Galileo: Heretic.* Translated by Raymond Rosenthal. Princeton: Princeton University Press.

REED, JOHN J.
1985. Sarah Moore Grimké and Angelina Emily Grimké. In *American Reformers,* edited by Alden Whitman, pp. 379–82. New York: H. W. Wilson.

REICHENBACH, HANS
1938. *Experience and Prediction.* Chicago: University of Chicago Press.

REID, IVAN
1977. *Social Class Differences in Britain: A Sourcebook.* London: Open Books.

REJAI, MOSTAFA, AND KAY PHILLIPS
1979. *Leaders of Revolution.* Beverly Hills and London: Sage Publications.
1983. *World Revolutionary Leaders.* New Brunswick, N.J.: Rutgers University Press.
1988. *Loyalists and Revolutionaries: Political Leaders Compared.* New York: Praeger.

RENSBERGER, BOYCE
1983. The nature-nurture debate I. *Science 83* 4 (April), pp. 28–37.

REYER, ALEXANDRE
1871. *Leben und Wirken des Naturhistorikers Dr. Franz Unger.* Graz: Leuschner and Lubensky.

RICHARDS, ROBERT J.
1987. *Darwin and the Emergence of Evolutionary Theories of Mind and Behavior.* Chicago and London: University of Chicago Press.

RICHET, DENIS
1989. Revolutionary *journées.* In *A Critical Dictionary of the French Revolution,* edited by François Furet and Mona Ozouf; translated by Arthur Goldhammer, pp. 124–35. Cambridge: Harvard University Press.

RICHMOND, PHYLLIS ALLEN
1954a. Some variant theories in opposition to the germ theory of disease. *Journal of the History of Medicine and Allied Sciences* 9:290–303.
1954b. American attitudes toward the germ theory of disease (1860–1880). *Journal of the History of Medicine and Allied Sciences* 9:428–54.

RIDLEY, JASPER
1985. *Henry VIII.* New York: Viking Press.

RIDLEY, MATT
1994. *The Red Queen: Sex and the Evolution of Human Nature.* New York: Macmillan.

ROAZEN, PAUL
1975. *Freud and His Followers.* New York: Alfred A. Knopf.

1985. *Helene Deutsch: A Psychoanalyst's Life.* Garden City, N.Y.: Anchor Press/Doubleday.

ROBERT, ADOLPHE, AND GASTON GOUGNY

1889–91. *Dictionnaire des parlementaires français.* 5 vols. Paris: Bourloton.

ROBERT, HENRY MARTYN

1876. *Pocket Manuel of Rules of Order for Deliberative Assemblies.* Chicago: S. C. Griggs.

ROBINSON, JOHN P., JERROLD G. RUSK, AND KENDRA B. HEAD

1972. *Measures of Political Attitudes.* Ann Arbor, Mich.: Institute for Social Research.

ROE, ANNE

1953. *A Psychological Study of Eminent Psychologists and Anthropologists and a Comparison with Biological and Physical Scientists. Psychological Monographs, no. 353.*

ROE, SHIRLEY A.

1981. *Matter, Life, and Generation: Eighteenth-Century Embryology and the Haller-Wolff Debate.* Cambridge: Cambridge University Press.

ROGER, JACQUES

1963. *Les Sciences de la vie dans la pensée française du XVIII*[e] *siècle: La génération des animaux de Descartes à l'Encyclopédie.* Paris: Armand Colin; 2d ed., 1971.

ROGERS, EVERETT M.

1962. *Diffusion of Innovations.* New York: Free Press.

1971. *Communication of Innovations: A Cross-Cultural Approach.* 2d ed. [of Everett 1962]. With F. Floyd Shoemaker. New York: Free Press.

1983. *Diffusion of Innovations.* 3d ed. New York: Free Press.

RONAN, COLIN A.

1969. *Edmond Halley: Genius in Eclipse.* Garden City, N.Y.: Doubleday.

ROODIN, PAUL A., AND GLEN M. VAUGHT

1972. Birth order and conservatism. *Psychological Reports* 31:814.

ROSEN, EDWARD

1984. *Copernicus and the Scientific Revolution.* Malabar, Fla.: Robert E. Krieger.

ROSENBERG, BENJAMIN GEORGE

1982. Life span personality stability in sibling status. In *Sibling Relationships: Their Nature and Nurture Across the Lifespan,* edited by Michael E. Lamb and Brian Sutton-Smith, pp. 167–224. Hillsdale, NJ: Lawrence Erlbaum.

ROSENBLATT, PAUL C., AND ELIZABETH L. SKOOGBERG

1974. Birth order in cross-cultural perspective. *Developmental Psychology* 10:48–54.

ROSENTHAL, ROBERT

1984. *Meta-Analytic Procedures for Social Research.* Newbury Park, Calif.: Sage Publications; rev. ed., 1991.

1987. *Judgment Studies: Design, Analysis, and Meta-analysis.* Cambridge: Cambridge University Press.

1991. Parametric measures of effect size. In *Handbook of Research Synthesis,* edited by H. Cooper and L. V. Hedges, pp. 231–44. New York: Russell Sage Foundation.

ROSENTHAL, ROBERT, AND RALPH L. ROSNOW

1984. *Essentials of Behavioral Research: Methods and Data Analysis.* New York: McGraw-Hill; 2d ed., 1991.

1985. *Contrast Analysis: Focused Comparisons in the Analysis of Variance.* Cambridge: Cambridge University Press.

ROSENTHAL, ROBERT, AND DONALD B. RUBIN

1982. A simple, general purpose display of magnitude of experimenter effect. *Journal of Educational Psychology* 74:166–69.

ROSNOW, RALPH L., AND ROBERT ROSENTHAL

1988. Focused tests of significance and effect size estimation in counseling psychology. *Journal of Counseling Psychology* 35:203–8.

ROSS, HELGOLA G., AND JOEL I. MILGRAM

1982. Important variables in adult sibling relationships: A qualitative survey. In *Sibling Relationships. Their Nature and Significance across the Lifespan,* edited by Michael E. Lamb and Brian Sutton-Smith, pp. 225–49. Hillsdale, N.J.: Lawrence Erlbaum.

ROSS, LEE, AND RICHARD E. NISBETT

1991. *The Person and the Situation: Perspectives of Social Psychology.* Philadelphia: Temple University Press.

ROTHMAN, KENNETH J.

1986. *Modern Epidemiology.* Boston: Little, Brown.

ROUTH, C. R. N.

1964. *Who's Who in History.* Vol. 2: *England 1485 to 1603.* Oxford: Basil Blackwell.

ROWE, DAVID C.

1994. *The Limits of Family Influence: Genes, Experience, and Behavior.* New York and London: Guilford Press.

RUBIN, DONALD B.

1978. Multiple imputation in sample surveys—a phenomenological Bayesian approach to nonresponse. *The Proceedings of the Survey Research Methods Section of the American Statistical Association,* pp. 20–34. American Statistical Association: Arlington, Va.

1987. *Multiple Imputation for Nonresponse in Surveys.* New York: John Wiley & Sons.

1996. Multiple imputation after 18+ years. *Journal of the American Statistical Association* 91:473–89.

RUBIN, DONALD B., AND JOSEPH L. SCHAFER

1990. Efficiently creating multiple imputations for incomplete multivariate normal data. *Proceedings of the Statistical Computing Section of the American Statistical Association,* pp. 83–88.

RUBINS, JACK L.

1978. *Karen Horney: Gentle Rebel of Psychoanalysis.* New York: Dial Press.

RUDWICK, MARTIN J. S.

1970. The glacial theory. Review of *Studies on Glaciers,* by Louis Agassiz. *History of Science* 8:136–57.

1972. *The Meaning of Fossils: Episodes in the History of Palaeontology.* London: MacDonald; New York: Elsevier. 2d ed., Chicago: University of University Press, 1985.

1974. Miller, Hugh (1802–1856). *Dictionary of Scientific Biography* 9:388–90.

1985. *The Great Devonian Controversy: The Shaping of Scientific Knowledge among Gentlemanly Specialists.* Chicago and London: University of Chicago Press.

RUNCO, MARK A.

1987. Birth order and divergent thinking. *Journal of Genetic Psychology* 148:119–25.

RUNYON, WILLIAM MCKINLEY

1982. *Life Histories and Psychobiography: Explorations in Theory and Method.* New York: Oxford University Press.

RUSE, MICHAEL E.

1970. The revolution in biology. *Theoria* 36:1–22.

1971. Two biological revolutions. *Dialectica* 25:17–38.

1979. *The Darwinian Revolution: Science Red in Tooth and Claw.* Chicago and London: University of Chicago Press.

RUTTER, MICHAEL

1977. Separation, loss, and family relationships. In *Child and Adolescent Psychiatry: Modern Approaches,* edited by Michael Rutter and Lionel Hersov. Oxford: Blackwell.

1979. Maternal deprivation, 1972–1978: New findings, new concepts, new approaches. *Child Development* 50:283–305

1981. *Maternal Deprivation Reassessed.* 2d ed. Harmondsworth: Penguin.

RYAN, JOHN PAUL, AND C. NEAL TATE

1980. *The Supreme Court in American Politics: Policy Through Law.* 2d ed. Washington, D.C.: American Political Association.

SACK, ROBERT L., AND EMANUEL DE FRAITES

1977. Lithium and the treatment of mania. In *Psychopharmacology: From Theory to Practice,* edited by Jack D. Barchas, Philip A. Berger, Roland D. Ciaranello, and Glen R. Elliott, pp. 208–25. New York: Oxford University Press.

SALMON, CATHERINE

1996. Middleborns are different: Birth order and the psychology of kinship. Talk presented at the Human Behavior and Evolution Society meetings, Northwestern University, 28 June.

SALTUS, RICHARD

1992. Twinspeak: They often lag in verbal skills. *Boston Globe,* 11 May, pp. 25, 27.

SALVIN, OSBERT

1876. On the avifauna of the Galapagos Archipelago. *Transactions of the Zoological Society of London* 9:447–510.

SAMPSON, EDWARD E.

1962. Birth order, need achievement, and conformity. *Journal of Abnormal and Social Psychology* 64:155–59.

SAMPSON, EDWARD E., AND FRANCENA T. HANCOCK

1967. An examination of the relationship between ordinal position, personality, and conformity: An extension, replication, and partial verification. *Journal of Personality and Social Psychology* 5:398–407.

SANTILLANA, GIORGIO DE

1955. *The Crime of Galileo.* Chicago: University of Chicago Press.

SAUDINO, KIMBERLY J., SHIRLEY MCGUIRE, DAVID REISS, E. MAVIS HETHERINGTON, AND ROBERT PLOMIN

1995. Parent ratings of EAS temperaments in twins, full siblings, half siblings, and step siblings. *Journal of Personality and Social Psychology* 68:723–33.

SAUER, GORDON C.

1982. *John Gould the Bird Man. A Chronology and Bibliography.* Kansas City: University Press of Kansas.

SCARISBRICK, J. J.

1968. *Henry VIII.* London: Eyre & Spottiswoode.

SCARR, SANDRA, AND SUSAN GRAJEK

1982. Similarities and differences among siblings. In *Sibling Relationships: Their Nature and Nurture Across the Lifespan,* edited by Michael E. Lamb and Brian Sutton-Smith, pp. 357–381. Hillsdale, N.J.: Lawrence Erlbaum.

SCARR, SANDRA, AND KATHLEEN MCCARTNEY

1983. How people make their own environments: A theory of genotype → environmental effects. *Child Development* 54:424–35.

SCHACHTER, FRANCES FUCHS

1982. Sibling deidentification and split-parent identification: A family tetrad. In *Sibling Relationships: Their Nature and Significance across the Lifespan,* edited by Michael E. Lamb and Brian Sutton-Smith, pp. 123–52. Hillsdale, N.J.: Lawrence Erlbaum.

SCHACHTER, FRANCES FUCHS, GABI GILUTZ, ELLEN SHORE, AND MICHELLE ADLER

1978. Sibling deidentification judged by mothers: Cross-validation and developmental studies. *Child Development* 49:543–46.

SCHACHTER, FRANCES FUCHS, ELLEN SHORE, SUSAN FELDMAN-ROTMAN, RUTH E. MARQUIS, AND SUSAN CAMPBELL

1976. Sibling deidentification. *Developmental Psychology* 12:418–27.

SCHACHTER, STANLEY.

1959. *The Psychology of Affiliation: Experimental Studies of the Sources of Gregariousness.* Stanford: Stanford University Press.

SCHAFER, JOSEPH L.

1991. Algorithms for multiple imputation and posterior simulation from incomplete multivariate data with ignorable nonresponse. Ph. D. Dissertation, Department of Statistics, Harvard University.

SCHAMA, SIMON

1989. *Citizens: A Chronicle of the French Revolution.* New York: Alfred A. Knopf.

SCHEPER-HUGHES, NANCY

1992. *Death Without Weeping: The Violence of Everyday Life in Brazil.* Berkeley and Los Angeles: University of California Press.

SCHLUTER, DOLPH, TREVOR D. PRICE, AND PETER R. GRANT

1985. Ecological character displacement in Darwin's finches. *Science* 227:1056–59.

SCHNEIDER, HANS-GEORG

1992. *Paradigmenwechsel und Generationenkonflict: Eine Fallstudie zur Struktur wissenschaftlicher Revolutionen: Die Revolution der Chemie des späten 18. Jahrhunderts.* Frankfurt am Main: Peter Lang.

SCHOOLER, CARMI

1972. Birth order effects: Not here, not now! *Psychological Bulletin* 78:161–75.

SCHUBERT, DANIEL S. P., MAZIE EARLE WAGNER, AND HERMAN J. P. SCHUBERT

1976. A thousand references on sibling constellation variables: ordinal position, sibship size, sibling age spacing, and sex of sibling. *JSAS Catalog of Selected Documents in Psychology* 6, no. 1792.

1984. An additional 2,000 references on sibling constellation variables: ordinal position, sibship size, sibling age spacing, and sex of sibling. *Psychological Documents,* no. 2545.

SCHUBERT, GLENDON

1974. *The Judicial Mind Revisited: Psychometric Analysis of Supreme Court Ideology.* New York and London: Oxford University Press.

1983. Aging, conservatism, and judicial behavior. *Micropolitics* 3: 135–79.

SCHULTZE, JOHANNES

1957. Elisabeth, Kurfürstin von Brandenburg [1485–1555]. *Neue Deutsche Biographie* 4:443.

SCHWENNICKE, DETLEV

1980–91. *Europäische Stammtafeln.* New edition. 14 vols. Marburg: J. A. Stargart.

SCRIBNER, ROBERT W.

1986. *The German Reformation.* Atlantic Highlands, N.J.: Humanities Press International.

SCRIMSHAW, SUSAN C. M.

1978. Infant mortality and behavior in the regulation of family size. *Population and Development Review* 4:383–403.

1984. Infanticide in human populations. In *Infanticide: Comparative and Evolutionary Perspectives,* edited by Glenn Hausfater and Sarah Blaffer Hrdy, pp. 439–62. New York: Aldine.

SECORD, JAMES A.

1986. *Controversy in Victorian Geology: The Cambrian–Silurian Dispute.* Princeton: Princeton University Press.

1989. Robert Chambers and *Vestiges.* In *History, Humanity, and Evolution: Essays for John C. Greene,* edited by James R. Moore, pp. 165–94. Cambridge: Cambridge University Press.

1992. Edinburgh Lamarckians: Robert Jameson and Robert E. Grant. *Journal of the History of Biology* 24:1–18.

SEGAL, JEFFREY A., AND HAROLD J. SPAETH

1993. *The Supreme Court and the Attitudinal Model.* Cambridge: Cambridge University Press.

SEGAL, NANCY L.

1993. Twin, sibling, and adoption methods: Tests of evolutionary hypotheses. *American Psychologist* 48:943–56.

SEGALEÛ, MARTINE

1985. *Fifteen Generations of Bretons: Kinship and Society in Lower Brittany, 1720–1980.* Cambridge: Cambridge University Press.

SELIGMAN, EDMOND

1913. *La Justice en France pendant la révolution.* 2d ed. Paris: Plon-Nourrit.

SEYMOUR, WILLIAM

1972. *Ordeal of Ambition: An English Family in the Shadow of the Tudors.* London: Sidgwick & Jackson.

SHAKOW, DAVID, AND DAVID RAPAPORT

1964. *The Influence of Freud on American Psychology. Psychological Issues* 4, no. 1 (Monograph 13).

SHAPIN, STEVEN

1975. Phrenological knowledge and the social structure of early nineteenth-century Edinburgh. *Annals of Science,* 32:219–43.

1979a. Homo phrenologicus: Anthropological perspectives on an historical problem. In *Natural Order: Historical Studies of Scientific Culture,* edited by Barry Barnes and Steven Shapin, pp. 41–67. Beverly Hills and London: Sage Publications.

1979b. The politics of observation: Cerebral anatomy and social interests in the Edinburgh phrenology disputes. In *On the Margins of Science: The Social Construction of Rejected Knowledge,* edited by R. Wallis, pp. 139–78. Sociology Review Monograph no. 27. Keele, Staffordshire.

1981. Merton thesis. In *Dictionary of the History of Science,* edited by William F. Bynum, E. Janet Browne, and Roy Porter, pp. 262a–62b. Princeton: Princeton University Press.

1982. History of science and its sociological reconstructions. *History of Science* 20:157–211.

1988. Understanding the Merton thesis. *Isis* 79:594–605.

1993. Mertonian concessions. Review of *Making Science,* by Stephen Cole. *Science* 259:839–41.

SHAPIN, STEVEN, AND SIMON SCHAFFER

1985. *Leviathan and the Air-Pump: Hobbes, Boyle, and the Experimental Life.* Princeton: Princeton University Press.

SHAPIRO, BARBARA

1969. *John Wilkins, 1614–1672: An Intellectual Biography.* Berkeley and Los Angeles: University of California Press.

1974. Latitudinarianism and science in seventeenth-century England. In *The Intellectual Revolution of the Seventeenth Century,* edited by Charles Webster, pp. 286–316. London: Routledge & Kegan Paul. Originally published in *Past and Present* 40(1968):16–41.

SHARPE, R. BOWDLER

1893. *An Analytic Index to the Works of the Late John Gould. With a Biographical Memoir and Portrait.* London: Henry Sotheran.

SHERWOOD, JOHN, AND MARK NATAUPSKY

1968. Predicting the conclusions of Negro-White intelligence research from the biographical characteristics of the investigator. *Journal of Personality and Social Psychology* 8:53–58.

SHUTE, MICHAEL N.

1985. Henry Highland Garnet. In *American Reformers,* edited by Alden Whitman, pp. 332–34. New York: H. W. Wilson.

SIMON, EDITH

1963. *The Making of Frederick the Great.* Boston: Little, Brown.

SIMONTON, DEAN KEITH

1984a. *Genius, Creativity, and Leadership. Historiometric Inquiries.* Cambridge and London: Harvard University Press.

1984b. Is the marginality effect all that marginal? *Social Studies of Science* 14:621–22.

1984c. Scientific eminence historical and contemporary: A measurement assessment. *Scientometrics* 6: 169–82.

1987. *Why Presidents Succeed. A Political Psychology of Leadership.* New Haven and London: Yale University Press.

1988. *Scientific Genius: A Psychology of Science.* Cambridge and New York: Cambridge University Press.

1990a. *Psychology, Science, and History: An Introduction to Historiometry.* New Haven and London: Yale University Press.

1990b. Personality and politics. In *Handbook of Personality: Theory and Research,* edited by Lawrence A. Pervin, pp. 670–92. New York: Guilford Press.

1994. *Greatness: Who Makes History and Why.* New York and London: Guilford Press.

SIMPKINS, DIANA M.

1974. Malthus, Thomas Robert (1766–1834). *Dictionary of Scientific Biography* 9:67–71.

SINCLAIR, WILLIAM J.

1909. *Semmelweis: His Life and His Doctrine.* Manchester: University of Manchester Press.

SINGER, ELEANOR

1971. Adult orientation of first and later children. *Sociometry* 34:143–51.

SKINNER, G. WILLIAM

1992. Seek a loyal subject in a filial son: Family roots of political orientation in Chinese society. In *Family Process and Political Process in Modern Chinese History,* pp. 943–93. Taipei, Republic of China: Chiang Ching-kuo Foundation for International Scholarly Exchange.

SLATER, E.

1962. Birth order and maternal age of homosexuals. *Lancet* 13:69–71.

SMITH, COLIN

1976. *Carlos: Portrait of a Terrorist.* London: André Deutsch.

SMITH, DENIS MACK

1982. *Mussolini.* New York: Alfred A. Knopf.

SMITH, JOHN MAYNARD

1991. Dinosaur dilemma. Review of *The Dinosauria,* edited by David B. Weishample, Peter Dodson, and Halszka Osmälska; and *Dinosaurs, Spitfires, and Sea Dragons,* by Chris McGowan. *New York Review of Books,* 25 April, pp. 5–7.

SMITH, MERRITT ROE

1991. Industry, technology, and the "labor question" in 19th-century America: Seeking synthesis. *Technology and Culture* 32:555–70.

SMITH, PRESERVED

1911. *The Life and Letters of Martin Luther.* Boston and New York: Houghton Mifflin.

SMITH, THOMAS EWIN

1971. Birth order, sibship size and social class as antecedents of adolescents' acceptance of parents' authority. *Social Forces* 50:223–32.

SNOW, CHARLES P.

1961a. Either-or. *The Progressive* 24(February):24–25.

1961b. *The Two Cultures and the Scientific Revolution.* New York: Cambridge University Press.

SOBOUL, ALBERT

1980. Introduction to *Actes du Colloque Girondins et Montagnards,* edited by Albert Soboul. Paris: Societé des Études Robespierristes.

SOLOMON, MIRIAM

1994. Social empiricism. *Noûs* 28:325–43.

SOLOVYOV, VLADIMIR, AND ELENA KLEPIKOVA

1992. *Boris Yeltsin: A Political Biography.* Translated by David Gurevich in collaboration with the authors. London: Weidenfeld and Nicolson.

SOMIT, ALBERT, ALAN ARWINE, AND STEVEN A. PETERSON

1996. *Birth Order and Political Behavior.* Lanham, Md.: University Press of America.

SOMKIN, FRED

1973. Lubbock, Sir John (Lord Avebury) (1834–1913). *Dictionary of Scientific Biography* 8:527–29.

SONNERT, GERHARD

1995. *Who Succeeds in Science?: The Gender Dimension.* With the assistance of Gerald Holton. New Brunswick, N.J.: Rutgers University Press.

SONNERT, GERHARD, AND GERALD HOLTON

1996. Career patterns of women and men in the sciences. *American Scientist* 84:63–71.

SOUTHWELL, CHARLES

1840. *An Essay on Marriage; Addressed to the Lord Bishop of Exeter.* London: E. Roe.

ca. 1845. *The Confessions of a Free-Thinker.* London: Printed for the author.

SPENGEL, JOHANN WILHELM

1872. *Die Darwinische Theorie: verzeichniss der über dieselbe in Deutschland, England, Amerika, Frankreich, Italien, Holland, Belgien und Skandinavischen Reichen erschienenen Schriften und Aufsätze.* 2d ed. Berlin: Wiegant und Hempel.

SPINKA, MATTHEW

1968. *John Huss: A Biography.* Princeton: Princeton University Press.

SPITZ, LEWIS W.

1971. *The Renaissance and Reformation Movements.* 2 vols. St. Louis: Concordia Publishing House.

1973. Reformation. In *Dictionary of the History of Ideas: Studies of Selected Pivotal Ideas,* edited by Philip P. Weiner, vol. 4, pp. 66–69. New York: Charles Scribner's Sons.

1977. Psychohistory and history: An examination of Erikson's *Young Man Luther.* In *Psychohistory and Religion: The Case of Young Man Luther,* edited by Roger A. Johnson, pp. 57–96. Philadelphia: Fortress Press.

1985. *The Protestant Reformation, 1517–1559.* New York: Harper & Row.

SPURZHEIM, JOHANN G.

1838. *Phrenology, or the Doctrine of the Mental Phenomena.* 2 vols. 5th ed. Boston: Marsh, Capen and Lyon.

STANFIELD, JAMES FIELD

1813. *An Essay on the Study and Composition of Biography.* London: Sunderland.

STANNARD, DAVID E.

1980. *Shrinking History: On Freud and the Failure of Psychohistory.* Oxford and New York: Oxford University Press.

STEBBINS, ROBERT E.

1972. France. In *The Comparative Reception of Darwinism,* edited by Thomas F. Glick, pp. 117–63. Austin and London: University of Texas Press.

STEELMAN, LALA CARR, AND BRIAN POWELL

1985. The social and academic consequences of birth order: Real, artifactual, or both. *Journal of Marriage and the Family* 47:117–24.

STEIN, RICHARD S., ADELE B. STEIN, AND JEROME KAGAN

1970. The effects of ordinal position and identification on the development of philosophical attitudes. *Journal of Genetic Psychology* 117:13–24.

STEPHEN, LESLIE

1888. Dickens, Charles (1812–1870). *Dictionary of National Biography* 5:20–32.

1890. Godwin, William (1756–1836). *Dictionary of National Biography* 8:64–68.

1893. Martineau, Harriet (1802–1876). *Dictionary of National Biography* 12:1194–99.

STEWART, JOHN A.

1986. Drifting continents and colliding interests: A quantitative application of the interests perspective. *Social Studies of Science* 16:261–79.

1987. Drifting or colliding interests?: A reply to Laudan with some new results. *Social Studies of Science* 17:321–31.

1990. *Drifting Continents & Colliding Paradigms: Perspectives on the Geoscience Revolution.* Bloomington and Indianapolis: Indiana University Press.

STEWART, LOUIS H.

1977. Birth order and political leadership. In *A Psychological Examination of Political Leaders,* edited by Margaret G. Hermann, with Thomas W. Milbury, pp. 205–36. New York: Free Press; London: Collier Macmillan.

1992. *Changemakers: A Jungian Perspective on Sibling Position and the Family Atmosphere.* London and New York: Routledge.

STEWART, RALPH H.

1967. Birth order and dependency. *Journal of Personality and Social Psychology* 6:192–94.

STIMSON, DOROTHY

1917. *The Gradual Acceptance of the Copernican Theory of the Universe.* New York: Baker & Taylor; Gloucester, Mass.: Peter Smith, 1972.

1935. Puritanism and the new philosophy in 17th century England. *Bulletin of the Institute of the History of Medicine* 3:321–34.

1948. *Scientists and Amateurs: A History of the Royal Society.* New York: Henry Schuman.

STIPP, DAVID

1994. Family matters. *The Wall Street Journal,* 23 August, pp. A1, A5.

STONE, LAWRENCE

1979. *Family, Sex, and Marriage in England, 1500–1800.* Abridged ed. New York: Harper Torchbooks.

STOWE, HARRIET BEECHER

1852. *Uncle Tom's Cabin; or, Life among the Lowly.* Boston: John P. Jewett.

STRESEMANN, ERWIN

1975. *Ornithology: From Aristotle to the Present.* Edited by G. William Cottrell. Translated by Hans J. and Cathleen Epstein. Cambridge and London: Harvard University Press.

STRICKLAND, HUGH E.

1840. On the true method of discovering the natural system in zoology and botany. *Notices and Abstracts to the British Association for the Advancement of Science; at the Glasgow Meeting, August 1840.* Vol. 10:128–29. London: John Murray.

1844. Report on the recent progress and present state of ornithology. In *Report of the Fourteenth Meeting of the British Association for the Advancement of Science; Held at York in September 1844.* Vol. 14: 170–219. London: John Murray.

SULLIVAN, WALTER

1974. *Continents in Motion: The New Earth Debate.* New York: McGraw-Hill.

SULLOWAY, FRANK J.

1969. Charles Darwin and the voyage of H.M.S. *Beagle.* A thesis presented to the Committee on History and Science for the degree of Bachelor of Arts, Harvard College.

1979a. Geographic isolation in Darwin's thinking: The vicissitudes of a crucial idea. *Studies in the History of Biology* 3:23–65.

1979b. *Freud, Biologist of the Mind: Beyond the Psychoanalytic Legend.* New York: Basic Books.

1982a. Darwin and his finches: The evolution of a legend. *Journal of the History of Biology* 15:1–53.

1982b. *The* Beagle *Collections of Darwin's Finches (Geospizinae). Bulletin of the British Museum (Natural History) Zoology Series* 43, no. 2.

1982c. Darwin's conversion: The *Beagle* voyage and its aftermath. *Journal of the History of Biology* 15:325–96.

1983a. The legend of Darwin's finches. *Nature* 303:372.

1983b. Further remarks on Darwin's spelling habits and the dating of *Beagle* voyage manuscripts. *Journal of the History of Biology* 16:361–90.

1984. Darwin and the Galapagos. *Biological Journal of the Linnean Society* 21:29–59.

1985a. Darwin's "dogged" genius: His Galapagos visit in retrospect. *Noticias de Galapagos,* no. 42, pp. 7–14.

1985b. Darwin's early intellectual development: An overview of the *Beagle* voyage (1831–1836). In *The Darwinian Heritage,* edited by David Kohn, pp. 121–51. Princeton: Princeton University Press.

1991a. Reassessing Freud's case histories: The social construction of psychoanalysis. *Isis* 82:245–75.

1991b. Darwinian psychobiography. Review of *Charles Darwin: A New Life,* by John Bowlby (1990). *New York Review of Books,* 10 October, pp. 28–32.

1995. Birth order and evolutionary psychology: A meta-analytic overview. *Psychological Inquiry* 6:75–80.

In preparation (editor). *Testing Theories of Scientific Change.*

SULLOWAY, FRANK J., AND ADAMS, MARK B.
1970. Charles Darwin's voyage with H.M.S. *Beagle.* A series of six films and film guides. Cambridge, Mass.: Ealing Films.
SUOMI, STEPHEN J.
1982. Sibling relationships in nonhuman primates. In *Sibling Relationships: Their Nature and Significance across the Lifespan,* edited by Michael E. Lamb and Brian Sutton-Smith, pp. 329–56. Hillsdale, N.J.: Lawrence Erlbaum.
SUTTON-SMITH, BRIAN, AND B. G. ROSENBERG
1970. *The Sibling.* New York: Holt, Rinehart and Winston.
SWANSON, GUY
1967. *Religion and Regime: A Sociological Account of the Reformation.* Ann Arbor: University of Michigan Press.
SWARTH, HARRY S.
1931. *The Avifauna of the Galapagos Islands. Occasional Papers of the California Academy of Sciences,* no. 18.
SYDENHAM, MICHAEL JOHN
1961. *The Girondins.* London: University of London.
1965. *The French Revolution.* London: B. T. Batsford.
SYMONS, DONALD
1979. *The Evolution of Human Sexuality.* New York: Oxford University Press.
TANNER, EDWIN P.
1931. Franklin, William (1731–1813). *Dictionary of American Biography* 6:600–601.
TATE, C. NEAL
1981. Personal attribute models of the voting behavior of U.S. Supreme Court justices: Liberalism in civil liberties and economics decisions, 1946–1978. *American Political Science Review* 75:355–67.
TATE, C. NEAL, AND ROGER HANDBERG
1991. Time binding and theory building in personal attribute models of Supreme Court voting behavior, 1916–88. *American Journal of Political Science* 35: 460–80.
TAWNEY, RICHARD HENRY
1926. *Religion and the Rise of Capitalism: A Historical Study.* New York: Harcourt Brace.
TEMPKIN, OWSEI
1947. Gall and the phrenological movement. *Bulletin of the History of Medicine* 21:275–321.
THAGARD, PAUL
1989. Scientific cognition: Hot or cold? In *The Cognitive Turn: Sociological and Psychological Perspectives on Science,* edited by Steve Fuller, Marc de Mey, Terry Shinn, and Steve Woolgar, pp. 71–82. Dordrecht: Kluwer Academic.
THOMAS, ALEXANDER, AND STELLA CHESS
1977. *Temperament and Development.* New York: Brunner/Mazel.
THOMPSON, DOROTHY
1984. *The Chartists: Popular Politics in the Industrial Revolution.* New York: Pantheon Books.

THOREN, VICTOR E.
1990. *The Lord of Uraniborg: A Biography of Tycho Brahe.* With contributions by John R. Christianson. Cambridge: Cambridge University Press.

TODD, JOHN M.
1982. *Luther: A Life.* London: Hamish Hamilton.

TOLAND, JOHN
1976. *Adolf Hitler.* Garden City, N.Y.: Doubleday.

TOMAN, WALTER
1961. *Family Constellation.* New York: Springer.
1970. Birth order rules all. *Psychology Today,* December, pp. 44–49, 68–70.
1971. The duplication theorem of social relationships as tested in the general population. *Psychological Review* 78:380–90.
1988. Basics of family structure and sibling position. In *Siblings in Therapy: Life Span and Clinical Issues,* edited by Michael D. Kahn and Karen Gail Lewis, pp. 46–65.
1989. Family constellations and friendships systems. *Contemporary Family Therapy* 11:3–20.
1992. *Family Constellations.* 4th ed. New York: Springer.

TOMAN, WALTER, AND SIEGFRIED PREISER
1973. *Familienkonstellationen und ihre Störungen: Ihre Wirkungen auf die Person, ihre sozialen Beziehungen und die nachfolgende Generation.* Stuttgart: Ferdinand Enke.

TOOBY, JOHN, AND LEDA COSMIDES
1990a. On the universality of human nature and the uniqueness of the individual: The role of genetics and adaptation. *Journal of Personality* 58:17–68.
1990b. The past explains the present: Emotional adaptations and the structure of ancestral environments. *Ethology and Sociobiology* 11:375–424.
1992. Psychological foundations of culture. In *The Adapted Mind: Evolutionary Psychology and the Generation of Culture,* edited by Jerome H. Barkow, Leda Cosmides, and John Tooby, pp. 19–136. New York: Oxford University Press.
In press. Friendship and the banker's paradox: Other pathways to the evolution of adaptations for altruism. *Proceedings of the British Academy: Evolution of Social Behaviour Patterns in Primates and Man.* Edited by John Maynard Smith.

TOULMIN, STEPHEN
1972. *Human Understanding.* Princeton: Princeton University Press.

TRAVIS, RUSSELL, AND VANDANA KOHLI
1995. The birth order factor: Ordinal position, social strata, and educational achievement. *Journal of Social Psychology* 135:499–507.

TRIVERS, ROBERT L.
1972. Parental investment and sexual selection. In *Sexual Selection and the Descent of Man, 1871–1971,* edited by Bernard Campbell, pp. 136–79. Chicago: Aldine.
1974. Parent-offspring conflict. *American Zoologist* 14:249–64.
1985. *Social Evolution.* Menlo Park, Calif.: Benjamin/Cummings.

TRIVERS, ROBERT L., AND DAN WILLARD
1973. Natural selection of parental ability to vary the sex-ratio of offspring. *Science* 179:90–92.

TROELTSCH, ERNST
1913. *Zur religiösen Lage, Religionsphilosophie und Ethik.* Tübingen: J. C. B. Mohr.
1931. *The Social Teachings of the Christian Churches.* Translated by Olive Wyon. London and New York: Macmillan.

TUFTE, EDWARD R.
1983. *The Visual Display of Quantitative Information.* Cheshire, Conn.: Graphics Press.
1990. *Envisioning Information.* Cheshire, Conn.: Graphics Press.

TURNER, FRANK MILLER
1974. *Between Science and Religion: The Reaction to Scientific Naturalism in Late Victorian England.* New Haven and London: Yale University Press.
1978. The Victorian conflict between science and religion: A professional dimension. *Isis* 69:356–76.
1990. The Victorian crisis of faith and the faith that was lost. In *Victorian Faith in Crisis: Essays on Continuity and Change in Nineteenth-Century Religious Belief,* edited by Richard J. Helmstadter and Bernard Lightman, pp. 9–38. London: Macmillan; Palo Alto, Calif.: Stanford University Press.

ULMER, S. SIDNEY
1986. Are social background models time-bound? *American Political Science Review* 80:957–67.

USSHER, JAMES
1650. *Annales Veteris Testamenti, a prima mundi origine deducti.* London: J. Flesher.

VERGER, DON
1968. Birth order and sibling differences in interests. *Journal of Individual Psychology* 24:56–59.

VERNON, PHILIP EWART, ED.
1970. *Creativity: Selected Readings.* Harmondsworth: Penguin Books.

VICKERS, BRIAN
1993. *Appropriating Shakespeare: Contemporary Critical Quarrels.* New Haven and London: Yale University Press.

VISHER, STEPHEN SARGENT
1947. *Scientists Starred 1903–1943 in "American Men of Science": A Study of Collegiate and Doctoral Training, Birthplace, Distribution, Backgrounds, and Developmental Influences.* Baltimore: Johns Hopkins University Press.

VOCKELL, E. L., D. W. FELKER, AND C. H. MILEY
1973. Birth order literature 1967–1971: Bibliography and index. *Journal of Individual Psychology* 29:39–53.

VOGEL, CHRISTIAN
1992. Die Rolle der Familie im biogenetischen Geschehen. In *Fortpflanzung: Natur und Kultur,* edited by Eckart Voland, pp. 290–305. Frankfurt: Suhrkamp.

VOLAND, ECKART

1984. Human sex-ratio manipulation: Historical data from a German parish. *Journal of Human Evolution* 13:99–107.

1990. Differential reproductive success within the Krummhorn population (Germany, 18th and 19th centuries). *Behavioral Ecology and Sociobiology* 26:65–72.

VOLTAIRE (FRANÇOIS-MARIE AROUET)

1733. *Letters concerning the English Nation.* London: C. Davis and A. Lyon.

1734. *Lettres philosophiques.* Amsterdam: E. Lucas. Translated as *Letters on England,* by Leonard Tancock. Middlesex, England: Penguin Books, 1980.

1738. *Éléments de la philosophie de Newton.* Amsterdam: Étienne Ledet.

1835–38. *Oeuvres de Voltaire, avec des notes et une notice historique sur la vie de Voltaire.* 13 vols. Paris: Furne.

1877–85. *Oeuvres complètes de Voltaire.* 52 vols. Paris: Garnier Frères.

1953–1965. *Voltaire's Correspondence.* Edited by Theodore Bestermann. 107 vols. Geneva: Institut et Musée Voltaire.

VOLTAIRE (FRANÇOIS-MARIE AROUET) AND FREDERICK THE GREAT

1927. *Letters of Voltaire and Frederick the Great.* Selected and translated by Richard Aldington. London: G. Routledge & Sons; New York: Brentano's.

WADE, IRA O.

1969. *The Intellectual Development of Voltaire.* Princeton: Princeton University Press.

WALLACE, ALFRED RUSSEL

1855. On the law which has regulated the introduction of new species. *Annals and Magazine of Natural History* 26:184–96.

1859 [1858]. On the tendency of varieties to depart indefinitely from the original type. *Journal of the Proceedings of the Linnean Society (Zoology)* 3:53–62; reprinted in Darwin and Wallace (1958:268–79).

1869. *The Malay Archipelago: The Land of the Orang-utan and the Bird of Paradise; a Narrative of Travel with Studies of Man and Nature.* London: Macmillan.

1889. *Darwinism, an Exposition of the Theory of Natural Selection with Some of its Applications.* London: Macmillan.

1905. *My Life; a Record of Events and Opinions.* 2 vols. London: Chapman and Hall; New York: Dodd, Mead.

WALLER, NIELS G., BRIAN A. KOJETIN, THOMAS J. BOUCHARD, JR., DAVID T. LYKKEN, AND AUKE TELLEGEN

1990. Genetic and environmental influences on religious interests, attitudes, and values: A study of twins reared apart and together. *Psychological Science* 2:138–42.

WALLER, NIELS G., AND PHILLIP R. SHAVER

1994. The importance of nongenetic influences on romantic love styles: A twin-family study. *Psychological Science* 5:268–74.

WALTER, GÉRARD

1961. *Robespierre.* 2 vols. Paris: Gallimard.

WALTER, MAILA L.

1990. *Science and Cultural Crisis: An Intellectual Biography of Percy Williams Bridgman (1882–1961).* Stanford: Stanford University Press.

WARD, REGINALD SOMERSET

1934. *Maximilien Robespierre: A Study in Deterioration.* London: Macmillan.

WARNICKE, RETHA M.

1989. *The Rise and Fall of Anne Boleyn: Family Politics at the Court of Henry VIII.* Cambridge and New York: Cambridge University Press.

WARREN, JONATHAN R.

1966. Birth order and social behavior. *Psychological Bulletin* 65:38–49.

WEBER, MAX

1904. *Die Protestantische Ethik und der "Geist" des Kapitalismus.* Tübingen and Leipzig: J. C. B. Mohr.

1930. *The Protestant Ethic and the Spirit of Capitalism.* Translated by Talcott Parsons. London: George Allen & Unwin.

WEBER, PAUL

1984. The birth order oddity in Supreme Court appointments. *Presidential Studies Quarterly* 14:561–68.

WEBSTER, CHARLES

1966. Richard Towneley (1629–1707), and the Towneley group, and seventeenth-century science. *Transactions of the Historical Society of Lancashire and Cheshire* 118:51–76.

1976. *The Great Instauration: Science, Medicine and Reform, 1626–1660.* New York: Holmes & Meier.

1986. Puritanism, separatism, and science. In *God and Nature: Historical Essays on the Encounter between Christianity and Science,* edited by David C. Lindberg and Ronald L. Numbers, pp. 198–200. Berkeley and Los Angeles: University of California Press.

WEBSTER, RICHARD

1995. *Why Freud Was Wrong: Sin, Science and Psychoanalysis.* New York and London: HarperCollins.

WEDGWOOD, BARBARA, AND HENSLEIGH WEDGWOOD

1980. *The Wedgwood Circle, 1739–1897: Four Generations of a Family and Their Friends.* London: Studio Visa.

WEDGWOOD, JOSIAH

1929. *The Economics of Inheritance.* London: George Routledge & Sons.

WEGENER, ALFRED

1929. *Die Entstehung der Kontinente und Ozeane.* Braunschweig: Vieweg & Sohn; first edition, 1915. Translated as *The Origins of Continents and Oceans* by John Biram from the fourth revised German edition. New York: Dover, 1966.

WEINER, JONATHAN

1994. *The Beak of the Finch: A Story of Evolution in Our Time.* New York: Alfred A. Knopf.

WEINGART, PETER, JÜRGEN KROLL, AND KURT BAYERTZ

1988. *Rasse, Blut, und Gene: Geschichte der Eugenik und Rassenhygiene in Deutschland.* Frankfurt am Main: Suhrkamp.

WEIR, ALISON
1991. *The Six Wives of Henry VIII.* New York: Ballantine Books.
WEISS, PHILIP
1989. Conduct unbecoming? *New York Times Magazine,* 29 October, pp. 40–95.
WEISS, SHEILA FAITH
1987. *Racial Hygiene and National Efficiency: The Eugenics of Wilhelm Schallmayer.* Berkeley and Los Angeles: University of California Press.
WELLS, KENTWOOD D.
1973. The historical context of natural selection: The case of Patrick Matthew. *Journal of the History of Biology* 6:225–58.
WENKE, ROBERT A.
1989. *The Art of Selecting a Jury.* 2d ed. Springfield, Ill.: Charles C. Thomas.
WEST, S. STEWART
1960. Sibling configuration of scientists. *American Journal of Sociology* 66:268–74.
WESTFALL, RICHARD S.
1958. *Science and Religion in Seventeenth-Century England.* New Haven and London: Yale University Press.
1971a. *Force in Newton's Physics: The Science of Dynamics in the Seventeenth Century.* London: Macdonald; New York: Elsevier.
1971b. *The Construction of Modern Science: Mechanisms and Mechanics.* New York: John Wiley & Sons; Cambridge: Cambridge University Press, 1977.
1980. *Never at Rest: A Biography of Isaac Newton.* Cambridge: Cambridge University Press.
1985. Scientific patronage: Galileo and the telescope. *Isis* 76: 11–30.
WESTMAN, ROBERT S.
1975a. The Melanchthon circle, Rheticus, and the Wittenberg interpretation of the Copernican theory. *Isis* 66:165–93.
1975b. Ed. *The Copernican Achievement.* Berkeley and Los Angeles: University of California Press.
WHITMAN, ALDEN, ED.
1985. *American Reformers.* New York: H. W. Wilson.
WHITTERIDGE, GWENETH
1971. *William Harvey and the Circulation of the Blood.* London: Macdonald; New York: Elsevier.
WIGGINS, JERRY S.
1979. A psychological taxonomy of trait-descriptive terms: The interpersonal domain. *Journal of Personality and Social Psychology* 37:395–412.
WILKINSON, LELAND
1990. *SYGRAPH: The System for Graphics.* Evanston, Ill.: SYSTAT.
WILKINSON, LELAND, AND MARY ANN HILL
1994. *Using SYSTAT.* Evanston, Ill.: SYSTAT.
WILLIAMS, GEORGE C.
1966. *Adaptation and Natural Selection: A Critique of Some Current Evolutionary Thought.* Princeton: Princeton University Press.
1975. *Sex and Evolution.* Princeton: Princeton University Press.

WILLIAMS, GEORGE HUNSTON
1962. *The Radical Reformation*. Philadelphia: Westminster Press.
1992. *The Radical Reformation*. 3d ed. Vol. 15 of Sixteenth Century Essays and Studies. Kirksville, Mo.: Sixteenth Century Journal Publishers.

WILLIAMS, L. PEARCE
1965. *Michael Faraday: A Biography*. London: Chapman & Hall; New York: Basic Books.
1971. Faraday, Michael (1791–1867). *Dictionary of Scientific Biography* 4:527–40.

WILLIAMS, WESLEY C.
1971. Chambers, Robert (1802–1871). *Dictionary of Scientific Biography* 3:191–93.

WILLIAMS-ELLIS, AMABEL
1966. *Darwin's Moon: A Biography of Alfred Russel Wallace*. London and Glasgow: Blackie.

WILSON, ALEXANDER
1970. *The Chartist Movement in Scotland*. New York: Augustus M. Kelley.

WILSON, ARTHUR M.
1972. *Diderot*. New York: Oxford University Press.

WILSON, DAVID SLOAN
1996. Adaptation and individual differences. Talk presented at the Human Behavior and Evolution Society meetings, Northwestern University, 29 June.

WILSON, EDWARD O.
1971. *The Insect Societies*. Cambridge: Harvard University Press.
1975. *Sociobiology: The New Synthesis*. Cambridge: Harvard University Press.
1978. *On Human Nature*. Cambridge: Harvard University Press.

WILSON, GEORGE, AND ARCHIBALD GEIKIE
1861. *Memoir of Edward Forbes*. Cambridge and London: Macmillan; Edinburgh: Edmonston and Douglas.

WILSON, LEONARD G.
1970. *Sir Charles Lyell's Scientific Journals on the Species Question*. New Haven and London: Yale University Press.

WINKLER, MARY G., AND ALBERT VAN HELDEN
1992. Representing the heavens: Galileo and visual astronomy. *Isis* 83:195–217.

WINSOR, MARY PICKARD
1979. Louis Agassiz and the species question. *Studies in the History of Biology* 3:89–117.

WINTER, DAVID G. *The Power Motive*. New York: Free Press.

WOLF, FREDERIC M.
1986. *Meta-Analysis: Quantitative Methods for Research Synthesis*. Beverly Hills, Calif.: Sage Publications.

WOLFENSTEIN, E. VICTOR
1967. *The Revolutionary Personality: Lenin, Trotsky, Gandhi*. Princeton, N.J.: Princeton University Press.

WOODWARD, KENNETH L., WITH LYDIA DENWORTH
1990. The order of innovation: A study finds scientific rebels are born, not made. *Newsweek*, 21 May, p. 76.

WORKMAN, HERBERT B.
1926. *John Wyclif: A Study of the English Medieval Church.* 2 vols. Oxford: Clarendon Press.
WRENCH, GUY THEODORE
1913. *Lord Lister, His Life and Work.* London: T. Fisher Unwin.
WRENCH, SUSAN BLEISWEIS
1985a. Sojourner Truth. In *American Reformers,* edited by Alden Whitman, pp. 814–15. New York: H. W. Wilson.
1985b. Harriet Tubman. In *American Reformers,* edited by Alden Whitman, pp. 816–18. New York: H. W. Wilson.
WRIGHT, ROBERT
1994. *The Moral Animal: Evolutionary Psychology and Everyday Life.* New York: Pantheon Books.
WRIGLEY, E. A., AND R. S. SCHOFIELD
1981. *The Population History of England, 1541–1871: A Reconstruction.* Cambridge: Harvard University Press.
WURZBACH, CONSTANT VON
1884. Unger, Franz. *Biographisches Lexikon des kaiserthums Oesterreich* 49:44–61.
YOUNG, ROBERT M.
1970. *Mind, Brain and Adaptation in the Nineteenth Century: Cerebral Localization and Its Biological Context from Gall to Ferrier.* Oxford: Oxford Clarendon Press.
1972. Gall, Franz Joseph (1758–1828). *Dictionary of Scientific Biography* 5:250–56.
1985. *Darwin's Metaphor: Nature's Place in Victorian Culture.* Cambridge: Cambridge University Press.
ZAJONC, ROBERT B.
1976. Family configuration and intelligence. *Science* 192:227–36.
1983. Validating the confluence model. *Psychological Bulletin* 93:457–80.
ZAJONC, ROBERT B., AND JOHN BARTH.
1980. Birth order, family size, and decline of SAT scores. *American Psychologist* 35:662–68.
ZAJONC, ROBERT B., AND GREGORY B. MARCUS
1975. Birth order and intellectual development. *Psychological Review* 82:74–88.
ZAJONC, ROBERT B., HAZEL MARCUS, AND GREGORY B. MARCUS
1979. The birth-order puzzle. *Journal of Personality and Social Psychology* 37:1325–41.
ZANGWILL, OLIVER L.
1966. The consequences of brain damage. *International Journal of Neurology* 5:395–402.
ZIMBARDO, PHILIP G.
1977. *Shyness: What It Is and What to Do about It.* New York: Addison-Wesley.
ZIMBARDO, PHILIP G., AND MICHEL R. LEIPPE
1991. *The Psychology of Attitude Change.* Philadelphia: Temple University Press.
ZINNER, ERNST
1943. *Entstehung und Ausbreitung der Copernicanischen Lehre.* Erlangen: Kommissionsverlag von Max Mencke.

ZUCKER, KENNETH J., AND RAY BLANCHARD

1994. Reanalysis of Bieber et al.'s 1962 data on sibling sex ratio and birth order in male homosexuals. *Journal of Nervous and Mental Disease* 182:528–30.

ZUCKERMAN, HARRIET

1977. *Scientific Elite: Nobel Laureates in the United States.* New York: Free Press; London: Collier Macmillan.

ZUCKERMAN, MARVIN

1987. All parents are environmentalists until they have their second child. *Behavioral and Brain Sciences* 10:42–44.

1990. The psychophysiology of sensation seeking. *Journal of Personality* 58:313–45.

ZWEIG, STEFAN

1934. *Erasmus of Rotterdam.* Translated by Eden and Ceder Paul. New York: Viking.

ZWEIGENHAFT, RICHARD L.

1975. Birth order, approval-seeking and membership in Congress. *Journal of Individual Psychology* 31:205–10.

INDEX

Page numbers in *italics* refer to captions, charts, or tables.

ABOUT THE AUTHOR

Frank J. Sulloway is a Research Scholar at the Massachusetts Institute of Technology, in the Department of Brain and Cognitive Sciences. He has a Ph.D. in the history of science from Harvard University and is a former MacArthur Fellow. His book *Freud, Biologist of the Mind: Beyond the Psychoanalytic Legend* provides a radical reanalysis of the origins and validity of Freud's theories and received the Pfizer Award of the History of Science Society. In addition, Dr. Sulloway has written about the nature of scientific creativity, and, in this connection, has published extensively on the life and ideas of Charles Darwin. For the last two decades, Dr. Sulloway has also employed evolutionary theory to understand how family dynamics affect personality development, including that of creative geniuses. He lives in Cambridge, Massachusetts.